Alpheus Todd

On Parliamentary Government in England

Its Origin, Development and Practical Operation

Alpheus Todd

On Parliamentary Government in England
Its Origin, Development and Practical Operation

ISBN/EAN: 9783741141034

Manufactured in Europe, USA, Canada, Australia, Japa

Cover: Foto ©Thomas Meinert / pixelio.de

Manufactured and distributed by brebook publishing software (www.brebook.com)

Alpheus Todd

On Parliamentary Government in England

ON

PARLIAMENTARY GOVERNMENT

IN

ENGLAND:

ITS ORIGIN, DEVELOPMENT, AND PRACTICAL OPERATION.

BY

ALPHEUS TODD

LIBRARIAN OF THE LEGISLATIVE ASSEMBLY OF CANADA.

IN TWO VOLUMES.

LONDON:
LONGMANS, GREEN, AND CO.
1867.

TO THE

HONOURABLE JOHN ROSE, M.A., Q.C.

A MEMBER OF THE LEGISLATIVE ASSEMBLY OF CANADA

FOR THE CITY OF MONTREAL

This Volume is Inscribed

AS A TOKEN OF RESPECT FOR HIS PUBLIC CHARACTER

AND PRIVATE WORTH

AND IN

GRATEFUL ACKNOWLEDGMENT FOR MANY ACTS OF KINDNESS,

BY HIS OBLIGED FRIEND

ALPHEUS TODD.

PREFACE.

AN ATTEMPT by a resident in a distant colony to expound the system of Parliamentary Government, as administered in the Mother Country, may call for some explanation. I venture, therefore, to prefix to my work a few personal remarks.

More than twenty-five years ago, when in the service of the House of Assembly of Upper Canada, as an assistant in the Provincial Library, I was induced to compile a Manual of Parliamentary Practice for the use of the Legislature. The valuable treatise of Mr. May, on the 'Usage of Parliament,' had not then appeared; and no work then published was sufficiently elementary and comprehensive to be of any service to our colonial legislators in the performance of their parliamentary duties. My little volume, although the crude and imperfect production of a very young man, was received with much favour by the Canadian Parliament. At the first meeting of the Legislature of United Canada, in 1841, the book was formally adopted for the use of members, and the cost of its production defrayed out of the public funds.

It was in the same year, and immediately after the union of the two Canadas, that 'responsible government'

was first applied to our colonial Constitution. In carrying
out this new, and hitherto untried, scheme of colonial
government, many difficult and complex questions arose,
especially in regard to the relations which should subsist
between the popular chamber and the ministers of the
crown. Upon these questions, my known addiction to
parliamentary studies, together with my official position as
one of the librarians of the Legislative Assembly, caused
me to be frequently consulted. I speedily became aware
that then, as now, no work previously written on the
British Constitution undertook to supply the particular
information required to elucidate the working of 'responsible' or 'parliamentary' government. For, all preceding
writers on this subject have confined themselves to the
presentation of an outside view, or general outline, of the
political system of England. There is nowhere to be
found a practical treatment of the questions involved in
the mutual relations between the Crown and Parliament,
or any adequate account of the growth, development, and
present functions of the Cabinet Council. In the words
of Lord Macaulay (History of England, iv. 437), 'no writer
has yet attempted to trace the progress of this institution,
an institution indispensable to the harmonious working of
our other institutions.'

My own researches in this field enabled me to accumulate a mass of information which has proved of much
utility in the settlement of many points arising out of
responsible government. I was frequently urged, by
persons whose opinions were entitled to respect, to digest
and arrange my collections in a methodical shape. The
fact that the greater part of my notes had been collected
when engaged in the investigation of questions not of

mere local or temporary significance, but capable of general application, led me to think that, if the result were embodied in the form of a treatise on parliamentary government as administered in Great Britain, it might prove of practical value both in England and her colonies; and that in the constitutional states of continental Europe it might serve to make more clearly known the peculiar features of that form of government, which has been so often admired, but never successfully imitated. I therefore determined to avail myself of the resources of the well-stored library under my charge, and attempt the compilation of a work which, while trenching as little as possible on ground already worthily occupied by former writers, should aim at supplying information upon branches of constitutional knowledge hitherto overlooked.

I proposed at first to prepare, more especially for colonial use, a manual which should include a dissertation upon the peculiar features of 'Responsible Government' in the colonies. But I decided, after much reflection on the subject, to change my plan, and to confine myself to the exposition of parliamentary government in England. I arrived at this conclusion, firstly, from a conviction that the safest guide to the colonies, whose institutions are professedly modelled upon those of the mother country, will be found in a detailed account of the system which prevails in the parent state; and, secondly, because parliamentary government in our colonies is still in its infancy, and its success is as yet but problematical. 'The well-understood wishes of the people, as expressed through their representatives,' has indeed been the acknowledged maxim of colonial rule;

and, so far as they are applicable to colonial society, the principles of the British Constitution have, in the main, been faithfully carried out. But it is easy to foresee that some considerable modifications must at no distant day be introduced into the fabric of colonial government, to enable it to resist the encroachments of the tide of democratic ascendancy, which is everywhere uprising, and threatening to overwhelm 'the powers that be.' Most of the British colonies still enjoy the advantage of an immense extent of unoccupied territory, affording to industrious men of the humblest class the opportunity of becoming landowners, and of achieving a degree of comfort and independence which naturally inclines them to be supporters of law and order. Nevertheless, from an observation of the working of our municipal institutions in Canada, and of the characteristics and results of responsible government in the British dependencies generally, it is evident that the democratic element is everywhere gaining the mastery, and is seeking the overthrow of all institutions that are intended to be a check upon the popular will.

The great and increasing defect in all parliamentary governments, whether provincial or imperial, is the weakness of executive authority. It may be difficult to concede to the governor of a colony the same amount of deference and respect which is accorded to an English sovereign. But any political system which is based upon the monarchical principle must concede to the chief ruler something more than mere ceremonial functions. It is the tendency of the age in which we live to relax the bonds of all authority, and to deprive all rank and station, not directly derived from the people, of the influence which it has heretofore possessed. The hereditary dignity of the British Crown itself has, within the last half century, sustained considerable loss. In popular estimation in our own day the prerogatives of royalty are accounted as well-nigh obsolete; and whatever may be the degree of affection expressed towards the occupant of the throne, the sovereign of England is too often regarded as but little more than an ornamental appendage to the state, and her rightful authority either derided or ignored. These erroneous ideas, it need scarcely be said, are not shared by any who have participated in the direction of state affairs. But they are widely diffused, even amongst educated men. The true position of the sovereign in a parliamentary government may not appear to be capable of exact definition, because much will always depend upon the personal character of the reigning monarch. But in the treatment of this difficult question, I have endeavoured to reflect faithfully the views of the most experienced statesmen of the present day; and while I have elsewhere claimed for the popular element in our constitution its legitimate weight and influence, I have here sought to vindicate for the monarchical element its appropriate sphere; being convinced that the functions of the crown are the more apt to be unappreciated because their most beneficial operations are those which, whilst strictly constitutional, are hidden from the public eye.

In attempting to define the limits between the authority of the crown and that of the legislature under parliamentary government, I have never relied upon my own interpretations, but have always illustrated the matter in hand by reference to the best opinions recorded in the debates of Parliament, or in evidence before select committees of either House. Such testimony, for the most part from the lips of eminent administrators and politicians now living, or but recently deceased, is of the highest value, especially when it embodies information upon the usages of the constitution which had not previously appeared in print. It is in the abundant use of such valuable material, never before incorporated in any similar treatise, that the chief claim of my work to public attention must consist.

Notwithstanding these obvious advantages, I am deeply conscious of its many defects and shortcomings; and in submitting it to the favourable consideration of those to whom it is addressed, I can only plead, as an excuse for its deficiencies, an honest endeavour to supply a want which must have been often experienced, by men engaged in public life, both at home and abroad.

ALPHEUS TODD.

LIBRARY OF PARLIAMENT, OTTAWA, CANADA:
December 1866.

CONTENTS

OF

THE FIRST VOLUME

CHAPTER I.

GENERAL INTRODUCTION.

	PAGE
Definition of English Parliamentary Government	1
Constitutional principles established by the Revolution of 1688	3
Government by Prerogative defined, and contrasted with Parliamentary Government	3
Concentration of political power in the House of Commons under Parliamentary Government	7
Introduction of ministers of the Crown into the House of Commons	8
Influence of the Landed Aristocracy therein	9
Use and value of Nomination Boroughs	11
Incompatibility of an efficient Parliamentary Government with a purely democratic House of Commons	13
Necessity for a moderate preponderance of Executive authority in Parliament	14
Effect of the Reform Act of 1832 in lessening that authority	15
Probable results of further democratic Reform	16
Necessity for strengthening the authority of the Executive in a Reformed House of Commons	19
Earl Grey's plan for conserving and strengthening Executive authority in connection with further Parliamentary Reform	20
Arguments in favour of strengthening the authority of the Crown in Parliament	23
Objection to allowing ministers of the Crown to hold seats in the House of Commons *ex officio*	26
Relative position of the two Houses of Parliament in the English political system	26
The House of Lords	27
The House of Commons	30
Peculiar advantages of Parliamentary Government	32
Subjects proposed to be considered in the following treatise	35

XIV CONTENTS OF THE FIRST VOLUME.

CHAPTER II.

HISTORICAL INTRODUCTION. PART I.

	PAGE
Origin of our Representative Institutions	35
Government by Prerogative prior to the Revolution of 1688	36
Origin of the principle of Ministerial Responsibility	37
Meaning of the Maxim 'The king can do no wrong'	40
Increasing recognition of Ministerial Responsibility from the Revolution of 1688	40
Case of the Partition Treaties	42
Constitutional provisions in the Act of Settlement	43
William III. as a constitutional monarch	44
Development of Ministerial Responsibility under the Hanoverian dynasty	46
Character and conduct of George III.	48
His irregular practice of consulting with 'friends,' instead of with his responsible Ministers	49
His dismissal of the Coalition Ministry in 1783	52
Mr. Pitt's first Administration	54
Lord Grenville's Administration	56
Its disagreement with the King on the Roman Catholic Question	57
Political influence of George III.	58
Influence of 'the great governing families'	59
Reign of George IV.	61
Case of Queen Caroline	62
Reign of William IV.	65
Effects of the Reform Bill of 1832	65
Abrupt dismissal of the Melbourne Ministry, and short-lived Administration of Sir R. Peel, in 1835	67
Return of Lord Melbourne to office	69
Reign of Queen Victoria	70

CHAPTER III.

HISTORICAL INTRODUCTION. PART II.

Constitutional Annals of the successive Administrations of England from 1782 to 1860; giving a brief account of the circumstances attending their appointment, resignation, or dismissal, with a notice of the various Constitutional questions, illustrative of Ministerial duty or responsibility, which arose within that period	72
1. Marquis of Rockingham's Administration (March 1782)	73
2. Earl of Shelburne's Administration (July 1782)	75
3. Duke of Portland's Administration (April 1783)	76
4. Mr. Pitt's first Administration (December 1783)	77
5. Mr. Addington's Administration (1801)	80
6. Mr. Pitt's second Administration (1804)	83

CONTENTS OF THE FIRST VOLUME. xv

	PAGE
7. Lord Grenville's Administration (1806)	88
8. Duke of Portland's Administration (1807)	90
9. Mr. Perceval's Administration (1809)	93
10. Earl of Liverpool's Administration (1812)	100
11. Mr. Canning's Administration (April 1827)	108
12. Lord Goderich's Administration (August 1827)	111
13. Duke of Wellington's Administration (1828)	114
14. Earl Grey's Administration (1830)	118
15. Viscount Melbourne's first Administration (July 1834)	122
16. Sir R. Peel's first Administration (November 1834)	123
17. Viscount Melbourne's second Administration (1835)	125
18. Sir R. Peel's second Administration (1841)	139
19. Lord John Russell's first Administration (1846)	144
20. Earl of Derby's first Administration (February 1852)	146
21. Earl of Aberdeen's Administration (December 1852)	148
22. Lord Palmerston's first Administration (1855)	150
23. Earl of Derby's second Administration (1858)	151
24. Lord Palmerston's second Administration (1859)	154
25. Earl Russell's second Administration (1865)	158
26. Earl of Derby's third Administration (1866)	160
Tabular view of Ministries and Parliaments from 1782 to 1860	162

CHAPTER IV.

THE SOVEREIGN.

Supremacy of the Sovereign in the State	167
Responsibility of Ministers for all acts of the Crown	169
Public acts of the Crown to be transacted through the medium of Responsible Ministers	170
Development of the principle of Ministerial Responsibility	174
Extent of royal interference in affairs of state since the Accession of Queen Anne	176
Character and public conduct of George I. and II.	177
" " " George III.	180
" " " George IV.	184
" " " William IV.	185
" " " Queen Victoria	187
Right of the Sovereign in regard to appointments in the royal household	188
Right of the Sovereign to employ a private secretary	191
Constitutional position of a Prince Consort	195
Prince Albert, his character and public services	199
Constitutional position of the Sovereign of Great Britain	201
Personal and moral influence	201
Ceremonial and social functions	204
Opinions of eminent statesmen on this subject	205
Lord Brougham	205
Earl Grey	208
Earl Derby	208

CONTENTS OF THE FIRST VOLUME.

	PAGE
Circumstances under which the influence of the Crown is increased or diminished	210
Right of the Sovereign to select the Ministers of State	210
Constitutional limitations thereto	211
Circumstances under which Parliament may advise the Crown in the choice of its Ministers	212
Restrictions upon the Crown in the choice or dismissal of individual Ministers	217
Free choice of the Crown in regard to the Prime Minister	219
Restrained only by the necessity for obtaining the confidence of Parliament in the new Administration	223
Proceedings upon the formation of a new Cabinet	224
The Prime Minister empowered to select his colleagues in office	226
During a ministerial interregnum, the Sovereign may consult any Peer or Privy Councillor	226
That whilst a Ministry is in office, it should receive the unreserved support of the Sovereign	227
Formal appointment and resignation of Ministers	228
Dismissal of Individual Ministers not ordinarily noticeable by Parliament	229
Cabinet councils not attended by the Sovereign	229
The Prime Minister the channel of communication between the Sovereign and the Ministry	230
The Sovereign to be consulted on all important acts of government	230
Mode in which the daily transactions of Government are communicated for the Royal approbation	231
Epistolary form in which Ministers address the Sovereign	232
Exercise of the Royal authority in Privy Council	233
Mode of obtaining the Sign-Manual to official papers	233
Circumstances under which the Royal functions may be delegated	234
Absence of the Sovereign from the Realm	234
Necessity for the Royal Sign-Manual to every act of delegation	235
Proceedings during the illness of George III.	235
Parliamentary authority to dispense with the Royal Sign-Manual in certain cases	238
Royal Prerogative in respect to Suits-at-Law against the Crown	239
Petitions of Right	239
Personal Immunity of the Sovereign before all earthly tribunals	242

CHAPTER V.

THE ROYAL PREROGATIVE IN CONNECTION WITH PARLIAMENT.

The Royal Prerogative generally	244
In relation to Parliament itself	246
In matters of Administration	252
1. General principles which govern the relations between Parliament and Ministers of the Crown in matters of Administration. Precedents	253—256

CONTENTS OF THE FIRST VOLUME.

	PAGE
II. Practice of Parliament in the appointment of Select Committees to Inquire into Administrative Questions	270
III. Practice in regard to the granting or withholding, by the Executive, of information desired by Parliament	278
IV. Circumstances which may require the interposition of Parliament to restrain the illegal exercise of Executive authority in relation, more particularly, to:—	284
(1) Orders in Council and Royal Proclamations	285
(2) Minutes of Committees of Council, and other Departmental Regulations	291
(3) Contracts entered into on behalf of the Crown	291
(4) Illegal or oppressive Acts by particular Ministers	293
In matters Ecclesiastical	304
(1) As concerns the Church of England in the Mother Country	305
(2) The position of the Church of England in the Colonies	308
(3) The position of the Church of England in Foreign Countries	317
(4) The obligations of the Act of Uniformity	318
In respect to the Army and Navy:—	
Their levy and maintenance	320
Their direction and control	321
Precedents	330
In respect to Martial Law	341
In Pardoning Offenders	343
Precedents	348
In the Administration of Justice	352
Precedents	358
Cases of erroneous convictions	364
In granting Honours and Rewards	366
Thanks voted by Parliament to individuals	368
In granting Charters of Incorporation, &c.	372
In creating Offices; appointing to Office; and in the control of Persons in Public Employ	375
In the remuneration of Persons in Office	395
Precedents	408
In matters of Supply and Taxation	427
I. (a) Restrictions upon Parliament in matters of Supply	428
Necessity for the consent of the Crown before proceeding upon any matter which involves public expenditure	429
Practice of the Lords less stringent	433
Abstract Resolutions on pecuniary questions	435
Addresses of House of Commons for the Advance of Money	436
Informal expressions of opinion in Parliament upon Money Questions	437
Precedents	438
I. (b) Restrictions upon Parliament in matters of Taxation	444
Motions concerning Taxation should emanate from Ministers of the Crown	444
Abstract Resolutions concerning particular Taxes	445
Precedents	446

VOL. I.   a

	PAGE
Inquiries of Ministers in regard to Taxation	451
Right of the Commons to amend or reject proposed Duties	451
11. Privileges of Parliament in the grant of Supplies, and in the control of the Public Expenditure	452
(a) Parliamentary control over the grant of Supplies	453
No Supplies to be used but such as are granted by Parliament	454
No Public Money to be advanced, or Debts remitted, by the Crown, without consent of Parliament	455
Relative position of the two Houses in regard to questions of Supply and Taxation	457
Paper Duties case	459
Practice of combining all the Budget Resolutions in one Bill	464
Appointment of Committee of Supply	465
Introduction of the Budget into the House of Commons	466
Public Revenues, whence derived, and how payable	467
Entire Public Revenue at the disposal of Parliament	471
Annual Estimates of probable Expenditure to be submitted to the House of Commons	473
Supplementary Estimates	474
Motions for a Revision of the Estimates by Committees of the House of Commons	475
Motions for a general Reduction of the Public Expenditure	478
Contents of the Estimates	480
Proceedings on the Estimates in Committee of Supply	482
Votes 'on Account'	484
Effect of debates in Committee of Supply upon the Public Expenditure	489
Items in the Estimates negatived	490
Introduction of Bills involving Public Expenditure otherwise than upon Supply Resolutions	491
Public Contracts made by Government, whereby expenditure will be incurred in excess of any Parliamentary Grant, require the consent of the House of Commons	493
Precedents	497
Right of the Commons to refuse a grant of Supply	508
Resolutions reported from Committee of Supply and agreed to by the House	509
Committee of Ways and Means	510
Effect given to Supply Votes in anticipation of the Appropriation Act	511
When Taxes may be voted in ordinary Committees of the whole House	512
Duties may be either annual or permanent	512
Immediate effect given to Resolutions concerning Taxes, or Stocks	513
All Financial Operations of Government, which affect the Public Debt, to be submitted to Parliament	515
Right of the House of Commons to revise or control the Financial Propositions of Ministers	517

CONTENTS OF THE FIRST VOLUME.

xix

	PAGE
Money Bills Defined	525
Origin and present form of the Appropriation Act	529
Its progress through Parliament	530
Speaker's Speech, on presenting Money Bills for the Royal Assent	531
Votes of Credit	532
Prorogation of Parliament before the passing of an Appropriation Bill	532
(b) Parliamentary control over the Issue and expenditure of Public Money	534
Exercised by means of three distinct Tribunals:—	
(1) The department of Exchequer and Audit	535
Functions of the Exchequer	536
Union of the Exchequer and Audit Offices	537
Its control over the issue of Public Money	540
Its inability to prevent the misapplication of Money after it has been issued	545
Necessity for allowing the Government some discretionary powers of expenditure in unforeseen cases	546
True remedy against unjustifiable Expenditure	546
Cases of unauthorised Expenditure by Government, and Proceedings in Parliament thereon	547
Funds from which such Expenditure has been defrayed	550
'Treasury Chest,' and 'Civil Contingencies' Funds	550
Secret Service Fund	551
Increasing strictness of Parliament in regard to any Expenditure that has not been duly voted and applied	552
Cash Account of the Paymaster-General	554
Payment of Salaries out of Revenue Receipts	555
(2) Functions of the Treasury in controlling the Public Expenditure	559
The Treasury is responsible for all Public Expenditure	560
No Department to exceed any Vote in their Estimates without consent of the Treasury	560
The Treasury empowered, by the Appropriation Act, to sanction Transfers of Surpluses to meet Deficiencies in Votes for Army and Navy Services	561
Difficulties of enforcing Treasury control, especially in the case of Naval Expenditure	564
New Appropriation Clause: requiring the sanction of Parliament to Transfers of Surpluses	567
Proceedings under this Clause	568
Expenditure for Civil Services	569
Unexpended Balances, at the end of the year, to be surrendered to the Exchequer	570
Difficulties of enforcing this rule	572
(3) Application of the system of Audit to the Public Accounts	573
(a) Ordinary duties of the Board of Audit	573
Unable to prevent unauthorised Expenditure	574
Is a Board of Verification, not of Control	574

CONTENTS OF THE FIRST VOLUME.

	PAGE
Recent Amalgamation of this Board with the Comptroller of Exchequer's Office	575
Departmental Audit	576
Administrative Audit	577
(b) Origin, nature, and operation of the Appropriation Audit	578
Not yet applied to the Miscellaneous Civil Service Expenditure	581
Schemes proposed to effect this end	581
Advantages of for applying the Appropriation Audit to all the Public Expenditure	585
Mode of conducting this Audit	586
Result reported to the House of Commons	587
No action hitherto taken by the House on such Reports	587
(4) Standing Committee on Public Accounts	589
Origin of this Committee	590
Its Appointment, Duties, and efficient Service	592
Its Reports from 1861 to 1866	593
Its active labours a guarantee for the constitutional control of the House of Commons in all Financial Concerns	596
In matters wherein the Sovereign represents the State in dealings with Foreign Powers:—	
1. The right of declaring War, and making Peace	598
2. Intercourse with Foreign Powers	601
3. The right of making Treaties	606
4. Interference in the Domestic Concerns of Foreign Nations	611
Concluding Remarks	620

ON

PARLIAMENTARY GOVERNMENT

IN

ENGLAND.

GENERAL INTRODUCTION.

THE PRINCIPLE of a constitutional or parliamentary go- *Definition* vernment is essentially different from either that of a re- *of parliamentary* public or of a despotism. A constitutional king is not *government.* responsible to the people, but he is bound by the laws; he is not free to govern as he pleases, but must rule in conformity to the recognised usages of the constitution, and in subjection to the fundamental laws of the realm, which regulate and define the rights and privileges of all classes and estates therein.

Society, like the family, is of divine appointment; and headship, in either case, has a divine origin. In a parliamentary government, rule and authority must receive the sanction of popular consent, though it does not necessarily emanate from the will of the people. The obligation of a king to rule righteously is as great as that of a people to obey those who have the rule over them. It is indeed more difficult to control and punish a sovereign who may abuse his office than to call people to account for treason and rebellion. But in a parliamentary government the kingly power is subjected to such rigid limitations and restraints that its abuse is difficult, if not impossible. The axiom that the king can do no wrong, is necessary for the protection of the monarchy from injurious aspersion or attack; but it is rendered innocuous, as a means of oppression or misrule, by the recognition of the doctrine that ministers of state are responsible for every exercise of kingly authority. These ministers have been permitted to share, with their sovereign, in all the functions of royalty, on condition that they assume a full responsibility for the same, before the Parliament and people. By this means, the services of statesmen in whom the country has confidence, and who represent the varying needs of the age, and its progressive intelligence, are secured on behalf of the empire; while the equilibrium of the state is duly preserved, amidst the recurrent changes of its actual rulers, by the permanence of the monarchical principle in the person of the sovereign. Such is the theory and practice of the British constitution.

'Since the establishment of parliamentary government, the ordinary description of the British constitution, as one in which the executive power belongs exclusively to the crown, while the power of legislation is vested jointly in the sovereign and the two Houses of Parliament, has ceased to be correct, unless it be understood in a legal and technical sense. It is the distinguishing feature of parliamentary government that it requires the powers belonging to the crown to be exercised through ministers, who are held responsible for the manner in which they are used, who are expected to be members of the two Houses of Parliament, the proceedings of which they must be able generally to guide, and who are considered entitled to hold their offices only while they possess the confidence of Parliament, and more especially of the House of Commons.'[*] Through the instrument-

---
[*] Grey on Parl. Government, 4.

ality of the cabinet, as a connecting link between the crown and Parliament, a close union, an intimate reciprocal action, has been effected between the executive and legislative powers. It is this which has given peculiar vitality to English parliamentary government.[a]

The great and leading principles of the British constitution, as now interpreted, are therefore the personal irresponsibility of the king, the responsibility of ministers, and the inquisitorial power of Parliament. For the complete recognition of these cardinal principles, the nation is indebted to the statesmen who effected the Revolution of 1688.[b] *Revolution of 1688.*

Prior to that epoch, the government of England was mainly carried on by virtue of the royal prerogative, that is to say, by the king in person, with the advice and assistance of ministers appointed by himself, and who were responsible to the sovereign alone for the ordinary conduct of public affairs; whilst they were amenable to Parliament for any direct abuse of their functions. Under this system, Parliament had no voice in the selection of ministers of the crown, and whenever they entertained adverse opinions in regard to questions of administration, they had no means of making those opinions known, except by retrospective complaint and remonstrance. This occasioned frequent contests between the crown and the Parliament, which sometimes ended in civil war. *Government by prerogative.*

While the sole executive authority of the realm was possessed by the king—in whom, together with his

---

[a] See Bagehot on the Cabinet, Fortnightly Review, No. 1, p. 9.

[b] We have the great Lord Camden's authority for asserting that 'The Revolution restored this constitution to its first principles: it did no more. It did not enlarge the liberty of the subject, but gave it a better security. It neither widened nor contracted the foundation, but repaired and perhaps added a buttress or two to the fabric.'—*Howell's St. Trials*, xix. 1058. To the same effect, it has been well observed by a recent political writer, that, 'Prior to 1688, the theory of our constitution was, that the crown was limited, and that its powers were checked by the Houses of Parliament; but this theory was not always recognised by the king in practice. The Revolution of 1688 brought the theory and practice into harmony. Since that time the crown has never attempted to govern without Parliament.'—*Edinb. Rev.* vol. cix. p. 275.

ministers and officers of state, was vested the exclusive right of administering the laws of the land—the legislative authority was divided between three co-ordinate powers, the King, the House of Lords, and the House of Commons. Each of these branches of the one Parliament enjoyed an equality of rights, and had a deliberate choice of assent or dissent to every legislative measure.

Balance of powers in the constitution.

So long as this form of government prevailed, it was customary to assume as an axiom, that the well-being of the English commonwealth consisted in the preservation of the balance of power between these co-ordinate branches of the supreme Parliament, so that any abuse of authority on the part of one, might admit of correction by the interposition of the authority of another branch. For example, the power of the two Houses of Parliament to frame laws was presumed to be held in check by the king's negative, which could always be interposed to prevent the adoption of an unwise or unnecessary statute. Again, the arbitrary exercise of the king's right of veto was itself restrained by the power which Parliament possessed of refusing a grant of supplies for the service of the crown. On the other hand, freedom of speech, though nominally conceded to Parliament from a very early period, was not invariably respected by the crown. In some instances, even the Tudor monarchs went the length of charging the Speaker of the Commons to forbid members from meddling with matters of state. Occasionally we read of free-spoken representatives being cited before the Privy Council, interrogated and reprimanded, or sent to the Tower. In self-defence, the Commons adopted a standing order for the exclusion of strangers during debate, and making it punishable to repeat out of doors what had passed within.[a] And in order to maintain the due independence of the legislative chambers, it

---

[a] Macaulay, Hist. of Eng. vol. iii. p. 543; Park's Dogmas, p. 104; May, Parl. Prac. c. 4.

was held to be an infringement of constitutional privilege for the king to take the initiative in legislation by submitting any Bills to the consideration of the two Houses—save only acts of grace and pardon—or even for the sovereign to take formal notice of any resolution or proceeding of Parliament which did not affect the interests of the crown, until the same had been regularly communicated to him for his concurrence.*

This was the doctrine and usage of the English constitution which prevailed before the era of parliamentary government; and notwithstanding the fundamental alterations that have since taken place in constitutional practice, this is still the theory of the British government, as expounded by Blackstone, Paley, De Lolme, and other text-writers of a later date. And yet how strikingly is this theory at variance with the recorded facts of our Parliamentary history for the past century and a half! While for many generations the forms of the ancient constitution of England have continued unchanged, the principle of growth and development has been at work, and has silently effected numerous and important alterations in all our governmental institutions. For instance, the prerogative of the crown to veto obnoxious measures presented for its sanction by the Legislative Chambers has never been invoked since the reign of Queen Anne. The undoubted right of the Commons to withhold supplies from the crown has not been exercised in a single instance since the Revolution of 1688. All important public bills are now submitted to Parliament by ministers of the crown, with the avowed sanction and express authority of the sovereign; and it has become a recognised and prominent part of the functions of the king's ministers that they shall be able to lead and control the two Houses of Parliament, and to carry on the government therein, by themselves undertaking the oversight

Contrast between the theory and practice of the constitution.

* Hats. Prec. vol. ii. p. 356.

and direction of the entire mass of public legislation. Moreover, the exercise of every branch of the royal prerogative is now subjected to free criticism in both Houses of Parliament; and although the standing orders for the exclusion of strangers are still retained, they are practically a dead letter; and so much publicity is allowed to the debates and proceedings as to justify the saying that 'the entire people are present, as it were, and assist in the deliberations of Parliament.'[1] As a natural consequence of these momentous changes, harmony has been established between the executive and legislative powers, in place of the jealousy and spirit of antagonism which usually characterised the former system.

A proof of vital changes in the constitution.

This wide discrepancy between theory and practice—between the ordinary functions of the several branches of the legislature as defined in our old constitutional text-books, and the modern usages in respect thereto, affords unmistakeable proof that the constitution itself has really undergone a material alteration within the last 150 years, albeit these changes, for the most part, have been unnoticed by political writers. Formerly the obsolete privileges above enumerated were regarded as so many proofs of an admirable system of 'checks' and 'balances of power,' whereby the different parts of our complex political system were maintained in equipoise. They now remain as mere indications of ancient landmarks, which have ceased to be effectual restraints in the existing development of our institutions.

Dormant powers of the crown and Lords.

And here it may be remarked, parenthetically, that because the crown and the House of Lords are precluded by modern constitutional usage from making direct use of the powers which originally appertained to them as distinct and independent branches of the legislature, it must not, therefore, be assumed that they are but of small account in their separate and individual capacity. Their ancient rights, though dormant, have never been

---

[1] May, Const. Hist. vol. i. p. 420.

disallowed; but are still held in reserve, in case of any sudden or violent attack upon their new mode of operation. This may surely be affirmed of the royal veto, in the present state of our constitutional system, although, as a matter of constitutional practice, the system of parliamentary government has fortunately done away with the necessity for collisions between the crown and the people on questions of public policy or internal administration, and has caused all such matters to be decided within the walls of Parliament by the relative strength of existing political parties. The same principle holds good in regard to the two Houses of Parliament. While no formal alteration has taken place in the original limits of authority between the two co-ordinate and co-equal chambers of the legislature, and it is now generally conceded that the proper function of the House of Lords is not to take a prominent part in the initiation of public Bills, but to control, revise, and amend the measures of legislation which have received the sanction of the House of Commons,—nevertheless, if need be, it would be perfectly competent for the House of Lords to claim its ancient privileges, and to assume a more active share in the origination of measures which concern the general welfare of the community.

The principal change effected by the development of the English constitution since the Revolution of 1688 has been the virtual transference of the centre and force of the state from the crown to the House of Commons. Instead of prerogative government we now have parliamentary government. Instead of the will of the crown being either paramount, or else engaged in direct conflict with the other branches of the legislature, we now find the constitutional influence of the crown, and of the great landowners, exerted in the House of Commons, through the instrumentality of members who obtain seats therein, expressly in order that they may uphold and carry out that influence. The introduction of members into the *House of Commons under parliamentary government.*

House of Commons for such a purpose, however at variance it may be with the abstract idea of popular representation, has, indeed, become essential and of vital consequence to the maintenance of monarchical institutions in Great Britain. Curtailed in the exercise of their original rights, as independent branches of the legislature, it has become impossible for the crown and the nobles to retain their legitimate share in the government of the country unless they are both fairly represented in that assembly wherein the supreme political power of the state is now concentred. This result has been attained by the growth of a system under which each of the three co-equal elements of the crown, the aristocracy, and the commonalty,—representing respectively the principles of authority, of stability, and of progress,—have been effectually, if not formally, incorporated into the Commons' House of Parliament.

Introduction of ministers therein.

By the introduction of the king's ministers into Parliament, which was accomplished in the reign of William III., the monarchical element in the constitution began to make itself felt in the House of Commons. The great advantages of this step were not at first appreciated, even by its promoters; but they gradually became apparent in the harmonious working of the machinery of government. As a natural consequence, it necessitated a recourse by the rival factions on both sides to a system of party organization, in order to give strength and consistency to their endeavours. 'For parliamentary government is essentially a government by means of party, since the very condition of its existence is that the ministers of the crown should be able to guide the decisions of Parliament, and especially of the House of Commons; and all experience proves that no popular assembly can be made to act steadily under recognised leaders except by party organization.'[*] Seats in the House of Commons for the king's

Party government.

---

[*] Grey, Parl. Govt. new ed. 1864, p. 10. See further, as to the benefits of party, Austin, Plea for the Constitution, p. 34; Park's Lectures, pp.

ministers and their adherents were obtainable from the first by means of various small boroughs, which were under the direct control of the Treasury, and of other boroughs which were subject to the influence of certain great families or wealthy proprietors, who were willing to dispose of the same in support of an existing administration. Thus the government for the time being were always able to command from forty to fifty seats in a new Parliament, in addition to the natural strength of the party they represented.[h]

In like manner, the holders of landed property throughout the country, and especially the great hereditary aristocracy, were able, in their own behalf, to control many of the smaller constituencies. The commanding influence thus exercised by the crown, and the landed gentry of the kingdom, over the election of members of the House of Commons, appears at first sight to be a departure from the strict rule of representation in a popular assembly. The case however assumes a very different aspect when it is considered that property, not numbers, has been hitherto the acknowledged basis of representation in the House of Commons.[i] It is true that the direct interference of peers (as such) at elections is declared by a standing order to be a high breach of the privileges of the House of Commons;[j] nevertheless, it has been admitted by the most eminent constitutional authorities, including the names of Lord John Russell, Sir Robert Peel, and Lord

Property, not numbers, represented in the Commons.

61, 128; Fraser's Magazine, August, 1863; Mr. Disraeli's speeches, in Hans. Deb. vol. cliii. p. 1304; ibid. vol. claxiv. p. 1291; and see the Edinburgh Review, vol. cviii. p. 277, in reply to an article in the Westminster Review for April, 1858, condemnatory of party government. The arguments against party government are summed up in Lord Brougham's Essay on the Effects of Party, in his Hist. Sketches of the Statesmen of the Time of George III.

[h] Grey, Parl. Govt. new ed. p. 227.
[i] See Russell, Eng. Const. new ed. 1865, pp. xxxi.–xxxvi. The registered electors of Great Britain are 1,045,000, out of a population of rather over twenty million persons. Edinburgh Rev. July, 1865, p. 281. It is estimated that by the existing suffrage the working class are able to command more than one fourth of the whole borough constituency.—Hans. Deb. vol. clxxxii. pp. 1238, 1110.
[j] S. O. H. of C. Nos. 410, 417.

Palmerston, that there is 'a customary and due influence' exercised by landlords over their tenantry, in the choice of members to serve in the House of Commons, which is perfectly legitimate, and will always exist. Occasional complaints have been made to the House, under peculiar circumstances, of the infringement of the standing order by peers, but the House has always evinced great reluctance to proceed thereon. For, in fact, the influence which is exercised by peers is mainly that which rightfully appertains to them as the guardians and representatives of vast hereditary estates, and it is impossible to dissociate the individual peer from the landed proprietor.[1] In a monarchical government, property must necessarily be in the hands of the few; and 'the law-maker must be a possessor of property, because the end of all legislation is the security of property.'[1] The extent to which the influence of property prevails in England at the present time is very considerable, notwithstanding the disfranchisement of so many small boroughs by the Reform Bill. This influence is more or less exerted in every constituency; but it is only in the counties and in certain of the smaller boroughs that it usually affects the result of the elections. The larger manufacturing towns and cities are generally under the control of the commercial or manufacturing interests. Nevertheless, it has been computed in a work which has recently appeared, upon the 'Great Governing Families of England,' that the thirty-one families therein enumerated 'supply at this moment one clear fourth of the English House of Commons.'[m]

---

[1] See Mirror of Parl. August 6, 1832, p. 3588; Hans. Deb. vol. lxxxiii. p. 1167; ibid. vol. xcv. pp. 1047, 1854; ibid. vol. clix. p. 1583; ibid. vol. clxxiv. pp. 833, 946; May's Parl. Prac. ed. 1863, p. 601, n.; Macmillan's Magazine, April, 1865, p. 476; and Lord Palmerston's speech on the Ballot, Hans. Deb. June 10, 1853.

[l] Letter to Mr. Bright, by Henry Drummond, M.P., 1858, p. 36. It is remarkable that even in the United States, where a nearly universal suffrage prevails, the landed interest is so powerful, owing to the almost universal possession of property, that 'the great mass of the farmers, when they choose to exert themselves, are able to overrule the mob of the cities, and decide the policy of the nation.'—*Goldwin Smith*, in Macmillan's Mag. April, 1865, pp. 418, 424.

[m] Sanford and Townsend's Great Governing Families of England, 2 vols.

And here it may be well to notice the important services which have been heretofore rendered to the state through the instrumentality of the smaller or nomination boroughs. Some of the ablest and most uncompromising advocates of parliamentary reform have freely admitted that we are indebted to these boroughs for the introduction into the House of Commons of many of its most eminent and useful members, who could not otherwise have obtained entrance there; and for the representation in Parliament of various classes and interests which would else have failed to acquire the weight and influence therein to which they are justly entitled. The nomination boroughs have also served to redress, in however irregular a manner, the balance of authority between the several branches of Parliament, which would else have been overthrown by the increasing power of the Lower House. This is emphatically true of the legitimate authority and influence of the crown in the House of Commons, which has been maintained, under our parliamentary system, chiefly by means of the control exercised by government over certain of the smaller constituencies.* For, as a general rule, nearly all our ministers of state, and eminent politicians of the class out of which ministers are necessarily chosen, have been indebted to the small boroughs for a seat in Parliament. Even when able to command a county constituency, ministers of the crown have generally preferred to represent small boroughs, on account of the comparative immunity thereby obtained from the incessant demands upon their time and attention on behalf of their constituents, which is so great a tax upon members who represent populous constituencies.

London, 1865, pp. 3–20. In the new House of Commons, chosen in 1865, including four Irish Peers, there were no less than 134 members of noble families (chiefly sons of noblemen) elected, and 83 other members who were connected by marriage or close relationship with noble families. This gives a total of one-third of the House of Commons connected with the peerage.—*Macmillan's Mag.* Feb. 1866, p. 314.

* Grey, Parl. Govt. p. 105; Russell, Eng. Const. pp. xxxv. xlix.; Austin, Plea for the Const. p. 28.

Thus, when Mr. Canning was appointed Foreign Secretary, and leader of the House of Commons, in 1822, he retired from the representation of Liverpool, and was elected for the borough of Harwich, considering that the duties entailed upon him as member for that great commercial town were incompatible with the faithful discharge of his functions as a minister of state.[a] In like manner, Sir Robert Peel, Lord Palmerston, Lord Stanley, Sir G. Grey, Sir Stafford Northcote, and other noted parliamentary leaders, have almost invariably sat for small boroughs, and have refused to represent large constituencies. Again, statesmen of the highest eminence who, through their connexion with great governing families, have obtained seats for counties, have not seldom been obliged to resort to boroughs in order to retain a seat in Parliament when they have chanced to incur the displeasure of their numerous electors. For example, in 1835, Devonshire rejected Lord John Russell, and compelled him to seek a refuge in Stroud; in 1834 Lord Palmerston was defeated in Hampshire, and afterwards sat for Tiverton; in 1852 Sir G. C. Lewis was defeated in Herefordshire, and was obliged to have recourse to Radnor; in 1847 Macaulay was defeated at Edinburgh, and kept out of Parliament for five years. It has been computed that out of some sixty-three members, in the last House of Commons, who either held, or were qualified to hold, the highest administrative offices, by far the greater proportion represented small constituencies. The more populous boroughs only contributed one-fifteenth of this governing element.[b] In fact, it is notorious that there has been, of late years, a decided and increasing disposition on the part of large boroughs to make choice of local celebrities, or persons of limited reputation, to represent them in Parliament, in place of electing men possessed of statesmanlike qualities,

---

[a] Stapleton, Canning and his Times, p. 334. And see Grey, Parl. Govt. new ed. p. 121.
[b] See Fraser's Magazine, August, 1865, p. 181.

or administrative experience.* If, therefore, the few remaining small boroughs are disfranchised, it will become indispensably necessary to find some other mode of entrance into the House of Commons for the great statesmen to whom the administration of public affairs is or may be entrusted.

It has been justly observed that 'the history of the world affords, as yet, no example of the permanent success of parliamentary government with a legislature formed on the strict principles of popular representation.'[r] The House of Commons owes its success as an active part of the supreme authority, and its peculiar excellences, to 'what are regarded as defects and departures from principle in our representative system;' and 'it is chiefly by means of these defects that the ministers of the crown have been enabled to obtain the authority they have exercised in the House of Commons.'* Able to rely upon the support of a certain number of stedfast adherents, every administration in turn has hitherto possessed, in general, sufficient power to conduct the government of the country consonantly to the best and most enlightened opinions, even though in opposition to popular prejudices, or superficial ideas which might temporarily prevail throughout the kingdom. The policy of an administration charged with the government of the British empire must indeed, of necessity, be a reflex of the best-informed

Peculiar excellences of our representative system.

---

* See illustrative tables, in Edinb. Review, vol. cvi. pp. 273–277, and speeches by Mr. Gladstone and Mr. Disraeli, &c., Hans. Deb. vol. clxxxiii. pp. 488, 874, 904, 1285, 1883, 1904.

r Grey, Parl. Govt. p. 67. 'Parliamentary government is a machine of the most exquisite delicacy.' 'America during the last five years has only repeated to the world the lesson that had already been taught by France, that, if you will have democracy, you must have something like Cæsarism to control it. The feeble and pliable executive of England is wholly unsuited to such an electoral body. A government that yields, and must yield, to the slightest wish of the House of Commons, is only possible so long as that House of Commons is the organ of an educated minority. Such an instrument of government has never yet, in the history of the world, been worked by a legislature chosen by the lower class.'—Quar. Review, January, 1880, p. 270.

* Grey, Parl. Govt. pp. 67, 68. And see Lord Dudley's speech in Knight's Hist. of Eng. vol. viii. p. 282.

14   GENERAL INTRODUCTION.

Control of public opinion.

opinion of the nation.' But this opinion 'is expressed, not by the clamorous chorus of the multitude, but by the measured voices of all classes, parties, and interests. It is declared by the press, the exchange, the market, the club, and society at large. And it is subject to as many checks and balances as the constitution itself; and represents the national intelligence rather than the popular will.'" And, after all, it should be remembered that while public opinion, in a free state, must ultimately determine into whose hands authority shall be entrusted, and what shall be the general policy of government, it is chiefly within the walls of Parliament that the contest for power between the rival candidates for office is conducted; and that one of the most important functions of Parliament is that of being 'an instrument for the instruction of the nation, and for enabling it to arrive at just and wise conclusions on matters affecting its welfare.'" How essential, therefore, is it that Parliament should consist of the most intelligent, educated, and enlightened men that are to be found in the whole community!

Importance of a strong government.

In order that the ministry may be in a position to devise and recommend to Parliament a policy that shall commend itself to the highest intelligence of the country, it is essential that they should have sufficient strength in the popular assembly to enable them to withstand the pressure of temporary political excitement. Prior to the passing of the Reform Bill, in 1832, there was no impediment of this kind, but thoughtful politicians foresaw, as an inevitable consequence of that measure, that parliamentary government would become more and more difficult

---

' Macaulay, Hist. Eng. vol. iii. p. 643; May, Const. Hist. vol. i. p. 430.
" May, Const. Hist. vol. ii. p. 253; see also Park's Dogmas, pp. 88, 97.
' Grey, Parl. Govt. pp. 27–37. And see some weighty observations in Bagehot's Papers on the Constitution, in Fortnightly Review, vol. i. pp. 15, 320; vol. iv. p. 277. The custom which has grown up within the present generation of members meeting their constituents, during the recess, to address them upon the political topics of the day, and to invite inquiry and discussion upon the course taken by their representatives in Parliament, is 'one of the most powerful and beneficial engines for the creation of a moderate, temperate, tolerant, yet clear and definite public opinion.' — *Ibid.* vol. iv. p. 60.

and embarrassing. Special attention was bestowed upon this subject by Mr. J. J. Park, who at that period filled the chair of English Law and Jurisprudence at King's College, London. In a course of lectures on the theory and practice of the constitution, delivered before that institution, Mr. Park pointed out with great force and perspicuity the altered relative position of 'King, Lords, and Commons,' by the establishment of parliamentary government, to which attention has been directed in the preceding pages. And in a petition to the legislature which he drafted when the Reform Bill was under consideration, Professor Park strongly urged the necessity for making legislative provision to ensure 'a moderate preponderance of the influence of the crown in the Houses of Parliament, so as to preserve the government there carried on from factious intrigue, and daily and capricious opposition, and to reserve that opposition for occasions of real misconduct or misjudgment.' *

Authority of the crown in parliament.

But the Reform Bill became the law of the land. Its immediate effect was to place the representation of the people upon a wider basis, by introducing the commercial and manufacturing classes—which, ever since the peace of 1815, had been growing in wealth and importance—to a share of political power. So far, this great measure has been just and beneficial in its operation. At the same time, by increasing the weight and influence of the House of Commons in public affairs, while it diminished the means previously at the disposal of the crown for exercising a constitutional control over the proceedings of Parliament, it has served to render parliamentary government a more onerous undertaking. Nevertheless, with the assistance of the few small boroughs that escaped disfranchisement, it has not been found impracticable, albeit increasingly difficult, to carry on the Queen's government in the Reformed Parliament. Owing to the conservative spirit which has generally animated that assembly, the

Weakened by the Reform Act.

---

* Park's Lectures on the Dogmas of the Constitution, p. 147.

traditions of the monarchy have been hitherto respected, and the balance of the constitution, though obviously jeopardized, has not been overthrown. To the influence of the same spirit we may attribute the fact that the various schemes for an extension of the electoral franchise which have been propounded within the last few years have met with no favour from Parliament, and have not excited much interest throughout the nation. But from the pertinacity with which further changes in a democratic direction have been urged by a small but energetic class of politicians, there is little doubt that ere long an additional instalment of parliamentary reform will be conceded by the legislature. The preservation of the English constitution, in its integrity, will entirely depend upon the principle on which the forthcoming Reform Bill shall be based. The highest constitutional authorities, not only in England but even in the United States, have concurred in declaring that the suffrage should be regarded as a privilege or trust bestowed on the voter, to be exercised for the benefit of the nation, and not as a personal right.* On this ground it becomes the duty of the state to limit its possession to those who are most competent to make use of it for the general good. More than twenty years ago it was pointed out, by an able writer, that the ultimate result of further political changes in the representation of the people must be the adoption of a very widely extended, if not universal suffrage. The advanced reformers will be satisfied with nothing less. And this will occasion a political revolution, by which is meant, 'not a violent anarchical movement, but a change in the depositaries of power.' As the labouring classes form the great majority—probably nineteen-twentieths of the population—such a constitution would give them irresistible influence. The House of

marginal note: Will be jeopardized by further democratic Reform.

---

* Compare an article in the North American Review for July, 1865, on 'The Democratic View of Democracy' (pp. 111-116) with Russell, Eng. Const. p. xxxi.; Tremenheere, The Franchise a Privilege, and not a Right; Lord Palmerston on the Ballot, in Hans. Deb. vol. clxxx. p. 420.

Commons, even now, while it is returned by less than one-tenth of the people, is the preponderating power in the British empire. Returned by universal suffrage, representing, not as now a fraction, but the whole of our population, it would trample on the crown and the House of Lords. The British empire would be governed by the agricultural labourers in the country, and by the artisans in towns.'' And as a natural consequence of the transfer of political power to a class of men who are destitute of political foresight, and naturally prone to urge the adoption of schemes that promise to promote their immediate benefit, without considering their effect upon other classes in the community, there is cause to apprehend that the whole social fabric of the empire would be endangered. Time and the event can alone determine upon the accuracy of these prognostications. Some, indeed, contend that the progress of education and general enlightenment would avert many, if not all, of the evils anticipated from entrusting the masses with political power. But the experience afforded by the working of democratic institutions in Australia, in America,' and in France under the Empire,² does not justify this conclusion. On the contrary, we have every reason to fear that a wide extension of the suffrage to a class who are less instructed, and less capable of apprehending political questions, than those who are now enfranchised, must have a downward tendency. Rival parties will bid against each other for the support of this new portion of the national constituency; and in order to obtain it must adopt their views, and pander to their prejudices. Thus, by sure degrees, the interests of the nation will be subjected to the ultimate control of 'its more ignorant, instead of its more edu-

<small>Consequences of transferring political power from the middle to the lower classes.</small>

' N. W. Senior's Essays, vol. i. p. 340. Hans. Deb. vol. clxxxii. pp. 013, 2108.

' See Tremenheere's English and American Constitutions compared; Park's Dogmas, p. 140; Austin's Plea, p. 38; and particularly Grey's Parl. Govt. new ed. pp. 155-184.

² See Edinb. Review, July, 1865, p. 272; Fraser's Magazine, August, 1865, p. 158; Hans. Deb. vol. clxxxii. p. 2110.

cated classes—of its lowest instead of its highest intellects.'[b] The transference of power to a class of men who, however estimable they may be in their proper place, are full of misapprehensions concerning the province and purposes of government, and are ignorant of the causes which determine their own economical condition, must be fraught with the greatest peril to the noble institutions of England, which have been the safeguard of liberty, and are the admiration of the world.[c]

Effects of democratic reform upon the authority of the crown in Parliament.

But to return to considerations which are of more immediate concern at the present time. Whatever may be the general character of the next Reform Bill, one thing is certain, namely, that it will result sooner or later in the disfranchisement of the few remaining small boroughs, and their absorption into larger constituencies. The disastrous consequences of any such change may be easily inferred from the explanations already given as to the assistance rendered by the small boroughs to the work of parliamentary government. It is already but too evident that the weak point in our political system is the feebleness of executive authority. Mr. Pitt foresaw what is now happening when he said, 'the part of our constitution which will first perish is the prerogative of the king, and the authority of the House of Peers;'[d] and Mr. Disraeli has observed, with equal truth, that 'in this age the elements of governing are daily diminishing, the power of governing nations is every day weakening.'[e] Anticipating,

---

[b] See Fraser's Magazine for August, 1865, p. 158.

[c] For a careful statement of the main arguments against any further reform of Parliament, in a decidedly democratic direction,—pointing out the probable effects of certain specific changes, and showing how a deterioration in the House of Commons would necessarily re-act upon the national character,— see Professor Austin's Plea for the Constitution, London, 1859, pp. 10–42. See also Report of the Lords' Committee, in 1860, upon the probable result of a reduction of the franchise; Mr. Horsman's speech, Hans. Deb. vol. clix. p. 1574; and for an exposure of the revolutionary aims openly avowed by the acknowledged organs of the working classes at the present time, see an article in the Quarterly Review for January, 1866, on 'The Coming Session.'

[d] Stanhope's Life of Pitt, vol. i. p. 133. And see Sir R. Peel's remarks on the effects of the Reform Bill, Hans Deb. vol. clxxxii. p. 1050.

[e] Hans. Deb. vol. clxx. p. 430.

therefore, that the growing demand for a further reform of Parliament must speedily be granted, and that this will inevitably lead to further democratic encroachment, it should be the endeavour of practical statesmen to devise some plan to strengthen the authority of the ministers of the crown in Parliament *pari passu* with the concession of a reformed and extended franchise. But such an attempt, to be successful, must be urged upon proper grounds. It should distinctly claim for the monarchical and aristocratic elements in our constitution as their right, that they should be adequately represented in that branch of the legislature which has now become the source and centre of political power. No considerations of mere expediency would warrant the recognition of such a demand. No attempt to increase the authority of the crown in the House of Commons merely because it was abstractedly desirable, would be likely to succeed. But if it could be shown that—unless we are willing to admit the right of the crown, and of the landed gentry, to a proportionate influence in the councils of the reformed popular assembly—we must be prepared to acquiesce in the curtailment of their just share in the control of public affairs, in the overthrow of the principles of English constitutional monarchy, and in the virtual establishment of a democratic form of government, the bulk of the nation would, it is presumed, be prompt to acknowledge the justice of such a concession, and to discern in it, moreover, a reasonable solution of a great political problem.

Necessity for conserving the monarchical and aristocratic elements in our constitution.

Thus far, we have seen, the landed proprietors of England, the natural guardians of law and order, have no cause to complain of being inadequately represented in the House of Commons. It is true that, since the Reform Bill of 1832, the landed interest is no longer supreme; and that the commercial and manufacturing interests have acquired a share of power, to which, by their growth and development, they had become justly entitled. But although, by this great measure, the House of Commons became a truer representation of the people, the groundwork of our electoral system was not changed. And so long as property is acknowledged to be the rightful basis of representation, there is no fear but that the aristocratic element in our constitution will be duly conserved. But should ever the theory of representation according to population find favour and acceptance, the influence of the aristocracy in the Commons' House of Parliament will be materially diminished, if not altogether annihilated.[f] This contingency, indeed, has not yet arrived; but the danger is so imminent, and the practical difficulties of government are so increasingly apparent, that our statesmen are becoming impressed with the necessity for strengthening the authority of the crown in Parliament, in connection with any further extension of Reform.

<small>Earl Grey's suggestions on this behalf.</small>

In a new edition of his admirable essay on 'Parliamentary Government,' which has recently appeared, Earl Grey has examined this question with much acuteness and sagacity. Without referring to the theory propounded by Professor Park, and apparently in ignorance of it, his lordship has nevertheless proposed, in his suggestions for a new Reform Bill, certain constitutional changes bearing upon this subject, which only lack the authority they would derive from a recognition of the claims of the crown and the nobles to a legitimate influence in the House of Commons, to entitle them to the highest consideration.

After a thorough practical discussion of the growing

---

[f] In a paper read by Professor Leone Levi, before the British Association, in September 1865, on the Statistics of Representation, it is computed that if representation in England were based upon population, 'for every 100 votes there should be given 4 to the upper, 32 to the middle, and 64 to the working classes. If, on the other hand, it were in proportion to the amount of taxes paid by each, of every 100 votes 83 should be given to the upper classes, 13 to the middle, and 4 to the working classes.' This will afford some idea of the vast social revolution which would be effected by the introduction of representation according to population into the electoral system of England.

evils attending the present working of parliamentary government,—owing to the weakness of executive authority, and the increase of democratic ascendancy in the House of Commons,—Earl Grey proceeds to show that if the representation is enlarged, by admitting any considerable number of the working classes into the constituency, it will be necessary to guard against the dangers that may be apprehended from such a step; and more especially from the probable result of disfranchising the few remaining nomination boroughs, which, he asserts, have 'answered purposes of the highest importance in our constitution.'[a] In connection with any further measure of parliamentary reform, his lordship contends that provision should be made,—1. For the representation of minorities; 2. For the apportionment of a certain number of seats in the House of Commons to members representing universities, the learned professions, and the principal industries and trades; 3. For the election by the House itself, of from twelve to fifteen *life members*, to be chosen by a 'cumulative vote,'[b] in batches of three at a time, from amongst the leading men of different political parties; 4. For the election, by the House, at the commencement of every Parliament, and for the duration of the Parliament, of a limited number of persons, to be proposed for membership in a list which should be framed and submitted to the House by the existing administration. This would afford an opportunity for the introduction into political life of young men of talent, who could be trained for the future service of the state; it would provide seats for such holders of political offices as were required to be

---

[a] Grey, Parl. Govt. p. 106.
[b] By a 'cumulative vote' is meant the principle of giving to every elector as many votes as there are members to be chosen by the constituent body, with the option of giving all his votes to a single candidate, or of dividing them amongst the several candidates proposed. By this process minorities would have a fair opportunity of ensuring the election of their favourite men. This mode of voting has received the approval of Mr. J. Stuart Mill. (See his Rep. Govt. p. 141.) It has also obtained the qualified support of Earl Russell—Eng. Const. Introd. p. li. And see Earl Grey's Parl. Govt. p. 280.

present in the House of Commons, but could not otherwise find entrance therein; and it would confer upon the ministry the inestimable benefit of a compact body of staunch supporters, who, while they contributed to uphold the authority of the crown, were themselves approved of by the suffrages of the House of Commons. The selection of this class of members being made by lists, a majority of the House, acting in concert, would have the power of naming the whole; and the lists being presented for the sanction of the House by ministers, the agreement thereto would be a question of confidence. Finally, his lordship proposes that members of the House accepting parliamentary offices should be relieved from the necessity of being re-elected by their respective constituencies.[1]

<small>Objections to Earl Grey's proposals.</small>

The acknowledged reputation of Earl Grey as a political philosopher, and his practical experience in the art of government, demand for these suggestions a respectful consideration. At the same time, it is worthy of remark, that other men, whose opinions are equally entitled to respect, have differed from him in regard to certain portions of his scheme. Thus, Professor Austin strenuously denounces the introduction of an electoral qualification consisting in the mere possession of intelligence and knowledge, apart from property.[2] Earl Russell contends that a graduated franchise—as a means of 'averting the dangers of universal suffrage, and of unlimited democracy,' would be an 'invidious' novelty.[3] And the *Saturday Reviewer* protests against the 'elaborate complications of electoral machinery which are recommended by Lord Grey and Mr. Hare, in order to afford artificial protection to the minority, as being fit only to serve as intellectual amusements;' declaring with great justice

---

[1] Grey, Parl. Govt. pp. 204–240.
[2] Plea for the Constitution, pp. 21, 22. And see some pithy remarks to the same effect in Henry Drummond's Letter to Mr. Bright (London, 1858), p. 35.
[3] On the English Govt. new ed. p. li.

that 'the minority is more or less effectually protected at present by the limitations of the franchise, by the dissimilarity of different constituencies, and by their great inequality in numbers.'¹ This, indeed, is undeniable, so long as the interests of the minority continue to be secured indirectly and unconsciously by the number and variety of the constituencies into which the electoral body is divided; but in proportion as constituencies become homogeneous, and approach to one uniform standard, the necessity of some direct provision for the representation of minorities will undoubtedly be felt.²

But these objections are only aimed at those recommendations of Earl Grey which are designed to create a counterpoise to the diminution of aristocratic or territorial influence in the House of Commons, which must inevitably follow from any extensive measure of parliamentary reform; they do not at all affect the integrity of his plan for obtaining a moderate increase of the power of ministers in Parliament, which he declares has already become 'a matter of urgent necessity.'³ 'Our constitution brings the whole conduct of the government under the

His plan for increasing the strength of ministers in Parliament.

---

¹ Saturday Review, February 25, 1865. The objections to the principle of the representation of minorities are very admirably put in a paper by Mr. J. Boyd Kinnear, in the Fortnightly Review for February 15, 1866, p. 40, &c. And see the weighty arguments against the system proposed, by Mr. Hare and Mr. Mill, of 'plurality of votes,' by which the several classes of society should exercise a power proportional to their station in life, and their education, in the Edinb. Review for July, 1865, p. 277. On the other hand, the argument in favour of plural votes is ably stated in Fraser's Magazine for August, 1865, p. 145.

² See a valuable article in Fraser's Magazine for August, 1865, p. 155.

³ In the new edition of his Essay, his lordship has pointed out with great force and clearness the growing evils arising from the want of sufficient power in the House of Commons on the part of Ministers. Parl. Govt. pp. 99-104, 220-220, 232. The subject may be further illustrated by an anecdote which was told by Lord Brougham in the House of Lords, in 1847. In conversation with Bishop Burnet, King William III. once remarked that he had no very clear opinion whether a monarchical or a republican form of government was the best; for he saw many reasons in favour of both. 'But,' said his Majesty, 'I am quite sure which of all governments is the worst, and that is a monarchy without due power vested in the executive; anything is better than that.' 'So say I,' added Lord Brougham, 'of an impotent ministry; give me any ministry rather than that.' Hans. Deb. vol. ci. p. 814.

virtual control of the House of Commons: unless therefore ministers, as its leaders, are enabled to exercise in that chamber an authority that cannot easily be shaken, and to command a majority on all ordinary occasions, it is obvious that the policy of the government must fall under the direction of a fluctuating majority of the House; and their measures will necessarily be ruled by popular passion and feeling, instead of by reason and prudence.' For the requirements of government continually demand the aid of legislation; whether for the grant of money, or for the amelioration of existing institutions. A strong government, enjoying the confidence of Parliament, is able to rely upon its concurrence in all acts which may be deemed advisable for the public good. But if those who have been entrusted with the administration of public affairs are unable to control the legislation of Parliament, so as to bring it into unison with their own policy, good and stable government will be impossible. In such a case, 'the law-makers and tax-imposers are sure to quarrel with the tax-requirers.' The executive is crippled by not getting the laws it needs, or the money it wants; and becomes unfit for its name, since it cannot execute what it may decide upon: while the legislature becomes demoralized, by attempting to assume the reins of government without being itself responsible for the consequences of its own acts, and by venturing to intrude upon matters which are beyond its province to determine.* But where the balance of power between the component parts of the supreme authority is duly preserved, these evils will have no existence. Parliament, on the one hand, will be able to fulfil its proper function, of exercising a vigilant control over every act of administration, and being prompt to interpose upon every occasion of abuse or misgovernment; and, on the other hand,

Evils resulting from a weak ministry.

Benefits of a stable administration.

---

* See Bagehot on the English Constitution, Fortnightly Review for May 15, 1865, p. 13, and for March 15, 1866, p. 263. For examples of the increasing weakness of the executive in the House of Commons, see Hans. Deb. vol. clxxxii. pp. 158, 2168.

the responsible servants of the crown, while always dependent upon an enlightened public opinion for the approval of their conduct, and subject to dismissal if they fail to secure the confidence of Parliament in their general policy, will nevertheless, so long as they retain that confidence, be in possession of 'sufficient power to act according to their own deliberate judgment, instead of being compelled to follow the shifting currents of the popular will.'[y]

This has been the practical working of parliamentary government in England, at least until the present day, when we are beginning to experience the injurious effects of weak administrations. A result so excellent, however, has not been attained without considerable alloy. In the gradual development of the constitution, the separate rights of other estates of the realm, which have become absorbed into the House of Commons, have only been preserved by means of anomalous and corrupt practices and departures from principle in our representative system, which no one would willingly see perpetuated.[z] In the event of Earl Grey's suggestions for preserving the just weight and influence of the crown in a reformed legislature being approved by Parliament, the necessity for continuing a system which, while it is admirable in practice, is nevertheless open to such serious objections, would be done away with, and the full benefits of an equitable parliamentary government could be secured with the sanction and authority of law.

Under the altered circumstances herein contemplated, it is probable that as a general rule the sovereign would select her leading ministers in the House of Commons either from the life members, or from amongst the members chosen by the House at the commencement of every Parliament. This would be very preferable to the plan that has been suggested by some writers, of authorising

Ministers in the House of Commons.

---
[y] Grey, Parl. Govt. pp. 236, 238.   [z] See Park's Dogmas, p. 50.

Ought not to sit ex-officio.

ministers, who are required by the public service to have seats in the House of Commons, to sit in that assembly by virtue of their offices. Such an arrangement, however convenient, would be a great innovation upon the acknowledged principles of the constitution, and might occasion very serious consequences. By ceasing to combine the character of member of Parliament with that of servant of the crown, and holding their seats in the latter capacity only, much misapprehension as to the true position of ministers would naturally be engendered. It might appear as though the crown, whom alone they professed to represent, was a power apart from, if not antagonistic to the legislature. The prevalence of any such idea would materially jeopardise the harmonious action of the three branches of Parliament.*

It now only remains to point out the position occupied by the Houses of Lords and Commons, respectively, in the English political system.

Influence of county families.

The Revolution of 1688 placed the control of the government of England in the hands of the great county families; and from that period until 1832 the power of the peerage was immense. This power was exercised, however, not so much in their own Chamber as indirectly towards the sovereign, and over the county and borough elections. Their influence at court, and their authority as landed proprietors in the constituencies, generally made them virtually supreme over every successive administration. Consequently, the fate of a cabinet was virtually determined by the relative strength of the rival factions into which the leading families of England were divided. But the Reform Bill of 1832 deprived them of the greater portion of this power, and transferred it to the middle class. The landed interest is still, indeed, very influential in the House of Commons, but it is no longer dominant,

---

* See Austin's Plea for the Constitution, p. 2d, n.; also the opinions of the first Earl Grey and of Lord Althorp to the same effect, Hans. Deb. vol. cxlvii. p. 603; and Bagehot, in Fortnightly Rev., vol. vi. p. 51d.

as heretofore. The commercial and manufacturing interests, which have attained to such enormous magnitude within the present century, now possess their due share of political power.

In their own House, however, the Lords continue to exercise the just weight and influence which belong to them, not only as representing the great bulk of the landed property of the kingdom, but on account of the high personal qualities for which, as a class, they are eminently distinguished. For cultivation, refinement, moral worth, active and intelligent interest in the welfare of those dependent upon them, and for general sympathy in the progress of the whole community, the aristocracy of England will favourably compare with that of every other nation in Christendom.¹ As an independent branch of the legislature, they undoubtedly possess a very substantial power, which serves as a positive check upon the Lower House when it has been induced to act with unwise precipitation.²

Position of the House of Lords.

But the increasing importance of the House of Commons, since the establishment of parliamentary government, has materially modified the relations between the two Chambers, and lessened the authority which theoretically appertains to the House of Lords as a co-ordinate and co-equal branch of the imperial legislature. Though entitled, equally with the Commons, to express their opinion upon all acts of administration, and their approval or otherwise of the general conduct or policy of the cabinet, they are powerless, by their vote, to support or overthrow a ministry against the will of the House of Commons. 'To place upon the House of Lords the weight and responsibility of controlling the executive government of this country, would soon put that House in a position which they have never hitherto occupied, and which they could not safely maintain.'³ Nevertheless, the

---

¹ See Hans. Deb. vol. cxliii. p. 600; vol. clix. p. 1571; also ibid. vol. clxli. p. 2137.
² See Grey, Parl. Govt. p. 64.
³ Lord John Russell, in Hans. Deb. vol. cxii. p. 105.

censure of the policy of a government by the House of Lords is 'a matter of very great importance,' and can only be c unterbalanced by the formal approval of the same policy by the House of Commons.' It is true that the Grey ministry resigned, in 1832, in consequence of the rejection of the Reform Bill by the House of Lords; but this was an instance of parliamentary obstruction to a measure of vital importance, which the administration had pledged themselves to carry through the legislature. After an ineffectual attempt to form a new ministry, the former cabinet was reinstated in office, and succeeded in obtaining the consent of the Lords to their measure of reform.

The Lords seldom initiate legislation. In the fulfilment of their legislative functions, the Lords have long ceased to take the initiative in the introduction of great public measures. Bills which concern the improvement of the law, and certain private Bills of a semi-judicial character, appropriately commence with the Lords; and recently it has been arranged that a fair proportion of ordinary private Bills shall be first introduced in the Upper House, with a view to facilitate the despatch of private business. But as a general rule, the Commons are not disposed to receive very favourably Bills which do not originate with themselves. The province of the House of Lords appears more properly to be that of controlling, revising, and amending the projects of legislation which emanate from the House of Commons. In the discharge of this onerous and important duty the House of Lords have maintained their independence, and vindicated their responsible position as a branch of the legis-

---

* Lord John Russell, in Hans. Deb. vol. cxii. p. 105; May, Const. Hist. vol. i. p. 467. See precedents: Mirror of Parlt. 1830, pp. 1705, 1737, 1803; Hans. Deb. (Lords) August 24, 1841; Hans. Deb. (1850) vol. cxii. pp. 105, 634, 721; censure of foreign policy of ministers by the Lords, on July 8, 1864; a similar vote of censure proposed in the Commons on July 4, negatived July 8, 1864.

* May, Parl. Prac. ed. 1863, p. 603.

* See Lords' Debates, in Hans. vol. cxix. pp. 246, 517; Lord Derby's opinion, ibid. vol. xcvii. p. 833; vol. clix. p. 2130; vol. clxi. p. 182. And see Bagehot, in Fortnightly Review, Feb. 1, 1866, pp. 604, 607.

lature. Witness their successful defence of the revenues of the Irish Church, their valuable amendments to the Municipal Corporations Bill, their protracted resistance to the introduction of Jews into Parliament, and their spirited opposition to the repeal of the Paper Duty.⁷ A second Chamber, independent of popular election, active, vigilant, and powerful, is, indeed, of vital necessity to a well-regulated state.⁸ And it is generally conceded by the best political writers, that whatever may be the theoretical objections to the constitution of the House of Lords, it has fulfilled the functions which belong to an Upper Chamber of the legislature with signal and singular success.⁹ In fact, 'as a legislative body, the Lords have great facilities for estimating the direction and strength of public opinion. Nearly every measure has been fully discussed before they are called upon to consider it. Hence they are enabled to judge, at leisure, of its merits, its defects, and its popularity. If the people are indifferent to its merits, they can safely reject it altogether; if too popular, in principle, to be so dealt with, they may qualify, and perhaps neutralise it, by amendments, without any shock to public feeling. At the same time, they are able, by their debates, to exercise an extensive influence upon the convictions of the people. Sitting like a court of review upon measures originating in the Lower House, they can select from the whole armoury of debate and public discussion the best arguments, and the most effective appeals, to enlightened minds.'¹⁰ It may be regarded, however, as a settled constitutional principle, which has been endorsed by the highest authority, that it is not the duty of the House of Lords to continue a persistent oppo-

<small>Important services of the House of Lords.</small>

---

⁷ See May, Const. Hist. vol. 1. p. 204.

⁸ The arguments in favour of two legislative chambers have been ably stated in Creasy's Eng. Const. p. 198; and Mill, Rep. Govt. c. 13, Of a Second Chamber. See also the debates in Parliament on the Australian Government Bill, in 1850; and in the House of Commons on the New Zealand Constitution, June 4, 1852.

⁹ Grey, Parl. Govt. p. 64.

¹⁰ May, Const. Hist. vol. i. p. 203.

sition to measures that have been repeatedly passed by the House of Commons with large and increasing majorities; especially when public opinion out of doors has been unmistakeably expressed to the same effect.*

Culpable indifference of the Peers to their legislative duties.

A serious defect has been noted in the conduct of the great majority of the hereditary peers of England, and one which has seriously impaired, if not endangered, their political influence, namely, their indifference to the discharge of their legislative duties. The quorum of the House of Lords is but three, a number palpably inadequate for a numerous deliberative assembly, and the average attendance of peers is very incommensurate with the number of those whose privilege it is to take part in the proceedings of this august body.* But with such a large proportion of members who are fitted by natural gifts, high cultivation, and political experience acquired in other fields of labour for a parliamentary career, there is no reason why the House of Lords, if sufficiently alive to their responsibilities, should not possess and permanently retain the confidence of the nation, as an essential part of the legislature, and a main safeguard of constitutional liberty.

Position of the House of Commons.

But ever since the days of Walpole, the House of Commons have been steadily gaining political ascendancy. Nominally co-equal with the crown and the Lords, as a constituent part of the legislature, they have gradually attained to a position which enables them to compel the adoption, sooner or later, of any policy, or any legislative measure, upon which they are agreed. Witness the Roman Catholic Emancipation Act, which was carried against the deliberate will of George IV., the Reform Act, the repeal of the Corn Laws, and the Jewish Oaths Bill, against the deliberate will of the House of Lords.

---

* Lord Stanley (Earl of Derby) on Free Trade, Hans. Deb. vol. lxxxvi. p. 1175; Earls Grey and Lyndhurst on the Jewish Oaths Bill, *ibid.* vol. cxlix. pp. 1421, 1771; and see Mr. Horsman's speech, *ibid.* vol. clix. p. 1573; Creasy, Eng. Const. p. 380.

* See May, Const. Hist. vol. i. p. 269; Saturday Review, August 5, 1861; Hans. Deb. vol. clxxx. p. 1031.

These, and other important acts of legislation, though disapproved of either by the crown or by the Peers, were nevertheless acquiesced in by them, to avert more serious consequences. Again, it devolves upon the House of Commons practically to determine in whose hands the government of the country shall be placed. By giving their confidence to one party and by refusing it to another, by extending it to certain men and refusing it to certain other men, they plainly intimate to the sovereign the statesmen who should be selected to conduct the administration of public affairs, and to advise the crown in the exercise of its high prerogatives.* In 1835, William IV. was compelled to accept the resignation of Sir Robert Peel, who, at the earnest solicitation of the king, had attempted to carry on the government, and to recall to his councils the Melbourne administration, which he had previously summarily dismissed, on account of the inability of Sir Robert Peel to obtain the confidence of the House of Commons. In deciding the fate of a ministry, the House of Lords, we have already seen,† are practically powerless. The Grey Ministry (in 1830—1834), which was remarkably strong both at home and abroad, was throughout opposed in the Lords by a decided and constantly increasing majority. On the other hand, the Derby administrations, in 1852 and 1858, though approved and sustained in the Upper House, were speedily broken up because they could not command a majority in the Commons. And the Palmerston ministry in 1864, when their foreign policy was censured by the House of Lords, were able to set at nought this hostile vote, in consequence of obtaining a small majority, upon a similar question, in the Lower House. These examples are sufficient to prove the great and preponderating authority of the House of Commons. That this authority has not been abused, is due to the spirit of moderation which has generally pervaded the councils of that assembly, and also

They decide the fate of ministers.

---

* Russell, Eng. Const. new ed. p. xlviii.   † *Ante*, p. 27.

to the legitimate influence of the crown and of the hereditary aristocracy, which, happily for the equilibrium of the constitution, still finds expression within its walls.

These preliminary observations upon the system of parliamentary government in England will, it is hoped, afford some idea of its true character, and serve to explain the chief points of contrast between our modern political institutions and those which were in operation prior to the Revolution of 1688.

Parliamentary government.

It must be evident to the student of history, that parliamentary government is no recent political device, but that it owes its origin to the growth of foundation principles in the English constitution; and that the transition, from the ancient method of government by prerogative to that which now prevails, has been a gradual and legitimate development. Whether the modern system is, in every respect, the most perfect or the best adapted to the wants and wishes of the nation, it is not the object of the present writer to inquire. He is not concerned with the special advocacy of any particular form of government; but it has been his aim to describe the actual working of representative institutions in England as they now exist. He has not refrained from noticing, as opportunity offered, the peculiar defects of parliamentary government, and the dangers to which he conceives that system to be exposed. On the other hand, he is bound in fairness to point out its peculiar merits and advantages, whereby it has become so popular at home, and a model for imitation in so many countries abroad. These advantages have been admirably stated by Rowlands, in his work on the English Constitution, in the following terms:—

Its peculiar advantages.

The value [of parliamentary government] in bringing the monarchy into unison with the freedom demanded and obtained by the other institutions of the government and by the people, cannot be too highly estimated. It has changed the vague, precarious, and irresponsible authority of the ancient monarchs for an executive council, nominated by the monarch from the peers and representatives of the people, but acting under the direct influence of the House of Commons, and accountable there for all its proceedings. It has relieved the king from the burden, and from the moral as well as actual responsibility, of directing or conducting the state affairs; and whilst he retains his high position as chief of the state, and the power of impressing his views of government on his ministers when in office, and of selecting new ministers when a change is required, he is not involved in the fluctuating fortunes of the rival statesmen who from time to time become his servants as ministers of the crown. With respect to the people, it has opened the road to the highest offices of the state to the ambition of all who can raise themselves to distinction in the House of Commons; and thus it places political power of the highest order in the most eminent and distinguished of the people themselves.[a]

To this it should be added, that in times of difficulty a parliamentary constitution possesses additional advantages over every other form of government. If the statesman at the helm should prove deficient in vigour or sagacity, upon emergencies arising that were not contemplated when he was originally placed in office, he can be promptly removed, and replaced by one more fitted for the occasion; and this can be effected, through the interposition of Parliament, without the necessity for resorting to any extreme measures, and without disturbing the ordinary course of public affairs.[b]

As a suitable introduction to the more practical part of this treatise, it is proposed, in the two following chapters, to give a brief outline of the leading events in the annals of England which tend to elucidate the origin and progress of our present political institutions; together with a summary of the constitutional history of the successive administrations of England from 1782 to our own day.

Subjects embraced in this treatise.

---

[a] Rowlands, Eng. Const. p. 438. See further, as to the advantages of parliamentary government over the system which it superseded, Grey, Parl. Govt. p. 314.

[b] Thus, upon the sudden crisis of the Crimean War, and as the result of parliamentary interposition, the respectable but too pacific premier Lord Aberdeen was compelled to give place to Lord Palmerston, in whom the nation had confidence as a vigorous war minister. It was said of the House of Commons, on this occasion, that they had 'turned out the Quaker, and put in the pugilist.'—*Bagehot on the Cabinet, Fortnightly Review*, No. I, p. 20.

We shall next consider the precise position of the sovereign in relation to parliamentary government. The leading prerogatives of the crown will be then separately reviewed, and the limits of the control which may be rightfully exercised by the two Houses of Parliament over the administration of the same, by responsible servants of the crown, will be explained and illustrated. The origin, history, and duties of the cabinet council, and the political functions of the several members who compose the administration, will next engage our attention. Finally, the duties which devolve upon members of the government, in the conduct of public business in Parliament, will be briefly described.

In treating upon the various and important questions contained in this work, due regard will be paid to the recorded opinions of eminent statesmen who have spent their lives in the practical exposition of our parliamentary system; and numerous precedents will be adduced, at every stage of the inquiry, not merely to corroborate the doctrine advanced in the text, but to illustrate the manner in which the principles and practices of parliamentary government have been gradually developed, and become incorporated as recognised parts of the British constitution.

HISTORICAL INTRODUCTION.

PART I.

CHAPTER I.

THE ORIGIN AND PROGRESS OF PARLIAMENTARY GOVERNMENT.

In the compilation of this chapter, the author would disclaim any pretensions to originality or research. The circumstances which gave rise to the existing political institutions of England have been thoroughly investigated by Hallam, Macaulay, May, and other authors of established reputation. No account of these events can be complete which does not mainly rely upon the facts elicited, and the conclusions arrived at, by these able commentators. It has therefore seemed preferable to the present writer, when, in the course of the following pages, he has occasion to avail himself of the labours of his predecessors, to quote their own words, rather than to attempt to rewrite the narrative, in phrases less accurate and perspicuous.

It was customary with the older writers upon the constitution of England to trace the rise of our representative system to the institutions which existed amongst the Anglo-Saxons; but the elaborate researches of Palgrave, Sir James Mackintosh, Hallam, Sir W. Betham, and of the learned men to whom we owe the Reports of the Committees of the House of Lords upon the Dignity of a Peer of the Realm, have shown this to be a fallacy. The Anglo-Saxons undoubtedly possessed a well-ordered government, which afforded to the people a large amount of personal liberty. Their local assemblies were, in

Rise of our representative system.

theory at least, extremely democratic; but 'there is no trace among the Anglo-Saxons, either of representative commoners or of a peerage like the modern.'*

Without entering into the difficult question of the origin of the English Parliament, it may suffice to state the general result arrived at by the labours of the learned writers above mentioned, that prior to the reign of Henry III., although the sovereign occasionally convened councils and asked their advice, which he followed or not, as he thought fit, there existed no deliberative legislative assembly in England, and that it was not until the fifteenth year of the reign of Edward II. that it was declared and enacted that the legislative authority of the realm should be in the king, with the advice and consent of the lords spiritual and temporal and commons in Parliament assembled. 'This may be considered,' says Sir William Betham, 'the first successful and effectual attempt to settle a free constitutional government. The assembly was afterwards modified from time to time until the reign of Henry IV., about which time it obtained the division into two distinct Houses, as it has since continued.'*

Government by prerogative.
During this period, and more or less until the epoch of the Revolution of 1688, the government of the country was carried on by virtue of the king's prerogative. So long as the House of Commons was merely regarded as a machine for granting money, with no substantial voice in general legislation, or the conduct of public affairs, the will of the monarch was supreme, if not indisputable. The ordinary revenues of the crown, irrespective of parliamentary supplies, sufficed for its customary expenditure, and it was only when more money was wanted, for extraordinary purposes, that it became necessary to apply to Parliament. When a meeting of Parliament took

---
* Mackintosh, Hist. of England, vol. i. p. 75; Park's Lectures, pp. 64-78
* Betham, Feudal and Parl. Dignities, pp. 11-13.

place, the influence of the king and his nobles was generally paramount. If grievances could not otherwise be redressed, a grant of supply, conditional upon their removal, had to be resorted to. This method, though often effectual, occasionally led to collisions between the crown and Parliament. Until the reign of Henry VIII. or Elizabeth, this was the practical shape of the English political system, the king, the Lords, and the Commons each acting upon their own view of their peculiar interests. The contest between Charles I. and his Parliament was an indication of a coming change. During that memorable struggle for pre-eminence, the king took his stand upon his prerogative, while the Commons, who had begun to appreciate their power, contended for popular rights. Various attempts were made by the king to win over to his cause his most formidable opponents in the House of Commons, but he had not discovered the secret of making them his ministers, and using them as the channels of his influence, while they continued to retain the confidence of their own party. Charles I. never promoted any parliamentary leader to office until he had lost all power and popularity amongst his former associates by an avowed desertion to the separate party of the king. Consequently, these attempts proved wholly unavailing to bring about a cordial co-operation between the crown and the Commons, and the terrible catastrophe of the downfall of the monarchy naturally ensued.* But it is a remarkable circumstance, that in the Grand Remonstrance, which was addressed by the House of Commons to Charles I. in 1641, the principle of ministerial responsibility is distinctly referred to, as a method of conciliating the favour of Parliament, and of protecting the king from evil counsellors. It was proposed in this able document that thenceforth such counsellors, ambassadors, and other

Government by the Stuart kings.

Origin of ministerial responsibility.

---

* Edinb. Review, vol. xiv. p. 300, &c.

ministers only should be employed as were able to retain the confidence of Parliament.[d] The king, however, had previously declared that he would neither separate the obedience of his servants from his own acts, nor suffer them to be punished for executing his commands.[e] Conciliation, therefore, was impossible, and both king and Parliament were driven to the commission of violent and unwarrantable deeds.

The restoration of the monarchy under Charles II. was too hastily effected to admit of needful constitutional restrictions being imposed, to prevent the recurrence of former grievances. Accordingly, during the reigns of Charles II. and James II. the nation was continually suffering under, or struggling against, the exercise of the king's prerogative—against the claim, on the part of the king, to an indefensible right of power, neither responsible nor to be resisted, and from the effects of which there was no legal remedy.[f]

Control of the Commons over the supplies.

Meanwhile, the influence of the House of Commons began to make itself felt in matters heretofore presumed to be beyond the jurisdiction of Parliament. It was during the Long Parliament (temp. Charles II. 1661-1679) that the practice of appropriating the supplies granted to the crown to distinct and specific services was first introduced. This was not accomplished without difficulty. Clarendon and the old court party inveighed against it as an invention derogatory to the honour of the crown; but the king himself acquiesced in the views of the Commons, considering it the most likely way of ensuring their ready compliance with his demands. On a later occasion, however, the unworthy House of Commons that sat in 1685, not content with a needless augmentation of the revenue, took credit with the king for not having appropriated the supplies. But from the Revolu-

---

[d] See Forster's Debates on the Grand Remonstrance, pp. 272, 273.
[e] Campbell's Chancellors, vol. ii. p. 532.
[f] Coxe's Walpole (Pownall's Paper), vol. iii. p. 610.

tion, the system of appropriation was made a regular part of the scheme of government, which was then established for the better securing the rights, liberties, and privileges of the English nation. Once recognised as an undisputed principle, the appropriation of the supplies necessarily led to the preparation by the crown of estimates of the sums required, and of the services to which it was proposed to apply the same. Thus the House of Commons succeeded in obtaining, not merely a general control over the public revenues, but an authoritative voice in respect to the details of public expenditure.*

In reviewing the character and conduct of the Sovereigns of the houses of Tudor and Stuart, Hallam remarks that they were the master movers of their own policy, albeit not always with as much ability as diligence; that they were not very susceptible of advice, but always sufficiently acquainted with the details of government to act without it.^b In a word, they ruled by virtue of their prerogative, and with the aid of ministers of state who had no necessary connection with Parliament, and were only amenable thereto for high crimes and misdemeanors.^c Hence arose frequent altercations and struggles between the crown and Parliament, which sometimes could only be decided by an appeal to the sword. Although, in the main, the people were contented and prosperous, and the great principles of constitutional liberty continued to advance, yet the security for the public welfare depended too much upon the personal character of the monarch, and his ability to rule with foresight and beneficence. Herein consisted the peculiar weakness of government by prerogative. When the exercise of the royal authority fell into bad hands, or irreconcilable differences arose between the crown and the Parliament, there was no adequate security against misrule,

Weakness of prerogative government.

---

^a Park's Dogmas, Lecture XIII. p. 388. Hatsell, vol. III p. 202.   ^b Park's Dogmas, p. 41.
^c Hallam, Const. Hist. vol. iii.

and no remedy to prevent national discontent from fermenting into open rebellion. Two revolutions within the space of half a century, and a dynasty of kings sent into permanent exile for the continued infraction of popular rights, proved the necessity for a vital change in the practice, if not in the theory of the constitution.

Revolution of 1688.
Upon the occurrence of the Revolution of 1688, the attention of the most eminent statesmen was directed to the endeavour to bring the executive and legislative powers into more harmonious action. This was mainly effected by a more distinct recognition than heretofore of the doctrine of ministerial responsibility to Parliament. But it was only by slow degrees, and as the result of political experience painfully acquired on all sides, that this doctrine became fully accepted.

Meaning of the maxim 'the king can do no wrong.'
It has always been a leading maxim of the British constitution that 'the king can do no wrong.'[a] He is to be accounted as responsible to God alone for the righteous exercise of authority over the people of his realm. It is not meant by this doctrine that the king is above the laws, and that all his acts are necessarily just and right. As an individual he is independent of, and not amenable to, any earthly power or jurisdiction; but all his acts are, nevertheless, controlled by the law; and 'the body politic is reared upon the basis, that the law is above the head of the state, and not the head of the state above the law.'[b] The maxim that 'the king can do no wrong,' while it sounds like a moral paradox, is, in fact, but the form of expressing a great constitutional principle, that no mismanagement in government is imputable to the sovereign personally; whilst, on the other hand, it is equally true, that no wrong can be done to the people for which the constitution does not provide a remedy."[c]

---

[a] See Bowyer, Const. Law, p. 130; Broom's Legal Maxims, p. 40. And Maurice's paper, Do Kings reign by the Grace of God? in Tracts for Priests and People, second series, p. 85.

[b] See Smith's Parl. Remembrancer, 1801, pp. 197-200.

[c] See Amos, English Constitution in the Reign of Charles II. pp. 11-10; Cox, Eng. Govt. p. 416.

These seeming anomalies are reconciled by the important axiom that the king can perform no act of government of himself, but that all acts of the crown must be presumed to have been done by some minister responsible to parliament." This principle, now so well understood, was not recognised in its entirety until a comparatively recent period; for while it is a necessary corollary from the principles of government established by the Revolution of 1688, we find it first asserted, without exception or qualification, in the reign of George II.[b] At the same time, it has always been acknowledged, with more or less distinctness, that the king's ministers were answerable for all acts of government that could in any way be traced to their advice or co-operation. Either by parliamentary censure, or impeachment, or by ordinary process of law, unworthy ministers have, from a very early period, been called to account for complicity in acts of misgovernment. But this mode of redress was invariably doubtful and uncertain. In the days when the collective responsibility of the administration for the acts of each individual minister formed no part of the theory of government, it was not easy to ascertain upon whom to affix the responsibility for any particular offence. So long as a minister of state retained the favour of his sovereign, it was difficult, if not impossible, to convict him of misconduct, or make him amenable for misdeeds agreed upon in secret, and which were perhaps commanded by the king himself; so that opposition to a suspected favourite commonly took the shape of intrigues to displace him from power, or gave rise to open resistance to the crown itself.

Ministerial responsibility fully asserted.

---

[a] See Chap. IV. On the Sovereign.
[b] By the Duke of Argyle, in the House of Lords, in 1739; Parl. Hist. x. 1138. See Hallam, Const. Hist. iii. 315, n. And in a debate in the House of Commons, on February 13, 1741, Sir John Barnard thus expressed himself: 'The king may, it is true, exercise some of the prerogatives of the crown without asking the advice of any minister; but if he does make a wrong use of any of his prerogatives, his ministers must answer for it, if they continue to be his ministers.'—*Parl. Hist.* vol. xi. p. 1203.

The necessity for some constitutional provision to require that the advisers of the crown, through whose agency all affairs of state are conducted, should be publicly known—in order that they might be held accountable to Parliament for the advice they had given to the sovereign, and for the consequences of acts which had been brought about through their own instrumentality—

Case of the Partition Treaties. was strikingly exemplified in the case of the Partition Treaties, which occurred in 1698. The House of Commons were of opinion that these treaties were highly injurious to the public interests, and it was proposed to impeach Lord Somers, who, as Chancellor, had affixed to them the great seal. Somers, in his defence, alleged that he had opposed the treaties, but that he had put the great seal to one of them by the king's command, considering that he was bound to do so. Dissatisfied with this explanation, the Commons resolved upon his impeachment. They also determined to impeach the Earl of Portland, Lord Orford, and Lord Halifax, who, as prominent members of the administration, were held responsible for advising this objectionable measure. But it proved that these noblemen had had nothing to do with the matter, and that the treaties had been negotiated by the king himself. Lord Somers was acquitted by the House of Lords, notwithstanding the unwarrantable nature of his defence, in trusting for the justification of his conduct to the king's command; an excuse which was entirely at variance with the true principles of responsible government, and which, if recognised as sufficient, would deprive Parliament of all control over the executive administration.* The proceedings against the other members of the ministry were equally unsuccessful, it being impos-

---

* Contrast the conduct of Lord Somers in this particular with that of his successor in the chancellorship, Lord Hardwicke, who, on two occasions when required by George II. to put the great seal to conventions concluded by the sovereign himself, positively refused to do so, solely because he deemed the treaties in question to be injurious to the interests of England. See Harris's Life of Hardwicke, vol. ii. pp. 50, 323; vol. iii. p. 520.

sible to prove that they had been parties to the obnoxious treaty.* Foiled in their attempt to bring home to anyone responsibility for this act of arbitrary power, the House of Commons set about the adoption of measures to prevent a repetition of the offence. This they endeavoured to effect by the introduction of a clause into the Act of Settlement which provided, that after the accession of the House of Hanover, 'all matters relating to the well-governing of this kingdom, which are properly cognisable in the Privy Council by the laws and customs of this realm, shall be transacted there, and all resolutions taken thereupon shall be signed by such of the Privy Council as shall advise or consent to the same.' This provision was meant to compel the discussion of all state affairs in full Privy Council, and to discriminate between the responsibility of those who promoted and those who opposed each resolution, by requiring all who voted for it to sign their names thereto. It was, however, soon perceived that such a system would cause infinite delay and embarrassment in governing the kingdom; while doubtless it was also obnoxious to the ministry, who were not as yet prepared to assume such a definite responsibility, involving with it prospective anticipations of impeachment and disgrace.* Accordingly, in the following reign, before the time when it was to have come into operation, it was formally repealed.

Responsibility of Privy Councillors.

Another clause in the Act of Settlement,—which appears to have been framed in connexion with the foregoing,—declared that no pardon under the great seal should be pleadable to an impeachment by the Commons. This salutary provision still remains in force, and is calculated to increase the sense of individual responsibility of ministers. It has been interpreted by Blackstone as designed to prevent the royal pardon from being available

Impeachment of ministers.

---

* Hallam's Const. Hist. vol. iii. p. 253; Campbell's Chancellors, vol. iv. pp. 150–158.
* 12 & 13 Will. III. c. 2, § 4.
* Creasy, English Const. p. 312.
* 4 & 5 Anne, c. 8.

pending an impeachment, and in bar to its progress; but not to restrain a pardon after the conclusion of the trial."

Although the Act of Settlement proved abortive to ensure the direct accountability of the advisers of the crown to Parliament, yet that result was gradually brought about by the course of events, in a way that was quite unforeseen by the politicians and statesmen who effected the Revolution.

William III. had been summoned to the throne of England by the two Houses of Parliament, in order that he might rule as a constitutional sovereign. The rights and liberties of the subject, for infringing which King James had forfeited his crown, had been declared by Parliament in a document which was presented to the Prince of Orange upon his assumption of the government. They had afterwards been embodied in the Bill of Rights, as part of the fundamental laws of the kingdom, and the motive and condition of the revolution-settlement. The king, on his own part, was sincere in his resolve and endeavour to discharge his sacred obligations with fidelity. But owing to the natural reserve of his disposition, and his large capacity for administration, he relied much less upon the advice of his ministers than would now be expected of a constitutional king. In fact, according to the testimony of Hallam, William was eminently his own minister, and was better fitted for that office than any of those who served him.' In all domestic matters, as a general rule, he was wont to consult his ministers," and to govern through their instrumentality; but he still preserved in his own hands the supreme control. Questions of war and diplomacy, however, the king reserved to him-

* Warren's Black. Com. Abridged, p. 648.
* Hallam, vol. iii. pp. 252, 388.
* In 1701, when the reign of William III. was drawing to a close, it was made the subject of complaint by Lord Sunderland, in a letter of advice addressed to Lord Somers, that his Majesty evinced too much neglect and distrust of his cabinet; the remonstrance was summed up in these significant words: 'It would be much for the king's service if he brought his affairs to be debated at that council.'—*Parl. Hist. of Eng.* vol. iv. p. 134.

self; and his advisers, conscious that they were less versed in military and foreign affairs than their royal master, were content to leave with him the command of the army, and to know only what he thought fit to communicate about the instructions which he gave to his own ambassadors, or concerning the conferences which he held with the ambassadors of foreign princes.* We have seen the consequences of this policy in diplomatic affairs in the matter of the Partition Treaties; but so deep-seated was the conviction that military affairs were a branch of the prerogative that belonged exclusively to the king himself, that it was not until the year 1806 that it was fully conceded that the management of the army, in common with all other prerogatives, was subject to the supervision of ministers.ʸ

To William III., however, is due the credit of the formation of the first administration avowedly constructed upon the basis of party, in order that it might carry on the king's government in conformity with the general political views of the majority of the House of Commons. This ministry was composed of statesmen who had seats in one or other of the Houses of Parliament; thereby supplying a defect in the scheme of government, the want of which in the plan propounded in the Act of Settlement was sufficient to account for the failure of that projected reform. The history of this remarkable transaction, which constitutes such a memorable epoch in our political annals, is reserved for another chapter, in which it is proposed to treat, with more detail, of the origin and development of the cabinet council. Suffice it here to state, that during this reign the distinction between the cabinet and the privy council,—and the exclusion of the latter from deliberation upon all affairs of state, except of the most formal description,—was fully established, and that the king's ministers were first introduced into Parliament for

His first parliamentary administration.

---

* Macaulay, vol. v. p. 123.   ʸ May, Const. Hist. vol. i. p. 87.

the avowed purpose of explaining, defending, and carrying out the measures of government; thereby practically asserting a constitutional principle, which it was reserved for another generation to bring to maturity, that ministers are responsible to Parliament for every act of the crown in the conduct of public affairs.

<small>Hanoverian dynasty.</small>

Henceforward (to use the words of May) a succession of monarchs arose, less capable than William, and of ministers gifted with extraordinary ability and force of character, who rapidly reduced to practice the theory of ministerial responsibility. Under the sovereigns of the House of Hanover, the government of the state was conducted throughout all its departments by ministers responsible to Parliament for every act of their administration, without whose advice no act could be done, who could be dismissed for incapacity or failure, and impeached for political crimes; and who resigned when their advice was disregarded by the crown or their policy disapproved by Parliament. With ministers thus responsible, 'the king could do no wrong.' The Stuarts had strained prerogative so far that it had twice snapped asunder in their hands. They had exercised it personally, and were held personally responsible for its exercise. One had paid the penalty with his head; another with his crown; and their family had been proscribed for ever. But now, if the prerogative was strained, the ministers were condemned, and not the king. If the people cried out against the government, instead of a revolution there was merely a change of ministry. Instead of dangerous conflicts between the crown and the Parliament, there succeeded struggles between rival parties for parliamentary majorities; and the successful party wielded all the power of the state. Upon ministers, therefore, devolved the entire burthen of public affairs; they relieved the crown of its cares and perils, but, at the same time, they appropriated nearly all its authority. The king reigned, but his ministers governed.[a]

<small>The cabinet.</small>

During this period in our political history, the cabinet council began to assume a definite shape and organisation, distinct from the privy council, whose functions it had for the most part superseded; and the direct interference of the sovereign in public affairs gave way to the constitutional authority of ministers of the crown, exercised in the name and on the behalf of their royal master. These innovations upon the ancient usages of the constitution, which were none the less important because they had

---

[a] May, Const. Hist. vol. I. pp. 5, 6.

been gradually and silently effected, merit, and will hereafter obtain, a more ample consideration.*

Making use of their undoubted prerogative of selecting their own ministers, it had been customary for the sovereigns of England, anterior to the Revolution, to choose men to fill the high offices of state upon personal grounds, without regard to their general agreement upon political questions. Party as well as parliamentary government originated with William III., who, in 1696, constructed his first parliamentary ministry upon an exclusively Whig basis. But the idea was unhappily abandoned by the king in his subsequent administrations, and it was not until the House of Hanover ascended the throne that ministers were, as a general rule, exclusively selected from amongst those who were of the same political creed, or who were willing to fight under the same political banner. Queen Anne was inclined to favour the Tories, and in 1710 she authorised the appointment of a decidedly Tory ministry: upon the accession of George I., however, the Whig party obtained possession of the government, and continued for a long time to maintain the upper hand, compelling the king to sacrifice his personal inclinations in favour of their party leaders.*

The reigns of the first three Georges were characterised by the strife of rival factions to obtain possession of office, and to coerce the sovereign, by the united influence of the great families, to choose his ministers exclusively from amongst themselves. George I. and his successor succumbed to the necessity of conciliating the aristocracy, who by their wealth and territorial possessions had obtained supremacy in the councils of Parliament. But subjection to Whig control in any shape was peculiarly irksome to George III., who being naturally fond of power, determined when he became king to use his prerogative to the fullest possible extent. Accordingly, when he succeeded to the throne he immediately endea-

* See Chapter IV. on the Sovereign, and Vol. II. ch. I, on the Cabinet Council.   * May, Const. Hist. vol. i. p. 7.

voured 'to loosen the ties of party, and to break down the confederacy of the great Whig families. His desire was to undertake personally the chief administration of public affairs, to direct the policy of his ministers, and himself to distribute the patronage of the crown. He was ambitious not only to reign, but to govern. His will was strong and resolute, his courage high, and his talent for intrigue considerable. He came to the throne determined to exalt the kingly office; and throughout his long reign he never lost sight of that object.'[a] The constant aim of the king was to be, in effect, his own minister. 'When ministers not of his own choice were in office, he plotted against them and overthrew them; and when he had succeeded in establishing his friends in office, he enforced upon them the adoption of his own policy.' The king's tactics were frequently at variance with the principles of constitutional government, but credit is due to him for his conscientious and intelligent activity in the promotion of the public weal. 'That he was too fond of power for a constitutional monarch, none will now be found to deny; that he sometimes resorted to crafty expedients, unworthy of a king, even his admirers must admit. With a narrow understanding and obstinate prejudices, he was yet patriotic in his feelings, and laboured earnestly and honestly for the good government of his country. If he loved power, he did not shrink from its cares and toil. If he delighted in being the active ruler of his people, he devoted himself to affairs of state even more laboriously than his ministers. If he was jealous of the authority of the crown, he was not less jealous of the honour and greatness of his people. A just recognition of the personal merits of the king himself enables us to judge more freely of the constitutional tendency and results of his policy.'[b]

The foregoing description of George III. is taken from the first chapter of May's 'Constitutional History.' It

---

[a] May, Const. Hist. vol. i. p. 10.   [b] Ibid. pp. 13, 14.

vividly portrays the chief points in the character of that monarch, upon whom such various judgments have been passed. By some he is regarded as the model of a 'patriot king,' whilst others point him out as a bigoted, selfish monarch, obstinate, and wholly regardless of constitutional rights when opposed to his own policy or prejudices. But whatever opinion we may entertain of his personal character, we have no right to judge his proceedings by the strict rule of parliamentary government as it is now interpreted; for that system was still in its infancy when George III. was king, and the usages of the constitution in that day warranted a more direct and extended interference in the details of government by the occupant of the throne than would now be deemed expedient or justifiable. Further consideration, however, will be bestowed on this subject when treating of the office of sovereign in relation to parliamentary government. We must now proceed to notice certain particulars of the king's public conduct, which claim particular attention on account of their bearing upon the history and development of ministerial responsibility.

George III., during at least the earlier part of his reign, was in the frequent habit of conferring secretly upon public affairs with noblemen and others who were not members of the cabinet, but who were personally devoted to the king, and willing to aid him in carrying out his own peculiar views. His object in this was evidently to create a new party, faithful to himself, and dependent entirely upon his will. He succeeded; and the party came to be known as 'the king's men,' or 'the king's friends.' Instead of relying upon the advice of his responsible ministers, the king often took counsel with those whom Burke describes (in his 'Thoughts on the Cause of the Present Discontents') with some oratorical exaggeration as his 'double,' or 'interior cabinet.' It is said that his first speech to Parliament was not even submitted for the approval of his ministers, but was drawn

The 'King's friends.'

up, by the king's command, by ex-Chancellor Hardwicke, who, when in office, had had much experience in the preparation of royal speeches, and in whose skill and judgment his Majesty had peculiar confidence. One important paragraph is known to have been written by the king himself, and the whole speech was forced upon the ministry, who consented, very reluctantly, to adopt it as their own.* 'This "influence behind the throne" was denounced by all the leading statesmen of the day,—by Mr. Grenville, Lord Chatham, the Marquis of Rockingham, the Duke of Bedford, and Mr. Burke. Occasionally denied, its existence was yet so notorious, and its agency so palpable, that historical writers of all parties, though taking different views of its character, have not failed to acknowledge it. The bitterness with which it was assailed at the time was due, in great measure, to political jealousies, and to the king's selection of his friends from an unpopular party; but on constitutional grounds it could not be defended.'† From his accession to the throne in 1760, up to at least the year 1765, George III. was more or less guided by Lord Bute, who, whether in or out of office, continued to be his chief adviser.‡ After the retirement of Lord Bute from the king's secret counsels, his Majesty still had a numerous party of friends, some of whom held office in the government or household, but who severally 'looked to the king for instructions instead of to the ministers.' 'But the greater part of the king's friends were independent members of Parliament, whom various motives had attracted to the personal support of the king. They formed a distinct party, but their principles and position were inconsistent with constitutional government. Their services to the king were not even confined to counsel or political intrigue, but were made use of so as to influence

---

* Harris, Life of Hardwicke, vol. iii. p. 231.
† May's Hist. vol. i. pp. 11, 12.
‡ Ibid. pp. 22, 27, 30; and see Parl. Deb. vol. xvi. p. 9.

the deliberations of Parliament. The existence of this party, and their interference between the king and his responsible advisers, may be traced, with more or less distinctness, throughout the whole of this reign. By their means the king caballed against his ministers, thwarted their measures in Parliament, and on more than one occasion effected their overthrow.'[b]

By the encouragement which he afforded to these irregular practices, it is undeniable that George III. violated a foundation principle of the constitution, and hindered the progress of parliamentary government, which, when faithfully carried out, should foster and promote reciprocal confidence between the sovereign and his responsible advisers. We are not prepared to assert, however, that under no circumstances whatever is the sovereign justified in seeking advice from others than those who form part of his recognised administration. Every peer of the realm is an hereditary councillor of the crown, and is entitled to offer advice to the reigning monarch. The king, moreover, is at liberty to summon whom he will to his Privy Council; and every privy councillor has in the eye of the law an equal right to confer with the sovereign upon matters of public policy. The position and privileges of cabinet ministers are, in fact, derived from their being sworn members of the Privy Council. It is true that by the usages of the constitution cabinet ministers are alone empowered to advise upon affairs of state, and that they alone are ordinarily held responsible to their sovereign and to Parliament for the government of the country. Yet it is quite conceivable that circumstances might arise which would render it expedient for the king, in the interests of the constitution itself, to seek for aid and council apart from his cabinet. Such an occasion, it may be urged, was found in the events which led to the dismissal of the Coalition

Who may advise the king.

---

[b] May, Const. Hist. vol. i. pp. 31, 47, 57, 70, 84, 88, 98; Massey, Geo. III. vol. i. pp. 67, 144, 242.

Dismissal of the Coalition Ministry, in 1783.

ministry of Fox and North in 1783. It will be remembered that the Bill for the government of India, which had been drawn up by Mr. Fox, had been formally sanctioned by his Majesty, and passed triumphantly by the influence of the ministry through the House of Commons, before the true character of the measure was understood, either by the sovereign or by the country at large. The eyes of the king were opened to the real scope and tendency of the Bill by ex-Chancellor Thurlow, who availed himself of his privilege as a peer to obtain access to the king, and to advise him what course he should pursue at this juncture. As soon as the Bill reached the Upper House, George III. authorised Lord Temple, one of his 'friends,' to oppose it, and even to use his name to defeat it in that chamber. Succeeding in this, the king then dismissed his ministers, and empowered Mr. Pitt to form a new administration. In taking office, Mr. Pitt, as he was constitutionally bound to do, justified to the country the removal of his predecessors, and assumed entire responsibility for the same. Only by such a course, indeed, was it possible that the conduct of the king could be condoned, in a constitutional point of view. Even so, it must be admitted that the course he pursued in this emergency was unusual, extreme, and most undesirable to establish as a precedent; more especially in regard to the mode in which he brought about the rejection of the India Bill—namely, by the use of his own name to influence the proceedings of the legislature. For the crown cannot take notice of business actually depending in Parliament without a breach of privilege, and an infringement of the independence which belongs to both branches of the legislature, as component parts of the supreme power of the state.[1] But the question is, not whether the king chose the best course that was open to him to thwart the designs of the unscrupulous men who had obtained con-

---

[1] Bowyer's Const. Law, pp. 135, 130; Hatsell's Precedents, vol. ii. pp. 352–356.

trol, both in the ministry and in Parliament, but whether we are warranted in so far limiting the exercise of personal authority on the part of the sovereign as to deny him the right to interfere when his ministry are about to consummate an act which, in his opinion, is fraught with danger to the constitution, and perilous to the well-being of the community. It may be urged that, having lost confidence in his ministers, the king should have immediately dismissed them; but events were scarcely ripe enough for such a step. For, while the right of the sovereign to dismiss his ministers is unquestionable, constitutional usage prescribes that it should be exercised on grounds which can be justified to Parliament;[1] and as the king had agreed to the introduction of the India Bill, although in ignorance of its true character, and it had already passed the House of Commons, he could scarcely venture to dismiss his ministry on that account until he had succeeded in unmasking their designs, and in bringing about their defeat on the measure in the House of Lords. To assist his judgment and afford him substantial help at this crisis, the king naturally had recourse to the advice of trusty friends, on whose fidelity he could rely. There is no question that, in a constitutional point of view, any peer or privy councillor who may advise the crown becomes himself responsible to Parliament for such advice, and should be prepared to admit and assume the same, in order that, in the words of Lord North,[b] 'advice and responsibility might go hand-in-hand.' The king, however, having succeeded, with the assistance of his friends, in arresting the further progress of the obnoxious Bill, determined to entrust the reins of government to Mr. Pitt, who, while he could not vindicate in every particular the means made use of in bringing about the change of ministry, nevertheless assumed the responsibility of that change

Advice and responsibility must go together.

---

[1] See May's Hist. vol. i. p. 122.
[b] Parl. Hist. vol. xxiv. p. 201; and see Ibid. vol. xxiii. p. 678.

before Parliament and the country.[1] Thus the authority of the sovereign was rescued from the meshes of political intrigue in which it had become involved; partly by the machinations of the ambitious men who had then the upper hand, and partly by reason of the king's own irregular acts; and the chariot of the state proceeded once more along the beaten tracks, duly subjected to constitutional control.

<small>Mr. Pitt's first administration.</small>

The position of Mr. Pitt, on accepting office, was one of peculiar difficulty. He had to contend almost single-handed against an overwhelming majority of the House of Commons, marshalled by Fox, North, Sheridan, and other able politicians, who were indefatigable and unscrupulous in their endeavours to effect his overthrow. But he resolutely determined to maintain his ground as the king's minister, and to abstain from a dissolution of Parliament, though this was repeatedly urged upon him by his Majesty, until he could be satisfied that there was a decided reaction in the country in his favour, indications of the commencement of which began to be speedily manifested. He therefore boldly continued the struggle from December 22 to March 24, notwithstanding reiterated votes of want of confidence, and every hindrance (short of an actual refusing of the supplies, from which even the factious Opposition shrank) that the ingenuity of his opponents could devise.

Meanwhile, 'the loyalty of the people was aroused, and they soon ranged themselves on the side of the king and his ministers. Addresses and other demonstrations of popular sympathy were received from all parts of the country; and the king was thus encouraged to maintain a firm attitude in front of his opponents. The tactics of the two parties in Parliament, and the conduct of their

[1] See Stanhope's Life of Pitt, vol. i. pp. 153-155. Massey's George III. vol. iii. p. 224. See also Lord Campbell's account of these transactions, in his Lives of the Chancellors, vol. v. p. 665. This sound constitutional lawyer does not hesitate to express his approval of the king's conduct in this emergency.

leaders, were also calculated to convert public opinion to the king's side. Too much exasperated to act with caution the Opposition ruined their cause by factious extravagance and precipitancy. They were resolved to take the king's cabinet by storm, and without pause or parley struck incessantly at the door. Their very dread of a dissolution, which they so loudly condemned, showed little confidence in public support. Instead of making common cause with the people, they lowered their contention to a party struggle. Constitutionally, the king had a right to dismiss his ministers, and to appeal to the people to support his new administration. The Opposition endeavoured to restrain him in the exercise of this right, and to coerce him by a majority of the existing House of Commons. They had overstretched the legitimate limits of their power, and the assaults directed against prerogative recoiled upon themselves.'*

The private letters of the king to Mr. Pitt, at this period, show us the light in which his Majesty regarded the conduct of the House of Commons towards the minister of his choice. Writing to Mr. Pitt shortly before the dissolution of Parliament, the king says, 'he [Mr. Pitt] will ever be able to reflect with satisfaction, that in having supported me, he has saved the constitution, the most perfect of human formation.'* And, on another occasion, the king refers to his own course as 'calculated to prevent one branch of the legislature from annihilating the other two, and seizing also the executive power.'* While it is necessary that the king's government should be carried on in harmony with the House of Commons, a due regard to the royal prerogative certainly requires that, in the first instance, the choice of the crown, in selecting the ministers of state, should be respected, and no hasty or factious opposition be directed

---

* May's Hist. vol. I. p. 71, 72.
* Tomline's Life of Pitt, vol. i. p. 321. * Ibid. p. 203.

against them, until they have given proof of incapacity or unfitness for the duties they have been selected by the crown to discharge. This the Parliament of 1784 were unwilling to allow; and accordingly when, at the fitting moment, the king and his minister appealed to the people, the result of the dissolution was the return of a large majority in favour of the new minister, who thus commenced a long lease of power, secure alike in the good will of the people and of the crown. In Mr. Pitt, George III. found a minister after his own heart, of high ability, unswerving integrity, and firmness of purpose. Nevertheless, the king never surrendered, even to his favourite minister, the unrestricted exercise of the prerogative, but himself shaped the general policy of his government, and personally influenced the distribution of patronage, both in Church and State.[p]

Fox and Grenville ministry.
After the death of Mr. Pitt, in 1806, the king was obliged to accept of an administration taken chiefly from the Whig party, in whom he had no confidence. The ministry of 'All the Talents,' under the presidency of Lord Grenville and Mr. Fox, was forced, by political considerations, upon the king. Before the arrangements were completed, a difficulty arose on a point of prerogative. During the negotiations, 'Lord Grenville proposed to his Majesty some changes in the administration of the army; by which the question was raised whether the Control of the army by ministers. army should be under the immediate control of the crown, through the commander-in-chief, or be subject to the supervision of ministers. The king at once contended that the management of the army rested with the crown alone; and that he could not permit his ministers to interfere with it, beyond the levying of the troops, their pay and clothing. Lord Grenville was startled at such a doctrine, which he conceived to be entirely unconstitutional, and to which he would have refused to submit.

---

[p] May, vol. i. pp. 75, 85.

For some time it was believed that the pending ministerial arrangements would be broken off; but on the following day Lord Grenville presented a minute to his Majesty, stating that no changes in the management of the army should be effected without his Majesty's approbation.' To the doctrine thus expressed the king assented; and thus the sole remaining branch of the public service, heretofore considered as to a certain extent exempted from ministerial interference, was brought under ministerial control.ⁿ

Lord Grenville's ministry was then completed, but it was of very brief duration. The death of Mr. Fox, which speedily followed that of his great rival, led to several changes in the cabinet, and the following year a difficulty occurred between the king and his ministry, which led to their dismissal.ʳ Anxious to make a concession in favour of religious liberty, the ministry brought in a Bill respecting Service in the Army and Navy, which contained a clause removing certain disabilities on officers, being Roman Catholics or Dissenters. At first the king did not oppose the measure, but being stirred up by some of his friends, and the opponents of the ministry, he openly denounced it, authorising his friends to make known his adverse sentiments, and directing some of them to vote against it. Thus we find him, as on former occasions, ready to lend himself to an irregular interference with the freedom of debate. The ministry, however, averted further opposition by the withdrawal of the Bill. But at the same time, they were indiscreet enough to record, in a minute of council, their right to avow their opinions, should a petition for Roman Catholic relief be presented to Parliament; and to submit to his Majesty, from time to time, this question, or any subject connected with it.ˢ The ministers, however, were required by the king, not

marginal note: Quarrel between the king and his ministers.

---

* May's Hist. vol. I. p. 87, quoting Ann. Reg. 1800, 20; Sidmouth's Life, vol. ii. p. 410.
ʳ Hans. Deb. March 20, 1807.
ˢ *Ibid.* vol. ix. pp. 231-247; May's Hist. vol. I. p. 89.

only to withdraw the latter reservation, but to substitute for it a written declaration, pledging themselves never again to bring forward the measure they had abandoned, or to propose anything connected with the Roman Catholic question. To this they refused to assent; whereupon the king dismissed them from office, and proceeded to form a new administration under Mr. Perceval and the Duke of Portland.[1]

The circumstances attending this change of ministry underwent a full discussion in Parliament; and attempts were made in both Houses, by friends of the ex-ministers, to procure a vote in justification of their conduct; but through the influence of the new administration the attempt was defeated. The point at issue will hereafter engage our attention, when the relations between a constitutional sovereign and his responsible advisers are discussed. Meanwhile it is worthy of remark, that May, in reviewing this transaction, condemns alike the conduct of ministers in their hasty and unauthorised minute, and the conduct of the king in endeavouring to exact a pledge from his cabinet that they would never again obtrude their advice upon him in regard to the Roman Catholic claims. He also distinctly asserts that the incoming ministers were responsible for the conduct of the king concerning the pledge, as though they had themselves advised it.[2]

Personal influence of George III.

From this time until the close of the reign of George III. no further question arose which affects the history of ministerial responsibility. The king's 'own power, confided to the Tory ministers who were henceforth admitted to his councils, was supreme. Though there was still a party of "the king's friends," his Majesty agreed too well with his ministers, in principles and policy, to require the aid of irresponsible advisers."[3] The personal influence of the king was, indeed, very considerable throughout the

---

[1] See the National Review, vol. xiv. p. 328.
[2] May, Const. Hist. vol. i. pp. 90, 97.
[3] Ibid. p. 69.

whole of his reign, and was a great source of strength to such ministers as enjoyed his favour. It was, on the contrary, a continual cause of difficulty to ministers who were so unfortunate as to incur his disapprobation.*

In reviewing the history of this reign, we cannot fail to notice the ease with which the successive administrations who held office were able to control the House of Commons, and to carry on the government in connection therewith. This was mainly attributable, no doubt, to the number of seats in that House which were virtually in the nomination of the crown, or in the hands of the leading aristocratic families, from amongst whom the members of the cabinet were, at that time, exclusively chosen.

Strength of ministers in Parliament.

The great governing families of England have always been divided in their political opinions. Had they been of one mind, their influence would have been irresistible. As it was, the Whigs and Tories were continually struggling for the mastery. Sometimes the heart of the nation would incline to favour the traditions of the monarchy, embodied in the Tory creed; again, the ideas of progress which were the battle-cry of the Whigs would be in the ascendant. George III., as we have seen, was strongly biassed on behalf of the Tory party; and no wonder, for the ' great Tory peers and patrons of boroughs, who, by their influence in counties and their direct power of nomination, commanded the votes of a large section of the House of Commons, were willing, in general, to support any ministry which the king appointed, and to permit all the influence of the crown to be exercised in its favour, provided that their own personal wishes respecting the distribution of patronage received due attention. They contented themselves, as politicians, with a barter of power for patronage; they gave the former and received the latter. The great

Influence of the great governing families.

---

* Sir G. C. Lewis, in Edinb. Rev. vol. cx. p. 62.

Whig lords, however, made a harder bargain with the crown. They insisted upon selecting the king's ministers before they consented to support them. They required that an administration should be formed of members of their own party, whose names should be proposed by their own leaders.'[a]

Between the oligarchies of the two great parties, says Sir G. C. Lewis, 'there was this great difference, that whereas the Tories submitted themselves absolutely to the will of the king, the Whigs gave him only a conditional support; they insisted on his government acting upon their political principles, and being formed of persons who would carry those principles into effect, though they might be unpalatable to the crown. The king chafed at the oligarchy of the Whig houses, because the Whigs put a bit in his mouth; whereas the Tory party was a quiet beast of burden, which he could ride or drive as he pleased. The real contest in those days was, not between aristocracy and democracy, but between aristocracy and monarchy. The plan of Reform advocated by Mr. Pitt, in 1780, was mainly directed to emancipate Parliament from the influence of the crown, exercised through the nomination boroughs, and to prevent the king from bartering patronage for seats. He sought thus to diminish the influence of the crown in the House of Commons, which, in the words of Dunning's famous resolution of April 6, 1780, 'had increased, is increasing, and ought to be diminished.' But ere long this desirable object was attained by other means. The labours of Edmund Burke in the cause of economic reform, the abolition of sinecure offices, and the reduction of the pension list within reasonable limits, sufficed to curtail the excessive and unwarrantable abuse of crown patronage. For this reason, principally, Mr. Pitt refrained from any further advocacy of Parliamentary

_{Mr. Pitt's plan of parliamentary Reform.}

---

[a] Sir G. C. Lewis, in Edinb. Rev. vol. ciii. p. 308.

Reform. When the question was revived by Lord John Russell, after the Peace, and made a ministerial question by the Grey administration, it had entirely changed its aspect. The influence of the crown was no longer formidable; and the measure of 1831 was aimed at the diminution of the power of the aristocratic proprietors of close boroughs, by the same means which Pitt proposed to employ to diminish the power of the crown.'[?]

George IV., when Prince of Wales, had been the bosom friend of Fox and Sheridan, and it was supposed that upon his accession to the throne he would promote the Whigs to place and power. But when, in 1811, during the incapacity of his father, he became prince regent, he evinced a remarkable and increasing indifference to the principles and persons of the Whig leaders. After the death of the old king, he made no change in his policy, but continued to repose confidence in the ministers of whom his father had approved. So that, during the whole of this reign, the Tories maintained their ascendancy in the cabinet and in the legislature. Indifferent to the exercise of political power, and chiefly concerned in gratifying his taste for pomp and luxury, George IV. rarely attempted to interfere with his ministers, except in matters personally affecting himself, such as the Civil List, or the conduct of the queen, when he could be very resolute and determined.' So far as general politics were concerned, he usually acquiesced in the views of his constitutional advisers, and co-operated with them in their measures for the public good. But at the same time he appears to have taken a lively interest in the progress of state affairs, if we may judge from the active correspondence he kept up with his ministers.[*] From defects of personal character, the regal influence of George IV. was

Character of George IV.

[?] Sir G. C. Lewis, in Edinb. Rev. vol. ciii. pp. 310-315.
[b] Campbell's Chancellors, vol. vii.
[*] See Stapleton's Canning and his Times, pp. 410, 437, 445.

limited to the strict exercise of the prerogative; and his personal influence was so small, that it was even difficult for his ministers to bear the weight of his unpopularity, and to uphold the respect due to the crown, when it encircled the head of such an unworthy sovereign.* On one point of public policy, however, he attempted to make a stand, in behalf of his own sense of right. He had always strenuously opposed the Roman Catholic claims, and the ministry had gone with him in resisting them. But at length it became apparent that any further opposition to the political emancipation of Roman Catholics was fraught with danger to the empire, and ministers accordingly advised the passing of a Relief Bill. The king, at first, refused his consent; but ministers were firm, and obliged him to give way. For George IV. had not his father's spirit, and could not persevere in opposing an act which he nevertheless considered to be contrary to his coronation oath, and a dereliction of his duty as a Protestant king.

Case of Queen Caroline.

The domestic relations of George IV. were, it is well known, extremely unhappy; and they led, in 1820, to serious difficulties between the king and his ministers, which threatened to terminate in an open rupture, a catastrophe which was only averted by the patience and good sense of ministers themselves. Some account of these events will afford a valuable illustration of the ministerial *status* during this reign. The queen having, when Princess of Wales, disgraced herself by levity of conduct, and exposed herself to the charge of adulterous practices, the king determined to apply to Parliament for a divorce, and if possible to proceed against his guilty consort for high treason. The cabinet, however, were not in favour of such severe measures. In a minute dated February 10, 1820, ministers communicated to the king their opinion, individually as well as collectively, that a proceeding against the queen for high treason was

---
* Sir G. C. Lewis, in Edinb. Rev. vol. cx. p. 62.

out of the question; and that to attempt to procure a divorce might seriously prejudice the interests of the crown and of the monarchy, inasmuch as, bearing in mind the king's own conduct, it would be impossible to establish a case sufficient to justify the grant of a divorce by Act of Parliament. They agreed, however, to propose certain measures to prevent personal annoyance to his Majesty by the return of the queen to England, and were willing to justify the king in omitting her name from the Liturgy, and refusing to allow her to be crowned. The king replied to this memorandum at considerable length, reiterating his objections. On February 14, the cabinet re-stated to the king their unanimous opinion that, whatever other measures they might agree to propose, they could not recommend the introduction of a Bill of Divorce; whereupon the king yielded, being 'ready, for the sake of decorum and the public interest, to make this great and this painful sacrifice of his personal feelings.'*

A few weeks afterwards we learn, through a private letter from Lord Chancellor Eldon to his daughter, that the king 'has been pretty well disposed to part with us all, because we would not make additions to his revenue.'* Upon which transactions a recent historian justly remarks, 'These minor troubles have a happy capacity for adjustment in a constitutional monarchy, when responsible ministers possess the requisite degree of firmness.'* The king was well aware that he could not ask his advisers to advocate any measures affecting himself individually, but such as they could properly submit for the sanction of Parliament, upon their own personal responsibility; and that, had he taken upon himself, under such circumstances, to dismiss his ministry for refusing to be subservient to his wishes, he would have found it difficult, if not

---

* See Stapleton's Canning and his Times, pp. 266-274.
* Twiss, Life of Eldon, vol. ii. p 362.
* Knight's Hist. of England, vol. viii. p. 105.

impossible, to induce any one to take their places, and assume the responsibility of his act. Notwithstanding the criminatory evidence obtained against the princess in 1806, and again in 1819, ministers determined to take no active measures against her unless she should obtrude herself upon public notice by demanding to be regarded as Queen of England. She imprudently decided upon this course, and in the summer of 1820 left the continent, where she had been residing for several years, and made her appearance in London, for the purpose of prosecuting her claims. On the day of her arrival in London, a message from the king was presented to both houses, communicating certain papers respecting the conduct of her Majesty since her departure from the kingdom, and recommending them to the immediate and serious attention of Parliament. In the House of Lords, on motion of Lord Liverpool (the prime minister), these papers were referred to a committee of secrecy, upon whose report a Bill of Pains and Penalties for the degradation of the queen, and for her divorce from her husband, was introduced by his lordship. After evidence taken at the bar, the second reading of this Bill was carried by a majority of 28. In committee a motion was made to expunge the divorce clause, which, though unsuccessful, was voted for by all the ministers present, nine in number. By this proceeding they preserved their consistency, and maintained their independence of the personal influence of the king. On November 10, the third reading of the Bill was carried by a majority of nine only; whereupon Lord Liverpool arose, and announced that the measure would be abandoned. In the state of excitement which prevailed throughout the country on the question, and the feeling which existed against the king, the attempt to carry the Bill through the House of Commons, after such a close division in the Lords, would have been most disastrous, and would probably have resulted in the overthrow of the administration, whose popularity had been already diminished by the degree of assistance they had rendered to the king on this occasion.'

The reign of William IV. has been rendered memorable by the passing of the Reform Bill; a measure to which the king was at first opposed, but which was ultimately carried through Parliament with a high hand by his own personal exertions. Impressed with the necessity for Reform, to save the country from revolution, and to avert the perils anticipated by the defeat of the Bill in the House of Lords, the ministry extorted from the king a pledge to create a sufficient number of peers to turn the scale in favour of Reform; but a dread of the consequences of such an arbitrary proceeding induced the king, without the knowledge of his ministers, to cause a circular letter to be addressed to the Opposition peers, urging upon them to drop all further resistance to the Bill, so that it might pass without delay, and as nearly as possible without alteration.^g This unconstitutional interference with the independent deliberations of the House of Lords was even more irregular and unsound in principle than the creation of additional peers; but it was a less obvious evil, and it had the desired effect.^h

William IV. and the Reform Bill

The Reform Bill became law, through the active interposition of the crown, and with the reluctant assent of the House of Lords. It has effected an important revolution in the English political system. Professedly based upon a 'careful adherence to the acknowledged principles of the constitution, by which the prerogatives of the crown, the authority of both Houses of Parliament, and the rights and liberties of the people, are equally secured,'ⁱ it has contributed, in its consequences, to increase the

Effects of the Reform Bill

---

^f For a succinct narrative of all the proceedings in this memorable case, both in and out of Parliament, see Sir G. C. Lewis's article in Edinb. Rev. vol. cix. pp. 162-173, 188-190.

^g Roebuck's Hist. of the Whig Ministry, vol. ii. pp. 331, 334.

^h May's Hist. vol. i. p. 120.

ⁱ The king's speech at the opening of Parliament, in June 1831. And see Earl Russell's comments thereon, in the new edition of his Essay on the English Const., Introd. p. lii.

power of the House of Commons, not only by lessening the aristocratic influence of the proprietors of close boroughs, but also by diminishing the strength of the crown in that assembly. The disfranchisement of constituencies, in England alone, which formerly returned 143 members, the distribution of seats to various localities hitherto unrepresented, and the general extension of the franchise, have been the means of emancipating a large proportion of voters from the direct influence of the landed gentry, and of introducing into the House of Commons a body of independent members, who cannot be relied upon as the staunch supporters of any political party, but who think and act for themselves. This has brought about a silent but material change in the relations between Parliament and the ministers of the crown. The stable administrations of former days have passed away, and no government can now expect to continue in office by dint of mere party strength. The House of Commons has become more difficult to control, from the lack of a sufficient number of members upon whose support an existing ministry could generally depend, and from the necessity of conciliating the goodwill of divers important and independent interests, which are now represented therein.[1] Nevertheless, as we have already remarked,[b] the influence of 'the great governing families of England,' though materially reduced, is still powerful over many constituencies. And while the representation of the people has been made more direct and efficient, rank and hereditary property have been permitted to retain a fair proportion of legitimate influence in that chamber which has become the source and centre of political authority.[1] To this we owe it that the complex machinery of parliamentary government has continued in successful operation, and that the House of Commons has been hitherto preserved from the evil effects of democratic ascendancy.

Increasingly difficult to control the House of Commons.

[1] See Edinb. Rev. vol. xcv. p. 225.
[b] Ante, p. 10.
[1] See May, Const. Hist. vol. i. p. 355, vol. ii. p. 84.

Two years after the passing of the Reform Bill, the prerogatives of the crown were again called into activity, in a manner which seemed to revive the political history of 1784. Lord Grey's government had lost the confidence of the king. The retirement of several members of the cabinet on the question of the appropriation of the surplus revenues of the Church of Ireland excited the apprehension of the king as to the safety of the Irish Church, and, without consulting his ministers, he gave public expression to his alarm, in replying to an address of the prelates and clergy of Ireland.* 'The ministry, enfeebled by the loss of their colleagues, by disunion, and other embarrassments, soon afterwards resigned; notwithstanding that they continued to command a large majority in the House of Commons. They were succeeded by Lord Melbourne's administration, which differed little in material politics and parliamentary strength. But this administration was distasteful to the king, who had, meantime, become a convert to the political opinions of the Opposition.'*

Taking advantage of the removal of Lord Althorp from the leadership of the House of Commons, and from the office of Chancellor of the Exchequer, owing to his accession to a peerage by the death of his father, the king suddenly dismissed his ministers, and consulted the Duke of Wellington upon the formation of a government from the Tory party, who were in a decided minority in the House of Commons. The propriety of this act has been questioned by May, for the reason that 'all the usual grounds for dismissing a ministry were wanting. There was no immediate difference of opinion between them and the king upon any measure or question of public policy; there was no disunion among themselves, nor were there any indications that they had lost the confidence of Parliament. But the accidental removal of a single minister—not necessarily even from the govern-

Dismissal of his ministers by William IV.

---

* An. Reg. 1834, p. 43.   * May, Const. Hist. vol. i. p. 120.

ment, but only from one House of Parliament to the other—was made the occasion for dismissing the entire administration. It is true that the king viewed with apprehension the policy of his ministers in regard to the Irish Church; but his assent was not then required to any specific measure of which he disapproved, nor was this the ground assigned for their dismissal. The right of the king to dismiss his ministers was unquestionable; but constitutional usage has prescribed certain conditions under which this right should be exercised. It should be exercised solely in the interests of the state, and on grounds which can be justified to Parliament—to whom, as well as to the king, the ministers are responsible. But here it was not directly alleged that the ministers had lost the confidence of the king; and so little could it be affirmed that they had lost the confidence of Parliament that an immediate dissolution was counselled by the new administration. The act of the king bore too much the impress of his personal will, and too little of those reasons of state policy by which it should have been prompted; but its impolicy was so signal as to throw into the shade its unconstitutional character.'*

Ministry of Sir R. Peel, in 1834.

The Duke of Wellington advised that the formation of the new administration should be entrusted to Sir Robert Peel; and as that statesman was abroad at the time, he himself accepted the office of First Lord of the Treasury, together with the seals of office as Secretary of State, which, there being no other secretary, constituted his grace Secretary for the Home, Foreign, and Colonial Departments.

Upon the arrival of Sir R. Peel, he immediately waited upon the king, and accepted the proffered charge. And 'so completely had the theory of ministerial responsibility been now established that, though Sir R. Peel was out of the realm when the late ministers were dismissed

---

* May, Const. Hist. vol. i. pp. 122, 123.

—though he could have had no cognisance of the causes which induced the king to dismiss them—though the Duke of Wellington had been invested with the sole government of the country without his knowledge, he yet boldly avowed that, by accepting office after these events, he became constitutionally responsible for them all, as if he had himself advised them.' He did not attempt, like the ministers of 1807, to absolve himself from censure for the acts of the crown, and at the same time to denounce the criticism of Parliament, as an arraignment of the personal conduct of the king, but manfully accepted the full responsibility which had devolved upon him.' '

A dissolution of Parliament was at once determined upon; its result proved, upon the whole, unfavourable to Sir Robert Peel, for, although his own supporters were largely increased, yet a majority against his ministry was returned. For a while he endeavoured, with great tact and consummate ability, to carry on the government, but he was confronted at every turn by a hostile and enraged majority in the House of Commons, and compelled to succumb. After several previous discomfitures, he was defeated on a resolution affirming that no measure on the subject of tithes in Ireland could be satisfactory that did not provide for the appropriation of the surplus revenues of the Irish Church.' He then resigned, and Lord Melbourne's administration, with some alterations, was reinstated. But it is remarkable that the appropriation of Irish Church property to other uses, which was a favourite project of the Whigs at this time, and the immediate occasion of the change of ministry, was afterwards abandoned, and the resolution of the House of Commons, upon which Sir Robert Peel resigned, remains a dead letter on the Commons' Journals.

Replaced by the old Whig ministry.

The failure of the efforts of William IV. in favour of the Tory party was complete, and it affords 'an instructive

---

' Hans. Deb. 3rd ser. xxvi. pp. 210, 220.
' May, vol. I. p. 125.
' Com. Jour. vol. xc. p. 208.

illustration of the effects of the Reform Act, in diminishing the ascendant influence of the crown. In George III.'s time, the dismissal of a ministry by the king, and the transfer of his confidence to their opponents—followed by an appeal to the country—would certainly have secured a majority for the new ministers. Such had been the effect of the dissolutions in 1784 and 1807. But the failure of this attempt to convert Parliament from one policy to another, by royal prerogative and influence, proved, that, with the abolition of the nomination boroughs, and the extension of the franchise, the House of Commons had emancipated itself from the control of the crown; and 'that the opinion of the people must now be changed before ministers can reckon upon a conversion of the Parliament.'*

Waning authority of the crown.

Reign of Queen Victoria.

Lord Melbourne's ministry continued in office during the rest of the king's reign, and on the accession of our present gracious queen, in 1837, she confirmed them in their places, and gave them her entire confidence. In 1839, however, they were obliged to resign office, on account of their inability to carry on the government with success. Sir Robert Peel was then charged with the formation of a new ministry. Acting upon the advice of Lord Melbourne, her Majesty was induced, on this occasion, to insist upon retaining the ladies of her household, notwithstanding the change of ministry. This decision of the queen compelled Sir Robert Peel to relinquish the task entrusted to him, and the Melbourne administration were reinstated. But being defeated upon a vote of want of confidence in the House of Commons, in 1841, they again resigned, when Sir R. Peel was sent for, and fully empowered to make such alterations as he thought fit in the composition of the royal household. More particulars in regard to this transaction will be found in the chapter which treats of the position and privileges of the sovereign.

* May, vol. I. p. 127. See also Edinb. Rev. for Jan. 1862. art. viii.

'From this time,' says May, 'no question has arisen concerning the exercise of the prerogatives or influence of the crown which calls for notice. Both have been exercised wisely, justly, and in the true spirit of the constitution. Ministers enjoying the confidence of Parliament have never claimed in vain the confidence of the crown. Their measures have not been thwarted by secret influence and irresponsible advice. Their policy has been directed by Parliament and public opinion, and not by the will of the sovereign, or the intrigues of the court. Vast as is the power of the crown, it has been exercised, through the present reign, by the advice of responsible ministers, in a constitutional manner, and for legitimate objects. It has been held in trust, as it were, for the benefit of the people. Hence it has ceased to excite either the jealousy of rival parties or popular discontents.'[1]

---

[1] May, Const. Hist. vol. I. p. 135.

HISTORICAL INTRODUCTION.

PART II.

CHAPTER I.

ANNALS OF THE ADMINISTRATIONS OF ENGLAND, FROM 1782 TO THE PRESENT DAY.

It is proposed in the following chapter to give a brief account of the circumstances attending the appointment, resignation, or dismissal, of the several administrations of England, from 1782 to the present time; together with a mention of the various constitutional questions, illustrative of ministerial duty or responsibility, which arose in connection with the same.

The year 1782 a constitutional epoch. In selecting the year 1782 as our starting-point, we do so because it is the date of an important epoch in constitutional history. It marks the first introduction of the practice, since universally recognised, of the simultaneous change of the whole ministry upon the enforced retirement of the cabinet. Prior to that time, there had been frequent instances of partial alterations in the cabinet, with a view to conciliate the favour of Parliament, but it was not until the downfall of Lord North's administration, in 1782, in consequence of its having lost the confidence of the House of Commons, that the necessity for a complete change in the ministry, under such circumstances, was freely acknowledged. Moreover, previous to this occasion, there had been but one example—that of Sir Robert Walpole, in 1741—of the retirement of a prime minister on account of a defeat in the House of Commons.[a]

---

[a] Particulars of this case will be found in the chapter on the 'Cabinet Council.'

1. *Rockingham Administration.—March* 1782.

In March 1782, upon the resignation of the North administration, the Marquis of Rockingham[b] was appointed First Lord of the Treasury. The history of the formation of this ministry is remarkable. The North administration, after a successful career of twelve years, came to an end in consequence of its growing unpopularity in the House of Commons. The House had passed resolutions denouncing the great and increasing influence of the crown, and in favour of peace with the revolted American colonies. George III. was strongly averse to the recognition of American independence; and Lord North, though personally inclined towards conciliation, is said to have remained in office 'to carry into effect the personal wishes of the sovereign, which he preferred to the welfare of the state.'[c] But the House of Commons had become impatient at the continuance of the war, and it was evident that the war ministry were losing ground. A direct vote of want of confidence had indeed been negatived by a bare majority of nine; but Lord Surrey had given notice of a similar motion, for March 20, 1782, which it was anticipated would pass. With some difficulty Lord North induced the king to forestall this defeat, by accepting the resignation of ministers; an event which was communicated to the House on the day the debate was to have begun.[d] The king made several

---

[b] For an account of the political career of this nobleman, who was twice prime minister of England, see an article (by Sir G. C. Lewis) in the Edinburgh Review, vol. xcvi. p. 110. Since this chapter has been written, the able and instructive articles in the Edinburgh Review, to which frequent reference has been made, with the assumption that they proceeded from the pen of Sir G. C. Lewis, have been collected into a volume by Sir Edmund Head, and published under the title of 'Essays on the Administrations of Great Britain, from 1783 to 1830, contributed to the Edinburgh Review by the Rt. Hon. Sir G. C. Lewis. Longmans, 1864.'

[c] Russell's Memorials of Fox, vol. i. p. 247.

[d] See Mahon, Hist. of Eng. vol. vii. p. 206.

1782. attempts to induce the Whig party to take office upon his own terms, but without success. He was at length obliged to authorise Lord Rockingham to form an administration upon the basis of the independence of America, and a curtailment of the influence of the crown. The list of the new cabinet, before being submitted to the king, received the approval of the leading Whigs. The king refused to see his new premier until he was actually in office, and conducted the ministerial negotiations through Lord Shelburne, who was appointed Home Secretary, and at whose suggestion Mr. Dunning (with the title of Lord Ashburton) was added to the cabinet, without previous communication with Lord Rockingham. The contest in which the North administration had been overthrown was a struggle of the king's personal will, backed by the influence of the crown, against the independent portion of the House of Commons. When the result was known, Fox openly treated it as a victory of the Commons over the king; declaring in his place in Parliament that the new ministers must remember that they owed their situations to the House. The king, though fully sensible that he had sustained defeat, was prudent enough to tolerate for a time a ministry composed for the most part of men whom he regarded as his personal enemies. The only member of the late ministry who remained in office was Lord Chancellor Thurlow, who retained his place at the express desire of the king, and who showed his independence of his new colleagues by opposing them in council.[e] But the new ministry were very short-lived; within four months of their appointment they were dissolved, by the death, on July 1, of the premier, Lord Rockingham.[f]

---

[e] Knight, Hist. of England, vol. vi. p. 439.

[f] Sir G. C. Lewis, in Edinb. Rev. vol. xcix. pp. 18–22.

2. *Shelburne Administration.—July* 1782.

Two days afterwards, Mr. Secretary Fox advised the king to appoint some member of the Rockingham party as premier; but his Majesty refused, and gave the appointment to Lord Shelburne, whereupon Fox, Burke, Sheridan, and others of their friends, resigned office. Nevertheless the new ministry was decidedly Whig, and professed the same principles as their predecessors. Mr. Pitt, the new Chancellor of the Exchequer, and leader of the House of Commons, was, at this time, accounted a good Whig. Fox, after his resignation, continued in opposition, and soon afterwards entered into his famous Coalition with Lord North, which immediately placed the government in a very perilous position. The comparative strength of parties in the House of Commons was estimated to afford the ministry 140 votes, Lord North 120, Fox 90, and the residue uncertain. Preliminaries of peace, which recognised the independence of the American colonies, had been agreed upon by the government, and presented to Parliament. It was decided that their acceptance should be a test question between the new Coalition and the ministry. Accordingly, a motion of censure upon the terms of the preliminaries was proposed by Lord J. Cavendish, on February 21, and agreed to by the House of Commons, by 207 to 190 votes. Three days afterwards, the ministry resigned. Owing to the difficulties of the situation, there was a ministerial interregnum, which extended to the beginning of April. In the interim, the king made an unsuccessful attempt to induce Mr. Pitt to form a government; and the Commons, on March 24, passed an address, praying his Majesty to form a strong and united administration, which was graciously received, and responded to through Earl Ludlow.[f] On March 31, a motion was made for a further address upon

---

[f] Adolphus, Geo. III. vol. iii. pp. 450, 464, 469.

the subject; but the House being of opinion that it was premature to interpose again with their advice so soon after his Majesty's gracious reply to their former address, the motion was withdrawn.[b]

3. *Duke of Portland's First Administration.—April* 1783.

1783.

At length, on April 2, 1783, the celebrated 'Coalition Ministry' was formed, under the nominal presidency of the Duke of Portland. It included Lord North and Mr. Fox, heretofore such bitter and, as was supposed, irreconcilable opponents. The other cabinet offices were chiefly filled by followers of Fox, who was himself the virtual prime minister.[i] The Coalition was unpopular with the nation on public grounds, and was vehemently assailed both in and out of Parliament. Lord North and his friends attempted to vindicate their conduct by arguments of expediency.[j] The king himself resented the Coalition for personal reasons. He had long entertained a great aversion to Fox, which was aggravated by the friendship that had sprung up between Fox and the Prince of Wales. Lord North was formerly a favourite with the king, but he now looked upon him as a deserter to the enemy's camp. He therefore resolved to take the earliest opportunity of ridding himself of his obnoxious advisers. Nothing remarkable occurred during the remainder of the session in which the ministry was appointed. But, on the reassembling of Parliament, in the autumn of 1783, the king's speech announced that the treaties of peace had been signed. Mr. Pitt, as leader of the Opposition, reminded ministers that these treaties were substantially identical with the preliminary articles, upon which they had turned out their predecessors in office.[k] Early in the

---

[b] Parl. Hist. vol. xxiii. pp. 687-700.
[i] Russell's Memorials of Fox, vol. ii. p. 35.
[j] For the principal arguments for and against the Coalition, see Adolphus, vol. iii. pp. 400-404; Edinb. Rev. vol. xcix. p. 10.
[k] Parl. Hist. vol. xxiii. p. 1140.

session, Mr. Secretary Fox introduced his famous India Bill. Its principal feature was that it vested the government of India, for four years, in a commission of seven persons, named in the Bill, and not removable by the crown, except upon an address from the two Houses of Parliament. Pitt denounced the plan as dangerous to the constitution,[1] and a violation of the chartered rights of the East India Company. But though the measure was unpopular in the country, the Coalition were sufficiently strong to carry it through the House of Commons without difficulty. In the Lords it obtained a different reception. Lord Temple, at the instigation of the king himself,[*] brought about its rejection, in that House, on December 17, by 95 to 76 votes. On the following day, the king dismissed the ministry, and again appealed to Pitt to assume the reins of government.

4. *Mr. Pitt's First Administration.*—December 1783.

On December 19, 1783, Mr. Pitt's first administration was formed. Earl Temple, who had been appointed a Secretary of State, advocated an immediate dissolution of Parliament. But Pitt would not agree to this, being of opinion that the time had not yet come when the country could be appealed to with success. Accordingly Temple resigned, on the 22nd instant, leaving the youthful premier to bear the brunt of the severest contest ever waged in

---

[1] A protest—signed by Lord Rockingham, the Duke of Portland (the present head of the administration), Lord Fitzwilliam, and other peers—to a Bill for the management of the East India Company's affairs, in 1773, contained the following passage, which, from its striking applicability to Mr. Fox's Bill, was much quoted at the time:—'The election of executive officers in Parliament is plainly unconstitutional, and an example of the most pernicious kind, productive of intrigue and faction, and calculated for extending a corrupt influence in the crown. It frees ministers from responsibility, while it leaves them all the effect of patronage.' See Adolphus, vol. iv. p. 59 n.; Lords' Journals, June 10, 1773. See Edinb. Rev. vol. cvii. p. 678.

[*] See *ante*, p. 52; Knight's Hist. of Eng. vol. vii. p. 138.

1783. Parliament. For though Pitt possessed the unlimited confidence of the king, and the support of the House of Lords, yet a powerful majority of the House of Commons was arrayed against him. His cabinet consisted of seven persons, all of whom, save himself, were peers.[a] His only assistant in the House of Commons was his friend Dundas. He was assailed at once by every imaginable device of a hostile Opposition—votes of want of confidence, censures upon the government, obstructions and defeats in every shape.[b] But he stood firm; and though frequently urged by his supporters, and even by the king himself, to dissolve Parliament, he refrained from doing so until he considered that the country was prepared to sustain him. It was not until March 24 that the prorogation took place, to be followed by an immediate dissolution. But such was the inveteracy of the Opposition that Pitt was obliged to prorogue before the passing of an Appropriation Act. Upon the reassembling of Parliament, however, it appeared that the amount of unauthorised expenditure had been very small, so that no objection was urged, or indemnity sought for, in regard to the same.[c] The sense of the country, in reference to the great issues involved in the contest between Pitt and the Coalition, had been expressed at the time by numerous addresses to the king. It was afterwards unmistakably pronounced by the return of a House of Commons which gave a triumphant support to the new administration. Above 160 members lost their seats at this election, nearly all of whom were Oppositionists. Upon the meeting of Parliament, an amendment was moved to the address in answer to the royal speech, to rescind the paragraph which expressed approval of the late dissolution; but it

---

[a] Stanhope's Pitt, vol. I. p. 165.
[b] See a list of the defeats of Pitt, in the House of Commons, from his acceptance of office, in December 1783, to the dissolution of Parliament, in March 1784. Mirror of Parl. 1841, pp. 1052, 1054.
[c] 3 Hats. Prec. 208; see also post, p. 633.

was negatived by a majority of more than two to one.[a] In the course of this session, Pitt introduced his India Bill, which was carried by a majority of 271 to 60. It created a Ministerial Board of Control for the affairs of India, to act in concert with the Court of Directors of the East India Company. This system of 'double government' continued in operation until after the great mutiny of 1857, when, by the Act 21 and 22 Vict. c. 106, the government of India was assumed by the queen herself, acting through a responsible Secretary of State. Mr. Pitt's majority in the House of Commons continued unshaken during the whole period of his administration, which lasted upwards of seventeen years. The unpatriotic conduct of Fox and his followers, in regard to the French Revolution and consequent war between England and France, contributed largely to the popularity of the government.[b] The course pursued by Fox reduced his party so low that, near the end of the century, it was jocularly estimated that the entire Opposition could have been held in one hackney-coach.[c] The retirement of this ministry, in 1801, was not purely voluntary, but was brought about by differences with the king in regard to the Roman Catholic claims. Mr. Pitt, in order to facilitate the passing of the legislative Union between Great Britain and Ireland, had intimated his readiness to propose the removal of the Roman Catholic disabilities from office-holders and members of Parliament. A proposition to this effect was discussed in the cabinet for about six months previous to its being communicated to the king, notwithstanding the known repugnance of his Majesty to any legislation upon the subject. When the desire of his

1784.

1801.

---

[a] Knight, vol. vii. pp. 140-143; Adolphus, vol. iv. pp. 103, 117.
[b] See Edinb. Rev. vol. ciii. pp. 343-345; Ibid. vol. cvii. p. 140.
[c] 'I heard old George Byng say, at the dinner given to him to celebrate the fiftieth anniversary of his having sat for Middlesex, alluding to those times, "It has been asserted that the Whigs would all have been held in one hackney-coach. This is a calumny. We should have filled two."'—Campbell's Lives of the Chanc. vol. v. p. 614.

1801. ministers to submit to Parliament some measure of relief became known to the king, by a letter from Mr. Pitt, dated January 31, 1801, informing him that, unless the royal sanction thereto was granted, he must resign his office, the king at once declined to discuss the proposition. He nevertheless urged Mr. Pitt not to leave his service. But Pitt would not yield. So the king declared that he should form a new administration.¹ Canning, who was in office at the time, is said to have strongly advised Pitt not to give way on this occasion; for that, for three years back, so many concessions, as he termed them, had been made, and so many important measures overruled, from the king's opposition to them, that government had been weakened exceedingly; and if in this instance a stand was not made, Pitt would retain only a nominal power, while the reality would pass into the hands of those who influenced the king's mind and opinion out of sight." The causes of this change of ministry were very briefly stated to Parliament; and Mr. Pitt's explanations were neither full nor satisfactory." This reticence was evidently resorted to in order to avoid bringing the royal name too prominently forward in connection with these events;" but it naturally gave rise to much misapprehension at the time, and it was not until after the death of Pitt that the whole truth transpired.

5. *Addington Administration.*—1801.

Mr. Addington, who at that time was Speaker of the House of Commons, was empowered by the king to form a cabinet as soon as the correspondence between his

---

¹ The best account of these transactions is given in Massey's George III. vol. iv. pp. 537–570. See also Sir G. C. Lewis's papers, in Edinb. Rev. vol. ciii. pp. 340–357, and vol. cvii. p. 134.

* Malmesbury, Diaries, vol. iv. p. 4.
* Parl. Hist. vol. xxxv. pp. 915, 997, 1112.
* *Ibid.* p. 1121.
* Parl. Deb. vol. ix. p. 232; Quar. Rev. vol. cxii. p. 369.

Majesty and Mr. Pitt had terminated. But before the outgoing ministers had their audiences to deliver up their seals, the king, in consequence of the agitation produced by the change of ministry, was seized with a return of his mental malady. He was unable to attend to business until about March 10, when he was sufficiently recovered to sign documents and give audiences to some of his ministers. Pending the completion of the new arrangements which were thus unavoidably delayed, Mr. Pitt continued to conduct the public business in the House of Commons, performing the official duties of the Chancellor of the Exchequer, although he had formally resigned that office on February 5.[f] On the 16th instant, he moved the House into Committee of Supply, for the purpose of enabling him to open the budget. The motion was opposed on the ground that 'the responsibility of the former ministers was at an end,' and the incoming ministers were as yet absent from their places; and that therefore 'further proceedings on the estimates should be delayed until the new ministers, by taking their seats, have assumed responsibility.' This was resisted by Mr. Pitt, who said that 'when there arises a change among his Majesty's ministers, it must be left to his Majesty to determine when the new arrangements shall be formed; and it is contrary to the spirit of the constitution for the House to assume any right of determination on a subject

---

[f] Parl. Hist. vol. xxxv. p. 950. But his resignation was not legally complete until the appointment of his successor; he was therefore competent to transact official business. (See 2 Hatsell, p. 304; Parl. Deb. vol. xvi. p. 735.) The king did not receive the seals of office from Mr. Pitt until March 14; and he gave them to Mr. Addington on that day. In order to facilitate the new arrangements, Mr. Addington vacated his seat in Parliament, by accepting the Chiltern Hundreds, on February 19; but owing to the king's illness it became impossible to confer upon him his ministerial office previous to his re-election for Devizes. Accordingly, on March 10, a new writ for Devizes was again ordered, upon the acceptance by Mr. Addington of the offices of First Lord of the Treasury and Chancellor of the Exchequer. The result of these delays was that it was March 25 before Mr. Addington again took his seat in the House. Sidmouth's Life, by Pellew, vol. i. pp. 294, 315.

of this kind.' He also contended that the perilous state of the country, in its foreign relations, demanded that there should be no delay in granting the supplies, and 'that every department of the public service should be accelerated to the greatest possible degree.' If the new ministers were not responsible for framing the estimates (a responsibility from which he himself would not shrink), they would be undoubtedly responsible for expending the money. He claimed, moreover, that there was no ground to 'call for the interference of the House, either from a change of measures or of men.' Until the appointments of the new ministers 'were publicly notified, it was inconsistent with the constitution to come to any determination. In no previous instance had it been attempted to be denied, that, according to the constitution, his Majesty had the sole right of nominating his ministers, and that the House had no right to form any resolution till their conduct came to be judged of by the acts of their administration. Even in 1784 this general principle had never been attempted to be denied in the abstract.'* Adverting to his having refrained from entering into explanations as to the cause of his own resignation, Mr. Pitt observed that it appeared to him to be a new and not very constitutional doctrine, that 'a man must not, in compliance with the dictates of his conscience, retire from office without being bound to give to this House, and to the public, an account of all the circumstances that weigh in his mind and influence his conduct. Where this system of duty is established, I know not.'* The motion for going into Committee of Supply was then put and agreed to, without a division. On February 18, Mr. Pitt introduced the budget, which excited no opposition. The

---

* Parl. Hist. vol. xxxv. pp. 960–
962.
* Ibid. p. 960. See also p. 1121,
for further remarks from Mr. Pitt on
this point, showing that the reciprocal duty between a sovereign and
his ministers may sometimes render
it impossible to afford full explanations to Parliament of the causes
which have led to the resignation or
dismissal of a ministry.

House continued to sit, and to debate various public political questions up to March 17, when the new administration were formally inducted into office. But even then, owing to the unsettled condition of the king's mind, a further delay of several weeks took place before the ministry was entirely completed.[b]

Mr. Addington's administration was constructed upon an avowedly 'anti-Catholic' basis. It had been formed, at the outset, 'with the concurrence of Mr. Pitt, who wished all his private and personal friends to remain in office.'[c] It began its career upon March 14, 1801, the day when the king transferred the seals of office from the outgoing to the incoming premier. Ministers had no sooner taken their seats in the House of Commons, when, on March 25, Mr. Grey moved for a committee of the whole to consider the state of the nation. His speech was an elaborate attack upon the conduct and policy of the preceding ministry, and a condemnation of the existing one, because of their presumed incompetency to fill their places properly; and because it had been avowed, on their behalf, that their principles were similar to those of their predecessors in office. Mr. Pitt defended himself and his late colleagues, and claimed for the new ministry, at the outset of their career, 'a constitutional confidence;' in other words, 'that, unless some good reason were assigned to the contrary, the House was bound, by the best principles of policy, as well as by the true spirit of the constitution of this country, to wait to see the conduct of the ministers of the crown, before they should withhold their confidence.'[d] The new premier expressed himself to the same effect, saying, 'In what degree the confidence of the House might be supposed to extend to his Majesty's present ministers, it was not for him to conjecture. They only asked, however, for that portion of

---

[b] Adolphus, vol. vii. pp. 450, 458; Edinb. Rev. vol. cvii. pp. 135-138.
[c] Rose, Diary, vol. I. p. 292.
[d] Parl. Hist. vol. xxxv. p. 1115.

it which should be constitutionally reposed in persons duly appointed by his Majesty, unless it was precluded by their antecedent conduct and characters.'* The House then divided on Mr. Grey's motion, which was negatived by a large majority. A similar motion, proposed to the House of Lords on March 20, met with a similar fate. Nevertheless it was evident that the new administration did not possess the confidence of either House of Parliament to the same extent as their predecessors. Conscious of this, Mr. Addington, in March 1803, made overtures to Mr. Pitt, offering him the selection of a new premier, if he would consent to serve with himself in the capacity of Secretary of State. Pitt would not listen to this arrangement. He was then offered the premiership, on condition that there should be no extensive changes in other offices. But neither would he agree to this, although he and his friends were tired of bolstering up a feeble government.' Accordingly, Addington continued at the helm for another year, when it became notorious that he had lost his hold upon both Houses. In the Commons, ministerial majorities on important divisions were gradually reduced; while in the minority were found most of the leading men

1803.

---

* Parl. Hist. vol. xxxv. p. 1160.
' Knight, vol. vii. p. 424; Edinb. Rev. vol. cvii. pp. 144–147. Commenting on these transactions, Sir G. C. Lewis pointedly remarks:—'It appears that the king's consent to the negotiation, however necessary an element in the business, had never been procured by Addington; so that, in fact, no distinct offer, by competent authority, was made to Pitt. Addington assumed to act as plenipotentiary, but had not full powers to treat. . . . It is remarkable that the latter should have ventured to make the offer, or that the former should have been willing to entertain it, without the king's express authority being previously obtained]. It was not a mere question of changing a cabinet office, as to which a prime minister might properly make a preliminary arrangement, subject to the king's confirmation. It was practically a negotiation for a complete alteration of the character of the government; and the whole discussion proceeded on the assumption that Addington and Pitt were between them to settle who was to be the new prime minister.' After he had received Pitt's final answer, Addington took an opportunity to mention the matter to the king. But he represented Pitt's conduct in such an unfavourable light, as to excite the king's anger; and when, shortly afterwards, he gave the king copies of the correspondence, his Majesty refused to read the letters, and remarked that 'it was foolish business, which was begun ill, conducted ill, and terminated ill.' Ibid. p. 148.

of all parties, including Pitt, Fox, and Sir Francis Burdett. On April 22, 1804, Mr. Pitt wrote to the king, intimating that he could no longer refrain from direct opposition to the ministerial measures; a determination which he immediately carried out, by opposing, on April 25, the government plan for military defence, and developing a scheme of his own. On a division, ministers were sustained by a small majority. But, taking into account the gradual decline of his own numbers, and the increasing strength of his opponents, Mr. Addington deemed it expedient to resign. Upon his informing the king of this resolution, there was an immediate resumption of intercourse between his Majesty and Mr. Pitt. At first, communications were conducted through Lord Eldon (the Lord Chancellor);[r] but, on May 6, the king himself wrote to Mr. Pitt, requiring of him, as a necessary preliminary to his return to office, that he would never agitate or support Roman Catholic emancipation, or the repeal of the Test Act; and that in the new ministry (wherein the king hoped Mr. Pitt would include as many of his Majesty's present servants as possible) Mr. Fox should be excluded. Mr. Pitt had previously determined that he would not again press the Catholic claims upon his royal master, whether he should be in or out of office. This resolution had been made known to the king so long ago as March 1801; so that, while he contrived on this occasion to evade giving the formal pledge which his Majesty required, he was nevertheless able to satisfy his sovereign as to the policy he would advocate in the event of his return to power.[s] Although yielding to the necessity of the case, in recalling Mr. Pitt, the king was reluctant to part with Mr. Addington. Before taking the

---

[r] Lord Eldon's share in these transactions gave rise to an imputation that he intrigued for the return of Pitt to power, and for his own retention in office; but there seems no ground for this opinion. Edinb. Rev. vol. cvii. p. 157; Quar. Rev. Oct. 1862, p. 375.

[s] Knight, vol. vii. p. 431; Parl. Deb. vol. ix. p. 254; Edinb. Rev. vol. cvii. pp. 150–157.

final step, he offered his faithful premier a dissolution of Parliament, if he thought it would insure the stability of his administration. But this was declined; for, while Mr. Addington did not doubt his ability to restore and retain his ascendancy in the House of Commons, he felt that he could not command a majority in the Lords without resorting to the extreme and dangerous measure of creating a batch of peers.¹ He therefore resigned office on May 10, 1804.

6. *Mr. Pitt's Second Administration.*—1804.

1804.   Mr. Pitt, when invited to communicate with the king in regard to the existing state of public affairs, sent his Majesty a letter, on May 2, through Lord Eldon, containing a plan for the formation of a new government, which should comprehend the leaders of all political parties. The king, who was greatly troubled at this time by the resignation of his favourite Addington, and not at all willing to re-admit Pitt to office, gave a discouraging reply. But on May 7, after Pitt had satisfied the King that he would no longer agitate him by renewing his advocacy of the Roman Catholic claims, he had an audience of his Majesty, and succeeded, with some difficulty, in obtaining leave to treat with Lord Grenville and his friends, and with the friends of Mr. Fox; but the king positively refused to admit Mr. Fox himself into the cabinet, though pressed to receive him by Pitt. The Grenville party, however, declined to accept office without Fox, and Pitt was compelled to make other arrangements. The new cabinet consisted principally of peers; Lord Castlereagh being the only one, besides Pitt, who was a member of the House of Commons.² Pitt took his seat, after his re-

---

¹ Adolphus, vol. vii. p. 708.   ² Edinb. Rev. vol. cvii. pp. 158, 159.

election, on May 18, 1804. But he found himself less strong in the confidence of the House than heretofore. A severe and mortifying trial overtook him in the following session. His friend and colleague, Lord Melville (First Lord of the Admiralty), was accused, in the Tenth Report of the Commissioners of Naval Inquiry, with a misappropriation of public money when he held the office of Treasurer of the Navy. A motion, inculpating him of this offence, was carried in the House of Commons by the Speaker's casting vote, notwithstanding the opposition of Pitt. A few days afterwards, Mr. Pitt informed the House that Lord Melville had resigned his ministerial office; and that he had advised the king to erase his name from the list of the privy council.[k] In the autumn of 1805, Pitt again endeavoured to overcome the king's objections to Mr. Fox, but without success; and he was obliged to abandon the idea of meeting Parliament with any accession of administrative or parliamentary strength.[l] But it was fated that he should never meet Parliament again. His health, which had been long failing, suddenly gave way, and he died on January 23, 1806, at the early age of forty-eight. After Mr. Pitt's decease, the junction of political parties, which he had latterly striven to bring about, though frustrated by the king's refusal to admit Mr. Fox into the cabinet, was accomplished. The critical state of our continental relations induced the leading politicians to sink minor differences in a general union, and to agree to the formation of a Coalition government on a wide and comprehensive basis.[m]

1805.

1806.

---

[k] Edinb. Rev. vol. cvii. p. 105. Articles of impeachment were exhibited against Lord Melville; and he was tried by the House of Lords, but pronounced not guilty. He was then restored to his place in the privy council; but never afterwards held office, though invited to do so by the Portland administration. Ibid. vol. cviii. p. 300.
[l] Ibid. vol. cvii. pp. 107, 108.
[m] Ibid. p. 171.

7. *Lord Grenville's Administration.*—1806.

1806.

After an ineffectual attempt on the part of the king to induce Lord Hawkesbury (the Home Secretary) to form a new ministry, which should represent as nearly as possible the principles of the late cabinet, his Majesty was induced, by the retiring ministers, to send, on January 26, for Lord Grenville, and empower him to form a comprehensive administration, which, it was understood, should include Mr. Fox. From the eminent statesmen of which this ministry was composed, it became known as 'All the Talents.' Fox was appointed Foreign Secretary, and leader of the House of Commons. The only terms which the new ministers made with the king related to the management of the army. They contended for the principle that the army should cease to be subject to the direct control of the crown through the commander-in-chief, and should be brought into subordination to the cabinet. This proposition was resisted by the king, but his objection was removed by an agreement that no change should be introduced into the government of the army without his Majesty's approbation.* Upon the question of the Roman Catholic claims the ministry were divided, and had no declared policy. With a view to strengthen their political position, Lord Ellenborough, the Chief Justice of the King's Bench, had been admitted to a seat in the cabinet. This arrangement was open to grave constitutional objections, and became the subject of animadversion in both Houses of Parliament. Although the appointment was successfully defended at the time, it was generally condemned by public opinion, and no similar appointment has since been made.* On September 13, 1806, Mr. Fox died, an event which weakened the ministry in Parliament very materially. But the

---

* Sir G. C. Lewis, in Edinb. Rev. vol. cviii. pp. 200-202 ; and see *ante,* p. 50.

* See a full discussion of this question, in Vol. II. c. 1.

changes of office proposed by Lord Grenville, and assented to by the king, preserved the balance of power in the Coalition government.* In the following month the Parliament was dissolved; and in the new House of Commons the ministry were able to command a large majority. However, their downfall was near at hand. True to their avowed principles when in opposition, they drafted a Bill to remove certain civil disabilities of Roman Catholics and Dissenters who held commissions in the army or navy. They sought and obtained permission from his Majesty to submit this measure to Parliament. But the king's consent was given with great reluctance; and, as it afterwards proved, with a misapprehension as to the extent of relief proposed to be granted. This misapprehension was shared in by some members of the cabinet itself. When the ministerial intentions were fully explained, one of their number (Lord Sidmouth) tendered his resignation, and the king declared his decided opposition to the Bill; which, meanwhile, had been introduced, and read a first time in the House of Commons. The ministry anxiously disavowed any intention to deceive their royal master, or to go beyond the authority they presumed he had given them to initiate legislation on this subject; and the king himself fully acquitted them of any such design. In order to satisfy his Majesty's scruples, the ministry, on March 15, passed a cabinet minute, which they communicated to the king, and in which they agreed to withdraw the Bill, but nevertheless recorded their opinion that it was their right and duty to propose, at any time, such measures for the relief of their Roman Catholic fellow-subjects as they might deem to be called for by the condition of Ireland. The king resented this declaration, and insisted that it should be withdrawn. But, not content with this, he endeavoured to exact from the ministry a pledge that they would never, under any

1807.

---

* See Edinb. Rev. vol. cviii. p. 302.

circumstances, propose in cabinet any measure of concession to the Roman Catholics, or in relation thereto. They very properly refused to give any such assurance; whereupon, on March 24, they received their dismissal.⁶ On the day previous, Lord Howick (Foreign Secretary) informed the House of Commons that, although ministers had not received the royal commands to deliver up the seals of office, the king had thought proper to send for persons not employed as his servants, and was engaged in arrangements for a new administration.⁷ On the 25th instant, after the dismissal, his lordship gave notice that as, on the morrow, the House would be moved to adjourn for several days, he would take the opportunity to give explanations respecting the change of ministry. A similar notice was given by the late premier in the House of Lords. At the time appointed, the explanations were made, and a short debate thereupon arose in both Houses. In the course of the debate, notice was given (in each House) of intended motions in regard to the circumstances attending the dismissal of the ministry.⁸ Parliament then adjourned until April 8.

6. *Duke of Portland's Second Administration.*—1807.

1807. Meanwhile the Duke of Portland, who had been charged by the king to form a new ministry, appears, on March 25, 1807, to have succeeded in that undertaking; although no formal announcement of his success seems to have been communicated to Parliament.⁹ But, on the following day, new writs were moved for, in the Commons, on behalf of the members of the incoming administration who had seats in that House. On April 9, the new ministers being present, Mr. Brand moved to resolve, 'That it is

---

⁶ Knight, vol. vii. pp. 478–480. Parl. Deb. vol. ix. pp. 266–270.
⁷ Parl. Deb. vol. ix. p. 174.
⁸ *Ibid.* pp. 260, 279.
⁹ *Ibid.* p. 187. For an account of the new ministerial arrangements, see Edinb. Rev. vol. cviii. p. 308.

contrary to the first duties of the confidential servants of the crown to restrain themselves by any pledge, expressed or implied, from offering to the king any advice which the course of circumstances may render necessary for the welfare and security of any part of the empire.' There was a general acquiescence by members in this doctrine, but it was objected to as being 'an abstract proposition,' and therefore inexpedient and inconvenient for the House directly to affirm. Accordingly, an amendment, that the other orders of the day be read, was proposed on behalf of ministers, and agreed to. During the debate, Mr. Perceval (the Chancellor of the Exchequer) stated that, 'to the best of his knowledge and belief, the king had no adviser on the point of requesting the pledge;'[a] a remark which called forth emphatic declarations 'that there was not a moment in the king's life, from his accession to his demise, when there was not a person constitutionally responsible for his actions;' that it was 'of the greatest importance to his Majesty that the doctrine of responsible advisers should be strictly maintained;' and that, although the king, in dismissing a ministry, in the exercise of his undoubted prerogative, might appear to be acting without advice, yet that the incoming ministry did themselves assume the responsibility of the dismissal of their predecessors. The king being irresponsible by law, if the ministers should also claim, for whatever reason, to be absolved from responsibility, there would be no security for the people against the evils of bad government.'[b] In the House of Lords, on April 13, the Marquis of Stafford made a motion similar in effect to that submitted to the House of Commons by

---

[a] Parl. Deb. vol. ix. p. 328. He admitted, however, that he 'approved of what had been done, and was ready to be responsible for it' (p. 316); a declaration in which Mr. Secretary Canning expressed his full concurrence (p. 346). But, a few days afterwards, Mr. Perceval reiterated his denial of the doctrine, that ministers who accepted office were legally responsible for the change of government (p. 473).

[b] Ibid. pp. 285, 320, 335, 362, 380.

Mr. Brand, except that it was prefaced by a preamble, expressive of regret at the changes which had taken place in his Majesty's councils. It was met on behalf of ministers by a motion to adjourn, which was carried. On April 15, Mr. Lyttleton moved, in the House of Commons, 'That this House, considering a firm and efficient administration as indispensably necessary, in the present important crisis of public affairs, has seen, with the deepest regret, the late change in his Majesty's councils.' The friends of the motion acknowledged the right of the king to choose his own advisers, but insisted that the House had the privilege of giving its opinion on the fitness of the persons selected to fill the situations to which they were appointed.* But the House were not prepared to limit the exercise of the prerogative so far as to refuse a fair trial to the king's ministers. The debate was in substance a repetition of the former discussion; but it was signalised by an able speech from Sir William Grant (the Master of the Rolls), in which he commented severely on the attempt of the late ministers to expose the king to odium because he had thought fit to dismiss them. He remarked that many ministers had been dismissed from office without any cause assigned, but that never until now had any one come to Parliament to complain of his sovereign. 'Lord Somers was removed without a shadow of complaint; did he demand an investigation of the cause? When Godolphin's administration was removed by Queen Anne, did they complain to Parliament? In 1757, the dismissal of Mr. Pitt and Mr. Legge produced a great ferment; but was anything said about that dismissal in Parliament? If a minister were to secure himself the right of enquiry into the causes of his removal, he would approximate his situation to that of a judge, or any other officer, for life. Of a change in administration, Parliament had no constitutional knowledge,

---

* Parl. Deb. vol. ix. p. 472.

and on such change could found no enquiry.'ᵃ An amendment, on behalf of ministers, to pass to the orders of the day, was then put and carried. Notwithstanding that by these votes the new government was fully sustained by majorities in Parliament, advantage was taken of the popular feeling in favour of the king's act in dismissing his ministers upon 'Protestant grounds,' to dissolve Parliament at the end of its first session. The main issue raised by this appeal to the country was the propriety of the conduct of his Majesty in changing his advisers; proceeding, as it did, from a conscientious conviction that a due regard for the maintenance of the principle of Protestantism in the constitution demanded such a proceeding. This was distinctly enunciated in the royal speech at the prorogation of Parliament.ᵇ The elections went in favour of ministers, and their majority was largely increased in the new House of Commons. Upon the meeting of Parliament, amendments to the address, in answer to the speech from the throne, were proposed in both Houses, condemning the dissolution, as having been resorted to upon 'groundless and injurious pretences;' but they were negatived by large majorities.ᶜ The Duke of Portland, we have seen, was the nominal head of this ministry; but its most influential member was Mr. Spencer Perceval, the Chancellor of the Exchequer.

9. *Mr. Perceval's Administration.*—1809.

On October 30, 1809, the Duke of Portland died. After an ineffectual attempt to induce Lord Grenville to form an extended and combined administration, he was succeeded by Mr. Perceval as premier.ᵈ The new cabinet

1809.

ᵃ Parl. Deb. vol. ix. p. 474.
ᵇ *Ibid.* p. 552. Mr. Canning and Lord Castlereagh laid themselves open to attack for sanctioning the 'No Popery.' cry on this occasion; notwithstanding their own convictions in favour of Roman Catholic emancipation. See Edinb. Rev. vol. cviii. p. 312.
ᶜ *Ibid.* pp. 583-658.
ᵈ Knight, vol. vii. p. 526. Edinb.

consisted of ten persons, seven of whom were peers. In December following, the Marquis Wellesley was appointed Foreign Secretary, an office which he continued to hold until February 19, 1812, when he resigned, because his 'general opinions for a long time past, on various important questions, had not sufficient weight in the cabinet to justify' his remaining in the government. He had chiefly objected to the narrow and imperfect scale on which the war in Spain had been conducted. His views on this head had been always overborne in council by Mr. Perceval. In announcing his intention to retire from office, he declared that he should have no objection, in any future ministerial arrangements that might be determined upon, to serve *with* Mr. Perceval, provided the principles he contended for were carried out; but that 'he never again would serve *under* Mr. Perceval in any circumstances.'[b] A few weeks afterwards, this administration was deprived of its main-stay, by the assassination of the premier, on May 11, in the lobby of the House of Commons. Then came a struggle for power, which left the country virtually without a government for about a month. The prince regent,[c] after the death of Mr. Perceval, being desirous of continuing the administration

---

Rev. vol. cviii. p. 323. Mr. Perceval held the two offices of First Lord of the Treasury and Chancellor of the Exchequer in conjunction. The Chancellorship of the Exchequership had been offered, on this occasion, to Mr. Milnes and to Lord Palmerston, but declined by each. *Ibid.* p. 324 *n.*

[b] Parl. Deb. vol. xxiii. pp. 307–370. Mr. Perceval was desirous of appointing Lord Sidmouth Foreign Secretary in place of Lord Wellesley; but the prince regent, who had at this time a personal repugnance to Lord Sidmouth, positively refused his consent. Edinb. Rev. vol. cviii. p. 342. But, a year after, his lordship became a member of the cabinet. *Ibid.* p. 345.

[c] Contrary to general expectation, the Prince of Wales, upon his assumption of the regency, in February 1811, addressed a letter to Mr. Perceval, stating that it was not his intention to remove the existing ministers from office. This step, he added, was prompted exclusively by filial duty and affection. Edinb. Rev. vol. cviii. p. 340. A year afterwards, when the restrictions on the regent expired, he still continued Mr. Perceval as minister. He did, indeed, invite the co-operation of Lords Grey and Grenville, but they could not consent to form a junction with their political opponents. *Ibid.* pp. 342–343. The death of George III., which took place on January 29, 1820, was not followed by any important political consequence.

upon its existing basis, authorised Lord Eldon (the chancellor) to ascertain whether the cabinet were willing, if called upon by his royal highness, to carry on the government under any one of their colleagues whom his royal highness might select. The cabinet replied that they would be perfectly willing to do so, but that under the existing circumstances of the country they considered that the result would be very doubtful. They appeared to think that at any rate it was advisable to invite the co-operation of the leading Whig statesmen before venturing to act without them.[a] Accordingly, the prince regent, who was anxious to strengthen, as much as possible, his present ministry by the introduction therein of public men who coincided with the general principles on which the government of the country had been hitherto conducted, authorised the Earl of Liverpool (then Colonial Secretary) to negotiate with Lord Wellesley and Mr. Canning with a view to their joining the administration. A communication was therefore addressed by Lord Liverpool, with the consent of his colleagues, to these gentlemen, on May 17. But it was declined by them upon the ground that they could form part of no ministry that was not prepared to adopt a less restrictive policy towards the Roman Catholics. Lord Wellesley furthermore objected to the manner in which the war was carried on, as evincing but little improvement since he withdrew from the ministry on that account.[b] Notwithstanding this failure, the remaining members of the existing administration were unwilling to retire from office,[c] being confident of their ability to carry on the government, if only they could succeed in replacing their able and popular chief, and could agree together on a definite line of policy. But their continuance in office was not satisfactory to the

---

[a] Twiss, Life of Eldon, vol. i. p. 403.
[b] Parl. Deb. vol. xxiii. Appx. p. l.
[c] On May 20, Mr. Nicholas Vansittart was appointed to the office of Chancellor of the Exchequer, and a new writ moved for in the House of Commons. He took his seat on June 10.

1812 House of Commons. Accordingly, on May 21, Mr. Stuart Wortley moved the adoption of an address to the prince regent, praying him to take measures for the formation of 'a strong and efficient administration.' The motion was resisted on the ground that it was 'an unconstitutional and unprecedented interference with the prerogative of the crown.' 'The House had interfered when an administration had been formed and found inefficient; but they never had come forward with their previous advice. It was their duty to watch over and control the crown; but there was no doctrine in the constitution better understood than that they had no right to interfere with the crown in the nomination of its servants.'[a] An amendment was moved, 'that the other orders of the day be read.' Mr. Wilberforce adverted to the case of 1784[b] as deciding the question, 'whether the House should have a previous negative on the appointment of the ministers of the crown. It had then been determined that it should not, and that it was only when either or both of the Houses of Parliament had had experience of some of the measures of ministers, that, if they could not confide in the administration, it became their duty to address the throne, and express their judgment.'[c] But Mr. Canning drew a proper distinction when he said that he perfectly concurred in the general doctrine laid down, that it is the exclusive prerogative of the crown to nominate its own ministers; that the case must be urgent indeed to authorise the interference of the House; but that he could not forget that Parliament had a double character. 'The House of Commons is a Council of Control, but it is likewise a Council of Advice;' and a case of 'transcendent importance' might arise, in which it would be 'competent for the legislature, by the timely interposition of advice, to prevent the necessity of control.'[d] This distinction

---

[a] Parl. Deb. vol. xxiii. p. 250.
[b] See *ante*, p. 78.
[c] Parl. Deb. vol. xxiii. p. 258.
[d] Ibid. p. 207.

was agreed to by the Foreign Secretary (Lord Castlereagh), who nevertheless contended 'that the House was not by circumstances justified, at this moment, to interfere.' Mr. Wortley's motion, however, was agreed to by a majority of four, and the address was ordered to be presented to the prince regent by the mover and seconder. It received a gracious reply from his royal highness. Viewing the address as tantamount to a declaration of their own inefficiency, the remaining members of the ministry immediately placed their offices at the prince regent's disposal, and it was understood that they merely continued in office until his royal highness should signify his pleasure as to any future arrangement.[k] At this juncture the prince regent laid his commands on the Marquis Wellesley to form a plan of administration, and submit the same for his approval. Accordingly, on May 23, the marquis requested Mr. Canning to be the medium of communication between himself and Lord Liverpool, for the purpose of inviting his lordship, with such of his colleagues as might be willing, to assist in the formation of a new ministry, on the basis of an early adjustment of the Roman Catholic claims, and the prosecution of the war with vigour. This overture was also declined. Simultaneously with his appeal to Lord Liverpool, Lord Wellesley addressed himself to Lords Grey and Grenville to the same effect, informing them, however, that he considered himself on this occasion as being merely the instrument for executing the prince regent's commands, and that he neither claimed nor desired for himself any station in the projected administration. On May 26, while this

---

[k] Lord Liverpool. Parl. Deb. vol. xxiii. pp. 332, 357. During the whole of this ministerial interregnum, and until (on June 8) he was formally commissioned by the prince regent to form an administration, Lord Liverpool appears to have been regarded, on all sides, as the temporary head of the ministry. He was its chief mouthpiece in Parliament, the recognised organ of his colleagues, and the one whom, it was understood, they were desirous should be appointed to the premiership. Memoirs of Lord Liverpool, pp. 415–427.

1812. negotiation was still pending, the prince regent revoked Lord Wellesley's general commission. But subsequently his lordship received more precise and definite powers, so that on June 1 he was able to inform Lord Grey that he had been fully commissioned to become the premier of an administration, to be formed on the basis above mentioned, and that he had been specially authorised to invite the co-operation of Lords Grey and Grenville, with permission to those noble lords to recommend four or five persons for seats in the cabinet, together with Lords Moira and Erskine, and Mr. Canning, who, it had been agreed, should form part of the same. In reply, Lords Grey and Grenville declined to participate in a government to be formed on the basis of 'the supposed balance of contending interests.' They considered that such a principle would 'establish within the cabinet itself a system of counteraction inconsistent with the prosecution of any uniform and consistent course of policy;' which could only be productive of weakness and disunion, and would be utterly opposed to the object of the House of Commons in recommending the formation of a strong and efficient administration. They furthermore objected to the nomination, on behalf of the prince regent, of Lords Moira and Erskine, and Mr. Canning, to seats in the cabinet, not on the plea that it was an unconstitutional exercise of power on the part of his royal highness, but because 'the first and vital principle of a cabinet was the mutual confidence of its members, and the total absence of everything like jealousy among them;' and this could only be insured when the parties invited to form a government were empowered 'to arrange the cabinet among themselves.'[1] On June 3, Lord Wellesley acquainted the prince regent of his failure in this undertaking, and was informed that the task would be entrusted to other hands. On June 5, Lord Moira, as the confidential friend of

---

[1] Parl. Deb. vol. xxiii. p. 428.

the prince regent, endeavoured to bring about a political understanding with Lords Grey and Grenville, but they refused to enter into 'unauthorised discussions.' Next day Lord Moira again addressed their lordships, acquainting them that he had the prince regent's instructions to take steps towards the formation of a new ministry, with special authority to invite their lordships' co-operation. On the following day, a meeting took place between these noblemen, in the presence of Lord Erskine, at which Lord Moira stated that he had received his commission 'without any restriction or limitation whatever being laid by the prince on their considering any points which they judged useful for his service,' or as to the filling up of any place in the cabinet. This announcement was favourably received, but their lordships desired to know, at the outset, whether the liberty to be accorded to them in filling up offices in the new ministry extended to the consideration of new appointments to those great offices in the household which have been usually included in political arrangements made on a change of ministry. To this Lord Moira replied that he had no commands from the prince regent on this head; but that, for his own part, he could not concur in this exercise of power on the present occasion, because he should deem it, on public grounds, peculiarly objectionable. Their lordships answered that, on similar grounds, 'it appeared to them indispensable that the connection of the great offices of the court with the political administration should be clearly established in its first arrangements.' A decided difference of opinion as to this point having been thus expressed on both sides, the conversation ended here, with mutual declarations of regret." In the subsequent explanations in Parliament on this point, it was admitted that a new administration had a right to claim the removal of these officers of the household; but its exercise, under existing circumstances, was

---

" Parl. Deb. vol. xxiii. Appx. pp. xx-xlii.

deemed inexpedient and impolitic. The prince regent himself appears to have been quite willing to part with all these functionaries; but Lord Moira, who was his adviser on this occasion, decidedly objected to such a proceeding.º After his unsatisfactory interview with the Whig noblemen, Lord Moira relinquished the task entrusted to him, and advised the prince regent to have recourse once more to the assistance of his former servants; whereupon the old ministry was reconstituted under the premiership of Lord Liverpool.º

10. *Lord Liverpool's Administration.*—1812.

1812. During the progress of these protracted negotiations the House of Commons continued sitting, and frequent attempts were made to invoke its interference, in the shape of remonstrances and appeals, in respect to the proposed ministerial arrangements, but without success. On May 30, after the failure of Lord Wellesley's first overtures to Lord Liverpool, and to Lords Grey and Grenville, Mr. Martin, of Galway, gave notice that he would, on June 3, move an address to the prince regent beseeching him to carry into effect his gracious declaration, in reply to the address of the House on May 21, and proceed without delay to appoint a strong ministry, 'possessing more of the confidence of the people than that which had lately been in existence.'ᵖ But on June 1, Mr. Canning informed the House that the Marquis Wellesley had been empowered to form a new administration. Mr. Wortley then proceeded to enquire of Mr. Ponsonby whether any proposal had been made to him, or to those who acted with him in Parliament, to form part of the ministry; what reply had been given, and what conditions made. After some altercation on the

---

º Parl. Deb. vol. xxiii. pp. 398–430, 453. And see Edinb. Rev. vol. cviii. pp. 337–340.

º Twiss, Life of Eldon, vol. i. p. 400.

ᵖ Parl. Deb. vol. xxiii. p. 312.

point of order, these questions were permitted to be put, they being according to precedent, and unobjectionable in principle, 'as tending to explain the conduct and clear the characters of public men.'⁴ It was then proposed that the House should go into committee to sanction a contract for a loan of a million and a half of money for the service of Ireland. This was objected to, on the ground that there was no responsible minister to answer for the same. But it was replied that the contract had been approved by the late premier, and that 'the Irish Chancellor of the Exchequer (the Right Hon. W. Fitzgerald) was before the House, and in a responsible situation.' Whereupon the resolution was agreed to.⁵ On June 2, Mr. Martin, on being questioned whether he meant to proceed with the motion of which he had given notice for the morrow, answered that, as he was satisfied with the commission given to Lord Wellesley, it was highly improbable, though not impossible, that he should bring forward his motion.⁶ On June 3, the Marquis Wellesley informed the House of Lords that he had resigned the authority given him by the prince regent to form a new ministry, and that he had received permission to disclose all the circumstances attending his endeavours in that behalf, and would be ready, when called upon, to communicate them to the House. But he advised

---

⁴ Parl. Deb. vol. xxiii. pp. 313–316.

⁵ Ibid. pp. 317, 318. A few days before, objection was taken to the regularity of the House of Commons proceeding to vote a pecuniary provision for the family of the late lamented premier, on the ground that, as he united in his own person the offices of First Lord of the Treasury and Chancellor of the Exchequer, by his decease the country was left 'without an administration.' To this it was replied that no objection could be taken to the proceeding in point of form, inasmuch as the proposition 'had been regularly introduced to the House by a message from the throne, brought by a minister of the crown,' and there was no rule of the House requiring that such a proposition should be submitted by a Chancellor of the Exchequer. The House then proceeded to pass resolutions, based upon the prince regent's message on behalf of the family of Mr. Spencer Perceval, and in their liberality and respect for the memory of the murdered minister voted to increase the amount of the provision recommended by the crown. Ibid. pp. 109, 211, 217.

⁶ Ibid. p. 331.

1812. their lordships not to press for such disclosures at present, as it would be highly detrimental to the public interests.[1] After some debate, the House appeared in favour of delaying the explanations, and adjourned for two days. In the Commons, on the same day, Mr. Canning stated the fact of Lord Wellesley's non-success. Whereupon Mr. Martin began to question Mr. Ponsonby on the subject; but a member interposed, and declared that, if the attempt were persisted in, he would move to take the sense of the House upon it. This induced Mr. Martin to forbear, and also to abandon the motion of which he had given notice.[2] On June 5, Earl Grey informed the House of Lords of the failure of the negotiations entered into by Lord Wellesley with himself and Lord Grenville, attributing it to the fact that the prince regent had intimated his pleasure that 'four individuals expressly named should occupy seats in the cabinet;' whilst Lord Grey and his friends were merely invited to propose eight or nine other persons for this position. In reply Lord Moira stated that, 'with regard to the nomination of individuals, it was to be understood to be a mere statement of a wish' on the part of his royal highness, who presumed that the persons indicated would be generally acceptable.[3] On the same day, in the Commons, upon the reception of the Report of the Committee of Ways and Means, objection was taken that the House was placed in the dilemma of either withholding the necessary supplies, or of granting them without a responsible minister. But the distinction was drawn that no opposition ought to be made on this ground 'till the last stage of each financial measure, by which time it was to be presumed an efficient administration would be formed.'[4] General Gascoyne then gave notice that on the next sitting day he would move an address to the

---

[1] Parl. Deb. vol. xxiii. p. 333.
[2] *Ibid.* p. 334.
[3] *Ibid.* pp. 343–345. See also his remarks at p. 380. A fuller explanation of the cause of the failure of this negotiation has been already given in this narrative; *ante*, p. 198.
[4] *Ibid.* p. 352.

prince regent, expressing regret at the failure of the efforts to form a government, and a wish that no further delay should take place. It was then agreed, with some reluctance, to adjourn the House (from Friday) till Monday; an opinion of Mr. Pitt having been quoted that, in a crisis like the present, 'time should be measured not by days, but by hours,' and that 'the House should sit as often as it possibly could, and exert its vigilance over the proceedings of public men.'* But an end was about to be put to these protracted difficulties. On Monday, June 8, the Earl of Liverpool informed the House of Lords that he had been appointed First Lord of the Treasury, and had received authority to complete an administration as soon as possible. Lord Moira took this opportunity to state that the task confided to him of endeavouring to ' conciliate the differences of public men, and to form an administration which should possess the confidence of the country, had been unsuccessful.' Lord Wellesley then proceeded to give his hitherto deferred explanations as to the causes of the failure of his attempts in the same direction; and a discussion ensued between the various noble lords interested therein.' On the same day, the House of Commons was informed, by Lord Castlereagh, of the commission given to Lord Liverpool; and members were urged to postpone the discussion of important questions until the new ministry was formed. Strong objections were made to any further delay, but ultimately the motions were put off, though the House continued to sit every day."

On June 8, 1812, as we have seen, the Earl of Liverpool announced to Parliament that he had been appointed First Lord of the Treasury, with authority to complete the administration as soon as possible. The new ministry was substantially the same as the previous

---

* Parl. Deb. vol. xxiii. p. 354.   * Ibid. pp. 391-38..
' Ibid. pp. 350-380.

1812 one, the principal difference being that—although the premier's own opinions were decidedly opposed to emancipation—it was agreed that the cabinet should consider the Roman Catholic claims as an 'open question,' while Mr. Perceval's administration, on the other hand, had been distinctly 'anti-Catholic.'[a] On this ground of similarity to its predecessor—which nevertheless had enjoyed the confidence of Parliament—the new administration was immediately assailed in the House of Commons. On June 11, Mr. Stuart Wortley, being of opinion that a stronger government might have been formed, notwithstanding the failure of the recent negotiations, proposed an address to the prince regent, expressing regret that the address of May 21, which had been so graciously received by his royal highness, had not led to the appointment of an administration that was 'entitled to the support of Parliament, and the confidence of the nation;' and entreating that such a ministry might be formed without delay.[b] To this an amendment was moved by Lord Folkestone, representing that the new administration was essentially the same as the one that had already experienced the disapprobation of the country, and whose management of public affairs had been so prejudicial to the national interests; and imploring the appointment of men of wisdom, firmness, and prudence, in the present emergency of the state.[c] A second amendment, of a similar purport, was also submitted by Lord Milton.[d] After considerable debate, it became apparent that the sense of the House was opposed to these propositions, viewing them as attempts to dictate to the head of the executive in regard to the choice of his servants. It was urged, on behalf of the ministry, by Lord Castlereagh, that an interference by the House, under existing circumstances, would be unprecedented

---

[a] May, Const. Hist. vol. ii. pp. 304, 374; An. Reg. 1827, p. 61.
[b] Parl. Deb. vol. xxiii. p. 380.
[c] Ibid. p. 403.
[d] Ibid. p. 400.

and unwarrantable. He claimed for the new administration 'the constitutional support of Parliament, till their actions should show them to be unworthy of it.' The several motions were then put and negatived; two of them without a division, and the third by a majority of 125.* The administration, thus vehemently assailed at the outset of its career, and presumed to be incapable of weathering even the current session, proved to be one of the most durable and successful cabinets ever known. Lord Liverpool, though not a man of remarkable abilities, was prudent, sagacious, and conciliatory; well fitted for the eminent position to which he had attained, and admirably adapted to cope with the peculiar evils of the times.' He was ably sustained by his colleagues in office, some of whom were greatly his superiors in intellect, but who, nevertheless, were willing to acknowledge his supremacy in council. With these advantages Lord Liverpool was enabled to continue at the helm of the state for upwards of fourteen years. During the whole of this period the cabinet continued without any material change of policy, and without any important additions of individual strength—except the return of Mr. Canning to office, in 1816, and his promotion to the leadership of the House of Commons, in September 1822; the entrance of the Duke of Wellington into the ministry, as Master-General of the Ordnance, in 1819; of Mr. Peel, as Home Secretary, in 1822; and of Mr. Huskisson, as President of the Board of Trade, in 1823. At length, on February 17, 1827, Lord Liverpool was seized with an attack of paralysis, which, though not fatal at the time, was of such severity as to render his retention of office impossible.* Six weeks afterwards, as soon as returning consciousness permitted, he tendered his resignation to the king; and his situation was such as to give

1812.

1827.

---

* Parl. Deb. vol. xxiii. pp. 397–404.
f Sir G. C. Lewis says that 'he performed the most important function of a prime minister, that of keeping his cabinet together.' Edinb. Rev. vol. cx. p. 70.
ᶠ He died on Dec. 4, 1828, aged 58 years.

1827. the sovereign no alternative but to accept it. During the long interval which elapsed between the seizure of Lord Liverpool and his resignation of office, the administration was left virtually without a head. Nor did his final retirement solve the difficulty. The men who had been content to act in subordination to Lord Liverpool, out of respect to his personal worth and integrity of purpose, were by no means willing to yield the pre-eminence to one of their own number. They were not disposed themselves to retire from office; but they required a chief, in whose political views they could coincide, and, above all, one who should be able to form a cabinet that would regard the Roman Catholic claims as an open question, upon a similar system of compromise to that which had been agreed upon by Lord Liverpool's administration. Both Mr. Peel and Mr. Canning were well qualified to fill the vacant post; but the former was the recognised leader of the anti-Catholic party, and the latter had been equally conspicuous for his advocacy of emancipation. Neither of these statesmen, moreover, could be expected to serve under the other. Such were the difficulties wherein his Majesty was involved. The king's first attempt was to consult Mr. Canning (on March 27), in his capacity of a privy councillor, upon the reconstruction of the ministry. Mr. Canning recommended that a cabinet should be formed whose members would unite in opposing Roman Catholic emancipation, a policy which was in conformity with the acknowledged sentiments of his Majesty, and with the existing state of public opinion on the question. In giving this disinterested advice, Mr. Canning expressed his own readiness to retire from office rather than be an obstacle to such an arrangement. But this offer was rejected by the king, who desired to retain Mr. Canning in his service, and to place a peer of anti-Catholic opinions at the head of the ministry. Mr. Canning, however, objected to the 'superinduction of an anti-Catholic first minister over his head;' he was, in fact, desirous of placing Mr. Robinson, whose views on the

Catholic question agreed with his own, at the head of the Treasury, and of retaining his place as Foreign Secretary, with the understanding that he should be the virtual premier. But this scheme proved to be impracticable. Other plans were then devised, but it was found impossible to agree upon anything which would allow the prominent members of the Liverpool cabinet to continue to act in concert. The latter part of February, and the whole of March, were consumed in these fruitless negotiations. All this time the old ministry nominally continued in office, although it was understood that they merely held their places until their successors should be appointed. The Liverpool administration was accordingly regarded as virtually defunct.[b]

During this ministerial interregnum, on March 30 it was moved in the House of Commons, by the Chancellor of the Exchequer, that the report of the Committee of Supply (being resolutions granting money which was required in order to carry on the public service) be brought up. Mr. Tierney opposed the motion, alleging that there was no administration to be responsible for such expenditure. Admitting the undoubted privilege of the king to choose his own ministers, he claimed for the House of Commons that it had a right to know to whom the administration had been entrusted before it separated for the Easter holidays. He therefore moved to defer the consideration of the report until May 1. Mr. Secretary Canning replied that the delay which had arisen in filling up the office of premier had resulted from a hope that Lord Liverpool's illness might prove but transitory, and that ministers were ready to assume as much responsibility for the same as for any other act of their administration. But no further delay would take place, inasmuch as the king, regarding the premier's recovery as hopeless, had authorised the formation of a new

---
[b] Annual Register, 1827, pp. 60-60; Sir G. C. Lewis, in Edinb. Rev. vol. ca. pp. 71-77.

1827. ministry. Under these circumstances, he claimed that the necessary supplies should be granted, otherwise the House would affix a stigma upon those who still remained in office, which would be equivalent to a vote of censure, and would strike at their existence as a ministry. Mr. Tierney then asked for an assurance that some definitive arrangement with respect to the administration would be entered into before the House adjourned for the holidays. This Mr. Canning refused to give; whereupon Mr. Tierney declared that he must persist in his amendment, and resist any further grant of money until he knew in whose hands the government of the country had been placed. The Chancellor of the Exchequer reminded the House that they had already been informed that the proposed grant was merely sufficient to enable the government to be carried on until after the recess. No more money would be asked for until a new administration was formed; otherwise he admitted that 'it would have been the imperative duty' of the House to oppose the same. The original motion was then put, and agreed to on division.[1] The want of agreement amongst the great party leaders with whom negotiations for a new ministry had been entered into induced Sir Thomas Lethbridge to give notice of a motion for an address to' the king that he would be pleased to take into consideration, in the appointment of his ministry, 'the great importance of unanimity in any cabinet on questions affecting the vital interests of the empire.' On April 6, however, the day on which this motion was to have been brought forward, the king came to town, professedly in order to take decisive steps to put an end to this protracted disorganisation of the cabinet, and Sir T. Lethbridge, by the advice of his friends, determined not to press his motion, although invited to proceed with it by Mr. Secretary Canning. The king had now finally determined that the new

---

[1] Parl. Deb. N. S. vol. xvii. pp. 157-171.

ministry, like its predecessor, should consider the Catholic claims as an 'open question,' and also that Mr. Canning should be premier, notwithstanding his previous prominence as the strenuous advocate of emancipation.[J]

11. *Mr. Canning's Administration.—April* 1827.

It was on April 10, 1827, that Mr. Canning, who held at the time the office of Secretary of State for Foreign Affairs, was commissioned by the king to prepare a plan for the reconstruction of the administration under his own presidency. The policy he intended to pursue in reference to the Roman Catholic question is uncertain, and has been made the subject of controversy between his friends and opponents. A new writ was moved for, on behalf of Mr. Canning, on April 12; and at the same time it was moved to adjourn the House for the Easter holidays, until May 1. This motion was opposed by Mr. Tierney, who desired that the House should know of whom the new ministry would be composed before it adjourned for so long a period. In reply, Mr. Wynn stated that undoubtedly some difficulties had occurred in the formation of a ministry, but that an arrangement was now in progress, and would certainly be completed before the time of adjournment had expired. The motions were then agreed to without a division. As soon as he was in a position to do so, Mr. Canning made overtures for assistance in the formation of a ministry to his colleagues in office; but for the most part they were either civilly or contemptuously rejected. Nearly the whole interval of the adjournment was spent in further negotiations. Disappointed in the support of his former associates, Mr. Canning was obliged to make new alliances, and his administration was finally completed by a Coalition with the Whigs, between whom and

[J] Annual Register, 1827, p. 00.

1827. himself there had been heretofore a decided political antagonism.* Explanations were given in the House of Commons by the retiring as well as by the incoming ministers on May 1, and in the House of Lords on the day following. The new premier was assailed by an inveterate hostility in both Houses of Parliament; and attacks upon the new ministry were continued throughout the session. The principles of the Coalition were vehemently attacked,¹ and the Opposition made repeated attempts, by enquiries of ministers, to elicit further particulars than had been already communicated in regard to the circumstances which had attended the formation of the ministry; and particularly whether certain appointments had been made provisionally, with the intention of a future rearrangement of ministerial offices. But Mr. Canning refused to give any further explanations, or 'to answer a single question relative to the late transactions, unless it were brought forward as a motion.' He considered it to be beneath the dignity of the House to waste its time in irregular and extraneous discussions. It should revert to the old usage of Parliament, and submit by formal motions such questions as it might be desirable for the House to entertain."' This incessant exhibition of party spirit hindered the progress of public business, and prevented the passing of any important measures. The principal events of the fragment of the session which succeeded the formation of Mr. Canning's ministry were, the personal alienation of Mr. Peel from the government, and the insertion of a hostile amendment in the Corn-law Bill, upon motion of the Duke of Wellington, which led to the abandonment of the Bill by the government.* At length, on July 2, Parliament was prorogued; but within six weeks of that period

---

* Annual Register, 1827, p. 103; pp. 607, 653, 1028. Edinb. Rev. vol. cx. p. 75.
¹ Parl. Deb. N. S. vol. xvii. (Lords) pp. 548, 853, 1083, (Commons),
" Ibid. pp. 832-834.
* Edinb. Rev. vol. cx. p. 70.

the great and gifted minister was no more. The labours and anxieties of office had brought him to an untimely grave.*

12. *Lord Goderich's Administration.—August* 1827.

The death of Mr. Canning led to the placing of Lord Goderich, early in August, at the head of the administration; otherwise the composition of the cabinet was but slightly altered. Mr. Herries was introduced into it as Chancellor of the Exchequer, in the room of Mr. Canning; but this appointment was so distasteful to the Whig section of the cabinet, that the Marquis of Lansdowne waited upon the king to resign the seals of the Home Department. Mr. Herries was objected to on political grounds, and also because he was supposed to be a nominee of the king. But on its being explained that his appointment had not been recommended by the king to the prime minister, but *vice versâ*, the Whigs consented to remain in office.* The new premier lacked the energy and decision of character that had enabled Mr. Canning to reconcile the discordant materials of which his cabinet was composed; accordingly, the dissensions which were unavoidable amongst such ill-assorted companions became more virulent, and rendered the ministry weaker and more helpless the nearer they approached to the meeting of Parliament. The Whigs, though seemingly reconciled to the presence of Mr. Herries, only tolerated him, and strove to diminish the just influence of his office by assuming the control of matters that were clearly within the jurisdiction of the finance minister. In so doing, they overthrew the

---

* Knight, vol. viii. p. 208.
* Annual Register, 1827, p. 102; 1828, p. 2. Lord Lansdowne himself consented to remain in office on condition that he might have the royal authority for stating that it was solely in submission to the express desire of his Majesty that he did so. Edinb. Rev. vol. cx. p. 78 n.

government. The occasion which led to this result appeared trivial and unimportant, but it truly indicated the hostility which prevailed between the rival parties in the cabinet. Mr. Canning, on opening the budget in 1827, had avowed the necessity for a thorough scrutiny into the financial condition and resources of the country, and had pledged himself to propose to the House, in the ensuing session, the appointment of a finance committee. Desirous of carrying out this engagement, the new cabinet began, towards the middle of November, to turn their attention to the formation of this committee. Mr. Tierney (the Master of the Mint), and his Whig friends in the cabinet, forthwith intrigued to get Lord Althorp fixed upon as the government nominee for the chairmanship of this committee. They succeeded in obtaining the premier's consent to his appointment, Lord Goderich being under the impression that the Chancellor of the Exchequer was a consenting party thereto. When he learnt that the proposition had not been communicated to Mr. Herries, he desired that he should be consulted upon it immediately. When Mr. Herries became aware that a matter so intimately connected with his own department had been arranged without his knowledge, he was naturally indignant. He was also of opinion that the appointment was objectionable on its own merits. Accordingly, he sought an interview with the premier on November 29, at which he made known to his lordship the strong objections he entertained, both on public and private grounds, to Lord Althorp's nomination, and to the proceedings of his colleagues in reference thereto. Lord Goderich received the communication with considerable agitation; admitted the wrong that had been done; and agreed that no time should be lost in removing the objections which had been stated.[*] Mr. Herries subsequently made a protest, in writing, against the nomination

---

[*] Annual Register, 1828, p. 7.

of Lord Althorp; after which the matter seems to have remained in abeyance for about a month, during which interval the government was in the agonies of dissolution from other causes. The premier, in fact, tendered his resignation to the king. But about December 19, the ministerial difficulties were tided over for a while. Whereupon, Mr. Herries again addressed the premier respecting the chairmanship of the Finance Committee, and offered to resign his office, so as to enable the government to appoint their own nominee. Hearing of this, Mr. Secretary Huskisson informed the premier that, unless Lord Althorp's appointment were persisted in, he would himself resign. Some further correspondence took place between the parties concerned, but without leading to any better understanding. Accordingly the premier, being unable to restore harmony in the cabinet, waited upon the king on January 8, and tendered his own resignation. Thus perished the Canning Coalition 'before it had been able to acquire a character, or gain that hold on public confidence which had been forfeited by the sudden reconciliation of the ancient enemies of whom it was composed.'[1] The dispute between Mr. Herries and Mr. Huskisson may have been the last straw that broke the camel's back; but, if so, it must have been already sinking under the pressure of accumulated burdens. The new ministry had scarcely been in existence more than five months, and was dissolved without ever having met Parliament; a circumstance wholly unprecedented in our political annals.[2]

---

[1] Annual Register, 1828, p. 11.
[2] A full account of the transactions which led to the downfall of this ministry will be found in chapters i. and ii. of the Annual Register for 1828.

13. *The Duke of Wellington's Administration.*—1828.

1828.   On January 8, 1828, the king sent for Lord Lyndhurst (the Lord Chancellor) and the Duke of Wellington, who was Commander-in-Chief, and entrusted the formation of a new ministry to the latter. Whereupon his grace resigned the office of Commander-in-Chief, and took that of First Lord of the Treasury.¹ There was no difficulty or delay in the construction of this government. It consisted, as nearly as possible, of men who had formed part of Lord Liverpool's administration, with the exception of the Whigs brought in by Mr. Canning, who were excluded upon this occasion. Parliament was not in session when these events took place. It met on January 29, and new writs were immediately issued for the re-election of such members of the new ministry as had seats in the House of Commons. The only representative of government remaining in the House during this interval was the Secretary-at-War (Lord Palmerston), who had uninterruptedly continued in office, during successive administrations, since 1809; and who had been re-appointed, with a seat in the cabinet, by the Duke of Wellington.² Notwithstanding the absence of the other cabinet ministers, and of their colleagues in office, the House proceeded with the debate upon the Address in answer to the speech from the throne, on the principle that the absence of ministers 'by no means takes from the House the right, or abridges the right, of free discussion.' But at the same time it was generally admitted that 'it would be inconvenient and unsatisfactory to attempt to enter upon questions intimately connected with disputable measures, in the absence of those whose duty it is to sustain those measures.'³ Lord John Russell went

---

¹ Hans. Deb. N. S. vol. xviii. p. 61.
² Lord Palmerston was first introduced into the cabinet by Mr. Canning, in 1827.
³ Hans. Deb. N. S. vol. xviii. pp. 44, 49, 61.

further, and said that while 'he certainly saw symptoms of danger in the formation of the government, he would not make up his mind definitively until he saw it act;' for that 'it was but fair to wait for the measures of a new ministry before the House decided upon its character.'* Ministerial explanations were not given to the House of Commons until February 18, although the principal cabinet ministers had taken their seats several days previously. The delay, however, appears to have arisen from accidental causes." This ministry, like its immediate predecessors, was composed of a combination of men of different political opinions, especially in regard to the Roman Catholic claims, which it had been expressly stipulated by the king should be treated as an open question.' Ere long, however, the followers of Mr. Canning (five in number) seceded from the cabinet, and the Duke of Wellington embraced the opportunity to replace them by men whose political principles were more akin to his own.' At this juncture the government were defeated in the House of Commons by the adoption of a resolution in favour of the Roman Catholic claims. Sir R. Peel, who was then Home Secretary, afterwards declared that it was his wish and intention to decline to remain in office as minister for the Home Department and leader of the House of Commons, 'being in a minority on the most important of domestic questions.' The threatened danger to the ministry, from the retirement, upon totally distinct grounds, of the Canningites, 'and the real difficulty of constructing, from any combination of parties, any other government at that time,' induced him not to insist upon his own resignation at this moment." In the interval between the close of the

* Hans. Deb. N. S. vol. xviii. p. 67.
' Ibid. pp. 450, 463, 588. Lord Palmerston having been requested, in the debate on the Address, to give some account of the recent cabinet changes, declined doing so, 'until the parties principally concerned shall be present.' Mirror of Parl. 1828, p. 21.
' Peel's Memoirs, vol. i. p. 12.
" Knight, vol. viii. p. 234; Guizot's Peel, p. 37.
" Peel's Memoirs, vol. i. p. 103.

session, and the next meeting of Parliament, it became apparent, from events which transpired in Ireland, that the repeal of the Roman Catholic disabilities could no longer be delayed, consistently with the preservation of the public peace. Accordingly the ministry determined to give way, and on January 12, 1829, Mr. Peel submitted to the premier a memorandum, setting forth in much detail his reasons for believing that the Roman Catholic claims could no longer be treated as an open question; and that the consent of the king should be sought to a consideration of the question by a united cabinet. In this memorandum his colleagues concurred. A copy of it was communicated to the king by the Duke of Wellington; and on the following day his grace, Sir R. Peel, and the four other ministers who had hitherto opposed these claims, had each a separate interview with his Majesty, at which they succeeded, after much difficulty, in obtaining his consent to a re-consideration of the question, in connection with the existing state of Ireland. But it was understood that the king was not bound to adopt the conclusions of his advisers, whatever they might agree upon. The draft of the royal speech at the opening of Parliament contained a paragraph which implied an intention on the part of government to adjust this question. When it was submitted to the king he gave an unwilling consent to this passage. Afterwards, upon notice being given to the House of Commons of the introduction of the Bill itself, the king sent for the premier, the Lord Chancellor, and Mr. Peel, and insisted that it should contain no alteration in the terms of the oath of supremacy. The ministers declared that it must necessarily do so. Much unavailing argument ensued, which ended in ministers tendering their resignation, and in the king accepting the same. But in a few hours the king changed his mind, and wrote to the Duke of Wellington that he anticipated so much difficulty in the attempt to form a new administration, that he had decided to recall his late advisers, and authorise them to proceed with the measure they were about to submit to Parliament.ᵇ This impediment being removed, the Bill was introduced and speedily became law.ᶜ No further ministerial difficulties occurred until after the accession of William IV., when the breaking out in France of the three days' Revolution of July 1830 gave an impetus to the advocates of parliamentary reform in England. At this juncture the dissolution of Parliament (consequent upon the demise of the crown) took place; and the elections were held under the sympathetic excitement caused by the 'three glorious days of July,' which naturally produced a House of Commons unfavourable to the Wellington ministry, and prepared to adopt measures of reform. In the month of September the country sustained an unexpected loss in the melancholy death of Mr. Huskisson, which occurred at the opening of the Liverpool and Manchester railway. Soon after this event, the Duke of Wellington invited Lord Palmerston to enter the cabinet, promising also a seat to two of his political friends. But his lordship declined office, unless Lords Grey and Lansdowne were included in the arrangement. This put an end to the matter, as it involved a complete re-modelling of the cabinet, which the duke did not contemplate.ᵈ Upon the assembling of Parliament, in the following October, it speedily became apparent that a crisis was at hand. The downfall of the ministry was precipitated by a declaration from the Duke of Wellington that no reform was necessary. Great excitement arose in the public mind upon this question. On November 15, the ministry were defeated in the House of Commons on a

---

ᵃ Knight, vol. viii. pp. 235-238; Peel's Memoirs, vol. i. pp. 294-360; Sir G. C. Lewis, in Edinb. Rev. vol. cx. pp. 82-94.

ᵇ This abandonment of their former political convictions on the part of ministers gave great offence to the Tory party, who contended that emancipation, if unavoidable, should at all events have been submitted to Parliament by a Whig and not a Tory administration. See May's Const. Hist. vol. ii. p. 50. See also the case of Sir R. Peel and the Corn Laws, in 1846. Ibid. p. 74.

ᵈ Edinb. Rev. vol. cx. p. 98.

motion to refer the civil list estimates to a select committee. The next morning they resigned. It was afterwards admitted, both by the Duke of Wellington and Sir Robert Peel, that their retirement on this question was only a pretext, and that the real reason was a wish not to 'expose his Majesty and the country to the consequences that might result from the government going out on the success of the question of parliamentary reform.'*

14. *Earl Grey's Administration.*—1830.

1830.

On November 16, 1830, the king sent for Earl Grey, and entrusted him with the formation of a ministry. On the 22nd instant, his lordship informed the House of Lords that he had succeeded in the undertaking, and briefly explained the principles upon which his administration would be conducted. As soon as the state of the public business would permit, Parliament was adjourned until February 3. A committee of four members of government, two of whom were of the cabinet, was directed to prepare the details of a Reform Bill, upon principles laid down by the premier. Their report was adopted by the cabinet, and submitted for the approval of the king, on January 30, a day already memorable in English history as being the anniversary of the execution of Charles I. The king is said to have given a reluctant consent to the measure. It was introduced into the House of Commons on March 1, by Lord John Russell (notwithstanding that he only filled a subordinate place in the ministry and had no seat in the cabinet), as an acknowledgment of his former efforts in the cause of parliamentary reform. The second reading of the Bill was carried, on March 21, by a

---

* Knight, vol. viii. p. 245. In other words, the retirement of this ministry arose from its weakness and want of public confidence. See Mirror of Parl. 1-11, pp. 2005-06; and see Sir G. C. Lewis, in Edinb. Rev. vol. cx. p. 57.

majority of one only, in a remarkably full House. This was a forerunner of defeat, which speedily followed. On April 19, upon a motion that the number of members for England and Wales ought not to be diminished, the ministry were beaten by a majority of eight. On April 21, they were again defeated, in the House of Commons, on a question of adjournment. They immediately waited upon the king, with a tender of resignation, unless his Majesty would grant them a dissolution of Parliament. The king was not easily persuaded to this step, but ministers represented to him that the continuance of the existing House of Commons was incompatible with the peace and safety of the kingdom, and that without a dissolution they could not remain in office. Accordingly, at three o'clock on April 22, the king came down and prorogued Parliament, ' with a view to its immediate dissolution.' Meanwhile, rumours of his Majesty's intentions had gone abroad, and a motion was actually under discussion in the House of Lords for an address to the king, praying that he would be pleased to refrain from this exercise of his undoubted prerogative. Had the prorogation been deferred for another day, it is probable that both Houses would have agreed to address the king against the dissolution—a circumstance which would have rendered the exercise of the royal prerogative extremely difficult.' The new Parliament was assembled on June 14, and it was soon apparent that the appeal to the people had been successful. The Reform Bill passed the Commons on September 21, by upwards of 100 majority. In the Lords a different fate awaited it. On the morning of Saturday, October 8, the motion for the second reading of the Bill was negatived by a majority of 41. On the following Monday, the House of Commons resolved that they adhered to the principle and leading

---

' Knight, vol. viii. pp. 270-278.

1831. provisions of the Reform Bill, notwithstanding its rejection by the other House, and that they had unabated confidence in the ministry by whom it had been promoted. On October 20, Parliament was prorogued, with a speech from the throne stating that its attention must necessarily be directed, at the opening of the ensuing session, to the important question of parliamentary reform. Parliament re-assembled on December 6, and a Reform Bill was again introduced, which passed the Commons by a large majority. This time the second reading was carried, in the Lords, by a majority
1832. of nine; but a defeat in committee showed the impossibility of success in the present temper and condition of the House. The creation of a new batch of peers for the express purpose of carrying the Bill was openly advocated out of doors; but the ministry shrank, at first, from having recourse to such an extreme proceeding. But when it became clear that a direct and apparently insurmountable obstacle to the passing of a Reform Bill was to be found in the existing condition of the House of Lords, they at length determined upon this step. On May 8, they tendered to the king their advice that he should exercise his prerogative to create a sufficient number of peers to insure the safety of the Bill. But his Majesty refused to do so. Thereupon the ministry resigned. Their resignation was announced to both Houses on the following evening. Next day, the House of Commons passed an address to the king, expressing their deep regret at this event, and imploring him 'to call to his councils such persons only as will carry into effect, unimpaired in all its essential provisions,' the Reform Bill recently agreed to by the House. Meanwhile, the Duke of Wellington had been authorised to form a new administration; but, after conferring with Lord Lyndhurst and Sir Robert Peel, he abandoned the task. The king then recalled his late advisers, and most reluctantly gave them a written permission 'to create such a number of

peers as will be sufficient to insure the passing of the Reform Bill; first calling up peers' eldest sons. (Signed) William R. Windsor, May 17, 1832.' But at the eleventh hour, the necessity for this extreme proceeding was avoided, by the temporary withdrawal from the House of a sufficient number of the Tory peers to give the ministry a decided majority upon the Bill, during its further progress through Parliament. The Opposition were induced to take this course by the personal interference of his Majesty, through his Private Secretary; an interference which was in itself irregular and unconstitutional, however it may have tended to avert the difficulties of an alarming crisis.* After this, the Reform Bills for England, Scotland, and Ireland became law without further impediment. Parliament was then dissolved, in order that the new representative system might be put into immediate operation.

The new Parliament, though composed of various discordant elements, fully sustained the ministerial policy. But on May 27, 1834, a resolution was proposed in the House of Commons in favour of the reduction of the temporalities of the Irish Established Church. This led to the secession of four members of the cabinet, who were unable to agree with their colleagues upon the manner in which this question should be met. The vacancies in the ministry were filled up; but very soon another difficulty arose. Lord Althorp, the Chancellor of the Exchequer, determined to retire from the cabinet, on account of a disagreement respecting the form in which the Irish Coercion Bill should be framed and submitted to Parliament. He had himself previously acquainted Mr. O'Connell that certain objectionable clauses would not be included therein. Nevertheless a majority of the cabinet, including the premier, had insisted upon their insertion. These conflicting opinions

* Knight, vol. viii. p. 299; May. vol. i. p. 120.

between ministers were of so grave a character that a compromise was deemed to be incompatible with personal honour, or a sense of public duty.[b] The ministry had been considerably weakened by the former resignations, and the loss of Lord Althorp was the finishing stroke. Accordingly, on July 8, Lords Grey and Althorp together waited upon the king, and formally tendered their resignations. On the following day, Earl Grey informed the House of Lords of the break-up of his administration.[i]

15. *Lord Melbourne's First Administration.*—*July* 1834.

1834.

On July 14, 1834, Viscount Melbourne announced to the House of Lords that he had been entrusted with the formation of a new ministry. He was instructed by the king, in the first instance, to endeavour to obtain the services 'of all those who stand at the head of the respective parties in the country,' and for that purpose was directed by his Majesty to enter into communication with the Duke of Wellington, Sir R. Peel, Mr. Stanley, and other parliamentary leaders. But these negotiations proved abortive,[j] and the king was obliged to consent to the formation of another Whig ministry, which was, in fact, a reconstruction of the previous one. On July 17, Lord Althorp informed the House of Commons that he had resumed his former office, and that the new administration was complete. The Irish Coercion Bill, then before the House of Lords, was dropped, and a new and less restrictive measure was brought forward by Lord Althorp, and became law.[k] But the duration of

---

[b] See Peel's Memoirs, vol. ii. p. 10.
[i] Ibid. p. 1; Knight, vol. viii. p. 545. This ministry, before its retirement, had lost the confidence of the king, on account of their known views with respect to the Irish Church. Without consulting his ministers, the king gave public expression to his own opinions, in replying to an address of the prelates and clergy of Ireland. May, Const. Hist. vol. i. p. 120.
[j] Peel's Memoirs, vol. ii. pp. 1-13.
[k] Knight, vol. viii. p. 540.

this ministry was very brief. By the death of his father, Lord Althorp inherited a seat in the House of Peers. This necessitated the appointment of a new Chancellor of the Exchequer and leader of the House of Commons. Whereupon Lord Melbourne, both verbally and by letter of November 12, 1834, made known to the king the posture of affairs, and sought his commands as to the filling up of the vacant offices; indicating, at the same time, his desire that the lead of the House of Commons should be conferred upon Lord John Russell. The king, however, had by this time become a convert to the principles of the Opposition; he accordingly informed the premier that in his opinion the loss of Lord Althorp from the Commons had so materially weakened the government in that House as to render it impossible for them to continue to conduct the public affairs; particularly when it was remembered that they were in a minority in the other House. Under these circumstances, his Majesty was prepared to consider the administration at an end.[1]

16. *Sir Robert Peel's First Administration.*—*Nov.* 1834.

Immediately after the dismissal of the Melbourne administration the king sent for the Duke of Wellington, and requested him to undertake to form a government. The duke earnestly recommended that his Majesty's choice might fall upon Sir Robert Peel, on account of the peculiar difficulties presented by the existing state of the House of Commons. The king consented, but remarked that he had given the preference to the duke because of the absence of Sir R. Peel from England. It was then agreed to summon Sir R. Peel home at once. In the interim, as it was necessary to take possession of the government, the Duke of Wellington assumed the temporary charge of the seals of the secretariat, and of the office

1834

---

[1] Peel's Memoirs, vol. ii. pp. 21, 22; May, Const. Hist. vol. i. p. 121.

of First Lord of the Treasury, being of opinion that 'nothing would be more unfair than to call upon Sir R. Peel to put himself at the head of a government which another individual should have formed.'[a] Anxious to place his services at his sovereign's disposal in this difficult crisis, Sir R. Peel unhesitatingly agreed to accept the proffered task, although he 'greatly doubted the policy' which had led to the breaking up of Lord Melbourne's government, and 'entertained little hope that the ministry about to replace it would be a stable one—would command such a majority in the House of Commons as would enable it to transact the public business.' He was well aware that by his acceptance of office he became 'technically, if not morally, responsible for the dissolution of the preceding government, although he had not the remotest concern in it.'[b] He was also fully sensible of the hazard he incurred in meeting a House of Commons wherein his personal followers were in a large minority, with but a doubtful prospect of improving his position by a dissolution of Parliament. Nevertheless he did not shrink from the endeavour to respond to his sovereign's appeal, being persuaded that Parliament would 'so far maintain the prerogative of the king as to give to the ministers of his choice, not an implicit confidence, but a fair trial.'[c] After weighing the counterbalancing advantages of an immediate dissolution of Parliament, or of an attempt to carry on the government, in the first instance, with the existing House of Commons, Sir Robert decided in favour of a dissolution, upon grounds of public policy, which are explained in his memoirs.[d] A new Parliament was accordingly convened for February 19, 1835, but the

---

[a] Peel's Memoirs, vol. ii. p. 20. For observations upon this act of the Duke of Wellington, see post, Vol. II. c. 1 on the Cabinet.

[b] Ibid. p. 31. It is noticeable, in proof of the superior correctness of Sir R. Peel's views of his constitutional position, that the Duke of Wellington had previously written to him to say that he did not think the new ministers were 'at all responsible' for the king's quarrel with their predecessors; it being 'an affair quite settled' when his Majesty sent for the Duke. Ibid. p. 21.

[c] Tamworth Manifesto, Ibid. p. 67.

[d] Ibid. pp. 43-68.

result of the elections, while it largely increased the number of Conservative members, had failed to place the new ministry in a position of sufficient strength to enable them to carry on the government. At the outset of the session the ministry were defeated on the choice of a Speaker, and upon an amendment to the Address, censuring the dissolution of Parliament.

In the debate upon the Address in the Lords, Lord Chancellor Eldon defended the change of ministry, and consequent dissolution of Parliament, on the ground that the previous secession (in May 1834) of four cabinet ministers had so weakened the government, that when Lord Althorp was obliged to vacate his seat and office in the Commons, it became probable that any re-construction 'was not likely to be permanent, but would be liable to be broken up, at a time when it might be productive of much more mischief than the breaking of it up at that moment was calculated to occasion.' In the Commons, Lord John Russell argued the question against the change of ministry with great force and ability, contending that there had been no sufficient cause to justify the exercise of the prerogative in dismissing the late ministry and in dissolving Parliament. He also complained of the new cabinet for not having met Parliament before its dissolution, in order to ascertain whether they would be allowed a fair trial, or be met with a factious Opposition against the opinion of the country; in which case a dissolution might have been properly advised. It was furthermore contended, by Lords Morpeth and Stanley, that 'it is the right and privilege of the House of Commons to express its opinion and judgment, and even to offer advice to the sovereign, as to the circumstances under which, and the mode in which, he may have been advised to exercise his undoubted prerogative of choosing the ministers of the crown.' The Opposition, however, confined themselves

---

* Knight, vol. viii. p. 365.
* Mirror of Parl. 1835, p. 35.
* Ibid. p. 84.
* Ibid. p. 74.

1835'.
to moving an amendment to the Address in answer to the speech, to represent the regret of the House that the progress of certain important reforms, which had engaged the attention of the late Parliament, should have been interrupted and endangered by the unnecessary dissolution of a Parliament earnestly intent upon the rigorous prosecution of such measures. This amendment was carried against ministers. It elicited a reply from the king, expressing regret that the House did not concur with him as to the policy of the appeal he had recently made to the sense of his people, and expressing a confident trust that the success of no good measures would be injuriously affected thereby. Shortly after this reply was communicated, Sir Robert Peel took an opportunity of informing the House that he did not intend to resign on account of his defeat upon the Address, but should persevere, and submit to the consideration and approval of Parliament the measures contemplated in the speech from the throne.* But further defeats awaited him. He was obliged to propose Mr. Bernal for the chair of the Committee of Ways and Means, from inability to secure the election of any one in the confidence of the government. The first diplomatic appointment made by the new ministry, that of the Marquis of Londonderry, as ambassador to the court of St. Petersburg, 'could not have been persisted in,' and was resigned, in consequence of the interference of the House of Commons. In fact, they met with continual hindrance in the conduct of public business, and had not 'the weight and authority to check, through the opinion and voice of a majority, the vexatious opposition of individual members.'* At length, after several minor defeats, they were left in a minority upon a motion of Lord John Russell, in regard to the appropriation of the temporalities of the Irish Church, and the adjustment of the Irish tithe question.* Anticipating defeat upon this

---
* Mirror of Parl. 1835, pp. 140, 148.   * Knight, vol. viii. p. 350.
* Peel, Memoirs, vol. ii. pp. 87, 88.

important motion, Sir Robert Peel wrote to the king on March 29, intimating that the pending debate would necessarily assume the ground of want of confidence in the administration. Following upon a succession of votes adverse to the views of ministers, there was a 'great public evil in permitting the House of Commons to exhibit itself to the country free from any control on the part of the executive government, and usurping, in consequence of the absence of that control, many of the functions of the government.' This state of things 'might be tolerated so long as there was a rational hope of converting a ministerial minority into a majority, or of making an appeal to the people with a prospect of decided success.' But Sir Robert Peel entertained the apprehension that 'from continued perseverance in the attempt to govern by a minority, it would be difficult for an administration, however composed, to recover a control over the House of Commons; that the House of Commons, having been habituated to the exercise of functions not properly belonging to them, will be unwilling to relinquish it; and that the royal prerogatives and royal authority will inevitably suffer from continued manifestation of weakness on the part of the executive government.'¹ On April 7, Lord John Russell's motion was decided against ministers by a majority of 27. Next day, Sir Robert Peel informed the House that he and his colleagues had resigned office, in consequence of that vote, regarding it as tantamount to a declaration by the House of want of confidence in the government; and believing that, 'in conformity with the constitution, a government ought not to persist in carrying on public affairs, after a fair trial, against the decided opinion of a majority of the House of Commons;'² notwithstanding that it may enjoy, as upon this occasion, the confidence

---

¹ Peel, vol. ii. pp. 91-93. For further explanations by Sir R. Peel of his position at this time, see Mirror of Parl. 1841, sess. 2, pp. 158, 159, 211.
² Mirror of Parl. 1835, pp. 817, 818.

and favour of the crown, and possess a working majority in the House of Lords.'

17. *Lord Melbourne's Second Administration.*—1835.

1835.   On April 18, Viscount Melbourne announced in the House of Lords that, by command of the king, he had formed a new administration. Both Houses adjourned until May 12, to enable the ministers in the Commons to go for re-election. No event occurred to affect the stability of this administration until after the death of King William IV., and the accession of Queen Victoria 1837. in 1837. Reposing entire confidence in the men whose opinions harmonised with those in which she had been educated, her Majesty continued the Melbourne ministry in office as her constitutional advisers. But on May 1839. 6, 1839, the ministry sustained a moral defeat upon their Bill to suspend the constitution of the Island of Jamaica, the second reading of which was made an occasion for a trial of party strength. It was carried by a majority of five only, in a full House. Upon the following day, Lord John Russell informed the House of the resignation of ministers; alleging that it had taken place on account of their not possessing such support in the House of Commons as would enable them efficiently to carry on the public business.* Internal weakness, however, was the true ground of their fall. Having attained to power through a combination of parties of the most diverse political aims and aspirations, they were unable to act with vigour and determination. In their attempts to carry out the principle in respect to the Irish Church, by the assertion of which they had driven Sir R. Peel from power, they signally failed. The Whigs had pledged themselves to connect the settlement of the tithe question with the appropriation of the surplus revenues of the Established

---

* Mirror of Parl. 1841, p. 2032.   Lord John Russell's remarks, in *Ibid.*
* *Ibid.* 1839, p. 2301; and see 1841, p. 2120.

Church in Ireland. But the Conservatives were determined to resist that principle, and having a large majority in the House of Lords, their resistance was effectual. After several attempts to induce the Lords to give way, the victory gained in 1835 was abandoned in 1838 by the surrender of the appropriation scheme by ministers themselves. This was a moral defeat to the Whig ministry, which largely contributed to turn the scale of popular favour against them.* Their inability to control legislation in Parliament in conformity with their avowed convictions was notorious. Hence arose the necessity for their resignation at this juncture.

At the suggestion of the Duke of Wellington, to whom her Majesty applied for counsel upon this occasion, Sir Robert Peel was entrusted with the formation of a new ministry. The next day he submitted to the queen a list of the persons whom he proposed to associate with himself in office, which was approved of by her Majesty. But a difficulty occurred in reference to the ladies of the bedchamber. Sir Robert Peel was of opinion that the continuance in attendance upon the person of the sovereign of ladies who had been originally appointed upon the recommendation of the Whig ministry, and who were nearly all related to the leaders of the opposite political party, was likely to prove prejudicial to the interests of his government. His objection appears to have chiefly applied to the wife of the Lord Lieutenant of Ireland, and to the sister of the Secretary for Ireland, on account of the widely different views of policy towards that country which were entertained by himself and by his predecessors in office. He accordingly respectfully urged upon the queen the propriety of making some change in the appointment of ladies to fill the great offices of her household. Her Majesty replied that it was repugnant to her feelings to

---

* May, Const. Hist. vol. ii. pp. 485–487.

1839. make any such change, and that she considered such a course to be contrary to usage, and one that she could not adopt. This answer was framed upon the advice of Lord Melbourne, to whom the queen had again applied, after she had verbally informed Sir R. Peel that she could not accede to his request. Upon the receipt of this reply, Sir Robert immediately relinquished the trust which had been committed to him. Her Majesty then reinstated her former ministers, requesting them, at the same time, to sustain her in the course she had taken. Accordingly a cabinet council was held on the following day, at which a minute was agreed upon, approving of that course, and assuming full responsibility for the same. Nevertheless it is now generally conceded that Sir R. Peel was right upon the abstract constitutional question;[c] and upon his return to office, in 1841, no difficulties were raised to the making of such changes amongst the ladies of the household as he thought fit to recommend; and the principle he then contended for has since been universally acknowledged to be correct.[d] Although the 'bedchamber question' brought back Lord Melbourne's ministry it was only for a few months.

They continued in office, but not in power, being unable to conduct the government with credit or success in the face of a vigorous and united Opposition, through whom they were subjected to frequent defeats in both Houses of Parliament.[e] At length, on May 27, 1841, after the ministry

---

[c] Knight, vol. viii. p. 420; Mirror of Parl. 1839, p. 2415.
[d] May, Const. Hist. vol. i. p. 132. For a fuller account of these transactions, see post, p. 200.
[e] Abstract of defeats sustained by the Melbourne administration in the two Houses of Parliament, from its formation in April 1835 to March 1840. Read to the House of Lords by the Marquis of Londonderry, who 'pledged his honour for its accuracy.' Mirror of Parl. 1840, p. 2310:—

Ministers in a minority	In Commons	In Lords
In Session of 1835	4	11
,, 1836	11	18
,, 1837	9	5
,, 1838	21	4
,, 1839	8	11
,, 1840 (up to Mar.)	5	—
	58	49
		58
Total defeats		107

had sustained a defeat upon the important question of the sugar duties, and had still declared their intention of proceeding with the business of the country,' Sir Robert Peel moved a vote of want of confidence, which embraced two propositions: (1) that 'her Majesty's ministers do not sufficiently possess the confidence of the House of Commons to enable them to carry through the House measures which they deem of essential importance to the public welfare;' (2) that 'their continuance in office under such circumstances is at variance with the spirit of the constitution.' He based his first proposition upon their repeated defeats and obstructions in the attempt to carry on the public business. He defined the 'spirit of the constitution' to mean the system of parliamentary government which has prevailed since the accession of the house of Hanover, which implies that the ministers of the crown should have the confidence of the House of Commons, and which has placed 'the centre of gravity in the state' in that House. He defended his second proposition by reviewing the history of the principal prime ministers from the days of Sir Robert Walpole to recent times, showing that they had invariably yielded to the necessity implied by a withdrawal of the confidence of the House of Commons, and abdicated their functions as servants of the crown. The seeming exception in the case of Mr. Pitt, in 1783, he met by showing that the protracted hostility of the House of Commons against that minister (and which he resisted until he could take

---

Number of Bills introduced by the said ministry, and not passed through Parliament:—

In Session 1836 20
    ,,   1837 21
    ,,   1838 34
    ,,   1839 28
                      —
        Total 112

' Mirror of Parl. 1841, p. 1843. Although afterwards, and before the vote was taken on the want of confidence motion, Lord John Russell stated that it had been the intention of ministers to appeal to the country as soon as possible when they found themselves defeated upon the sugar duties, Sir R. Peel replied that he had submitted the motion of want of confidence because he could not, and did not, know the intentions of government with respect to a dissolution. Ibid. pp. 2129, 2137.

the sense of the people by a dissolution of Parliament) did not arise from want of confidence in his measures, having commenced before he took his seat on the Treasury benches, but from a suspicion that he owed his appointment to an unconstitutional proceeding—that is to say, to secret influence, by whose agency the previous administration had been overthrown. Mr. Pitt, however, resisted the attempt of the majority of the House of Commons, on the ground that it was irregular to endeavour to control the prerogative of the crown in the choice of its ministers, by denouncing them without waiting to see their acts.[a] In reply, Lord John Russell acquiesced in the general principle that ministers ought to possess the confidence of the House of Commons, and admitted that, if the House should 'continue to refuse its confidence' to them, it would be 'impossible for them to continue in office,' provided there is 'a ministry capable of being formed to succeed them.'[b] His lordship contended, however, that isolated defeats of a government possessing the general confidence of the crown and of Parliament, although they be upon questions of great importance, do not involve the necessity for resignation. For example: Lord Sunderland was defeated upon the Peerage Bill, a measure recommended by royal message; Lord North did not resign when Dunning carried against him his famous resolution against the influence of the crown. Mr. Pitt was defeated, on different occasions, on the Westminster scrutiny, on parliamentary reform, on his proposition for a general fortification of the coasts, on his French commercial treaty, on his proposition concerning the trade of Ireland, on the impeachment of his friend and colleague, Lord Melville, and also his India Bill, which was one of the principal measures of his administration; and yet, in none of these cases, did he feel called upon to resign.[c] Again, Lord Liverpool was de-

[a] Mirror of Parl. 1841, pp. 1923–1945, 2110.
[b] Ibid. pp. 2110, 2120.
[c] Ibid. pp. 1970, 1971, 2030, 2095.

feated upon the Bill of Pains and Penalties against Queen Caroline, and, in 1816, on the question of the renewal of the property-tax, the loss of which occasioned a deficiency of twelve millions of revenue.¹ And the Duke of Wellington was defeated upon a motion for the repeal of the Test and Corporation Acts, which was carried against ministers in the House of Commons.* In none of these instances did a resignation ensue. The friends of the ministry, however, pressed this point too far when they proceeded to state that it mattered little whether government were able to carry their legislative measures so long as they were not censured by Parliament for the exercise of their administrative functions. Lord Stanley and Sir R. Peel concurred in declaring this to be a most unconstitutional and dangerous doctrine.¹ Lord John Russell's views on this subject were more cautiously and correctly expressed. He called attention to the fact that in recent times, and especially since the passing of the Reform Bill, the country and the constitution, in its practical development, have required more at the hands of ministers than formerly. Up to the time of Mr. Pitt, his lordship observed, 'the usages of the constitution did not require that those at the head of the government should bring forward legislative measures, and, indeed, for the greater part of the last century, did not even require them to take a uniform and consistent part either in supporting or opposing measures submitted to Parliament.' Nowadays, 'what with the necessity for legislation, the difficulty which individual members experience in carrying through Bills, the great changes so long delayed, and which (after the passing of the Reform Bill) it became indispensable to make, suddenly, and on various

---

Upon the rejection of the India Bill, Mr. Fox said, 'I readily agree that the failure of any Bill proposed by a minister afforded no ground for that minister's dismissal from office; this is a sound doctrine.' This remark was quoted, with approval, by Lord John Russell. *Ibid.* p. 2110.

² Mirror of Parl. 1841, pp. 2030, 2005.

³ *Ibid.* p. 2121.

⁴ *Ibid.* pp. 2110, 2134.

subjects—from all these causes an expectation has arisen that the government should bring forward measures on matters which excite public attention, and do their best to carry them through the House.' 'In this case,' he added, 'I think it is unreasonable to expect that a government should possess the same uniform and general support, on the part of the House of Commons, which was required when ministries had merely acts of administration to perform.' 'If, on the one hand, new duties have been imposed on ministers, and you require them to carry through Parliament measures which they deem of essential importance, so, on the other hand, you must make a fair allowance for the effect of discussion and the expression of the deliberate opinions—first, of members of this House, and, secondly, of our constituents—which will inevitably occasion the alteration of some measures and the rejection of others.' As a case in point, he instanced an alteration, suggested by Sir R. Peel, when at the head of only a small minority, in an important government measure, and to which the government, after due consideration, acceded.[a]

Adverting to the probability of a dissolution of Parliament, Lord John Russell remarked that the ministry had uttered no threats or menaces on the subject. He considered that ' a dissolution, like other prerogatives of the crown, is one in which the House has a right, in certain cases, to interfere. But I think the only ground upon which it can properly interfere is when this House can say that the course of legislation and administration is proceeding harmoniously, and likely to continue to lead to beneficial results, ... and that a dissolution would be a needless and wanton interference with the course of business. Such was the ground taken by Mr. Fox, in 1784, when an Address was moved against the dissolution of Parliament.' 'Such was the ground that we took, when, in 1835, we moved and

---

[a] Mirror of Parl. 1841, pp. 2120-2122.

carried a vote of censure against Sir R. Peel for the advice he gave to the crown for the dissolution of that Parliament.' He then added that it had been asserted by no one that the present Parliament, if not sooner dissolved, was likely to continue to its natural term with benefit to the country, or with improvement to its legislation.*

Upon the whole, Lord John Russell resisted the motion, as ' not rightly founded in precedent, and, above all, ill-suited to the present condition and state of our constitution.' If it meant that the ministry were not entitled to advise a dissolution of Parliament, it was an unjustifiable interference with the royal prerogative. If not so intended, he was prepared to admit that ministers would not think it right, after the decision of the House on the sugar question, to continue in office with the existing Parliament any longer than would suffice to prepare for the speedy assembling of a ' new Parliament to decide upon the whole question at issue.' With this admission, ' where is the necessity and where the justification of the resolution?'*

In reply, Sir R. Peel acknowledged that no minister who is obstructed by a powerful Opposition, upon the first formation of his government, is bound to resign after his first defeat. He did not consider it the duty of a minister, having met with obstructions upon his financial propositions, at once to resign. He should not feel himself bound to resign on any single defeat, being of opinion that ' the propriety of resignation depends on a combination of circumstances.'* He also admitted the existence of an alternative, in the case of a ministry who had lost the confidence of the House of Commons, between resignation and dissolution, saying, ' if there be a clear intention forthwith to dissolve Parliament, that may be a vindication of the government, but the dissolution ought to be immediate. The House of Commons has no other

---

* Mirror of Parl. 1841, pp. 2127-2129.   * *Ibid.* pp. 2129, 2130.
              * *Ibid.* p. 2133.

mode of marking its sense of the unconstitutional tenure of power than by passing some such resolution as that which I have proposed, and which I most properly submitted because I could not, and did not, know the intentions of government with respect to a dissolution.' In conclusion, Sir Robert Peel said that he had selected this course 'less with a view to any party advantage than to the vindication of the just authority of the House of Commons, and to uphold the great principles of the constitution.'*

On division, upon June 4, Sir R. Peel's resolution was agreed to by a majority of one. At the next meeting of the House, Lord John Russell announced the intention of ministers to advise a dissolution of Parliament as soon as practicable. He also declared that, under existing circumstances, he should not introduce an important motion, of which he had given notice, respecting the Corn Laws. He added that it could not be denied that the only method of solving the doubt implied by the adoption of the aforesaid resolution was ' to let the country itself decide the question thus gravely submitted to them. Until this decision shall be given, I think it would not be proper that any further party struggle should take place.'' Whereupon Sir R. Peel said that, a dissolution having been determined upon, he would throw no impediment in the way of completing the public business, provided it should take place with the least possible delay, and no measure be proposed meanwhile that was not imperatively required. It was also necessary, and according to precedent, that ' the new Parliament should be called together without delay.' He apprehended that there could be no constitutional objection to giving the House an assurance to this effect, inasmuch as in 1807, in 1820, and in 1831, the crown, in proroguing Parliament, intimated that 'a new Parliament' should be convoked 'forthwith,'

* Mirror of Parl. 1841, pp. 2137, 2142.   ' Ibid. pp. 2162-2164.

or 'without delay.' Lord John Russell, under the peculiar circumstances of the case, gave these assurances; but he 'did not think, on ordinary occasions, any guarantee should be called for from, or given by, the advisers of the crown,' in respect to the exercise of this prerogative.*

Agreeably to promise, the ministry postponed the consideration of the Corn Law and Poor Law Bills; but they pressed forward a Bill for the improvement of the administration of justice in the Court of Chancery, on the ground that all parties were agreed upon its principle. This Bill, however, proposed to create two new judicial offices, the patronage of which would be in the hands of the Lord Chancellor. Sir R. Peel, although favourable to the passing of the Bill, was unwilling that it should go into operation at this juncture. Accordingly, on motion of Sir E. B. Sugden, a clause was added to the Bill, postponing its operation for four months. Whereupon Lord John Russell refused to proceed with the Bill, declaring that this decision affixed a stigma on the Lord Chancellor, 'as unfit to advise the disposition of offices relating to the administration of justice;' that it was 'a violent infringement of the prerogative of the crown, and an unfair interference with the executive government.'* Sir R. Peel repudiated the idea that the action of the House in this matter was any infringement of the royal prerogative. He said that, in the present position of ministers, there was no other alternative than 'resignation or immediate dissolution;' in other words, a dissolution as soon as the exigencies of the public service would allow; and that ministers had no right to bring forward any contested motion whatever, or to ask of the House any act implying confidence in themselves, such as would be implied by the devolution of any new authority; that for the House to acquiesce in any such demand would be inconsistent with its former declaration of want of confidence in

---

Mirror of Parl. 1841, pp. 2165, 2160.   * Ibid. pp. 2227, 2228.

ministers; and that they, in preferring the same, did not 'do homage to the principles of representative government.' Lord John Russell's motion, to give the Chancery Bill a 'three months' hoist,' was then agreed to without a division.*

After completing the necessary business, Parliament was prorogued on June 22, and dissolved upon the following day. The 'cry' with which ministers went to the hustings was not that of confidence in themselves, but in favour of 'cheap bread,' and the modification of the Corn Laws.† This roused the agricultural interests, and a large majority against ministers was returned to the new House of Commons; they nevertheless determined to meet Parliament, upon the ground that they could not constitutionally infer the opinions of members from anything save their voices in Parliament. This determination, although undoubtedly a correct one, placed them in the disagreeable position of advising a royal speech which could not fail to give dissatisfaction.

Upon the meeting of the new Parliament, which took place on August 19, amendments were proposed to the Address in both Houses, asserting a want of confidence in the advisers of the crown. In the Lords, the constitutionality of this course was defended by the Duke of Wellington. In the Commons, attention was drawn to the fact that, since the elections, Lord John Russell had informed his constituents that the ministry would 'take the first opportunity of asking for a clear and decided judgment, upon their policy. This intention, however, was forestalled by the proposed amendment. Sir R. Peel, in commenting upon the result of the elections, observed that it was 'a great constitutional principle, that the favour and support of the crown ought not to

---

* Mirror of Parl. 1841, p. 2231. Subsequently, in regard to the Bribery at Elections Bill, Lord John Russell showed his willingness to carry out the understanding that all opposed measures, not being of urgent necessity, should be dropped. See *Ibid.* pp. 2258, 2282.

† *Ibid.* p. 2142; Annual Register, 1841, pp. 143-116.

maintain, for a long and indefinite period, a government in existence against the will of the representatives of the people. It compromises the prerogatives of the monarchy so to retain power, because it exhibits those prerogatives without their just influence. It exhibits the House of Commons as wanting in its just influence, when it can thwart the measures and censure the acts, but cannot decide the fate of a ministry.' In reply, Lord John Russell complained of the insufficient reasons assigned on behalf of the motion, but had no fault to find with the motion itself. The proposed amendment was carried by large majorities in both Houses. The royal answer was as follows:—' Ever anxious to listen to the advice of the Parliament, I will take immediate measures for the formation of a new administration.' In communicating the same, upon August 30, Lord John Russell announced the resignation of ministers, adding the assurance that their duty to the sovereign and to the country had, in their conviction, rendered it incumbent upon them ' to continue the struggle to the present moment.'*

18. *Sir Robert Peel's Second Administration.*—1841.

Immediately upon the resignation of the Melbourne ministry, her Majesty sent for Sir Robert Peel, and charged him with the formation of a new administration. On September 8, the arrangements were complete, and the new writs were moved for in the House of Commons. On September 16, the Prime Minister made a statement to the House of his general policy. But it was very brief and reserved, and afforded no indication of the course he intended to pursue upon the great questions of commercial and financial policy that were agitating the public mind. He claimed for his ministry that time should be afforded to them to consider those measures which they might deem it expedient to submit to Parliament on these

1841.

---

* Mirror of Parl. 1841, sess. ii. pp. 20–52, 68, 74, 164, 211, 222, 230.

important subjects.* Sir Robert Peel had, in fact, undertaken a most difficult task. 'He was obliged to be at once a Conservative and a Reformer, and to carry along with him, in this double course, a majority incoherent in itself, and swayed, in reality, by immovable and untractable interests, prejudices, and passions.'† Elected as the champion of agricultural Protection, one of his first acts was to obtain the consent of his colleagues to a material change in the Corn Laws, and to the removal of the prohibition which existed against the importation of foreign cattle and meat. But this, while it failed to conciliate the advocates of free trade, was not effected without occasioning serious dissatisfaction amongst his own supporters. Sir R. Peel states, in his 'Memoirs,' that the Duke of Buckingham resigned his seat in the cabinet rather than become a party to these measures; and that it was no easy matter to induce the remaining members of the government to accede to them.‡ Twice, during the session of 1844, and before the complete development of his intended policy in respect to the Corn Laws, the existence of Sir Robert Peel's administration was seriously jeopardised by votes of the House of Commons. First, upon the question of the hours of labour in factories, and afterwards, upon the question of the sugar duties, a majority of the House affirmed certain propositions which were regarded by the ministry as injurious to the commercial prosperity of the country, and opposed to the principles of public policy which they were resolved to maintain. Upon each of these defeats, Sir Robert informed the House that, unless its decision were reconsidered and reversed, he should feel it to be his duty to resign office. This appeal was successful upon both occasions; and the government were sustained by the adoption of resolutions in accordance with their views.* At length, in October

---

* Knight, Hist. of Eng. vol. viii. p. 492; Mirror of Parl. 1841, sess. ii. p. 272.
† Guizot, Peel, p. 60.
‡ Memoirs, vol. ii. p. 100.
* Knight, vol. viii. pp. 515–517.

1845, a more alarming peril arose. The Irish potato crop had failed, and it became necessary to adopt measures to supply the immense deficiency thereby occasioned in the ordinary food of the people. On October 31, Sir Robert Peel laid before the cabinet a memorandum containing various suggestions calculated to meet this emergency. In the discussions which ensued upon this communication, it became evident, however, that grave differences of opinion existed, both as to the necessity for adopting any extraordinary measures, and as to the shape which such measures should assume.[b] The cabinet separated, to meet again in a week. Upon their re-assembling, it appeared that a considerable majority of his colleagues differed from the premier, three only being willing to give him their support. Sir Robert, however, decided not to resign his office, and thereby dissolve the government, but to afford his colleagues an opportunity of reconsidering the whole subject.[c] The discussions in the cabinet were accordingly resumed; and, upon December 2, Sir Robert Peel submitted to them a project for the settlement of the Corn Law question, but which failed to obtain their concurrence. He then, on December 5, waited upon the queen, and tendered his resignation.[d] Whereupon her Majesty sent for Lord John Russell, and commissioned him to form a government. With a view to facilitate a just and comprehensive settlement of this momentous question, Sir Robert Peel conveyed, through her Majesty, an offer of his support, and that of those of his late cabinet who agreed with him, to any ministry that might be formed for the purpose of settling the question; provided their measure should be founded upon certain defined principles, and be framed in

---

[b] Peel's Memoirs, vol. ii. p. 146.
[c] Ibid. p. 158.
[d] Ibid. p. 222. Lord Stanley, with others of his colleagues who differed from Sir Robert Peel, had authorised him to state that they would not undertake to form a government upon the principle of Protection. He therefore did not advise the queen to send for any of them. Ibid. pp. 229-241.

a cautious and conciliatory spirit. Lord John Russell acknowledged the liberality of this offer, but pressed for a further assurance that Sir Robert and his friends would pledge themselves to concur in a certain plan of adjustment, the outlines of which he offered to communicate. This Sir Robert Peel declined to do; objecting to 'concert, and to preliminary pledges, as calculated to dissatisfy the House of Commons, to embarrass all parties, and to diminish his ability to render efficient service.' While proffering a general support on the particular question, he would not 'relinquish his power of free and independent action.' In these conclusions, Lord John Russell expressed his concurrence.' But the Whig party were in a large minority in the Commons; and after several days spent in negotiations, it became evident that Lord John could not succeed. He failed, moreover, to obtain an agreement amongst his own friends in respect to the composition of his ministry, Lord Grey having decidedly opposed an appointment which Lord John Russell was desirous of making.' Accordingly, on December 20, he wrote to the queen, relinquishing the task. Sir Robert Peel was then recalled to power. He agreed to resume the office of first minister without previous concert with any one, a course which he had formerly taken in 1834. He met the cabinet the same evening, and told them that, whether supported or not, he was firmly resolved to meet Parliament as her Majesty's minister, and to propose such measures as the public exigencies required. This determined conduct had the effect of bringing the waverers back to their party allegiance, and, with the exception of Lord Stanley, all his former colleagues consented to support the prime minister." Immediately upon the assembling of Parliament, ministerial explanations of these transactions were given; and Sir Robert Peel boldly announced his intention to stand free

---

^c Peel's Memoirs, vol. ii. pp. 241, 242.   ^f Ibid. p. 247.
^s Ibid. pp. 249, 250.

from the trammels of party, declaring that he would not remain at the helm unless the ship of the state were allowed to pursue the course he thought she ought to take. He reserved to himself the marking out of that course, and claimed for himself the unfettered power of judging of those measures which he conceived it to be for the good of the country to propose.[b] By this speech he asserted his independence, not merely of his colleagues in office, but of the great party of which he was the acknowledged chief. In due course, Sir R. Peel communicated to Parliament his plan of financial and commercial reform. It excited strong opposition from his quondam supporters, but, nevertheless, it received the sanction of a majority in both Houses. But the Nemesis was at hand. During the progress of the Corn Law Repeal Bill, another measure for the Protection of Life in Ireland, which, at an early period of the session, had received the assent of the Lords, was brought under discussion in the Commons, and, by a combination of parties hostile either to the ministry or to the Bill itself, was defeated. Foreseeing that this Bill, so essential to the maintenance of the public peace in Ireland, would be rejected by the hostility of a factious Opposition, Sir Robert Peel, on June 21, transmitted a memorandum to the cabinet upon the position of the government. He elaborately discussed therein the alternatives of resignation or dissolution of Parliament, and, if the latter course were taken, the proper ground upon which to appeal to the country. He summed up by expressing a strong opinion in favour of immediate resignation, as being the most desirable step for the interests of his party, of the crown, and of the whole community; and as being more creditable than the

1846.

---

[b] Hans. Deb. vol. lxxxiii. p. 94. Sir R. Peel's conduct on this occasion, like that of the Duke of Wellington in regard to Roman Catholic emancipation, gave great offence to his party, who contended that it was a violation of one of the first principles of political morality. See May's Const. Hist. vol. ii. p. 74. For his own defence, see Peel's Memoirs, vol. ii. pp. 164, 221, 311–325.

1846. retention of office without power, or the advising of a dissolution with little prospect of securing a majority of members honestly and cordially concurring with the government in great political principles.' This memorandum Sir Robert Peel addressed, in the first instance, to the Duke of Wellington, and upon receiving his grace's reply—which, while coinciding, in the main, with his own views, differed somewhat as to the proper grounds for dissolving Parliament, should it be necessary to take that step—he circulated both papers amongst the cabinet ministers.¹ Sir R. Peel's suggestions met with unanimous approval.

On June 25, owing to a concerted union between the Whig and Protectionist parties for the purpose of displacing the government, the Irish Coercion Bill was rejected, on its second reading, by a majority of 73. Next day the ministry resigned. In communicating the fact of his retirement from office to the House of Commons, Sir R. Peel stated that, had he failed to carry his measures of commercial policy, he would have advised the crown to dissolve Parliament, but, having succeeded in passing them, he could not consent to advise a dissolution for the mere continuance of his own administration in office, unless he could reasonably anticipate that it would insure him the support of a powerful party, united to him by a general concurrence of views on all great questions, a result which, at this juncture, he did not consider probable. Moreover, he thought that the country, after its recent excitement, stood in need of repose.

19. *Lord John Russell's First Administration.*—1846.

On July 6, 1846, Lord John Russell was sworn in as First Lord of the Treasury. His cabinet consisted of the then unusual number of 16 persons. In February 1850, he narrowly escaped defeat upon the question of agricul-

---

¹ Peel's Memoirs, vol. II. pp. 288–297.   ¹ *Ibid.* pp. 298–308.

tural distress, being sustained by a majority of 21 only, in a House of 530 members. On this occasion a change of ministry was anticipated, but did not occur. On June 17, 1850, a resolution, proposed by Lord Stanley in the House of Lords, condemnatory of the foreign policy of ministers, in relation to the affairs of Greece, was carried, by a majority of 37. This was met by a counter-resolution, proposed by Mr. Roebuck, in the Commons, approving of the whole foreign policy of government, which was carried, on June 28, by a majority of 46. However, on February 13, 1851, upon another Protectionist motion, proposed by Mr. Disraeli, they obtained a bare majority of 14, in a House of 548 members, and, on the 20th instant, were defeated, upon a motion of Mr. Locke King, on a question of the extension of the franchise. On February 22, Lord John Russell resigned. But after ineffectual attempts on the part of Lords Stanley and Aberdeen, and of Lord John Russell, in connection with Lord Aberdeen and Sir James Graham, to form a ministry, her Majesty sent for the Duke of Wellington, to take counsel from him in regard to this political emergency; and ' paused for a while before she again commenced the task of forming an administration.'[1] At length, upon the advice of the Duke of Wellington, the Whig ministry were recalled to office. On December 22 following, the ministry were weakened by the retirement of Lord Palmerston, under circumstances which will be specially noticed in another chapter.[2] Explanations were given to the House of Commons, of this affair, by Lord John Russell, in the debate upon the Address, at the commencement of the session, on February 3, 1852. A few days afterwards, the ministry were defeated upon an amendment, proposed by Lord Palmerston, to the motion for leave to bring in a Bill to regulate the ' local militia.' The amendment consisted in the substitution of

---
[1] Lord John Russell, Hans. Deb. vol. cxiv. pp. 1038, 1075.
[2] See post, p. 231. And particularly Vol. II. c. I.

the word 'general' for 'local.' It was carried, on February 20, by 136 votes to 125. On February 23, their resignation was announced to both Houses.

20. *Lord Derby's First Administration.*—*Feb.* 1852.

1852.

Instead of sending for Lord Palmerston, as might have been anticipated, Her Majesty commissioned the Earl of Derby to form a ministry. He succeeded in the undertaking, and on February 27 the new Premier explained the intended policy of his cabinet in the House of Lords. This administration was confessedly in a minority, in the House of Commons, upon the great party questions." Nevertheless, they struggled through the session in which they had taken office, with the intention (which, for constitutional reasons, was hinted, rather than expressed) of dissolving Parliament in the ensuing autumn, and of then shaping their course of policy on the question of Free Trade, and the Corn Laws, according to the general sentiment of the country, as it might be expressed in the new Parliament. But they were not permitted to take this course without encountering strenuous opposition. On March 15, Lord John Russell warmly contended that the proposed delay in dissolving Parliament, and the attempt to conduct public business by Lord Derby's ministry, whilst in an admitted minority in the House of Commons, was unconstitutional and unprecedented." He was followed, at greater length, and to the same effect, by Sir James Graham. Afterwards, Mr. Gladstone and Lord Palmerston urged that, constitutionally, the new ministry were bound to give a distinct assurance that, as soon as the necessary business before Parliament could be despatched, the crown should be advised to appeal to the country." In the House of Lords, similar views were

---

* Hans. Deb. vol. cxix. p. 914.   * *Ibid.* p. 1007.
* *Ibid.* pp. 1090, 1105, 1111.

expressed by the Duke of Newcastle.* Lord Derby, in reply, said that he did not rely on the conduct of Mr. Pitt, in 1784, as a precedent, not regarding it as a very analogous case; but he defended his position by referring to the course adopted by Sir R. Peel, in 1835, when he was in a minority, in the House of Commons, upon his assumption of the reins of government, and failed to obtain a majority upon a dissolution of Parliament. He sustained several serious defeats in the new House, yet he would not resign, saying, 'I hold there is nothing unconstitutional, in the post I fill, and in the fulfilment of my duty, to persevere in the discharge of those duties to which my sovereign has called me, in defiance of the majority that is against me upon any abstract question, and in defiance of any declaration on the part of the House of Commons that I ought to bring forward a particular question, and settle it in a particular manner. I will perform my duty until the House shall, by its vote, refuse its sanction to some measure of importance which I think necessary to submit to its consideration.' Upon this constitutional doctrine, laid down in 1835, Lord Derby declared that he was prepared to abide in 1852. He could not consent to resign, as he and his party had not sought office, or brought about his accession to it; neither would he give any distinct pledge as to the time when he would advise a dissolution. He expressed, however, an anxious desire that an appeal to the country should be made at the earliest period possible, consistently with the public welfare. Furthermore, he said that he thought the new Parliament should be assembled before the close of the coming autumn, to 'pronounce its definitive and final decision.'ᵠ With this explanation, the leading statesmen in the House of Lords declared themselves to be satisfied. A similar announcement was made in the House of Commons, on the same day, by Mr. Disraeli, in reply to an

---

* Hans. Deb. vol. cxix. p. 1207.
ᵠ Lord Derby's speech, Hans. Deb. March 10, 1852.

enquiry by Lord John Russell. On March 22, Lord John Russell professed himself content with these explanations, and expressed his willingness to aid the government in completing the necessary business without delay.[r] The prorogation took place on July 1, and the dissolution of Parliament upon the same day. At the close of the session, Lord Derby 'gratefully acknowledged' that his ministry had met 'with no factious opposition,' and had 'encountered nothing but a fair, legitimate, and constitutional opposition in the other House of Parliament.'[s] The new Parliament assembled on November 4. The returns to the new House of Commons indicated the opinion of the country to be in favour of a continuance of the new commercial policy, and opposed to any return to the principle of Protection. Accordingly, on November 11, in the debate upon the Address, in answer to the speech from the throne, Lord Derby stated that he should bow to the decision of the country, thus unmistakably expressed, and should give his unequivocal adhesion to that policy.[t] Notwithstanding this frank avowal, the combination of parties proved too strong for the administration, and upon the introduction of the budget by the Chancellor of the Exchequer (Mr. Disraeli), a debate ensued upon the whole financial policy of the government, which resulted in a defeat of the ministry, on December 16, by a majority of 19. Next day their resignation was announced to both Houses of Parliament.

21. *Lord Aberdeen's Administration.—December* 1852.

1852. On December 27, 1852, Lord Aberdeen informed the House of Lords that, having been empowered by her Majesty to form a ministry, he had succeeded, in conjunction with Lord John Russell, in forming a Coalition Ministry, of Conservatives and Liberals, who would

---

[r] Hans. Deb. vol. cxix. p. 1400. [s] Lords' Debates, 30 June, 1852.
[t] Hans. Deb. vol. cxxiii. p. 53.

agree in 'the maintenance and prudent extension of Free Trade and the commercial and financial system established by the late Sir Robert Peel.' He then proceeded to state the outlines of the policy intended to be pursued by the new ministry. Both Houses were then adjourned until February 10. On that day, Lord John Russell, as leader of the government in the House of Commons, explained the measures intended to be submitted to Parliament. The Aberdeen ministry remained in office until 1855. Their downfall was occasioned by internal dissensions and notorious incompetency to meet the crisis of the war with Russia. It was preceded by the unexpected secession of Lord John Russell himself, who resigned on January 23, 1855, on account of his inability to resist a pending motion of Mr. Roebuck, for the appointment of a committee to enquire into the conduct of the war in the Crimea. This motion was carried, on January 29, by a large majority. It was regarded as a declaration of want of confidence in the government. Accordingly, on February 1, the resignation of ministers was announced to both Houses.* After the Premier had communicated this intelligence to the Lords, the Duke of Newcastle took the unusual course of explaining to the House his personal motives for his conduct in office, and for his resignation. On February 5, Lord John Russell (in the Commons) entered into similar explanations, in answer to certain remarks from the Duke of Newcastle on the aforesaid occasion. Meanwhile, ineffectual attempts had been made, both by Lord Derby and by Lord John Russell, at the command

1855.

---

* The announcement was made, in the Commons, by Lord Palmerston, the Home Secretary. The resignations had actually taken place before the meeting of the House on the previous sitting (January 30), and would have been formally made known upon the moving of the adjournment on that day, on account of 'the present state of public affairs,' but for the accidental circumstance of the Lords having adjourned over that day. The Premier having a seat in the Lords it was necessary that the formal announcement of resignation should proceed first from him. Hans. Deb. vol. cxxxvi. pp. 1233, 1261.

of the queen, to form a new administration; and Lord John Russell took this opportunity to explain the causes of his failure. This elicited some observations from the Chancellor of the Exchequer; but no debate arose upon either occasion.

22. *Lord Palmerston's First Administration.*—1855.

On February 6, 1855, both Houses were informed that her Majesty had empowered Lord Palmerston to form a ministry. In the Commons (upon the motion to adjourn), a short debate took place, in which dissatisfaction was expressed at the delay in the formation of a new ministry, and hints were thrown out that, if further delay occurred, it might become expedient to address the crown on the subject. On the 8th, Lord Granville informed the House of Lords that Lord Palmerston had succeeded in the task entrusted to him. His lordship briefly explained that no change of policy was intended by the incoming administration, which was, in fact, a reconstruction of the preceding one, with some partial changes, and re-distribution of offices." Lord Derby took this opportunity to enter into explanations in regard to his own failure to construct a cabinet, which gave rise to a short debate. But the ordinary ministerial explanations were deferred until the appearance of Lord Palmerston in the House of Commons, after his re-election. Until this took place, with the partial exceptions above noted, there was no political discussion in either House, although the House of Commons sat, for the transaction of ordinary and unopposed business, on January 30, February 2, 5, 6, 7, 8, and 9, when they adjourned until the 16th instant. Meanwhile, the Chancellor of the Exchequer (Mr. Gladstone), the Commissioner of Public Works (Sir W. Molesworth), and the President of the Board of Control (Sir C. Wood)

---

* Hans. Deb. vol. cxxxvi p. 1330. An. Register, 1855, p. 38.

resumed their offices as members of the new administration. Nevertheless, while taking part in the debates, they refrained from asserting their official position during this interregnum, and in the absence of their chief. In proposing a vote on account in supply, on behalf of the Army, upon February 7, the Chancellor of the Exchequer said: 'I presume the government are of opinion that it would be the wish of the House that we should not proceed with any business, except such as is of absolute necessity, in order that those who have accepted office, or who have changed their offices, in her Majesty's government—at least the principal members of it—may have an opportunity of submitting themselves to their constituents for their re-election.'[*] Upon the re-assembling of the House, on the 16th instant, Lord Palmerston was present, and entered into the ordinary ministerial explanations.[*] By a resolution of the House of Commons, on March 3, 1857, the Palmerston ministry were censured for the 'violent measures resorted to at Canton in the late affair of the *Arrow*.' The House of Lords, however, approved of their conduct and policy upon the Chinese question, and upon other questions the House of Commons gave them a general support. They therefore resolved to appeal to the country by a dissolution of Parliament. They were influenced in this determination by the probability that it would be difficult to form a strong government to work with the existing House of Commons, which had already lasted five years,

---

[*] Hans. Deb. vol. cxxxvi. p. 1300.
[*] On February 22, it was announced that Mr. Gladstone, Mr. Sidney Herbert, and Sir J. Graham, had retired from the new cabinet; they were speedily replaced, however, by Sir G. C. Lewis, Lord John Russell, and Mr. Vernon Smith. The ex-ministers made their explanations on the following day, alleging their strong objections to the proposed committee of enquiry into the state of the army before Sebastopol, as the ground of their retirement. With the consent of the Premier, and his new colleagues, the committee was appointed. (Hans. Deb. vol. cxxxvi. pp. 1733, 1857.) On July 16, Lord John Russell resigned office, on account of animadversions in Parliament, and out of doors, upon his conduct as Minister Plenipotentiary at Vienna, Sir E. Bulwer-Lytton having given notice of motion for a vote of censure upon him. Ann. Reg. 1855, p. 151.

within which period there had been three different administrations.ʸ The Chinese question excited very little interest at the hustings, but the name of 'Palmerston' was the rallying cry at almost every constituency. The result of the elections was the return of an increased majority of members to support the administration of that popular nobleman.ᶻ But ere long a still more difficult bone of contention arose. At the commencement of the year 1858, there was much excitement in England and France in consequence of the discovery of a nefarious plot, against the life of the Emperor of the French, by a foreign refugee resident in London. This occasioned a diplomatic correspondence between the two governments, and led to the introduction, by Lord Palmerston, of a Bill into Parliament to amend the law in relation to the crime of conspiracy to commit murder. But certain expressions in a despatch from the French minister for Foreign Affairs, impugning the sacred right of asylum, and the sufficiency and enforcement of the existing law applicable to the case, gave offence to the House of Commons. While they were willing to agree to any amendment that might be required to satisfy the ends of justice, they disclaimed the right of the French government to dictate upon a matter of internal legislation; and they considered that the objectionable portions of the despatch in question should have been formally answered by the Foreign Secretary before the initiation of further legislation upon the subject.ᵃ These opinions were embodied by Mr. Milner Gibson in an amendment which, on February 19, he proposed to the second reading of the Bill, and which was carried by a majority of 19 (234 to 215) against the government. On this occasion it was clear that the feeling of the country con-

1858.

ʸ Hans. Deb. vol. cxliv. pp. 1885, 1894.
ᶻ Ann. Reg. 1857, pp. 83, 84.
ᵃ 'To the measure itself, apart from the circumstances under which it was offered, no valid objection could be raised; and three years later, its provisions were silently admitted to a place in our revised criminal laws.'—May, *Const. Hist.* vol. ii. p. 304. 24 & 25 Vict. c. 100, § 4.

curred with the majority of the House of Commons; and notwithstanding the general support afforded by the House to the ministry, and the fact that the only party in Parliament which was capable of assuming office was neither strong in numbers nor high in popular favour, it was evident a vote of censure so emphatic left the ministry no alternative but to resign.[b] Accordingly, at the next meeting of the House, Lord Palmerston announced their retirement from office.

23. *Lord Derby's Second Administration.*—1858.

On February 22, 1858, it was intimated that the Earl of Derby had been sent for and commissioned to form a new administration. Although unable to command a majority in the House of Commons,[c] the noble earl consented to take office, and succeeded in constructing an efficient cabinet. On March 1, he made his ministerial statement in the House of Lords, and both Houses then adjourned for eleven days, to admit of the new ministers, in the Commons, going for re-election. Shortly after this recess (on March 15), Lord Malmesbury (the Foreign Secretary) laid on the table of the House of Lords a correspondence that had taken place between her Majesty's ministers, since their accession to office, and the French government, which correspondence, he stated, had terminated in all honour and good feeling on both sides. On May 11, a breach was made in the ministerial ranks by the resignation of Lord Ellenborough (the President of the Board of Control), on account of complaints in Parliament that he had unwisely and precipitately published a secret despatch to the Governor-General of India, animadverting upon a proclamation about to be issued in India. On March 1, 1859, Mr. Walpole (the Home Secretary), and Mr. Henley (the President of the Board of Trade)

1858.

1859.

---

[b] An. Reg. 1858, p. 50.
[c] See Hans. Deb. vol. cliv. p. 111. In fact, only one-third of the members of the existing House of Commons were supporters of the government. *Ibid.* p. 123.

1859. informed the House of Commons that they had retired from the ministry, on account of their objections to some of the provisions of the government Reform Bill. Owing in part to the forbearance of their political opponents, and also to a general disposition, both in and out of Parliament, to give the Conservative ministry a fair trial, they were permitted to carry on the government without obstruction, or factious opposition, until the introduction of this measure. The scheme of Reform propounded on the part of the Conservatives excited, however, great hostility for various and widely different reasons. Lord John Russell skilfully availed himself of the prevalent dissatisfaction to forestall the committal of the Bill—at which stage the ministry expressed their readiness to consider any proposed amendments of detail, and to endeavour to make their measure generally acceptable—by moving an amendment upon the second reading, condemnatory, in general terms, of its principle. On March 31, this amendment was carried against the government.

On April 4, ministers announced their intention of appealing to the country by a dissolution of Parliament. In communicating this intention to the House of Lords, the Premier adverted to some remarks which had fallen from Lord Palmerston, in a recent debate in the other House, to the effect that the ministry, notwithstanding this defeat, 'should be permitted neither to retire, nor to dissolve, nor to withdraw the Bill,' but should remain in their places, 'to do our bidding.' Repudiating the idea that he could consent to occupy such an ignominious and unconstitutional position, his lordship proceeded to enquire where any authority could be found to justify any restriction upon the prerogative of the crown to dissolve Parliament at any time and upon any occasion.[d] He asserted that ever since the memorable case of 1784—' which re-

---

[d] On April 6, Lord Palmerston took occasion to disclaim this construction of his former remarks. See *post*, p. 150.

coiled upon the heads of its authors—there has been no
attempt to interfere with the prerogative of the crown to
dissolve Parliament when and for what reason it thought
fit.' He then declared that, with the unanimous consent
of his colleagues, he had assumed the responsibility of
advising the Queen, unless she preferred to accept their
resignation of office, to dissolve the present Parliament,
'so soon as it could be done consistently with the discharge of those duties, and the performance of that
amount of business which is indispensable before a dissolution can take place;' and that her Majesty had been
pleased to sanction this appeal to the judgment and decision of the people. But in regard to the issue upon
which the ministry would go the country, Lord Derby
distinctly stated that it should be wholly irrespective of
the merits of their Reform Bill, or of the general question
of Parliamentary Reform. The appeal would be made
'on a much larger and broader question,' as to whether
the country would support the ministry in whom the
Sovereign had bestowed her confidence, and who had
endeavoured, by their public conduct, to deserve the
confidence which the House of Commons had withheld.[*]
In reply, Lord Granville, as leader of the Opposition,
complained of Lord Derby for not stating 'exactly the
policy upon which the appeal' to the country was to be
made.' On the same day, a similar statement was made
to the House of Commons by the Chancellor of the Exchequer (Mr. Disraeli). He remarked that, 'ever since the
commencement of the session, the government had found
itself frequently in minorities, and that, too, in many instances, on subjects of no mean importance.' But while
regarding their position as a painful one, they had hitherto
refrained from making it the subject of a communication
to the House, for various reasons, arising out of the state
of parties, of the foreign relations of the crown, and of

[*] Hans. Deb. vol. cliii. pp. 1280-1291. [†] Ibid. p. 1208.

1859. their desire to fulfil their pledge to introduce a Reform Bill. But they considered the vote on the second reading of that measure to be a censure upon the government, which virtually deprived them of all authority. They had accordingly advised the Queen to dissolve Parliament, in hopes that, by 'recurring to the sense of her people, a state of affairs might be brought about which might be more conducive to the public interest.' He characterised the intended dissolution as an 'appeal to the country on our personal position.'[a] In reply, Lord Palmerston acknowledged the right of the government to advise the dissolution, saying, 'we recognise the right of the crown upon any occasion to appeal from the House of Commons to the country. We may think it more or less advisable to make that appeal, but when such an intention is announced, I am persuaded that this House will concur with government in accelerating as much as possible the moment for dissolving,' with the understanding 'that Parliament must meet at the earliest moment at which the writs are returnable.' He also admitted that 'the government may say that the question put to the country is whether it has entire confidence in them, or whether it prefers any other combination of men; although he contended that practically the question of Reform would be the issue that the country would decide.[b] On April 6, Lord Palmerston entered into personal explanations in reply to what fell from Lord Derby on the 4th instant. He denied the construction put by the Premier upon his remarks on a former occasion, and declared that no one who knew anything of the British constitution could question the prerogative of the crown, upon the advice of responsible ministers, 'to dissolve Parliament at any period of the year, or in any state whatever of the public business that they may think a fit opportunity of so doing.' Nevertheless, 'it is obvious that the advisers of the crown

---

[a] Hans. Deb. vol. cliii. pp. 1302-1307.   [b] Ibid. pp. 1310, 1311.

cannot, without great inconvenience to the public service, recommend the Sovereign to dissolve Parliament, and carry that recommendation into effect, unless the House of Commons makes itself a party to the transaction, accelerates its proceedings, and concurs in the temporary expedients which are necessary in order to place the public business in a position in which a dissolution would not be attended with inconvenience.' For it would have been perfectly constitutional for the House, under existing circumstances, to refuse to be a party to the abrupt and premature termination of the session, and to interpose their advice between that tendered to her Majesty by her responsible ministers and the act of dissolution, by an 'address to the crown, praying that it would neither dissolve nor prorogue Parliament until the House had had the opportunity of considering another Reform Bill, to be presented by the Government;' or 'to address the crown to dismiss the present ministers.'[2] His lordship, however, would not advise the House to adopt either of these courses, but thought it far better to 'accept the challenge of her Majesty's ministers, and appeal to the sense of the people' without delay. Some further discussion ensued as to the issue upon which the government intended to go to the hustings. The Opposition persisted in asserting that the issue for the country to decide was the propriety of their Reform policy; but the Home Secretary (Mr. Sotheron-Estcourt) maintained that 'the real question at issue for the country to consider was whether the government should be carried on by the present ministers, or whether power should be transferred to other hands.'[1] The prorogation of Parliament took place on April 19, 1859, and the dissolution on the 23rd. The new Parliament assembled on May 31. On the motion for an Address in answer to the speech

---

[1] Hans. Deb. vol. cliii. p. 1415. And see Sir G. Grey's remarks on this point, p. 1410.
[2] Ibid. p. 1420. This was in fact the issue which the Derby government put to the people, and which was decided against them. See ibid. vol. cliv. pp. 111, 117.

from the throne, an amendment was proposed, in the House of Commons, on June 7, representing that the present advisers of her Majesty did not possess the confidence of this House, or of the country. After three nights' debate, the amendment was carried, by a majority of 13. The division upon this question was the largest on record. There were 638 members present out of 654.[a] The ministry thereupon immediately resigned office; but their resignation was not formally announced to both Houses until June 17.[1] At this juncture the queen first commissioned Earl Granville to form a ministry, but as soon as that nobleman found 'that a better and a stronger arrangement might be made, he at once requested her Majesty to absolve him from the task.'[m] Lord Palmerston was then commanded to undertake it.

24. *Lord Palmerston's Second Administration.*—1859.

On June 17, the Houses were informed that Lord Palmerston had been empowered to form an administration. On June 22, the new writs were ordered; and an adjournment took place until the 30th instant, on which day the new Premier made his ministerial statement to the House of Commons. This ministry lasted for upwards of six years, and was finally broken up by the death of Lord Palmerston, which occurred on October 18, 1865.

25. *Earl Russell's Second Administration.*—1865.

A few days after the decease of the veteran Lord Palmerston, which occurred on October 18, 1865, being within two days of the completion of his eighty-first year, Earl Russell, the Secretary of State for Foreign Affairs, and the most experienced and prominent member of the administration, who had already once before filled the office

---

[a] Hans. Deb. vol. cliv. p. 410. An. 423, 431.
Reg. 1859. Chronicle, p. 81.   [m] *Ibid.* p. 457.
[1] Hans. Deb. vol. cliv. pp. 422.

of Premier, was called upon by the queen to assume that position. The lead of the House of Commons was assigned to Mr. Gladstone, the Chancellor of the Exchequer. A few minor alterations were made in the *personnel* of the government, and two new members introduced therein, namely, Mr. Forster, as Under-Secretary of the Colonies, and Mr. Göschen, first as Vice-President of the Board of Trade, and, after a few weeks, as Chancellor of the Duchy of Lancaster, with a seat in the cabinet.[a] Otherwise, the political character of the new ministry resembled that of Lord Palmerston, although in the loss of that gifted and popular statesman it failed to acquire the same amount of confidence and respect from the various parties into which the House of Commons was divided. Three months before Lord Palmerston's death, a general election had taken place, and the returns to the new Parliament appeared to have somewhat added to the strength of ministers, and to have given them a majority of about seventy over their political opponents.

A Reform Bill was promised in the speech from the throne, at the opening of Parliament. Some delay occurred in the production of this measure, and when at length it was brought in, it consisted of a part only of the government scheme, in the shape of a Bill for the reduction of the franchise. It was stated that the necessary complement, of a Bill for the re-distribution of seats, would not be introduced until the following session. This arrangement produced great dissatisfaction in the House, and ministers were at length obliged to bring in their Seats Bill without further delay, in order that the complete scheme of Reform might be discussed in Committee of the whole House. After several minor discomfitures on the question of Reform, ministers were defeated on May 28, on a motion, which was carried against them, for an instruction to the committee on the Bill to provide therein

1866.

---

[a] Annual Register, 1865, p. 150.

for the better prevention of bribery and corruption at elections.* They were again defeated, in committee, on June 18, by a resolution to amend the 5th clause (concerning the occupation franchise for borough voters) by striking out the words 'clear yearly,' with a view to the insertion of 'ratable' instead thereof.† Regarding this decision as equivalent to a vote of want of confidence, ministers immediately tendered their resignations. The queen was, at the time, at Balmoral Castle, in Scotland, a circumstance which occasioned some delay. But, on learning the intentions of ministers, her Majesty expressed her desire that they would not persist in retiring from office in the existing state of public affairs, especially upon the Continent—where a war between Austria, Italy, and Prussia, was on the eve of taking place—and declared her opinion that a mere defeat upon a question of detail, which was capable of adjustment, did not call for such serious consequences. In deference to this opinion the matter remained in abeyance until the queen, on her return from Scotland, should be able to confer personally with her ministers. On June 26, the Premier and the Chancellor of the Exchequer had an audience with the queen, at Windsor Castle, at which her Majesty was informed that ministers persevered in tendering their resignations. They were accordingly accepted; and full explanations of the grounds of their retirement from office were given, on that day, to both Houses of Parliament. Earl Russell's statement, in the House of Lords, gave rise to speeches from Earls Derby, Granville, and Grey, upon the ministerial crisis. Mr. Gladstone's statement, in the House of Commons, elicited no remarks from any other member.

26. *Earl of Derby's Third Administration.*—1866.

1866. On June 28, the House of Commons was informed that the Earl of Derby had received the queen's commands to

---

* Hans. Deb. vol. clxxxiii. p. 1344.   † ibid. vol. clxxxiv. p. 670.

form an administration.[a] Adjournments of both Houses took place from time to time, until July 6, when new writs were moved for in the House of Commons on behalf of the incoming administration. But no observations were made upon this occasion. On Monday, July 9, however, the new premier, the Earl of Derby, made his ministerial statement to the House of Lords. He said it had been the wish of the Queen, and his own endeavour, that he should be able 'to form a government composed, no doubt, in the main, from the Conservative party, but formed on an enlarged basis, capable of including within it some persons either opposed to us, or who had been supporters, or even members, of the late government.' By 'enlarged basis' his lordship meant, 'enlarged, not as to principles, but as to persons,' and not 'a government of coalition;' by which he understood 'a government of men of different parties, in which each, to a greater or less extent, sacrifices his individual opinions for the purpose of obtaining united political strength.' Being unsuccessful in his attempt to obtain any such 'extraneous aid,' Earl Derby proceeded to form a ministry from the ranks of the Conservative party, which was accepted by the Queen. His lordship then explained the general principles upon which he proposed to carry on the government. He was followed by Earl Russell, who commented upon one or two topics of the premier's speech; but no further discussion took place.[b] After the return of the new ministers, who had vacated their seats in the House of Commons by accepting office, the business of the session was brought to a speedy termination, and Parliament was prorogued upon August 10. Although the Conservative party was in an acknowledged minority in the House of Commons, ministers met with no factious or ungenerous opposition in winding up the public business.

1866.

---

[a] But it was on Tuesday, June 20, that the Queen intimated her desire to the Earl of Derby that he should form a ministry. Hans. Deb. vol. clxxxiv. p. 734.
[b] Ibid. pp. 726—750.

TABULAR VIEW OF THE ADMINISTRATIONS OF GREAT BRITAIN FROM 1782 TO 1844.

N.B.—The numbers refer to the preceding 'Narrative of Administrations,' which describes the political history of each Ministry.

No.	Name of Prime Minister	Political Character of the Ministry	Date of Appointment	Date of Resignation or Dismissal	Cause of Retirement of the Ministry	Dissolutions of Parliament during this period	Reasons for which Parliament was dissolved
1	Marquis of Rockingham	Whig	1782 March	1782 July 1	Death of the premier	[Existing Parliament first met on Oct. 21, 1780]	
2	Earl of Shelburne	Whig	1782 July 8	1783 Feb. 24	Vote of censure by House of Commons on February 21, 1783		
3	Duke of Portland (His first administration)	Coalition	1783 April 2	1783 Dec. 18	Dismissed by the king on account of Fox's India Bill		
4	William Pitt (His first administration)	Tory	1783 Dec. 19	1801 Feb. 5; but owing to the king's illness he remained in office until the middle of March	Disagreement with the king on account of the Roman Catholic claims	1784, March 25 1790, June 10 1796, May 20	Observations and defeats of ministers in the House of Commons. On account of the near approach of its natural term of existence. For the same reason as the preceding dissolution. N.B. This Parliament was declared by proclamation, issued under the authority of certain statutes, and delivered in open Parliament on December 31, 1800, to be continued as the first Parliament of the United Kingdom of Great Britain and Ireland.—(*Parl. Hist.* vol. xxxv. p. 951.)

#	Name	Party			Reason		Notes
5	Henry Addington	Tory	1801 March 17	1804 May 10	Weakness of the ministry in the House of Commons	1802, June 29	On account of the near approach of its natural term of existence, the king offered Mr. Addington a dissolution of Parliament before his resignation of office, but the offer was declined.
6	William Pitt (His second administration)	Tory	1804 May 10	1806 Jan. 23	Death of the premier	1805, Oct. 24	On account of the failure of the negotiations for peace with France, and in order to strengthen the hands of the government in the prosecution of the war.—(Parl. Deb. vol. viii. p. 21.)
7	Lord Grenville	Whig	1806 Jan. 28	1807 March 24	Dismissed by the king for refusing to give a pledge on the Roman Catholic question		
8	Duke of Portland (His second administration)	Tory	1807 March 24	1809 Oct. 30	Death of the premier	1807, April 27	Though the new ministry were fully sustained in the House of Commons, yet Parliament was dissolved, in order to take the sense of the country upon the conduct of the king in changing his advisers. The ministerial majority was thereby largely increased.
9	Spencer Perceval	Tory	1809 Nov. –	1812 May 11	The death, by assassination, of the premier	1812, Sept. 29	For no consideration affecting the state of parties.
10	Earl of Liverpool	Tory	1812 June 8	1827 March 27	The resignation, occasioned by severe illness, of the premier. He was seized with paralysis on February 17, 1827, but did not resign his office for about six weeks. During this interval, and from thence until April 10, the ministry was virtually without a head	1818, June 10 / 1820, Feb. 28 / 1826, June 14	On account of the near approach of its natural term of existence. On account of the demise of the crown (George III.) On account of the termination of its ninth session.

TABULAR VIEW OF THE ADMINISTRATIONS OF GREAT BRITAIN—continued.

No.	Name of Prime Minister	Political character of the Ministry	Date of Appointment	Date of Resignation or Dismissal	Cause of Retirement of the Ministry	Dissolutions of Parliament during this period	Reasons for which Parliament was dissolved
11	George Canning	Coalition	1827 April 10	1827 Aug. 8	The death of the premier		
12	Lord Goderich	Coalition	1827 Aug. —	1828 Jan. 8	Internal dissension in the cabinet		
13	Duke of Wellington	Coalition at first, afterwards Tory	1828 Jan. 8	1830 Nov. 16	Ministerial defeat in House of Commons on November 15, 1830, on the Civil List	1830, July 24	The demise of the crown by death of George IV.
14	Earl Grey	Whig	1830 Nov. 16	1834 July 8	Internal dissensions in the cabinet. N.B. This ministry resigned on May 8, 1832, because the king would not consent to create a batch of peers, in order to carry the Reform Bill in the House of Lords. The Duke of Wellington was empowered to form a new ministry, but failed in the attempt. On May 17 the king recalled the Grey Ministry, and gave them written authority to create as many peers as might be necessary to ensure the passing of the Reform Bill	1831, April 22 1832, Dec. 3	On account of defeat of ministers in the House of Commons on the Reform Bill. To admit of the enlarged representative system being put into immediate operation.
15	Viscount Melbourne (His first administration)	Whig	1834 July 14	1834 Nov. 12	Dismissed by the king, who disapproved of the politics of ministers		
16	Sir Robert Peel (His first administration)	Tory	1831 Nov. —	1835 April 8	Inability to control the House of Commons, and consequent ministerial defeats in that House	1834, Dec. 30	With a view to obtain a House of Commons that would give the king's new ministers 'a fair trial.'

17	Viscount Melbourne. (His second administration) Whig	1835 April 18	Vote of want of confidence by House of Commons; followed up, after the dissolution of Parliament, by a similar vote in both Houses, in answer to the Speech from the Throne. N.B. This ministry resigned on May 7, 1839, nominally because of their inability to carry the Jamaica Constitution Bill in the House of Commons by more than five majority on its second reading, but really on account of internal weakness. Sir Robert Peel was empowered to form a ministry; but as the Queen refused to alter the Ladies of the Bedchamber to be changed, he relinquished the undertaking. The old ministry were then reinstated in office	1841, June 28	On account of the vote of House of Commons on June 4, 1841, against ministers. But the immediate cause was not that of confidence in themselves, but advocating a modification of the corn laws.
18	Sir Robert Peel. (His second administration) Conservative	1841 Aug. 30	Ministerial defeat in House of Commons on June 25, 1846, on the Irish Coercion Bill. N.B. This ministry was dissolved on December 5, 1845, by the resignation of Sir R. Peel, on account of the refusal of his colleagues to agree to his plan for the settlement of the corn laws; whereupon Lord John Russell was commissioned to form a government, but could not succeed. Sir R. Peel was then recalled to power, and his former colleagues agreed to support his policy, with the exception of Lord Stanley, who did not again take office		
19	Lord John Russell. (His first administration) Whig	1846 July 6	Defeat in House of Commons on February 20, 1852, on Militia Bill. N.B. This ministry resigned on February 23, 1851, on account of their weakness in the House of Commons, and especially their recent defeat on a motion of Mr. Locke King for the extension of the franchise. Several attempts were made to form a Conservative or a Coalition government, but without success. At length the Whig ministry were recalled to office	1847, July 23	On account of the termination of the seventh session of this Parliament.

TABULAR VIEW OF THE ADMINISTRATIONS OF GREAT BRITAIN—continued.

No.	Name of Prime Minister	Political Character of the Ministry	Date of Appointment	Date of Resignation or Dismissal	Cause of Retirement of the Ministry	Dissolution of Parliament during this period	Reason for which Parliament was dissolved
20	EARL OF DERBY (His first administration)	Conservative	1852 Feb. 26	1852 Dec. 17	Ministerial defeat in House of Commons on December 16, 1852, on the Budget	1852, July 1	To take the sense of the country on the question of free-trade and the corn laws.
21	EARL OF ABERDEEN	Coalition	1852 Dec. 27	1855 Feb. 1	Internal dissensions, incompetency, and defeat in the House of Commons on January 29, on appointment of Sebastopol Committee		
22	VISCOUNT PALMERSTON (His first administration)	Whig	1855 Feb. 8	1858 Feb. 20	Rejection by the House of Commons on February 19, 1858, of the Conspiracy to Murder Bill, and vote of censure against ministers in reference to that measure	1857, March 21	On account of the vote of censure by the House of Commons on March 3, 1857, upon the conduct of affairs in China.
23	EARL OF DERBY (His second administration)	Conservative	1858 Feb. 23	1859 June 10	Vote of want of confidence by the House of Commons on June 9, 1859, in amendment to the Address in answer to the Speech from the Throne	1859, April 26	The ministerial Reform Bill having been rejected by the House of Commons on March 31, 1859, ministers resolved to appeal to the country. But the issue they raised at the hustings was upon the general policy of the government, irrespective of their views on the question of reform.
24	VISCOUNT PALMERSTON (His second administration)	Whig	1859 June 17	1865 Oct. 18	The death of the premier	1865, July 6	On account of the termination of the seventh session of this Parliament.
25	EARL RUSSELL (His second administration)	Whig	1865 Oct. —	1866 June 26	Ministerial defeat in the House of Commons on June 18, 1866, on the Representation of the People Bill		
26	EARL OF DERBY (His third administration)	Conservative	1866 July 6				

CHAPTER IV.

THE SOVEREIGN.

THE supreme executive authority of the state in all matters, civil and military, together with jurisdiction and supremacy over all causes and persons ecclesiastical in the realm, belongs to the sovereign of the British Empire, by virtue of his kingly office; for he is the fountain of all state authority, dignity, and honour, and the source of all political jurisdiction therein. He is also the head of the Imperial Legislature, which derives its existence from the crown, and a component part of every local legislature throughout his dominions. In all that concerns the outward life of the empire, and its relations with other countries or provinces, the sovereign is the visible representative of the state. It is his especial prerogative to declare war and to make peace, and also to contract alliances with foreign nations. Supremacy of the sovereign.

Preeminence, perfection, and perpetuity are acknowledged attributes of the Crown of England in its political capacity. The crown is hereditary, but in the eye of the law 'the king never dies.' The decease of a reigning monarch is usually termed his demise; which signifies that, in consequence of the disunion of the king's natural body from his body-politic, the kingdom is transferred or demised to his successor, and so the royal dignity remains perpetual.[a] Perpetuity of the kingly office.

After their accession to the throne in the natural order, the sovereigns of England are consecrated to their high

---

[a] Broom's Legal Maxims, 4th ed. pp. 48, 51.

Coronation.

office in the solemnity of a royal coronation at Westminster Abbey. This rite is performed by the Archbishop of Canterbury, assisted by other prelates of the English Church, in the presence of the nobility. By this solemn act the Divine sanction is imparted to the English monarchy, and the whole fabric of our political and social order is strengthened and confirmed.[b]

Personal irresponsibility of the sovereign.

From the supreme dignity and preeminence of the crown, it naturally follows that the king is personally amenable to no earthly tribunal whatsoever, because all tribunals in the realm are presumed to derive their authority from him, and none are empowered to exercise authority or jurisdiction over him. The royal person, moreover, is by law sacred and inviolable, and the sovereign is personally irresponsible for all acts of government.[c]

His subjection to the law.

But while the power of the sovereign is supreme in point of jurisdiction, it is neither absolute nor unlimited in extent; for it is a maxim of the common law, that although the king is under no man, yet he is in subjection to God and the law, for the law makes the king.[d] And though the monarch is not personally responsible to any human tribunal for the exercise of the functions of royalty, yet these functions appertain to him in his political capacity, are regulated by law, and must be discharged for the public welfare, and not merely to gratify his personal inclinations. For the king is bound to govern his people according to law.[e]

Succession to the Crown.

Succession to the Crown of England has always been hereditary; but even this right is held subject to limita-

---

[b] See Bagehot on the Eng. Const., in Fortnightly Review, Aug. 15, 1865, pp. 160, 164.
[c] Broom's Legal Maxims, 4th ed. p. 51; Bowyer, Const. Law, pp. 134-140; Atkinson's Papinian, p. 33.
[d] Broom's Legal Maxims, p. 48.
[e] Broom, Const. Law, p. 63. And see in De Lolme, book i. chap. viii., the manner in which the several prerogatives of the crown are limited and restrained by law, and their exercise subjected to the general control of Parliament. See also post, Chap. V., On the Royal Prerogative in connection with Parliament.

tion and control by the High Court of Parliament. Formerly the crown went to the next heir; but since the Act of Settlement the inheritance is conditional, being limited to heirs of the body of the Princess Sophia of Hanover, being Protestant members of the Church of England, and married only to Protestants.*

As a pledge and security for the rightful exercise of every act of royal authority, it is required by the constitution that the ministers of state for the time being shall be held responsible to Parliament and to the law of the land for all public acts of the crown. This responsibility, moreover, is not merely for affairs of state which have been transacted by ministers in the name and on the behalf of the crown, or by the king himself upon the advice of ministers, but it extends to measures that might possibly be known to have emanated directly from the sovereign. If, then, the sovereign command an unlawful act to be done, the offence of the instrument is not thereby indemnified; for though the king is not personally subject to the coercive power of the law, yet in many cases his commands are under its directive power, which makes the act itself invalid if it be unlawful, and so renders the instrument of its execution obnoxious to punishment.* The personal command of the king, says Lord John Russell, is no excuse for a wrong administration of power. Lord Danby was impeached for a letter which contained a postscript in the king's own hand, declaring that it had been written by his order. And although the king is the fountain of justice, a commitment by his own direction has been held to be void, because there was no minister responsible for it.* In a constitu-

Responsibility of ministers for acts of the Crown.

---

* 12 & 13 Will. III. c. 2.
* Broom's Legal Maxims, p. 54.
* 'A king, however limited his powers may be, is, in all modern constitutions, personally irresponsible. His command is no justification of any illegal act done by another, but no constitutional monarchy seems to supply any ordinary means of punishing an illegal act done by the king's own hands.'—E. A. Freeman, in National Review, November 1861, p. 6; and see Cox, Eng. Govt. pp. 30, 408–416.
* Russell, Eng. Const. p. 150. See Broom, Const. Law, pp. 244, 240, 615.

tional point of view, so universal is the operation of this rule, that there is not a moment in the king's life, from his accession to his demise, during which there is not some one responsible to Parliament for his public conduct; and 'there can be no exercise of the crown's authority for which it must not find some minister willing to make himself responsible.'¹ Accordingly, whenever the royal sign-manual is used, it is necessary that it should be countersigned by a responsible minister, for the purpose of rendering it constitutionally valid and authoritative.¹

If a peer of the realm desire to avail himself of his privilege of peerage to solicit an audience of the sovereign, to make any representations on public affairs, it is necessary that he should apply for an interview through the medium of the Secretary of State for the Home Department.ᵏ And all letters or reports on public affairs intended for the government of Great Britain must be addressed to the king's minister, not to the sovereign personally; that is to say, to the secretary of state to whose department their subject-matter would properly belong.¹

Communicates with foreign powers, &c. through ministers.

When Napoleon Bonaparte was First Consul of France, he disregarded this constitutional rule, and addressed a letter containing proposals of peace between France and England to the king himself; but it was acknowledged and answered by the Foreign Secretary. If it were fitting that the sovereign should receive such a communication without the interposition of a minister, there would be no reason why he should not deal with it on his own authority.ᵐ

In 1810 a violation of this rule was made the subject of parliamentary inquiry. Lord Chatham, being at the time a privy

---

¹ See Lords Erskine and Holland's speeches, in Hans. Deb. vol. ix. pp. 303, 414; Mr. Adam's speech, *ibid.* vol. xvi. p. 8****; Sir H. Nicolas, Pro. Privy Coun. vol. vi. p. cc.; and Grey's Parl. Govt. new ed. p. 329 s.

² Park, Lectures on the Dogmas of the Constitution, p. 33; Sir G. C. Lewis, in Hans. Deb. vol. clxv.

p. 1480. The sovereign's signature is first appended, afterwards that of the secretary of state. Rep. Com. on Pub. Accounts, 1865, Ev. 2080, 2185.

ᵏ Hans. Deb. vol. clxxx. p. 340.

¹ Lord John Russell, *ibid.*, vol. cxxx. p. 100.

ᵐ Canning and his Times, by Stapleton, p. 47.

councillor and a cabinet minister, accepted the post of commander *Official reports to be made through a minister.*
of the expedition to the Scheldt. On his return to England, he
presented to the king, at a private interview, a narrative, drawn up
by himself, of the conduct of the expedition, in which he criminated
one of his colleagues in the ministry, and brought serious charges
against an admiral who had been employed conjointly with himself
in the expedition. He did this unknown to any other cabinet
minister, and requested the king not to communicate the paper to
anyone, at least for a time. The document remained in the king's
possession for nearly a month, when Lord Chatham asked to have
it returned to him, in order that he might make some alterations in
it. Upon receipt of the paper, Lord Chatham expunged a paragraph
therein, and returned it to his Majesty. When the narrative again
reached his hands, the king directed that it should be forwarded to
the Secretary of State, for the purpose of making it an official paper.
It was afterwards transmitted to the House of Commons, when its
peculiar history transpired.[a] The House called for the attendance
of Lord Chatham at the bar, and questioned him as to whether he
had, on any other occasion, made such a communication to the king;
but he refused to answer, and, being a peer, could not be compelled
to do so. Whereupon, on February 23, on motion of Mr. Whitbread, the House agreed to an address to the king (on division,
against ministers), praying for copies of all reports or papers at any
time submitted to his Majesty by Lord Chatham relative to the
expedition to the Scheldt. During the debate Lord Chatham's
conduct was strongly reprobated by Mr. Canning and other constitutional authorities, who contended that whilst his lordship, as a
member of the cabinet, was equally responsible with the rest of his
colleagues for the wisdom or policy of the said expedition, yet that
in his capacity of commander he was responsible to the king,
through the secretary of state; and that he was bound to present
his report through the regular constitutional channel—namely, the
secretary of state, or the commander-in-chief of the army. His
position was compared with that of a minister at a foreign court,
who, on being appointed to office under the royal sign-manual, is
always formally instructed to conform to the orders and correspond
with the secretary of state through whom he has received his
appointment. Lord Chatham's instructions had been similarly prepared, and there was nothing in his peculiar position of privy
councillor and cabinet minister to justify his passing by the secretary of state, in communicating with his Majesty upon a public
matter.[b] In reply to their address, the king made known to the
House of Commons the circumstances under which he had received

---

[a] Parl. Deb. vol. xv. p. 482.   [b] *Ibid.* p. 581.

Lord Chatham's communication, and stated that no other reports or papers concerning the Scheldt expedition had been presented to him by that nobleman.* On March 2 Mr. Whitbread submitted to the House resolutions of censure upon Lord Chatham for his unconstitutional conduct. The previous question was proposed thereupon, on the part of the administration, and negatived. But an amendment, proposed by Mr. Canning, modifying the terms of censure, was accepted by Mr. Whitbread, and agreed to by the House. It was then moved that the resolutions be communicated to the king; but the opinion being generally entertained that the sense of the House in regard to this transaction had been sufficiently expressed by the recording of the resolutions upon the journals, and that it would not be consistent with the dignity of the House to proceed any further in the matter, this motion was withdrawn.⁴ In consequence of this vote of the House, Lord Chatham retired from the ministry, and was succeeded as Master-General of the Ordnance by Lord Mulgrave. A month elapsed after the formal resignation of Lord Chatham before his successor was appointed, during which interval, as is customary in respect to patent offices, his lordship continued to discharge the duties of the situation; abstaining, however, from advising in the cabinet, and from attending upon his Majesty with official reports, &c. Nevertheless, his continuing to perform official duty, under the peculiar circumstances of his position, gave rise to remarks in the House of Commons.ʳ But the constitutional law which he had infringed had been sufficiently vindicated by his enforced retirement from office, and any further proceedings would have been unnecessary.*

Secretary of state.

The recognised channel of approach to the person of the sovereign is by means of a secretary of state, and it is through such an officer that the royal pleasure is communicated in regard to acts of government. Whenever the sovereign is temporarily absent from his usual places of residence, it is necessary that a secretary of state should be in attendance upon him; and at every interview between the sovereign and the minister of any foreign court, it is the duty of the Secretary of State for Foreign Affairs to be present. Private communication between a king of England and foreign ministers is contrary to the

---

* Parl. Deb. vol. xv. p. 602.
ᵠ Ibid. vol. xvi. p. 12.*
ʳ Ibid. p. 735.

* Knight's Hist. of England, vol. vii. p. 527; Edinb. Rev. vol. cviii. p. 320.

spirit and practice of the British constitution. George III. invariably respected this rule. During the reign of his successor it was not so strictly adhered to; but upon the appointment of Mr. Canning as foreign secretary, he restored and maintained the constitutional usage.[1]

While the sovereign, as the fountain of justice and the source of all political authority and jurisdiction in the realm, is presumed to be personally present in every court of law, and especially in the High Court of Parliament, justice must be dispensed and laws enacted in the king's name, in strict conformity to the laws, usages, and customs of the constitution. And by the common law itself, and more especially since the formal recognition of the doctrine of ministerial responsibility, the sovereign of England is constitutionally debarred from the public exercise of any functions of royalty, except such as are necessary to express the royal pleasure in regard to acts of state which have been advised or concurred in by constitutional ministers. For example, although in the eye of the law the king is always present in all his courts, he is not above the law, and cannot personally assume to decide any case, civil or criminal, but must do so by his judges.[2] And when any judicial act is by any Act of Parliament referred to the king, it is understood to be done in some court of justice according to the law.[3] And though the sovereign may be present in the House of Lords at any time during the deliberations of that House, seated upon the throne, yet he may not interfere or take part in any of its proceedings, except when he comes in state for the exercise of the royal prerogatives. Up to the reign of Queen Anne it was customary for the sovereign to attend debates in the House of Lords as a

The king must always act through a minister.

---

[1] Stapleton, Canning and his Times, p. 433.
[2] Broom's Const. Law, pp. 145-148.
[3] Stephen's Blackstone, vol. ii. p. 485; 2 Co. Inst. p. 180; and see Fischel, Eng. Const. p. 238; and Lord Camden's Judgment in Shipley's case, wherein the king had been appealed to, as visitor of a college which was a royal foundation.

spectator, and his presence was duly recorded in the journals; but since the accession of George I. this questionable practice, which might be used to overawe the assembly and influence their debates, has been wisely discontinued.* And although the king is the acknowledged head of the military forces of the empire, no English monarch has taken the field in person since the siege of Dettingen by George II. 'A contrary practice,' says a recent writer on the English Constitution, 'would not accord with modern parliamentary usage.'ˢ

Development of ministerial responsibility.

The great principle of ministerial responsibility for every act of sovereignty, and its legitimate result, in limiting the personal action of the sovereign in state affairs to formal and representative occasions, is a natural consequence of the system of parliamentary government which was established by the Revolution of 1688. It is based upon the fundamental doctrine that the king himself 'can do no wrong,' a maxim the true meaning of which has been discussed in a former chapter.ʸ The doctrine of ministerial responsibility has been contended for, more or less emphatically, from an early period; although we do not find it distinctly asserted, according to the modern interpretation of it, until the reign of George II.ᶻ During the earlier part of the reign of George III. this doctrine continued in an unsettled state. In 1770 we find Dr. Johnson, who was a professed Tory, arguing that 'a prince of ability might and should be the directing soul and spirit of his own administration—in short, *his own minister*, and not the mere head of a party; and then, and not till then, would the royal dignity be sincerely respected.'ᵃ This passage seems to claim for the king that he should govern as well as reign. In Russell's 'Memorials of Fox,' under the date of 1778, it is stated that about this time Lord George

---

* May, Parl. Prac. ed. 1863, p. 425.
ˢ Fischel, Eng. Const. p. 136.
ʸ See *ante*, p. 40.
ᶻ *Ante*, p. 41. And see further on this subject, Vol. II. c. 1.
ᵃ Boswell's Johnson, vol. iii. p. 131.

Germaine asserted in the House of Commons 'that the king was *his own minister*, which Charles Fox took up admirably, lamenting that his Majesty was *his own unadvised minister*.'[b] But, as we have already seen in our introductory survey of the history of parliamentary government, the Whigs and Tories at this time differed radically in their ideas upon this point, and neither party held what is now considered to be sound doctrine on the subject. The Whigs arrogated to themselves the right of nominating all the king's ministers, not excepting the prime minister; whilst the Tories, going to the other extreme, claimed for the king, on his own personal responsibility, the right to select all the persons who should govern the state.[c] With these discordant ideas and rival claims, which are now admitted by all parties to be equally untenable, it is no wonder that the true principles of government should have been so frequently disregarded on every side. Ere long, however, they were amply vindicated. During the memorable debates of 1807, when the king dismissed his ministers because they refused to sign a pledge which he had no right to exact of them, more intelligent and enlightened opinions as to the relative position of the king and his ministers were expressed by all the leading statesmen in Parliament, of every creed. On this occasion we find it distinctly enunciated as incontrovertible maxims : '1. That the king has no power, by the constitution, to do any public act of government, either in his executive or legislative capacity, but through the medium of some minister, who is held responsible for the act ; 2. That the personal actions of the king, not being acts of government, are not under the cognisance of law.'[d] This is now universally accepted as sound doctrine.

---

[b] Russell's Fox, vol. I. p. 203.
[c] *Ante*, p. 50; and see Edinb. Review for 1811, an article by Mr. Allen, the well-known writer on the Royal Prerogative.
[d] Lord Selkirk, in House of Lords, Parl. Deb. vol. ix. p. 381; and Mr. Adam, in House of Commons, *ibid.* vol. xvi. p. 2****; and see Maky's William IV. vol. ii. p. 134.

The kingly office no fiction.

But if the exercise of personal power by the sovereign be thus limited and circumscribed, it may be thought that the monarchy of England exists only in name, and that the authority of the king is a mere legal fiction, to express the dominion exercised by certain public functionaries who have obtained possession of supreme power. Such an idea is very erroneous; for while the usages of the constitution have imposed numerous restrictions upon the crown in the conduct of state affairs, these restrictions have been established to secure good government and to protect the liberty of the subject, and not with a view to reduce the authority of the crown to a nullity.

Personal acts of government since Queen Anne's reign.

Before attempting to define the nature and limit of the authority which may be rightfully exercised by a reigning monarch, it may be profitable to glance over a few examples indicative of the extent of interference in affairs of state which has been claimed and exercised by English sovereigns since the accession of the House of Hanover. Our illustrations upon a subject so delicate, and upon which so little is recorded, will necessarily be very few. Nevertheless, they may serve to mark the growth of popular opinion on the subject, and to show how much, in this as in other matters, depends upon the force of individual character.

Queen Anne.

The dogma of the impersonality of the sovereign is the offspring of the Revolution of 1688, although, as we have already seen,* it found no favour, either in theory or practice, in the eyes of William III. It began to be asserted as a constitutional principle in the reign of Queen Anne, who, unlike the great Elizabeth, had no special administrative capacity, although she clung to the exercise of power with great tenacity. The weakness and inexperience of a female sovereign, combined with the acknowledged necessity for governing by means of a ministry acceptable to Parliament, gave increased weight

---

* *Ante*, p. 44.

to the advocates of this doctrine. Hallam tells us that Anne, like all her predecessors, kept in her own hands the reins of government, jealous, as such feeble characters usually are, of those in whom she was forced to confide. Obstinate in her judgment, from the very consciousness of its weakness, she took a share in all business, frequently presided in meetings of the cabinet, and sometimes gave directions without their advice.' In the impeachment of Lord Oxford by the Commons, for alleged treasonable acts, he alleged in his defence that he had acted under the immediate commands of the queen, in the matter specially complained of, using these words: 'My lords, if ministers of state, acting by the immediate commands of their sovereign, are afterwards to be made accountable for their proceedings, it may one day or other be the case of all the members of this august assembly'"—a species of defence similar to that urged by Lord Somers in the case of the Partition Treaty, but which would undoubtedly not be tolerated in the present day.

Throughout the reigns of the first two Georges, the principle of the royal impersonality continued to make progress,—but rather through the incapacity for the details of administration arising from the foreign education of both these monarchs, and the force of circumstances which compelled them to entrust to the leaders of the dominant Whig party authority which they felt incompetent to exercise, than because either the nation or the political philosophers of the day were prepared to accept it in theory.^b

George I. and II.

It is a fact that would be hardly credible, were it not so well attested, that George I., being incapable of conversing in English, as his chief minister, Sir Robert Walpole, was of conferring with him in French, they were compelled to hold communication with each other in the

---

' Hallam, Const. Hist. vol. iii. pp. 314, 315.
^d Parl. Hist. vol. vii. p. 105.

^b See Quarterly Review for April 1859, Art. 0.

Latin language.[1] It is impossible that, under such circumstances, the king could have obtained much insight into the domestic affairs of England, or become familiarised with the character of the people over whom he had been called to rule. 'We know, indeed, that he nearly abandoned the consideration of both, and trusted his ministers with the entire management of the kingdom, content to employ its great name for the promotion of his electoral interests. This continued, in a less degree, to be the case with his son, who, though better acquainted with the language and circumstances of Great Britain, and more jealous of his prerogative, was conscious of his incapacity to determine in matters of domestic government, and reserved almost his whole attention for the politics of Germany.'[2]

In describing the character and conduct of the first two Georges, Hallam intimates of both of them that they forced upon their ministers the adoption of a foreign policy adverse to the interests of England and directed to the aggrandisement of Hanover: but that, so far as domestic politics were concerned, they surrendered almost everything into the hands of their ministers, so that during their reigns 'the personal authority of the sovereign seems to have been at the lowest point it has ever reached.'[3] But, so far as regards George II., this conclusion is contradicted by the researches of later writers. Although this monarch, equally with his predecessor, rendered the interests of his British dominions subservient to those of his German principality, he was, nevertheless, fond of the exercise of arbitrary power, and unwilling to yield his prerogative into the hands of ministers. The recent publication of the Life of Lord Hardwicke, for many years one of the principal advisers of George II., has thrown great light upon the political history of this reign.

George II.

---

[1] Coxe's Walpole, vol. L p. 200; iv. p. 340.
[2] Walpole's Works, vol. iv. p. 476; [3] Hallam, vol. iii. pp. 389, 390.
and see Campbell's Chancellors, vol. [4] Ibid. p. 303.

On the occasion of certain ministerial changes, which had been brought about by the leading members of the cabinet in order to strengthen their position in Parliament, a curious conversation is reported to have taken place between Lord Chancellor Hardwicke and the king, in which his Majesty declared his aversion to the new men who had been introduced into the ministry, and asserted that he had been 'forced' and 'threatened' into receiving them. The chancellor deprecated the use of such language, saying that 'no means had been used but what have been used at all times—the humble advice of your servants, supported by such reasons as convinced them that the measure was necessary for your service.' After some further explanations, the chancellor observed, 'Your ministers, sire, are only your instruments of government;' to which the king replied, with a smile, 'Ministers are the king in this country.' But although the force of circumstances compelled the king to give way on this occasion, the 'Hardwicke Papers' afford frequent examples of his active and successful interference in the government of the country. The interests of Hanover, it is true, were ever uppermost in his mind; but he seems to have possessed great discernment of character, both in regard to the abilities of the men whom he selected for his ministers, and the degree of confidence he could safely repose in them. 'To a large extent,' says the biographer of Lord Hardwicke, 'he was not only the chooser of his own ministers, but the director also of all the most important measures propounded by them; and into every political step taken he seems to have entered fully, even to the very details. As a politician, his great fault, especially for a king, was his being so decided a partisan. He was the sovereign and the head, in fact, not of the English people, but of the Whig party.'

---

[1] Harris, Life of Hardwicke, vol. ii. pp. 100-106.   [2] Ibid. vol. iii. p. 222; and see p. 519.

George III.

Naturally ambitious and fond of power, George III. ascended the throne with a determination to exercise to the fullest possible extent the functions of royalty. Born a Briton, and prepared by careful training for the duties of his exalted station, he became at once popular with the country at large, who were ready to sustain him in any attempt to magnify his office. In the Introduction to this volume we have had occasion to dwell at considerable length upon the character of George III., and to point out several instances of his departure from the line of conduct which should characterise a constitutional king, and it is unnecessary to repeat our observations in this place. Regarded in the light of the present recognised relations between the sovereign and his responsible advisers, the conduct of George III. would call for unqualified censure, from his systematic endeavours to govern by the exercise of his personal authority, and to absorb in himself the power and patronage of the state. Such practices are incompatible with the theory of parliamentary government, and would be neither tolerated nor attempted in our own day. But before we condemn George III. for pursuing a policy at variance with our present political ideas, we should remember that the principle of royal impersonality was only beginning to be understood when he ascended the throne. Not only was this particular theory still unrecognised as a part of our constitution, but the practice of his immediate predecessors, who had voluntarily abstained, for various reasons, from continued personal interference with the details of government, had fallen into disfavour. The country was heartily sick of the victories of court intriguers, and the monopoly of power in the hands of certain 'Revolution families;' and the young monarch, in obeying his mother's emphatic exhortation of 'George, be a king!' did but respond to the popular will, although the experience of the first year of his reign should have sufficed to convince him of its unstable and misleading character.° The great error of George III. was his love of power, which continually led him to ignore the constitutional restraints of a limited monarchy. Notwithstanding his moral and exemplary life, his sympathies with the popular prejudices, and his genuine endeavours to govern for the good of all classes of his subjects,—his habitual interference in the smallest details of administration, and frequent disregard of the principles of responsible government, caused him to suffer during his lifetime from the violent attacks of political partisans, and has loaded his memory with an amount of calumny and misrepresentation from which it is only now beginning to recover.° But if we make allowances for the difficulties of his position, and the temptations to an exaggerated idea of his personal authority natural to a time when the sovereign was still permitted to govern as well as reign, we must acquit him of any intentional violation of the constitution; and at the same time allow that his integrity of purpose, and rigid adherence to the line of duty, according to his lights, entitle him to be regarded as 'a patriot king.' We may unreservedly condemn his unconstitutional acts, but should, nevertheless, remember that much that was faulty in his conduct was 'simply the natural result of a complicated position, still undefined, and the working of a spirit as yet inexperienced in government, and seeking with hesitation its course and its friends.'ᵖ

The following instances of the direct interference of George III. in the details of government have been

---

° Quarterly Review for April 1859, Art. 6.

° See Edison's Commentary on Lord Brougham's 'Character of George III.' (London, 1860). Lord Campbell says of George III., that he 'certainly was a prince possessed of very valuable qualities; and it is only fair to state that everything discovered concerning him since his death, has tended to raise our opinion both of his abilities and of his generosity.' — *Lives of the Chanc.*, vol. vii. p. 341.

ᵖ This felicitous phrase was applied by M. Guizot to the conduct of Louis Philippe after his elevation to the throne of France.—*Guizot's Memoirs*, vol. ii. p. 45.

His personal acts of government.

gathered from the pages of contemporary historians: some of them are rather inconsistent with modern ideas of the duties of a sovereign. Shortly after his accession to the throne, the king informed his ministers that it was his wish that Lord Holdernesse, then one of the secretaries of state, should retire upon the wardenship of the Cinque Ports, and that the Earl of Bute should be appointed secretary in his stead. With some reluctance the ministry acquiesced in this arrangement.[e] In 1792 his Majesty conferred upon Mr. Pitt the office of Lord Warden of the Cinque Ports, unsolicited by that minister, and with a declaration that he would receive no recommendation in favour of any other person.[f] It was with great difficulty that Mr. Pitt obtained the king's consent to confer a bishopric and deanery upon his tutor and friend, Dr. Pretyman;[g] and when Mr. Pitt recommended his friend and biographer, Dr. Tomline, for promotion to the see of Canterbury, the king insisted upon appointing Dr. Manners-Sutton, notwithstanding all the solicitations of his minister.[h] The king refused to confer a dukedom upon Earl Temple, although requested to do so by Mr. Pitt, and, moreover, declared his determination to grant no more dukedoms except to princes of the blood.[i] Several examples of the rightful exercise of kingly authority on the part of George III. are enumerated by Mr. Edison[j] in the work already quoted. E. g., upon the resignation of the elder Pitt, in 1761, the king expressed his concern at the loss of so able a minister, and made him an unlimited offer of any reward in the power of the crown to bestow. In 1781, when the commander-in-chief carried him a packet of military commissions to be signed, the king, on looking over the list, observed one

---

[e] Harris, Life of Hardwicke, vol. iii. p. 242; but see a different account of this transaction in Rose, Corresp., vol. ii. p. 191.
[f] Stanhope's Pitt, vol. ii. p. 160.
[g] Ibid. vol. i. p. 322; App. xx.
[h] Rose, Corresp. vol. ii. pp. 82-91.
[i] Stanhope's Pitt, vol. i. p. 104.
[j] Edison, George III., pp. 20, 44, 40.

person appointed captain over an old lieutenant. Referring to some private memoranda of his own, which contained particulars very much to the credit of the old veteran, his Majesty at once directed that he should be promoted to the vacant company, without purchase. And we have the authority of Mr. Wynn for stating that from the close of the American war until the breaking out of hostilities with France, the king's pleasure was taken by the Secretary-at-War upon every commission granted in the army. And throughout Mr. Pitt's administration, and indeed so long as his Majesty was capable of attending to business, 'every act and appointment was submitted to him, not nominally, but really for the purpose of his exercising a judgment upon it.'* A notable instance of the king's firmness occurred in 1780, during the prevalence of the great anti-popery riots in London. His Majesty was presiding at a Privy Council, to which all who had a right to sit had been summoned. Ministers were timorous and vacillating in advising the steps that should be taken to quell the disturbances, when the king interposed; and after taking the opinion of the Attorney-General, directed that an Order in Council should be drawn up for the guidance of the proper authorities in the emergency, to which he instantly affixed the sign-manual.ᵗ Lord Eldon often declared that he thought his old master George III. had more wisdom than all his ministers conjointly; and that he could not remember having taken to him any state-paper of importance which he did not alter, nor one which he did not alter for the better. This peculiar sagacity he attributed not so much to the natural qualities of the king, as to his immense opportunities of gaining knowledge by an experience in state affairs, which was far greater than that of the oldest of his ministers.ʸ

* Parl. Deb. (April 14, 1812), vol. xxii. p. 384.
ᵗ Adolphus, Reign of Geo. III., vol. iii. p. 144.
ʸ Campbell's Chancellors, vol. vii. p. 253 n.

George IV. George IV. had not the weight of personal character that belonged to his father. Naturally of an indolent disposition, he was called to the throne too late in life to become thoroughly acquainted with the duties of his office, or to care for burthening himself with the details of government. He was unpopular with the nation, having alienated from himself their respect and goodwill by his conduct as a prince. He was indifferent to the exercise of political power, except when his own feelings or interests were concerned, when he could be as imperative as his father. Otherwise he was not unwilling, for the most part, to leave the reins of administration, unchecked, in the hands of his responsible advisers.' 'It may accordingly be said, that from the beginning of his regency in 1811 to the close of his reign in 1830, the regal influence was limited to the strict exercise of the prerogative. George IV. had no personal influence: instead of his popularity supporting the ministry, the difficulty was for the ministry to support his unpopularity, and to uphold the respect for the crown when it encircled the head of such a sovereign.'[a]

A curious account of the differences between George IV. and his ministers in the matter of Queen Caroline has been already given in our introductory chapter.[b] On this occasion the king was most reluctantly obliged to yield his personal wishes to the exigencies of his position, and to permit his ministers to conduct that painful and embarrassing affair according to their own convictions of that which it might be feasible to ask the Parliament to sanction. But a circumstance is mentioned in Buckingham's 'Court of the Regency,' which shows that the king could stand upon his prerogative when he thought proper. Upon a vacancy occurring in the see of Oxford, Mr. Perceval, the prime minister, waited upon his royal master,

---
* May, Const. Hist. vol. i. p. 99.
a Sir G. C. Lewis, in Edinb. Rev. vol. cx. p. 62.
b Ante, p. 62.

with a recommendation that the bishopric should be conferred upon Dean Legge. The prince peremptorily refused, and declared his intention of appointing Dr. Jackson. Mr. Perceval urged that it had been 'the positive and declared intention' of the king to give the appointment to Dean Legge; whereupon the prince reiterated his determination 'to make his own bishop,' and desired that he might 'never more hear what were the king's wishes upon such subjects through a third person.'* Dr. Jackson was accordingly nominated to the see, but he held it only four years. On his death, which occurred in 1815, the bishopric was conferred upon Dean Legge.ᵈ

William IV. was a monarch of very amiable disposition, but deficient in strength of character. He ascended the throne at an advanced period of life, and found himself unable to cope successfully with the embarrassing questions which arose during his short but eventful reign. Averse to parliamentary reform, and fearful of its consequences, he nevertheless gave a reluctant consent to the great experiment. But ere long his mind underwent a reaction; he withdrew his confidence from the statesmen by whom that measure had been accomplished, and attempted to form a Tory government. But the endeavour proved abortive. He learnt to his chagrin that the preponderance of power was now so firmly established in the House of Commons, that the mere prerogative and influence of the crown were insufficient to effect a change of administration, unless seconded by the voice of that assembly, or by the unequivocal expression of popular opinion.ᵉ Two instances are referred to by May,ᶠ wherein William IV. took upon himself to interfere personally in political affairs without previous consultation with his ministers: once when, in the interest of ministers themselves, and in

William IV.

---

* Buckingham, Regency, vol. I. p. 172.
ᵈ Haydn, Book of Dignities, p. 303.
ᵉ See ante, p. 123; Bagehot, Eng. Const. Fort. Rev. Decem. 1, 1866, p. 810.
ᶠ May, Const. Hist. vol. I. pp. 119, 120.

furtherance of their public policy, he caused a circular letter to be addressed by his private secretary to the Opposition peers, urging upon them to cease from any further resistance to the Reform Bill, so as to permit the passing of that measure in the House of Lords without the necessity for creating a new batch of peers in order to carry the Bill—a stretch of the prerogative to which his Majesty had been induced by his ministers to consent, if necessary. This letter was circulated by command of the king, without the knowledge of his ministers, and was itself an unconstitutional interference with the freedom of Parliament. Again, in 1834, his Majesty gave public expression to his alarm for the safety of the Established Church in Ireland, in a remarkable reply to an address from the prelates and clergy of Ireland, which he delivered without first communicating with his responsible advisers.[a] But these were exceptional cases, arising out of the prevalence of political excitement, both at home and abroad, during the period in question, and by which the king himself was carried away to the commission of acts which were irregular and indefensible, however they may be excused by a consideration of the integrity of purpose and solicitude for the public welfare by which they were dictated. In the 'Posthumous Memoirs of Sir Robert Peel,' we have the assurance of that eminent statesman that 'His Majesty uniformly acted with scrupulous fidelity towards his advisers, whatever might be their political bias;'[b] and in the two Houses of Parliament, after the decease of William IV., the leading politicians, without respect to party, vied with one another in bearing testimony to his exemplary conduct as a constitutional sovereign.[c]

---

[a] This speech is said to have been delivered extempore, and to have been quite unpremeditated; but Maloy, in his Recollections of this reign (vol. II. p. 133), gives reasons for the belief that it was written for the king by some secret adviser.

[b] Peel's Memoirs, vol. ii. p. 10.
[c] Knight, History of England, vol. viii. p. 377. A solitary instance of the independent exercise of judgment by William IV., in a matter of prerogative, has come under our notice. It relates to Captain Marryat, the

Since the accession of our present Queen, the personal predilections of the sovereign in respect to an existing administration have never been brought into public view. While she has abated nothing of the legitimate influence and authority of the crown wherever it could be constitutionally exercised, her Majesty has scrupulously and unreservedly bestowed her entire confidence upon every ministry in turn with which public policy, or the preference of Parliament, has surrounded the throne.[1] 'It is well known,' says a recent political writer, 'that her Majesty has habitually taken an active interest in every matter with which it behoves a constitutional sovereign of this country to be concerned; in many instances her opinion and her will have left their impression on our policy;[2] but in no instance has the power of the crown been so exercised as to expose it to check, or censure, or embarrassment of any kind.[3] It may be asserted, without qualification, that a sense of general content, of sober heartfelt loyalty, has year by year been gathering around the throne of Victoria.'[4] The present writer would add to this his sincere conviction, that attachment to the person

---

celebrated novelist, and is mentioned in the memoir prefixed to the edition of his 'Pirate,' published by Bohn, 1841. When a member of the administration waited upon the king to recommend that the gallant captain might receive the royal licence to wear an order which had been conferred on him by the King of the French, his Majesty positively declined to comply with the request; assigning, as the ground of his refusal, his disapprobation of a book, on the Impressment of seamen, which had been written by Marryat.

[1] Lord John Russell, Hans. Deb. vol. cxxx. p. 182. This was in accordance with Prince Albert's idea of the duty of the Queen towards her ministers.—*Ibid.* vol. clxv. p. 44.

[2] For example, in the year 1861, at the suggestion of the late Prince Consort, the forbearance and firmness of our gracious Queen were exercised to require that the language of an important despatch—calling for the surrender, by the United States Government, of certain persons who had been illegally taken from the *Trent*, a British vessel, by an American ship-of-war—should be so modified, as to make the demand as conciliatory as possible, in order to avert the prospect of war with a kindred people. Earl Russell's statement in Hans. Deb. vol. clxxvii. p. 72.

[3] See Earl Russell's remarks, in reply to the Earl of Ellenborough, in Hans. Deb. vol. clxxv. p. 615.

[4] Edinburgh Review, January 1862, Art. viii; attributed to the Rt. Hon. W. N. Massey, author of the 'History of England under George III.'

and throne of our gracious Queen is not confined to the mother-country, but extends with equal if not greater intensity to the remotest bounds of her immense empire; and that few could be found, even in lands that owe her no allegiance as a sovereign, who would not willingly unite in a tribute of respect and admiration for Victoria, as a woman, a mother, and a queen.

During the present reign three questions, hitherto undetermined, and that intimately affect the personal rights of the sovereign, have been decided by constitutional authority. They will fittingly claim our attention before we proceed to define the present position of the crown in public affairs. They concern—

1. The appointment of Officers of the Royal Household.
2. The right of the Sovereign to employ a Private Secretary.
3. The constitutional position of a Prince Consort.

1. *As to the appointment of Members of the Household.*

Appointments in the Royal Household controlled by ministers.

Owing to the gradual introduction of the usages which have been incorporated by time into the unwritten law of the British Constitution, it was not until the end of the reign of George II. that it became customary to make alterations in the household establishment of our sovereigns upon a change of ministry.[a] But it is a fundamental principle of parliamentary government, that 'the responsible servants of the crown are entitled to advise the crown in every point in which the royal authority is to be exercised;'[b] and nothing could tend more to enfeeble an administration than that certain high offices, held during pleasure, should be altogether beyond their control. Accordingly, from the accession of George III. it became a recognised practice to concede this privilege to every successive administration.

---

[a] Parl. Deb. vol. xxiii. p. 412.   [b] Mr. Ponsonby, *ibid.* p. 431.

Thus we find that when George III. dismissed the North Ministry, in 1782, he was obliged to dismiss the Earl of Hertford from the office of Lord Chamberlain, which he had held for fifteen years; and to appoint the Earl of Effingham, whom he disliked, to be Treasurer of the Household. Even the aged Lord Bateman, who was the king's personal friend, was obliged to resign his office of Master of the Buckhounds.[p] Similar difficulties, in regard to appointments in the household, attended the formation of the Portland Ministry in the following year.[q]

In 1812, when negotiations were set on foot for the reconstruction of the ministry, after the assassination of Mr. Perceval, the premier, a question was raised as to whether the appointment of officers in the royal household should form part of the proposed ministerial arrangements, or should be left to the determination of the sovereign. Lords Grey and Grenville, having been invited by the Prince Regent to join the now administration, declined to do so unless the actual incumbents of these offices were first dismissed. The Prince Regent was advised by Lord Moira, who conducted the negotiations with the Whig leaders, to resist this stipulation; and, accordingly, the attempt at a reconstruction of the cabinet resulted in failure. But it has since come to light that the difficulty arose from the unskilful management of the dispute. The Prince Regent himself was quite willing to allow a change to be made in his household, and the officers of the household had all privately resolved to resign as soon as the new ministry had been completed, leaving their places at the disposal of the new cabinet. This intention had been made known to Sheridan, but, either from accident or design, he did not communicate it to his friends.[r] In the subsequent explanations in Parliament, it was admitted that an incoming administration had a right to claim the removal of the great officers of the household, although the exercise of such a right on the present occasion was, for special reasons, deemed inexpedient and impolitic.[s] The principal officers of the royal household are invariably chosen from amongst members of the two Houses of Parliament, and it is but reasonable that they should be expected to co-operate with their colleagues in the ministry. Moreover, from their habitual

---

[p] Fischel, Eng. Const. p. 520; as corrected by Haydn, Book of Dignities, p. 200; Adolphus, Geo. III. vol. iii. p. 348.

[q] Tomline, Life of Pitt, vol. i. p. 140 n.; Parl. Hist. vol. xxiii. p. 606. But during Mr. Pitt's administration, George III. (as he afterwards told Mr. Rose), 'insisted on having in his household such persons as he could, with comfort to himself, associate with occasionally.' (Rose, Corresp. vol. ii. p. 158.) This is a privilege which no minister, at any time, would have thought of denying to his sovereign.

[r] Campbell's Chancellors, vol. vii. p. 285; May, Const. Hist. vol. i. p. 106.

[s] Parl. Deb. vol. xxiii. p. 453.

attendance upon the person of the sovereign, they undoubtedly possess means of influence that ought not to be at the disposal of any persons who are unfriendly to the party in power.

Ladies of the Bedchamber.

Upon the resignation of the Melbourne Ministry in 1839, and before the difficulty arose between her Majesty and Sir Robert Peel respecting the Ladies of the Bedchamber, Lord Melbourne informed the Queen 'that it had been usual in later times, when an administration was changed, to change also the great officers of the household, and likewise to place at the disposal of the person entrusted with the formation of a new administration those situations in the household which were held by members of either House of Parliament.'[1] In claiming the exercise of this privilege, Sir Robert Peel, when called upon to form a ministry, assured her Majesty that he would not press the appointment of anyone who was not personally acceptable to her. At the same time he respectfully urged that, in view of the throne being filled by a female sovereign, the same principle should be held to apply to the chief appointments which were held by the ladies of her Majesty's household, including the Ladies of the Bedchamber. This was objected to by the Queen, who declared that she must reserve to herself the whole of these appointments, and that it was her pleasure that no change should be made in the present incumbents. Afterwards, by advice of the retiring ministers, her Majesty wrote to Sir Robert Peel, stating that she could not 'consent to adopt a course which she conceived to be contrary to usage, and which was repugnant to her feelings.' But, in point of fact, nearly all the ladies of the court were related to the Whig ministers or to their political adherents, having been selected by the Melbourne Cabinet when her Majesty's household was first organized; thus identifying the entire Court with the ministry of the day.[2] Under these circumstances it was impossible for Sir Robert Peel to persevere in the attempt to form a ministry. He therefore wrote to her Majesty, and stated that it was essential to the success of the commission with which he had been honoured, 'that he should have that public proof of her Majesty's entire support and confidence which would be afforded by the permission to make some changes in that part of her Majesty's household which her Majesty resolved on maintaining entirely without change.' The Melbourne Ministry were then reinstated in office, and they at once recorded their opinion on the point at issue in a minute of council, as follows: 'That for the purpose of giving to the administration that character of efficiency and stability, and those marks of the constitutional support of the crown, which are required to enable it to act usefully to the public service, it is reasonable that the great offices of the court, and situations in the household held by members of Parliament, should be included in the

---

[1] Mirror of Parl. 1839, p. 2411.   [2] May, Const. Hist. vol. i. p. 128.

political arrangements made on a change of the administration; but they are not of opinion that a similar principle should be applied or extended to the offices held by ladies in her Majesty's household.'

But two years afterwards, when it became necessary for the Queen to apply again to Sir Robert Peel to undertake the formation of a government, 'no difficulties were raised on the Bedchamber question. Her Majesty was now sensible that the position she had once been advised to assert was constitutionally untenable. The principle which Sir R. Peel applied to the household has since been admitted, on all sides, to be constitutional. The offices of Mistress of the Robes and Ladies of the Bedchamber, when held by ladies connected with the outgoing ministers, have been considered as included in the ministerial arrangements. But Ladies of the Bedchamber belonging to families whose political connexion has been less pronounced, have been suffered to remain in the household, without objection, on a change of ministry.'

2. *As to the right of the Sovereign to employ a Private Secretary.*

Until the reign of George III. none of the English monarchs ever had a private secretary. It naturally formed a part of the duty of the Principal Secretaries of State to assist the sovereign in conducting his official correspondence; but such were the habits of industry and attention to the duties of his exalted station which characterised George III., that it was not until his sight began to fail that he would permit another person to assist him in transacting the daily business of the crown. But in 1805 his Majesty became so blind, as to be unable to read the communications of his ministers. Averse to remain in London, where his infirmity would be more exposed to public observation, the king resolved to reside at Windsor. This rendered the appointment of a private secretary absolutely necessary. Accordingly, Colonel Herbert Taylor was appointed to the office, with a salary of 2,000*l.* per annum, which was paid out of funds at

Private Secretary to the king.

Herbert Taylor.

---

* Mirror of Parl. 1880, pp. 2415, 2421.
* May, Const. Hist. vol. i. p. 131. On the accession of the Derby ministry, in 1800, the Ladies of the Court remained unchanged, not having owed their appointments to political influence. And Lord Torrington continued in office as one of the Lords in Waiting, at the personal request of her Majesty. (*Guardian*, July 18, 1800, p. 701.)

the disposal of the crown, and never came under review in Parliament. Colorel Taylor discharged the duties of this delicate and confidential office, until the commencement of the Regency, with such integrity, prudence, and reserve, as to shield himself from every shadow of complaint. Nevertheless, the appointment itself was viewed with disfavour by many leading men in Parliament, who only refrained from calling it in question from motives of delicacy towards the afflicted monarch, whose loss of sight was attributable to his unceasing devotion to his public duties.* When the Prince Regent was called to the throne, he appointed his friend Colonel M'Mahon, who was at the time a member of the House of Commons and a privy councillor, to be his private secretary and Keeper of the Privy Purse, with the same salary as his predecessor, but with the important difference that it was to be paid by the Treasury, thereby rendering Colonel M'Mahon a public officer. This transaction gave rise to an animated discussion in the House of Commons. After the 'Official Gazette' had appeared, announcing the appointment, enquiries were made of ministers, on March 23, 1812, as to the facts of the case; and on April 14, Mr. C. W. Wynn moved for a copy of the appointment, for the purpose of founding upon it a resolution of censure, or a declaration of the inutility of the office. Mr. Wynn urged that the appointment was wholly unprecedented, except in the case of Colonel Taylor, which was purely a private affair, arising out of the king's infirmity; and that 'it was a most unconstitutional proceeding to allow the secrets of the council to pass through a third person,' thereby subjecting the advice of cabinet ministers to their sovereign ' to the revision of his private secretary.' Ministers opposed the motion, contending that the Prince Regent, who had not been trained to habits of business like his father, stood in need of the

(margin: Col. M'Mahon.)

---

* Parl. Deb. vol. xxii. pp. 121, 342, 361.

services of a private secretary to assist him in his private correspondence, and to relieve the bodily manual labour which the immense amount of public business requiring the attention of the crown unavoidably entailed. This office, moreover, was not one of responsibility, and would not encroach upon the province or responsibility of any minister. Ministers of the crown would still be the legal and constitutional organs through which all the public business must be transacted. On a division Mr. Wynn's motion was negatived, by a majority of 76. The Opposition, however, determined to renew the attack, on the special ground that the appointment, unlike that of Colonel Taylor, had been made a public one. But on June 15, Lord Castlereagh informed the House that the Prince Regent had been pleased to direct that Colonel M'Mahon's salary should be paid out of his privy purse. The Opposition then agreed to let the matter drop; and Colonel M'Mahon continued to hold the office until his death, which occurred in 1817.'

Both George IV. and William IV. had their private secretaries; Sir Herbert Taylor, the faithful secretary of George III., having been reappointed to this office by King William. We have the testimony of Lord Aberdeen, when prime minister, that no objection was ever made to these appointments, notwithstanding that ' these men must of necessity have known and were able to have given advice, or to have disclosed everything, if they had thought fit, although neither of them was a privy councillor.'* It is true that on one occasion, as we have seen, William IV. made his private secretary the medium of giving expression to his wishes to certain peers, in regard to their conduct upon a great public question, in a very

Sir Herbert Taylor.

' Parl. Deb. vol. xxiii. p. 470 ; Ann. Reg. 1817, p. 147. M'Mahon was succeeded, in his office of Keeper of the Privy Purse, by Sir Benjamin Bloomfield, who, in 1822, was replaced by Sir Wm. Knighton, who retained the office until the King's death, in 1830. (Sir B. C. Brodie's Works, vol. 1. p. 77.)
* Hans. Deb. vol. cxxx. p. 96. And see Nicolas, Pref. to Pro. Privy Coun. vol. vi. p. cxxxiv. n.

irregular manner;[a] and this circumstance may have led a recent German commentator on the English Constitution to state, that since the accession of her present Majesty it has been deemed expedient to dispense with the appointment of a private secretary, 'experience having shown that by such influence William IV.'s independence of the reigning parties had become too great.'[b] But no authority is given for this statement, and it does not agree either with the facts of the case, or with the declaration of Lord Aberdeen, above quoted.

Upon the accession of Queen Victoria, Lord Melbourne, who was then first minister of the crown, determined to act also as her Majesty's private secretary. This was avowedly a mere temporary arrangement, for it was undertaken in the hope—which, happily, was speedily realised—that her Majesty would very soon contract a marriage, which would enable the duties of private secretary to be appropriately transferred to the royal consort. Nevertheless, the assumption by the prime minister of such a position towards the Queen, under any circumstances, was truly characterised by Lord Aberdeen as an 'unconstitutional' proceeding;[c] being calculated to impair the free exercise of the royal judgment, under the plausible pretext of assisting the sovereign in the performance of her onerous functions. But we are safe in concluding that no such intention influenced Lord Melbourne upon this occasion, and that his sole desire was to afford to his royal mistress, in her youth and inexperience, the benefit of his matured acquaintance with the routine of government. After her Majesty's marriage with Prince Albert, his Royal Highness, with the sanction of the ministers of the crown, assumed the duties of the Queen's private secretary. He was peculiarly fitted for this office, not merely by his admirable personal qualities and high attainments, but from his position as husband and *alter*

Prince Albert as the Queen's Private Secretary.

---

[a] See ante, p. 180.
[b] Fischel, p. 521.
[c] Hans. Deb. vol. cxxx. p. 90.

ego of the Queen.[d] He acquitted himself of the duties which thus devolved upon him to the admiration of all parties, as well as to the inestimable benefit of his queen and country. Further remarks upon this painful topic must be reserved for our next section. Suffice it here to add, that whatever attempts may have been made to supply, in this respect, the great loss which her Majesty has sustained in the premature decease of her lamented consort, by the appointment of another private secretary, it is clear that there is no constitutional objection to such an office; and that the great and increasing amount of routine duty devolving upon an English sovereign at the present day, as well as a consideration of the altered position of the crown towards the members of the administration since the establishment of parliamentary government, alike justify and require the appointment.[e]

_{Right of the Sovereign to employ a Private Secretary.}

3. *The constitutional position of a Prince Consort.*

_{Prince Consort.}

The position of a queen-consort has been ascertained by the laws and customs of the realm. She has her own privileges and rights. She has important duties to perform as head of the court, in maintaining its dignity and respectability; and by her example and authority she is enabled to exercise a direct influence over the manners of society, and especially of the female portion of it. But the constitution has assigned no definite place to the husband of a reigning queen. The only precedent in English history, since the Revolution, of this peculiar and difficult position is that of Prince George of Denmark, the husband of Queen Anne; but this prince was destitute of the ability and strength of character which should have made him an active and efficient helpmate to his wife and sovereign.[c] It was reserved for Prince Albert, by the

---

[d] Hans. Deb. vol. cxxx. pp. 07, 105.
[e] Sir T. M. Biddulph, Master of the Household, now acts as the Queen's Private Secretary.
[c] Edinb. Rev. Jan. 1802, Art. viii.

Character and conduct of Prince Albert.

rare combination of admirable qualities with which he was endowed, to create for himself a position of preeminent usefulness, without trenching in the slightest degree upon the limits within which, as the husband of his sovereign, he was necessarily confined. Called to his exalted station at a very early age, he diligently applied himself to the study of our laws and institutions, in order that he might be qualified to afford to the crown efficient aid and counsel in the discharge of its onerous functions. On September 11, 1840, about eight months after his marriage, and a few days after the completion of his twenty-first year, Prince Albert was introduced, by her Majesty's command, to the Privy Council, and took his seat at the board, which he never afterwards failed to attend; and the rank conceded to him there was, naturally, immediately next to the sovereign. His Royal Highness was not a member of the House of Peers, and had therefore no place formally assigned to him for the public expression of his personal opinions upon political questions. In this respect his position was analogous to that of the Queen herself. As the consort of his sovereign, he was in fact her *alter ego*; and it was in this capacity, not merely from his being a member of the Privy Council, that he was constitutionally empowered to attend at every conference between the Queen and her ministers.[f] Generally present at such times, he always took part in the discussions with tact, ability, and discretion. As we have already seen, the prince, with the express sanction of the ministers of the crown, assumed the duties of the Queen's private secretary, and in that capacity was permitted to peruse all public despatches that were laid before the Queen, and all the confidential communications of ministers. Upon his retirement from office in 1841, Lord Melbourne took occasion to congratulate her Majesty upon 'the inestimable advantage she possessed in being

---

[f] Lord Campbell, in Hans. Deb. vol. cxxx. p. 105.

able to avail herself of the advice and assistance of her royal consort,' and asserted his conviction that she could not do better 'than to have recourse to him when it was needed, and to rely upon him with confidence.'[a]

In a work which has been lately published, by the express permission of the Queen herself, we have Prince Albert's own definition of his place and duties. He says the position of 'the consort and confidential adviser and assistant of a female sovereign' 'is a most peculiar and delicate one. Whilst a female sovereign has a great many disadvantages in comparison with a king, yet if she is married, and her husband understands and does his duty, her position, on the other hand, has many compensating advantages, and, in the long run, will be found even to be stronger than that of a male sovereign. But this requires that the husband should entirely sink his *own individual* existence in that of his wife; that he should aim at no power by himself or for himself; should shun all ostentation, assume no separate responsibility before the public, but make his position entirely a part of hers; fill up every gap which, as a woman, she would naturally leave in the exercise of her regal functions; continually and anxiously watch every part of the public business, in order to be able to advise and assist her at any moment, in any of the multifarious and difficult questions or duties brought before her—sometimes international, sometimes political, or social, or personal. As the natural head of her family, superintendent of her household, manager of her private affairs, sole *confidential* adviser in politics, and only assistant in her communications with the officers of the government, he is, besides the husband of the queen, the tutor of the royal children, the private secretary of the sovereign, and her permanent minister.'[b]

How thoroughly Prince Albert fulfilled the multifarious

---

[a] Hans. Deb. vol. cxxx. p. 97.   [b] Prince Albert's Speeches, &c., pp. 74, 76.

duties of his difficult and delicate position, which he has thus graphically described, is well known to the world, as well as to the British nation, who have never ceased to mourn his loss. The Queen herself, in a few lines which she has caused to be inserted in the work from which the above quotation has been made, bears her tender and touching testimony to 'the ever-present, watchful, faithful, invaluable aid which she received from the Prince Consort in the conduct of the public business;' thereby 'proclaiming the irreparable loss to the public service, as well as to herself and to her family, which the prince's death has occasioned.'[1]

The irreparable loss of his death.

Defence of his conduct.

The constitutionality of Prince Albert's position, as well as the wisdom and prudence with which he maintained it, have been recognised by all the leading statesmen of England who have held office during the last twenty years. At the opening of the session of 1854, an opportunity was afforded to the principal members of government and of the Opposition, in both Houses of Parliament, for the public expression of their sentiments on the subject, during the debate upon the address in answer to the speech from the throne. A portion of the press had recently indulged in unwarrantable attacks upon the prince, for 'interference' in politics, and especially in the affairs of the army. The prime minister, Lord Aberdeen, took the earliest opportunity of defending his Royal Highness from the unjust aspersions upon his character, and, at the same time, of defining his proper sphere of duty in regard to the executive government. He stated that Prince Albert had, with great self-denial and discretion, declined to accept the office of commander-in-chief of the British army, notwithstanding the urgent solicitations of the Duke of Wellington that he would consent to succeed

---

[1] Prince Albert's Speeches, &c., p. 67. His Royal Highness departed this life on the 14th December 1861, after a very brief illness. The best memoir of Prince Albert which has yet appeared, is to be found in the Annual Register for 1862, pp. 482–502.

him in that post; and that his alleged 'interference with the business of the army,' had been no more than his position as a field-marshal and colonel-commanding certain regiments, and one acting on behalf of a female sovereign, amply justified. The commander-in-chief, Lord Hardinge, corroborated this statement. Lords Derby and Campbell in the House of Peers, and Lord John Russell and Mr. Walpole in the House of Commons, expressed their entire satisfaction with this explanation, and their cordial approval of the conduct of Prince Albert in his position of confidential adviser of the Queen.* Full particulars of the circumstances under which his Royal Highness declined the honourable post of commander-in-chief, so earnestly pressed upon him by the Duke of Wellington, will be found in a memorandum prefixed to the collection of the prince's speeches above mentioned. The forbearance and self-denial exercised by Prince Albert upon this occasion reflects the highest credit upon him. He justly felt that the assumption of the charge of a great executive department would interfere with the performance of the duties which properly belonged to him as the consort of the sovereign, and which no one but himself could adequately fulfil.

We have further evidence, from the pen of one who should be well informed on the subject, as to the manner in which Prince Albert discharged the difficult task he had undertaken, during the whole course of his brief but well-spent life. He says that the prince's conduct uniformly exhibited proofs of a consummate judgment, and was characterised by a constant deference to the constitutional rights of the ministers of the crown. With strong political convictions, and a decided opinion on the political questions of the day, which he expressed and defended

---

* Hansard's Debates, in both Houses, for January 31, 1854. And see the eulogiums pronounced upon the Prince Consort, in both Houses of Parliament, on February 6, 1862, after his decease, and especially the speeches of Earl Russell and of Mr. Disraeli.

with great ability, his course was invariably straightforward and patriotic. 'His influence in public affairs was at once so genial and so salutary, that, like the pressure of the atmosphere, it was unfelt. He hit the exact mean on which authority rests in a free country, and he contributed to make the crown act as the adjusting balance of our institutions at home, and of our policy abroad.' He brought to the consideration of every question of foreign policy, and of every point of domestic administration, ' the principles of a statesman, rather than the interests of a politician; and as his position had placed him beyond the region in which men contend for political power, he sought, without distinction of parties or persons, to apply his dignified, liberal, and honest rule of life to the smallest as well as the greatest objects to which he turned his clear and comprehensive mind.'[1]

His services to the community.

With an intuitive perception of the widely-extended field—hitherto untrodden by royal footsteps—wherein his varied accomplishments, and the influences of his exalted station, could be suitably employed, Prince Albert took a prominent part in the encouragement of every social movement which sought to advance the industrial, educational, or moral interests of the people. He lent his aid and countenance to the promotion of science and the arts, and was always ready to foster every undertaking that gave promise of contributing to develope the resources of the empire, or of assisting her friendly and successful rivalry with other countries in the arts of peace.

The value of his life to the cause of monarchy.

The loss which the nation has sustained in the death of this illustrious man has, unhappily, deprived our enquiry into the constitutional standing of a prince-consort of its immediate practical value; nevertheless, the example of his life is of incalculable service to the cause of monarchy, as it serves to illustrate and define the *status* of the

---

[1] Right Hon. W. N. Massey, in Edinb. Review, Jan. 1862, Art. viii.

sovereign in the existing development of the British constitution, and also to exemplify the value and extent of the influence which may be rightfully exercised by one who is politically identified with the occupant of the throne, and who yet fills a personally irresponsible position,* without encroaching upon the province of responsible government.

We now proceed to define, more particularly, the constitutional position of the British sovereign. We have already seen that, in a system of parliamentary government, as it is administered in England, the personal will of the monarch can only find public expression through official channels, or in the performance of acts of state which have been advised or agreed to by responsible ministers; and that the responsible servants of the crown are entitled to advise the sovereign in every instance wherein the royal authority is to be exercised. In other words, the public authority of the crown in England is exercised only in acts of representation, or through the medium of ministers, who are responsible to Parliament for every public act of their sovereign, as well as for the general policy of the government which they have been called upon to administer. This has been termed the theory of Royal Impersonality. But the impersonality of the crown only extends to direct acts of government. The sovereign retains full discretionary powers for deliberating and determining upon every recommendation which is tendered for the royal sanction by the ministers of the crown; and, as every important act of administration must be submitted for the approval of the crown, the sovereign, in criticising, confirming, or disallowing the same, is enabled to exercise an active and intelligent control over the government of the country.

In the fulfilment of the functions of royalty, much must always depend upon the capacity and personal character

Constitutional position of the sovereign.

---

* Earl Derby and Mr. Disraeli, in Hans. Deb. vol. clxv. pp. 27, 60.

of the reigning monarch. It has been well observed, by a sagacious political writer, that 'a wise and able sovereign can exercise in the councils which he necessarily shares whatever authority belongs to his character, to his judgment, and, in the course of years, to his unequalled experience. A lifelong tenure of office, ensuring an uninterrupted familiarity with public business, gives a king a considerable advantage over even veteran ministers; and the undefinable influence of supreme rank is in itself a substantial basis of power.'* But in order to discharge his functions aright, it is indispensable that the sovereign should be ready and willing to labour, zealously and unremittingly, in his high vocation; otherwise he will be unable to cope with the multifarious and perplexing details of government, or to exercise that controlling power over state affairs which properly appertains to the crown. On the other hand, a sovereign who, from whatever cause, is indifferent to the exercise of his kingly functions, may neglect the administrative part of his duties, and, if he be served by competent ministers, the commonwealth will suffer no immediate damage. But, in such a case, the legitimate influence of the monarchical element in the constitution is impaired, and is rendered liable to permanent deprivation.* Moreover, while a sovereign may forego the active control of the affairs of state without apparent public loss, provided his ministers are able and patriotic, the moment political power falls into the hands of self-seeking and unscrupulous men, the nation is deprived of the check which a vigilant monarch alone can maintain—a check no less valuable because unseen, but which may suffice, upon an emergency, to save the country from the effects of misgovernment. For the

---

* Saturday Review, November 8, 1862. And see some weighty remarks in the same journal, for June 4, 1864, in an article on 'Foreign Influence.' See also, on the advantages derivable from the experience of a sagacious king. Bagehot, on the English Constitution, in the Fortnightly Review for October 15, 1865, pp. 005-000.

* See Bagehot's paper, above cited, pp. 010-012.

sovereign can always dismiss a ministry, and summon another to his councils, provided he does so not for mere personal considerations, but for reasons of state policy, which the incoming administration can explain and justify to the satisfaction of Parliament. This branch of the royal prerogative will hereafter engage our attention more fully.

Constitutional position of the sovereign.

It need scarcely be urged that the possession of a high personal character and a cultivated intellect are of vital consequence to the sovereign, to fit him for his rightful position in the secret councils of the state. They enable him to subject every recommendation of his ministers to the scrutiny of an intelligent and impartial mind, intent only upon the promotion of the public good; and should such a necessity unfortunately arise, a prudent and sagacious monarch can do much to moderate party asperities, rebuke selfish and unworthy aims, and encourage patriotism, by bringing to bear upon the ministers of the crown a healthy moral influence, similar to that which proceeds from an enlightened public opinion.

And on the wider field of national pursuits, while the individuality of the sovereign is debarred from active exercise, except through the agency of responsible ministers, the moral influence of the crown, as a means of promoting the public welfare, is of incalculable weight and value. It properly devolves upon the constitutional sovereigns of England to employ this powerful influence for the encouragement of public and private morality, for the advancement of learning, and for the diffusion of civilisation among their people.[p] The favour of the king is always an object of honourable ambition, and, when worthily bestowed, will nerve the arm and excite the brain to deeds which deserve a nation's gratitude, and bring renown upon the whole empire.

With such advantages resulting from monarchical rule,

---

[p] See Harrison on Civilisation, pp. 291-294.

THE SOVEREIGN.

Importance of the kingly office.

it were vain to imagine that, because the direct interference of the crown in acts of government is forbidden by the spirit of the constitution, therefore royalty has ceased to be anything but an empty phantom or a costly pageant. Though divested, by the growth and development of our political institutions, of direct political power, the crown has still retained immense personal and social influence for good or evil. 'The king's name is a tower of strength;' and without the blessing of headship, in the person of an hereditary sovereign, the time-honoured institutions of England would sink at once to the level of a democracy, and the good government of the country would be jeopardised, if not overthrown, by the strife and cupidity of rival factions contending for the mastery.*

Ceremonial functions.

One of the most important branches of the regal functions is that wherein the crown, as 'the symbol of national sovereignty,' appears in public for the performance of those acts of state which peculiarly appertain to the kingly office—such as the opening and proroguing of Parliament, the holding of public receptions, of ceremonials for conferring marks of distinction and royal favour upon particular persons, and the like. These duties, while they frequently entail heavy burdens upon the sovereign, cannot be intermitted—except for unavoidable causes, and for a limited time—without impairing the dignity and influence of the crown itself. The presence of the sovereign in the midst of his people, dispensing favours, or engaged in the performance of high acts of state, affords opportunity for the public expression of the loyalty or personal devotion of the people to their king. This elevated Christian sentiment is of the greatest value in uniting together the ruler and the subject, so that fidelity and attachment to the monarchy becomes a part of the national life.' But 'loyalty needs to be stimulated by external display, by

---

* See Cox, Eng. Govt. p. 634.
† On this point, see Austin, Plea for the Constitution, p. 37.

the pomp and circumstance of power, by all the kindly feelings which personal intercourse creates between sovereign and subject. If a sovereign omits to keep it alive by such means, he leaves unfulfilled that one function which no one else can perform in his stead." Moreover, notwithstanding the supreme political power which is concentrated in the hands of the prime minister for the time being, the court, presided over by the sovereign, is still the highest point in the social scale. No prime minister, or leader of a political party, can attempt to vie with his sovereign in this particular. The personal preeminence of the king invests himself and his surroundings with a dignity which is absolute and unapproachable. The most elevated position in English society is thereby withdrawn from the arena of political competition, which is an incalculable benefit to the whole community. Were it otherwise, 'politics would offer a prize too dazzling for mankind.' If, in addition to the immense advantages that at present attend upon a successful parliamentary career, 'the highest social rank was to be scrambled for in the House of Commons, the number of social adventurers there would be incalculably more numerous, and indefinitely more eager;' and an overwhelming preponderance would be given to a force which is 'already perilously great.' From all these disturbing influences, the political system of England has been preserved by the position assigned to the English monarch.

Social preeminence.

The foregoing definition of the true place and work of the sovereign in the British Constitution, as now administered, may be suitably illustrated by reference to the recorded opinions of eminent statesmen of our own day upon this topic. Lord Brougham, in his 'Historical Sketches,' has the following weighty remarks: 'The question is, Does the king of this country hold a real

---

* Saturday Review, March 20, 1861
* Bagehot, Eng. Const. in Fortnightly Review, August 15, 1865, pp. 109, 110.

<small>Lord Brougham on the kingly office.</small>

or only a nominal office? Is he merely a form, or is he a substantive power in our mixed and balanced constitution? Some maintain—nay, it is a prevailing opinion among certain authorities of no mean rank—that the sovereign, having chosen his ministers, assigns over to them the whole executive power. They treat him as a kind of trustee for a temporary use, to preserve, as it were, some contingent estate; or a provisional assignee, to hold the property of an insolvent for a day, and then divest himself of the estate by assigning it over. They regard the only power really vested in the crown to be the choice of ministers, and even the exercise of this to be controlled by Parliament. They reduce the king more completely to the condition of a state pageant, or state cypher, than one of Abbé Sieyes' constitutions did, when he proposed to have a grand functionary with no power except to give away offices; upon which Napoleon, then First Consul, to whom the proposition was tendered, asked if it well became him to be made a "Cochon à l'engrais à la somme de trois millions par an?"* The English animal, according to the Whig doctrine, much more nearly answers this somewhat coarse description; for the Abbé's plan was to give his royal beast a substantial voice in the distribution of all patronage, while our lion is only to have the sad prerogative of naming whomsoever the Parliament chooses, and eating his own mess in quiet.

'Now, with all the disposition in the world to desire that the royal prerogative should be restricted, and the will of the nation govern the national affairs, we cannot comprehend this theory of a monarchy. It assigns to the crown either far too much revenue, or far too little power. To pay a million a year, or more, for a name, seems absurdly extravagant. To affect living under a kingly government, and yet suffer no kind of kingly

---

* A hog to be fatted at the rate of 120,000*l.* a year.

power, seems extravagantly absurd. Surely the meaning of having a sovereign is, that his voice should be heard, and his influence felt, in the administration of public affairs. The different orders of the state have a right to look towards that high quarter all in their turn for support, when their rights are invaded by one another's encroachments, or to claim the royal umpirage when their mutual conflicts cannot be settled by mutual concessions; and unless the whole notion of a mixed monarchy, and a balance of three powers, is a mere fiction and a dream, the royal portion of the composition must be allowed to have some power to produce the effect upon the quality of the whole. It is not denied that George III. sought to rule too much—it is not maintained that he had a right to be perpetually sacrificing all other considerations to the preservation or extension of his prerogative: but that he only discharged the duty of his station by thinking for himself, acting according to his conscientious opinions, and using his influence for giving these opinions effect, cannot be denied.'... ' George III. set one example which is worthy of imitation in all times. He refused to be made a state puppet in his minister's hands, and to let his name be used either by men whom he despised, or for purposes which he disapproved. Nor could anyone ever accuse him of ruling by favourites; still less could anyone, by pretending to be the people's choice, impose himself on his vigorous understanding."

Again, in his 'Political Philosophy,' Lord Brougham interprets the British Constitution as intending that the opinions of the monarch should have a sensible weight, even against the most conflicting sentiments of the people and of the peers, and that the individual monarch should be a substantive part of the political system, as a check on the other branches.*

---

* Historical Sketches of Statesmen, in the Time of George III., first series, edit. 1839, pp. 12-14.

* Vol. iii. p. 302. But see Mr. Senior's comments upon this passage, in his Historical Essays, vol. i. p. 347.

Earl Grey on the kingly office.

In his Essay on Parliamentary Government,¹ Lord Grey thus expresses himself:—'There is a further safeguard against abuse, in its being requisite that the ministers of the crown should obtain its direct sanction for all their most important measures. The crown, it is true, seldom refuses to act upon the advice deliberately pressed upon it by its servants, nor could it do so frequently without creating great inconvenience. But the sovereigns of this country nevertheless may, and generally have exercised much influence over the conduct of the government; and in extreme cases the power of the crown to refuse its consent to what is proposed by its servants, may be used with the greatest benefit to the nation. A refusal on the part of the sovereign to sanction measures which the ministers persist in recommending as indispensable, is indeed a legitimate ground for their resignation: and if the question which leads to this is one on which they have the support of public opinion, they must in the end prevail. But if this high power is exercised with wisdom, and is reserved for great emergencies, the crown may generally calculate on the support of the nation in refusing to sanction measures improperly pressed upon it by its ministers, especially where the measures so urged involve an abuse of the royal authority for their own party objects.'

Earl Derby on the influence of the Sovereign.

And upon a recent occasion Lord Derby, from his place in Parliament, gave utterance to the following remarks:—'The people of this country are under a great mistake if they suppose that the sovereign does not exercise a real, salutary, and decided influence over the councils and government of the country. The sovereign is not the mere automaton, or puppet, of the government of the day. She exercises a beneficial influence and control over the affairs of the state; and it is the duty of the minister for the time being, in submitting any propo-

---
¹ New edition, pp. 5, 6.

sition for the assent of her Majesty, to give satisfactory reasons that such propositions are called for by public policy, and justified by the public interests. If the sovereign is not satisfied with the advice tendered to her, —if, either from the suggestions of her own mind, or from objections which may be suggested to her by [the Prince Consort], her Majesty is of opinion that she will not accept the advice of the responsible minister of the crown, the course of the crown and the minister is equally open. The course of the crown is to refuse to accept that advice of the minister, and the inevitable consequence to the minister would be the tender of his resignation.'*

'It is not to be supposed,' says Professor Austin, in reference to the control exercised over Parliament by means of the royal prerogative of dissolution, 'that the king is powerless because this power of control is seldom exercised. As his power depends, in the long run, on the rational attachment of the people to the royal office, the permanence of the power would be put in jeopardy if it were indiscreetly exercised. The power of the crown to control the Houses operates silently. It is rarely exercised in fact; but it could be exercised in fact if the exercise became necessary, and were sanctioned by the approbation of the country.'

Austin on the kingly office.

The weight of influence which properly appertains to the opinions of the sovereign, when constitutionally expressed, would naturally be exerted in such an emergency to place the government of the country in the hands of a minister whose policy was in accordance with the views entertained by the crown itself; but unless those views found a response from the nation at large, and were accepted by Parliament, they could not ultimately prevail. In the last resort, no opinions or policy can be carried out by the government of England but such as meet with the sober approval of Parliament and of the people.

---

* Hans. Deb. vol. cxxx. p. 103.   * Plea for the Constitution, p. 6.

Influence of the sovereign in political affairs.

It has been aptly pointed out, by a recent political writer, that the power of the sovereign in England is considerably increased when rival political parties are evenly balanced; and that 'it rises still higher when the competition between the various statesmen of all parties becomes close. For, though the rise and fall of parties is decided in the main by the constituencies, their power extends only in very rare cases to the careers of individual politicians. Unless a man be singularly eminent, the sovereign can place a ban upon him, and exclude him, if not from all office, at least from the highest office, without any great risk of a collision with the House of Commons or the people. Court favour, therefore, is no matter of tinsel, but an object of substantial importance to politicians; and the fear of losing it avails, to a certain extent, to mould their policy, whether they are in office or in opposition. If this species of influence were merely used to give a due weight to the personal opinions of the sovereign, there would be no reason to complain, and its exercise would be acquiesced in cheerfully.' The writer then adverts to the 'obscure favourites concealed under the shadow of the throne,' who, in the last century, gave rise to complaints of unauthorised advice and backstairs influence; but he adds, most truly, that 'in our day the sense of honour has become keener, and political combatants no longer consider stratagems of this kind legitimate.'⁷

This brings us to the consideration of the prerogative of the crown in the appointment of the ministers of state, by whom the government of the country is conducted.

Appointment of ministers by the crown.

From the high and commanding position occupied by the sovereign, it would be natural to infer that he should be free to secure the services of the wisest and ablest men to whom to entrust the administration of public affairs. Accordingly the British Constitution distinctly recognises the right of the sovereign to make choice of all his

---

⁷ Saturday Review, August 1, 1863, p. 142.

responsible ministers,[a] and the continuance of the royal confidence in an existing ministry is an essential prerequisite to its remaining in office.

Commenting upon the exercise of this branch of the royal prerogative, Lord Brougham has declared that it is in the 'unquestioned power of the crown to choose and to change its servants;' and that 'no one would think of questioning the foundation of this power, of objecting to its existence, or of wishing to restrict it,' provided only that it is exercised 'on grounds capable of being stated and defended.' The grounds upon which the sovereign may constitutionally dismiss a ministry he has thus defined: 'If they exhibit internal dissensions amongst themselves; if they differ from the sovereign, or from the country at large; if their measures are ruinous to the interests of the country, at home or abroad; or if there should exist a general feeling of distrust and disapprobation of them throughout the country.'[a]

Dismissal of ministers.

The personal discretion of the sovereign in regard to his ministers has been explained as follows:—'The sovereign exercises his opinion on the sentiments as well as capacity of his ministers; and if upon either he judges them to be incompetent, or in any degree unfit, it is the prerogative and, with perfect loyalty let me add, the duty of the crown to dismiss such ministers.'[b] For 'the king cannot be required to take advice from men in whom he cannot confide; and, were there no other reason, a diminution of confidence is a sufficient ground for a change in his Majesty's councils.'[c]

It is the undeniable right of either House of Parliament to advise the crown upon the exercise of this or any other of its prerogatives; but this right cannot be pressed so far as to render the sovereign 'accountable to Parliament for

Advice of Parliament on the appointment of ministers.

---

[a] Hallam, Const. Hist. vol. iii. p. 302. And see a resolution of the House of Lords, on February 4, 1784.
[b] Mirror of Parl. 1836, pp. 28, 29.
[b] Mr. Pitt, Parl. Hist. vol. xxxv. p. 1121.
[c] Lord Selkirk, Parl. Deb. vol. ix. p. 377.

his conduct in changing his advisers,' or as to entitle Parliament 'to question the motives of his Majesty for dismissing ministers who had lost his confidence.'[d] It has been contended, indeed, that 'it is the right and privilege of the House of Commons to express its opinion and judgment, and even to offer advice to the sovereign, as to the circumstances under which, and the mode in which, he may have been advised to exercise his undoubted prerogative of choosing the ministers of the crown.'[e] But such an interference with the free choice of the sovereign would be justifiable only in the extreme case, if we may suppose that such could occur, wherein the crown had selected unfit or improper persons as its advisers.[f] In all ordinary circumstances, the ministers chosen by the sovereign are entitled to receive from Parliament, if not 'an implicit confidence,' at the least 'a fair trial.'[g] This has been the established rule and practice of the constitution, as the following cases will show:—

King's ministers entitled to a fair trial.

When Mr. Pitt was appointed prime minister by George III., in 1783, in the face of a hostile majority in the House of Commons, he braved the fierce opposition with which he was encountered, and disregarded the factious obstructions of his foes, until he was in a position to dissolve Parliament and appeal to the people.[h] Adverting, nearly twenty years afterwards, to the conduct of the House of Commons upon this occasion, Mr. Pitt declared that amidst all the violence which characterised the proceedings of the House at the time, the 'general principle' of the sole right of the king to nominate his ministers 'had never been attempted to be denied in the abstract.' The hostility of the House to Mr. Pitt arose, according to

---

[d] Lord Selkirk, Parl. Deb. vol. ix. p. 377. 'The House of Lords have nothing to say to the changes which may take place in his Majesty's councils. It is his Majesty's prerogative to appoint his own ministers, and to change them as he pleases; and the House of Lords cannot take into consideration the special circumstances under which such changes have been made, except in particular cases, in which an administration has been removed in consequence of an address from this house.'—*Duke of Wellington.* Parl. Deb. N. S. vol. xvii. p. 455.
[e] Lords Morpeth and Stanley, Mirror of Parl. 1835, p. 74.
[f] Lord Selkirk's speech, Parl. Deb. vol. ix. p. 377. And see Adolphus, Hist. of Eng. vol. iii. p. 403 n.
[g] Sir R. Peel's Memoirs, vol. ii. p. 67.
[h] See *ante*, p. 77.
[i] Parl. Hist. vol. xxxv. p. 902.

Sir Robert Peel, from a suspicion that he owed his appointment to unconstitutional motives; that is to say, to the exercise of secret influence, by means of which it was notorious that the previous administration had been overthrown. But Mr. Pitt took his stand upon the principle that it was irregular for the House to endeavour to control the prerogative of the crown in the choice of its ministers, by denouncing them without waiting to see their acts.[k]

In 1801, after the retirement of Mr. Pitt from office, and the appointment of Mr. Addington to the premiership, an arrangement which was not satisfactory to Parliament, Mr. Pitt expressly claimed for the king 'the sole right of nominating his ministers,' and contended 'that the House had no right to form any resolution till their conduct came to be judged of by the acts of their administration.' He asserted, moreover, that the new ministers were entitled, at the outset, to 'a constitutional confidence;' in other words, 'that unless some good reason were assigned to the contrary, the House was bound, by the best principles of policy, as well as by the true spirit of the constitution, to wait to see the conduct of the ministers of the crown before they should withhold their confidence.'[l] The House of Commons acquiesced in this reasoning, and refrained from any attempt at disturbing the new ministry.

In 1807, after the dismissal by George III. of the Grenville Administration, and the appointment of the Duke of Portland's ministry, debates arose in both Houses of Parliament upon this event, and upon the circumstances which had given rise to it. The ex-ministers had a majority in both Houses. Their friends accordingly endeavoured to embarrass the new government by proposing resolutions expressive of regret at the change in the royal councils. But Parliament, while they were inclined to approve of the conduct of the late ministry in the matter which had occasioned their dismissal, refused to concur in resolutions of censure, or to take any steps which would appear like an attempt to limit the exercise of the prerogative by refusing to the new ministers of the crown a fair trial. Accordingly the resolutions were superseded in the Lords by a motion of adjournment, and in the Commons by a resolution to pass on to the orders of the day.[m] During the debate in the House of Commons, Sir William Grant took occasion to show that the attempt of the late ministers to convert Parliament into a court of appeal against the king's decision was unwarrantable and unprecedented.[n]

In 1834 Sir Robert Peel, by desire of King William IV., undertook the formation of a ministry, although his party was in a decided

[k] Mirror of Parl. 1841, p. 1037.
[l] Parl. Hist. vol. xxxv. pp. 962, 1115.
[m] See ante, p. 91.
[n] Parl. Deb. vol. ix. p. 474. See also the proceedings in the House of Commons after the death of Mr. Perceval: ante, p. 90.

minority in the House of Commons. A dissolution of Parliament ensued, but this did not add very materially to the strength of the new administration. Ministers sustained very severe defeats in the new House; nevertheless, Sir R. Peel refused to resign, saying, 'I hold there is nothing unconstitutional, in the post I fill, and in the fulfilment of my duty, to persevere in the discharge of those duties to which my sovereign has called me, in defiance of the majority that is against me upon any abstract question, &c. I will perform my duty until the House shall by its vote refuse its sanction to some measure of importance which I think necessary to submit to its consideration.'[o] He accordingly persisted in the attempt to maintain his position, in the face of repeated defeats in the Commons for nearly two months; when, being convinced of the evil of permitting the House of Commons to exhibit itself to the country free from any control on the part of the government, and believing that 'in conformity with the constitution, a government ought not to persist in carrying on public affairs, after a fair trial, against the decided opinion of a majority of the House of Commons,' he resigned, and a new ministry, whose views were in accordance with the opinions of the Commons, was appointed.[p] Earl Derby in 1852, in 1858, and in 1866, assumed the reins of government, by command of the Queen, with an adverse majority in the House of Commons. Upon each occasion the new ministry were treated with great forbearance by the House, and were permitted to remain in office without molestation or annoyance until they had developed their policy, and had shown themselves to be decidedly at issue with the House of Commons upon some great public question.[q]

Address to the crown on the formation of a ministry.

During the interval between the resignation or dismissal of a ministry, and the appointment of their successors, should it appear expedient to either House to tender advice to the sovereign in regard to the formation of a new ministry—whether it be to urge the appointment of a strong and efficient administration, or even to indicate the political character of a ministry that would prove acceptable to Parliament—it is perfectly constitutional to do so. But an administration once formed is entitled, as we have seen, to receive from Parliament favourable consideration and a fair trial.

In 1783, thirty-seven days (February 24 to April 2) elapsed between the resignation of the Shelburne Ministry and the ap-

---

[o] Hans. Deb. vol. cxix. p. 1276. Mirror of Parl. 1835, p. 817.
[p] Peel's Memoirs, vol. ii. p. 91; [q] See ante, pp. 149, 153, 161.

pointment of a Coalition Ministry, under the Duke of Portland. On March 24, the Commons passed an address to the king, praying him to form a strong and united administration. His Majesty sent a gracious reply to this address through Earl Ludlow,[a] expressing his earnest desire to do everything in his power to comply with the wishes of his faithful Commons.[b] On March 31, a motion was made for the adoption of another address, representing the urgent necessity which existed for the immediate appointment of an efficient and responsible administration; but after some debate, the motion, being regarded as premature, was withdrawn.[c]

Upon the break-up of the Perceval Administration, owing to the assassination of the premier, on May 11, 1812, four weeks elapsed before a new ministry, under the Earl of Liverpool, was appointed. On May 21, a motion was made in the House of Commons for an address to the Prince Regent, praying him to form a strong and efficient administration. It being known that the former colleagues of Mr. Perceval were desirous of remaining in office, and were in communication with the prince upon the subject, the motion was resisted by the friends of the late government, on the ground that it was an attempt to interfere with the crown in the choice of its servants, which was not justified by existing circumstances. The motion was nevertheless agreed to by a small majority, and the mover and seconder of the address were ordered to present it to his Royal Highness. The mover reported on the following day that the prince had promised that the address should receive his immediate and serious consideration. Viewing this address as equivalent to a declaration of their own inefficiency, the remaining members of the administration immediately placed their offices at the disposal of the Prince Regent. Negotiations were then commenced with the Whig party, but they proved unsuccessful; and the old ministry was reinstated in office, under the premiership of the Earl of Liverpool.[d] The new administration was vehemently assailed in the House of Commons, and motions were submitted to declare that it was essentially the same as the one in regard to which disapprobation had been expressed by the House and by the country. But after much debate it became apparent that the sense of the House was opposed to any proceedings that might appear like an attempt

---

[a] His lordship was Comptroller of the Household.
[b] Com. Journals, March 20, 1788.
[c] *Ibid.* March 31, 1788.
[d] See *ante*, pp. 94-103. During this interval, on May 30, and again on June 5, notice was given in the House of Commons for a further address to the Prince Regent, beseeching him to proceed without delay to appoint a strong ministry, in which the House could confide. But the House being informed that negotiations were in active progress, with every prospect of a successful termination, the motions were not made.—*Ibid.* pp. 100, 102.

to dictate to the crown in regard to the choice of its advisers. The leader of the government, moreover, claimed for the new ministry 'the constitutional support of Parliament till their actions should show them to be unworthy of it.' The several motions of censure were then put and negatived.*

A fortnight elapsed between the resignation of Lord Liverpool, on March 27, 1827, and the appointment of the Canning Administration. Meanwhile, after eight days had elapsed, notice was given, for April 6, of an address to the crown, to be pleased to appoint a ministry who were unanimous on questions of vital importance to the empire. But when the day arrived for bringing on this motion, it was withdrawn upon an intimation that the formation of a ministry was about to take place. Four days afterwards the Canning Ministry was appointed.*

Ten days elapsed between the resignation of Sir Robert Peel, in 1835, and the appointment of the Melbourne Ministry; and there was a similar interval between the resignation of the Derby Ministry, in 1852, and the appointment of their successors. Upon neither of these occasions was there any action taken by Parliament, although a change of ministry is ordinarily effected within one week.

But on February 1, 1855, the Aberdeen Ministry resigned, and the Palmerston Ministry accepted office on the 8th inst. Notwithstanding this short interval, on the motion to adjourn the House of Commons, on February 6, a short debate ensued, in which dissatisfaction was expressed at the delay in forming a ministry, and hints were given that, if much further delay occurred, it might be expedient to address the crown upon the subject.*

Upon the resignation of the Grey Ministry, on May 8, 1832, consequent upon their defeat upon the Reform Bill in the House of Lords, the House of Commons passed an address to the king on the 10th inst., expressing their deep regret at the retirement of ministers, and imploring his Majesty ' to call to his councils such persons only as will carry into effect, unimpaired in all its essential provisions,' the measure of Reform to which the House had recently agreed. The address was ordered to be presented by members of the Privy Council.¹ Four days having elapsed without the reception by the House of any reply to their address, the Speaker was questioned upon the subject. He could only state that the address had been placed in proper hands for presentation, and suggest that his Majesty, not having any responsible minister or confidential adviser, might think it better to delay sending an answer till he had

---

* See ante, pp. 104, 105.
* See ante, pp. 100–108.
¹ See ante, p. 150.

¹ Mirror of Parl. 1832, pp. 1070–1092.

such a minister, through whose hands it might be conveyed. This surmise was afterwards confirmed, and declared to have been the reason why no reply had been sent to the address, by the Chancellor of the Exchequer, upon his return to office.* For the king, having failed in the attempt to form a Tory administration, had been obliged to recall his late advisers.

Having vindicated the right of the sovereign to the free choice of his constitutional advisers, by whom the administration of the Government is to be conducted—a freedom which necessitates that they should be unreservedly accepted by Parliament at the outset of their career, and until they prove themselves by their general policy and public conduct to be undeserving of confidence—it remains to be seen to what extent the sovereign is at liberty to exercise his personal inclinations in the choice or dismissal of individual ministers. Personal inclinations of the sovereign in the formation of a ministry.

The cabinet, as will be hereafter more fully explained, is a committee of the Privy Council. The sovereign is empowered by his prerogative to summon whom he will to the Privy Council; and he is at liberty to dismiss any member thereof, at any time, who may incur his displeasure.* As every cabinet minister is necessarily a member of the Privy Council, the sovereign is thereby enabled to alter the composition of the cabinet council whenever he may think fit to do so. But by modern constitutional practice the freedom of choice possessed by the crown in the selection of its advisers has been subjected to important limitations.

Theoretically, it is presumed that the sovereign acts in this matter according to his own discretion. William III., it is notorious, allowed no interference with his own will in appointing whom he would to fill the high offices of state;* but the necessities of parliamentary government, coupled with the inferior capability of his immediate

---

* Mirror of Parl. 1832, pp. 2024, 2079.
* Several instances are given by May (Const. Hist. L pp. 20, 24), wherein George II. and George III. struck out the names of individuals from the list of privy councillors, for imputed misconduct.
* Macaulay, Hist. of England, passim.

successors upon the throne, soon entangled the reigning monarch in the meshes of party, and deprived him of free agency, even in the choice of his own ministers.

Nomination of ministers by the crown.

The Whigs, during the reign of the first three Georges, set up a claim to have the nomination of the prime minister, and to limit the choice of the sovereign in regard to his ministers generally to the members of certain leading aristocratic families. In this they were partially successful, the earlier sovereigns of the House of Hanover being unable to resist the strength of the party by whom this claim was supported. But George III., immediately upon his accession, endeavoured to free himself from such trammels, and to break down the great Whig oligarchy. As a matter of compromise, he succeeded in making good his right to appoint a portion of every administration, whilst the remainder were nominated by the leading statesmen who were invited to join the same. This arrangement appears to have continued in operation until a very recent date. It was not until the accession of Sir Robert Peel to office, in 1834, that we find the present constitutional practice distinctly enforced.

Thus, in 1782, George III. was allowed to nominate Lord Thurlow as Lord Chancellor and a member of the cabinet, whilst the Shelburne and Rockingham parties introduced five members each.[c] Thurlow was first appointed to the chancellorship in 1778, and continued to hold the office during successive administrations, until 1792, on account of the king's strong partiality for him. But the imprudence of this arrangement was afterwards manifested by Thurlow's own conduct, for he pertinaciously opposed the policy of his colleagues, and boasted of his independence on the ground that he was 'the king's friend.'[d] During Mr. Pitt's administration, the king, who had great confidence in that statesman, did not interfere at all in his arrangement of the political offices, though

---

[c] Parl. Deb. vol. xxiii. p. 413.   [d] Campbell's Chanc. vol. v. pp. 547, 611.

in regard to some of them he privately expressed his extreme disapprobation.* During the Regency, in 1812, the negotiations with Lords Grey and Grenville for the reconstruction of the ministry fell through, because the Prince Regent claimed the right to nominate three members of the cabinet (including the prime minister) himself. This claim was objected to by the Whig lords, not as being unconstitutional, but because they deemed it to be opposed to the spirit of mutual confidence and freedom from suspicion which ought to characterise the cabinet council, and which rendered it essential that parties invited to co-operate in forming an administration should be at liberty to arrange its *personnel* amongst themselves.[t] Upon the formation of Sir Robert Peel's administration, in 1834, he being abroad when the king resolved upon selecting him as premier, his Majesty appointed the Duke of Wellington to be secretary of state, and named Lord Lyndhurst for the office of chancellor. But it was distinctly understood that this was to be a mere *ad interim* arrangement; and upon the arrival of Sir Robert Peel in England, three weeks afterwards, one of his first acts was the formal recommendation to the king that the Duke of Wellington should be appointed foreign secretary, and that Lord Lyndhurst should be the chancellor.[a]

In regard to the selection of the prime minister himself, it is only within a very recent period that the free choice of the crown has been distinctly acknowledged. This is partly attributable to the fact that the office of premier was not regarded as conferring upon its possessor an absolute control over his colleagues in the ministry, until within the past century.[b] But, in proportion as its pre-eminence became apparent, its possession was naturally coveted by the great political parties.

Free choice of the prime minister by the crown.

It has been already noticed that from the accession of the House of Hanover, it was a fundamental article of

* Rose, Corresp. vol. li. pp. 156, 175.
t Parl. Deb. vol. xxiii. p. 428.
a Peel's Memoirs, ii. pp. 17, 27, 35.
b See *post*, Vol. II. c. I.

the Whig creed that the ministers of the crown, and especially the prime minister, should be nominated by the chiefs of the Whig party. Mr. Pitt, during the debates on the Regency, in 1788, publicly referred to this claim in the House of Commons, in presence of Mr. Fox, who did not attempt to deny it.[b] Its existence serves to explain many obscure passages of political history, wherein ministerial negotiations, otherwise promising, proved unsuccessful, because of the attempt to assert the independence of the crown in the choice of its first minister.[¹] It continued in operation until the time of the Regency, when Lord Wellesley, having been authorised by the Prince Regent to reconstruct the ministry, after the assassination of Mr. Perceval, failed in the endeavour, as we learn upon Whig testimony, mainly because that party had not been empowered to choose the premier, although they were invited to enter a cabinet to be formed upon their own political principles. In the debate upon the failure of these negotiations, Mr. Canning adverted to this doctrine, and claimed, on behalf of the constitution, that the crown should be unfettered in the choice of its ministers, save only by the advice and control of a free Parliament.[j] It is somewhat remarkable, however, that Mr. Pitt, who in 1788 had contended for the rights of the sovereign in this particular, should himself have been a party, in 1803, to a negotiation with Mr. Addington (the then prime minister) for his own return to power, as the head of the administration, without having previously obtained the consent of the king to the proposed arrangement. The correspondence between Pitt and Addington was presented to the king by the latter, after the scheme had proved abortive; but his Majesty refused to read it, caustically remarking that 'it

---

[b] Parl. Hist. vol. xxvii. p. 772.   pp. 202-207.
[¹] See historical precedents, cited   [j] Parl. Deb. vol. xxiii. p. 455.
in Stapleton's Canning and his Times,

was a foolish business, which was begun ill, conducted ill, and terminated ill.'[b]

The inability of the Prince Regent to reconstruct the ministry in 1812, in consequence of the obstinate adherence of the Whig leaders to their favourite maxim, requiring a surrender of the prerogative of the crown in the choice of its advisers as the condition of their support and co-operation, induced his Royal Highness to adopt the unprecedented and undignified course of commanding the members of the existing cabinet to elect their own first minister. Their choice fell upon Lord Liverpool, who in this way began his long and prosperous career as premier.[1] After the death of Lord Liverpool, in 1827, Mr. Canning was obviously the one who, from his position and influence, should have succeeded him in the premiership; but his known opinions in favour of Roman Catholic Emancipation made the king averse to placing him in such a prominent office. Accordingly, after a fruitless interview with Mr. Canning, his Majesty again resorted to his former expedient, and sent the following minute to the cabinet: 'That his Majesty is desirous of retaining all his present servants in the stations which they at present fill, placing at their head, in the station vacated by Lord Liverpool, some peer professing opinions upon whom his Majesty's confidential servants may agree, of the same principles as Lord Liverpool.' He afterwards sent a verbal message to Mr. Canning, leaving it to his *discretion* to make or withhold this communication to his colleagues. Mr. Canning, being of opinion that it was inexpedient to refer the selection of their chief to the suffrages of the cabinet, decided upon withholding it; while he at the same time privately made known to them its general purport, to which they responded by simply expressing their earnest desire for a

^{Choice of the premier by his colleagues in the ministry.}

---

[b] Sir G. C. Lewis, in Edinb. Rev. vol. cvii. p. 147. [1] Stapleton, Canning and his Times, p. 208.

speedy termination of the present embarrassing position of the government; whereupon the king allowed his proposal to drop. Several days were then spent in conferences between his Majesty and leading members of the cabinet, which terminated at last in the issue of the royal commands to Mr. Canning to prepare, with the least possible delay, a plan for the reconstruction of the administration. Thus commenced the premiership of Mr. Canning, which, in a few short weeks, was brought to a sudden and unexpected close by his premature decease.[m]

The prime minister to be the free choice of the crown.

It is now universally conceded that the prime minister— as *the* minister in whom the crown has placed its constitutional confidence, and who is responsible to his sovereign for the government of the whole empire—should be the free and unbiassed choice of the crown itself. Adverting to the circumstances attending his resignation of office in 1845, Sir Robert Peel said, in the House of Commons: 'I offered no opinion as to the choice of a successor. That is almost the only act which is the personal act of the sovereign; it is for the sovereign to determine in whom her confidence shall be placed.'[n] A retiring minister may, if requested by the sovereign, suggest that any particular statesman should be empowered to form a new administration, but such advice should not be obtruded upon the sovereign unasked. Being debarred by his own resignation, or dismissal from office, from the constitutional right to tender advice to the crown, he can only do so, if required, in the quality of a peer or a privy councillor; being still responsible, in that capacity, for any advice he may give to the sovereign.[o]

But while the doctrine is now fully established, that the sovereign has a free choice in the appointment of the

---

[m] Stapleton, Canning and his Times, pp. 540-580.
[n] Hans. Deb. vol. lxxxiii. p. 1004. See also Lord Derby, ibid. vol. cxxiii. p. 1701; and Massey's Geo. III. vol. iii. p. 213.
[o] See *ante*, p. 51.

prime minister, the selection of that functionary is nevertheless practically limited by the all-important fact, that no minister can, for any length of time, carry on the government of the country who does not possess the confidence of Parliament, and more especially of the House of Commons.[f] This circumstance has contributed to restrain the undue exercise of the royal prerogative, and to compel the crown, in all its dealings with an administration, to govern itself by considerations of high political expediency.[g] Ample security, moreover, that no changes of ministry will be effected by the authority of the crown but such as would commend themselves to the judgment of Parliament, is obtained by the operation of the constitutional rule which requires that whenever a change of ministry takes place in consequence of an act of the crown, the incoming ministers shall be held responsible to Parliament for the policy which occasioned the retirement of their predecessors in office.[r]

Necessity for ministers to possess the confidence of Parliament.

New ministers responsible for dismissal of their predecessors.

In 1807, when George III. dismissed the Grenville Ministry, because of their refusal to carry out his particular views in reference to the Roman Catholics, the incoming administration endeavoured to evade the responsibility which had devolved upon them in regard to the change of government: but it was emphatically asserted, by the best parliamentary authorities, 'that there was not a moment in the king's life, from his accession to his demise, when there was not a person constitutionally responsible for his actions;' and that although he might seem to be acting without advice when, in the exercise of his undoubted prerogative, he dismissed his ministers and appointed others, yet that the incoming ministers were themselves responsible for the dismissal of their predecessors.[s]

In 1834 William IV., having become a convert to Tory principles, came to the sudden determination of dismissing the Whig ministry of Lord Melbourne. It did not appear that either the interests of the state or the wishes of Parliament necessitated this proceeding; for there had been no immediate difference of opinion between the

---

[f] Bowyer, Con-t. Law, p. 137; Rowlands, Eng. Const. p. 434.
[g] See Prince Albert's opinion on this subject, quoted by Earl Russell, in Hans. Deb. vol. clxv. p. 44.
[r] Grey, Parl. Gort. 189, n.
[s] Commons Debates, April 9, 1807. And see the case of Lord Danby, cited by Lords Lauderdale and Holland, on this occasion, Hans. Deb. vol. ix. pp. 405, 414.

king and the cabinet on any point of public policy, nor had ministers lost the confidence of the House of Commons.¹ His Majesty, however, determined to entrust to Sir R. Peel the formation of a new ministry. Sir Robert was absent from England at the time, and was ignorant of the circumstances attending the dismissal of Lord Melbourne. When informed of the facts, he expressed great doubts of the policy which had occasioned the change of government. Nevertheless, so fully did he recognise the extent of his obligations in accepting office, that he boldly avowed his constitutional responsibility 'for the dissolution of the preceding government, although he had not the remotest concern in it.'" The late ministry had a large majority in the House of Commons, and one of Sir R. Peel's first acts was to appeal to the people. The new House, although more favourably inclined to the new minister, failed to put him in a sufficiently strong position to enable him to carry on the government; and, after a gallant struggle for several weeks against an adverse majority, Sir R. Peel was compelled to retire from office. The king had then no alternative but to recall to his councils the Melbourne Ministry, which he had before so summarily dismissed.

Formation of new ministry.

Upon the resignation or dismissal of a ministry, it is customary for the sovereign to send for the recognised leader of the Opposition, or for some other person of known weight and influence in either House of Parliament, who is capable of leading successfully the political party to which he belongs, and to authorise him to undertake the formation of a new administration." It is not essential, however, that the person selected to bring about the construction of a new cabinet should be the intended prime minister. It may be difficult at first to fix upon anyone suitable for this office with whom a new administration could be induced to co-operate. Under such circumstances some less prominent person could be chosen to negotiate for the formation of the ministry. Thus, in 1812, Lord Moira received a commission of this kind from the Prince Regent, with the understanding that he should receive some inferior office, together with a seat in the cabinet."

---

¹ May, Const. Hist. vol. i. p. 122.
" Peel's Memoirs, vol. ii. p. 31.
' See Fischel, Eng. Const. p. 517.
" Campbell, Chancellors, vol. vii.
p. 284. And see the Duke of Wellington's remarks on this point, in Hans. Deb. N. S. vol. xvii. p. 404.

We have already seen (*ante*, p. 218) that it has of late years become a settled principle that the political chiefs to whom the sovereign may confide the task of forming a ministry, are at liberty to select the individuals to compose the same, and to submit their names for the royal approval. This privilege is indispensable to the successful working of our parliamentary system, and, after a long struggle, it has been conceded to every political party which may, in turn, acquire the preeminence.[a] It is a constitutional necessity that the first minister of the crown should be able to assume full personal responsibility before Parliament for the appointment of every member of the administration. This he can only do when he has been empowered to advise the crown in regard to the selection of the persons who are to be associated with him in the functions of government. The sovereign has, indeed, an undoubted right to express his wishes in favour of the introduction or exclusion of particular persons, but by modern constitutional usage he has no authoritative voice in the selection of anyone but the prime minister. It is true that, in this as in other matters, the expression of a strong personal feeling on the part of the crown may have great weight in excluding a person from office, or including him, at least for a time; but even this consideration must ultimately yield to a regard for the public interests, and the sovereign must be prepared to accept as his advisers and officers of state those who have been selected for such functions by the premier.[b] In like

Prime minister empowered to choose his colleagues.

---

[a] See Sir G. C. Lewis, in Edinb. Rev. vol. cili. p. 313; Mr. Canning's letter of 1827, in Hans. Deb. N. S. vol. xvii. p. 457; Duke of Wellington's letter of 1828, in Peel's Memoirs, vol. i. p. 11; Sir R. Peel, Evidence, 283, Com. on Official Salaries, in 1850; and see Mill, Rep. Govt. p. 90.

[b] George III., it is notorious, had such a repugnance to Mr. Fox, that for a long time he absolutely refused to admit him into the cabinet. (See May, Const. Hist. vol. i. p. 83; Campbell, Chanc. vol. vii. p. 168.) In 1801, after entrusting the formation of a new ministry to Mr. Addington, and giving him full authority to make such arrangements for carrying on the public service as he should think fit, George III. expressed a 'wish' that he might be enabled to place the Great Seal in the hands of Lord Eldon, and place Sir Pepper Arden in the office of Chief Justice of the Common Pleas. (Pellew's Life of Sidmouth, vol. i. p. 296). Both these appointments were

manner, in the event of a vacancy occurring in an administration, whether from ordinary circumstances, or as the unavoidable result of differences between individual members of the same, it is the duty of the prime minister to take the pleasure of the crown in regard to the appointment of some one selected by himself to fill the vacant office.*

The king consults peers on the formation of a ministry.

If difficulties should occur in the formation of a ministry, it is always competent for the sovereign to send for, and take the advice of, any peer or privy-councillor of weight and experience in public affairs, whose counsel he might consider would be serviceable to him in the emergency.

Thus, upon the crisis arising out of the assassination of Mr. Perceval, in 1812, when it became necessary to reconstruct the cabinet of which he was the chief, the Prince Regent applied for and acted upon the advice of his brother, the Duke of Cumberland.* In 1827, during the interregnum occasioned by the break-up of the Liverpool Administration, on account of the death of the premier, and the delay in the formation of a new ministry by Mr. Canning, the Duke of Newcastle used his privilege as a peer to obtain an audience of the king, at which he threatened the withdrawal of the support of the Tory party from the government if his Majesty should select Mr. Canning as prime minister.[b] Upon the resignation of the Russell Ministry in 1851, after several ineffectual attempts on the part of

---

conferred agreeably to the king's desire. George IV. refused to allow the readmission of Mr. Canning into the cabinet, in 1821, after the death of Queen Caroline, although he had retired therefrom a few months previously, solely on account of his objections to taking part in the proceedings against the queen. A year afterwards, the premier (Lord Liverpool) renewed his appeal to the king on Mr. Canning's behalf, but still without success; until at length, through the intercession of the Duke of Wellington, his Majesty was induced, very reluctantly, to yield. (Stapleton, Canning and his Times, pp. 323, 368; Guizot's Peel, p. 23.) When the Wellington coalition ministry was about to be formed, in 1828, George IV., while expressing his wishes in regard to several statesmen, on the whole gave a *carte blanche* for the selection of any persons who had heretofore been in his service, except Lord Grey, whom he objected to receive again into the cabinet. (Peel's Memoirs, vol. I. p. 12.) Upon the reappointment of the Melbourne Ministry, in 1835, William IV. stipulated that Lord Brougham, who was personally displeasing to his Majesty, should not be replaced in the office of Lord Chancellor. (Howley, Brit. Const. p. 200; Ann. Register, 1835, p. 237.)

* Sir R. Peel, in Commons' Committee on Official Salaries, 1850, Evid. 285, 290.

* Campbell's Chancellors, vol. vii. p. 280.

[b] Stapleton's Canning and his Times, p. 592.

various statesmen to form a new administration, her Majesty sent for the Duke of Wellington, not for the purpose of entrusting the making of a cabinet to his hands, but in order that she might take counsel from him in regard to the existing state of affairs, determining also 'to pause awhile before she again commenced the task of forming an administration.'[e] Again, in 1852, upon the resignation of the Derby Ministry, her Majesty sent for the Marquis of Lansdowne for a similar purpose.[d] Both the Duke of Wellington and (after his death) the Marquis of Lansdowne, from their eminent position, acknowledged patriotism, and freedom from all selfish aims, were regarded by common consent as the personal advisers and referees of the Queen. In this capacity they often and successfully intervened to reconcile political adversaries and rival competitors for power, and afforded substantial assistance to the crown upon occasions of grave emergency.[e]

The act of the sovereign, in communicating with trusty counsellors in circumstances of political exigency, is in strict accordance with constitutional principle; and it is not to be confounded with the attempts made by George III., during the early years of his reign, to govern with the aid of secret and irresponsible advisers. For advice given to the sovereign upon any such emergency, the peer or privy-councillor is liable to be called to account by Parliament, should his counsel be followed by consequences that require parliamentary interposition.[f]

Once a ministry is formed, it becomes the duty of a constitutional monarch to give it his implicit confidence and support, co-operating heartily and sincerely with the members of his cabinet, so long as he may consider that the best interests of the empire are served by their continuance in office. Should he have reason to believe that those interests would be promoted by a change in his advisers, he is at liberty to insist that they shall give place to others, in whom he can repose more perfect trust: but he must always take care to assure himself beforehand that the proposed alteration in the ministry is

Mutual confidence between the king and his ministers.

---

[c] Hans. Deb. vol. cxiv. pp. 1039, 1076.
[d] Ibid. vol. cxxlii. p. 1702.
[e] Saturday Review, February 7, 1804, p. 108.
[f] See ante, p. 88.

one that will satisfy the nation, and will merit and secure the approbation of Parliament.^a

Formal appointment or resignation of ministers.

The several members of the administration are formally appointed to their respective offices by the sovereign, at a meeting of the Privy Council, specially holden for the purpose. They are introduced to the sovereign by the prime minister, when they receive the seals and symbols of office from the royal hands, which they are then permitted to salute. Upon the accession of a new sovereign, all the ministers deliver up the emblems of their different offices to the new monarch, at a meeting of the Privy Council; receiving them back again from the royal hands, if it is intended that they should continue in office.^b

When a minister of state wishes to resign his office, his intended retirement should be officially communicated to the sovereign, through the prime minister, as the regular channel of communication between the crown and the ministry. But, if necessary, a personal interview with the sovereign can be obtained by the retiring minister, at which he may formally deliver up his symbols of office, and inform the sovereign of the reasons which have induced him to withdraw from the royal service.^c

Dismissal of a minister.

It is always in the power of the crown, acting through its responsible advisers, to direct the dismissal from office of a minister of state, whether he be a member of the cabinet or not. And Parliament has no right to

---

^a 'Public opinion determines, in the last resort, to what hands authority shall be entrusted; for though the ministers are the servants of the crown, and are appointed by the sovereign, yet as the sovereign must choose ministers who can command the confidence of Parliament, it is practically the people who decide, through their representatives, by whom the power of government shall be wielded. There is, however, a vast difference in the effect produced by giving to the people, instead of the power of nominating their rulers by direct election, only an indirect control, through their representatives, over the selection of the ministers by whose advice the powers of the crown are exercised.'—(*Grey, Parl. Govt.* p. 25.) See also Mill on Representative Govt. p. 110.

^b Campbell's Chanc. vol. vii. p. 342.

^c Pellew's Life of Sidmouth, vol. iii. p. 335; Edinb. Review, vol. cx. p. 79, n.

interfere in any such case, unless it can be clearly shown that the prerogative had been exercised in an arbitrary and unreasonable manner.   *Not ordinarily subject to parliamentary control.*

Thus, in 1795, the government deemed it expedient to recall Earl Fitzwilliam from the lord-lieutenancy of Ireland, on account of his having favoured a policy in regard to Roman Catholic Emancipation, which was objectionable and embarrassing to the administration. This proceeding gave rise to much discussion in Parliament, and addresses were moved in both Houses, for copies of such correspondence as would show 'the motives and grounds of the recall' of the noble earl. The motion was opposed by ministers, as being unconstitutional and unprecedented. 'The power of nominating and dismissing his servants, without assigning any cause, * * * was vested in the crown, and was an indisputable part of the constitution.' Admitting 'that no prerogative could bar the inquisitorial functions of the House of Commons,' it was necessary, in order to justify enquiry into the exercise of this prerogative, that 'a special case should be made out of positive danger, or public misconduct or delinquency.' Ministers are sworn to secrecy in respect to the advice they gave to the sovereign, and they are all responsible to Parliament for the administration of the government. But 'if either House of Parliament were to enquire into the causes of dismissing ministers, the next step must be enquiring whether or not their successors were well chosen, and advising as to their appointment.' Before ministers could be called to account, 'substantive ground must be laid for a charge against them.'[k] In conformity with this doctrine, ministers refused to enter into particulars as to the reasons that occasioned the recall of Earl Fitzwilliam, explanations in regard to which would necessarily 'involve the discussion of cabinet secrets.' They were sustained in this determination by large majorities in both Houses of Parliament.[l]

The sovereign never attends at meetings of the cabinet council. Previous to the accession of the present dynasty, it was otherwise; and so long as it was consistent with the practice of the constitution for the monarch to take an active and immediate part in the direction of public affairs, it was fitting that no meeting of the cabinet should be held without his presence. But under the existing   *Cabinet councils not attended by the sovereign.*

---

[j] Mr. Pitt, the prime minister, in Parl. Hist. vol. xxxi. p. 1550.
[k] Lord Grenville, *ibid.* p. 1518.
[l] Parl. Deb. May 8 and 10, 1795; Adolphus, Hist. of Eng. vol. vi. p. 273. See also an account of the dismissal of Lord Palmerston, in 1851, from the office of Foreign Secretary, *post*, Vol. II. c. 1, On the Cabinet Council.

system of government, through responsible ministers, it is obvious that in order to enable the cabinet to arrive at impartial conclusions upon any matter, it is necessary that their deliberations should be private and confidential. The absence of the sovereign from the cabinet arose, however, in the first instance, from the accidental circumstance of the inability of George I. to express himself in the English language. The innovation once commenced soon commended itself as a suitable practice, in entire conformity with the new theory of constitutional government then in progress of development.

The sovereign and the prime minister.

The proper medium of communication between the sovereign and the administration is the prime minister; not merely on account of his position as head of the government, but especially because he is the minister who has been personally selected by the sovereign as the one in whom the crown reposes its entire confidence. He is bound to keep the sovereign duly informed of all political events of importance, including the decisions of Parliament upon matters of public concern. Formal decisions of the cabinet upon questions of public policy are also submitted to the sovereign by the prime minister, upon whom it devolves to take the royal pleasure thereupon.

When the crown should be consulted on state affairs.

It is not needful to consult the crown upon minor matters of administration: discretion, in such cases, is necessarily reposed in the official responsible head of every department of the state. But no important acts of government, which would commit the crown to a particular course or line of policy, should be performed by ministers without the previous knowledge and consent of the sovereign.[a] The cabinet council is frequently occupied in discussing important matters, which it would be premature to submit to the crown until some definite conclusions have been come to, or some line of policy

---

[a] May, Const. Hist. vol. i. p. 132.

agreed upon, in regard to the same. But so soon as the cabinet have arrived at a decision upon any important question which is intended to be the basis of future action, whether legislative or administrative, it becomes the duty of the prime minister to submit the same for the consideration of the crown. The neglect of this rule, on the part of Mr. Pitt, in the year 1800,—when the cabinet had agreed upon the expediency of a concession to the claims of the Roman Catholics,—occasioned his loss of office, and the withdrawal of the king's confidence.[a] And, in 1851, Lord Palmerston was removed from the office of Foreign Secretary, by command of the Queen, acting upon the advice of the prime minister, for an excess of authority as secretary of state, in writing an important despatch which had not been submitted for the approval of the sovereign, or the concurrence of the premier, before it was transmitted to its destination.[b] 'These events exemplify the effective control which the crown constitutionally exercises in the government of the country. The policy and conduct of its ministers are subject to its active supervision. In minor affairs the ministers have a separate discretion, in their several departments; but in the general acts of government, the crown is to be consulted, and has a control over them all.'[c]

To ensure a due observance, on the part of ministers, of their duty to the crown, provision has been made for the regular transmission of every important despatch, correspondence, report, or other paper, which it is material should be inspected by the sovereign, to the sovereign herself, either through the instrumentality of the prime minister, or, in certain cases, direct from one of the secretary of state's offices.[d] All despatches received by

Method of communicating with the crown.

---

[a] May, Const. Hist. vol. i. pp. 81, 82.
[b] Ibid. pp. 132-135. Full particulars of this case will be found in the chapter on the Cabinet Council.
[c] May, Const. Hist. vol. i p. 135.
[d] Despatch-boxes, containing official reports, correspondence, warrants, and others papers, for the royal approval or signature, are daily forwarded to the sovereign, in charge of queen's messengers, from the several offices of the Principal Secretaries of State,

a secretary of state, after perusal by the proper officer,—and, in important cases, all drafts of answers thereto,—are required to be forwarded, by the senior clerk of the particular department, first to the prime minister, then to the Queen (for the royal sanction, previous to their being despatched, in the case of important drafts), and afterwards to the other cabinet ministers.' Constitutional practice also requires that no political instruction should be sent to any British minister abroad, and no official note be addressed to any foreign diplomatic agent, without the draft being first submitted to the prime minister, in order that he may take the pleasure of the crown upon it. And if either the sovereign or the prime minister suggest alterations, they are either adopted, or the despatch is withheld.'

Interposition of the royal authority.

If any question should arise in the mind of the sovereign, in regard to anything contained in the official papers submitted for her consideration and approval, she would properly consult the prime minister thereupon.' And should it be necessary for the sovereign to interpose her authority, to correct or control the conduct of any particular minister, she would do so upon the constitutional advice and responsibility of the prime minister."

Etiquette in writing to the sovereign.

The mode in which ministers address the sovereign in epistolary communications is peculiar. It is the established etiquette for the minister to use the third person, and to address his sovereign in the second. When or by whom this epistolary form was introduced is unknown. Mr. Grenville's letters to George III., in 1765, are in the ordinary form.' But, twenty years later, we find Mr. Fox employing the phraseology which is now in use: '*Mr. Fox* has the

---

the First Lord of the Admiralty, and from the Prime Minister. The perusal and consideration of these papers forms an important part of the daily routine of the royal labours.

' See Report of Commons' Committee on the Diplomatic Service, 1861, pp. 74-76.

' Lord Palmerston, Hans. Deb. vol. cxix. pp. 106, 110. See further on this subject, in the Chapter On the Cabinet Council.

' Lord John Russell, Hans. Deb. vol. cxix. p. 91.

* Ibid. p. 99.

' Grenville Papers, vol. iii. pp. 4-15.

honour of transmitting to *your Majesty* the minute of the cabinet council assembled this morning at Lord Rockingham's, 18th May 1782.'"

When it is necessary that the authority of the crown should be exercised in public acts of government, a privy council is convened, from whence orders in council and proclamations are promulgated. According to modern usage, the Privy Council is regarded as a formal and not a deliberative assembly; for 'it would be contrary to constitutional practice that the sovereign should preside at any council where deliberation or discussion takes place.'" The commands of the sovereign in reference to affairs of state, whether they be issued at a privy council or otherwise, are communicated to the executive departments to whom it belongs to give effect thereto, through the medium of a secretary of state.' {Privy councils}

When it is necessary to obtain the royal sign-manual to any important document, the various secretaries and other ministers of state who may require it, in their respective departments, should make personal application for the same. But if the paper to be signed be of an ordinary and unimportant character, it may be transmitted to the sovereign in a departmental despatch-box.' It is the duty of the Lord Chancellor to attend upon the sovereign in order to obtain the sign-manual for the sanction of bills that have passed the two Houses of Parliament.° {Royal sign-manual}

If circumstances should occur that would render the personal exercise of the royal functions inconvenient or impossible, the powers of the crown may be delegated, for a time, to commissioners or other substitutes. The only exception appears to be in regard to the power of creating peers, which has never been made the subject of {Delegation of royal functions}

---

* Russell's Fox, vol. i. p. 361, quoted by Sir G. C. Lewis, in Edinb. Rev. vol. xcix. p. 25, n.
¹ Earl Granville, in Hans. Deb. vol. clxxv. p. 251. And see Vol. II. c. 2,
On the Privy Council.
' Hans. Deb. vol. cxl. p. 1047.
* *Ibid.* vol. clxv. p. 841.
° Campbell's Chanc. vol. vii. pp. 157-159.

delegation.[b] Neither can a commission be granted for the purpose of signifying the royal assent to bills in Parliament, except with respect to specified bills, which have passed both Houses at the date of the commission.[c]

Absence of sovereign from the realm.

The most general delegation by the crown of its political power has been that which has taken place from time to time in the appointment, by the sovereign, of Lords Justices and Guardians for the administration of the government during the absence of the sovereign from the realm. The powers granted to such persons have usually included every possible exercise of the royal authority, except that of assenting to bills in Parliament, and of granting peerages. But it has been customary to accompany the commission by instructions, requiring the commissioners not to exercise certain of the powers granted (particularly those for the pardon of offenders and the dissolution of Parliament) without special signification of the royal pleasure. During the long reign of George III., the sovereign was never absent from England; and his son and successor, George IV., went abroad once only, in the year 1821, when Lords Justices were appointed by his Majesty in Council. After the accession of the present Queen, her Majesty, in the year 1843, paid a short visit to the King of the French at the Château d'Eu; and again, in 1845, visited Germany. Upon both these occasions, the opinion of the law-officers of the crown was taken, as to whether there was any legal necessity for the issue of a commission appointing Lords Justices during her Majesty's absence. Each time the law-officers were clearly of opinion that it was unnecessary. The question then resolved itself into one of expediency; and considering the great facilities for speedy communication afforded by the general introduction of the railway system, and the circumstance that her Majesty would necessarily be accompanied by a secretary

---

[b] Cox, Eng. Govt. pp. 614 617.   [c] *Ibid.* p. 49.

of state, and could therefore perform any royal act required of her with as much validity and effect on the continent of Europe as if it were done in her own dominions, the ministry decided that it was quite unnecessary to advise the appointment of Lords Justices, 'really for no practical purpose.'[a] Royal visits abroad have since been of no infrequent occurrence, and as no appointment of Lords Justices has taken place upon such occasions, the practice may be considered to have fallen into desuetude.[b]

It is essential to the due execution of any powers by delegation from the crown, that a special authority, under the royal sign-manual, should be issued for the purpose. This was a difficulty that presented itself in the year 1788, arising out of the melancholy condition of George III., who was first attacked by insanity at that time.

Royal functions in abeyance during illness of George III.

The mental disorder which afflicted the king was of such a serious character, that it rendered it imperative upon Parliament to take immediate steps to supply the defect in the royal authority for so long a period as the king's illness might continue. Parliament then stood prorogued for a particular day, upon which, under ordinary circumstances, it is probable that it would not have assembled. But, taking advantage of the authority of the royal proclamation, ministers determined to meet Parliament without further delay, and deliberate upon the posture of affairs. After full enquiries had been instituted, by both Houses, into the state of his Majesty's health, they agreed to a resolution, that it was the right and duty of the Lords and Commons assembled in Parliament to provide for the exercise of the royal authority, in such manner as the exigency of the case might appear to require. It was then resolved, by both Houses, that it was expedient and necessary that letters-patent for opening Parliament should pass under the Great Seal. This was done accordingly;

---

[a] Lord Chancellor Lyndhurst, in Hans. Deb. August 7, 1845.   [b] Campbell's Chanc. vol. iv. p. 128, n.

and, so far as was possible, under these painful and unprecedented circumstances, the usual forms for the opening of Parliament were adhered to, notwithstanding the incapacity of the sovereign.[f] But in the proceedings had upon this occasion, the two leading statesmen, Pitt and Fox, with their respective followers, were at issue. Pitt contended that Parliament alone was competent to make good the deficiency in the executive authority; whilst Fox claimed for the Prince of Wales an inherent moral, if not legal, right to assume the crown, as though the king his father were actually dead. A succinct account of this memorable controversy, will be found in 'May's Constitutional History.'[g] It will suffice here to state the general results arrived at, so far as they establish an important point of constitutional law.[h]

Proceedings to supply defect in the kingly office.

It was argued by Mr. Pitt, who was then prime minister, that in conformity with the principles established by the Revolution of 1688, and by the Bill of Rights, the Lords and Commons represented the whole estates of the people, and were, therefore, legally as well as constitutionally, empowered to supply any deficiency in the kingly office, whensoever that should arise; that this assumption of power was not incompatible with the principle of an hereditary monarchy, but was essential as a safeguard of the throne itself against encroachment from any quarter. Having succeeded in obtaining the concurrence of

---

[f] Parl. Hist. vol. xxvii. p. 675, et seq.

[g] Vol. i. pp. 146–162. See also Sir G. C. Lewis, in Edinb. Rev. vol. ciii. p. 320.

[h] The decision of Parliament upon this great question was given exactly one hundred years after the determination, by the same authority, of another question, of still more importance, affecting the right of succession to the English throne—viz., the devolution of the crown upon the 'abdication' of James II., which took place in the year 1688. For those who are curious in such points, it may also be noted that exactly ten years elapsed between the births of the following statesmen, all of them among the most prominent characters of this remarkable era:—Mr. Fox was born in 1749; Mr. Pitt and Lord Grenville in 1759; the Duke of Wellington, Lord Castlereagh, and Napoleon Bonaparte, in 1769. (Sir G. C. Lewis, in Edinb. Rev. vol. cviii. p. 312, n.) Moreover, William IV. signed the draft of the Reform Bill on January 31, 1831, the anniversary of the martyrdom of Charles I.

Parliament to these conclusions, Mr. Pitt admitted that, as a matter of discretion, the Prince of Wales ought to be called upon to assume the Regency, with all necessary authority, unrestrained by any permanent council, and with a free choice of his political servants. But he contended that any power which was not essential, and which might be employed to embarrass the exercise of the king's authority, in the event of his recovery, should be withheld. This was strenuously opposed by Fox, who maintained that the Regent ought to possess the full authority and prerogatives of the crown, without any diminution. Parliament, however, agreed to the views propounded by Mr. Pitt, and the Prince of Wales consented to accept the Regency upon these terms. The proposed restrictions upon the exercise of the regal authority by the prince were defined and embodied in a bill, which it was intended should be passed by both Houses, and receive the royal assent 'by a commission to be ordered by the two Houses of Parliament, in the king's name.' The bill actually passed the Commons, but during its progress through the Lords the king's convalescence was announced, and the bill was dropped.

In 1801 the king was threatened with a return of insanity, and the premier, Mr. Addington, had determined to follow the precedent established in 1788, when, happily, the king's recovery rendered any such proceedings unnecessary.[1] But in 1810, the king's malady again showed itself, this time destined to remain, and to terminate only with his life. Mr. Spencer Perceval was prime minister at this juncture, and he decided to adhere strictly to the precedent afforded by the proceedings in 1788, in every essential particular.[1] The ministerial plan was warmly opposed in Parliament, but was carried, nevertheless, without alteration. The Opposition did not then maintain that the Prince of Wales, as heir-apparent,

Return of the king's malady.

---

[1] Pellew's Life of Sidmouth, vol. I. p. 347.   [2] Edinb. Rev. vol. cviii. p. 329.

succeeded of right to the Regency during the king's incapacity. But Mr. Lambe (afterwards Lord Melbourne) —upon the resolution that certain restrictions should be imposed upon the Regent—moved an amendment, 'That the entire royal power should be conferred upon him, without any restrictions.' This amendment was negatived, by a majority of 224 to 200. Lord Brougham remarks upon these two precedents that they 'have now settled the constitutional law and practice in this important particular.'[1]

Royal sign-manual, when dispensed with.

If at any time the sovereign should be unable, through physical infirmity, to append the royal sign-manual to the multifarious papers which require his signature, the intervention of Parliament must be invoked to give legal effect to the arrangements necessary under the circumstances. In the last year of the reign of George IV., an Act was passed authorising his Majesty to appoint one or more persons to affix his royal signature to papers, the state of the king's health being such as to render it painful and inconvenient for him to sign his own name.[1] And in 1862, with a view to relieve her Majesty from the excessive labour of signing every separate commission for officers of the army, marines, &c., after having already signed a 'submission paper' authorising the issue of such commission, an Act was passed empowering the Queen in Council to direct that the said commissions may be signed by the commander-in-chief and a secretary of state, and to dispense with the necessity for the royal signature being appended thereto.[m] The urgency for this relief will be apparent when it is stated that in 1862 her

---

[1] Sketches of Statesmen, vol. i. p. 170. Notwithstanding the authority of Lord Brougham, his successor, Lord Campbell, adheres to the Whig doctrine in regard to this question, and stoutly maintains that the Imperial Parliament had no right to interfere with the assumption by the Prince of Wales of the regal authority during the incapacity of the king, his father; but should have imitated the example of the Irish Parliament, in 1789, in acknowledging the right of the prince, and in addressing him to take upon himself the government as regent. (Campbell's Chanc. vol. v. p. 337, vi. 180, 583, vii. 90. See a debate in the House of Commons on the Regency question, on July 6, 1830.)

[1] 11 Geo. IV. & 1 Will. IV. c. 23.

[m] 25 Vict. c. 4. See the debates on this Bill, in Hansard, vol. clxv.; and ibid. vol. clxxvi. p. 2030.

Majesty was signing commissions of 1858, and that up to the time when an Order in Council was issued to permit the commander-in-chief and the secretary of state to sign on her behalf, there were 15,931 commissions remaining unsigned. The arrears are now cleared off; but the Queen still undertakes to sign first commissions, and these had so accumulated, that up to 1st June, 1865, there were 4,800 first commissions awaiting her signature. But arrangements have since been made to prevent the recurrence of such delays.*

The preeminence of the king, by virtue of his prerogative, is such that he cannot be sued in any court, either civilly or criminally. Nevertheless, the law has provided a remedy for injuries proceeding from the crown which affect the rights of property; as where it is alleged that the crown is in wrongful possession of property to which the subject has a legal title, or of money which by contract is due to the subject from the crown, and where there is an absence of an appropriate compulsory remedy against the crown.* It cannot be presumed that the crown would knowingly be a party to the injury of a subject, yet it might commit injustice by misinformation or inadvertency, through the medium of some responsible agent. It is therefore fitting that the subject should be authorised to represent to the sovereign, in a respectful manner, the nature of the alleged grievance, in order to enable a remedy to be applied. This remedy is by means of a Petition of Right, a mode of procedure the origin of which has been traced back to the stat. 14 Edw. III. c. 14, if not to Magna Charta itself.*

<small>Petition of Right.</small>

---

* Rep. Com. Pub. Accounts, 1865; Evid. 2010–2003, 2118–2127. Hans. Deb. vol. clxxx. p. 973.
* Attorney-General Palmer, Hans. Deb. vol. clxxvi. p. 2120.
* Broom, Const. Law, pp. 241, 726 (k); Cox, Eng. Govt. p. 410. For the present procedure see *Scott* v. *The Queen*, in Foster and Finlason's Nisi Prius Cases, vol. ii. p. 634. It has been held that a Petition of Right does not lie to recover compensation from the crown for damage to the property of an individual occasioned by the negligence of the servants of the crown (*Viscount Canterbury* v. *The Attorney-General*, 1 Phill. p. 306), nor to recover compensation for a

Petitions of Right.

The law in regard to Petitions of Right has been recently amended and simplified by the Act 23 & 24 Vict. c. 34. The object of this Act is to assimilate the procedure upon such petitions as much as possible to that which is adopted in cases between subject and subject, and to permit Petitions of Right to be entertained by any of the superior courts of law or equity at Westminster. It provides that any such petition shall be left with the secretary of state for the home department, in order that the same may be submitted for her Majesty's consideration. If she think fit, the Queen will grant her fiat that right be done, when the merits of the suit will be investigated by the proper court, and judgment given according to law.

It is a mistake to suppose that whenever a Petition of Right is presented, the sovereign should be advised to write upon it *soit droit fait*, whatever may be its prayer, leaving it to the courts to decide whether it contains any grounds for relief. By the law and constitution of England a suit cannot be maintained against the sovereign, without the express consent of the crown. That consent cannot properly be withheld when sufficient foundation or *primâ facie* groundwork for the claim put forth has, in the statement of facts on behalf of the petitioner, been adduced;[*] but it ought to be withheld, by advice of the attorney-general, where it is clear that no relief can be afforded. The attorney-general is answerable to Parliament for the advice he may give as to the granting or withholding of a Petition of Right, in like manner as he would be in respect to the granting of a writ of error, or a *nolle prosequi*.[t]

In the recent case of Mr. G. O'Malley Irwin, it was contended by

---

wrongful act done by a servant of the crown in the supposed performance of his duty (*Tobin v. The Queen*, Com. Bench Rep. N. S. vol. xvi. p. 310). Public officers are themselves personally liable under the law and constitution for any dereliction of duty. —*Attorney-General*, in Hans. Deb. vol. clxxvi. p. 2121.

[t] Broom's Legal Maxims, p. 81, n.
[*] Campbell's Chancellors, vol. vii. p. 408, n.

Sir Fitzroy Kelly (ex-attorney-general), in his place in Parliament, that 'it was not competent or consistent with the duty of any officer of the crown to advise the Queen to withhold her fiat to any Petition of Right, upon any ground, whether right or wrong, whether well or ill-founded. Such an interference was only to be justified in a case where a petition appeared to be founded on fraud, or upon gross and manifest error.' In reply, the solicitor-general (Sir Roundell Palmer) stated, that he was prepared to show that Mr. Irwin's petition 'had been presented in gross and manifest error, and that no minister could be justified in advising the crown to give its fiat to that so-called Petition of Right.'* Previous to this discussion in the House of Commons, Mr. Irwin brought an action in the Court of Common Pleas against Sir George Grey, the secretary of state for the home department, to recover damages for his having refused or neglected to present to her Majesty his Petition of Right in relation to certain claims upon the crown to the extent of 100,000l., for alleged damages sustained by reason of a prosecution against him in Ireland.' The case was tried before the lord chief justice and a special jury, in December 1862. Sir George Grey stated that he had presented Mr. Irwin's petition to the Queen, with the advice that it should not be granted; that he had acted on the advice of the then attorney-general, Sir R. Bethell, and that the plaintiff had been duly informed of the result. The lord chief justice then told the jury that if they believed the home secretary's statement—that he had presented the petition to the Queen, 'accompanied with certain advice which he, as a responsible minister of the crown, considered it to be his duty to give,' he had been guilty of no breach of duty,—it became their duty to give a verdict for the defendant. The jury at once declared that they believed the statement, and gave their verdict for the defendant accordingly.* Subsequently, the plaintiff moved for a new trial on the ground of misdirection, but took nothing by his motion, the court being of opinion that the question as to the nature of the advice given to the crown by the secretary of state ought not to have been answered. The only thing for the

---

Mr. Irwin's case

---

* Hans. Deb. vol. clxxii. p. 1.74. On July 20, 1854, a motion was made in the House of Commons for an address to the Queen that she would be pleased to grant her fiat to the Petition of Right of Mr. O'Malley Irwin, or to satisfy his claims without suit. But the attorney-general reviewed the facts of the case, showed that Mr. Irwin's claims were frivolous and untenable, and declared that if the law-officers had put their fiat on his petition, they would have adopted a different course to that pursued by their predecessors in office, and would have given advice the tendency of which must have been most pernicious. After a short debate, the motion was negatived.

* See comments on this case, in Tobin v. The Queen, Common Bench Rep. N. S. vol. xvi. p. 328.

* Dublin Evening Post, December 6, 1862. And see Index to The Times for 1863, verbo *Irwin, Mr.*

court to enquire into was whether the Petition of Right had been presented to the Queen by the home secretary, and advice tendered to her Majesty thereupon. But 'the advice he gave ought not to have been divulged.'[*]

The foregoing case has established the point that the advice to be given to the crown, by its responsible ministers, upon a Petition of Right, is discretionary; and that ministers are responsible for the same to the sovereign and to Parliament, but not to the ordinary courts of law.[w]

Personal immunity of the sovereign.

It has been already stated, as a constitutional principle, 'that the personal actions of the sovereign, not being acts of government, are not under the cognizance of law;' and that as an individual he is independent of, and not amenable to, any earthly power or jurisdiction.[x] A few remarks on this point will be appropriate. The best authorities have declared that there is no legal remedy obtainable by the subject for personal acts of tyranny and oppression on the part of the sovereign which have not been instigated by bad advisers, but have proceeded from the personal misconduct of the monarch himself. Should any such cases occur, so far as the ordinary course of law is concerned, they would be covered by the maxim which forbids the imputation of wrong to the sovereign,[y] and the erring prince must be left to the rebukes of his own conscience, and to his personal accountability to God alone. No decisions in regard to common criminal offences committed by any English king are to be found in the books; the jurists contending that the case of a sovereign being guilty of a common crime must be treated as the laws of Solon treated parricide,—it must be considered an impossibility.[z] It was truly observed by Locke, in his essay on 'Government,' that the inconveniency of some particular mischiefs that may happen

---

[*] See the case, in Foster and Finlason's Nisi Prius Cases, iii. 540.
[w] See also, to the same effect, the case of *Dickson* v. *Viscount Combermere and others*, Foster and Finla-son, vol. iii. p. 527.
[x] See *ante*, p. 108.
[y] Broom's Legal Maxims, p. 63.
[z] Fischel, Eng. Con-t. p. 129.

sometimes, when a heady prince comes to the throne, are well recompensed by the peace and public security which result from the person of the chief magistrate being set out of the reach of danger.[a]

The curious question, whether the sovereign is examinable as a witness, has been discussed by Lord Campbell, who asserts 'that the sovereign, if so pleased, might be examined as a witness in any case, civil or criminal, but that he must be sworn; although there would be no temporal sanction to the oath,' inasmuch as he is the fountain of justice, and no wrong may be imputed to him.[b]

The sovereign as a witness.

---

[a] Book II. section 205. And see Cox, Eng. Govt. pp. 408–410.
[b] Lives of the Chancellors, vol. ii. p. 527. How far the king is bound in his private capacity to undertake municipal charges or offices is said to be doubtful. George III. was nominated churchwarden of St. Martin's, and the parishioners absurdly threatened to bring an action to compel him to assume the functions! He accepted the office, and got himself represented by deputy. Fischel, p. 135, n. And see Cox, Eng. Govt. p. 248, n.

CHAPTER V.

THE ROYAL PREROGATIVE IN CONNECTION WITH PARLIAMENT.

Prerogative defined.

THE term Prerogative may be defined as expressing those political powers which are inherent in the crown, and that have not been conferred by Act of Parliament.[a] Nevertheless, the king's prerogative is a part of the law of the realm, and hath bounds set unto it by the laws of England.[b]

The prerogatives of the sovereign of Great Britain are of vast extent and paramount importance. In the crown is centred the whole executive power of the empire, the functions appertaining to the administration of government, and supreme authority in all matters—civil, judicial, military, and ecclesiastical.

The king is, moreover, the head of the legislature, of which he forms an essential constituent part; the generalissimo, or first in command, of the naval and military forces of the state; the fountain of honour and of justice, and the dispenser of mercy, having a right to pardon all convicted criminals; the supreme head of the national church; and the representative of the majesty of the realm abroad, with power to declare war, to make peace, and to enter into treaty engagements with foreign countries.

It is beside the object of the present writer to consider the prerogatives of the crown in their legal aspect: full information on this subject will be found in the works of Chitty and Bowyer on Prerogative. The present enquiry is confined to an investigation of the prerogative from a

---

[a] Cox, Inst. p. 592. [b] Coke, 3 St. Tri. p. 68.

constitutional point of view, in reference more particularly to the legitimate control of Parliament over the exercise of the same on the part of ministers of state. For it must be observed, of all the royal prerogatives, that they are held in trust for the benefit of the whole nation, and must be exercised in conformity with the constitutional maxim, which requires that every act of the royal authority should be performed by the advice of councillors who are responsible to Parliament, and to the law of the land.ᵉ This responsibility is now acknowledged to be thorough and complete; and as no public act of the sovereign is valid which is not performed under the advice of some responsible minister, so, on the other hand, for every exercise of the royal authority, ministers must be prepared to account to Parliament, justifying the same, if need be, at their own peril. *(marginal note: Responsibility of ministers for every exercise of the prerogative.)*

The advisers of the crown are responsible not merely for the legality, but also for the policy and wisdom, of every measure of government. Having so vast a trust reposed in them, they are bound to use their best endeavours, irrespective of all party claims or personal advantages, to administer the affairs of the kingdom for the public good, and for the honour and credit of their sovereign.

In conducting the necessary measures of government through the Houses of Parliament, it is the duty of ministers to shield the crown from personal obloquy, to avoid all reference to the expressed opinions of their royal master for the purpose of influencing the freedom of debate, and to assume themselves an entire responsibility for the administration of public affairs in all its details.

It is proposed, in the present chapter, to examine, in detail, the leading prerogatives of the crown, which are now exercised upon the advice of responsible ministers,

---

ᵉ See *ante*, p. 100; Lord Palmerston, Hans. Deb. vol. cliii. p. 1415.

and to point out the authority of Parliament in relation thereto. In every instance, after defining the limit within which the subjection of the prerogative in question to parliamentary supervision and control is justifiable, a selection of precedents will be given, in illustration of the views set forth in the text. Before entering upon this enquiry, however, it will be necessary to consider, briefly, the relations between the Crown and the Parliament itself.

Parliament.

The Parliament of Great Britain is composed of the king (or queen) and the three estates of the realm—to wit, the Lords spiritual, the Lords temporal, and the Commons. In its collective capacity, Parliament exercises supreme authority in and over the empire, to which the constitution has assigned no limit. In the words of Sir Edward Coke, the power of Parliament 'is so transcendent and absolute that it cannot be confined, either for causes and persons, within any bounds.'

Its dependence upon the crown.

From the supremacy of the sovereign in a constitutional monarchy, it necessarily follows, that while regular meetings of Parliament are indispensable, the legal existence of this high court results altogether from the exercise of the royal prerogative. It is summoned, by virtue of the king's writ, to meet for despatch of business, at whatsoever time [d] or place he may please to direct. It can only commence its deliberations at the time appointed by the king, and cannot continue them any longer than he may allow. The deliberations of Parliament may be cut short at any moment by the exercise of the royal power of prorogation, which quashes all proceedings pending at the time, except impeachments by the Commons, writs of error and appeals before the House of Lords, and

---

[d] In 1858, an informal discussion arose in the House of Commons, in which it was suggested that it would be desirable to have meetings of Parliament in the autumn, so as to secure a prorogation early in the summer. (Hans. Deb. vol. cli. pp. 1185, 1198). Next session, an address to the crown to this effect was proposed, and negatived, after a short debate.—*Ibid.* vol. clv. p. 51.

trials in progress before election committees. By a prorogation, all resolutions,[e] bills,[f] and other proceedings, pending in either House, are naturally terminated, and cease to have any further effect, except in so far as they may be continued in operation under the authority of an Act of Parliament. The statutable provision in regard to the meeting of Parliament merely requires that no longer a period than three years shall elapse between the determination of one Parliament and the issue of writs for another.[g] Nevertheless, by constitutional practice, the annual assembly of Parliament has become necessary. Supplies for the public service are annually voted, and

---

[e] Commons' Papers, 1861, vol. xi. p. 430. The only apparent exception to this rule is in the case of standing orders. By the custom of Parliament these are accounted to be in force, in succeeding sessions, until rescinded. They are considered as being declaratory of the law and practice of Parliament; and, without relying upon their absolute validity, the House agrees to adhere to their observance. (May, Parl. Prac. p. 182. Commons' Papers, 1850, Sess. 1, vol. iii. p. 37. Com. on the Jews' Act, Hans. Deb. vol. ciii. p. 402.)

[f] A proposal that a power should be given by statute, to either House of Parliament, of suspending (at any stage of proceeding) bills which shall have been passed by the other House, and of resuming such bills in the succeeding session at the precise stage where they had been dropped, was rejected by a committee of the House of Commons, in 1861, on account of 'the grave and numerous objections' to it, and particularly because 'this suspending power in either House of Parliament, if exercised at its own discretion, would be at variance with the prerogative of the crown.' (Commons' Papers, 1861, vol. xi. p. 430; and see Lord Redesdale's objections to this proposal, Hans. Deb. vol. clxi. p. 185.) But in the case of private bills generally, or of railway bills in particular, relief has been repeatedly granted to the parties concerned in promoting or opposing such measures, when a session of Parliament has been brought to a sudden and premature close, on account of the exigencies of political warfare. This was done by the adoption, in both Houses, of resolutions, permitting such bills to be re-introduced in the following session, and by means of pro formâ and unopposed motions advanced to the stages at which they severally stood when the prorogation took place. (See Com. Journals for 1841, vol. lxxxvi. pt. 2, p. 525. Mirror of Parl. 1841, pp. 2331, 2340. Hans. Deb. vol. cxliv. p. 2200; ibid. vol. cliii. pp. 1524, 1007.) It was suggested, in the session of 1865, that on account of the great mass of private business before Parliament, and the desirability of an early prorogation, with a view to an immediate dissolution, similar resolutions should be agreed to; but the case was not deemed sufficiently urgent and unexpected to warrant such a course, which should only be resorted to when the session has been brought to an abrupt and premature termination. (Hans. Deb. vol. clxxx. pp. 832, 851.)

[g] 16 Chas. II. c. 1; 6 & 7 W. & M. c. 2; 2 Hats. 262.

the Acts for the control of the army and navy are limited in their duration to one year, and must be renewed before the expiration of that time.[b]

Opening of Parliament.

In order to give life and existence to a Parliament, and to enable it to proceed to the execution of its functions, the personal presence or delegated authority of the crown is required for the formal opening of the session. At the beginning of every new Parliament, and of every session after a prorogation, the cause of summons must be declared to both Houses, either by the sovereign in person, or by commissioners appointed to represent him, in a speech from the throne: until this has been done neither House can enter upon any business.[c] The act of the Commons in choosing a speaker is no exception to this rule, for they are specially empowered to make choice of a presiding officer by command of the sovereign, who refrains from making known the purpose for which Parliament has been convened until the Commons are completely organised, by the election of their speaker.

Independence of Parliament.

But when once Parliament has been formally opened, by the declaration of the causes of summons, each branch of the legislature has a separate and distinct jurisdiction; and business may be entered upon by either House, in conformity with its recognised rules, usages, and customs, irrespective of the royal will and pleasure. It is an ancient and undoubted privilege of the two Houses of Parliament, after the speech from the throne has been delivered, to proceed upon any matter, at their discretion or convenience, without giving priority to the discussion of the topics included in the royal speech. As a deliberate assertion of this right, both Houses invariably read a bill a first time, *pro forma*, before they enter upon the consideration of the speech; and there are many instances of their postponing the consideration of the same in favour of other business for one or more days.[d]

---

[b] May, Parl. Prac. p. 520.
[c] 2 Hats. pp. 308, 327.
[d] Ibid. p. 300. May, Parl. p. 45.

Formal communications between the sovereign and Parliament, in the shape of royal speeches or messages, and the interposition of the authority of the crown to effect the adjournment, prorogation, or dissolution of Parliament—which heretofore emanated from the mere personal will of the reigning monarch,—are, under our present constitutional system, considered as the acts of the queen's responsible advisers. Ever since the introduction of ministers into Parliament, they have been held directly responsible for every exercise of the royal authority. The recognition of this principle has produced important changes in the relations between Crown and Parliament. While the outward ceremonial remains unaltered, a greater harmony and freedom both of action and intercourse has been brought about between the executive and the legislature. The sovereign is no longer called upon to perform ungracious acts towards his Parliament, or held individually accountable for a policy which is distasteful to that august body. If bills are introduced into either House that are disapproved of by the crown, the royal veto need not be invoked for their rejection; but after they have undergone the fullest and freest discussion, the constitutional influence of ministers generally suffices to control their fate.[1] If it be necessary, on the other hand, to propose for the acceptance of Parliament the adoption of unpopular measures, ministers are at hand to explain and defend them, upon their personal responsibility. And if it be impossible to continue to carry on the government successfully without appealing from the House of Commons to the constituent body, ministers of the crown are themselves responsible for the act of dissolution.

The opinions of either House of Parliament are

---

[1] The royal veto upon bills in Parliament has not been exercised for upwards of 150 years; nevertheless, its continued existence is undoubted, and circumstances might at any time arise that would justify the crown in resorting thereto. (See Hans. Deb. vol. cxl. p. 284.) And see *Bid.* vol. cli. p. 568, and *ante*, p. 7.

Resolutions of Parliament.

constitutionally expressed either by means of an address of advice or remonstrance to the crown, or by their agreement to a bill to add to, alter, or repeal an existing law. But no mere resolution of either House has any legal validity, except in so far as it records the opinion of the House upon some matter which comes within the sphere of its acknowledged authority, as a component branch of the legislature, to determine.

For example, either House of Parliament may resolve that its privileges have been infringed in a particular instance. But it cannot enforce a claim of privilege beyond the limits of acknowledged precedent.[1] It may declare the expediency of an alteration of the law in a given direction, but it can only give effect to its opinions by the regular method of parliamentary procedure—that is to say, by the introduction and passing of a bill, which is assented to by the other branches of the legislature.

Cannot dispense with an existing law.

No mere resolution of either House, or joint resolution of the two Houses, will suffice to dispense with the requirements of an Act of Parliament, even although it may relate to something which directly concerns but one chamber of the legislature. The effect of a parliamentary resolution in a matter of administration will be presently considered. But, first, it will be expedient to notice one or two cases explanatory of the principle above mentioned.

Jews in Parliament.

The House of Lords having repeatedly refused to agree to certain bills passed by the Commons for the admission of Jews to a seat in Parliament, in the year 1857 a select committee was appointed by the House of Commons, to consider whether the House had not the power of itself, under the Act 5 & 6 Will. 4, c. 62, to admit Jews to the privilege of membership, by substituting a declaration in lieu of the oath prescribed by law, which oath contained

---

[1] See the decisions of the Judges, cited in May, Parl. Prac. p. 102, &c.; also the proceedings in the case of *Stockdale* v. *Hansard* (ibid. p. 170), wherein the House of Commons laid claim to a privilege which the courts of law disputed; the matter was finally settled by the passing of an Act (3 & 4 Vict. c. 9), legalizing the action of either House of Parliament in regard to the main question at issue.

words ('upon the true faith of a Christian') that rendered it unsuitable to, and impossible to be taken by, a Jew. The committee was presided over by Lord John Russell, who, together with the attorney-general (Sir R. Bethell), was inclined to the opinion that the legal power to administer a declaration to a person objecting to take the oath, was possessed by the House of Commons,* although it was confessedly undesirable to use that power until all other constitutional remedies had been tried. But the majority of the committee was against this opinion, whereupon the committee agreed to report to the House as follows:—'The following resolution was proposed by a member of the committee: That, in the opinion of this committee, the House of Commons is included within the following words of the 8th section of 5 & 6 Will. 4, c. 62, that is to say, "All bodies now by law, or statute, or by any valid usage, authorised to administer or receive any oath" [may make order, &c. authorising and directing the substitution of a declaration in lieu of any oath]. Upon deliberation, the resolution passed in the negative.'ᵇ Notwithstanding the able arguments made use of to induce the House to assert a claim to settle this controversy by its own act, and the eminent men by whom this claim was advocated, the House of Commons refrained from the attempt. But the probability that a continued resistance on this point might lead to a serious conflict between the two Houses, and possibly between the courts of law and the House of Commons, induced the House of Lords, in 1858, to pass a Bill empowering either House to agree to a resolution admitting Jews to sit and vote, upon their taking a suitable declaration, in lieu of the oath imposed by law.ᶜ This compromise was agreed to by the other House, and the vexed question was thus finally determined, so far as the admission of Jews to a seat in the House of Commons was concerned. No such resolution, however, was ever adopted by the House of Lords. Nevertheless, by an Act passed in 1866, the oath required to be taken by members of both Houses of Parliament was altered, so as to omit the words 'on the true faith of a Christian,' thereby rendering a Jew eligible for a seat in either House.ᵈ

In 1866, when immediate legislation was called for, to stay the ravages of the cattle plague, and yet the question itself was beset with so many difficulties as to render it impossible for Parliament to

Cattle Plague.

---

* Thus, in 1833, Mr. Pease, a Quaker, was admitted by the House to sit and vote, upon making affirmation instead of the oaths directed to be taken by law. This course was adopted upon a general construction of the statutes permitting Quakers to make affirmation in lieu of being sworn (May, Parl. Prac. p. 190). But the introduction of Jews into Parliament in a similar way would have been a violation of the principle of Christianity, as recognised in all the statutes upon the subject of oaths.

ᵇ Commons' Papers, 1857, Sess. 2, vol. ix. p. 477; and see May, Parl. Prac. p. 193.

ᶜ Hans. Deb. vol. cli. p. 1372.

ᵈ 21 & 22 Vict. c. 49.

ᵉ 29 Vict. c. 19.

agree to a measure without patient and careful consideration of the whole matter, it was suggested by the Earl of Derby, that general resolutions should be adopted by both Houses of Parliament, authorising the government to deal with the subject by Orders in Council, upon certain main principles to be laid down in the resolutions, such orders to remain in force until Parliament had matured a Bill upon the subject. But Earl Russell (the premier) and Earl Grey both objected that this would be a dangerous and unwarrantable proceeding. Accordingly, it was not pressed upon the consideration of the House.[r]

Abstract resolutions, objectionable.

In the ordinary course of procedure, resolutions of either House of Parliament should be the embodiment of opinions, or facts, as a basis or preliminary step towards some proximate parliamentary action. Mere abstract resolutions upon any question, while they are too commonly regarded as allowable weapons in the exigencies of party-warfare, are undoubtedly open to grave objection. They are generally made use of to assert a principle, perhaps undeniable in itself, but which it would be impossible or inexpedient to carry out at the time. They have, accordingly, a tendency to fetter the present action of government, and to impede the current of useful legislation in future. Upon these grounds the most eminent statesmen have concurred in condemning them.[s] Upon the occasion of the debate on a question of this kind, in 1865, Mr. Gladstone said: 'I have never concealed my strong opinion that a resolution of this House, unless relating to a matter of grievance, or recommending the reduction of a burden oppressive to the community, does not demand great consideration from the government.'[t]

Prerogative of administration.

The prerogative that will first engage our attention is that which concerns the executive authority of the crown in the administration of public affairs. This prerogative is of such widespread and extensive operation, as to include, in a certain sense, every other. Our remarks in

---

[r] Hans. Deb. vol. clxxxi. pp. 441-445, 503.

[s] Lord Althorp and Lord Stanley (Earl of Derby), Mirror of Parl. 1836, p. 682; Sir R. Peel, *ibid.* 1840, p. 3524; Marquess of Lansdowne, Hans. Deb. vol. xciv. p. 177; Mr. Cardwell, *ibid.* vol. cxxv. p. 616; Mr. Disraeli, *ibid.* vol. cli. p. 126; Mr. Gladstone, *ibid.* vol. clxi. p. 1448.

[t] *Ibid.* vol. clxxviii. p. 58.

reference thereto, and the authorities cited, will accordingly be of general application, and will contribute, it may be hoped, to the solution of any question that may arise out of the constitutional relations between the Crown and Parliament.

Our comments upon this prerogative are divisible into four heads:—I. General principles which govern the relations between Ministers of the Crown and the two Houses of Parliament in matters of administration, with precedents illustrative thereof. II. The practice of Parliament in the appointment of Select Committees to enquire into administrative questions. III. Practice in regard to the granting or withholding, by the Executive, of information desired by either Houses of Parliament. IV. Circumstances which may require the interposition of Parliament to restrain the illegal exercise of executive authority; in relation (more especially) to (1) Orders in Council and Royal Proclamations: (2) Minutes of Committees of Council, and other departmental regulations: (3) Contracts entered into by Public Departments: (4) Illegal or oppressive acts by individual Ministers.

I. GENERAL PRINCIPLES WHICH GOVERN THE RELATIONS BETWEEN THE CROWN AND PARLIAMENT, IN MATTERS OF ADMINISTRATION.

Freedom of speech in Parliament is an essential part of the liberties of Englishmen. This privilege was guaranteed by the Bill of Rights, and it includes a license to discuss all matters affecting the public welfare, whether the same have been formally commended by the crown to the consideration of Parliament, or not. From the time of Edward III. to our own day, Parliament has freely exercised the right of tendering advice to the sovereign, unasked, upon matters the final determination of which appertained to the sovereign alone. The House of Lords, as representing the ancient Great Council of the realm, always possessed this right; and after the House of Commons arose, its position, as the Grand Inquest of the kingdom, justified it

Parliament may advise the crown in any matter.

in claiming similar privileges. The two Houses of Parliament collectively represent the whole community, and are the Great Council of the nation, while 'ministers are merely the council of the prince.'[a] They are, therefore, entitled to approach the sovereign with advice or remonstrance upon all affairs of state, and in regard to every grievance under which any subjects of the realm may be suffering. But it is equally necessary to remember that Parliament is designed for counsel and not for rule—for advice, and not for administration. There are some prerogatives into the exercise of which the Houses of Parliament must ordinarily refrain from intermeddling, lest their intrusion should be equivalent to an unwarrantable interference with executive functions.

Free exercise of executive functions.

The true responsibility of ministers depends upon their freedom in exercising the lawful authority of the crown. Without freedom of action there can be no genuine responsibility. It is this which renders it so essential to the successful working of parliamentary government that ministers should be sustained by a predominant party in the legislature, who are prepared, on general grounds of public policy, to approve their acts, and to assume a measure of responsibility for their conduct in office.[b] De Lolme, in anticipating the events that would be likely to destroy the fair fabric of the English constitution, strikingly remarks that, 'when the representatives of the people shall begin to share in the executive authority,' the government will be overthrown.[c]

How controlled by Parliament.

Great weight must necessarily be attributed to the opinions of either House of Parliament on public affairs; but, under ordinary circumstances, those opinions are constitutionally expressed by the degree of support they consent to afford to the ministers of the crown in the conduct of the government. If the Queen's ministers possess the confidence of Parliament, it is inexpedient and

---

[a] Rt. Hon. C. W. Wynn, Mirror of Parl. 1835, p. 1583.

[b] Edinb. Review, vol. cviii. p. 285.

[c] De Lolme, Const. book ii. ch. 10. And see Cox, Inst. p. 3.

unwise, as a general rule, to interfere with their decisions in regard to the details of administration, except in cases of manifest neglect or misconduct.

This doctrine is strongly insisted upon by the best constitutional authorities. Thus Earl Russell says: 'The two Houses of Parliament constitute the Great Council of the king, and upon whatever subject it is his prerogative to act, it is their privilege and even their duty to advise. Acts of executive government, however, belong to the king.'° And of the House of Commons, Burke says: 'It is their privilege to interfere, by authoritative advice and admonition, upon every act of executive government, without exception.'" In 1784 the House of Commons resolved (in conformity with the report of a select committee to search for precedents on the subject), 'That it is constitutional and agreeable to usage for the House of Commons to declare their sense and opinions respecting the exercise of every discretionary power which, whether by Act of Parliament or otherwise, is vested in any body of men whatsoever for the public service.'°

In 1788, on a motion for enquiring into the conduct of the Admiralty in a certain matter, Mr. Pitt (the prime minister), said : 'That the House had a constitutional power of enquiring into the conduct of any department of the government, with a view either to censure or punishment, was unquestionable ; and whenever a case was made out, strong enough to warrant a suspicion of abuse that deserved either censure or punishment, he should ever hold it to be the indispensable duty of the House to proceed to enquire.' Mr. Fox, on the same occasion, remarked, that 'it was the constitutional province and the undoubted duty of the House to watch over the executive departments, and, where they had cause to suspect abuse, to institute an enquiry, with a view either to censure or punishment.'° And, in 1863, Lord Derby

Right of enquiry.

° Russell, Eng. Const. p. 151.
' Quoted in Rowlands, Eng. Const. p. 400. See also Wyan, in Parl.
Deb. N. S. ii. 300.
° Parl. Hist. vol. xxiv. pp. 634-671.
° Ibid. vol. xxvii. pp. 277, 241.

declared it to be a position which could not be gainsaid, that 'every act done by the responsible ministers of the crown having any political significance is a fit subject for comment and, if necessary, for censure in either House of Parliament.' Earl Russell entirely coincided in this doctrine.[a]

The House of Commons, says May, 'has a right to advise the crown even as to the exercise of the prerogative itself; and should its advice be disregarded, it wields the power of impeachment, and holds the pursestrings of the state.'[b] Admitting, to the fullest extent, the truth of this proposition, it is evident that these extraordinary powers ought not to be evoked except upon a grave emergency: for, as a general principle, it is equally clear that Parliament should confide in the discretion of the responsible advisers of the crown, who are the trustees of the royal prerogative for the rightful administration of the same. So long as Parliament continues its confidence in ministers, it ought to be willing to leave the exercise of the prerogative in their hands, unfettered by restrictions in regard to its exercise, and should refrain from interference therewith, unless under circumstances of imperious necessity. The general responsibility of ministers for the wisdom, policy, and legality of the measures of government should be sufficient guarantee, in all ordinary cases, for the faithful discharge of the high functions entrusted to them. On a recent occasion, Lord Palmerston observed, that 'the ministry of the day were responsible for everything that was done in any department of the state;' and that while 'it was true that the House of Commons ought to have a control and supervision over every such department, its functions were those of

---

[a] Hans. Deb. vol. clxxi. pp. 1720, 1729.
[b] May, Const. Hist. vol. l. p. 458. In like manner, Canning defined the House of Commons to be a council of control, as well as a council of advice; and declared that in cases of adequate importance, especially where the prerogative was concerned, it should endeavour, by the timely interposition of advice, to prevent the necessity of control. (Parl. Deb. vol. xxiii. p. 207.)

control, not of administration.'[d] And Mr. Cobden, to the same effect, gave his opinion 'that the House can interfere with great advantage in prescribing the principles on which the executive government shall be carried on; but beyond that it is impossible for the legislature to interfere with advantage in the details of the administration of the country.'[e]

Any direct interference, by resolution of Parliament, in the details of government is inconsistent with and subversive of the kingly authority, and is a departure from the fundamental principle of the British constitution, which vests all executive authority in the sovereign, while it ensures complete responsibility for the exercise of every act of sovereignty. Experience has uniformly demonstrated the unfitness of large deliberative assemblies for the functions of government. The intrusion of parliamentary committees into matters which appertain to the jurisdiction of the executive government is equally to be deprecated, as it tends inevitably to the overthrow of all genuine responsibility, and the substitution instead of an arbitrary tyrannical power. During the reign of Charles I. the Long Parliament assumed, on the part of its committees, various executive functions; but this is admitted to have been a usurpation, and it is now acknowledged without dispute that all acts of administration belong exclusively to the crown.[f] Accordingly, no resolution of either House of Parliament which attempts to adjudicate in any case that is within the province of the government to determine, has of itself any force or effect. If it be intended merely to express the sense of the House upon some objectionable system or practice

Interference by Parliament in details of government.

---

[d] Hans. Deb. vol. cl. p. 1357; and *Ibid.* vol. clxix. p. 880. And see Professor Austin's observations on this point, *Plea for the Constitution,* p. 24.
[e] Hans. Deb. vol. clxxvi. p. 1000.
[f] Grey, Parl. Govt. new. ed. p. 9 n. 'Parliament does not interfere directly in carrying on the executive government; the supreme executive authority belongs to the crown, nor do the measures adopted by its ministers in the exercise of this authority require the previous sanction of Parliament.' — *Ibid.* p. 22. See Sir C. Wood, in Hans. Deb. vol. clxxv. p. 250. And see a curious case cited, *post,* p. 612.

of administration, or to complain of an existing grievance and suggest a remedy, Parliament is perfectly competent to approach the crown, by address, with advice upon the subject. It then becomes the duty of the government to give respectful consideration to the matter, but nevertheless to decide upon the course to be followed on their own responsibility. Sometimes, indeed, the government themselves invite the assistance of Parliament to institute, by means of select committees, enquiries into questions of administration, for the purpose of obtaining the fullest information to enable them to accomplish some desirable reform. But where the government deprecate interference, or refuse to concur in any such recommendation, the persistence of the House therein would either amount to an infringement of the royal prerogative, or it would be tantamount to a vote of censure upon the existing administration.

Limits of parliamentary control.

'The limits,' says May, 'within which Parliament, or either House, may constitutionally exercise a control over the executive government have been defined by usage upon principles consistent with a true distribution of powers in a free state and limited monarchy. Parliament has no direct control over any single department of the state. It may order the production of papers for its information; it may investigate the conduct of public officers, and may pronounce its opinion upon the manner in which every function of government has been or ought to be discharged; but it cannot convey its orders or directions to the meanest executive officer in relation to the performance of his duty. Its power over the executive is exercised indirectly, but not the less effectively, through the responsible ministers of the Crown. These ministers regulate the duties of every department of the state, and are responsible for their proper performance to Parliament as well as the crown. If Parliament disapprove of any act or policy of the government, ministers must conform to its opinion or forfeit its confidence. In this manner the House of Commons, having become the dominant power of the legislature, has been able to direct the conduct of the government and control its executive administration of public affairs, without exceeding its constitutional powers.'[a]

'Every measure of the ministers of the crown,' says Lord Grey, ' is open to censure in either House ; so that when there is just or even plausible ground for objecting to anything they have done or omitted to do, they cannot escape being called upon to defend their conduct. By this arrangement, those to whom power is entrusted are made to feel that they must use it in such a manner as to be prepared to meet the criticisms of opponents continually on the watch for any errors they may commit, and the whole foreign and domestic policy of the nation is submitted to the ordeal of free discussion.'[b]

Ministers accountable to Parliament.

The following cases may be adduced in illustration of the foregoing doctrine. They are entered in chronological order, a rule which will be generally observed in the series of precedents quoted in this chapter:—

In 1807 a Bill to abolish reversions was passed by the House of Commons, but failed to receive the sanction of the House of Lords: whereupon, on August 10, just before the prorogation, the Commons agreed to an address, nem. con., that his Majesty would be graciously pleased not to grant any office in reversion in any part of the empire until six weeks after the commencement of the next session of Parliament. To this request the king returned a favourable answer. In the following session a new Bill to suspend the granting of offices in reversion for a limited time was brought in, and received the royal assent (48 Geo. III. c. 50). Subsequently a law was passed, depriving the crown of the right to grant offices in reversion.[c]

Precedents. Reversions.

In 1836, on motion of Lord John Russell, then chancellor of the exchequer, the House of Commons passed an address to the king, that he would be pleased to take steps for the effectual discouragement of Orange lodges, and generally of all secret societies. This led to the immediate formal dissolution of the great Orange Society of the United Kingdom.[d]

Orange lodges.

---

[a] May, Const. Hist. vol. i. p. 457.
[b] Parl. Gov. p. 20.
[c] Rep. on Off. Salaries, 1850, p. 32.
[d] Mirror of Parl. 1836, pp. 300, 340. Ann. Reg. 1836, p. 10. And see post, p. 333.

260   THE ROYAL PREROGATIVE

Precedents. On May 17, 1836, on a motion for an address to the crown
Royal commission. that a certain royal commission might be required to report forthwith on a particular portion of their enquiry, Lord John Russell stated that such a proceeding, in regard to an enquiry which was not concluded, would be a very unusual course, and would be, in effect, 'taking out of the hands of the crown the direction of a commission appointed by it.' After a short debate the motion was withdrawn.[h]

Negro apprentices. On May 22, 1838, a resolution was carried against the government, by a majority of three, in favour of the 'immediate' termination of negro apprenticeship in the colonies.[i] The government declined to take any action in carrying out this resolution, and intimated their intention of opposing any Bill that might be introduced to give effect thereto:[m] whereupon the mover of the resolution declined to take any further action in the matter for the time being, but reserved his right to do so whenever he should think fit, leaving the resolution meanwhile to speak for itself.[n] This induced the government, on May 28, to submit to the House a motion that, for certain alleged reasons, 'it is not advisable to adopt any proceeding for the purpose of giving effect to the resolution of May 22.' After a long debate, this motion was agreed to by a majority of 72.[o]

Theatres in Lent. On February 18, 1839, Mr. Duncombe presented a petition to the House of Commons from the lessee, &c. of Drury Lane Theatre, complaining of the restrictions imposed by the lord chamberlain on theatrical performances in the city of Westminster during Lent. He then proposed an address to the Queen, that she would be pleased to direct the removal of these restrictions. This was opposed by government, and after a short debate was negatived on division. However, on February 26, Mr. Duncombe moved to resolve that, in the opinion of the House, the continuance of these restrictions was objectionable. Lord John Russell, on behalf of the government, deprecated an attempt by the House to declare by a resolution in what manner a discretionary power vested in an officer of the crown should be performed; but, notwithstanding, the resolution was agreed to on division.[p] Subsequently Mr. Duncombe complained that this resolution had been disregarded by government, and moved for correspondence on the subject, which was granted.[q] He then proposed (on March 11) a vote of censure on the Queen's ministers for assuming the responsibility of

---

[h] Mirror of Parl. 1836, p. 1521. See also Hans. Deb. vol. xlviii. p. 2083. And see *post*, p. 417.
[i] Mirror of Parl. 1838, pp. 4202–4218.
[m] *Ibid.* pp. 4221, 4244.
[n] *Ibid.* p. 4324.
[o] *Ibid.* p. 4481.
[p] *Ibid.* 1839, p. 625.
[q] *Ibid.* p. 800.

directing the lord chamberlain (who was authorised by statute to regulate theatrical entertainments in Westminster) to continue his obnoxious restrictions in manifest disregard of the resolution of the House. In reply, Lord John Russell justified the course he had pursued, declaring that, 'with every respect for the resolutions of the House, he was far from supposing that they could supersede the law of the realm, or dispense with the prerogative of the crown.'ᵉ The proposed vote of censure he regarded as quite uncalled for. The proper course would have been for the mover of the resolution to have followed it up with an address to the crown, which, if agreed to by the House, would have brought the matter under the notice of government, and necessarily elicited a reply; or he might have introduced a Bill into the House to carry out the principle embodied in the resolution. His lordship added, that the general question of licensing entertainments was under the consideration of government, and that some change in the present arrangements might hereafter be made.' After some further debate, the motion of censure was put and negatived. Before the commencement of Lent in the ensuing year, the lord chamberlain issued a new order, allowing all theatres under his jurisdiction to be open during Lent, except on Ash-Wednesday and in Passion-week. An astronomical lecturer, heretofore in the habit of lecturing during Passion-week at the theatres, petitioned the House, complaining that the new order prevented the continuance of his lectures: whereupon Mr. Duncombe moved an address to the Queen, that she would be pleased to direct that 'astronomical lectures' should be exempted from the operation of the new order. This motion, though opposed by the government, was agreed to on a division.' But no answer to the address was communicated to the House.

On March 22, 1842, a series of resolutions were proposed in the House of Commons, by Sir Charles Napier, in favour of the selection of naval officers, instead of civilians, as members of the Admiralty Board, and in favour of naval civil situations being filled by professional men. Sir Robert Peel, the prime minister, moved the previous question, and refused, as a minister of the crown, to make any promise as to what he would do in the matter; because, he added, 'it must be reserved as the prerogative of the crown, and I altogether protest against the House of Commons laying any restrictions upon the exercise of the royal prerogative with regard to any branch of the public service.' After some further debate the previous question was put and negatived.ᵉ

Precedents.

Admiralty Board.

ᵉ Mirror of Parl. 1839, p. 967.
ᵇ Ibid. pp. 957, 968.
ᶜ Ibid. 1840, pp. 2462-2485.
ᵈ Hans. Deb. (3) vol. lxi. pp. 1001-1070. See further on this subject in this chapter, section, Prerogative

Precedents.

Sunday labour in the Post-office.

On May 30, 1850, on motion of Lord Ashley in the House of Commons, an address to the Queen in favour of the total cessation of Sunday labour in the post-offices of the United Kingdom was agreed to. The ministry, though disapproving of the plan, advised her Majesty to comply with the wishes of the House.[v] Much public inconvenience resulted from this decision: accordingly, arrangements were entered into by newspaper agents and others for a general delivery of mailable matter on Sunday, which involved the employment of many extra hands on that day. Whereupon, on July 9, the House passed another address to a contrary effect, expressing an opinion in favour of a partial delivery of letters and papers through the Post-office on the Lord's Day. To this address her Majesty returned a favourable reply.[w]

Education in Ireland.

On June 17, 1856, an address to the Queen, in relation to education in Ireland, was passed by the House of Commons unexpectedly, and in opposition to the wishes of the government, by whom it was considered as tending to the subversion of the system of national education in operation in that country. By consent of the government, an opportunity was afforded to the House to reconsider the subject before the Queen's reply to the address should be given;[x] and a counter-resolution, expressing a decided opinion in favour of the maintenance of the existing system of Irish education, was agreed to.[y] In the course of the debate, Lord John Russell commented on the embarrassment resulting from the rule of the House permitting an address to be passed upon one deliberation; and said that he had been quite prepared to move for the rescinding of the vote, but was willing to accept the proposed resolution as a satisfactory equivalent.[z] On June 26 the Queen's reply to the address was sent down. It expressed an earnest desire to maintain the established system of education in Ireland, and a readiness to give to the wishes and recommendations of the Commons the consideration to which they were entitled.[a]

Royal commission.

On June 27, 1856, an address to the Queen for the issue of a royal commission to determine the site of the new National Gallery was carried against ministers, and contrary to the wishes of the principal leaders of the Opposition.[b] Whereupon the commission was issued by the crown.[c]

---

concerning the Army and Navy, amongst the *Precedents*.

[v] Hans. Deb. vol. cxi. pp. 484, 980. The majority in favour of this address is said to have been obtained owing to the absence, at a court ball, of many members who would have opposed it. (Edinb. Rev. July 1861, p. 74.)

[w] Hans. Deb. vol. cxii. pp. 1215, 1375. And see vol. cxlii. p. 1077.
[x] *Ibid.* vol. cxlii. pp. 1080, 1827.
[y] *Ibid.* pp. 1830, 1884.
[z] *Ibid.* p. 1842.
[a] *Ibid.* p. 1892.
[b] *Ibid.* p. 2151.
[c] *Ibid.* vol. cxlii. p. 510. And see *ibid.* vol. clxxi. pp. 201, 515.

In the session of 1860, upon the recommendation of the crown, the sum of two million pounds was granted by Parliament towards the construction of works for the defence of the royal dockyards and arsenals, and of the ports of Dover and Portland, &c. The entire cost of these fortifications, as originally estimated, was somewhat over five million pounds. But before they were completed their estimated cost amounted to nearly seven millions. Foremost in this great scheme of national defence was the construction of fortifications at Spithead, a roadstead in the vicinity of Portsmouth. Under the influence of the excitement occasioned by the news from America of the contest between the ironclad war-vessels, the Merrimac and the Monitor, the House of Commons, on April 4, 1862, resolved 'that it is expedient to suspend the construction of the proposed forts at Spithead until the value of iron-roofed gunboats, for the defence of our ports and roadsteads, shall have been fully considered;' and that on a future day (named) the House would go into committee to consider of authorising the funds appropriated for the construction of forts to be expended in building ironclad ships. (This committee, however, never sat, the order respecting it being allowed to drop.)[d] Meanwhile, in deference to the foregoing resolution, the government suspended the works at Spithead, although they thus incurred a heavy expense in indemnifying the contractors for losses sustained thereby. They also referred the question to the consideration of the Defence Commissioners, upon whose report they determined to suspend the further prosecution of the works until the result of certain experiments had been ascertained.[e] Adverting to the delay and expense attending this course, Lord Palmerston (the prime minister) took occasion to remark, 'that when the House of Commons takes into its own hands administrative details, and takes them out of the hands of the executive government, the probability is that such a course will be attended with increased expense and diminished efficiency.'[f] But as the government had merely consented to defer for a while and not to abandon the system of fortifications they had decided upon in 1860, another resolution was proposed, on June 23, 1862, as an amendment to a motion for the grant of a further

Precedents.
Fortifications.

[d] See Smith's Parl. Rememb. 1862, p. 130. For tokens of the change in the opinion of the House in regard to iron-plated wooden ships, see the debates on Mr. Lindsay's motions on the subject on February 20 and March 12, 1861.
[e] Hans. Deb. vol. clxvii. pp. 870, 883.
[f] Ibid. vol. clxvi. p. 1281. See also a debate in the House of Commons, on March 12, 1863, on a motion that 'it is not expedient to commence at the present time building wooden ships which are to be cased with iron armour-plates;' and Lord Palmerston's observations thereon, ibid. vol. clxix. p. 1385. The motion was negatived.

264   THE ROYAL PREROGATIVE

Precedents. sum in aid of the construction of fortifications: 'That considering the changes and improvements now in progress affecting the science of attack and defence, it is not at present expedient to proceed with the construction of the proposed forts,' &c.; 'and that in any general system of national defence this House is of opinion that the navy should be regarded as the arm on which the country must mainly depend.' After some debate this amendment was withdrawn, and the original motion put and agreed to.[a]

In 1863, on April 30, the House of Lords was informed, on behalf of the government, that the works on the Spithead forts, though not abandoned, had been suspended for the present. Subsequently, on July 9, in the House of Commons, in amendment to the second reading of a Bill to make further provision for the construction of these fortifications (including those at Spithead), a resolution was proposed in the House of Commons to postpone for the present any further expenditure upon the works for the defence of Portsmouth and Plymouth. This amendment was opposed by government, on the ground that, if agreed to by the House, it 'would be fatal to the whole Bill, and would stop all further progress of the works this year.' It was accordingly negatived, on division, by a large majority.[b] In the following session the House was informed that the contract at Spithead had been renewed in 1863, and the works recommenced upon a larger scale than had been originally anticipated.[c]

Education office: Inspectors' reports. On February 22, 1859, Mr. Cowper called the attention of the House of Commons to a circular from the Education Committee of the Privy Council, dated May 22, 1858, which directed that, instead of the annual reports of the inspectors of schools being published in full (as had been done from 1844 to 1858), relevant extracts only of such reports should be appended to a general report from the Education Committee to her Majesty. The new regulation had been made on account of certain objectionable matter which had appeared in a report, and which had been complained of by members of the House of Commons. Mr. Cowper contended that the Education Committee 'had it in their power to lay down the strictest rules with regard to the character and nature of the reports they desired to have sent up to them,' but asserted 'the expediency of allowing the original reports to appear unaltered and unabridged.' He concluded by moving that an humble address be presented to her Majesty, praying that the reports of school inspectors, when prepared in accordance with the instructions of the Committee of Council on Education, should continue to be laid before

---

[a] Hans. Deb. vol. clxvii. pp. 907-904.
[b] Ibid. vol. clxxii. pp. 441-490.
[c] Ibid. vol. clxxvi. p. 1871. See post, p. 401, note (n).

IN MATTERS OF ADMINISTRATION. 265

Parliament unaltered and unabridged. Mr. Adderley (Vice-Presi- Precedents. dent of the Education Committee) opposed the motion, on the ground that so much irrelevant matter had been introduced into these reports, that a new rule on the subject had become imperatively necessary, for economical reasons, as well as on the score of propriety. A specimen of the new form of report would shortly be submitted to Parliament, when, if it should appear objectionable, the House could 'agree to a resolution requiring, on its own responsibility, that the reports furnished to the executive should be published by them *in extenso*.' After some further debate, the motion was withdrawn, with the understanding that government would endeavour to meet the views of the House in this matter.[j] Accordingly, Mr. Adderley abandoned his plan of reducing the inspectors' reports under specific heads, and thenceforth permitted the reports to be printed without abridgment; but he nevertheless insisted on his right to strike out therefrom all superfluous and irrelevant matter.[k] But this concession failed to give complete satisfaction. On March 27, 1863, enquiry was made in the House of Commons, whether the reports of certain inspectors had been materially altered, or wholly suppressed, in the annual report from the Education Office; and if so, why so; and whether there was any objection to communicate such suppressed reports to Parliament. Mr. Lowe (who had succeeded Mr. Adderley as Vice-President of the Education Committee) replied that considerable difficulty had always been experienced in confining these reports within proper limits; that a new minute had been lately issued—embodying the substance of previous instructions—requiring the inspectors to confine their reports to the state of the schools they had examined, and to practical suggestions for the management and improvement of the same; that whenever a report contained irrelevant matter, it was sent back to the inspector, with an intimation that, unless it was altered in conformity to the minute, it would not be printed or laid before Parliament—(the particular passages objected to, however, were never specially indicated): that last year three reports had been returned to their authors, who had declined to amend them to the satisfaction of the Education Office, and there-

---

[j] Hans. Deb. vol. clii. pp. 690, 702, 714.

[k] *Ibid.* vol. clxxi. p. 727. Subsequently, in his evidence before the Commons' Committee on Education, in 1865, Mr. Adderley declared that the sum of the instructions to the inspectors which were issued up to the time he left office was, that their reports should be upon the facts which came within their inspection, and that their suggestions should be practical, and not abstract disquisitions upon educational philosophy: but he never meant to limit their suggestions to one side of the question. (Evid. pp. 61, 62.) The inspectors were then, and still are, at liberty to object to particular minutes, on the ground that they did not work well (*Ibid.* p. 65.)

Precedents.
Education office: inspectors' reports.

fore they had not been printed with the report of the department. This year a similar number had been sent back, including one from an inspector whose report had been rejected in 1862. He could not consent to lay these reports on the table, as this would be virtually offering a premium to the inspectors to disregard the rules of the department, and would be subversive of all discipline.[1] On June 11, 1863, a member complained to the House of Commons of the suppression of several reports from school inspectors, and enquired of the Vice-President of the Education Committee upon what conditions he would allow the publication of such reports for the information of the House. He argued that the House had a right to full information, and should be permitted to judge between the Education Office and the inspectors as to the suitability of the reports for publication. Mr. Lowe replied that it would be impossible to lay down any exact conditions under which the reports might be printed, but that, whenever they contained irrelevant or controversial matter in regard to questions decided upon by the department itself, they could not be allowed publicity. Mr. Adderley defended the conduct of the Education Office, and urged that if objection was taken thereto by any member, he should move for the particular report which he considered had been too stringently dealt with, instead of laying down a general proposition that would be disadvantageous to the public service. After some further debate the subject was dropped.[2] But on April 12, 1864, it was again revived, upon the motion of Lord R. Cecil, to resolve, 'that in the opinion of this House, the mutilation of the reports of her Majesty's inspectors of schools, and the exclusion from them of statements and opinions adverse to the educational views entertained by the Committee of Council, while matter favourable to them is admitted, are violations of the understanding under which the appointment of the inspectors was originally sanctioned by Parliament, and tend entirely to destroy the value of their reports.' His lordship cited, from a paper which was privately circulated amongst members during the debate,[3] cases in support of his position, and asked the House whether it could trust reports thus expurgated. Mr. Lowe denied any knowledge of the cases referred to, and repeated the arguments formerly adduced in justification of the department. He said, 'It is quite open to the House to express an opinion that the inspectors should report directly to Parliament, and not to the Privy Council, and thus exonerate us from all responsibility in the matter;' but so long as the present system prevails, departmental discipline must be enforced. He rejoiced to add, that the reports for the past year had all come

---

[1] Hans. Deb. vol. clxx. p. 24.
[2] Ibid. vol. clxxi. pp. 717-733.
[3] Lord Granville's speech in House of Lords, ibid. vol. clxiv. p. 1183; and Mr. Lowe's explanation, ibid. p. 1200.

in, and that it had not been necessary to return one of them to the inspectors. Secretary Sir George Grey said, that in the Home Office, and in other departments of state, similar regulations were enforced,* and that he considered it absolutely necessary that the head of a department should have such a power. Nevertheless, on division, the motion was carried against the government by a majority of eight. On April 18, Earl Granville (the President of the Committee of Council on Education) called the attention of the House of Lords to the foregoing resolution, and, as the official head of the department, assumed full responsibility for Mr. Lowe's acts. Moreover, he gave explanations of the routine pursued at the Education Office, which entirely corroborated Mr. Lowe's statements, and exonerated him from any suspicion of unworthy conduct. On the same day, Mr. Lowe informed the House of Commons that in vindication of his own honour, he had felt it necessary to resign his office;[p] and at the same time he entered into detailed explanations in disproof of the charges brought against him. The marks on the reports which had been privately circulated amongst members on the night of the adverse vote, had been made by subordinate clerks in the Education Office, without the knowledge or sanction of the official heads. They were intended to direct the attention of the secretary to particular passages. He himself had never, in any instance, struck out anything from an inspector's report, and had forbidden others to do so, or

---

* As, for example, in the case of factory inspectors. (See Hans. Deb. vol. clxxiv. p. 1501.)

[p] Mr. Lowe afterwards stated that he did not understand that the sending back a report to an inspector, to be corrected according to the regulations of the department, without marking any objectionable passage, could be regarded as 'mutilation.' 'The House resolved in a contrary sense, and I resigned my office, not because my department was censured, but because I considered, in fact, that the House gave me the lie in resolving, after the statement I had made, that I had mutilated.' He added that if he had supposed 'mutilation' to mean simply carrying out the official minute, according to his understanding of it, 'I should not have thought it necessary to resign my office; the department was censured, but that would not have concerned me: that would have been the Government's lookout. I considered that my personal honour was struck at, when, as I understood, the statement which I had made appeared to be disbelieved by the House.' (Rep. Com. on Education Inspectors' Reports, 1864, p. 57.) This view of the degree of official responsibility attaching to the office of Vice-President, was afterwards confirmed by Lord Granville, who declared that, as Lord President of the Council, he was technically the one who was bound to resign; whilst technically the Vice-President might have retained his office, notwithstanding the vote of censure passed on the department. But, in fact, Mr. Lowe's resignation was dictated by a sense of personal honour; Lord Granville wished to resign, but was induced by the premier to await the result of the reconsideration of the question by the House of Commons. (Rep. Commons' Com. on Education, 1866, p. 105.)

Precedents.
Education office: inspectors' reports.

even to mark objectionable paragraphs. Lord R. Cecil expressed his complete satisfaction with these explanations, and stated that, had they been given before the adverse vote was taken, it would not have been pressed, or agreed to by the House. Lord Palmerston passed a high eulogium on his retiring colleague, and intimated his intention to move for a committee to enquire into the question of fact involved in the charges which had been preferred against him: but the general feeling of the House appeared to be adverse to any further enquiry, after the satisfactory explanations given by Mr. Lowe. However, the resolution of April 12 being regarded by the government as conveying a grave and serious censure on a public department which was deemed unmerited, on May 12, upon motion of Secretary Sir George Grey, a select committee was appointed to investigate the matter, by enquiring into the practice of the Committee of Council on Education with respect to the reports of her Majesty's inspectors of schools. In deference to the wishes of the House, the government agreed that the committee should be nominated by the General Committee of Elections. On July 11 the committee made a report, which briefly reviewed the matter at issue, confirmed the statements made to the House by Mr. Lowe, and entirely exonerated him from the imputation of personal misconduct. After pointing out that the resolution of censure, which led to the resignation of Mr. Lowe, was passed from a 'want of information,' which 'was the cause of a double misunderstanding,' the committee declared that they had 'carefully considered the action of the department, and had come to the conclusion, that the supervision exercised in objecting to the insertion of irrelevant matter, of mere dissertation, and of controversial argument, is consistent with the powers of the Committee of Council, and has, on the whole, been exercised fairly, and without excessive strictness.' 'Some such power is essential to the effectual working of the department, so long as it retains its present constitution and functions.' In conclusion, the committee recommend, 'that all instructions which may hereafter from time to time be issued to the inspectors, either as to their general or tabulated reports, should be laid before Parliament.'* On July 25, Lord Palmerston moved that it be resolved, that having considered the foregoing report, the House was of opinion that the resolution of censure passed on April 12 should be rescinded. After a debate, in which the promoters of the vote of censure stated their willingness to agree to

---

* Report Commons' Com. on Education, Inspectors' Reports, 1864, pp. v. vi. The House was afterwards informed, 'that it was the unanimous opinion of the Committee that the resignation of Mr. Lowe was totally and entirely unnecessary.' (Hans. Deb. vol. clxxvi. p. 1804.)

this motion in the sense in which they understood it to be proposed—namely, as acquitting the department of being influenced by improper motives in the course it had pursued, whilst adhering to the opinion that the course was improper—the motion was agreed to without a division.

Precedents.

On June 16, 1863, a resolution was moved, in the House of Commons, to declare the opinion of the House that it was the duty of the government to carry the law into effect by immediately removing stake and hand weirs in certain rivers in Ireland; but no sufficient evidence of neglect of duty on the part of the authorities having been adduced, the motion was withdrawn.[r]

Rivers in Ireland.

The sovereign having determined, upon the advice of the Privy Council, and under the authority of the Act 3 & 4 Will. IV. c. 71, to constitute the West Riding of Yorkshire into a separate assize district, of which Leeds should be the assize town, an attempt was made in the House of Commons to obtain the nomination of the town of Wakefield instead of Leeds, by a motion, made on February 19, 1864 (previous to the formal issue of the Order in Council in favour of Leeds), for an address to the Queen, setting forth the claims of Wakefield to be the assize town, and praying that it might be selected for that purpose. The home secretary (Sir G. Grey) did not deny the right of the House to address the crown upon this subject, but urged that no sufficient cause had been given to justify an interference with the ordinary course prescribed by law, and to set aside the decision of the Privy Council. Upon a division, the motion was negatived. But on June 13, an address was carried in the House of Lords (against ministers), praying that the decision of the Privy Council, ordering the removal of the West Riding Assizes from York to Leeds, instead of to Wakefield, might be reconsidered. On June 17, the Queen's answer to this address was reported. It set forth that the assizes for the West Riding had been appointed to be held at Leeds on August 10, and that if it should hereafter appear expedient to appoint some other place for holding the said assize, the subject should be again referred for the consideration and advice of the Privy Council.[s]

West Riding of Yorkshire, assize town.

On March 22, 1866, a resolution was carried in the House of Commons, upon division, against the government: 'That in the opinion of this House, it is not expedient that the competition for the building of the New Courts of Justice should be limited to six architects only.' Subsequently the House was informed that, in consequence of this resolution, the number of competing architects had been extended to twelve.[t]

Plans for Palace of Justice.

---

[r] Hans. Deb. vol. clxxi. pp. 981-984.
[s] And see Hans. Deb., vol. clxxvi. p. 1893.
[t] Ibid. vol. clxxxiii. p. 181. See a further discussion on this subject, ibid. p. 1173.

II. Practice of Parliament in the Appointment of Select Committees to enquire into Administrative Questions.

Select Committees on public questions.

Reference has already been made [a] to the practice, which has been adopted of late years with increasing frequency, of appointing Select Committees of the House of Commons, or of the Lords, to take evidence, and report upon important public questions. These questions sometimes relate to matters which are strictly within the province of the executive government to determine; and it may be doubted whether the tendency of this practice is not to shift the labour and responsibility of administrative reforms more and more from those to whom it properly belongs; and to increase, in equal proportion, the power and influence of the House of Commons in details of government.[b]

When restricted in their enquiries within constitutional limits,[c] such committees are often very serviceable, in bringing members to a common agreement upon great public questions, upon which legislation, founded upon an impartial investigation of facts, is necessary. These

---

[a] See *ante*, p. 258.

[b] As a general rule, Parliament should not be called upon to appoint committees of enquiry into matters of administration, until application has been made to the department concerned to redress the grievance complained of. If no remedy could be thus obtained, it would be proper to appeal to the House. — Chanc. of Exch. in Hans. Deb. vol. clxxiv. p. 416.

[c] See some weighty observations, by Mr. Disraeli, on this point, in Hans. Deb., vol. clxi. pp. 1605–1608; by Mr. Cobden, *ibid.* vol. clxxvi. p. 1808; by Mr. Lowe, *ibid.* vol. clxxxii. p. 158. 'Nothing is more remarkable than the tender forbearance with which the House of Commons treats its own select committees; though, if their proceedings were strictly canvassed, there are perhaps few parts of our system of government which can less support criticism. As a means of enquiry and investigation, they are of the highest value, and they are constantly carrying on, with great success, the political education of Parliament and of the nation: but when they strain at executive authority they generally fail, nor can their judicial impartiality (except in peculiar cases) be entirely relied on.' —*Edinb. Rev.* vol. cviii. p. 280. For a humorous description of the manner in which such committees are sometimes organised, extracted from the 'Saturday Review,' see Fischel, p. 470.

committees are usually appointed either at the suggestion or with the direct approval of the government, and are composed of leading men from both sides of the House, including members of the existing and of former administrations, as well as others who, from their abilities, experience, or information, are specially qualified to serve thereon. 'Strong partisans on each side are knowingly and advisedly chosen, in order that truth might be elicited from the conflict of opposite and, it might be, interested opinions. If such committees consisted wholly of impartial men, their investigations would be most unsatisfactory.'* After taking evidence from every available source, the committee reports the same to the House, generally with observations embodying practical suggestions, which they submit for the consideration of the government. It then becomes the duty of the administration to consider these propositions, to subject them in turn to careful scrutiny, and, if necessary, to appoint either a royal commission,ʸ or a departmental committee of their own, to make further enquiries, in order to enable the government to decide, upon their own responsibility, to what extent, and in what way, the proposed reforms can be carried out, in conformity with the general principles upon which the public service is conducted.ᶻ

As a general rule, it is not customary to submit to the House motions for concurrence in the reports of such select committees, or any other resolutions founded thereupon. It is usual to leave with the government the initiation of any measures, be they legislative or otherwise, that may be required to carry out the recommendations of a public committee. Sometimes, however, a member of the committee (usually the chairman) submits to the House an abstract resolution on the matter, in order

Select Committees.

Result of their enquiries.

---

* Secretary Sir G. C. Lewis, Hans. Deb. vol. clxii. p. 1012.
ʸ For the practice in regard to the issue of royal commissions, see Vol. II. c. 3, The Administration in Parliament.
ᶻ Ibid. vol. clxi. p. 817; ibid. vol. clxviii. pp. 620–633; and Lord Palmerston, ibid. vol. clxxiii. p. 1239.

272 THE ROYAL PREROGATIVE

Select Committees.

to enforce the recommendations of the committee, or to elicit the views of the House upon the subject.¹

In illustration of the principles upon which it is usual to appoint these committees, of the proceedings consequent upon their labours, and of the conduct of government in respect to the same, the following cases may be consulted:—

Precedents.

Opening letters at Post-office.

On June 14, 1844, Mr. Duncombe presented a petition to the House of Commons from four persons, of whom Joseph Mazzini, the well-known Italian refugee, was one, complaining that their letters had been detained at the London post-office, broken open, and read. The home secretary (Sir James Graham) explained that Mazzini's letters only had been opened; and that this had been done by his express authority, under a warrant issued in conformity to an Act of Parliament. On June 24 Mr. Duncombe moved for a select committee to enquire into the operations of the Post-office Department in such cases. The motion was successfully opposed by Government, on the ground that they had merely exercised a right which had been constantly resorted to by their predecessors in office, and which had proved advantageous to the public interests, in the prevention and detection of crime. But on July 2 Mr. Duncombe again moved for a committee of enquiry; in amendment to which Sir James Graham himself proposed the appointment of a secret committee, to investigate the law in regard to the opening of letters, and the mode of its exercise—which was agreed to by the House. On July 4 a similar committee was appointed by the House of Lords. These committees were composed of some of the most eminent and impartial men in Parliament. A motion to include Mr. Duncombe upon the Commons' committee was negatived upon division.² Mr. Duncombe afterwards complained to the House, that while he had been invited to attend the committee to prefer his complaint against the home secretary, and to give in a list of witnesses in support of the same, he was not permitted to be present himself during the examination of witnesses. He then moved that it be an instruction to the committee to allow him to attend, and produce and examine witnesses in support of the case of the petitioners: but the motion was negatived. A motion to add Mr. Duncombe to the committee was ruled out of order by the Speaker, on the ground that a similar

---

¹ Anchors and Chains, Merchants' Service, Hans. Deb. vol. clxiv. pp. 235–242; Holyhead Harbour, *ibid.* vol. clxxii. p. 1330; Medical Officers in Unions (Ireland), *ibid.* vol. clxxvii. p. 1510; Bankruptcy Act of 1861, *ibid.* vol. clxxix. pp. 420, 1160.

² Hans. Deb. vol. lxxvi. p. 257.

motion had been already negatived by the House.[b] After due investigation, these committees reported. They fully exonerated Sir James Graham from blame in the discharge of his duty, and gave full particulars of the origin and exercise of the power of opening letters entrusted by statute to the secretary of state. They recommended no alteration of the law on this subject. A few days afterwards, Lord Radnor introduced into the House of Lords a bill to abolish the right of opening letters, but it did not proceed beyond a first reading:[c] so that the secretary of state still retains his accustomed authority whenever he may deem it advisable to exercise it.[d]

Select Committees Precedents.

On June 16, 1841, a select committee of the House of Commons, appointed to enquire into the present state of the national monuments and works of art in Westminster Abbey and in other public edifices, reported an opinion in favour of the opening of the English cathedrals, daily, to the public, for the inspection of their architectural beauties. On April 16, 1844, a motion was made to approve of this recommendation. Sir Robert Peel (the prime minister), while expressing himself favourable to the free admission of the public to such edifices, nevertheless opposed this motion as an attempt, by a mere resolution of the House, to control the lawful guardians of these institutions, who possessed rights independent of the House as an encroachment on the liberties of the people, and a dangerous endeavour to effect, by inadequate means, that which, if desirable, should be made the subject of legislation. The motion was accordingly withdrawn.[e]

Cathedrals.

A committee on Public Moneys, which sat during the years 1856 and 1857, made numerous recommendations, of more or less importance, in reference to the public finances, with a view to subject the public expenditure to a more rigid investigation and control on the part of the House of Commons. In their final report they stated, that they were 'aware that the important and extensive changes they have suggested cannot all be immediately carried into effect; but they believe that the continued attention of Parliament and of the executive government to the subject, will secure, at no distant date, all the objects embraced in their recommendations.'[f] In the session of 1861, the chancellor of the exchequer informed the House that the said recommendations had, in the interim, received the careful consideration of the government, and that he was prepared, in regard to most of them, to submit to Parliament bills, or resolutions, to carry the same into effect.[g]

Public Moneys.

---

[b] Hans. Deb. lxxvi. pp. 1010–1021.
[c] Ibid p. 1714; and see May's Const. Hist. vol. ii. p. 282.
[d] See Broom, Const. Law, pp. 615–617.
[e] Ibid vol. lxxiv. pp. 20–48.
[f] Sess. Pap. II. of C., 1857, Sess. 2, vol. ix. p. 572.
[g] Hans. Deb. vol. clxi. pp. 711, 1310. And see post, p. 601.

VOL. I.   T

THE ROYAL PREROGATIVE

Select Committee. Precedents.

Harbours of refuge.

In the years 1857 and 1858, a committee of the House of Commons was appointed to enquire into the policy of making further grants of public money for the improvement and extension of harbours of refuge on the coasts of Great Britain and Ireland. Pursuant to the report of this committee, a royal commission was appointed to complete the enquiry, which reported in the following year. While mutually agreed as to the necessity for the construction of these important works, the two tribunals differed as to their cost, and as to the mode of obtaining funds for the purpose. The committee recommended that two million pounds should be expended for this service, but suggested that three-fourths of the required amount, and three-fourths of the cost of maintaining these harbours, should be raised from passing tolls on shipping. The commission, on the other hand, adjudged that an outlay of four millions would be required to construct the works, and were of opinion, that inasmuch as the general interests of the community were concerned in the undertaking, the greater part, if not the whole, of this sum should be paid out of the Consolidated Fund; and that no passing toll should be levied either for the erection or maintenance of these harbours. On June 19, 1860, the House of Commons resolved that it was the duty of the government to adopt, at the earliest possible period, the necessary measures to carry into effect the recommendations of the commissioners. Some progress had been made by government in the construction of these harbours, but owing to the state of the public finances, and the large expenditure required for other extraordinary services, they had not felt warranted in incurring the whole of this enormous outlay.[b] Whereupon, on May 6, 1862, it was moved in the House of Commons to resolve, that it is the duty of the government to adopt measures to carry into effect the preceding resolution. But, after full debate and explanations from ministers, the motion was negatived upon division. Again, on April 17, 1863, it was moved to resolve, as the opinion of the House of Commons, that so much of the report of the commissioners on Harbours of Refuge, as concerned Waterford, Wick, and Padstow be carried into effect, but, after some debate, it was negatived without a division.[i] On April 26, 1864, a motion to declare the opinion of the House that the government ought to proceed with the construction of harbours of refuge, was negatived, on division. On June 13,

---

[b] Sir Morton Peto, in his work on Taxation (p. 316), observes that 'the case of the so-called harbours of refuge should be a lesson to us for the future. A great deal of money has been uselessly expended on very ill-conceived plans.'

[i] The whole case in regard to the harbours of refuge, is given in the correspondence between the Board of Trade and other public departments respecting said harbours, since the report of the Commons' Committee of 1857.—*Commons Papers*, 1864, vol. lv. p. 430.

1865, a motion that, in the opinion of the House, the government should adopt measures for the construction of some of the said harbours on the coast of Great Britain and Ireland, was negatived, on division.

On March 5, 1861, a motion was made in the House of Commons for the appointment of a select committee, to enquire and report whether any, and what, alterations may be advantageously adopted in regard to the defence of the British dependencies, and the proportions of cost of such defence as now defrayed from imperial and colonial funds respectively. The mover disclaimed any desire to invade the functions of the executive, but contended that the interference of Parliament in the settlement of this important question had become necessary, in consequence of the failure of a departmental committee, appointed by government in 1859, on colonial military expenditure, to agree in any recommendations on the subject. In reply, the under-secretary for the colonies deprecated the proposed committee, on the ground that the question being one of opinion and principle, and not of facts, was not a fit subject for enquiry by a parliamentary committee. He admitted that the report of the departmental committee had not been free from objection, but contended that the only proper way to treat the question was by negotiations, to be carried on by the imperial government with each of the colonies in their turn. Further debate ensued, from which it was evident that the sense of the House was in favour of the appointment of the committee. Accordingly, Lord Palmerston, while he expressed his agreement with the constitutional objections which had been urged against the motion, and felt bound to declare that its tendency was 'rather to transfer to a committee of the House duties and functions which properly belong to the responsible advisers of the crown,' nevertheless consented to the appointment of the committee.ʲ After taking voluminous evidence, the committee reported on July 11. Their labours have been justly characterised as being 'chiefly valuable in furnishing information, promoting discussion, and exhibiting the discordance and inconsistency of opinion on the subject, not as recommending any practicable policy.'ᵏ On March 4, 1862, on

---

ʲ Hans. Deb. vol. clxi. p. 1420. See the analogous case of the committee on the Board of Admiralty, noticed *ante*, p. 201.

ᵏ In an elaborate article in the Edinburgh Review for January 1862, analysing the evidence, and pointing out the different views of leading statesmen on this question. And see the observations of the colonial secretary (the Duke of Newcastle), on this report, in the House of Lords, in Hans. Deb. vol. clxiv. p. 1570; and of the secretary of war (Sir G. C. Lewis), on March 9, 1863, showing why the Government had been unable to carry out the recommendations of the committee, in effecting any material reduction in the number of troops in the colonies.

276 THE ROYAL PREROGATIVE

Select Committees. Precedents.

motion of the chairman of this committee, the House resolved, without division, 'That this House (while fully recognising the claims of all portions of the British Empire to imperial aid in their protection against perils arising from the consequences of imperial policy) is of opinion that colonies exercising the rights of self-government ought to undertake the main responsibility of providing for their own internal order and security, and ought to assist in their own external defence.' On March 21 following, another member of the committee, conceiving that this resolution did not go far enough, proposed the adoption of a resolution condemning the erection and maintenance of fortifications, out of imperial funds, in self-governed colonies, not being great naval stations. The administration, while acknowledging the correctness of this, as a general principle, considered it to be subject to certain limitations, rendering the assertion of the principle inexpedient. The motion was accordingly withdrawn.[1]

Inclosures in royal forests.

On March 3, 1863, a motion was made in the House of Commons for the appointment of a select committee, 'to enquire into the legality of inclosures in Waltham, Epping, and other forests in Essex, and to ascertain what steps ought to be taken to preserve the rights of the public, of the poorer foresters, and of the inhabitants of the metropolis, within the forests, as well as to enquire into their general management.' This motion was opposed by the attorney-general, on the ground that it would be a most inconvenient and dangerous precedent to erect a select committee into 'a court of judicature for the purpose of enquiring into and expressing an opinion with reference to the rights of individuals and of the crown,' or 'into any technical and strictly legal rights,' for which purposes a parliamentary committee was a manifestly defective and improper tribunal. Accordingly, at the suggestion of the attorney-general, the motion was withdrawn, and instead thereof a committee was appointed 'to enquire into the condition and management of the royal forests in Essex, and into any inclosures which may have taken place therein since the report of the commissioners of 1850; and to consider whether it is expedient to take any steps for preserving open spots in such forests.'[2] This committee reported on June 9. They recommended the continuance of the inclosure of Epping Forest; and that an adequate portion thereof should be set apart for the public, for the purposes of health and recreation; also, that any past encroachments on the forestal rights of the crown should be abated.[3]

—Hans. Deb. vol. clxix. p. 1281; and see *ibid.* pp. 1446-1457, 1770-1789; vol. clxx. p. 870.

[1] For further debates in the House of Commons on the military defence of Canada, see Hans. Deb. vol. clxxvi. p. 373.

[2] Hans. Deb. vol. clxix. p. 1024.

[3] Rep. of Com. on Royal Forests, 1863, p. iv.; Hans. Deb. vol. clxii.

On May 5, 1868, a private member moved, in the House of Commons, for the appointment of a select committee to enquire into the state of Holyhead Harbour, with a view to securing safe and efficient accommodation for vessels engaged in the Irish mail-service, and for passengers conveyed by them. On motion of the chancellor of the exchequer, the debate was adjourned until papers in relation thereto were distributed to members. It was resumed on May 12, when the motion was agreed to, notwithstanding the opposition of the government, who contended that the committee was unnecessary and inexpedient.* On June 1, upon motion that the committee do consist of certain specified members, the chancellor of the exchequer took exception to the list proposed, alleging that it was 'as far as possible from being an impartial committee.' He declined to take the 'invidious and annoying course of proposing that some of the names should be omitted, and replaced by others more impartially selected;' but he felt 'bound to say, even before the committee sits, that [the government] do not think the subject one that ought to be referred to its consideration, and that we shall not be able to look upon its finding as the verdict of an impartially constituted tribunal.'† The proposed list was nevertheless agreed to, without a division. But on June 4, a member of the committee, who was personally aggrieved by Mr. Gladstone's remarks, characterised them as being insulting and unparliamentary, and called upon that minister to move that he be discharged from the committee in order to take the sense of the House thereupon. An informal discussion then arose as to the purport of Mr. Gladstone's observations, which were further explained by himself. The Speaker, on being appealed to, acquitted Mr. Gladstone of unparliamentary language, and the

Select Committees. Precedents.

Holyhead Harbour.

---

p. 1055. This report contained recommendations which differed materially from the tenor of an address, passed by the House on February 13, 1849, condemning any more sales to facilitate inclosures of crown-lands within fifteen miles of the metropolis. (See further, on this point, Vol. II. c. 1, on the Cabinet Council.) See debates in the Commons, on June 3 and July 1, 1864, on the steps taken by government to carry out the recommendations of the committee. See also Hans. Deb. vol. clxxx. p. 481. In the session of 1865, another committee was appointed, to enquire into the best means of preserving, for the public use, the forests, commons, and open spaces in and around the metropolis. This committee reported, on June 20, their opinion that no more inclosures should take place within the metropolitan area; and that a new board should be appointed, to act as trustees for the preservation, for the use of the public, of forests, commons, and open spaces within that area. (Commons' Papers, 1865, vol. viii. p. 355. And see Commons' Papers, 1866, No. 172, p. 11.) In 1868, an Act was passed for the preservation of Epping Forest, &c., 29 & 30 Vict. c. 62.

* Hans. Deb. vol. clxx. pp. 1243, 1610.
† Ibid. vol. clxxi. p. 242.

subject was dropped.⁕ The committee reported on July 14.† Their report contained certain recommendations, to which, when discussed in the committee, the President of the Board of Trade had expressed his dissent. Accordingly, on July 23, the chairman moved to resolve, that the recommendation of the committee ought to be adopted. This motion was opposed by government, and negatived, without a division.‡

III. Practice in regard to the Granting or Withholding by the Executive of Information desired by either House of Parliament.

Information given to Parliament, or withheld.

The rule which forbids any encroachment by Parliament upon the executive authority of the crown has a further application, to which our attention must now be directed. It is imperative that Parliament shall be duly informed of everything that may be necessary to explain the policy and proceedings of government in any part of the empire; and the fullest information is communicated by government to both Houses, from time to time, upon all matters of public concern. Considerations of public policy, and a due regard to the interests of the state, occasionally demand, however, that information sought for by members of the Legislature should be withheld, at the discretion and upon the general responsibility of ministers. This principle is systematically recognised in all parliamentary transactions: were it otherwise, it would be impossible to carry on the government with safety and honour. Whenever it is declared, by the responsible servants of the crown, that any information sought for in Parliament could not be supplied without danger or inconvenience to the public service, the House refrains from insisting upon its production.† And if the government object to produce any documents, on the ground that they are of a private and confidential description, it

---

⁕ Hans. Deb. vol. clxxi. pp. 325–331.
† Commons' Papers, 1853, vol. vii. p. 223.
‡ Hans. Deb. vol. clxxii. p. 1330.

† Mirror of Parl. 1828, p. 100; 1833, p. 626; 1830, p. 671; 1827–8, p. 654. And see Lord Derby's remarks on this subject in Hans. Deb. vol. clxxiii. p. 1055.

IN MATTERS OF ADMINISTRATION. 279

is not usual to insist upon their being furnished,^a except under peculiar and imperative circumstances.^b Unless prepared to assert their want of confidence in the minister who is answerable for the department concerned, or in the government generally, the House ought not to embarrass the ministry by insisting on the production of documents which they feel it their duty to refuse.^c In like manner, if the government declare that a discussion on any particular subject could not take place without inconvenient and injurious consequences to the public service,^d or without eliciting expressions of opinion from the ministry, or from members generally, which it would be premature and prejudicial to make known,^e the debate ought not to proceed.

Information given and withheld.

It would, moreover, be highly irregular to communicate to Parliament copies of despatches issued by a secretary of state, until they had been either acted upon or forwarded to their destination;^f though this has sometimes been done by government, in the exercise of their own discretion.^g For further particulars in regard to the communicating of despatches to Parliament, see (*post*, p. 602) the section in this chapter concerning 'Intercourse with Foreign Powers.'

'The system of laying upon the table of the House

---

^a Mirror of Parl. 1834, p. 2774; 1835, p. 1034; 1838, p. 5060; 1840, p. 1130; Hans. Deb. (3), vol. clxiii. p. 822. But it must always be remembered that all public transactions of state are necessarily official; and that no public officer would be justified in withholding from official record and access, any document, emanating from himself in his official capacity, in relation to public affairs. See the case of Lord Chatham, *ante*, p. 171; and Parl. Deb. vol. xvi. p. 2****.

^b Mirror of Parl. 1831, p. 524.

^c *Ibid.* 1839, p. 700. When 'copies' of correspondence, &c. are moved for, by private members, it is customary to add, 'or extracts;' otherwise the Government will, ordinarily, refuse to produce the papers. (Hans. Deb. vol. clxxii. pp. 676–677.)

^d Hans. Deb. (3), vol. cxxviii. pp. 1420–1429.

^e Mirror of Parl. 1831, pp. 1100, 1184.

^f *Ibid.* 1833, p. 5824; 1840, p. 1710.

^g Hans. Deb. (3), vol. lxxxvii. p. 660. Thus, in 1854, the Government consented to lay before Parliament copies of instruction that had been, 'or hereafter might be issued,' to commanders of the Arctic Searching Expedition.—*Ibid.* vol. cxxxii. p. 488.

Departmental reports confidential.

reports from officers addressed to particular departments of the executive government is most objectionable.'[b] If the House were to insist upon the production of such documents, 'instead of the government getting what we get now, confidential reports, containing the most minute details of the opinions of officers, given frankly and freely, for the heads of departments, we shall have a system of reports framed for laying upon the table of the House of Commons, and these will be accompanied by "confidential reports for the head of the department alone." '[c] 'There have been cases in which reports of a confidential character from officers of the government have been laid upon the table of the House, to prepare the public mind, and also that of Parliament, to consent to some large measure, or perhaps some considerable vote of public money; but, generally, I think it is a course which the House ought not to sanction.'[d]

When papers are refused by ministers.

The administration have refused to concur in motions for the production of papers, whether by order or upon an address to the crown, on the ground that there was no public officer whose duty it was to furnish the required information.[e] Under these circumstances, 'it is particularly desirable that the House should make no such orders without, at the same time, determining by what means they shall be carried into execution.'[f]

Returns are sometimes refused on account of their voluminous character, and the length of time it would take to prepare them.[g] In order to obviate this objection, 'it is very desirable that members, before moving for very voluminous returns, should communicate with the department possessing the information, when it might be supplied in a much smaller compass.'[h] It is not customary,

---

[b] Lord C. Paget (Secretary to the Admiralty), Hans. Deb. vol. clxxvii. p. 93).
[c] Ibid. p. 1102; and see p. 1455.
[d] Mr. Disraeli, ibid. vol. clxxviii. p. 154.
[e] Mirror of Parl. 1830, p. 24; 1830–31, p. 50; 1831-2, p. 3254.
[f] Ibid. (The Speaker), 1830, p. 887.
[g] Ibid. 1837, p. 601.
[h] Ibid. 1829, p. 1000.

IN MATTERS OF ADMINISTRATION.

however, to object to motions for returns merely on account of the trouble and expense to individuals that would be occasioned by their production, notwithstanding that there may be no funds available for the remuneration of the persons employed in the execution of the order.[1] In fact, it has been the practice of Parliament to order from public officers, of various grades, returns which they were not required by law to furnish, and for which no remuneration was provided. 'That might be considered a customary right, exercised in the public interests;' and although, upon rare occasions, some remuneration has been given to the parties employed, in order to accelerate their labours, yet 'no public officer has any right to refuse to obey an order of the House until he shall be paid; the question of remuneration must not be raised between him and Parliament.' 'Every public officer holds his situation under the control of Parliament, and he is bound to give information.' It is for the executive government afterwards to decide whether he has any claim for compensation for such a service.[1]

Cost of furnishing returns to Parliament.

The queen's ministers are not only the rightful guardians of the prerogatives of the crown in Parliament, but it also devolves upon them to protect the liberty of the subject, and the interests of private individuals and associations, who have no direct representation therein, from the assumption by Parliament of arbitrary and unlawful authority. On this principle the government have uniformly resisted all attempts, on the part of either House, to obtain, whether by their own order or through an address to the crown, any documents or information concerning the affairs of private individuals,[b] unless proof

Papers concerning private affairs.

---

[1] See Mirror of Parl. 1830, Sess. 2, p. 601. To pay the expense of preparing returns to the Secretary of State or to Parliament out of county rates has been declared to be illegal. —*Ibid.* 1834, p. 3331; 1835, p. 245. See also *ibid.* 1841, p. 2014.

[1] *Ibid.* 1841, p. 2100; 1835, p. 1700. And see Hans. Deb. vol. clxxxii. pp. 1614, 1775.
[b] Mirror of Parl. 1830, p. 449; 1831, p. 109; 1833, p. 1014; 1834, p. 126. Thus, the Government will often require motions asking for in-

of delinquency, calling for parliamentary investigation, could be shown.¹ This rule includes the case of private educational institutions not being in the receipt of public money." It has even been held to apply to the affairs of private companies, and of 'public institutions who are not in receipt of assistance from public funds.'" But it was distinctly laid down by Sir Robert Peel and Lord John Russell, in the case of the Royal Academy, that the inquisitorial jurisdiction of Parliament could not be limited to such 'public institutions' only as were the recipients of public money; but that 'when an institution is established to assist in promoting the cultivation of the arts, or other strictly public object, it could not be denied that the House had a right to enquire into its affairs, even though it did not receive public aid.'° And on a later occasion it was declared, by Sir Robert Peel, that 'where Parliament has given peculiar privileges to any body of men' [as, for example, banks or railway companies], it has a right to ask that body for information upon points which it deems necessary for the public advantage to have generally understood.' The great point to be aimed at in such enquiries he considered to be, 'that while you extract all the information the public require to have, you should, at the same time, avoid all vexatious interference in the details of the business of the respective undertakings.'⁴

Marginal note: Private companies, &c.

formation affecting a particular class of individuals to be made numerical, instead of nominal, in order to screen private persons from unnecessary publicity.—*Hans. Deb.* vol. clxix. p. 1581.

¹ Mirror of Parl. 1831-2, p. 1237; 1840, p. 2053.

² *Ibid.* 1830, p. 873; 1840, p. 1772. On July 24, 1862, it was stated in the House of Commons, by the Secretary for Ireland, that Government had no authority to call for a certain educational return from the Roman Catholic Bishops in Ireland.—*Hans. Deb.* vol. clxviii. p. 737.

° Mirror of Parl. 1837-8, p. 3672; Hans. Deb. vol. lxxiii. p. 1759.

° Mirror of Parl. 1830, pp. 4238, 4503.

⁴ See the proceedings in the House of Lords, in regard to an order that the Corporation of the City of London should lay before the House a detailed account of their income and expenditure between certain years; the Corporation having applied to Parliament for an Act to enable them to increase their revenues, by imposing a tax on coals.—*Ibid.* 1820, pp. 1805, 1834.

⁴ *Ibid.* 1840, p. 4840. And see

It is 'the rule of Parliament, that no papers shall be laid on the table of either House, unless some sufficient reason have been stated for their production.' It is irregular to move for the production of papers merely to further the interests or views of private persons, or except for the purpose of founding, or facilitating, parliamentary proceedings.' Government have refused to grant papers, 'unless it be intended to found some proceedings upon them.'

Parliamentary ground for ordering papers.

The foregoing precedents, it is hoped, will serve to explain more clearly the constitutional position of Parliament in regard to the prerogative of administration. Without denying the abstract right of either House to address the crown upon any matter, they will show the great public inconvenience attending an attempt on the part of Parliament to interfere with the ministers of the crown in the details of government, the inexpediency of applications for documents which the responsible advisers of the crown consider it imperative to withhold, and the unwarrantable nature of any intrusion by Parliament into the private affairs either of individuals or of corporate bodies, without just cause. So long as any existing government retain the confidence of Parliament, it is unsafe and unwise, as a general principle, to interfere with them in matters of administration. Those who are directly responsible for the conduct of public affairs are they who possess the necessary information for the proper discharge of the

Summary in regard to this prerogative.

Mirror of Parl. 1829, p. 825. See further, in regard to the principle in question, showing the respect entertained by both Houses for private rights, *ibid.*, 1837, pp. 787, 997, 1030; 1838, p. 5400; 1839, p. 3421. Hans. Deb. vol. lxxiv. p. 26; vol. cxxxi. pp. 135, 786; vol. clvi. p. 1103. And on the general question of the power of Parliament to compel the production of documents, see Smith's Parl. Remembrancer, 1860, p. 20.

' Lord Melbourne, Mirror of Parl. 1838, p. 5387.
* *Ibid.* 1831, p. 2248; 1833, p. 547.
' *Ibid.* 1839, p. 4422. But see the following cases, wherein Members of Parliament, being in possession of valuable statistical or other information, obtained orders, or addresses, for the production of the same, to one or other of the Houses of Parliament.—*Ibid.* 1830, Sess. 2, p. 410; 1838, p. 5273; 1839, p. 4372.

same. Parliament exercises a direct control over the ministers by whom all public affairs are transacted. It has a right to enquire into every grievance or abuse of power, whether on the part of those ministers or of any other public functionary. It may also express its opinion in regard to any act of the government; and it not unfrequently happens that the mere declaration of opinion in Parliament upon some objectionable departmental regulation, unaccompanied by any formal motion, suffices to induce the government to modify their plans, conformably to the views entertained by the House.* But all this is very different from an attempt on the part of the legislature to usurp the functions of the executive, or from the endeavour by the House of Commons to compel the adoption of their opinions upon a question of administration, irrespective of those of the government or of the other Chamber; a proceeding which must tend to destroy the harmony which should exist between the different powers in the state, and to transfer the executive authority from the hands of responsible ministers into those of an irresponsible and uncontrollable democracy.

IV. CIRCUMSTANCES UNDER WHICH PARLIAMENT HAS A RIGHT TO INTERFERE, IN ORDER TO RESTRAIN THE ILLEGAL EXERCISE OF EXECUTIVE AUTHORITY.

Abuse of executive authority.

While Parliament is constitutionally debarred from interfering, by order or resolution, with the ordinary routine of government, except for the purpose of expressing an opinion as to the expediency of any particular proceeding, or line of policy—it is otherwise if the crown itself attempts to encroach upon the functions of Parliament, and endeavours to accomplish by its own action that which cannot lawfully be effected, except

---

* See the case of the Treasury discussed in the House of Lords on Warrant respecting unpaid letters, February 22 and 24, 1850.

with the sanction and co-operation of Parliament. It *Abuse of executive authority.*
then becomes the duty of Parliament to interpose, and to
call to account the ministers of the crown who are
responsible for the abuse or excess of executive authority.
In like manner, if any individual minister is guilty, in his
official capacity, of any illegal or oppressive act, it is the
privilege of the injured party to apply to Parliament for
redress; and the matter of complaint being substantiated,
Parliament will hold the offending minister personally
responsible for his misconduct.

There are three forms of procedure, of ordinary
occurrence in the administration of public affairs by the
ministers of the crown, which are liable to be perverted
into the instruments of tyranny and misgovernment, if
they are not strictly confined within constitutional limits.
These are—1. Orders in Council and Royal Proclamations;
2. Minutes of Committees of Council, and other Departmental Regulations; 3. Contracts entered into by Public
Departments. The proper limits of executive authority in
relation to each of these administrative acts will be
briefly explained. We shall then proceed to point out,
fourthly, the responsibility which devolves upon individual
ministers of state for personal acts of misconduct in their
official capacity.

1. *Orders in Council and Royal Proclamations.*

It is a fundamental law of the English Constitution, *Orders in Council.*
that the sovereign can neither alter, add to, nor dispense
with, any existing law of the realm.

This important point was first established beyond dispute in the reign of James I., by the proceedings in
Parliament upon the case of Bates, an English merchant,
who refused to pay a duty on currants imported into the
country from abroad, which duty was sought to be levied
by the sole authority of the king. The Court of Exchequer, in 1606, sustained the claim of the crown; but

Taxation by the crown illegal.

when the matter was discussed in the House of Commons, it was shown that this decision was contrary to the provisions of the Great Charter, and therefore void. It was further alleged that the sovereign could not, without the assent of Parliament, impose a duty on any article of merchandise imported into or exported from the country; or, in fact, any duty whatsoever, either upon foreign or domestic commodities, whether in time of war or peace. The conclusions arrived at upon this occasion were embodied in a Petition of Grievances, which was addressed by the House of Commons to the king, in the year 1610, and favourably received by his Majesty.*

This important doctrine was confirmed, in the following reign, by the celebrated case of ship-money; wherein it was established that the sovereign cannot, without the consent of Parliament, assess or levy ship-money upon the subject.*

The mode whereby the Stuart sovereigns sought to enforce their illegal claims of levying taxes upon the people, in derogation of the legislative functions of Parliament, was by the issue of royal proclamations and orders emanating from the Privy Council. At that period the Privy Council was the great governing body in the State, by means of which the will of the sovereign was promulgated and enforced. The king's government was carried on through the instrumentality of Orders in Council, and by the issue of royal proclamations, which were put into execution by the subordinate officers of the crown.

All this has been changed by the development of the authority of Parliament, and the recognition by the monarchs of England of the constitutional principles embodied in the Bill of Rights. The ancient prerogative of the crown in legislating by Orders in Council, has been

---

* See the case, and the proceedings in relation thereto, in Broom's Constitutional Law, pp. 217-305.
* See ibid. pp. 300-370, 404-408.

materially curtailed, and it is an admitted principle that the crown has no right, by a mere Order in Council, either to sanction a departure from the requirements of an existing law, or to interfere with the established rights or privileges of any class of persons within the realm. It is competent to the crown to declare and enforce, by proclamation, the execution of any existing law, but it is not within the power of the crown either to add to, alter, or dispense with any law of the land.*

<small>Dispensing power.</small>

Following the example of the Church of Rome, the sovereigns of England, from an early period, claimed the right to dispense with the laws of the land, by the issue of proclamations, and by making grants or decrees, ' *non obstante* any law to the contrary.' In this way they assumed a power, *virtute coronæ*, to dispense with existing laws, or with the penalties consequent upon a breach of them; or else they undertook to dictate to the people in respect of matters indifferent, and in regard to which perfect liberty of action ought to have been allowed.' The current of authority indicates that the prerogative of dispensing by *non obstante* with Acts of Parliament was, subject to certain restrictions, recognised in former times as vested in the crown, and was repeatedly exercised during the sixteenth and seventeenth centuries. The use and abuse of this prerogative occasioned repeated conflicts between the Crown and Parliament and the courts of law, and eventually cost King James II. his crown.' This branch of the royal prerogative was finally annihilated by the Bill of Rights, which declared that ' the pretended power of suspending of laws, or the execution of laws, by regal authority, without consent of Parliament, is illegal;' and that ' the pretended power of dispensing with laws, or the execution of laws, by regal authority, as it hath been assumed and exercised of late, is illegal.'

---

* Broom's Constitutional Law, p. 374.
' Cases cited. *ibid.* pp. 375–390.
* *Ibid.* pp. 404–507.

'Since then no one has presumed to advocate the existence of a dispensing power, under any circumstances whatever, as inherent in the crown.'[a]

Orders or proclamations.

From the epoch of the Revolution of 1688, whenever the crown has ventured, upon occasions of public emergency, to issue royal proclamations or Orders in Council, which appeared to sanction any departure from the laws of the land, the necessity for such a proceeding on the part of Government has been narrowly investigated by Parliament; and when it has been shown to have been illegal, although justifiable, acts of indemnity have been passed, to exonerate all persons who have advised or carried into execution the same.[b] Legislation of this kind is a parliamentary acknowledgment of the principle that, in times of danger or emergency, the crown, acting under the advice of responsible ministers, may properly anticipate the future action of Parliament, by a temporary suspension of certain classes of statutes.[c] Abstractly, the crown has no constitutional right to issue any such orders or proclamations; but, in the words of Sir Robert Peel, 'Governments have assumed, and will assume, in extreme cases, unconstitutional power, and will trust to the good sense of the people, convinced by the necessity to obey the proclamation, and to Parliament to indemnify the issuers.'[d]

Orders in Council.

Nevertheless, with the important limitations above referred to, considerable powers still remain to be exercised by the sovereign in council. 'A large proportion of what may be called the details of legislation rests upon the authority of Orders in Council, some of which are issued by her Majesty in virtue of her prerogative, while others derive their force from the provisions of Acts of Parliament.' As examples of the variety and importance of the subjects to which this form of quasi-legislation is

---

[a] Broom's Constitutional Law, pp. 507, 508.
[b] *Ibid.* pp. 379, n. 508, n.
[c] Cox, Eng. Govt. p. 29. Campbell's Chancellors, vol. v. p. 207.
[d] Peel's Memoirs, vol. ii. p. 131.

applicable, it may be stated that orders in council, or royal proclamations which are usually issued in pursuance of the same, are promulgated for the assembling, prorogation, and dissolution of Parliament; for declaring war; for confirming or disallowing the Acts of Colonial Legislatures; for giving effect to treaties; for extending the terms of patents; for granting charters of incorporation to companies or municipal bodies; for proclaiming ports, fairs, &c.; for deciding causes on appeal; for creating ecclesiastical districts; for granting exemptions from the law of mortmain; for the regulation of the Board of Admiralty, and of appointments to offices in the various departments of state; for creating new offices, and defining the qualifications of persons to fill the same; and for declaring the period at which certain Acts of Parliament (the operation of which has been left by the legislature to the discretion of the queen in council) shall be enforced.*

It is difficult to draw the line between what may and what may not be accomplished by an order in council. As a general rule, all orders in council restricting trade, unless issued under the authority of an Act of Parliament, or justified by reference to cases coming within the prerogative of war,—and all orders suspending the operation of any statute,—would require an Act of Indemnity. But when duly informed by the crown of the proceedings had upon any such occasion, Parliament has always been willing to indemnify the government for the timely exercise of authority for the public welfare, although it may have led to an overstepping of the constitutional limits of executive power.

When they require the sanction of Parliament.

According to modern practice, whenever it is necessary that orders in council should be issued to carry out the provisions of an Act of Parliament, it is customary to insert in any such Act a clause requiring that 'every order

When to be communicated to Parliament.

---

* Report on the Privy Council xxvii. p. 253. Rep. on Misc. Exp. 16. Office, Commons' Papers 1854, vol. 1847-8, vol. xviii. pp. 371, 377.

in council' under the same shall be laid before both Houses of Parliament within thirty days after the making thereof, or, after the next meeting of Parliament, should the order have been issued in the recess.[d]

Proclamations. So far as proclamations, as distinct from orders in council, are concerned, it is an indisputable branch of the royal prerogative to issue proclamations in reference to the existing state of the law, warning those who may be likely to commit offences, encouraging respect for the law, and offering rewards for the apprehension of offenders. These documents are regarded as solemn expressions of the royal will, and are invariably issued upon the advice of responsible ministers. They are usually based upon orders in council, and are intended to promulgate decisions arrived at by the sovereign in council. Their exact force has been a matter of dispute, which even now cannot be precisely determined, since it labours under the uncertainty which affects all questions bearing on the limits of the prerogative. The best established opinion is, that while a proclamation cannot make a law, it can add force to a law already made.[e] When the sovereign declares war against a foreign power, proclamations are usually issued, materially altering the ordinary laws relating to trade, and imposing rules for the conduct of trade with neutrals or belligerents.[f] Proclamations are also issued to fix the mode, time, and circumstances of putting into execution certain laws, the operation of which has been left to the discretion of the executive government;[g] or, for the purpose of making formal declaration of existing laws and penalties, and of the intention of government to enforce the same; or, to appoint and direct the keeping of a day of observance, whether as a fast or thanksgiving. But 'proclamations have only a binding

---

[d] See Acts 28 and 29 Vict. c. 112, sec. 3, c. 124, sec. 11, c. 125, sec. 20.
[e] Dicey on the Privy Council, 44. And see Hallam, Const. Hist. vol. i. p. 337.
[f] See Cox, Inst. Eng. Govt. 28.
[g] Ex. gra. 6 Geo. IV. c. 78. Municipal Corporations Act of 1835. Health of Towns Act of 1848.

force when they are grounded upon and enforce the laws of the realm.'ʰ The king cannot authorise by proclamation the creation of an offence which is not a crime by the existing law; 'for if so, he might alter the law of the land by his proclamation.'ⁱ

2. *Minutes of Committees of Council, and other Departmental Regulations.*

The responsibility of ministers to Parliament necessarily implies the right of either House to express its opinion as to the legality or expediency of any particular act of administration; and to proceed to call to account any minister of state, or department of government, who may have exceeded the limits of constitutional authority in the execution of public duty.ʲ

Minutes of Council.

In the working of constitutional government, experience has proved that certain subordinate powers of legislation must be entrusted to almost every leading department of state. So long as these powers are exercised with the knowledge of Parliament, and in direct subjection to its control, they can be more advantageously discharged by responsible ministers than if it were obligatory that they should emanate from Parliament itself.ᵏ But while it is necessary from time to time to issue minutes of council, departmental regulations, and other formal directions from the governing heads of the principal executive departments, in reference to many matters of administration which require to be determined by

Departmental regulations.

ʰ Coke, 3 Inst. 102.
ⁱ Bowyer, Const. Law, p. 173. Knight's Pol. Cyclop. vol. iv. p. 503.
ʲ See the debate in the Lords May 12, and in the Commons June 25, 1817, upon the circular letter of the Secretary of State for the Home Department (Lord Sidmouth) to the Lords Lieutenants of counties, respecting the authority and duties of magistrates, in regard to blasphemous or seditious libels; which letter was alleged to have been an interference with the ordinary course of justice, and an assumption by the executive of legislative power. May, Const. Hist. vol. ii. p. 188.
ᵏ See the Evidence of the Right Hon. R. Lowe, H. A. Bruce, and C. B. Adderley, and of Earl Granville, before the Commons' Committee on Education in 1865, pp. 42, 43, 56, 59, 60, 64, 141.

competent authority, it is also important that whenever either the expenditure of public money, or other great public interests are concerned in the matters thus disposed of, an opportunity should be afforded to Parliament of expressing its opinion in regard to the same, before any action is taken thereon by the government.

Minutes of the Education Committee.

This distinction was involved in the circumstances attending the issue, by the Committee of Privy Council on Education, in 1861, of a revised code of rules for the administration of the parliamentary grants for promoting education in England, as will appear from the following narrative. Having prepared a new code, effecting extensive alterations in the existing system of education as administered by the privy council, the government laid before Parliament the minute of council establishing the revised code, on August 6, 1861, being the very day of the prorogation,[1] but without giving any explanations on the subject. However, as the new regulations were not to come into operation until after the next meeting of Parliament, when they were liable to be objected to by either House, it was probably deemed unnecessary to comment upon them on their first introduction. During the recess, the new code was subjected to considerable criticism, and elicited formidable opposition in many quarters. The complaints against it received full attention from the government, who, shortly after the re-assembling of Parliament, laid before both Houses another minute, containing several modifications of the new code. These changes, however, were not sufficiently comprehensive to satisfy the opponents of the measure. Accordingly, a discussion took place in each House upon the subject, wherein exception was taken, not merely to the re-revised code itself, but also to the mode of its adoption by the government.[m] In the House

---

[1] Commons' Journal, 116, p. 427.

[m] Shortly after the adoption of the order in council of April 10, 1859, creating a separate department of the privy council as a body to superintend the distribution of the moneys voted by Parliament for educational purposes, the proceedings of government in the matter were called in question in both Houses. On June 14, an address was moved in the House of Commons, praying for the revocation of the said order. After several nights' debate, this motion was negatived by a majority of five only, in a full House (Mirror of Parl. 1859, p. 3105.) On July 5, in the House of Lords, a series of resolutions were agreed to, and embodied in an address to the Queen, deprecating the conferring of such important powers upon the Committee of Council without the consent of Parliament, and praying that no steps may be taken with respect to the establishment of any plan of national education without affording to their lordships an opportunity of fully considering the proposed measure. (Ib. p. 3382.) On July 11, an answer was returned to this address, expressing her Majesty's regret that the House of Lords 'should have thought it necessary to take such a step on the present

of Lords, on February 17, 1862, Lord Derby called upon the ministry to embody the principles and leading details of the scheme in a series of resolutions, to be submitted to both Houses, in order to afford opportunity for mature deliberation thereupon. But this they declined to do. Mr. Walpole, who led the attack upon the code in the House of Commons, condemned the government for not having submitted it to Parliament in a series of distinct propositions, instead of as a whole. He said that 'he wished to raise the question whether, when any alteration is made in a system of education which the country has adopted, accepted, and acted on, it is to be in the power of any government, at any future period, by its own mere motion, and without the concurrence and sanction of Parliament, to alter that system, fundamentally and entirely, in the manner they are now attempting to do. In 1839, this question was much agitated, and discussed in this House. There was then an attempt to introduce normal and industrial schools. That attempt was defeated; and one of the great objections urged against it was the manner in which the attempt was made. The House was told, and told truly, that the power which the committee of council asserted to itself was a power essentially beyond that which the constitution gave to any department in the state. It was the assertion by a body necessarily political in its character—necessarily fluctuating in its nature, which would be irresponsible, and therefore despotic—of an authority and power which does not belong to any minister, and which ought only to be entrusted to both Houses of Parliament.' With these views, Mr. Walpole submitted to the House a series of resolutions, condemnatory of certain parts of the revised code, for the purpose of obtaining, in committee of the whole House, a full discussion of the scheme, and the introduction of considerable changes therein. With the general principle of the code—as an endeavour to simplify the machinery for administering the grants of public money for the promotion of popular education, and an attempt to test the results of such education—he entirely concurred; but he considered the mode of effecting these objects, as set forth in the code, to be quite unpalatable to Parliament and to the country. In asking the House to adopt this course, he likened it to the proceeding in committee upon a government bill, the principle of which has been agreed to by the House, but which is subject to amendment of details at that stage of its progress. And in order to prevent a proceeding so objectionable as the present from being drawn into

Revised code of Education.

---

occasion;' and assuring their lordships that annual reports of the proceedings of the newly appointed Committee of Education would be laid before Parliament, 'so that the House would be enabled to exercise its judgment upon them.' (Mirror of Parl. 1839, p. 3815.)

precedent by the government, Mr. Walpole appended two resolutions to his series, requiring the re-printing of the code in the January of each year, should any material alteration therein be proposed, and in a form to point out distinctly the intended changes; and declaring that, in the event of any revision or material alteration being proposed by the department at any time, it shall not be lawful to take any action thereon until the same shall have been submitted to Parliament, and laid on the table of both Houses for at least one calendar month." By these resolutions it was his object to maintain, that the committee of council, whilst entrusted with important administrative functions, had no legislative authority, but must submit for the sanction of Parliament all material changes in the national system of education before attempting to enforce them. Secretary Sir George Grey, on behalf of the government, acquiesced in the course suggested by Mr. Walpole, and also in the principle involved in the last two resolutions.° Whereupon the House went into committee on the proposed resolutions. Three days afterwards, the Vice-president of the Education Committee announced that the government were prepared to make important alterations in the new code, in order to render it more acceptable to Parliament and to the country. To afford time for the due consideration of these amendments, no further action was taken in the House on the subject until May 5, when Mr. Walpole stated that the conduct of the government had been so conciliatory and satisfactory, that he was prepared to abandon his resolutions, and to accept the revised code in its amended shape. Thus ended a severe and protracted contest, wherein the right of Parliament to exercise a constitutional control over the executive government, in a matter which seriously affected a large portion of the community, was amply recognised and sustained.

Educational minutes to be laid before both Houses of Parliament.

It is now distinctly admitted that the Education Depart-

---

* As to the proper construction to be given to these resolutions, see Hans. Deb. vol. clxxi. p. 1042. In order to bring the language of the minutes in this particular 'in accordance with the sense and spirit' of Mr. Walpole's resolutions, the government submitted to the House of Commons, February 17, 1865, a new rule, to the same effect, which while it recognised the power of the department to alter the minutes, restrained any action upon such alterations until the documents had been laid before Parliament. Supplementary regulations on minor points, not included in the code, are laid on the table every year, with the report of the Education Department. Hans. Deb. vol. clxxvii. p. 327.

° Debate in House of Commons, March 25, 1862. In compliance with the foregoing resolutions, the code was reprinted January 1863; and a new minute of some importance having been issued in the following May, the same was immediately submitted to Parliament, to lie upon the table for one month before it became law. See Commons' Debates, June 15, 1863. Hans. vol. clxxi. pp. 952-954.

ment are bound to apply for the sanction of Parliament not merely to any minute which involves the expenditure of public money, but to any minute which affects any modification in the departmental regulations which have been previously submitted to Parliament.* To assist the judgment of the Commons in regard to any new minutes, a practice has been recently introduced under which the member who represents the department in the House calls the attention of members to the changes effected by the new minutes, when he lays them upon the table.† At this stage, however, no debate can take place, as there is no question before the Chair.

Minutes of Education Committee.

How submitted for the approval of the House of Commons.

In illustration of the manner in which the sense of the House of Commons has been taken in reference to new minutes of the Committee of Council on Education, when they have been laid upon the table, the following cases may be cited.

On May 5, 1863, two resolutions were submitted to the House, by a private member, to declare the expediency of modifying the regulations of the code in certain particulars. After a long debate, one of these resolutions was withdrawn and the other negatived.

On March 8, 1864, a resolution was proposed for the modification of the rules in regard to aid to schools for the working classes. After some debate, the government agreed to accept this resolution. On the 2nd June following, the mover, being of opinion that the new minute which had been issued in conformity with the said resolution did not meet the case, proposed another resolution, to declare the inadequacy of the minute to remove the objections entertained against the former minute; but the

---

* Rep. Commons' Committee on Education, 1864. Evid. 453, &c. Hans. Deb. vol. clxxvii. p. 327. It is also understood that no important changes in the system of national education in Ireland should be introduced, before they had been communicated to Parliament, although it is entirely within the province of the Irish Education Commissioners to alter or modify their rules, without any action on the part of government. *Ib.* vol. clxxxiii. p. 1031.

† Rep. Commons' Com. on Education, 1865, pp. 43, 60, 141.

motion was negatived. On June 30 another resolution, condemnatory of the new minute, was proposed; but the Speaker ruled that it was out of order, being similar in substance to the one previously negatived.'

A departmental regulation discussed in House of Commons.

In further illustration of the propriety of parliamentary interference in any case where the requirements of law appear to have been disregarded by a mere departmental regulation, see the discussion in the House of Commons on April 3, 1865, upon a member calling attention to the conduct of the Chief Commissioner of Police in refusing to allow the Metropolitan police to flog juvenile offenders under the order of magistrates, although they were required to inflict such punishment by law.'

3. *Contracts entered into by Public Departments.*

Public contracts.

An important question has arisen of late years with regard to contracts, to be entered into between any department of the executive government and other parties, for the performance of any work or service which has been authorised by Parliament to be undertaken. It is manifest that the responsibility of entering into such contracts properly rests upon the executive alone. But it is equally clear that the government have no constitutional authority to make a contract which shall be binding on the House of Commons,' by whom the necessary funds for carrying on the contract must be supplied; and that if any contract be entered into by any executive department for work to be performed, the cost of which will exceed the amount already voted by Parliament for the service to be contracted for, such contract should expressly state that payments on behalf of the same would be made 'out of moneys to be voted by Parliament;' and, in addition thereto, a copy of said contract should be laid upon the table of the House of Commons for one

---

' See the comments of Lord R. Cecil on this case, in his argument to show the inadequacy of the control of Parliament over minutes of Committee of Council on Education. Hans. Deb. vol. clxxvii. p. 900.

' Hans. Deb. vol. clxxviii. p. 710;

and in regard to framing the Articles of War, see *Ibid.* vol. clxxxiv. p. 2055.

' See Smith's Parl. Rememb. 1860, p. 75. Judgment of the Court of Queen's Bench in the Churchward case, 1865, cited *post*, p. 501.

month previous to its going into operation, in order to afford an opportunity to the House to express its disapproval thereof, if it should think fit to do so. *Public contracts.*

The principle of the control of Parliament, and especially of the House of Commons, over contracts, was first established, in the years 1859 and 1860, by a committee of the House of Commons appointed to enquire into certain transactions arising out of existing contracts for postal and telegraphic services. The proceedings of this committee, and of the House upon its reports, will come under review, in another part of this chapter (p. 493, &c.), in connection with the privileges of Parliament in matters of Supply. It will suffice here to state the conclusions arrived at, as the result of this enquiry, for the purpose of ensuring that due notice shall be given to Parliament of any contracts to be hereafter entered into by government, which may involve prospective expenditure to an amount beyond that which has been actually voted by Parliament for any specified service.

By a standing order, adopted by the House of Commons on March 4, 1861, it is provided that 'the Chairman of the Committee of Ways and Means shall make a Report to the House previously to the second reading of any private Bill, by which it is intended to authorise, confirm, or alter any contract with any department of the government, whereby a public charge has been or may be created; and such Report, together with a copy of the contract, and of any resolution to be proposed in relation thereto, shall be circulated with the Votes two clear days at least before the day on which the resolution is to be considered in a committee of the whole House, which consideration shall not take place until after the time of private business; nor shall the Report of any such resolution be considered until three clear days at least after the resolution shall have been agreed to by the Committee.'[*] *Standing order concerning contracts.*

---

[*] Commons' Journals, 1861, p. 80. Standing Orders, 1862, No. 78.

Mail and telegraph contracts.

Moreover, in the case of new contracts for the conveyance of mails by sea, or for the purpose of telegraphic communications beyond sea, it has been resolved by the House of Commons that such contracts shall not be binding until they have lain on the table of the House for one month,' without disapproval; unless sooner approved of by a resolution of the House."

In the year 1863, special resolutions were passed by the House of Commons,—approving of contracts which had been laid upon the table,—before the expiration of the month.' But this was done under peculiar and exceptional circumstances. As a general rule, it has been agreed, that 'the House should not be asked to share in the responsibility of the details of mail contracts,' and that it is 'far better that they should come into legal force on the sole responsibility of the executive, after an opportunity of rejecting them (by their remaining for one month upon the table) had been afforded to the House, than that the House should be called upon to affirm them by a positive vote.'

In the event of any such contract being disapproved of, it is of course necessary that a substantive resolution should be proposed in relation thereto. Thus, on March 20, 1863, a resolution was moved to declare that the House was not prepared to grant a sum of money to the Galway Packet Company, whose contract had expired, but was proposed to be renewed. The motion was negatived, on division. On July 21, on the motion of the Secretary to the Treasury, it was resolved (without debate) that the new contract with this company be approved.

Though confined, in the letter, to a particular class of contracts, the above-mentioned resolution,—requiring

---

' This must be understood to mean one month during which Parliament is in session. See Hans. Deb. vol. clxix. pp. 704, 806.

" Commons' Journals 1860, p. 413.

' Com. Jour. 1863, pp. 380, 404.

' The Chancellor of the Exchequer (Mr. Gladstone). Hans. Deb. vol. clxxii. p. 1201.

that Parliament shall be notified of the intention of the government to enter into contracts which involve prospective expenditure, not limited to the service of the current financial year,—embodies a principle which is of general application. In the proceedings of the House of Commons, in the years 1862 and 1863, in granting supplies for the purpose of constructing fortifications on the British coast, this principle was emphatically asserted, and notwithstanding the opposition of government, a clause was introduced into the Bill for providing funds for this purpose, declaring that whenever a contract shall be entered into by government which involves the expenditure of a greater amount than has been actually granted for such service, such contract shall not be binding until it has lain for one month on the table of the House of Commons without disapproval, or has been formally approved of within that period. This clause was agreed to by both Houses, and forms part of the statute.[a]

What contracts require the approval of the House of Commons.

4. *Illegal or oppressive acts by individual Ministers.*

If a minister of the crown be guilty of any abuse of authority, or dereliction of duty, he is personally liable, under the law and constitution, for his conduct.[a] But, in determining the liability of a public functionary for damage caused by his act to a fellow-subject, a seeming conflict between principles is noticeable, and an anxiety in the breast of the law on the one hand to assist the suitor, who perchance complains of wrong, and on the other to protect the officer who, inflicting an apparent injury, has perchance but done his duty.[b] Any direct infringement of the law of the land by a minister or officer of the executive government would render the offender liable, in a court of justice, to precisely the same consequences as if he were a private person. Nor would it be

Responsibility of ministers for illegal acts.

---

[a] 25 and 26 Vict. c. 78, sec. 2. See Smith's Parl. Rememb. 1862, p. 149.

[a] Attorney-General, in Hans. Deb. vol. clxxvi. p. 2121.
[b] Broom, Const. Law, p. 525.

any justification, in an English court of law, to plead the command of the sovereign as the warrant for an unlawful act.° It may be stated, as a general principle, that in assuming on behalf of the crown a personal responsibility for all acts of government, ministers are privileged to share, with the crown, in a personal immunity from vexatious proceedings, by ordinary process of law, for alleged acts of oppression or illegality in the discharge of their official duties, and are responsible to Parliament alone for acts of misconduct in their official capacity. Nevertheless, the courts of law have established certain rules which, so far as they go, afford protection to the subject against the abuse of executive authority. Thus it has been determined that general warrants, issued by a secretary of state to search for and seize the author—or the papers of an author—(not named) of a seditious libel, are illegal.ᵈ Also, that a warrant, issued by a secretary of state, to seize the papers of the author (named) of a seditious libel, is illegal.ᵉ

Immunity of ministers in courts of law.

Apart from the security afforded to the subject by these decisions, the law accords to persons who are clothed with an official character a peculiar protection. On grounds of political expediency all such persons are preserved from liability to actions at law. Whether the alleged liability arises out of contract or out of tort, or from any matter of private and individual complaint against a minister of the crown, for acts done, or directed to be performed by him, in his official capacity, the ordinary tribunals of justice will afford him special immunity and protection.ᶠ But if ministers of the crown think fit, for reasons of public policy, to take upon themselves the responsibility of

---

ᶜ See *ante*, p. 109.
ᵈ Leach v. Money; 10 St. Trials, p. 1001. Wilkes v. Wood, *Ib.* p. 1153.
ᵉ Entick v. Carrington, *Ib.* 1030. Broom's Const. Law, 525–017. See the proceedings in relation to General Warrants, Parl. Hist. vol. xvi. p. 207.
Hans. Deb. vol. lxxvii. pp. 005, 900.
ᶠ Broom, Const. Law, pp. 017–023, 720. See also the case of Luby v. Lord Wodehouse, showing that the Lord-Lieutenant of Ireland was not to be held liable at law for an act done by him in his official capacity. *Ib.* p. xxv.

directly infringing an existing law, they are bound to apply to Parliament for an Act of Indemnity, to relieve themselves, and those who have followed their directions in the particular matter, from the legal consequences of their conduct.*

The constitutional remedy against a minister of state who may be guilty of injustice or oppression in the exercise of his administrative functions, is by an appeal to Parliament; and more especially to the House of Commons. Attempts to obtain redress, under such circumstances, by resort to the courts of law, are unavailing; inasmuch as such complaints are not properly cognisable by these tribunals, which have no jurisdiction to coerce or otherwise control high public functionaries. Whereas, the House of Commons, as the grand inquest of the nation, is fully competent to investigate every case of ministerial abuse or misconduct, and to visit upon the offender the consequence of his misdeeds.*

In theory of law, the judgment and decision upon every matter of state is that of the sovereign, who acts, according to his discretion, upon advice given him by a responsible minister, who is sworn to keep the king's counsel secret, and who may not disclose elsewhere the nature of the advice given, without his sovereign's express permission. Nor is this secrecy enjoined merely as a personal privilege or protection to the sovereign or the minister, to be waived as they may think fit; it is founded upon constitutional principle and public policy, which unite in recognising the importance of entire and unfettered freedom in any advice to be given to the sove-

---

* Admitting the civil irresponsibility of the supreme power (including ministers of state) for tortious acts, it cannot be denied that its agents, the minor functionaries of government, are responsible to the law for illegal proceedings, beyond the legitimate scope of their derived authority, just the same as they are indictable for corrupt practices or misdemeanor in office. But the government is morally bound to indemnify its agent for the consequences of its own acts, otherwise a public servant might have to answer to the law for acts *bonâ fide* done by him, on behalf of the public, which, in contemplation of law, injuriously affected others. See Broom's Const. Law, pp. 243, 019-023, 71.

* See Hans. Deb. v. 180, pp. 1019-1022.

reign, and the necessity for preserving the king's counsellors from being harassed by actions on false pretences of malice or corruption.

Every minister is directly responsible to Parliament for his conduct in office, and for the advice he tenders to his sovereign; but he is responsible to no other tribunal. If he be put upon his trial by Parliament, it is right that he should be at liberty to disclose the secrets of the council chamber, so far as they may affect his personal responsibility for the acts under review; and permission to that end is invariably accorded by the sovereign. But it is not right for a minister to disclose before a jury, or before an ordinary court of law, the counsels of the crown, because these tribunals have no power to follow up the matter, and to sit in judgment upon the advice given to the sovereign by her ministers, or upon the acts of the sovereign consequent upon such advice. And even if, on any particular occasion, permission to divulge the advice given by a minister should have been granted by the sovereign, for the purpose of evidence in a court of law, it is very doubtful whether the court would be justified in allowing the disclosure to be made. In the case of Irwin *v.* Grey, where the secretary of state for the home department had been summoned as a witness, the court would not permit him to be questioned as to the advice he had given to his sovereign; and the case was stopped by the judge, with the concurrence of the court.[a]

Council secrets not to be divulged in a court of law.

In the case of Dickson *v.* Combermere and others, General Peel, the secretary of state for war, who was one of the defendants, attended and gave evidence before the Court of Queen's Bench in defence of an official act of his own, which had led to the removal of the plaintiff from the lieutenant-colonelcy of a regiment of militia. This evidence involved the disclosure of advice he had tendered to the Queen in regard to the removal of Colonel Dickson; and he informed the court that he had obtained her Majesty's permission to divulge the same. But after he had given his testimony, the chief justice informed the jury that the secretary of state was respon-

---

[a] Foster and Finlason, Nisi Prius cases, vol. iii. p. 630.

sible to his sovereign and the country for the recommendations he *Legal im-*
had made to the sovereign in this matter, and not to them; and *munity of*
that, unless they were of opinion that he had dishonestly and cor- *cabinet*
ruptly abused the power entrusted to him, they could not hold him *ministers.*
accountable for his conduct. The plaintiff's lawyer at once admitted the correctness of this decision, and withdrew the case so far
as General Peel was concerned.¹ In charging the jury upon the
case of the other defendants, who were high military functionaries,
acting under the immediate direction of the secretary of state for
war, the chief justice stated that unless the jury were of opinion
that the matters of complaint against Colonel Dickson, which occasioned his removal from office, had been maliciously and unreasonably put forward, with a view to his oppression and injury, and
without probable cause, they must find for the defendants. And
that even if they thought that General Peel, in recommending the
sovereign to displace Colonel Dickson, had acted harshly and
wrongfully, they could not on that account set Colonel Dickson right
by returning a verdict in his favour. Accordingly, a verdict was
returned for the defendants. The reporter, in commenting upon this
case, points out very forcibly, that according to the analogy of the
decision arrived at in the above-mentioned case of Irwin v.
Grey, as well as upon general grounds of constitutional reasoning,
the court ought not to have permitted the disclosure by General
Peel of the advice he had tendered to his sovereign in his capacity
of privy councillor. The arguments adduced by the Reporter in
support of this position are elaborate and convincing, and amply
justify his conclusion that 'the secretary of state, by reason of his
high office and dignity and the proximity of his position to that of
the sovereign, is protected from all liability by action and all responsibility save to his sovereign or to Parliament, for acts done
by him in his office as Secretary, or by way of advice to the sovereign as cabinet minister.'²

This view of the immunity which attaches to privy *Legal im-*
councillors and high functionaries of state, in the perfor- *munity of*
mance of their official duty, is corroborated and applied *nate*
to all responsible ministers of the crown, who are en- *officers of*
trusted with the direction of any particular department of *state.*
government, by the decision in the case of Gidley v. Lord
Palmerston.

This was an action brought to recover, from the secretary-at-

¹ Dickson v. Viscount Combermere, 578–585.
&c. Foster and Finlason, vol. iii. pp. ² *Ibid.* pp. 633, 634, n.

war, a certain sum of money claimed by a retired clerk of the War Office, as a part of his annual retired allowance, and which, though voted by Parliament for such service, had been withheld by Lord Palmerston, the secretary-at-war, for the purpose of liquidating certain liabilities incurred by the said Gidley, to persons for whom he had acted as agent. The court gave judgment for the defendant, declaring that 'on principles of public policy, an action will not lie against persons acting in a public character and situation, which, from their very nature, would expose them to an infinite multiplicity of actions; that is, to actions at the instance of any person who might suppose himself aggrieved: and though it is to be presumed that actions improperly brought would fail, and it may be said that actions properly brought should succeed, yet the very liability to an unlimited multiplicity of suits would, in all probability, prevent any proper or prudent person from accepting a public situation at the hazard of such peril to himself.'ᵃ

Having shown that it is an established principle in our constitutional system that ministers of the crown are accountable to Parliament alone for personal acts of misconduct, or dereliction of duty, in the discharge of the important functions entrusted to them, it will be our duty, in a subsequent chapter, to point out the course to be pursued to substantiate before Parliament any just ground of complaint against an individual minister, and to investigate the principles which have heretofore governed Parliament in the determination of such questions.

The next prerogative of the crown to engage our attention is that which relates to the government of the Established Church.

Prerogative in matters ecclesiastical.

'All jurisdiction within the realm, spiritual as well as temporal, is derived from the sovereign alone;' that is to say, all jurisdiction which is of a coercive character, and which can be enforced by an appeal to any tribunal or court of justice. Spiritual authority which is exercised merely *in foro conscientiæ* cannot be enforced in a court of law. Accordingly, by the laws of the realm no person can be consecrated to the office of bishop in the Established Church of England without

---

ᵃ 3 Bro. and Bingham, p. 287. And see the comments on this decision, in 3 Foster and Finlason, p. 535, n.

the license of the crown for his election to that office, and the royal mandate, under the Great Seal, for his confirmation and consecration. Moreover, 'the power of pronouncing judgment in *foro exteriori*, coactive judgments, having effects recognised by the temporal law, depends always (for its exercise by any ecclesiastical tribunal) on the temporal power.'¹

Our remarks in regard to this prerogative will admit of the following arrangement:—1. A consideration of the position of the Church of England in the mother country; 2. Its position in the colonies; 3. Its position in foreign countries; 4. The obligations of the Act of Uniformity.

1. *The position of the Church of England in the Mother Country.*

The crown is the legal head of the Church established in the realm of England; the interpreter of the meaning intended to be conveyed by the Thirty-nine Articles, the Liturgy, and other recognised formularies of the Church; and the depository of the ultimate appellate jurisdiction in all causes and matters ecclesiastical." All appellate authority which, previous to the Reformation, was exercised over members of the Established Church by the Pope, is now by statute vested in the Crown of England; and every court, ecclesiastical or civil, held in England must be held in the name and under the authority of the Sovereign.³

Legal position of the Established Church.

The kingdom of England and Wales is divided into twenty-eight dioceses, including that of Sodor and Man; the respective limits of which have been defined by Act

---

¹ Stat. 26 Geo. III. c. 84. Statement by Dr. Phillpotts, Bishop of Exeter, in his correspondence with the Rt. Hon. T. B. Macaulay, published by Murray in 1861, p. 7. See also Edinb. Review, January 1865, p. 153. Hans. Deb. vol. clxxxii. pp. 304-307.

² Royal Declaration prefixed to the Thirty-nine Articles.

³ 25 Henry VIII. cap. 10. 1 Eliz. cap. 1. 10 Charles I. c. 11. 13 Charles II. c. 12. See debate in House of Lords, June 3, 1850, on the Bishop of London's Bill in regard to Appeals to the Privy Council from Ecclesiastical Courts. The Lord Chancellor's speech, in Hans. Deb. vol. clxviii. p. 226. And the Bishop of Oxford's speech, *Ibid.* vol. clxxxiv. p. 518.

of Parliament." The crown has no power, by its mere prerogative, to create new dioceses, in any part of the kingdom. It must have recourse, for such a purpose, to the supreme authority of parliament. The Crown, as legal head of the Church, may command the consecration of a bishop to an existing see, but it has no right to create a new ecclesiastical corporation, whose status and authority should be recognised by the community at large. Accordingly, when four new bishoprics were constituted by Henry VIII., the assistance of Parliament was invoked to give effect thereto." And in our own day, when the bishoprics of Manchester and Ripon were constituted, and ecclesiastical jurisdiction conferred upon the bishops, it was under the provisions of an Act of Parliament.'

Supremacy of the the Crown.

The sovereign of this realm, as supreme head on earth, or 'supreme governor of the Church of England,' has authority to control its 'external polity.' All ecclesiastical synods or convocations of the Church must be convened, prorogued, dissolved, restrained, and regulated by the queen. No convocation of the bishops and clergy of the Church of England can assemble except by the express authority and command of the crown. Such authority has usually been given at the summoning of every session of Parliament, and it is now agreed that the convocations, or provincial synods, of the two provinces of York and Canterbury (which are the ancient ecclesiastical councils of the archbishops) are of right to be assembled concurrently with Parliament. By writs directed to the archbishops, respectively, the crown exercises the right of summoning and of proroguing convocation.' But by the Act of Submission, the clergy have renounced the right to enact any new canons, constitutions, or ordinances, 'unless the king's most royal assent and license may to them be had, to make, promulgate, and execute

Convocations.

---

* Act 6 and 7 Will. IV. c. 77.
' 31 Henry VIII. c. 9. This Act is not found in the ordinary edition of the statutes, but it is cited in the judgment of the privy council in the case of Bishop Colenso.
* 6 and 7 William IV. c. 77.
' Trevor on Convocations, pp. 120, 155.

the same.'ᵃ It has indeed been claimed, on behalf of the bishops of the Church of England, that they are at full liberty to assemble ordinary diocesan synods, to deliberate upon questions of faith and practice, but not to proceed to enact new canons, &c., without the previous license of the crown.' But this is very doubtful;" at any rate, 'it is admitted that diocesan synods, whether lawful or not, unless with the license of the crown, have not been in use in England for above two centuries.'" {Diocesan Synods.}

So far, at least, as convocation is concerned, all jurisdiction that may be exercised by convocation must be subject to the authority and control of the sovereign. By virtue of the queen's writ of summons, convocation is empowered to deliberate upon matters affecting the interests of religion and of the Church. It is well known that, from the time of Bishop Hoadly until a very recent period, it was the regular practice for the crown to interpose and stop the deliberations of convocation by a prorogation, immediately after they had formally assembled. But of late years a different policy has prevailed, and it has been deemed expedient that an opportunity should be afforded to the Church in convocation to enter upon the free discussion of all ecclesiastical questions. Nevertheless, convocation is still debarred from 'alleging or putting in use any existing ordinance or canon,' or, in other words, from passing any judgment, opinion, or sentence, without express license and authority from the crown. No ordinance or sentence agreed upon in convocation has any legal validity until it has received the sanction of the crown; and if any attempt be made to enforce the same without such sanction, the parties concerned would incur the penalties of a præmunire." {Convocation.}

ᵃ Stat. 25 Henry VIII. c. 10. See Hans. Deb. vol. clxxix. p. 1280; vol. clxxx. p. 1100.
' Joyce's Sacred Synods, p. 40; Pro. Church Congress, York, 1866.
" See arguments in Moore's Privy Council Cases, N. S. vol. L p. 434; and Bishop of Melbourne's Memorial, Commons' Papers, 1864, v. xliv. p. 142.
ᵛ Moore, P. C. Cases, N. S. vol. i. p. 404.
" Lord Chancellor Westbury, in

2. *The position of the Church of England in the Colonies.*

Church of England in the Colonies.

The principle of constitutional law which requires that the prerogative of the crown in matters ecclesiastical shall be exercised within the limits prescribed by Parliament, applies with equal force to the erection of episcopal sees in the colonies of the United Kingdom; although, the Church of England cannot claim to be regarded as the Established Church in any British colony.

In crown colonies, that is to say, colonies which have been acquired by conquest or cession, and which do not possess representative institutions, the legislative power being exercised by the crown, through orders in council, bishoprics may be constituted, and a measure of ecclesiastical jurisdiction conferred, by the sole authority of the crown. This has been done in the crown colonies of Ceylon, Sierra Leone, St. Helena, and the Mauritius, and also at Gibraltar. In all these places episcopal sees have been established by the authority of the crown, which have a legal connection with the Church in the mother country. But even in the case of crown colonies, it should be remarked, that since the repeal of the Act 1 Eliz. c. 1,* which enabled the sovereign to appoint persons who could execute all manner of ecclesiastical jurisdiction in any country belonging to the English crown, there is no power in the crown alone to create any new or additional ecclesiastical tribunal with coercive jurisdiction within the realm.' 'It is a settled constitutional principle or rule of law, that although the crown may by its prerogative establish courts to proceed according to the common law, yet that it cannot create any new court

---

reference to the Synodical Judgment by the Convocation of Canterbury upon 'Essays and Reviews.' Hansb. vol. clxxvi. p 1544. Attorney-General (Sir R. Palmer), Ib. vol. clxxx. p. 600.

* By the Act 16 Car. I. cap. 11. And see 13 Car. II. c. 12.

' Judgment of Privy Council, in Bishop (Colenso) of Natal v. the Bishop of Cape Town, delivered March 20, 1865. See Annual Register, 1865. p. 200. And see Moore's Privy Council Cases, N. S. vol. i. p. 430. Arguments in case of Long v. the Bishop of Cape Town.

to administer any other law; and it is laid down by Lord *Colonial Church.* Coke in the Fourth Institute, that the erection of a new court, with a new jurisdiction, cannot be without an Act of Parliament." The Church of England in a crown colony is prohibited from making any regulation which is at all at variance with the ecclesiastical law of the Church in the mother country.ᵃ And on the other hand, the power of the crown in any such colony must be exercised within the limits prescribed by constitutional law. Notwithstanding the opinion which has been expressed by some eminent authorities,ᵇ that the position of episcopal sees in the crown colonies is not affected by the judgment of the privy council in Bishop Colenso's case, it is extremely doubtful whether the power of the crown in colonies of this description is not shown by that decision to be limited to the issue of letters patent, sufficient in law to establish personal relations between the bishop and his clergy, as ecclesiastics; and not to extend to confer upon the bishop so appointed, under the authority of letters patent, any coercive legal authority whatsoever. If this be so, it is evident that additional statutory power is necessary in order to clothe the Church, even in crown colonies, with the authority required to maintain her in a proper state of efficiency. It is most probable, however, that in any future legislation on this subject by the Imperial Parliament, the congregations of the Church of England in all the British colonies will be placed on an equal footing, and will be rendered legally independent of the Church in the mother country.

As respects new settlements, not being crown colonies or colonies which have received representative institutions, we are no longer in any doubt,ᶜ it having been

---

* Judgment of Privy Council in Bishop Colenso's case.
ᵃ Case of the Diocese of Colombo; in Correspondence relative to Colonial Bishoprics, No. I, presented to Parliament in May 1866, p. 10.
ᵇ Bishop of London, Hans. Deb. vol. clxxxiv. p. 511. Lord Carnarvon (Col. Secretary), *Ib.* p. 603.
ᶜ See Act 6 and 7 Vict. c. 13. Certain bishoprics in the East Indies were authorised to be established by the Imperial Acts, 53 Geo. III. c. 155, s. 49, and 3 and 4 Will. IV. c. 85,

Colonial Bishops.

decided, in the case of the Bishop of Natal, that the crown (subject to the special provisions of any Act of Parliament) stands in the same relation to such a settlement or colony as it does to the United Kingdom; and although it may authorise the consecration of a bishop in and for the benefit of the Church of England in any such colony, and thereby establish 'personal relations' between the said bishop and his clergy, it has no power to assign him any diocese, or to give him any diocesan jurisdiction, or coercive legal authority therein, without a special Act being first passed by the legislature, authorizing the issue of letters patent for that purpose. 'No metropolitan, or bishop, in any colony having legislative institutions can, by virtue of the crown's letters patent alone (unless granted under an Act of Parliament, or confirmed by a colonial statute), exercise any coercive jurisdiction, or hold any court or tribunal for that purpose. Pastoral or spiritual authority may be incidental to the office of bishop, but all jurisdiction in the Church, where it can be lawfully conferred, must proceed from the crown, and be exercised as the law directs; and suspension or deprivation of office is a matter of coercive legal jurisdiction, and not of mere spiritual authority.'[4]

Case of Bishop Colenso.

The foregoing definition of the legal status of a bishop of the Church of England, in a colony or dependency of the British crown, is taken from the recent judgment of the privy council in the case of Dr. Colenso, bishop of Natal, who was deprived of his episcopal functions—after a formal trial, and condemnation for heretical opinions, before a synod of the Church in South Africa—by his

---

sec. 93. In 1824, a bishop was appointed in Jamaica, by letters patent; but his legal status and authority were defined and established by an Act of the colonial legislature, which was confirmed by the crown. And there are bishoprics in Antigua, Barbados, and Guiana, which have been recognised and confirmed by Acts of the Imperial Parliament, or of the local legislatures.

[4] Privy Council Judgment, Bp. of Natal v. Bp. of Capetown. Judgment of Master of the Rolls, on Bp. Colenso's salary, Nov. 6, 1866. And see Long v. the Bp. of Capetown, decided June 24, 1863, in Moore's Privy Council Cases, N. S. vol. I. p. 411.

metropolitan, Dr. Gray, the bishop of Capetown. Upon the appeal of Bishop Colenso to the privy council, the decision of the metropolitan was set aside, upon the ground of want of the necessary authority and jurisdiction to determine upon the case. In reviewing the legal position of the parties concerned, the privy council pronounced the opinion that while the sovereign had undoubted right, by virtue of her prerogative, to give style, title, dignity, and precedence, in all parts of her dominions, yet that she had no power to issue letters patent professing to create episcopal sees, or to confer diocesan jurisdiction, or coercive legal authority, in colonies that were in possession of representative institutions,—or wherein the Church of England had not been established by law. Representative institutions had been granted to Natal in 1847, and to Capetown in 1850, consequently the letters patent of Drs. Gray and Colenso, which were issued in 1853, without the necessary authorisation, were null and void for any legal purpose whatever.

The comprehensive effect of this judgment of the privy council will be better understood by referring to a speech of the Attorney-General, who stated, in answer to a question put to him in the House of Commons, on the 27th March, 1865, that he understood the aforesaid decision to have determined, (1), that no legal dioceses are created by letters patent in the colonies possessing representative institutions, or in which the Church of England had not been previously established by law; (2), that the letters patent heretofore illegally issued for the erection of episcopal sees in such colonies do not create any legal identity between the Episcopal Church presided over by these bishops, and the United Church of England and Ireland; (3), that these letters patent do not introduce into those colonies any part of the English ecclesiastical law; (4), that they confer on the bishops no legal jurisdiction or power whatever; and add nothing to any authority which the bishops may be legally capable of acquiring by the

Effect of the judgment of the Privy Council.

312　THE ROYAL PREROGATIVE

Colonial Bishops.

voluntary principle, without any letters patent or royal sanction at all. The maximum operation of these letters patent seems to be, to incorporate the bishops and their successors, not as an ecclesiastical corporation in the colony, whose status, rights, and authority the colonies would be required to recognise; but simply as a common legal corporation, which it is in the ordinary prerogative of the crown to create, and for which no statutory powers are required. It was further stated, by the Secretary of State for the Colonies, that until the very important subject brought under the notice of the government by the recent decision of the privy council had been fully considered, no letters patent nominating successors under the existing illegal patents to bishops who might die or resign would be issued to any colony.[e] On May 30, the Colonial Secretary informed the House of Commons that, upon the advice of the law officers of the crown, the government had decided that, under existing circumstances, no letters patent to bishops ought to be issued to colonies having representative institutions. In filling up a recent vacancy in the diocese of Rupert's Land, the following course had been pursued; a letter had been addressed by the Archbishop of Canterbury to the Colonial Secretary, upon which her Majesty had been pleased to issue a mandate to the archbishop authorising him to consecrate a bishop, but no letters patent would be issued purporting to convey jurisdiction conferred by the crown.[f]

Canadian Episcopate

The clergy and laity of the Church of England in Canada have, ever since the year 1857, been permitted to elect their own bishops, without the special license of the crown; and no letters patent are issued to the bishops of

---

[e] Hans. Deb. vol. clxxviii. p. 270.
[f] Ib. vol. clxxix. p. 1100. See the Correspondence, and form of mandate in Corresp. rel. to Colonial Bishoprics, No. 1, 1864, p. 19. It was afterwards decided by the Colonial Secretary, with the advice of the crown law officers, that 'a mandate from the crown is not necessary to enable colonial bishops to perform the act of consecration.' Case of the Bishop of Niagara, Lond. Guardian, Decem. 10, 1862, p. 1200.

the Canadian Church, who derive their civil rights from an Act of the colonial legislature.ᵉ 'In order effectually to legalize the election of Canadian bishops,' the crown lawyers opined in 1856, that an imperial statute 'would be requisite.' But the imperial government believed that the practical purpose which it was sought to attain might be secured without the obvious inconveniences attendant on direct legislation, if they adopted the course of recommending her Majesty to be guided, as a general rule, in filling up any vacancy which might occur, by such representation as she might receive from the clergy and laity of the diocese, duly assembled.ʰ

The authority presumed to have been conferred upon a colonial bishop, by his letters patent, 'to perform all the functions appropriate to the office of a bishop in a colony, does not confer power to convene a meeting of clergy and laity, to be elected in a certain manner prescribed by him, for the purpose of making laws binding upon churchmen. Such a meeting is not a synod, and its acts are illegal, if they purport, without the consent of the crown or the colonial legislature, to bind persons beyond its control, and to establish new courts of justice.'ⁱ

Colonial Diocesan Synods.

In the year 1855, application was made to the Imperial Parliament, by a joint address from both Houses of the Canadian legislature, for the repeal of such imperial statutes as impeded the clergy and laity of the Colonial Church from meeting in synod, and from electing their own bishops; but after consulting the law officers of the crown, the Secretary of State for the Colonies recommended that the powers sought for should be conferred by an Act of the Canadian legislature, as had already been done in the colony of Victoria.ʲ Whereupon a

---

ᵉ Canada Stat. 19 and 20 Vict. cap. 141. Mr. Secretary Cardwell, in Hans. Deb. vol. clxxviii. p. 270.

ʰ See Journals, Leg. Assembly, Canada, 1850, pp. 259-260. Commons' Papers, 1856, vol. xliv. p. 120.

Ibid. 1857, Sess. 2. vol. xxviii. p. 97.

ⁱ Case of Lang v. the Bishop of Capetown, in Brodrick's Judgments of the Privy Council, p. 201.

ʲ See authorities cited above, in note (h).

provincial statute was passed to enable the members of the Church of England in Canada to hold synods, and to elect their own office bearers, which being reserved for the royal sanction, was afterwards ratified by the queen in council.[1]

Zealand Episcopate

In view of the altered position of the Church of England in the colonies of Great Britain, by reason of the aforementioned judgment of the privy council, in the case of the Bishop of Natal,—which denies that the Church is a part of the constitution in any colonial settlement, and repudiates its claim to be recognised by the law of any colony otherwise than as 'the members of a voluntary association,'—the five bishops of the Anglican Church in New Zealand petitioned the queen, in the year 1865, that they might be permitted to surrender their letters patent (which had been issued by the crown after the colony had received representative institutions), and allowed to rely in future upon the powers inherent in their office for perpetuating the succession of their order within the colony, and securing the due exercise of their episcopal functions, in conformity with a church constitution agreed upon in 1857, 'by voluntary compact' between the bishops, clergy, and laity of the United Church of England and Ireland in New Zealand.

The bishops stated, in their petition, that their Church constitution had been recognised by an act of the New Zealand legislature, in 1858, which sanctioned the assembling of a general synod, and made regulations in regard to the holding of Church property. That a general synod had since assembled triennially, and had framed rules for enforcing discipline within their body, and had established a tribunal to determine whether such rules had been violated or not, and what should be the effect of their violation; in conformity with the judgment of the privy council, in the case of Long v. the Bishop of Capetown, which declared that the members of the Church of England in a colony 'may adopt rules for enforcing discipline within their body which will be binding on those who, expressly or by implication, have assented to them.'[2]

In order to prevent any failure of justice, as the result of this new relation between the Church authorities and the parties who may be subject to them, the bishops submit that the course of procedure, in all questions that may arise between any of the members of the Anglican Church in New Zealand,—whether bishops, clergy,

---

[1] Can. Stat. 19 and 20 Vic. c. 141. Amended, in order to remove doubts in regard to the representation of the laity in the synods, by the Act 22 Vict. c. 139.

[2] Brodrick's Judgments, p. 310.

or laity,—who have bound themselves by voluntary compact, under the authority of the general synod, should be that which was pointed out by the judgment of Lord Lyndhurst, in 1835, in the case of Dr. Warren,* viz. :—

The Church in New Zealand.

1. That the question be tried and decided according to the rules of the synod, as agreed to by the bishops, clergy, and laity.
2. That on petition of either party the Supreme Court of the colony would have authority to inquire into 'the regularity of the proceedings, and the authority of the tribunal, and, on those grounds merely,' to affirm or annul the decision.
3. That from any such decision of the Supreme Court of the colony an appeal would lie to the privy council, upon the same grounds.

The bishops are of opinion that such a mode of procedure would satisfy all the ends of justice, and secure the liberty of the subject, without its being necessary to appeal direct to the crown, in any litigated case, as had been done with such unsatisfactory results in the controversy between the Bishop of Capetown and the Bishop of Natal.

In order, therefore, that all doubts as to their status, both ecclesiastical and temporal, may be removed, the bishops pray,

1. That the surrender of their letters patent, now declared to be null and void, may be accepted.
2. That the royal mandate under which they were consecrated may be declared to have been merely permissive, and to have no further effect or legal consequence.
3. That the inherent right of the bishops in New Zealand to fill up vacancies in their own order by the consecration of persons elected in conformity with the regulations of the general synod, without letters patent, and without royal mandate, may be recognised: following therein the precedent already established in the case of the missionary bishop for the islands of the Western Pacific, who was consecrated by the bishops of New Zealand, without letters patent or royal mandate, after communication with the Secretary of State for the Colonies, and the Attorney-General of New Zealand.

On April 24, 1866, the Colonial Secretary (Mr. Cardwell) informed the House of Commons, in reply to a question from a member, that the foregoing memorial of the New Zealand bishops had been accompanied by a minute from the New Zealand ministry, objecting to the creation of corporations within the colony by the act of the crown without their advice, and also to any arrangement by which any quasi jurisdiction of the bishops in New Zealand should receive any authority from the crown. On the other hand, the

---

* See Brodrick and Fremantle's Judgments of the Jud. Com. P. C. 308 n, 311.

Archbishop of Canterbury approved of the petition from the New Zealand bishops, but was of opinion that, since the judgments of the privy council therein cited, 'the quasi judicial decisions of the governing powers in the colonial churches could only be regarded as proceedings "in *foro domestico*," which ought not to be liable to be reviewed, on appeal, by the judicial committee of the privy council.'[a] Under these circumstances, and considering the difficulties arising out of the decision of the privy council in the case of the Bishop of Natal, the government had decided to consult parliament before any further action was taken. Meanwhile, they were unable to recommend the filling up of a vacancy in the see of Nelson, New Zealand, although such vacancy had existed for several months.

Colonial Bishops Bill

On May 15, the promised Colonial Bishops Bill was introduced.[c] It permitted the surrender of his letters patent from the crown by any bishop exercising episcopal functions in any of the British colonies. It rendered valid ordinary episcopal acts done by any bishop, lawfully chosen, and consecrated, by the free and voluntary consent of his clergy and people, without the necessity for any letters patent, royal mandate, or license. It authorised any bishop of the Church of England to consecrate, within the United Kingdom, a bishop for the Church in the colonies, or elsewhere beyond the limits of the United Kingdom, upon receiving a royal license in lieu of a mandate for that purpose: and declared that no such mandate or license shall be necessary for any such consecration elsewhere than within the United Kingdom. All questions of law respecting the status, rights, and duties of a colonial bishop to be determinable, where there is no ecclesiastical court, by ordinary courts of law in the colonies. The remaining clauses of this Bill related to the relations between the Established Church in the mother country and the colonial bishoprics, so far as regards the performance of episcopal acts or clerical functions by persons ordained in the United Kingdom, or in any of its dependencies. Owing to the change of ministry in the latter part of this session, the Colonial Bishoprics Bill was unavoidably withdrawn. But, on July 13, the new Colonial Secretary expressed his general agreement with the principle of this Bill, and intimated that the government would be prepared to submit a similar measure to Parliament in the ensuing session.[d]

---

[a] See the petition, minute of New Zealand Cabinet thereon, and the Archbishop's letter, &c., in the 'Correspondence relative to Colonial Bishoprics,' presented to Parliament, in May 1866, No. 1, p. 1.

[c] Hans. Deb. vol. clxxxiii. p. 1032.

[d] Ib. vol. clxxxiv. p. 805.

3. *The position of the Church of England in Foreign Countries.*

Inasmuch as the whole collective legal powers of a bishop of the Church of England, as distinguished from his spiritual powers, are derived from the crown, in conjunction with Parliament, it follows that no such authority and jurisdiction can be granted out of the queen's dominions, except as the result of a special arrangement with the governing power of a foreign country; and that the authority of Parliament must be invoked to enable the crown to dispense with the requirements indispensable to the ordinary appointment and consecration of bishops within the realm. Thus, in 1786, after the independence of the revolted American colonies had been established, an act was passed empowering the Archbishop of Canterbury or York, with such other bishops as they shall think fit to assist, to consecrate citizens or subjects of foreign states to the episcopal office, according to the form of consecration in the Church of England. This act dispensed with the necessity for the royal license for the election, and of the royal mandate for the confirmation and consecration of such bishops; but it forbad any such consecration without the royal license having been first obtained for the performance of the same.[q] Subsequently, in the year 1841, the provisions of this Act were extended so as to admit of bishops so appointed to exercise spiritual jurisdiction over the ministers of British congregations of the Church of England in foreign countries, as well as over such other Protestant congregations as may be desirous of placing themselves under their authority.[r] In 1862, the Bishop of Oxford submitted a Bill to the House of Lords, to authorise the appointment and consecration of bishops for heathen and Maho-

Church of England abroad.

---

[q] 26 Geo. III. c. 84.
[r] The Jerusalem Bishopric Act, 5 Vict. c. 6, and see the form of license from the crown in Stephen's Ecclesiastical Statutes, vol. ii. p. 2150, n.

medan countries, with a view to the spread of the Gospel among the heathen, and to dispense with the necessity for any license from the crown, to enable the archbishops to proceed to consecrate such bishops. The Bill was opposed by the Lord Chancellor, as being an attempt to 'assail and remove the supremacy of the crown;' and because it was necessary, in order 'to maintain the constitution of the country in Church and State, that no act should be done by which dignity is conferred, except under special authority emanating from the sovereign, as the source of all authority, temporal and spiritual.' Moreover, there was no necessity for the Bill, as the power and authority required had been already given by the Acts of 26 Geo. III. and 5 Vict. aforesaid; and there was no difficulty in obtaining the license of the crown to proceed under those statutes. The Bill was accordingly withdrawn.*

In 1861, the bishops of the Anglican Church in New Zealand, after communication on the subject with the Secretary of State for the Colonies, and the Attorney-General for New Zealand, consecrated a missionary bishop for the islands of the Western Pacific, without letters patent, or any mandate from the crown.

4. *The obligations of the Act of Uniformity.*

Act of Uniformity. By the Act 13 and 14 Car. II. cap. 4, commonly called the Act of Uniformity, the use of the Book of Common Prayer thereunto annexed is made binding upon the clergy of the Church of England; and they are expressly forbidden to make use of any other form or order than what is prescribed and appointed to be used in and by the said book. A declaration of assent and consent to the said Book of Common Prayer is required to be made by all officiating ministers of the Church, together with other declarations for the maintenance of the established

---

* Hans. Deb. vol. clxviii. pp. 223-234.

religion and government in Church and state. This Act, however, is limited in its operation to the 'kingdom of England, dominion of Wales, and town of Berwick-on-Tweed.'¹ A similar Act was passed by the Irish Parliament.² In conformity with the general spirit of liberality, and increased freedom of action in regard to ecclesiastical questions, which characterizes enlightened public opinion at the present day, it would appear that Parliament is not inclined to insist upon the literal observance of this statute. Thus, on August 7, 1862, inquiry being made of the government, in the House of Commons, whether a certain injunction issued by the Bishop of Oxford to his clergy was in conformity with the Act of Uniformity, the Attorney-General evaded a direct answer to the question, and inclined to regard the subject-matter of the injunction 'as one that concerned the bishop and his clergy, and not the government.'³

<small>Act of Uniformity.</small>

In 1865, pursuant to the recommendations of a royal commission appointed to consider the terms of subscription to the Articles and Liturgy of the Established Church by persons admitted to holy orders therein,—which were previously of a very stringent character,—Parliament adopted a new form of subscription, couched in general terms," professedly in order to quiet the conscientious scruples of a large body of the clergy, and to admit of a greater latitude of opinion, in regard to many questions of faith and practice, concerning which the Church has not pronounced authoritatively, or does not consider it to be of essential importance that her ministers should be entirely agreed upon.³

<small>New terms of clerical subscription.</small>

The next branch of the royal prerogative that will

---

¹ But see the previous Act on the same subject, of 1 Eliz. c. 2, which applies to the whole of 'the Queen's dominions,' and which has not been repealed.
² 17 and 18 Car. II. c. 6.
³ Hans. Deb. vol. clxviii. p. 1213.

But see a valuable note on this point in Smith's Parl. Rememb. 1862, p. 180.
ⁿ By Act 28 and 29 Vict. c. 122.
³ Hans. Deb. vol. clxxix. p. 1883 (Archbishop of York). Ib. vol. clxxx. p. 656 (Attorney-General Palmer).

In relation to the Army and Navy.

engage our attention is that which concerns the maintenance and control of the army and navy. The existence of a military force, of greater or less extent, for purposes of protection and defence against the enemies of the state is essential to the well-being of every community. All military authority and command within the realm is necessarily centred in the sovereign; a prerogative which, by the declaratory Act 13 Car. II. c. 6, was expressly confirmed. The dependence of the army upon the crown, absolutely and without any qualification, is essential to the safety of the monarchy, and has ever been regarded as the undisputed right of the occupant of the English throne.[f] Nevertheless, at the revolution of 1688, this prerogative was subjected to such constitutional restraints that it is impossible it should be exercised to the detriment of English liberty. It was declared by the Bill of Rights 'that the raising or keeping a standing army within the kingdom, in the time of peace, unless it be with consent of Parliament, is against law.' This consent to the continued existence of a standing army is given only for the period of one year at a time, by a formal resolution of the House of Commons fixing the number of men of which the army shall consist. This resolution is embodied in the preamble of the annual Mutiny Act, which recites the aforesaid provision of the Bill of Rights, and enacts that 'whereas it is adjudged necessary by her Majesty and this present Parliament that a body of forces should be continued for the safety of the United Kingdom, the defence of the possessions of her Majesty's crown, and the preservation of the balance of power in Europe,'—the said force shall consist of such a number of men. Having declared the assent of Parliament to the existence of an army, to be composed of a limited number of soldiers, the Act proceeds to provide for the discipline of the force by authorising military offenders to be punished accord-

---

[f] See Com. Inst. Eng. Gov. t. 594.

ing to military law, instead of by the slow and complex process of the civil courts.

The first Mutiny Act was passed in 1689. It has since been renewed every session, with the exception of the interval between 1698 and 1701, when it appears not to have been enacted. In the years immediately following the revolution, the Mutiny Acts dealt exclusively with the matter of discipline, and the parliamentary sanction to the continuance of the army itself was given by resolution of the House of Commons in Committee of Supply, determining the number of men to be employed, and voting the money required for their maintenance and support. On two occasions during the reign of William III., the House of Commons reduced the number of the standing army by their resolutions in this committee, and one of these instances occurred at the time when there was no Mutiny Act in operation.[1] By modern practice, the numbers of men to be employed both in the army and navy are annually fixed by resolutions in Committee of Supply, and afterwards included, in respect to the army, in the Mutiny Act, and in respect to the navy, in the Act of Appropriation; thus obtaining, for the resolutions of the Commons in limitation of the amount of force to be in the hands of the crown, the consent of the other branches of the legislature.[2]

Mutiny Act.

---

[1] Hallam, vol. iii. pp. 189, 190.
[2] It is a direct infringement of the constitution, and a violation both of the Bill of Rights and of the Mutiny Act, for the government to raise more men for the land and sea forces than have been voted by Parliament. 'It is the practice of the War Office, however, to regard the number of men voted, not as a maximum number for any time during the year, but for an average upon the whole year; considering that if they made the average correct for the whole year, the vote of the House had been complied with.' (Secretary Sir G. Lewis, Hans. Deb. vol. clxv. p. 974.) Upon occasions of great emergency the government have assumed the responsibility of increasing the army or navy beyond the numbers actually voted, and have afterwards applied to Parliament to make good the deficiency in the supplies granted for this service. Ibid. vol. clxiv. pp. 1481-1493. But see Smith's Parl. Rememb. 1860, p. 254, and 1862, p. 39. And Report to Commons on Public Accounts, 1862, Evid. 976; and 1864, Evid. 1009-1029. In 1858, when the government of India was assumed by the British crown, clauses were inserted in the

Standing army.

It is worthy of remark that the declaration of the Bill of Rights, as to the illegality of maintaining a standing army without the consent of Parliament, is expressly confined to 'the time of peace.' Moreover, the Mutiny Act, in conferring extraordinary powers for the discipline of the army, is construed to imply that, except 'in time of peace,' the enforcement of martial law upon military men is not illegal. Accordingly, the royal prerogative in respect to the embodiment and control of an army for the defence of the kingdom in time of war remains unimpaired by these constitutional restrictions, and is still the same as it was by the common law. What that law allowed is, however, no longer material to inquire, inasmuch as the monarchs of England, ever since the revolution, have been satisfied to rely upon the authority of the Mutiny Act for the enforcement of discipline in the army both in war and peace, and have been equally dependent at all times upon the necessity of obtaining from Parliament, year by year, the supplies required for the prosecution of any war in which Great Britain might be engaged.[b] Moreover, when, during the American war, the question was raised in Parliament whether it was legal to allow regiments to be levied and maintained by individuals, without the sanction of Parliament, the weight of authority was against it, though ministers inclined to a contrary opinion. The principal objection to the practice was a very formidable one, namely, that it is of the very

---

new India Bill to prevent the use of the Indian army out of India, except upon sudden emergency; and requiring that, whenever it should be so made use of, the expense thereof should be defrayed out of moneys to be voted by Parliament, and not out of the Indian revenues. 21 & 22 Vic. c. 106, sec. 55, 56. Hans. Deb. vol. cli. pp. 1007, 1008, 2008. And see Ibid. vol. clxxii. p. 1201, vol. clxxvii. p. 1821, and Smith's Parl. Rememb. 1858, p. 40. See also, on the constitutional question of the employment of troops on the Indian establishment in other countries, the Report of the Commons' Committee on Mortality of Troops (China), 1860, p. xi.

[b] See an able article in the Saturday Review, Oct. 25, 1863, pp. 505–507.

essence of Parliament to judge of the necessities of the state, and make provision accordingly; and that any measure to that end, without the previous concurrence of Parliament, tended to supersede its authority and strip it of its rights.' It is, however, one of 'the ancient rights and liberties' of Englishmen to 'have arms for their defence, suitable to their condition, and as allowed by law;' and the fundamental laws of the kingdom have repeatedly affirmed the obligation of every Englishman to have a knowledge of the use of arms.[d] The formation of Volunteer rifle corps takes place under the direct authority of Acts of Parliament, which permit the sovereign to accept offers of military service from the people, under certain conditions.[e] The Volunteer movement, which has assumed such importance in England at the present time, originated in the spring of 1859, when General Peel, the then Secretary for War, issued two circulars, the first of which declared the readiness of government to accept the services of Volunteer corps, offered under the old Volunteer Act of the 44 George III., and the other made known the principles upon which the government was prepared to accept the same. In 1862, a royal commission was appointed to inquire into the condition of the Volunteer force, and to report whether any measures were necessary in order to ensure its stability, and increase its efficiency as an auxiliary arm of national defence. In reporting various recommendations for this purpose, the commissioners lay down the constitutional rule, that 'if it be desirable that any positive limit should be placed upon the total number of the force, the duty and responsibility of deciding that question must rest exclusively with the responsible advisers of the crown.'[f] In conformity with this principle, the Secretary of State

Volunteer corps.

[c] Parl. Hist. xix. 025. Campbell's Chancellors, V. 443.
[d] See Smith's Parl. Rememb. 1850, pp. 108–112.
[e] Stats. 44 Geo. III. c. 54; 60 Geo. III. c. 1.
[f] Commons Papers, 1862, vol. xxvii. p. 10.

for War shortly afterwards issued a circular forbidding the enrolment of additional Volunteer corps.

Such being the well-ascertained rights of the crown in regard to the levy and maintenance of a military force for the protection and defence of the empire, it remains to consider the extent of the royal prerogative in the direction and control of the same, and to inquire how far the Houses of Parliament are constitutionally empowered to interfere therein.

Responsibility of ministers for the control of the Army and Navy.

We have already seen [a] that this was the last of the prerogatives to be surrendered into the custody of responsible ministers. Even of late years there have been those who have contended that the administration of the military and naval forces of the kingdom should be left to the unquestioned control of the executive, and that any attempt at interference with the same, by either House of Parliament, under any circumstances, ought to be resisted as unconstitutional.[b] But sound doctrine forbids any distinction to be drawn between the exercise of the royal authority over the army and navy, and over other branches of the public service; upon all alike it is equally competent for either House of Parliament to tender its advice, and there can be nothing done in any department of state for which some minister of the crown is not accountable to Parliament. Were any exception to be allowed in the case of the army and navy, it would necessarily follow that the responsibility for their management would fall upon the sovereign directly; but this would be contrary to the constitutional maxim which declares that the king can do no wrong, and is not personally amenable to any earthly tribunal whatsoever.[1] It has been suggested that the Commander-in-Chief, and not the advisers of the crown, should be held singly responsible for all acts of military administration. But, as Lord Grey pertinently remarks,

---

[a] *Ante*, p. 60.
[b] See Mr. Sheil's remarks, in Hans. Deb. vol. lxxv. p. 1280.
[1] See *ante*, p. 40.

this would not materially lessen the inconvenience. 'The holder of that office would stand in a most unsafe position, if he could not depend upon the support of the ministers of the crown in case of his measures being questioned in Parliament; and they cannot be expected to give this support unless the officer who trusts to it communicates with them in the performance of his duties, in such a manner as to enable them to guard against his taking, or omitting to take, any step for which they will not be prepared to defend him.'[1] The mismanagement of our forces during the early part of the Russian war, in 1854-55, sufficiently demonstrated the necessity for a more direct and undivided responsibility than had previously been recognised in the conduct of interests of such importance to the security of the empire. There was also afforded signal proof of the advantages accruing from constitutional oversight, on the part of the House of Commons, into the manner in which the military departments were organised and controlled, by the improved system of administration which resulted from the investigations of Parliament into the conduct of the war in the Crimea.

<small>Commander of the Forces.</small>

The complete responsibility of ministers for the efficient control of the military force having been established beyond dispute, it is a necessary consequence that they are accountable to Parliament for the same. But as the command of the army and navy is the peculiar privilege and strength of the executive power, and cannot be surrendered to Parliament without a virtual overthrow of the monarchy, it is essential that the scrutiny of Parliament into the exercise of this prerogative should be conducted with the utmost discretion, lest the constitutional limits of inquiry and counsel should be overstepped, and the functions of executive authority be

---

[1] Grey, Parl. Govt. 8-10, n.; and see a debate in the Commons on military organisation, on June 1, 1858; and especially the observations of Mr. Sidney Herbert and of Lord Palmerston. Hans. Deb. vol. cl. pp. 1340, 1357.

encroached upon. The constitutional security against the abuse of this prerogative is found in the general responsibility of ministers, and the necessity for the sanction of Parliament to the continued existence of the army and navy, by the annual appropriations for the support of these services, and the annual renewal of the Mutiny Acts.[k]

Parliamentary control over this prerogative.

Parliament has an unquestioned right to interfere, by enquiry, remonstrance, and censure, in all cases of abuse, whether on the part of individual military officers, or of executive departments.[l] It has a right to inquire into the causes and consequences of any disasters that may befall our arms in the prosecution of contests against the queen's enemies.[m] It has a right to discuss and advise upon all general questions affecting the well-being of the army and navy, their internal economy or efficiency; but this right should be exercised with the utmost discretion, and with great forbearance.[n]

It is essential to the constitution of a military body that the crown should have the power of reducing to a lower grade, or of altogether dismissing, any of its officers from service in the army or navy at its own discretion, and, if need be, without assigning any reason for the act; such power being always exercised through

---

[k] Bowyer, Eng. Const. 484. Discipline in the army and amongst the Royal Marine forces is maintained by annual Mutiny Acts, but the discipline of the navy is enforced by certain rules and articles first enacted by Parliament soon after the revolution, but since new-modelled by various statutes. The existing code of naval discipline is contained in the stat. 29 & 30 Vict. c. 109.

[l] See the debate and proceedings in the House of Commons on June 16, 1848, on a motion to resolve that the practice of appointing naval officers as dockyard superintendents, and of limiting their term of office to five years, is inexpedient.

[m] The cases cited, by Messrs Walpole and Disraeli,—in urging inquiry into the condition of the army before Sebastopol,—of similar inquiries instituted by the two Houses of Parliament during the American revolutionary wars, and the subsequent naval and military operations in Europe,—including the case of the Walcheren expedition in 1810. Hans. Deb. vol. cxxxvi. pp. 1811-1816, 1857.

[n] Hans. Deb. vol. lxxxix. p. 1089. *Ibid.* (Lord Stanley) vol. clxvii. p. 211. *Ibid.* vol. clxiv. p. 625. *Ibid.* (Lord Palmerston) vol. clxix. p. 751.

a responsible minister, who is answerable for the same, if it should appear to have been exercised unwarrantably, and upon an insufficient ground.* And it would be a dangerous assumption of power for either House of Parliament to interfere in a matter affecting the discipline or command of the army or navy, in any individual instance:² or, to institute an inquiry into the causes which affect the promotion of particular officers:³ or, into the bestowal of military rewards or punishments to particular persons:⁴ or, to review the decisions of courts-martial, and the action of the military or naval authorities in relation thereto:⁵ except in cases where

---

* Hans. Deb. (Lord Hardwicke) vol. clxx. p. 382. Ibid. (Lord Palmerston) vol. clxxx. p. 456. It was decided by the Court of Queen's Bench, in the case of Dickson v. Viscount Combermere and others (Foster and Finlason, Nisi Prius Cases, iii. 527), that the discretionary power of the crown to remove officers of the army or militia is so absolute, that even if an officer had been tried by a court of inquiry and acquitted, the crown was justified in removing him from office upon the advice of a minister responsible to Parliament. See later cases to a similar purport, in Broom's Const. Law, p. 724. See also a discussion (in the Lords) on April 20, 1863, and (in the Commons) on May 19, 1863, on naval courts of inquiry.

² Mirror of Parl. 1847, p. 801. Ibid. 1841, p. 825. Hans. Deb. (Lord Lucan's case) vol. cxxxvii. p. 1393. See Macaulay's speech, Ibid. vol. lxxxiv. p. 800. General Peel's speech, Ibid. vol. clxxiv. p. 76.

³ Mirror of Parl. 1837, p. 574. Ibid. 1839, p. 2810. Proposed address for the retirement of old naval officers with a view to the promotion of young and active men. Hans. Deb. vol. lxix. p. 483; and see Ibid. vol. cxxxvii. p. 1191, vol. clxiv. p. 876. But in 1853, a committee of inquiry was appointed by the House of Commons into the case of Lieut. Englednc, it being alleged that he owed his restoration to the service to corrupt influences. Commons' Papers, 1852-3, vol. xxv. p. 47].

⁴ Macaulay, in Mirror of Parl. 1841, p. 1697. Duke of Wellington, in Hans. Deb. vol. lxxxii. p. 720. Case of Captain King (Army Prize Money), Parl. Deb. vol. xxiii. p. 1046; see also Hans. Deb. vol. lxxiv. p. 58, vol. clxiv. p. 934, vol. clxvii. p. 703; and the discussions on Lieut.-Col. Dawkins' case, Ibid. vol. clxxix. pp. 642, 870, vol. clxxx. p. 450.

⁵ Mirror of Parl. 1831-2, p. 2056. Ibid. 1834, p. 2121. Ibid. 1835, p. 2344. Ibid. 1841, p. 835. Hans. Deb. vol. clxxi. pp. 974, 1046. See observations in the House of Commons on the conduct of the Board of Admiralty in censuring a naval officer, after he had been fully acquitted by a court-martial. Ibid. vol. clxvii. p. 703. In 1863, the House of Commons were induced, under peculiar circumstances, to require papers to be laid before them touching the court-martial upon Colonel Crawley; but on March 15, 1864, it was resolved, after a long debate, that the production of any further papers in this case was inexpedient. The legal immunity of commanding officers in the army or navy in bringing their subordinates to trial by court-martial, is established by the case of Sutton v. Johnstone, 1 T. R. 493; see Broom, Const. Law, p. 650.

either malversation, corrupt motives, or similar improper conduct is distinctly chargeable. Neither should either House of Parliament assume the right of inquiring into the most suitable and efficient weapons for use in the army and navy, unless invited by the government to institute such an investigation.[t]

Parliament has a right to call for full information in regard to military matters, for the purpose of enabling it to vote with discretion and intelligence upon the naval and military estimates. But this right must not be held to justify an unseasonable interference in respect to the details of military administration. For example, it is an 'invariable rule, founded on the best possible reasons, never to publish instructions sent to naval and military officers, until the operations to which they referred were completed, and not often in that case:'[u] or, to present papers concerning a rebellion or war in which the country is engaged, until peace is restored:[v] or, to make public reports from military officers in the colonies to the military authorities at home, except at the discretion of the government:[w] or, to give information as to the mode in which honours are distributed in the army.[x]

If it be necessary at any time to institute minute inquiries into matters connected with the internal economy of the army or navy, such inquiries, it has been authoritatively stated, 'ought to be made by a com-

---

[t] Hans. Deb. vol. clxiii. pp. 1500-1581. In 1854, the House of Commons appointed a select committee on the cheapest, most expeditious, and efficient mode of providing small arms for the service; and in 1863, a committee to inquire into the results of recent experiments in various kinds of improved ordnance. These committees were appointed with the sanction of government; nevertheless, the result of their labours was most unsatisfactory. See a debate in the Commons, on March 2, 1865, on a motion for a committee to consider of navy armaments; which was negatived.

[u] Lord Palmerston, Hans. Deb. vol. clxxii. p. 650.

[v] Hans. Deb. vol. cil. pp. 1185, 1333.

[w] Mirror of Parl. 1837-8, p. 1528. And see ante, p. 280.

[x] Mirror of Parl. 1837, p. 603. But verbal explanations may be asked for on such points: see Hans. Deb. vol. clxxviii. p. 1648. Ibid. vol. clxxix. p. 47.

mission emanating from the crown and reporting to the crown, which report might afterwards be communicated to the House of Commons for any purposes which the House might require. But I think this House is not the authority which ought properly to institute any inquiries of this kind.'" It is perfectly competent, however, for Parliament to address the crown to appoint a commission for such a purpose.'

Occasionally, the administration will avail itself of some formal motion to explain to Parliament the circumstances attending the exercise of the royal prerogative in particular matters connected with naval or military administration. Thus, on June 7, 1861, on motion for going into Committee of Supply, the attention of the House was directed to the recent appointment of an officer to the colonelcy of a regiment, whose claims to such a distinction appeared to have been quite insufficient. The Under Secretary for War explained the circumstances of the appointment, and justified it. After a few remarks from other members, the subject was dropped.' Again, on June 5, 1862, inquiry was made in the House of Commons why a certain officer had been permitted to retire on half-pay, contrary to the Queen's Regulations. It was replied, that it was competent for the crown to dispense with its own rules when an exceptional case occurred, and that in any such case the Secretary for War was responsible

Ministerial explanations on this head.

---

* Lord Palmerston, Hans. Deb. vol. cxxxvii. p. 1241. [And see his speech on promotion and retirement in the navy. *Ibid.* vol. clxix. p. 740.] This opinion was afterwards corroborated by Mr. Disraeli. *Ibid.* vol. clxi. p. 1889; vol. clxx. p. 875. See a debate on a change in the system of promotion among army medical officers. *Ibid.* vol. clxxxiii. p. 585.

' Hans. Deb. vol. clxiii. p. 794. But while upon many definite and abstract questions, such as the pay of the navy, the manning of the fleet, or harbours of refuge, the labours of a royal commission are exceedingly useful, commissions ought not to be appointed to do the work of existing departments of state, who possess every facility for obtaining proper information upon matters of detail, and who are responsible for their conduct to Parliament. *Ibid.* (Ironclad Ships), vol. clxx. pp. 915–919.

* Hans. Deb. vol. clxii. p. 701.

to Parliament.^a And see on April 20, 1863, a debate in the House of Lords, on a question put to the First Lord of the Admiralty in regard to the proceedings of a naval court of inquiry, which resulted in the censure of Lord Elphinstone, the captain of H.M.S. Vigilant, for alleged neglect of duty. On May 19, a similar (informal) discussion took place on the same subject in the House of Commons.

Precedents of inquiries by Parliament.

Having endeavoured to define the rights of the two Houses of Parliament in regard to the exercise of this branch of the royal prerogative, the following precedents are submitted in further illustration of the subject:—

Kempenfeldt expedition.

In 1782, after the failure of the Kempenfeldt expedition, the causes thereof were discussed in both Houses of Parliament. On January 24, on motion of Mr. Fox, a committee of the whole House was appointed, with the concurrence of ministers, 'to inquire into the causes of the want of success of his Majesty's naval forces during this war, and more particularly in the past year.' After this committee had examined various papers laid before them, Mr. Fox, on February 7, moved, 'That it appears to this committee that there was gross mismanagement in the administration of naval affairs in 1781.' This was intended as a direct censure upon the Earl of Sandwich, the First Lord of the Admiralty, and was to have been followed up by an address for his removal from office, but the motion was negatived. It was again proposed, in the House itself, on February 20, but was again rejected.^b

Conduct of the Board of Admiralty.

In 1788, the Board of Admiralty, having, in their discretion, promoted certain captains to the rank of admiral, passing over others whom they adjudged to be disqualified for promotion, the House of Lords was moved, on February 20, to address the king on behalf of the naval captains who were thus neglected. The motion was opposed by the ministry, on the ground that Parliament ought to 'place a due confidence in the First Lord of the Admiralty, and suffer him to exercise the discretion that belonged to his situation, unmolested by their interference. The responsibility lay with that officer and the Board, and there the discretion ought to rest likewise. Whenever a complaint was formally made of breach of trust, or of improper conduct in any responsible member of the administration, the House had a right to institute an inquiry, and, upon sufficient

---

^a Hans. Deb. vol. clxvii. pp. 400, 420; and see *Ibid.* vol. clxix. pp. 1000, 1788.   ^b Parl. Hist. vol. xxii. pp. 878–940.

proof of the facts alleged, to address his Majesty to remove the President's
minister so misconducting himself. That was the constitutional
power of Parliament, and one of its most important and salutary
privileges; but it was widely distinct from that or the other House
taking upon themselves to exercise the functions of executive
government.'[a] The mover disclaimed any intention of interfering
with the prerogative, which he admitted would be 'highly indecent
and improper,' but founded his motion on the assumption that the
merits of deserving officers 'had been overlooked.' Nevertheless,
the motion was negatived without a division. On the following
day, Mr. Bastard moved, in the House of Commons, an address to
the king to be pleased to confer some mark of royal favour on
Captains Balfour and Thompson, two of the officers in question, and
who had already received the thanks of the House for gallant
conduct. This was resisted by the ministry as an attempt to transfer
the patronage of the navy from the crown, by whom it was exercised
through responsible ministers, to the Commons, by whom it would
be exercised without responsibility or control; 'for who shall call to
account the representatives of the people.' Such a usurpation
would be destructive to public liberty, and to our free institutions,
'for no axiom is more obvious than that this constitution is dissolved
from the instant that executive authority is assumed by the
representatives of the people.'[b] The sense of the House being
manifestly against the motion, it was withdrawn. On April 18,
however, Mr. Bastard renewed it in another shape. He moved
for the appointment of a committee to inquire into the conduct of
the Admiralty, in the late promotion of admirals. Mr. Pitt, the
premier, fully acknowledged the constitutional right of the House
to inquire into the conduct of any department of government, with
a view either to censure or punishment, 'whenever a case was made
out strong enough to warrant suspicion of abuse;' but he denied
that sufficient grounds for inquiry had been adduced in the present
instance. Mr. Fox expressed his concurrence in this view of the
constitutional position of Parliament, and observed that 'no one
held more sacred the power of the prerogative, with regard to the
distribution of military honours and rewards, than he did; nor was
any one more aware that the House of Commons was by no means
a proper place for canvassing military promotions.' Had this motion
been for an address to the crown, he could not have voted for it;
but being for inquiry into alleged abuse, in a case in which he saw
very strong grounds for suspecting partiality and oppression on the
part of the First Lord of the Admiralty, he should vote for it.
Nevertheless, the question was negatived. Undeterred by his
second defeat, Mr. Bastard once more renewed the subject, by
moving, on April 29, to resolve 'that it is highly injurious to the

---

[a] Parl. Hist. vol. xxvii. p. 16.   [b] Ibid. p. 28.

Precedents naval service of Great Britain to set aside, in promotions of flag officers, officers of distinguished merit and approved service, who are not precluded from such promotion by any orders of his Majesty in council.' The mover declared his object to be to induce the House to lay down a permanent rule for the guidance and protection of naval officers, and to prevent arbitrary and capricious promotions. The motion was characterised as being an uncalled for attempt to fetter the discretion of the Admiralty Board, and an implied censure on the First Lord, which had neither been shown to be merited, nor substantiated by evidence. The previous question was put thereon, and negatived.

Walcheren expedition.
Our next precedent refers to an event which is very memorable in English history; namely, the disastrous expedition to Walcheren, in 1809. This expedition had been sent out in order to divert the attention of Napoleon from the reinforcement of his armies on the Danube, which had hitherto proved too powerful for the resistance of Austria, and also for the purpose of attacking the naval armaments and establishments in the Scheldt, which were daily becoming more formidable to the security of Great Britain. The chief command of the expedition was given to Lord Chatham, a cabinet minister. Although partially successful, in the demolition of the docks and arsenals at Flushing, such gain was more than counterbalanced by the unfortunate occupation of the island of Walcheren. This island proved exceedingly unhealthy, and after sustaining severe losses and privations, the troops were obliged to evacuate it, and the remains of this ill-fated expedition were brought back to England. At the ensuing session of Parliament, resolutions of censure upon ministers, for the military operations of the preceding year, were moved, as amendments to the address, in both Houses. It was pertinently remarked, however, that ministers ought not to be condemned without previous inquiry; and these motions were negatived. But, on January 26, 1810, Lord Porchester moved, in the House of Commons, that a committee of the whole House be appointed to inquire into the policy and conduct of the late expedition to the Scheldt. It was contended, by ministers, that this inquiry should not be instituted until the papers on the subject had been communicated to Parliament. But the House would admit of no delay, and the motion was agreed to by a majority of nine. Soon afterwards, the papers relating to this expedition were laid before Parliament.*
The inquiry then proceeded, by the examination of witnesses at the

---

* The discovery among the documents of a narrative of the expedition, which had been privately submitted by Lord Chatham to the king, led to interesting discussions on the constitutional questions involved in this proceeding; and ultimately to the censure of his lordship, and his consequent resignation of office. But this point has been fully considered in a former chapter. See ante, p. 171.

bar. After its termination, Lord Porchester, on March 26, submitted a series of resolutions, setting forth the principal facts adduced in evidence, and declaring ministers responsible for the heavy calamities which had attended the failure of the expedition, and which called for the severest censure of the House upon them. After protracted debates, the resolutions were negatived, and counter-resolutions, proposed by General Cranford, were agreed to, on divisions which gave ministers a majority of from 23 to 51.[f] This result was unexpected, and was attributed, not so much to the exertions of the government in influencing votes, as to the preponderance of their arguments in debate.[g]

Precedents

On August 4, 1835, Mr. Hume complained to the House of Commons of the conduct of Field-Marshal H. R. H. the Duke of Cumberland, for having, contrary to the express orders of the Commander-in-Chief, taken part in promoting the establishment of Orange lodges in the army. Whereupon the House agreed to certain resolutions on the subject, and to an address to the king, directing his Majesty's attention thereto. In reply the king assured the House that he would take the most effectual means to discourage and prevent every attempt to introduce secret societies into the army. The Home Secretary (Lord John Russell) also informed the House that he had communicated copies of the address and reply to the Duke of Cumberland, and had been assured by his royal highness that he had taken steps to bring about the immediate dissolution of the Orange institution in Great Britain and Ireland.[h]

Secret societies in the Army.

On May 3, 1836, Sir William Molesworth moved for the appointment of a committee to inquire into the conduct of the Commander of the Forces, in appointing Lord Bradenell to the lieutenant-colonelcy of the 11th Light Dragoons. His lordship, it seems, had about two years previously been removed from the command of a regiment, on account of his having been censured by a court-martial before which he had appeared as prosecutor. Under these circumstances, it was assumed that his re-appointment to a similar position was improper. In reply, it was shown that the military authorities were of opinion that Lord Bradenell had been sufficiently punished for his past conduct, and that there were no objections to his being reinstated; that there was no cause for imputing misconduct to the Commander of the Forces, and therefore no parliamentary ground for the proposed inquiry. It was also urged that the re-appointment of this nobleman was simply an act of discipline, not of patronage, and that any interference in such an act by the House of Commons would be unprecedented and unwarrantable. After some further debate the motion was withdrawn.[i]

Conduct of Commander of the Forces.

---

[f] Parl. Deb. vol. xvi. p. 422.
[g] Sir G. C. Lewis, in Edinb. Rev. vol. cviii. p. 527.
[h] Com. Journ. vol. xc. pp. 534, 552; Hans. Deb. vol. lxx. p. 619.
[i] Mirror of Parl. 1836, p. 1300.

Precedents Crimean expedition.

The disasters which befell the British expeditionary force in the Crimea, at the commencement of the war with Russia, in 1854, were of such magnitude that the state of the army, and the general conduct of the war, engaged the serious attention of Parliament at its next meeting, and animated debates took place in both Houses. On January 26, 1855, Mr. Roebuck moved, in the House of Commons, for the appointment of a committee to inquire into the condition of our army before Sebastopol, and into the conduct of those departments of the government whose duty it had been to minister to the wants of the same. This motion, although of a very stringent character, and involving a censure on the government for their management of the war, was strictly within the limits of constitutional inquiry.[j] Before the debate commenced, Lord John Russell, the President of the Council, and leader of the House of Commons, announced his resignation of office, on account of his inability to resist the proposed investigation. He admitted that the inquisitorial power was a most valuable parliamentary privilege, and acknowledged that the motion for inquiry could only be opposed on one of two grounds, either that existing evils were not of sufficient magnitude to call for investigation, or that means had been taken to remedy them. As he could assert neither of these propositions, he had determined to resign his office.[k] After these explanations, the debate began. The motion was opposed by the ministry, on the ground that it went beyond mere inquiry, and was an unconstitutional attempt to take the control of the expedition out of the hands of the government; that to grant the committee would be detrimental to the public interests, and would tend to paralyse the action of the executive, both at home and abroad, at a most critical period.[l] Being thus strenuously opposed by government, the question virtually assumed the shape of non-confidence in the ministry, and when by a large majority the House affirmed the necessity for inquiry, the ministry resigned.[m] They were succeeded by a ministry under the premiership of Lord Palmerston, who had filled the post of Home Secretary in the previous (Lord Aberdeen's) administration, and who, retaining the objections he had formerly expressed to the proposed committee of inquiry, urged upon the House to

---

[j] See Hans. Deb. vol. cxxxvi. pp. 1811-1816, 1857. On June 17, 1864, Sir J. D. Hay moved to resolve that her Majesty's government, in landing forces on the Gold Coast for the purpose of waging war against the King of Ashantee, without making any sufficient provision for preserving the health of the troops to be employed there, have incurred a grave responsibility; and that this House laments the want of foresight which has caused so large a loss of life. The government regarded this motion as a vote of censure, and opposed it accordingly. After a long debate, it was negatived by a majority of seven. See also post, p. 340.

[k] Hans. Deb. vol. cxxxvi. p. 900.

[l] Ibid. pp. 1010, 1051, 1202, 1225.

[m] Ibid. p. 1234.

abandon it, and to repose confidence in the new executive, who Precedents would pledge themselves to introduce such administrative improvements as were necessary for the vigorous prosecution of the war.* The House of Commons, however, having agreed to appoint the committee, were unwilling to forego the inquiry; and at length Lord Palmerston reluctantly consented to its being nominated, without any limit to its original scope and purport.* The first report of the committee was a recommendation that they should be made a committee of secrecy, but this proposition, not meeting with general acceptance, was disagreed to by the House.* After a protracted investigation, the committee made several reports, disclosing grievous mismanagement on the part of the authorities at home and abroad, in the conduct of the war, and making several recommendations for the improvement of the military organisation, &c. On July 17, 1855, Mr. Roebuck moved the following resolution, based upon the information elicited before the committee: 'That this House, deeply lamenting the sufferings of our army during the winter campaign in the Crimea, and coinciding with the resolution of their committee, that the conduct of the administration was the first and chief cause of the calamities which befell that army, do hereby visit with severe reprehension every member of that cabinet whose counsels led to such disastrous results.' The government met this motion by proposing the previous question, contending that the House had not the means of judging correctly of the Crimean expedition; that the result of the inquiry had been inconclusive, and confessedly incomplete, inasmuch as the committee were precluded, from motives of state policy, from more thorough investigations and criticisms, owing to the war having been conducted in concert with our ally, the Emperor of the French; and that the present ministry were not responsible for the original disasters, which occurred before their acceptance of office, and had since been remedied, at least to a very considerable extent. In reply, Mr. Whiteside urged that, according to the doctrine of ministerial responsibility, Lord Palmerston, having been a member of Lord Aberdeen's government, and having, since the recent ministerial changes, consented to the present inquiry, was in fact still responsible for the past transactions; and that he, in common with the other members of the late government who could be shown to have been concerned in such mal-administration (and who were now out of the ministry), ought to suffer the penalty of exclusion from office. This view of the position of Lord Palmerston was denied by Lord John Russell, the Attorney-General, Sir G. Grey, and others, who contended that the responsibility for the acts com-

* Hans. Deb. vol. cxxxvi. p. 1424.   * Ibid. p. 2088, vol. cxxxvii. pp.
* Ibid. p. 1805.   19–63.

Precedents Crimean expedition.

plained of lay with the ministry of Lord Aberdeen, which having been virtually condemned by the House of Commons, had resigned office, and that Lord Palmerston was now the head of an entirely new administration, and could not be held responsible for the conduct of his predecessors. It was admitted by Lord John Russell that, agreeably to the dictum of Macaulay, the member of an existing cabinet who differs from the rest on a vital point is bound to resign: but that 'while he retains his office, he is responsible even for the steps which he has tried to dissuade his colleagues from taking.'[t] Further than this, he was of opinion the doctrine of ministerial responsibility could not be applied, and it certainly did not justify the condemnation of the head of one ministry for the acts of a preceding ministry, because he happened to form part of the same. In this view the House concurred, and after two nights' debate, the motion for the previous question was carried by a large majority.[v] Reviewing the question dispassionately, it is evident that the decision of the House was correct, and that the responsibility of Lord Aberdeen's administration terminated upon their enforced resignation of office. If, as the result of parliamentary investigation, further proceedings against any particular member of that ministry should have appeared to be advisable, they should have taken the shape of a parliamentary impeachment, or of a criminatory address to the crown, against the offending individual, and not that of an endeavour to affix a continuance of ministerial responsibility for past acts upon a member of a new administration.

Board of Admiralty.

On July 24, 1860, Sir John Pakington moved, in the House of Commons, for an address to her Majesty for the appointment of a royal commission to consider the existing system of promotion and retirement in the royal navy; and the pay and position of the several classes of naval officers. The motion was opposed by government on the ground that, admitting grievances to exist, it would be better to trust to the Board of Admiralty, as the responsible department, to effect the necessary improvements, rather than to unsettle the navy by appointing an irresponsible commission, whose recommendations might excite hopes that could not be realised. The motion was negatived on division. On June 12, previous, Admiral Duncombe had moved for the appointment of a select committee to inquire into the constitution of the Board of Admiralty, and the various duties devolving thereon. Being opposed by government, the motion had been withdrawn, but with the declared intention, on the part of the mover, to renew it in the following session. Accordingly, on March 1, 1861, the motion was

[t] Hans. Deb. vol. cxxxix. p. 1080.
[v] Commons Debates, July 17 and 19, 1855.

again made. Meanwhile, on February 28, a discussion had arisen *Precedents* upon a series of resolutions in favour of a reform in the naval administration, and a reorganisation of the Board of Admiralty, which were proposed by Sir J. Elphinstone, but, after a short debate, were withdrawn. Anxious to conciliate the House upon the question, the government decided to agree to the appointment of a committee on the Board of Admiralty; not because they anticipated that an enquiry would prove any great change in the composition of the Board to be necessary, but because it might 'possibly detect faults,' and 'prove that many misconceptions exist with regard to this great branch of the public service.'¹ They undertook, moreover, to 'give every possible assistance, in order that the enquiry might reach every detail and branch of the Admiralty.'¹ The committee was accordingly appointed. Four days afterwards, Sir J. Elphinstone moved for the appointment of another committee to consider the question of promotion and retirement in the Royal Navy, and *Promotion* the pay and position of naval officers. This motion was agreed to *and retire-* by a small majority, notwithstanding the opposition of government.² *ment in* But a week afterwards, this order was rescinded, without a division, *the Navy.* upon the motion of Lord Palmerston (the Premier), the House being 'fully agreed as to the inexpediency' of referring the question of paying the Navy to a select committee. So far as concerned the other portion of the enquiry, Lord Palmerston moved that it be an instruction to the committee on the Board of Admiralty to consider the present system of promotion and retirement in the Royal Navy, and to report their opinion thereon: which was agreed to.³ The committee, however, after examining a number of witnesses, merely reported the evidence, without expressing any opinion upon the matters referred to them.⁴ No motion for the reappointment of the committee was made in the following session,⁵ a circumstance which has been generally attributed to a growing impression that the administration of naval affairs had become more satisfactory within the last two years, and that no radical errors existed which called for the interference of Parliament.⁶ On June 9, 1863, however, the reappointment of the committee was moved for; but being opposed by government, the motion was withdrawn, on an adjourned debate, upon June 24. But on February 24, 1863, Sir John Hay moved for an Address to the Queen on the position of officers of the Navy in respect to promotion and retirement, declaring the same to be unsatisfactory at present, and setting forth the principles

¹ Hans. Deb. vol. clxi. pp. 1266, 1267.
² Ibid. p. 1213.
³ Ibid. pp. 1452–1480.
⁴ Ibid. pp. 1885–1880.
⁵ Commons Papers, 1861, vol. v.

¹ Hans. Deb. vol. clxv. pp. 626–638, 1863.
² Ibid. p. 630, vol. clxix. p. 754, vol. clxxi. p. 607. But see vol. clxix. pp. 603, 700. And see post, Vol. II. c. 2, section, The Board of Admiralty.

Precedents upon which it should be amended. Lord Palmerston opposed the motion, asserting it to be 'not altogether consistent with a proper regard for the legitimate functions of the House;' first, because 'it was a dangerous course for the House to assume to itself administrative functions,' and also because 'it is not expedient for the House to address the crown to make an increase in any department of the public expenditure. It is for the executive government, upon its own responsibility, if it should see fit so to do, to propose to Parliament such additions to that expenditure as they may deem necessary for the public service, and it is for this House to adopt or reject them, as it pleases.' The noble lord, however, contented himself with proposing, as an amendment to the question, a resolution that this House, having on March 13, 1861, instructed a select committee to consider the present system of promotion and retirement in the Royal Navy, is of opinion that its decision should be suspended until the subject shall have been accordingly considered and reported upon; and that a select committee be appointed to consider the said system, and to report their opinion thereon to this House. Sir John Hay accepted this alternative, and the amendment was agreed to without a division.[a]

Regimental promotions. On June 11, 1861, a motion was made in the House of Commons, for an Address to the Queen, to be pleased to take into consideration the position of certain army colonels who had been promoted to that rank for distinguished services during the Crimean war, but whose case had been overlooked in the framing of some new regulations in respect to regimental promotions, 'whereby their prospects in the service had been materially injured.' This motion was agreed to without a division, the government having admitted that the claims of these officers had been unintentionally overlooked, and consented to appoint an official departmental committee to consider the same.[b] This committee reported against the claims of these officers, and the government confirmed their decision. The question was still pressed upon the attention of government by questions and motions in the House of Commons,[c] and on April 28, 1863, a motion for an Address to the crown to issue a royal commission for the further investigation of the matter was proposed. Lord Palmerston deprecated the interference of the House with the detailed management of the Army, because that is no part of the constitutional functions of the House of Commons, 'and was calculated to lead to very objectionable results;' but he promised, if the motion were withdrawn, that a commission should be issued. Mr. Disraeli defended the motion as strictly regular, and as being no infringement of 'the constitutional practice, entirely recognised,

---

[a] Hans. Deb. vol. clxix. pp. 751- 781. See a further motion, by Sir L. Palk, on the subject of pay, &c. of naval officers, on June 3, 1864.
[b] *Ibid.* vol. clxiii. pp. 604-614.
[c] *Ibid.* vol. clxix. pp. 282, 1047.

that it is not the business of Parliament to interfere with the government of the Army,' inasmuch as the proposed proceeding was by an Address to the crown. The motion, however, was withdrawn, in faith of the promise made by the Premier.[c] *Precedents*

On May 15, 1863, a motion for papers relating to the condition of regimental quartermasters, 'though to a certain extent connected with the discipline of the Army,' was admitted to be very proper for the consideration of the House of Commons, 'involving as it did essentially a financial question.'[d] On June 21, 1864, an Address was agreed to by the House of Commons (with the consent of the government) for an enquiry into the condition, pay, and allowances, of regimental quartermasters. *Quartermasters.*

On March 3, 1864, a resolution was proposed in the House of Commons to declare that the discontinuance of the assembling of the yeomanry cavalry for the customary training, during the present year, was inexpedient, and would be detrimental to the efficiency of the force. The Assistant Secretary for War declared that the government had been obliged to take this step, in order to reduce the Army Estimates; but that they did not consider it would have the effect of materially diminishing the efficiency of the force. Upon division, the motion was negatived by a majority of one.[e] But the government, having been enabled to effect an unexpected saving upon the estimate for the cost of prosecuting the war in New Zealand, afterwards submitted to the House a vote for the training of the yeomanry, which was agreed to by a large majority.[f] *Yeomanry Cavalry*

On May 2, 1865, a member called the attention of the House of Commons to petitions from certain officers of the late East India Company's army, complaining of a breach of faith on the part of the government, in the reduction of that force, and its amalgamation with the Army of the Queen. The case of these officers had been already discussed in Parliament; upon a motion for a committee of enquiry, the government had agreed to appoint a royal commission, who had reported upon the alleged grievances. The government had undertaken to redress such grievances as might be substantiated before the commissioners. Nevertheless, it appeared that the result of their decision upon the several matters of complaint was regarded by many as being partial and inadequate. Accordingly, an Address to the crown—praying for the redress of all the grievances admitted to exist by the commissioners, which had arisen by a departure from the assurances contained in certain Acts of Parliament—was proposed and carried (against ministers); the Secretary of State for India contending that, as a whole, the condition of the officers of the Indian army had been considerably *Indian Army Officers.*

[c] Hans. Deb. vol. clxx. pp. 873–870.   [e] Ibid. vol. clxxiii. pp. 1376–1388.
[d] Ibid. p. 1770.   [f] Ibid. vol. clxxv. p. 45.

Precedents benefited by the action of government. On May 9, an answer was received to the aforesaid Address, stating that directions should be given for further enquiry into this matter, in order that 'ample redress' should be afforded wherever it might appear to be necessary. On May 15, the case of the officers of the late Indian army was fully debated in the House of Lords, upon the presentation of a petition from an officer in a Bombay regiment. It was then stated by the Secretary of State for War that, in deference to the opinion of the House of Commons, it was the intention of the government to appoint a new commission to investigate whether the grievances pointed out by the first commission had, or had not, been removed.^e On June 29, the House of Commons was informed that the new commission had been appointed, and had commenced their labours.^h Their report, dated September 14, 1865, was laid before Parliament in the following session. On August 6, 1866, Lord Cranbourne, the Secretary of State for India, informed the House of the conclusions arrived at by the new Derby administration, for the remedy of the grievances under which the officers of the local army of India had so long laboured. These conclusions were afterwards embodied in two despatches from the Secretary of State to the government of India, dated August 8, 1866.ⁱ

Mortality of troops in China. On March 20, 1866, with the consent of the government, a select committee was appointed by the House of Commons 'to enquire into the mortality of the troops in China, the causes which led to it, and into the conduct of those departments of the government whose duty it has been to administer to the wants of those troops.' This was no party question, but arose out of certain unfortunate occurrences, in regard to which the Under-Secretary for War stated that the government, whilst they were willing to take the responsibility upon themselves, considered it more advisable that the subject should be investigated by a committee.^j This committee reported, on July 24, the evidence they had taken on this subject, together with their opinion upon the facts before them. The main conclusion at which they arrived was to the effect that, during the summer of 1865, the troops stationed in China were overcrowded in barracks, and had very defective hospital accommodations, which occasioned much sickness and loss of life. They acquitted the War Department of blame in regard to these unfortunate occurrences, but recorded their belief that fuller instructions explanatory of the views of the imperial authorities respecting the needful arrangements for the proper care of the troops, 'so far from limiting the

---

^f Hans. Deb. vol. clxxix. p. 240. On the same day the House of Commons was informed of the intention to appoint this commission. *Ibid.* p. 297.

^h *Ibid.* vol. clxxx. p. 926.
ⁱ Commons Papers, 1866, No. 530.
^j Hans. Deb. vol. clxxxii. p. 647.

discretion of the general officer in command, would have enlightened *Precedents* and strengthened him in its exercise.'[k]

The military law, as exercised under the authority of Parliament, and by virtue of the annual Mutiny Act, together with the Articles of War, is not to be confounded with that other branch of the royal prerogative which invokes the exercise of martial law under certain peculiar circumstances. *Martial Law.*

In the emergency of invasion and insurrection or rebellion, when the ordinary authorities, in any part of the realm, are unable to quell disturbances, and enforce the operation of law by means of the customary legal tribunals, the crown is entitled, by virtue of its ancient prerogative, to proclaim martial law. This power being invoked either by the Sovereign or her representative, in any particular district, colony, or place, within the realm, the ordinary laws of the land are therein suspended for a time. It is the undoubted prerogative of the crown to declare a state of war, and our common law of treason, of which one of the overt acts is levying war against the crown, acknowledges that there may be a state of war between subjects and their Sovereign; as, for example, wherever there is an armed insurrection or rebellion, against which the constituted authorities of the country with such aid as can be afforded by the military power, acting in aid of and under the civil power[l] are unable to cope. Under such circumstances, the crown

---

[k] Report, p. xii. Commons Papers, 1849, No. 412.

[l] The legality of the employment of troops, under the authority of the civil magistrate, and upon the responsibility of the Secretary of State for the Home Department, has been sometimes impugned, as being equivalent to the introduction of martial law and military government. But this doctrine has found no favour with the best constitutional authorities, and it is quite inapplicable to an army which, like that of Great Britain, owes its very existence to Parliament, and is directly subordinated to the control of the civil power. It has been held, moreover, that, in cases of emergency, the executive government may issue a proclamation empowering the military authorities to act for the suppression of riots, without waiting for directions from a civil magistrate. See Parl. Hist. ix. 1280. Queen's Regulations and Orders for the Army, edit. 1855, p. 207. Prendergast, Law of the Army, p. 13. Finlason, Martial Law, pp. iv. 20. May, Const. Hist. vol. ii. p. 127.

may proclaim martial or military law, until the rebellion is suppressed, and the ordinary power of the law can be peaceably enforced.

Martial Law.

When once martial law has been proclaimed, either by the Sovereign or her representative, an entirely absolute discretion is vested in the military authorities in regard to their proceedings for the restoration of peace and good order. For martial law is a lex non scripta, and 'is built upon no settled principles, but is entirely arbitrary in its discretion. It ought not therefore to be permitted in time of peace, when the king's courts are open for all persons to secure justice according to the law of the land.' Nevertheless, even in time of peace, martial law may be proclaimed and exercised whenever the ordinary legal authorities are unable to maintain the public peace, and suppress violence and outrage; and it may be continued in force until the disturbances are effectually quelled, and peace and safety restored.[m]

Ministers responsible for the same.

But ministers of the crown, through whose instrumentality resort should be had under any circumstances to martial law, are responsible to Parliament for their conduct, and must be able to justify the necessity for their acts under penalty of censure, removal from office, or impeachment, if it should prove upon investigation that their proceedings had been uncalled for or unwarrantably severe.[n]

Jamaica case.

In 1865, a royal commission was appointed to enquire into the circumstances under which martial law was proclaimed by Governor Eyre upon the breaking out of an insurrection in the island of Jamaica. In consequence of the report of this commission, Governor Eyre, who had previously been suspended, was removed from office, on account of his having sanctioned an excessive and unjustifiable severity in the suppression of the insurrection; although, at the

---

[m] Hale, Hist. Common Law, p. 34; and see Finlason on Martial Law. Hans. Deb. vol. clxxxiv. p. 1007

[n] See Hans. Deb. vol. clxxxiv. pp. 1804, 1880. For able arguments on the constitutional restrictions upon the crown in proclaiming martial law, see the Law Magazine for November 1867, p. 170, on Martial Law in Australia; and articles on the Jamaica case, in The Jurist, for January 6, April 7, June 30, July 21 and 28, 1866. And see the evidence given by the Attorney-General for Jamaica, in papers laid before Parliament on the Jamaica case in 1866

same time, praise was awarded to him for the skill, promptitude, and vigour, he had manifested during its early stages; to the exercise of which qualities its speedy termination was, in a great degree, to be attributed. This report was laid before Parliament; and its conclusions met with general approval.*

We have next to consider the prerogative of mercy, which is a peculiar attribute of royalty, and is vested, by statute, in the Sovereign of England.ᵖ All criminal offences are either against the queen's peace or against her crown and dignity. She is, therefore, the proper person to prosecute for all public offences and breaches of the peace. Hence her prerogative of pardon, for it is reasonable that that person only who is injured should have the power of forgiving. But this, like every other prerogative of the British crown, is held in trust for the welfare of the people, and is exercised only upon the advice of responsible ministers. It is, moreover, subject to the control of Parliament, which has more than once interfered by statute to limit and restrain the effects of a royal pardon.

Prerogative of mercy.

The exercise of the prerogative of pardon is strictly confined to criminal offences, wherein the crown is a prosecutor, and does not extend to cases of private wrong.ʳ Hence Parliament has no right to address the crown for the release of a prisoner confined in gaol on a civil suit, or for contempt of court, as it is beyond the power of the crown to discharge such a person. Any such application by Parliament would be invoking the exercise of an unconstitutional and arbitrary power, in violation of law and order.ˢ Undue severity in cases of this description, if not capable of being redressed by the ordinary legal tribunals, can only be remedied by a special Act of Parliament.ᵗ

Is confined to criminal offences.

---

* Report of Jamaica Com. 1866. Hans. Deb. vol. clxxxiv. p. 1763.
ᵖ Stat. 27 Henry VIII. c. 24. And see C. J. Holt, King v. Parsons, 1 Showers, 283.
ʳ Petersdorff, Abridgment, ed. 1864, vol. vi. p. 43.
ˢ See *Ibid.* Bowyer, Const. Law, p. 172. Cox, Inst. 615 n.
ᵗ Case of John Thorogood, Mirror of Parlt. 1840, pp. 3898, 4001, 4935, 5008. Broom's Leg. Max. 4th ed. p. 65.
ᵘ See May, Const. Hist. vol. ii. pp. 275-278.

Royal pardons.

Until a very recent period, all royal pardons were granted under the great seal, upon the advice of the Privy Council. In compliance, generally, with the recommendation of the judge who presided at the trial, the Privy Council assembled to deliberate upon the case. Occasionally discussions arose on the question whether the crown should be advised to remit the sentence or not, in which the king himself took part. But since the commencement of the present reign, this practice has fallen into desuetude, and the administration of the prerogative of mercy has devolved upon the Secretary of State for the Home Department, who is considered as being directly and solely responsible for the same.* The agreement of the Privy Council having become unnecessary, this body is no longer consulted; but the practice is now regulated by the Act 6 Geo. IV. c. 25, under which pardons, whether free or conditional, may be granted by a warrant under the sign-manual, countersigned by a Secretary of State, without the necessity for a more formal instrument.' Thus the Home Office, which was originally employed as a medium of enquiry, for the information of the Sovereign, has gradually developed into a court of review in all criminal cases. Although it should rather be regarded as a court of mercy than as a court of appeal, because the cases wherein the Secretary of State sits as a court of review to re-try the prisoner, and to set aside verdicts, are exceedingly rare. For the most part the facts of the trial are not re-opened, there being seldom any doubt of the correctness of the verdict. The question generally is, whether it is a fit case for the interposition of the prerogative of mercy as a matter of grace. This is a question that no mere legal tribunal could decide, and it is one that suitably belongs to the crown, acting upon the advice of a responsible minister to determine."

---

* Hans. Deb. vol. clxxiv. p. 1181. Ibid. vol. clxxv. p. 252. See an article in the Westminster Review, for April 1864, on the Prerogative of Pardon.

' Parl. Deb. N. S. vol. xii. p. 1103.
" Evidence of Sir George Grey, Home Secretary, and of the Right

In the exercise of this prerogative, the Secretary of State is called upon to pay regard to the moral aspect of the case, as contrasted with the legal; and he is also obliged to consider, to some extent, the popular feeling in the community at large.* The royal prerogative may be exercised more than once in reference to the same case; thus, where a person has been sentenced to death for a capital crime, and the punishment has been commuted to one of penal servitude for life, the prerogative may be subsequently interposed for the mitigation of the sentence. But this is only done in cases of an exceptional character.†

Whenever the crown is memorialised, through the Home Secretary, for the remission of a capital sentence, if any circumstances are stated in the memorial which ought to have an influence upon the decision, or any new facts alleged, apparently in favour of the prisoner, it is invariably sent to the judge, unaccompanied by any expression of opinion, for his report thereon. Frequently the Home Secretary and the judge confer together upon the case. Besides which the Secretary has always the benefit of the ability and experience of the permanent Under-Secretary of State, in addition to any other information he may require to assist him in finally adjudicating upon the case. With this aid, he is in a position to assume full and sole responsibility for the advice he may tender to the Sovereign in every such instance; and although dissatisfaction is occasionally expressed in regard to the decisions of the Home Office when the prerogative of mercy is invoked, the current of enlightened opinion is decidedly opposed to any change in the present practice.‡

Lord Brougham, in his treatise on the 'British Constitution,' dwells at considerable length, and with great sagacity,

Margin note: Exercise of this prerogative.

---

* Hon. S. Walpole, ex-Home Secretary, before the Capital Punishment Commission, in 1865. See Commons Papers, 1866.
† Lord Chancellor, and others, in debate on Hall's case, Hans. Deb. vol. clxxiv. pp. 802, 860.
‡ Hans. Deb. vol. clxxxiv. p. 403.
* See the summary of the evidence on this subject, in the Report of the Commission on Capital Punishment, in 1865, pp. xvii.–xix.

upon the principles which should influence the executive government in the exercise of the prerogative of pardoning or commuting the sentences of criminals. He sums up his observations with the following weighty words: 'It seems hardly necessary to add that no interference of parties interested, politically or personally, should ever be permitted with the exercising of this eminent function of the executive government. Absolute monarchies offer to our view no more hideous features than this gross perversion of justice. Nor do popular governments present a less hateful aspect when they suffer the interference of the multitude, either by violence, or through the press, or the debate, or any other channel in which clamour can operate, to defeat the provisions of the law.'[a]

It is only under very exceptional and extraordinary circumstances that any interference by either House of Parliament with the exercise of this prerogative is justifiable. It was said by Macaulay, that 'he would rather entrust it to the hands of the very worst ministry that ever held office than allow it to be exercised under the direction of the very best House of Commons;'[b] and by Sir Robert Peel, that he would leave this prerogative in the hands of the executive, considering that it was the right and duty of the House to interfere only 'if there be a suspicion that justice is perverted for corrupt purposes.'[c]

But while direct interference with the discretion of the crown in the exercise of the pardoning power is only warranted in extreme cases of manifest injustice, it is competent for Parliament to receive petitions from or on behalf of criminals under sentence, and, if sufficient cause is shown to justify enquiry, to appoint committees for that purpose. A Mr. Palmer, who was condemned for seditious practices, by the High Court of Justiciary, in Scotland, in 1794, petitioned the House of Commons complaining of

---

[a] Brougham, Bt. Con. 330–342. [b] Hans. Deb. (3) vol. lxxxiv. p. 802.
[c] Mirror of Parl. 1835, p. 1581.

the illegality and undue severity of his sentence. The reception of his petition was at first opposed by Mr. Pitt, as being irregular and unjustifiable, but after an adjourned debate on the question, it was agreed to without a division.[d] Since then no objection has been offered to the reception of petitions from or on behalf of prisoners complaining of their sentences, of their treatment by the court, or in prison, and praying relief, or for the remission of their sentences.[e]

It has not been unusual for enquiries to be made of the administration in Parliament as to the circumstances attending the imposition or remission of sentences imposed either at the assizes or by local criminal courts having summary jurisdiction, so as to afford the ministry an opportunity of explaining erroneous impressions in the public mind.[f] But the government exercise their own discretion as to whether they deem it expedient to reply to such questions or not. On one occasion, an answer was refused to be given to a question of this kind, because it would be likely to lead to debate; and because, 'as a general principle, it would be inconvenient and unusual to lay before the House the grounds on which that discretion proceeds which dictates leniency or severity on the part of the responsible advisers of the crown.'[g]

Enquiries of ministers.

---

[d] Parl. Hist. vol. xxx. pp. 1440-1401.

[e] See Index to Public Petitions, House of Commons; and see the proceedings on a motion for an Address to the crown for the removal of a state prisoner from one place of confinement to another, 'where he may not be subjected to the treatment which he now endures.' Mirror of Parl. 1840, p. 3534.

[f] Mirror of Parl. 1835, p. 2511; Ibid. 1837-8, p. 240. Hans. Deb. vol. clxiii. pp. 1824, 1825. Ibid. vol. clxiv. pp. 1734, 1824.

[g] Mirror of Parl. 1840, p. 1702. A similar reply was given in the House of Lords, on August 4, 1842, in the case of W. Hardman. Hans. Deb. vol. clxviii. p. 1187. On March 28, 1862, enquiry was made in the House of Lords in the case of Watson and others, convicted for a criminal offence, as to whether, under the peculiar circumstances attending it, the Home Secretary was disposed to recommend the prisoners to the royal clemency. It was replied that the newspaper report of the trial was not strictly correct, and that 'up to that time no petition on behalf of these men had been received by the Secretary of State.' Ibid. vol. clxvi. p. 231. On April 24, 1863, a debate arose in the House of Commons on a motion for papers touching the remission of the sentence of Jessie Maclauchlan for the Glasgow murder. The Home Secretary Sir George Grey was willing to produce the papers,

Precedents

The following precedents may be adduced to confirm and illustrate the doctrine above set forth.

Muir, Palmer, and others.

In 1794, upon the conviction of Muir, Palmer, and others, for seditious practices in Scotland, under a law peculiar to that kingdom, and which was more stringent than the English law on the same subject, they were sentenced to transportation for fourteen years. Their case was warmly espoused by the Whig party, and Lord Stanhope, in the House of Lords, moved for an Address to the king, representing that it was the intention of the House to proceed at once to examine into the circumstances of the condemnation and sentence, and praying that meanwhile execution of the sentence might be stayed. This motion was characterised by the Lord Chancellor and other law lords as being unprecedented and unwarrantable, an improper interference with the course of criminal justice, and a departure from the constitutional course which permitted persons aggrieved by a sentence themselves to petition the crown for redress. The motion was negatived on division, the mover alone voting for it.[b] Soon afterwards, the question was submitted to the House of Commons, by Mr. Adam, a learned Scotch advocate, who, in a most elaborate speech, attempted to prove the illegality of the trials, and contended that the sentences imposed had been unjustifiable and excessively severe. He moved for various documents in support of his allegations, and also for an Address to the king, in which he recapitulated his reasons for regarding the sentences as illegal and oppressive, and prayed that, in consideration thereof, his Majesty would be graciously pleased to exercise the royal prerogative of mercy on behalf of the prisoners. This was opposed by the ministry, who maintained the legality and propriety of the sentences, and defended the conduct of the judges. On division the motions were negatived by large majorities.[c]

but feared that thereby 'a dangerous precedent might be established.' He added, that it would 'be highly inconvenient for the public interest, if this House is to become a court of appeal in criminal cases.' *Ibid.* vol. clxx. p. 606. The motion was withdrawn, but afterwards the government laid the papers on the table. Commons Papers, 1863, vol. xlix. pp. 265, 271, 403. See also Hans. Deb. vol. clxiv. p. 1270.

[b] Parl. Hist. vol. xxx. p. 1209.

[c] *Ibid.* pp. 1480-1570. Commons Journals, vol. xlix. pp. 313-315. In 1840 a case occurred of a similar description. Messrs. Frost, Williams, and Jones, having been convicted of treason, were sentenced to transportation. It was contended by some that the law had been strained against the prisoners, and that they were entitled to pardon, as an act of right and justice. Accordingly on this ground, and irrespective of any reference to the prerogative of mercy, the House of Commons was moved to address the crown to grant them a free pardon. This view was declared, on the part of the government, to be wholly unfounded, and proof was adduced of the legality of the sentence; whereupon the motion was negatived by a large majority.—Mirror of Parl. 1840, pp. 1087-1607.

On July 11, 1820, Lord John Russell moved an Address to the king, for the liberation of Sir Manasseh Lopez, then in prison under sentence of the Court of King's Bench, for bribery and corruption, at the suit of the House of Commons.¹ The Home Secretary (Lord Castlereagh) opposed the motion, saying that 'whether the law should have its execution was the peculiar prerogative of the crown, and the responsible servants of the crown could not be justified in recommending the interposition of the royal mercy upon the mere suggestion of that House (he spoke it with perfect respect) any more than upon the application of the humblest individual of the land.'ᵏ After some discussion the motion was withdrawn. Nevertheless, the strong expression of feeling in the House in favour of Lopez, on account of his advanced age, and the extenuating circumstances attending his case, led to the mitigation of his sentence, and he was shortly afterwards released, having been in custody only eight months, instead of the two years for which he was condemned.¹

On April 13, 1829, the Earl of Clancarty moved in the House of Lords, for certain documents in the case of Mr. Macdonnell, who had been sentenced to imprisonment for libel, but had been pardoned, in the king's name, by the Lord Lieutenant of Ireland, under circumstances which, it was currently reported, did not warrant any abridgment of his term of imprisonment. The papers asked for would explain the facts of the case. The Duke of Wellington (the Premier) opposed the motion. He stated that cases of this kind, though not entirely exempt from the inquisition of Parliament, ought to be least liable to enquiry by either House of any of the royal prerogatives; that, in the present instance, no sufficient parliamentary ground had been shown to warrant the House in departing from its 'usual practice and principles not to enquire into the exercise of this branch of his Majesty's prerogative.' The Duke was followed by the Lord Lieutenant himself, who justified his conduct towards Mr. Macdonnell, alleging that the matter had been thoroughly investigated before the royal clemency had been extended to him. The motion for papers was negatived without a division.ᵐ

On August 6, 1839, Lord Brougham proposed, in the House of Lords, some resolutions respecting the administration of criminal justice in Ireland, more particularly in respect to the principles which should guide the exercise of the prerogative of mercy, and declaring the mode in which this prerogative ought to be ad-

Precedents Sir M. Lopez.

Lord Lieutenant of Ireland.

Lord Brougham's resolutions.

ʲ Commons Journals, vol. lxxiv. p. 500.
ᵏ Parl. Deb. N. S. vol. ii. p. 371.
ˡ Mirror of Parl. 1841, p. 1804.
ᵐ Ibid. 1829, p. 1255. But see the case of Walter Hall, convicted of murder in 1812, and afterwards pardoned. Papers explanatory of the case were moved for in the House of Commons, and granted by the government, but no further proceedings were had thereon. Parl. Deb. vol. xxiii. pp. 407, 634.

ministered. Notwithstanding the opposition of government, these resolutions were agreed to. On the following day, Lord John Russell (the Premier) adverted to this vote, and stated that the proposed practice in the mode of exercising the prerogative of mercy was utterly inconsistent with that which had been hitherto pursued by Secretaries of State in their recommendations to the crown, and from which it would be exceedingly inconvenient to depart; and that it was not his intention to make any alteration whatever. If, instead of resolutions, a Bill had been passed, then of course he would be bound to obey the law. Meanwhile he should consider himself justified in adhering to the present practice.[a] Accordingly upon an enquiry being made of the ministry, at the next session, whether a certain commutation of sentence had taken place in conformity with principles set forth in the aforesaid resolutions, they declined to give any answer. At the same time it was observed that, if a formal motion were made on the subject, the government would be prepared to discuss the question.[b]

<small>*Precedents resolutions.*</small>

<small>*Chartist prisoners.*</small>

On May 25, 1841, Mr. Duncombe proposed an Address to the queen, praying her to take into her merciful consideration the cases of all persons confined in England and Wales for political offences; referring specially to those misguided men who had been led astray by Chartist leaders (now undergoing sentence of banishment), and were suffering the penalties of the law. Viewing the object of the motion to be an attempt to obtain from the crown, through the interposition of the House of Commons, a remission of the sentences of these prisoners, Sir Robert Peel (although at the time in Opposition) strenuously opposed it. He urged that the consideration of such cases should be left 'exclusively with the crown;' that the government, in exercising the prerogative of mercy, 'ought not to be influenced by any opinion which the House of Commons might express;' and he asserted it to be a dangerous precedent for the House to 'fetter the discretion and judgment of the crown by expressing any recommendation on such subjects.' Acting on this principle, when Secretary of State, he had himself resisted a motion for an Address for the remission of the remaining term of Mr. Hunt's imprisonment in Ilchester gaol; which was an attempt to induce the House to depart from that which had been its unvaried practice ever since the Revolution, namely, that nothing but 'circumstances of an overwhelming nature should tempt the House to interfere with this most important prerogative.' Lord John Russell (the Colonial Secretary) also opposed the motion, and pointed out the general ill effects of such an interference on the part of the House, although admitting that there might be exceptional cases. The

---

<small>* Mirror of Parl. 1839, p. 4801.   † Parl. Deb. N. S. vol. vii. p. 34.
* Ibid. 1840, pp. 1702, 1717.</small>

IN PARDONING OFFENDERS. 351

motion for the Address was negatived by the casting vote of the Speaker, who stated that he considered the proposed vote was an interference with the royal prerogative.[q]

On March 10, 1840, Mr. Duncombe proposed an Address to the Queen, that she would be graciously pleased to consider the recent petitions to Parliament in favour of a restoration from exile of the state prisoners Frost, Williams, and Jones; but Macaulay, Sir Robert Peel, Lord John Russell, and other leading statesmen, while admitting the abstract right of the House to advise as to the exercise of this or any other prerogative, all concurred in opposing the motion, as being of a dangerous tendency, and a departure from the rule imposed upon themselves by the discretion of former Houses of Commons, of non-interference with the exercise of certain prerogatives, which should be left to the unfettered discretion of the crown. The Address was negatived by a large majority.[r]

On June 30, 1864, it was moved, in the House of Lords, to resolve that, considering the extent to which agrarian outrages prevail in certain counties in Ireland, and the difficulty which exists in obtaining convictions for such offences, this House is of opinion that the power of the Lord Lieutenant of Ireland to remit the whole or a portion of the sentences of persons convicted of such crimes should be exercised with greater care and circumspection; and this House observes with regret that the Lord Lieutenant ordered the release of certain prisoners (therein named) under sentence for an agrarian offence, upon grounds which appear to be insufficient. The motion was opposed by the government, on the ground that nothing should induce the House to agree to such a motion unless it could be distinctly shown 'that there had been a very gross want of discretion in the administration of the prerogative of mercy, or that the person exercising it had been influenced by some corrupt motives.'[s] The sense of the House was evidently against the motion, and it was withdrawn.

In 1838, however, a case occurred of sufficient gravity and importance to give rise to discussions, in both Houses of Parliament, as to the circumstances under which the prerogative of mercy had been exercised, and which led to the appointment of a committee of enquiry by the House of Commons. A person of the name of Thom had been convicted of perjury, and sentenced to transportation for six years. Shortly after conviction, it was discovered that he was insane; he was thereupon transferred to a lunatic asylum,

Precedents

Frost, Williams, and Jones.

Lord Lieutenant of Ireland.

Thom's case.

---

[q] Mirror of Parl. 1841, pp. 1894–1903. See also ISD, p. 1715.
[r] Hans. Deb. (3) vol. lxxxiv. pp. 881-921. See also, the case of the Dorchester prisoners, Mirror of Parl. 1835, p. 1508; and the case of the Canadian prisoners, Hans. Deb. (3) vol. lxvi. p. 237.
[s] Hans. Deb. vol. clxxvi. p. 489.

Precedents where he remained four years, when he received a free pardon, and was discharged. Not long afterwards, his insanity assumed a more violent aspect, and he became concerned in a riot, which led to serious loss of life, he himself also being killed. This sad catastrophe was brought under the notice of Parliament, and documents explanatory of the case were called for in both Houses. A motion for the appointment of a committee of enquiry into the circumstances attending the discharge of Thom was submitted to the House of Commons, the mover commenting severely upon the conduct of the Secretary of State (Lord John Russell) in exercising the prerogative of mercy in favour of such a dangerous character. His lordship made a satisfactory explanation, but acquiesced, on the part of government, to the appointment of a committee of enquiry.¹ The committee reported merely the minutes of evidence they had taken, which sufficed to acquit the government of any blame in the transaction,² and no further discussion or proceedings took place in the matter.

Prerogative in administering justice and preserving the public peace.
The next prerogative which claims our attention is that which appertains to the king as the fountain of justice, and general conservator of the peace of the realm. So far as the maintenance of the public peace is concerned, the appointment and jurisdiction of officers to preserve the same are principally regulated by statutes, which are administered under the general supervision and responsibility of the Home Secretary.*

' By the fountain of justice, the law does not mean the author or original, but only the distributor. Justice is not derived from the king, as from his free gift, but he is the steward of the public, to dispense it to whom it is due. He is not the spring, but the reservoir, from whence right and equity are conducted by a thousand channels to every individual.' It is an undoubted prerogative of the crown to erect courts of judicature; nevertheless, the crown alone cannot erect a court, or enable it to proceed, otherwise than according to the common law. Thus the co-

---

¹ Mirror of Parl. 1838, pp. 4502, 5117, &c.
² Sess. Papers, II. of C. 1837–8, vol. xxiii. p. 353. For a circumstantial narrative of the career of Thom, *alias* Sir William Courtenay,

see Knight's Hist. of Eng. vol. viii. pp. 412–417.
* Com. Inst. 502; and see *post*, Vol. II. c. 2, On the Home Secretary's Office.

operation of Parliament is indispensable to enable the crown to erect a court of civil law, a court of equity, or a new court with a new jurisdiction." Moreover, the expense attending the administration of justice must necessarily be defrayed out of moneys which have been voted by Parliament. When any new courts of justice are required, it is usual to establish them by statute, so that Parliament, having concurred with the crown as to the necessity for the same, are morally bound to appropriate the needful supplies for their establishment and support."

The great function of Parliament has been declared to be 'the maintenance of the law and the redress of grievances.' In an official report from the pen of Edmund Burke, that eminent and philosophical statesman claims for the Commons of Great Britain, in Parliament assembled, that it is 'one of their principal duties and functions to be observant of the courts of justice, and to take due care that none of them, from the lowest to the highest, shall pursue new courses unknown to the laws and constitution of this kingdom, or to equity, sound legal policy, or substantial justice.' The express power which is given to the two Houses of Parliament by the Acts 12 & 13 Will. III. c. 2, and 1 Geo. III. c. 23 to address the crown for the removal of judges from office, who are otherwise declared to be irremovable, points in like manner to the duty that devolves upon Parliament to watch the course of the administration of justice. In the words of Sir Robert Peel, Parliament 'has not only the right to address the crown for the removal of a particular judge, but, in cases of misconduct, it has the right

---

* Bowyer, Const. Law. pp. 170, 171, 480.
* Hans. Deb. vol. clxl. pp. 510-512; and see Smith's Parl. Rememb. 1861, p. 18.
* 4 Inst. 9, 11. Rot. Parl. 1 Hen.
* Report on Lords' Proceedings on Mr. Hastings' Trial. Commons Journals, vol. xlix. p. 617.
* Smith's Parl. Rememb. 1860, p. 232.

of exercising a superintending control over the manner in which they discharge their duties, and to institute enquiries relative thereto.'ᵇ 'The judges of the land act under responsibility; and any misconduct of which they may be guilty may be enquired into, and animadverted upon, by either House of Parliament.'ᶜ

Limits of parliamentary interposition.

But in the discharge of these high inquisitorial functions, Parliament has prescribed for itself certain constitutional rules and limitations, to prevent undue encroachment upon the independence of the judicial office, which is in itself one of the main bulwarks of English liberty. And it devolves upon the advisers of the crown, as those who are peculiarly responsible for preserving the purity of justice inviolate, to guard against the intrusion of party influences in any proceedings of Parliament in matters affecting the administration of the law.

Criminative charges in Parliament.

It is, in the first place, the invariable practice of Parliament never to entertain criminative charges against anyone, except upon the ground of some distinct and definite basis. The charges preferred should be submitted to the consideration of the House in writing, whether it be intended to proceed by impeachment, by address for removal from office, or by committee, to enquire into the alleged misconduct, in order to afford full and sufficient oppor-

---

ᵇ Hans. Deb. (3) vol. lxvii. p. 1081. See the discussions in both Houses of Parliament in regard to the fitness of Chief Justice Lefroy to continue to preside over the Court of Queen's Bench in Ireland, when over ninety years of age. (*Ibid.* vol. clxxvii. p. 1020; vol. clxxxiii. pp. 353, 778.) His lordship resigned his seat on the bench very soon afterwards, when the Derby administration took office. (*Ibid.* vol. clxxxiv. p. 835.)

ᶜ Lord Chancellor Campbell, Hans. Deb. vol. clxiii. p. 824. See informal discussions in the House of Commons on certain expressions used by an Irish Judge in open court. (Mirror of Parl. 1830, pp. 3025-3027, and Hans. Deb. vol. clxxviii. p. 193.) Enquiry respecting the language and demeanour of a Vice Chancellor, in open court, in a recent case. (Hans. Deb. vol. clxxii. p. 871.) Enquiry respecting the undue severity of certain sentences passed by the Dy. Asst. Judge of the Middlesex Sessions. (*Ibid.* vol. clxxv. p. 1001.) See a debate in the House of Lords, on May 28, 1860, in regard to undue severity alleged to have been exercised by the local government of Bombay towards one of the judges of the Court of Small Causes therein, whose conduct on the bench had been complained of by a solicitor of the court.

tunity for the person complained of to meet the accusations against him.[a]

It is also highly irregular to bring into discussion, in either House of Parliament, any matters, whether they relate to civil or criminal cases, which are undergoing judicial investigation, or are about to be submitted to to courts of law; as it leads to the imputation of a desire to interfere with the ordinary course of justice.[e] This observation applies with additional force to the House of Lords, which, being itself the highest court of judicature, should carefully refrain from prematurely and prejudicially discussing the merits of a case that has been assigned, by law, to the consideration of another tribunal.[f] If, upon grounds of public policy, it should be expedient to institute a debate on a question of this kind; the House should nevertheless refrain from asking for papers to be laid before them, in any case that is waiting for trial or undergoing judicial investigation.[g]

<small>Matters sub judice.</small>

Complaints to Parliament in respect to the conduct of the judiciary, or the decisions of courts of justice, should not be lightly entertained. 'If there is a failure in the administration of justice, from whatever cause, affecting any judge, both Houses of Parliament may address the crown, to remove that judge from office.'[h] But it has been well remarked, by Lord Palmerston, that 'nothing could be more injurious to the administration of justice than that the House of Commons should take upon itself

<small>Conduct of judges not to be lightly impugned.</small>

---

[a] Case of the Bishop of Bath and Wells, 1852. Hans. Deb. vol. cxxii. pp. 405, 613, 644–663. Case of Chief Justice Monahan, Hans. Deb. (H. of Lords) June 10, 11, and 13, 1861; and again, Ibid. vol. clxxviii. p. 100; and see Mr. Wynn's observations in Parl. Deb. N. S. vol. xiii. p. 1240.

[e] Mirror of Parl. 1831, pp. 230, 523. Hans. Deb. vol. clxiv. p. 560; vol. clxv. p. 135; vol. clxvi. p. 100. Case of the seizure of the 'Alexandra,'

Ibid. vol. clxx. p. 709. Parliament cannot constitutionally entertain matters which come within the province of a jury to determine. Foster and Finlason, Nisi Prius Cases, vol. III. p. 500, n.

[f] Mirror of Parl. 1831, p. 523. 1831-2, p. 1101.

[g] Case of the so-called 'Confederate Rams.' Hans. Deb. vol. clxxiii. p. 905.

[h] Secretary Sir G. Grey, Ibid. vol. clxxxiii. p. 703.

the duties of a court of review of the proceedings of an ordinary court of law;' it should only interpose in cases 'of such gross perversion of the law, either by intention, corruption, or incapacity, as make it necessary for the House to exercise the power vested in it of advising the crown for the removal of the judge.'¹ The proper proceedings in such an extreme case will claim our consideration in a future chapter.

Bribery practices.

By the Act 26 Vict. c. 29, section 9, the duty of considering a report from an election committee (when the House have ordered the evidence to be printed) or from a royal commission, charging certain persons with bribery or treating, is assigned to the Attorney-General, who is empowered, at his discretion, to institute the necessary proceedings against the offending parties.ʲ In proceedings, in cases of bribery, and other misconduct arising out of parliamentary elections, it has been usual for the House of Commons to take the initiative, and to order the Attorney-General to prosecute the offenders.ᵏ When that officer is about himself to institute a prosecution

And other indictable offences.

against individuals for offences against the purity of election, under the statute, constitutional usage has permitted the House to interpose with an address to the crown, praying that such a prosecution may be relinquished.ˡ But in other cases, where there is ground for believing, from investigations of parliamentary committees, that indictable offences have been committed, the initiative in criminal proceedings should be left to the executive government.ᵐ And even in matters arising out of parliamentary elections, the House has no right 'to con-

---

¹ Hans. Deb. vol. cxl. p. 1501; and see Sir R. Peel's speeches in the case of Baron Smith, Mirror of Parl. 1834, pp. 152, 312.

ʲ See Hans. Deb. vol. clxxi. p. 1042; ibid. vol. clxxxiii. p. 1400.

ᵏ See the principles which should govern the House in ordering such prosecutions, as laid down by Mr. Wynn, in Mirror of Parl. 1841, pp. 2277-2282; and see Hans. Deb. vol. lxiii. pp. 810-843, vol. cxxvi. p. 1051. Commons Journals, vol. lxxxvi. p. 770.

ˡ Hans. Deb. vol. clviii. pp. 1752-1750.

ᵐ Case of the Directors, &c. of the West Hartlepool Harbour and Railway Company. Hans. Deb. vol. clxxi. pp. 1204-1302.

stitute itself into a court of appeal from any description of judicial authority,' or to interfere, by resolution, with the course of judicial proceedings." Otherwise, it would be impossible to avoid the suspicion that the administration of justice had been encroached upon for political purposes.

Parliament, however, has a right to demand full information upon all matters affecting the administration of justice, and papers on this subject, when moved for, are usually granted as a matter of course; unless the application be made with a view to an irregular and unconstitutional interference with the ordinary course of law.°

But it is not the practice of either House of Parliament, as a general rule, to ask for copies of legal opinions given by the law officers of the crown to the executive government (or furnished to a public corporation °), nor is it customary for government to lay them before Parliament should they be applied for.° They are considered confidential communications." The like rule applies with respect to communications between law officers of the crown concerning particular trials; or the judge's notes taken at a trial;° or coroners' notes, which, as they partake of a judicial character, can only be produced with the consent of the officer himself.° Opinions given by

Information to be laid before Parliament.

Confidential communications.

° Hans. Deb. vol. clviii. p. 1752; vol. clix. pp. 146, 201.
° Mirror of Parl. 1837, p. 2182. Hans. Deb. vol. clxv. pp. 372, 543.
° Hans. Deb. vol. cii. p. 1169.
° Mirror of Parl. 1830, pp. 387, 1877-1879; 1840, p. 2120. Hans. Deb. vol. lxxiv. p. 508; Ibid. vol. clxi. p. 542; Ibid. vol. clxix. pp. 1328-1881. A similar doctrine was laid down in Lower Canada, as appears by the reply of his Excy. Governor Gosford, to an address of the House of Assembly, on December 11, 1835, for copies of legal opinions, wherein he states that such communications were 'confidential;' and, 'except in peculiar cases, should be held sacred.'

° See a case in which, under peculiar circumstances, an opinion was presented to Parliament, the law officer himself acquiescing therein. Mirror of Parl. 1831, p. 2111, and see Hans. Deb. vol. clxxxiv. p. 40. It is not even usual for a minister to state to the House the substance of an opinion given by the crown law officers; though this may be done at the discretion of the government. Hans. Deb. vol. clxxii. pp. 250, 434.
° Mirror of Parl. 1830, pp. 527, 1067-1088. In another case, however, copies of 'judges' notes' were ordered. Ibid. 1834, p. 1243; but see Hans. Deb. vol. clxxi. p. 800.
° Mirror of Parl. 1841, p. 2207.

judges to the government on a bill pending in parliament ought not to be produced for the purpose of influencing the House in its legislative capacity, or to form the groundwork of legislative enactment."

The duty of Parliament in reference to abuses which may occur in the administration of justice, will receive further illustration from the following precedents.

Precedents

Prerogative Court.
On July 17, 1828, Mr. Hume presented to the House of Commons a petition complaining of abuses in the Prerogative Court, and especially of the misconduct and malversation in office of the presiding judge. He went into a detailed account of the alleged abuses, and concluded by remarking that it was doubtful whether the government should not themselves institute an enquiry therein, in preference to an investigation by a committee of the House. During the debate which ensued, it was shown that the charges in the petition were destitute of foundation, whereupon the motion that the petition do lie on the table was negatived.* On the following day, upon motion of Mr. Hume, a return of the amount of fees allowed and received in this court, during certain periods, was ordered, with a view to determine the existence of certain of the abuses attributed to the officers of the court.

Police Force.
On June 27, 1833, a petition was presented to the House of Commons from the inhabitants of two villages near London, complaining of the employment of the Metropolitan Police Force as spies, and asking protection against the evils resulting from such a practice. The petition was referred to a select committee, which on August 6 reported to the House three resolutions, declaring that the conduct of a certain policeman named Popay had been deserving of 'most grave and decided censure;' also, 'solemnly deprecating any approach to the employment of spies, in the ordinary acceptation of the term, as a practice most abhorrent to the feelings of the people, and most alien to the spirit of the constitution.'

Baron Smith.
On February 13, 1834, Mr. Daniel O'Connell brought before the House of Commons a complaint against Sir William Smith, one of the barons of the Court of Exchequer in Ireland, for 'neglect of duty as a judge, and for the introduction of political topics in his charges to grand juries. In proof of these accusations, he quoted from various returns on the table of the House, and from certain of the judge's charges; and concluded by moving that a select committee be appointed to enquire into the conduct of Mr. Baron

---

* Mirror of Parl. 1833, p. 2550.
* Ibid. 1828, pp. 2584–2597.
* Ibid. p. 2623.

* Commons Journals, 1833, pp. 517, 641. Commons Papers, 1833, vol. xiii. p. 401.

Smith in respect to these accusations, which was agreed to. On February 21, however, it was represented to the House that a *primâ facie* case, sufficient to justify the removal of Baron Smith from the bench, by a proceeding under the statute, had not been made out; and that Parliament had no constitutional right to institute an enquiry into the conduct of a judge with any other view than that of addressing the crown, under the provisions of the statute for his removal; else 'would the independence of the judicial bench be a mockery, and the Act of 1 Geo. I. no better than waste paper.' It was accordingly moved, that the order for the appointment of the committee be discharged; which, after a long debate, was concurred in by the House.

Precedents

On March 23, 1841, Lord Mahon submitted to the House of Commons a resolution, 'That in the opinion of this House the large increase in the number of convicts to be permanently confined in the hulks of Great Britain, although sentenced to transportation, in pursuance of the minute of the Secretary of State for the Home Department, dated January 2, 1839 [which declared, That convicts sentenced to seven years' transportation, shall be, as far as practicable, employed in the hulks and dockyards at home and at Bermuda], is highly inexpedient.' This resolution was chiefly intended to restrain an 'undue extension of the prerogative of the crown,' which nevertheless was exercised in accordance with the letter of the law. The Secretary of State was by law empowered, at his discretion, to retain in confinement at home any persons who might be sentenced to transportation. But this authority had been confessedly granted for the purpose of enabling the Secretary to 'distinguish between particular cases; that in cases of early youth, of extreme old age, or any other special circumstances, he might inflict imprisonment at home upon those to whose offences the law had affixed the punishment of transportation.' Moreover, the hulk system, as a mode of secondary punishment, had proved injurious to the criminal, and had been expressly condemned by a committee of the House of Lords in 1835. With a view to prevent an undue extension of the hulk system, Lord Mahon asked the House to adopt the above resolution. In reply, Lord John Russell (Colonial Secretary) admitted that the hulk system was objectionable, but did not think it advisable that the House should come to any resolution on the subject; he therefore moved the previous question. After a debate, Lord Mahon determined to press his motion, when it was carried, against the government, by a majority of twenty-one. A month afterwards, Lord John Russell intimated that it was the intention

Hulk system.

---

* Mirror of Parl. 1834, p. 123.   Deb. vol. clxxiii. p. 1030.
* *Ibid.* p. 304; and see Lord   * Mirror of Parl. 1841, p. 909.
Chelmsford's observations in Hans.   * *Ibid.* p. 982.

260   THE ROYAL PREROGATIVE

Precedents of government to continue, to a limited extent, the transportation of criminals; and to establish penitentiaries for criminals retained in this country, instead of sending them to the hulks.[c] It was subsequently stated, in the House of Lords, that the hulk system had been abandoned, in consequence of the foregoing resolution.[d]

Baron Gurney. On May 11, 1843, Mr. Duncombe presented to the House of Commons a petition from W. Jones, a prisoner in the Leicester County Gaol, complaining of the conduct of Baron Gurney, during his trial before that judge, on a charge of sedition, whereby Jones alleged that he had been deprived of an opportunity of vindicating his innocence to the jury. In such a case the law afforded no remedy, and an application to the crown for a remission of the sentence had been unsuccessful. Wherefore Mr. Duncombe moved that an address be presented to her Majesty, to be pleased to take this case into her merciful consideration. In reply, the Home Secretary (Sir James Graham) showed that there was no sufficient ground for impugning the conduct of the judge, and that it was inexpedient for the House to advise the crown in regard to the exercise of its prerogative of mercy, 'unless circumstances strongly warranted the adoption of such a course.' After some further debate, the motion was withdrawn.[e]

Irish Judge. On February 28, 1856, a motion was made in the House of Commons for a copy of a judgment recently delivered in an Irish court of law, and papers showing further proceedings consequent thereupon. The mover alleged that the judge had manifested incapacity at this trial, which had led to grievous consequences to the parties interested therein. In reply, Lord Palmerston denied that there had been any abuse in the administration of the law in this case, which could justify interference on the part of Parliament. He stated that the judgment complained of had been confirmed by a superior court, and 'was at this moment the subject of a judicial proceeding pending in the highest court of appeal.' The question was negatived, without a division.[f]

The Deacles. The point involved in the preceding case had already been decided by the House of Commons in the case of the Deacles, in 1831. Those parties had a grievance against a magistrate, which had been

---

[c] Mirror of Parl. 1841, p. 1288.
[d] Hans. Deb. vol. clxix. p. 850; and see a debate in the House of Commons, on March 9, 1863, on Transportation and Penal Servitude, wherein the manner in which the Home Secretary had exercised the discretion, vested in him under certain Acts of Parliament, of granting tickets of leave to criminals under sentence, as fully discussed, upon a motion for an address to the crown to enforce the existing law against criminals. After a lengthy discussion, the motion was withdrawn.
[e] Hans. Deb. (3) vol. lxix. pp. 180-200.
[f] Ibid. Case of Talbot v. Talbot. Hans. Deb. vol. cxl. pp. 1551-1561.

submitted to the examination of a court of law. The decision of **Precedents** the court was adverse to the Deacles; whereupon they petitioned the House of Commons for the appointment of a committee to investigate their complaint. Although both parties were desirous of a parliamentary enquiry, the House refused to grant the committee, on the ground that it was not according to usage to enquire into a matter which had already undergone judicial examination, and could be submitted, on appeal, to a higher court.[a]

On May 6, 1844, a motion was made in the House of Lords to **Irish** condemn the appointment of a certain person to the office of stipen- **magistrates** diary magistrate in Ireland, on account of his having published intemperate and extreme opinions upon public political questions. This motion was regarded as a censure upon the Lord Lieutenant, for having made this appointment, and upon the imperial government for having acquiesced therein. But the charge of unfitness for office not having been substantiated, the motion was negatived without a division.

On July 16, 1844, a motion was made, in the House of Lords, for copies of memorials addressed to the Irish government, recommending the restoration of Mr. Alexander O'Driscoll to the commission of the peace, who had been dismissed therefrom on account of violent and unbecoming conduct, and yet, within six months afterwards, had been reinstated. At first, the government opposed this motion, defending the right of the Irish Lord Chancellor to act as he had done in this case; but on hearing the facts elicited in debate, in proof of Mr. O'Driscoll's unfitness for office, acquiesced in the motion for papers. No further proceedings, however, took place in the House of Lords, in reference to this appointment; but on July 23, a motion was made in the House of Commons, for an address to her Majesty, praying for the removal of Mr. O'Driscoll from the Commission of the Peace. In reply, the government admitted that this subject 'was a very proper one for the House to consider;' and that 'there might be circumstances in which it would be the duty of the House to address her Majesty to remove a magistrate from the Commission of the Peace,' but the Irish Secretary said, 'he thought that when a member called upon the House thus to interfere with the prerogative of the crown, exercised by its highest law officer, he ought to be prepared to show that the power had been exercised either corruptly or mischievously.' After some further debate, the motion was negatived.[b] Having soon afterwards again misconducted himself, further enquiry was insti-

[a] Mirror of Parl. 1831, pp. 2213, 2344, 2463; see also the debate on Mr. Hunt's motion on March 15, 1832, for a committee to enquire into the loss of life at the Manchester Riots, in 1819; which, for a similar reason, was opposed by government, and negatived.

[b] Hans. Deb. vol. lxxvi. pp. 1310–1320.

tuted by the Lord Chancellor of Ireland into Mr. O'Driscoll's conduct, which led to his final dismissal from the magistracy.[1]

In 1861, a case occurred in reference to an Irish magistrate, which gave rise to much discussion out of the walls of Parliament, and which strikingly exemplifies the limits of parliamentary interference in matters affecting legal rights. Mr. Adair, an Irish landlord, and a magistrate for the county of Donegal, evicted a number of tenants from his estate, in punishment for the murder of his steward, being unable to discover the perpetrator of the deed. The attention of the Irish government having been directed to this highhanded proceeding, a correspondence ensued with Mr. Adair, in which he defended the course he had pursued, in the interests of life and property, denying that he had done anything that could not be justified. The government remonstrated with him for what he had done, but admitted that he had not transgressed the limits of the law, or exceeded his rights as a landlord. The case excited a strong feeling of indignation throughout Ireland, and great sympathy for the suffering tenantry. During the progress of these events, the attention of the House of Commons was called to the subject, on two occasions, by enquiries of the ministry as to whether they were cognizant of what had occurred, and whether they intended to recommend the removal of Mr. Adair from the Commission of the Peace. To this the government replied, that while they had not hesitated to express to Mr. Adair their disapproval of his conduct, they did not feel justified in removing him from the magistracy, as he had not exceeded his legal rights.[2] Not satisfied with this explanation, a motion was made on June 24, in the House of Commons, for an address to the queen, for an enquiry into the conduct of Mr. Adair, in reference to these transactions, 'with a view to consider whether it is fitting he should continue to hold her Majesty's commission.' The government opposed the motion (waiving the 'technical plea that it was beyond the province of the House') on the ground that nothing had occurred which would justify the exercise of the prerogative in the dismissal of Mr. Adair from the magistracy; and the question was negatived.[3] A few days afterwards another member moved to resolve ' that it is expedient that a full and efficient enquiry should be instituted into all the circumstances attending these transactions.' Lord Palmerston,

---

[1] Hans. Deb. vol. lxxx. pp. 827, 857, 1100. See also a discussion in the House of Commons, on February 26, 1846, on a motion for papers respecting the dismissal of Lord Lucan from the Commission of the Peace, and his subsequent restoration thereto, and appointment to the lord-lieutenancy of the county of Mayo. The government defended the conduct of the Irish authorities, but agreed to the production of the papers, that the facts might be fully known.

[2] Ibid. vol. clxii. pp. 623, 846.

[3] Ibid. vol. clxiii. p. 1513.

however, while admitting that it was right to discuss the matter, in **Precedents** order to elicit the opinions of the House upon the case, resisted the motion, as being an attempt to induce the House to exercise its powers in a manner not justified by constitutional principles. He asserted that 'it would be a most dangerous and outrageous abuse of the power of the House if it interfered with the private transactions of any individuals, within the limits of their legal rights. If they have done anything beyond the limits of the law; if, from any motives whatever, they may have exceeded their power, the law itself will correct the evil. But it is not necessary for this House to interfere unless the government has had a duty to perform, and has neglected to perform it.'[1] On division, the motion was negatived by a large majority. Undeterred by this defeat, the general question was soon afterwards revived, in a different shape. On July 5, it was moved that a committee be appointed to enquire into the causes and circumstances of certain evictions which had lately taken place in another part of Ireland. These evictions, unlike those at Derryveagh, had not resulted from a suspicion of Ribbonism, but were apparently owing to religious dissensions; it being alleged, on the one hand, that they had all occurred because the tenants refused to send their children to the Protestant schools, while by others this statement was denied upon oath. The Chief Secretary for Ireland opposed the motion, on general principles, without entering into particulars concerning it. He remarked that every argument that had been urged against the interference of the House in the Derryveagh case, was still more applicable to the present. 'Such an enquiry would be wholly without profit; it would not tend to elevate the character of the House; but it would make the House for the first time usurp the functions of the tribunals in a way that had undoubtedly never been done before. The powers of this House are without limit; but they are limited by our own sense of discretion, and guided by the precedents of former generations, and I believe that no precedent can be produced of the House having acted in a manner so contrary to its functions, and so inconsistent with its prudence.' Whereupon, without further debate, the question was negatived.[a]

On June 20, 1862, a motion was made in the House of Commons **Jurors.** for the appointment of a committee to enquire into certain irregularities concerning jurors at the last assizes at Tyrone. The government admitted that the conduct of the high sheriff had been blameable, but did not think that a sufficient case had been made out to justify the proposed enquiry. The question was accordingly negatived.

On June 15, 1866, it was moved to resolve, that the treatment of prisoners in the Limerick gaol, under the Habeas Corpus Suspension

[1] Hans. Deb. vol. clxiv. pp. 243-252.   [a] Ibid. pp. 413-435.

(Ireland) Act, has been unnecessarily severe and unconstitutional; and that it is the duty of the government to prevent the continuance of the same. After explanations offered by the Chief Secretary for Ireland, which were deemed satisfactory by the House, the motion was withdrawn.*

Erroneous convictions.
In the administration of justice it is unavoidable but that erroneous convictions will sometimes occur, and that circumstances afterwards brought to light will prove that an innocent person has been unfortunately condemned. While the government are bound to afford every facility to enable one who has thus unjustly suffered to re-establish his innocence, the principle has never been acknowledged that such persons are entitled to claim pecuniary compensation, either from the government or from Parliament.

Of Mr. W. H. Barber.
In 1858, however, a case occurred of extraordinary hardship. A Mr. W. H. Barber was convicted of forgery, and transported to Norfolk Island, where, it appears, he was subjected to peculiar indignities by the authorities. It was afterwards proved that he was wholly innocent of the charges brought against him and he was released. He then petitioned the House of Commons, setting forth his sufferings, and soliciting redress. On June 15, 1858, with the consent of the crown, this petition was referred to a select committee, 'to consider and report whether any, and what steps should be taken in reference thereto.' The committee unanimously agreed that every allegation in the petition was true, and that Mr. Barber had endured incredible hardships and persecutions, which entitled him to the favourable consideration of the government. Whereupon a sum of 5,000l. was included in the estimates as a compensation to this gentleman. Shortly afterwards, a change of ministry ensued; but the new administration retained this item in the estimates, in deference to the judgment of their predecessors in office, and the money was voted by Parliament. This amount, however, did not satisfy Mr. Barber. He considered himself entitled to a further sum of 9,700l., to indemnify him for his personal expenses in proving his innocence before the courts of law, and in regaining his original position. Accordingly, on June 11, 1861, the member who formerly introduced the matter to the notice of the House of Commons, submitted another motion, to declare that the strong claims of Mr. Barber to the favourable consideration of the crown, referred to in the aforesaid report of the committee in 1858, have not been satisfied; and that the circumstances set forth in a recent petition from himself to the House of Commons are entitled to the

---

* Hans. Deb. vol. clxxxiv. p. 491.

consideration of the government. But the Home Secretary (Sir George Grey) opposed the motion, on the ground that Parliament was not bound to award pecuniary compensation to persons who had been improperly convicted; and that it was only the exceptional circumstances of Mr. Barber's case which had induced the government to consent to the grant already made to him, and which was sufficient to cover every reasonable demand he had against the public. The question was accordingly negatived.[o]

On April 28, 1863, a petition was presented to the House of Commons by Mr. W. Bewicke, representing the loss and injury he had sustained in consequence of having been tried and convicted of firing a loaded pistol at four sheriff's officers, with intent to kill or do bodily harm, and sentenced to four years' imprisonment. His accusers were afterwards found guilty of having conspired falsely to charge Mr. Bewicke with the crime; whereupon he received the queen's pardon. But meanwhile his property had become forfeited, as that of a felon, and had been sold by auction. The net produce of the sale was afterwards paid over to him, but Mr. Bewicke's loss on the property had been very considerable, and he had also been at great expense in prosecuting and bringing to justice his false accusers. He therefore prayed the House to grant him relief and compensation. On July 21, Mr. H. Berkeley moved, that in the opinion of the House, the grievances suffered by Mr. Bewicke are such as entitle him to the consideration of government. The Home Secretary (Sir George Grey) opposed the motion. He admitted that it was a case deserving of commiseration, but the law provided no means of indemnity, and it would be an injurious precedent to vote compensation from the public purse. On division, the motion was negatived by a majority of two.[p] On April 29, 1864, Mr. Berkeley moved for a committee to consider of an address to the queen, praying her to direct adequate compensation to be made to Mr. Bewicke for his sufferings and losses, and declaring that the House would make good the same. The Home Secretary and Attorney-General resisted the motion, but expressed the willingness of government to agree to the appointment of a select committee to enquire into the special circumstances of the case, and as to whether Mr. Bewicke sustained much loss by the sale of his property at auction. After a division, in favour of the main motion, a committee of enquiry into the allegations of the petition presented in 1863 was appointed. On June 17, the committee reported their opinion that Mr. Bewicke was not entitled to any compensation, having failed to prove that there had been a miscarriage of justice in his case,

Erroneous conviction of Mr. Bewicke.

---

[o] Hans. Deb. vol. clxii. pp. 944-952.   [p] Ibid. vol. clxxii. p. 1175; and see Smith's Parl. Rem. 1863, p. 160.

through the default of the persons charged with the administration of the law. They also declared their inability to accede to the proposition, that persons who have been convicted in due course of law by evidence subsequently proved to be false are entitled to compensation out of the public purse. But in view of the loss sustained by the sale of his property, under forfeiture, they ventured to suggest, for the favourable consideration of the crown, whether the full value of such property at the time of forfeiture should not be restored to Mr. Bewicke, minus the net produce of the sale already paid over to him.^q

Prerogative in granting honours.

The next branch of the royal prerogative to which our attention will be directed is that which regards the sovereign as the fountain of honour.

Presuming that none can judge so well of the merits and services of the subjects of the realm as the crown itself, by whom they are employed, the law has entrusted to the king the sole power of conferring dignities and honours, or otherwise rewarding his faithful servants; in confidence that he will make use of the same in behalf of none but those who deserve distinction or reward.^r But this prerogative, like every other function of royalty, is exercised upon the advice of responsible ministers.

No interference with this prerogative by either House of Parliament should ordinarily take place, for the obvious reason that if it were understood that the goodwill and recommendation of Parliament was the road to honorary distinction, there would be an end to all true responsibility; and the favour of private members would be sought after instead of the approbation of the crown.^s

Advice of Parliament thereon.

Nevertheless, exceptional cases may arise, and have arisen, to justify the Houses of Parliament in approaching the sovereign with their advice and recommendations in regard to the exercise of this prerogative, and on behalf of meritorious public servants, whose claim to the favour of the crown had been either overlooked or disregarded.

---

^q Commons Papers, 1861, vol. v. p. 547.
^r Bowyer, Const. Law, p. 174.
^s Hans. Deb. vol. cxxxix. p. 1532.

Thus, on June 3, 1845, Mr. Hume moved an address to the queen, that she would be pleased to grant such a pension as she should think proper to the right hon. Sir Henry Pottinger, as a reward for his eminent public services, especially in China. The premier (Sir Robert Peel) deprecated the interference of the House in this matter, and said it was a question 'whether the House should make a precedent of a special grant, usurping the prerogative of the crown to reward public servants.' Considering, however, the peculiarly exceptional circumstances of the case, he stated that he would not oppose the motion, but would take upon himself to advise her Majesty to make a suitable provision for this distinguished man. Whereupon the resolution was agreed to, *nem. con.*[t]

And, in 1857, the government having been tardy in recognising the value of the public services of Sir John M'Neil and Colonel Tulloch, upon a commission of enquiry into the state of the army in the Crimea, and having tendered to them an inadequate reward, the House of Commons passed an address, 'praying that some especial mark of approbation might be conferred upon them' by the crown, in consideration of their able services on that occasion. The ministry yielded to the general wish of the House, did not oppose the address, and advised a favourable reply to it.[u]

On June 16, 1865, Mr. Hanbury Tracy called the attention of the House to the dissatisfaction prevailing in military circles, in regard to recent appointments to and promotions in the Order of the Bath, upon a motion for a copy of any regulations altering the constitution of the order. After a short debate, and explanations from the prime minister on the subject, the motion was withdrawn.[v]

By constitutional usage, it is customary, in the case of Speakers of the House of Commons, on their final retirement from the chair, to address the crown to confer upon them 'some signal mark of royal favour.' This is responded to, on the part of the sovereign, by their elevation to the peerage, and by a message to the House of Commons recommending that pecuniary provision may be made for the support of the dignity.[w] The creation

Precedents

Speakers of House of Commons.

---

[t] Hans. Deb. vol. lxxx. pp. 1340, 1391, 1404. See also the case of the officers, &c. engaged in the battle of Navarino; where the government were induced to allow them head-money, at the urgent appeal of the House of Commons. Mirror of Parl. 1834, pp. 2268, 2859. And the case of those engaged in the Chinese war, which was successfully resisted by the government. Hans. Deb. vol. lxxxii. p. 641.

[u] *Ibid.* vol. cxliv. pp. 2240, 2300.

[v] *Ibid.* vol. clxxx. p. 400; and see *Ibid.* p. 748, in regard to the claims of certain troops in India to the Indian mutiny medal.

[w] Rt. hon. C. M. Sutton, Mirror of

Peerages. of Peers is a peculiar and incommunicable privilege of the Sovereign, over which Parliament has no control; saving that it must be exercised upon the advice of responsible ministers.'

Life Peerages. In 1855, the question of the creation by the crown of peerages for life was elaborately discussed in the House of Lords. It was not contended that the sovereign was debarred from conferring this description of honour upon any of her subjects, but merely that, in conformity to the usage and practice of the constitution, since it has been defined and settled in its best days—namely, from the revolution of 1688 downwards—the patent creating a life peerage did not entitle the recipient thereof to sit and vote in Parliament.' This point having been decided by the House of Lords, after an examination of precedents, Lord Wensleydale, who had been created a baron 'for and during the term of his natural life,' did not attempt to take a seat in that House; until shortly afterwards when he was created an hereditary peer.

Votes of Thanks by Parliament. The usage of Parliament also permits of the adoption, by either House,' of resolutions of thanks to officers of the army or navy and others, who have rendered military service, for meritorious conduct in their official capacity. Various rules have been prescribed by precedent in respect to votes of this description. In the first place, it has been customary that all such motions should emanate from a member of the administration, acting on behalf of the crown, as the source and fountain of honour.' This rule has not been without exception, though it is worthy of notice that motions for votes of thanks which have proceeded from private members have rarely been successful.

Parl. 1831-2, pp. 3407, 3486, 3502. Rt. hon. C. S. Lefevre, Hans. Deb. vol. cxliv. pp. 2120, 2271, 2900.

' May, Const. Hist. v. 1. c. V. Mirror of Parl. 1830, p. 1705. And see Bagehot, Eng. Const. in Fortnightly Rev. Dec. 1, 1861, p. 820.

' Hans. Deb. vol. clviii. pp. 1457, 1480.

' Votes of thanks 'should be proposed in both Houses, and with such a concurrence of opinion that there could be no doubt of their being unanimously passed.' Rt. hon. B. Disraeli, Hans. Deb. vol. cxlix. p. 252.

' Parl. Hist. vol. xxxiii. p. 3. Hans. Deb. vol. cxlix. p. 265.

For example, on June 20, 1794, Mr. Secretary Dundas having moved a vote of thanks to the officers and men engaged in the expedition to Corsica, Mr. Sheridan proposed an amendment to restrict the same to certain officers enumerated; but his amendment was rejected.[b] Again, on March 3, 1797, Mr. Keene moved an amendment to a proposed vote of thanks to Sir John Jervis, to substitute an address to the crown to confer some signal mark of royal favour upon Sir John; but he was compelled to withdraw it. On August 10, 1803, however, Mr. Sheridan moved a vote of thanks to the Volunteer and Yeomanry Corps, which was carried nem. con.[c] On February 14, 1828, Mr. Hobhouse proposed a vote of thanks to the officers engaged in the battle of Navarin; but the previous question being proposed thereon, he withdrew his motion.

Votes of thanks.

It is contrary to the practice of Parliament to propose thanks to officers, by name, who are under the rank of general or commodore, or who are not in chief command in the action;[d] but 'the several officers, non-commissioned officers, and privates' engaged, are often thanked collectively.[e] After the suppression of the Indian mutiny, thanks were voted, collectively, to the gallant civilians, who had voluntarily performed military service on that occasion, with courage and self-devotion.[f] Thanks were also voted, on December 15, 1854, to 'General Canrobert and the French army, for their gallant and successful co-operation with her Majesty's land forces' in the Crimean campaign; and Field-marshal Lord Raglan was desired to convey to them the resolution.

It is usual to await the conclusion of operations before voting thanks in Parliament; and not to propose them after a brilliant exploit, which has left the operations or the victory incomplete.[g] And they are only voted for successes, and could not therefore be given to General

---

[b] Commons Journals, vol. xlix. p. 742.
[c] See also the proceedings on July 11, 1808.
[d] Peel, in Mirror of Parl. 1841, p. 222.
[e] See general indices, Commons Journals. And see Hans. Deb. (3) vol. cxxxvi. p. 324.
[f] Hans. Deb. (3) vol. cxlviii. p. 827.
[g] Peel, Hans. Deb. (3) vol. lxxi. p. 553.

Votes of thanks

Williams for his gallant defence of Kars, as that fortress was ultimately surrendered.[h]

It has not been customary to give the thanks of Parliament for victories, however brilliant, meritorious, or complete, unless they took place against a power with whom Great Britain was, at the time, in a state of formal recognised war.[i] Of late years, however, and especially in the case of military operations in India, this has not been insisted upon.[j] In proposing thanks for successes in India, it has been the uniform practice to confine the expression of the same to the military operations and arrangements, keeping out of view the question of the policy and origin of the war, for which the government are alone responsible.[k]

Votes of thanks are always confined to the survivors; there is no precedent of resolutions of approval being adopted in regard to the conduct of deceased officers, of whatsoever rank or merit.[l] In 1854, however, a general resolution of appreciation, sympathy, and condolence, was adopted in reference to the heroes who fell in the Crimean campaign.[m]

If names intended to have been included in a vote of thanks are accidently omitted, or if errors occur therein, they may be subsequently corrected, on motion to that effect.[n] Or, the order may be discharged, so as to admit of one more complete being adopted.[o]

In 1843, when it was proposed to include the name of Sir Henry Pottinger, plenipotentiary and envoy extraordinary to China, in a vote of thanks for successful operations during the war with that country, Sir R. Peel said, 'there is no instance in which a diplomatic agent of

---

[h] Hans. Deb. vol. cxli. pp. 1847, 1878.
[i] Mirror of Parl. 1828, p. 180.
[j] Hans. Deb. (3) vol. lxxii. pp. 512, 571.
[k] Mirror of Parl. 1840, p. 801. Hans. Deb. (3) vol. lxvi. p. 200.
[l] Peel, in Hans. Deb. (3) vol. lxxxiv. p. 421.
[m] *Ibid.* vol. cxxxvi. p. 520. Mirror of Parl. 1840, pp. 814, 1137. *Ibid.* 1841, p. 490. Hans. Deb. (3) vol. cxxxvi. p. 424.
[n] Mirror of Parl. 1840, pp. 1100, 1302.

the government has received the thanks of Parliament for the successful completion of any negotiation however important, or of any treaty however advantageous to the interests of the country;' adding, 'I think it of great importance to adhere in these matters strictly to precedents .... which, I think, have been founded upon good sense; otherwise, every omission that we happened to make in a vote of this nature would imply a censure.'[b] This principle was afterwards explained and enforced by Lord Palmerston, who said that 'Parliament seemed to have systematically avoided votes of thanks to negotiators, and most properly, because a negotiator was a person acting under the instructions of his government. The government had a majority in Parliament, and a vote of thanks to their negotiator was, in fact, a vote of thanks to themselves.'[c] But, in the same year, Lord Brougham proposed in the House of Lords,[f] and Mr. Hume in the House of Commons,[s] a vote of thanks to Lord Ashburton, envoy-extraordinary to Washington, for the manner in which he had conducted the negotiations which resulted in the Treaty of Washington. Sir Robert Peel, on the part of the government, acquiesced in this motion, viewing it as an exception to the general rule, on the distinct ground that such strong censure had been cast upon Lord Ashburton and the treaty, by leading public men, that it was due to his lordship to take the sense of Parliament upon his conduct. He said, moreover, that unprecedented as the proposed vote undoubtedly was, many precedents existed for insisting upon a distinct expression of opinion on the part of the House, in cases where, as in the present instance, a motion of condemnation had been made.[t] His views, however, as to 'the danger of establishing, or rather continuing such a pre-

---

[b] Hans. Deb. (3), vol. lxvi. pp. 572, 573.
[c] Ibid. vol. lxviii. p. 1237.
[f] Ibid. p. 641.
[s] Ibid. p. 1150.
[t] Ibid. p. 1217.

Prerogative in granting charters.

cedent,' in other cases, remained unchanged." The vote was agreed to in both Houses. It was acknowledged, in the House of Lords, by Lord Ashburton, from his seat in the House.'

The granting of charters to corporations, conferring upon them certain exclusive rights, privileges, and immunities, is also a matter of prerogative, and is exercised by order in council. In former times, this prerogative was of very wide extent, and implied an absolute legislative power on the part of the crown, by virtue whereof charters of liberties were granted to the people, both at home and abroad; which were all, more or less, in the nature of public laws. The growth and progress of our political institutions, however, have gradually restrained the authority of the crown in this particular within recognised limits, and now no charter conferring political power or franchise in Great Britain or her colonies can be granted by the crown, without the concurrence of Parliament.

And the crown cannot create corporations with powers which transcend the law. Thus, it may not create a corporation to enjoy a monopoly, nor with power to tax the rest of the community. When a corporation is to be created with privileges of this description, the authority of the legislature must be invoked to supply the deficiencies of the royal prerogative."

Corporations for local and municipal purposes must be created in the mode prescribed by law for the exercise of that portion of the royal prerogative, and with the incidents legally essential to their nature.* For example, her Majesty has been expressly empowered by statute,

---

* Hans. Deb. vol. lxviii. p. 1241. See also *Ibid.* vol. lxxx. p. 1387.
† On one occasion General De Lacy Evans, a member of the House of Commons, in acknowledging the thanks of the House, from his seat, proceeded to comment at length, and with severity, upon errors in the speech of the mover of the vote of thanks, describing the services of the army. Hans. Deb. (3) vol. cxxxvi. p. 1205.
" Bowyer, Const. Law. p. 412.
* *Ibid.* and see statutes cited therein.

on petition of the inhabitant householders, to grant, with the advice of her privy-council, a charter of incorporation, according to the provisions of the Municipal Corporation Act, to any town, whether already incorporated or not.[7]

The crown has ever exercised, and still retains, the prerogative of incorporating universities, colleges, companies, and other public bodies, and of granting to them, by charter, powers and privileges not inconsistent with the law of the land.[8] But public associations for commercial purposes ordinarily require powers which can only be conferred by legislation. Even long-established institutions, such as the Bank of England, which were originally created by royal charter, have of late years derived their extraordinary privileges, like other public companies, from Acts of Parliament.[9]

In 1864, the charter of the Queen's University in Ireland was surrendered, and a new charter which materially altered the constitution of the university, was granted by the crown without any previous communication to Parliament upon the subject, and without the intentions of government having been made known to any one, except the members of the senate of the university.[a] In 1866, the government decided upon the grant of a supplemental charter, granting additional powers to the Queen's University, and also upon making certain alterations in the constitution of the Queen's Colleges in Ireland. Being questioned upon the subject in the House of Commons, ministers stated that, whether or not they were compelled by law to do so, it was their intention to place clearly before Parliament their opinions in regard to university education in Ireland, and the advice they should tender to the crown in relation thereto. They intimated their intention of raising the question by asking the House to vote certain sums for scholarships to be opened to candidates from the Queen's Colleges, &c. in order that the House might have an opportunity of expressing its opinion upon the proposed

Queen's University, Ireland.

---

[7] 5 and 6 Will. IV. c. 76, § 141; 1 Vict. c. 78, § 49. And see Bowyer, 340 n.

[8] See the proceedings in the House of Commons in reference to the granting of a royal charter of incorporation to the University of London. Mirror of Parl. 1833, pp. 1842, 2740. Also the debate upon a resolution moved on July 9, 1861, to declare that the royal commission of the Great Exhibition of 1851 (which had been created by royal charters that were recognised by an Act of Parliament) should be determined. Hans. Deb. vol. clxxii. pp. 254-280.

[9] Knight's Political Cyclop. ii. 404.

[a] Hans. Deb. vol. clxxiv. p. 801.

Queen's University, Ireland.

measures of university reform.[c] Ultimately, however, the government took a different course. Having given full publicity to their intention in regard to the Queen's University, and no objection having been made to the same by either House of Parliament, they proceeded to issue a supplemental charter, to enable the senate of the Queen's University to confer degrees upon all persons who might pass their examinations without regard to the place of their education. But as certain difficulties had arisen in obtaining the consent of the existing corporation to these changes, the government announced their intention of submitting a Bill to Parliament to give effect to the reforms proposed in the management of this institution.[d] At this juncture the Russell administration resigned on account of a defeat in the House of Commons upon the Reform Bill. But two days after they had decided upon their resignation of office a warrant was issued directing the Great Seal to be affixed to the new charter; and a week afterwards a queen's letter was issued, appointing six additional members to the university senate, apparently in order to insure the acceptance of the charter by that body. The university senate, however, postponed the consideration of the new charter until a future day, in order that explanations might be elicited from the late ministers in regard to their proceedings in the matter. The decision of the senate was arrived at upon the motion of Sir R. Peel, M.P., who was a member of that body. As soon as the House of Commons reassembled for business, after the appointment of the new ministry, Sir R. Peel gave notice of an enquiry to be made of the late government in respect to the non-fulfilment of their promise to afford the House an opportunity of challenging the policy of the government concerning university education in Ireland, before the crown had committed any formal act on the subject.[e] Accordingly, on July 10, Sir R. Peel called the attention of the House to the circumstances under which the new charter had been issued, and intimated that if a satisfactory explanation of their conduct were not given by ministers, he should move an address praying the crown to annul the charter. In reply, it was contended by Sir G. Grey, Mr. Fortescue, and Mr. Gladstone (members of the late government) that ministers had duly informed Parliament of their policy and intentions in this matter, their object being, not to associate Parliament beforehand in the responsibility of any measures which might be taken, but to afford to the House such information as should enable it, if so minded, to prevent them. The new Attorney-General (Sir H. Cairns) acquitted the ex-ministers of any intention to deceive the House in this matter, but was nevertheless of opinion that the House had been thrown off its

---

[c] Hans. Deb. vol. clxxxi. pp. 811, 907.
[d] Ibid. vol. clxxxiv. pp. 720, 861.
[e] Ibid. p. 755.

guard by language calculated to mislead. He also contended that the late ministers had no right to issue the charter and appoint the new members of senate after they had tendered their resignations, and when their functions were actually 'in abeyance.' The new Chancellor of Exchequer (Mr. Disraeli) concluded the debate by remarking that the whole question of Irish education should be seriously considered by government, and their policy thereon communicated to Parliament upon a fitting opportunity.[f]

Prerogative in regard to officers and public officers.

The crown, besides being the fountain of dignity and honours, is likewise entrusted by the constitution with the sole power of creating such offices, for carrying on the public service, or maintaining the dignity of the state, as may be required. It has also, by virtue of the prerogative, a right to make choice of all persons to be appointed to fill places of trust and emolument under the crown; to determine the amount of remuneration to which they shall be respectively entitled; and to dismiss them from office, according to its discretion.

Every office and employment in the public service derives its authority either directly or indirectly from the crown; and in the eye of the law is accounted honourable, because implying a superiority of abilities; and being always presumed to be filled by the person best qualified for the same. Offices are in the gift of the crown, because the law supposes that no one can be so good a judge of the merits and qualifications of public officers as the sovereign by whom they are employed.[g]

As the king may create new titles, so may he create new offices, but with this restriction, that he cannot create new offices with new fees annexed to them, nor annex new fees to old offices; for this would be a tax upon the people, which cannot be imposed but by Act of Parliament.[h] Neither may the crown grant ancient

---

[f] *Ibid.* p. 142, &c. The supplemental charter was accepted by the senate of the university, by a vote of 11 to 9, on October 6, 1860, the six new members all voting in the majority. But a few days later, the convocation of the university resolved that its acceptance was inexpedient.

[g] Bowyer, Const. Law, 147.

[h] 2 Inst. 533. Com. Dig. Preroy. D. 3.

Abuse of patronage.

offices in other manner and form than has been usual, unless with consent of Parliament;[1] nor create an office that is inconsistent with the constitution, or prejudicial to the subject, though without fees.[2] Neither can a judicial office be granted for a term of years, or in reversion. Ministerial offices, however, are not subject to this rule.[3]

In former times, and even so recently as the reign of George III., the patronage of the crown was oftentimes shamefully abused. Persons were appointed to places of trust and emolument, or removed therefrom, on mere political grounds, and in furtherance of political intrigues. Even persons holding non-political offices, such as lord-lieutenants of counties, or having commissions in the army and navy, were not unfrequently dismissed by order of the king, for votes given in Parliament.[4] Sinecure offices, gifts of places in reversion, and secret pensions for political services to the court were multiplied; and the illegitimate influence of the crown was thereby greatly increased. But chiefly through the patriotic labours of Edmund Burke, in the cause of economic reform, these evils were exposed and remedied. Acts of Parliament were passed in the early part of the reign of George III. to abolish sinecures, to regulate the grant of offices, and to reform abuses connected therewith. Since the commencement of the present century, a marked improvement has taken place in the practice of governments, and in the tone of public opinion, respecting the distribution of patronage. No minister would now venture to incur the

---

[1] Chitty, Prerog. 81.
[2] Ibid. 81. Bowyer, 175.
[3] Com. Dig. Officer, B. 7.
[4] See May, Const. Hist. i. 24, 20, 40, 41. See the debate in the House of Lords, on March 6, 1780, for an address to the king, to be informed 'by whose advice the Marquis of Carmarthen and the Earl of Pembroke had been dismissed from the office of lord-lieutenant, by reason of their conduct in Parliament.' The motion was opposed by the ministry, as intrenching upon the king's prerogative of choosing his own servants, and was negatived. And see the case of Earl Fitzwilliam, who was removed from the lord-lieutenancy of Yorkshire, for taking part in the proceedings of a political meeting against the government, at a time of great political excitement. Edin. Review, vol. cix. p. 180.

responsibility of abusing the prerogative, in the choice and dismissal of servants of the crown, by such acts as were committed with impunity less than a century ago. Public opinion has gradually brought the exercise of these powers of administration under the control of certain rules, which, though for the most part enforced by no written law, are yet practically acknowledged by the government, and have put an end to many abuses.

The most important rule of modern times, in regard to the civil servants of the crown, is that whereby they have been divided into two classes—political and non-political; the former consisting of cabinet ministers and other members of the administration, and the latter of the remaining members of the civil service. The principle upon which this division is made, is that certain officers have duties to perform of a decidedly political character, or are otherwise so intimately connected with the person of the sovereign as to afford peculiar facilities for influencing the royal mind. All such functionaries, as a general rule, have seats in one or other of the Houses of Parliament, and are required to co-operate with their colleagues in office in furthering the policy of the government. And they necessarily relinquish their offices upon a change of ministry.

Political and non-political officers.

The non-political servants of the crown may be considered as virtually ineligible to a seat in Parliament. They have been, for the most part, excluded from the House of Commons by express statutes; but even where there is no positive prohibition, the fact of a person holding a permanent official appointment under the crown operates as an indirect disqualification for political life, inasmuch as every successive ministry in England is formed upon party principles, and 'no administration

Non-political officers.

---

* Grey, Parl. Govt. new ed. 285.
* See further on these points, vol. ii. c. 2, 'On the Cabinet Council.'
* See Papers on the Civil Service, Commons Papers, 1854-5, vol. xx. p. 400.
* See vol. ii. c. 2.

could act with colleagues who were members of the House, unless they were willing to act as members of the same party.' Their exclusion from the political arena is the price they pay for their tenure of office, being virtually that of good behaviour. For whether they were originally appointed for political reasons, or otherwise, nevertheless, 'as a general rule, the civil servants who do not sit in Parliament, hold their offices technically and legally during the pleasure of the crown, but are in practice considered as having a right to remain in undisturbed possession of them, so long as they continue to discharge their functions properly. This principle is so universally recognised, that the dismissal of a person holding a permanent office is never heard of now, except for misconduct.'

'The distinct line drawn between permanent and political offices, together with the complete establishment of the practice of regarding the former as held during good behaviour, has diminished the evils incidental to changes of administration.' 'By allowing these transfers to affect only a comparatively small number of high offices, and by retaining the great majority of the public servants permanently in their situations, the experience and traditional knowledge they possess of the business of the several departments of the state are rendered still available for the conduct of affairs.'

Contrast this picture with the results of the system which prevails in the United States of America, where some thousands of offices are periodically transferred from

---

* Report on Board of Admiralty, 1861, p. 43. See the case of the dismissal of Earl Howe, in 1831, from the office of Lord Chamberlain to Queen Adelaide, on account of his having voted against the Reform Bill in the House of Lords. Enquiry having been made of the ministry respecting this act, the Chancellor of the Exchequer stated that it would be contrary to his duty as a minister of the crown to give any reason for the exercise of his Majesty's undoubted prerogative of dismissing any of his servants. Mirror of Parl. 1831, p. 3127.

' Grey, Parl. Govt. new ed. 287. And see Papers on reorganisation of Civil Service. Commons Papers, 1854-5, vol. xx. p. 103.

* Grey, Parl. Govt. new ed. 288, 289.

the adherents of one party to that of another, upon the accession of every new president! This practice has had a most pernicious influence upon the public welfare in that country. On the part of the *employés* themselves, it has encouraged every species of political profligacy, diminished the sense of personal responsibility, and fostered a careless indifference to the obligations of office, whilst its emoluments are greedily sought for, and too often fraudulently increased. It has deprived the state of the services of men of character and qualifications, hindered the progress of departmental improvement, and compelled every successive batch of *employés* to acquire the merest rudiments of official routine, when they should be profiting by the traditions and experience of office to bring their several departments into the highest possible condition of efficiency. The demoralising effects of this system upon the whole community are beginning to attract serious attention, and one of the ablest and most respectable organs of public opinion in America has announced that a vital change in this particular has become essential to the maintenance of their republican institutions. After pointing out the nature and extent of the evil, at the present time, the writer urges the necessity of adopting the usage of Great Britain in regard to office-holders, declaring that 'we must have a general rule for the selection of *employés*; their tenure of office must be made dependent on their good behaviour; there must be promotion as a reward for fidelity and ability, and pensions as a refuge for old age. In other words, some inducement must be held out to honest and competent men to enter the public service, to remain in it, and behave well in it.'* This is a striking testimony to the superior advantages of the British system.

Evils of the American system, of frequent change of employés

The principle which regulates the choice of persons to

---

* North American Review, July 1855, pp. 122-124. See also, in regard to the working of the American system, Grey, Parl. Govt. new ed. pp. 165, 201.

fill political offices under the British crown, will be explained in another part of this treatise." It is, moreover, immaterial to our present enquiry. In selecting individuals to fill subordinate places of honour and emolument, a great responsibility devolves upon the existing administration. Public opinion will no longer tolerate the prostitution of offices for political services that so often disgraced our history in former times. It is now an admitted necessity, that every one appointed to an office of trust, however small, should be qualified for his post, otherwise the choice will bring discredit upon the government, and may lead to the withdrawal of public confidence and parliamentary support from those who are accountable for the same. But so long as this principle is not lost sight of, it is acknowledged to be the privilege of an administration to give the preference, in appointments to office, to their political friends and supporters; for among the powers that are required to enable a government to perform its functions with efficiency, there are few more essential than that of reward." 'The patronage of the crown,' says May," 'has ever been used to promote the interests and consolidate the strength of that party in which its distribution happened to be vested.' It is true that the offer of places, as a corrupt inducement to vote at elections, has long been recognised by the legislature as an insidious form of bribery." But while carefully avoiding the committal of any offence against the law, the patronage of the crown within certain limits —to be presently noticed—has been systematically, though not invariably,' distributed by the ministry of

Appointments to permanent officers.

Political patronage.

---

* See vol. ii. c. 1.
* Grey, Parl. Govt. p. 311. Rowland's Eng. Const. 497.
* Const. Hist. vol. ii. p. 91.
* 2 Geo. II. c. 24; 49 Geo. III. c. 118, &c. Rogers on Elections, 316–347.
* See the exceptions hereinafter noticed. And it is worthy of remark that the Earl of Shelburne (formerly prime minister), a staunch Whig, accepted the Marquisate of Lansdowne from the hands of Mr. Pitt; continuing in opposition, notwithstanding; though he took but little part in politics after his retirement from office. (Edin. Rev. vol. xcix. p. 42.) And in November 1858, during the Derby administration, the Right Hon. W. E. Gladstone, M.P., was

the day, 'as a means of rewarding past political service, and of ensuring future support. The greater part of all local patronage has been dispensed [by the secretary to the treasury] through the hands of members of Parliament, supporting the ministers of the day. They have claimed and received it as their right; and have distributed it, avowedly, to strengthen their political connection." Very recently, on May 24, 1860, the Lord-Lieutenant of Ireland (Lord Carlisle) was called upon in the House of Lords to defend an appointment he had made to a lieutenancy in an Irish county. While vindicating the propriety of his choice, he admitted that if he had had recourse to persons differing in political sentiment from the government, he might have found one or two persons more eligible for the post; but, he added, 'I think it due to those who concur in political opinion with her Majesty's government, whenever I have to assign stations of honour and distinction, unless there is some strong reason to the contrary, to give the preference to those who entertain the opinions and support the principles to which I myself owe the position I hold, and the power I possess of dealing with such matters at all.' 'This,' he continued, 'has been the general practice in this country;' in proof of which assertion he cited several notable examples.* On June 26 following it was moved in the House of Commons to resolve that 'fitness has not been primarily considered in certain appointments made by the Lord-Lieutenant of Ireland;' but it being conclusively shown that this charge was wholly destitute of foundation, the motion was negatived without a division.

appointed Lord High Commissioner Extraordinary to the Ionian Islands, from a sense of his peculiar fitness for the post, and notwithstanding his being a leading member of the Opposition.

* And see Hans. Deb. vol. clxxii. p. 854. Earl Grey, in his essay on Parl. Govt. now ed. p. 48, points out the tendency to encourage corruption, and especially that kind of corruption which consists in the misuse of patronage as 'inherent in the system of parliamentary government.' For further particulars as to the usage of ministries in the distribution of the patronage of the Crown, see vol. ii. c. 2. On the office of Prime Minister.

* Hans. Deb. vol. clviii. pp. 1044–40.

Non-political appointments.
In the Church.

We now proceed to notice the exceptions to this practice, which are both numerous and important.

In the first place, in the disposal of the ecclesiastical patronage of the crown, it is not the rule that it should be generally given to partisans of the existing government. Appointments to bishoprics, and other dignified offices in the Church, and to the more valuable livings in the gift of the crown, are usually made upon the recommendation of the prime minister, and he is careful to consult the general interests of the Church, in such nominations, without reference to mere political or sectional opinions.[b] The Lord Chancellor has the distribution of a very large amount of inferior Church patronage, which he is free to dispose of 'according to his notions of what is due to religion, friendship, or party.'[c]

In the army and navy.

In the appointment, or promotion, of naval and military officers, and of persons employed in the civil branch of the Admiralty, political distinctions are almost invariably overlooked. It is universally recognised as the duty of those who are entrusted with the patronage of the crown, to be guided in the distribution of promotion and professional employment in the army and navy by the rules of the service and the merits of the case.[d] Any minister would incur inevitable disgrace who should be actuated by political or party preferences on such occasions, and should select inferior men, because of their political opinions.[e] Promotion in militia regiments is, as a general rule, conducted on the principle of seniority.[f]

---

[b] See Rep. on Off. Salaries, 1850. Lord John Russell's Evid. 800, 1282. His lordship stated that, with regard to bishops, he thought the minister generally recommended persons who agreed with him in political opinion, they having seats in the House of Lords. But, of late years, a stricter impartiality has been observed in the selection of persons for this high office.

[c] Lord Campbell's Lives of the Chancellors, vol. i. p. 20.

[d] Grey, Parl. Govt. p. 100.

[e] Mr. Grey and Mr. Fox's speeches, in Parl. Deb. vol. iv. pp. 342, 358. And see Admiral Seymour's Evidence before Committee on Navy Promotion, Commons Papers, 1863, vol. x. p. 71, and Index to Report, p. 480.

[f] Hans. Deb. vol. clxxii. p. 1472.

So, also, with regard to vacancies in judicial offices. With the exception of the office of Lord Chancellor, which is political and ministerial, and of the posts of Chief Justice of the Common Pleas and of the Queen's Bench, which are usually conferred upon the law officers of the crown, no such principle would be permitted to prevail in England, as that seats upon the bench should be given to political partisans.[a] In Ireland, it is true, a greater laxity on this point has prevailed; and while the Derby administrations, in 1852 and 1858, afforded examples of promotion from the Irish bar of political opponents of the government, yet 'no doubt, in Ireland, promotions to the bench have been made in general, by both sides, on party grounds.'[b]

As respects civil service nominations, for minor appointments to office, Lord Palmerston has testified that they are 'often given without regard to political considerations.'[c]

So, also, in regard to promotions in the civil service; stringent regulations have been adopted and enforced by government to discountenance attempts on the part of public officers to obtain promotion by means of political influence. Circulars have been addressed to members of

---

[a] Hans. Deb. vol. clxxiii. p. 205. Lord Lyndhurst was made Chief Baron of the Exchequer in 1831, upon the recommendation of his political rival Lord Brougham, who then held the Great Seal. Lord Campbell, when Lord High Chancellor, appointed Colin Blackburn to be a judge of the Court of Queen's Bench, although he was of opposite politics, and was only known to the chancellor by his professional reputation. (*Macmillan's Magazine*, November 1864, p. 18.) And on July 3, 1865, the Attorney-General stated in the House of Commons that Lord Chancellor Westbury had exercised his judicial patronage without regard to the interests of party; and that he had selected a political opponent (Mr. Montague Smith, a conservative member of the House of Commons) to fill the last vacancy upon the bench, and another conservative gentleman to be Chief Registrar of the Court of Bankruptcy, because he considered them to be the most qualified persons for the said offices. In the appointment of County Court Judges he had also striven to select men for their merit and qualification, without regard to personal or party considerations. Hans. Deb. vol. clxxx. p. 1124.

[b] Hans. Deb. vol. clxxiii. p. 205.
[c] *Ibid*, vol. clxxii. p. 908.

Parliament by the head of the principal administrative departments, calling attention to orders in council, which strictly forbid the endeavour to interest members of Parliament in applications for office, or in promotions, and declaring that any attempt to obtain promotion by political or other indirect influence will be punished.¹ On the other hand, numerous public servants are forbidden by law (*post*, p. 391, n.) to exercise the elective franchise, lest they should be subjected to undue political influence by their official superiors. In other cases, where the franchise is not restrained, care has been taken to prevent its independent exercise from being interfered with.ᵏ These measures, coupled with the general adoption of the system of competitive examinations, in appointments to office, have done much to prevent the abuse of patronage for party purposes.

Crown patronage, its extent and distribution.

The entire patronage of the crown in Great Britain has been computed at about 105,000 offices.¹ After excluding the different classes of appointments in regard to which, as we have seen, the influence of party is but small, there still remains a considerable amount which is regarded as being available for distribution amongst the friends and supporters of the existing administration. Patronage of this description is generally exercised through the instrumentality of the parliamentary secretary to the treasury, or the political secretary of the department concerned.ᵐ It includes direct appointments to minor and subordinate offices, and nominations, under the competitive examination system. The principal members of the ministry are careful to hold themselves aloof from such transactions, lest their position should be compro-

---

² Rep. of Commons Committee on the Board of Admiralty, 1861, pp. 59, 65, 90, and see *post*, p. 397.

ᵏ See *post*, p. 392, n.

¹ Hans. Deb. vol. clxxii. p. 850. Of this number, it is stated that the *employés* of the civil service amounted, in 1862, to 49,161. In 1822, they were only 18,500. *Ibid.* vol. clxxvi. p. 1914.

ᵐ Commons Papers, 1854–5. On the Civil Service, vol. xx. p. 112.

mised thereby.ᵃ But in every branch of the public service the political head of the department must be held responsible, if not for every individual appointment, at any rate for the regulations under which the patronage is bestowed.ᵇ

Reference has already been made to the system of competitive examinations, which was introduced for the express purpose of doing away with abuses in regard to patronage.

Competitive examinations for civil service.

From time immemorial the constitution of the civil service of the crown has been regulated by royal orders in council.ᵇ By the same authority a change has recently been effected, and the principle of competitive examinations for appointments in the civil service established, by an order in council of May 21, 1855.ᶜ Its adoption in the various parts of the service has been gradual. In some departments open competition is the rule, in others a limited competition among three candidates. The civil and medical services of India, the scientific corps of the army, and some civil departments of the state, are supplied through open competition, and have ceased to afford patronage to ministers. But where limited competition prevails it has rather served to increase than diminish the amount of political patronage. Thus, formerly, when a vacancy occurred in a subordinate public office, the

---

ᵃ Commons Papers (Rep. on Dockyard appointments), 1852-3, vol. xxv. pp. 300, 344, 303.
ᵇ Ibid. Report, p. xii.
ᵇ See Sir James Stephen's letter on the reorganisation of the Civil Service, in Commons Papers, 1854-5, vol. xx. p. 81.
ᶜ Hans. Deb. vol. cxxxviii. p. 2157, vol. cxxxix. p. 642. See also debates in the House of Commons, on April 1, 1862, and July 17, 1863, wherein the objections to the new system were very forcibly urged. The government upon both occasions explained the extent to which the system had been already adopted, and showed that the principle of competitive examinations was being gradually introduced throughout the public service. But Lord Grey, in the new edition of his Parliamentary Government, points out the peculiar abuses which have arisen in the working of the competitive system, and strenuously condemns it, as being 'radically wrong,' and calculated to obtain in general a less efficient class of public servants than those appointed by government under the old system. (Pp. 200-310.)

patronage Secretary of the Treasury disposed of it upon the recommendation of a member of Parliament supporting the existing government. Now he can give nominations to three members for each vacancy, or, if he chose, could present them all to one member, to be distributed according to his discretion.¹

The existing arrangements in regard to competitive examinations for civil service appointments were explained by Lord Palmerston on May 29, 1862, as follows: The candidates for each examination are, in the first place, questioned upon a standard test to ascertain whether they possessed what might be called a *minimum* of the acquirements necessary for the vacant office. It was then usual to select three candidates for every vacancy, to subject these to a competitive examination, and confer the post upon the one who proved to be the best qualified.²

<small>Responsibility for appointments to office.</small>

But whether it be discharged upon the mere discretion of ministers or with the assistance to be derived from an organised system of preliminary examinations, 'there is no act,' says a recent political writer, 'which more imperatively requires to be performed under a strong sense of individual responsibility than the nomination to employments.' 'Besides, the qualifications which fit special individuals for special duties can only be recognised by those who know the individuals or who make it their business to examine and judge of persons from what they have done or from the evidence of those who are in a position to judge.' Combating the notion which has been entertained by some in favour of nominations to office by a popular assembly, Mr. Mill thus proceeds: 'When those conscientious obligations are so little regarded by

---

¹ May, Const. Hist. vol. ii. p. 92; Cox, British Commonwealth, p. 117; Hans. Deb. vol. clxvi. p. 338.

² Hans. Deb. vol. clxvii. p. 93. For an instance of evasion of the rules of the Civil Service Commissioners, on the part of the Board of Admiralty, in favour of a clerk who had been placed in that department without having obtained the usual certificate, see Report of Committee on Public Accounts, 1862, Evid. 601, 1541.

great public officers, who can be made responsible for their appointments, how must it be with assemblies who cannot? Even now the worst appointments are those which are made for the sake of gaining support or disarming opposition in the representative body: what might we expect if they were made by the body itself? Numerous bodies never regard qualifications at all.' 'When appointments made by a popular body are not decided, as they almost always are, by party connection or private jobbing, a man is appointed either because he has a reputation, often quite undeserved, for *general* ability, or oftener for no better reason than that he is personally popular.'*

Even the officers and servants attendant upon the two Houses of Parliament are not appointed by the Houses themselves," but either (as in the case of the principal officers) by letters-patent from the crown, or by the Clerk, Sergeant-at-Arms, or Usher of the Black Rod, or by the Speaker, according to the department to which the particular office may belong." The House of Commons appoint their Speaker and the Chairman of the Committee of Ways and Means; the House of Lords their Chairman of Committees, and the examiners of standing orders for private bills." By the Act 15 & 16 Vict. c. 57, authorising the issue of a commission to enquire into corrupt practices at elections of members of the House of Commons, upon a joint address of both Houses of Parliament to the crown, it is provided that the commissioners shall be persons 'named in such

Parliamentary officers.

' Mill on Representative Govt. pp. 94–90. See also Austin's Plea for the Constitution, p. 31. And see the observations of the Attorney-General and of Mr. Walpole on a proposal that certain new judicial offices, to be created by statute, should be placed, in the first instance, at the option of persons already holding certain other judicial offices. Hans. Deb. vol. clxxvii. p. 311. *Ibid.* vol. clxxviii. p. 525. And see *post*, p. 418.

* See, in regard to the appointment of Clerk of the House of Commons, Hans. Deb. vol. cxiv. p. 139. And of Clerk Assistant of the House of Lords, *ibid.* vol. xcvii. p. 456.
* *Ibid.* vol. cxl. pp. 268, 447. Commons Papers, 1847–8, vol. xvi. p. 45; *Ibid.* vol. xviii. pp. 90, 104, 111. *Ibid.* 1856, vol. li. p. 1.
* Hans. Deb. vol. cxiv. p. 43. S.O. H. of Lords, in May, Parl. Prac. p. 030.

address,' such persons having the standing at the bar, &c. indicated by the Act. It is customary for the commissioners to be named in the resolution for the address, which is first introduced into the House of Commons.*

<small>Representation in Parliament of every public department.</small>

As a necessary consequence of the division of the civil service into political and non-political officers, and of the acknowledged supremacy of the members of the administration over all the subordinate *employés*, it is required by our parliamentary system that every branch of the public service should be represented, either directly or indirectly, in the Houses of Parliament. This duty is performed by the political heads, who are themselves solely responsible for every act of administration down to the minutest details of official routine. Having entire control over the public departments, they are bound to assume responsibility for every official act, and not to permit blame to be imputed to any subordinate for the manner in which the business of the country is transacted, except only in cases of personal misconduct, for which the political chiefs have the remedy in their own hands.'

<small>Subordination of all permanent officers to some political head.</small>

'It is no arbitrary rule,' says Lord Grey, 'which requires that all holders of permanent offices must be subordinate to some minister responsible to Parliament, since it is obvious that without it, the first principle of our system of government—the control of all branches of the administration by Parliament—would be abandoned.'* But the control of Parliament, as will hereafter appear, is general, and does not admit of any direct interference with the subordinate officers of government.

So strict is the rule of ministerial supremacy as to forbid any orders to be given to any public servant of the crown, by either house of Parliament, except through the regular channel of official communication, namely, a Secretary

---

<small>* Hans. Deb. May 1, 1860, wherein four such addresses were voted.
† For further particulars on this head, see vol. II. c. 1, on the Cabinet Council.
‡ Grey, Parl. Govt. new ed. p. 300.</small>

of State, or other officer who may be authorised to convey the royal commands.[a]

So, also, as regards the dismissal of persons from public employ; the crown possesses by virtue of its prerogative an absolute legal power to dismiss any of its servants, on the advice of its responsible ministers.[b] Such a power 'is indispensable, in order to give to the latter that authority over those by whose agency and assistance they carry on the public business, without which they could not justly be held accountable by Parliament for the manner in which affairs are conducted.'[c] This rule, however, is subject to an important exception in the case of those offices which are held 'during good behaviour,' a tenure which has been applied by Acts of Parliament to the judges (whether their jurisdiction be local or general), the Comptroller of the Exchequer, the auditors of the public accounts, and certain other functionaries, whose position is one that makes it desirable that they should be independent of the crown, holding their offices for life, and being removable (except in the case of certain officers of inferior grade) only upon addresses from the two Houses of Parliament.[d]

Absolute power in the crown to dismiss all public servants:

With certain exceptions.

But while every government must necessarily possess the abstract right of dismissing any of its servants who may hold their offices 'during pleasure,' whenever they consider that such a step is required by the exigencies of the public service, it has nevertheless been recognised as a rule that persons holding non-political offices under the crown should only be dismissed for incompetence or mis-

Dismissals only occur for incompetence or misconduct.

---

[a] Case of Sir Baldwin Walker, in House of Commons, Hans. Deb. March 8 and 22, 1861.
[b] Chitty on Prerog. 82. See the case of Earl Howe in Mirror of Parl. 1831, p. 3127. As regards officers in the navy, army, or militia, see ante, p. 326.
[c] Grey, Parl. Govt. new ed. p. 320.
[d] Broom, Const. Law, 791. See also in regard to Clerks of the Peace who hold office *quamdiu bene se gesserint*, Hans. Deb. vol. clxxiii. p. 708, and stat. 27 and 28 Vict. c. 65. For the precise legal effect of this tenure, see Hans. Deb. vol. clxxx. pp. 295, 304.

conduct.'* Dismissals on other grounds are highly objectionable and inexpedient; more especially if they spring from political considerations. Doubtless, an active interference in politics, on the part of a non-political office-holder, would be a case of 'misconduct' sufficient to justify his dismissal. It is a well understood rule of constitutional government, that all such functionaries 'should abstain from taking an active part in political contests,' observing a strict neutrality therein. If a contrary practice prevailed, it would inevitably follow that the opposite party, on succeeding to power, would retaliate on those who had assisted to uphold a rival ministry; and thus a repetition of vindictive and extensive changes amongst government *employés* would occur, that would prevent the growth of experience in office, and destroy the efficiency of the public service.

Case of Mr. Beales.

In August 1866, the Lord Chief Justice of England, Sir Alexander Cockburn, dismissed, or rather declined to reappoint, as usual, Mr. Edmund Beales, as revising barrister for the county of Middlesex, on account of his having taken 'a very active and leading part in a political agitation of no ordinary character,' having for its object the endeavour to bring about a radical reform of Parliament. Revising barristers are annual appointments, but it is customary to nominate the same person year by year, unless for some special reason; so that declining to reappoint, in the present instance, was equivalent to dismissal. The Chief Justice conveyed his sentiments to Mr. Beales on this occasion, in an explanatory letter, wherein he stated that he was 'very far from thinking that to entertain or to express decided political opinions ought to be considered as disqualifying a member of the bar from holding office as a revising barrister. In making these appointments,' his lordship added, 'I have looked only to the fitness of the candidates, and have never stopped to enquire what were their political views. But, on the other hand, I must say I do not think it desirable that a gentleman holding what, in the view of many persons, would be deemed extreme opinions, and occupying a prominent position in the political warfare of the day—whether on the one side or the other—should be appointed to decide judicially on the claims of persons to vote in the election of members of Parliament.' Mr. Beales remonstrated against his removal, as being, in his opinion, uncalled

---
* Grey, Parl. Govt. p. 247.

for and unjustifiable, but acknowledged the kindly and friendly spirit in which his lordship had acted towards him.[f]

All public *employés*, whatever may be their private convictions on political questions, are bound to discharge their duties towards their official superiors for the time being honestly and faithfully, affording to them all the assistance in their power. But this assistance is necessarily limited to the sphere of official obligation, and does not require the surrender of private opinions, or justify an intermeddling, on behalf of their employers, in political strife. While, on the one hand, the practice of depriving persons of subordinate offices simply on account of their political views, is destructive of all efficient administration—as the example of the American Republic has strikingly shown—on the other hand, it is manifestly unreasonable that any public servant should be permitted to continue in active opposition to the existing government.[g]

Fidelity in the public service.

It is not easy to define the extent of 'misconduct,' of this description which should properly subject a permanent officer of the crown to dismissal. During a period of great political excitement the government may be constrained to act with more severity towards public servants who may take an active part in politics,[h] than at ordinary times.

All interference in politics objectionable.

---

[f] See the correspondence in the Jurist, Sept. 1, 1860, p. 340. And see the action taken by the government in 1841, upon complaint of Clerks of Justices of the Peace in Scotland, acting as 'political agents.' Mirror of Parl. 1841, p. 2210.

[g] Despatches of the Colonial Secretaries (Lord Grey and the Duke of Newcastle) to the Lieutenant-Governor of Nova Scotia in 1848 and in 1860, in respect to the control and dismissal of public officers in that colony; quoted in the Toronto *Globe* of September 22, 1860. Despatch from the Duke of Newcastle to the Governor of Jamaica, prohibiting public officers from writing offensive letters in the newspapers. Commons Papers, 1860, vol. xlv. p. 503; and see Hans. Deb. vol. clxii. p. 722. Also correspondence between the Duke of Newcastle, the Lieutenant-Governor of New Brunswick and his ministers, respecting dismissals from office for political reasons; in New Brunswick Assembly Journals, 1862, pp. 102-109.

[h] Even the mere exercise of the political franchise by a subordinate servant of the crown, though not prohibited, may be considered, as a general rule, to be inexpedient. (See Grey on Parl. Govt. new ed. p. 235.) All persons engaged in the management or collection of the public revenue are, by statutes passed in the last century, expressly disquali-

Dismissal of Earl Fitzwilliam.

For example, in 1819, when party feelings ran very high, Earl Fitzwilliam, an amiable and loyal nobleman, was summarily dismissed from his office of Lord-Lieutenant of the West Riding of Yorkshire, because he had joined in calling a meeting of freeholders to consider of petitioning the king, and the two Houses of Parliament, upon the existing state of public affairs, in terms supposed to reflect upon an answer recently given by the prince regent to an address from the City of London.[1] The ministry being interrogated in Parliament in regard to this dismissal, justified it on the ground that 'it was essential to the due administration of public affairs, and to the dignity of the crown, that none of its servants should hold opinions of it derogatory to its honour and character.'[2]

It has been suggested that the relations between the subordinate class of public functionaries and the executive government should be regulated by statute, so as to prevent a possible abuse of power on the part of the

---

fied from voting at parliamentary elections. So strictly is this enforced that country postmasters, who may not receive more than 4l. a year from the state, are disfranchised. And by more recent enactments, all persons connected with the police or constabulary force, in town or country, are prohibited from exercising the elective franchise. (Rogers on Elections, ed. 1859, pp. 103–104.) With these exceptions, however, no one is forbidden to vote by reason of his holding an office under the crown, or because he may be in receipt of a fixed income from the public revenue (Hans. Deb. vol. clxix. p. 524). On the contrary, the tendency of recent departmental regulations has been to secure a greater degree of independence than formerly to the public servant in the exercise of the political franchise. Witness the fact that Mr. Ferrand, a political opponent of the government, was elected a member for the borough of Devonport, in February 1863, against one of the Lords of the Admiralty, although the constituency comprises a large number of employés in the Admiralty Dockyards, whose votes turned the scale in favour of Mr. Ferrand (ibid. p. 784). At the general election in 1865, Devonport returned two Opposition members; but, upon petition, they were both unseated for bribery practices (ibid. vol. clxxxiii. p. 643). A recommendation of the royal commission on dockyards in 1860, in favour of disfranchising the dockyards was not approved of by the government at the time (ibid. vol. clxxi. p. 670). Nevertheless, by the 11th clause of the new Reform Bill, introduced by Mr. Gladstone in 1866, it was directed that the dockyard labourers should be disfranchised, avowedly in order to protect members from the undue influence on the part of constituents who are dependent upon government for their daily wages. See the debates on the conduct of these labourers, and their proposed disfranchisement in the session of 1866, and especially vol. clxxxi. p. 1870; vol. clxxxii. pp. 68, 72, 1177. It has been estimated that the number of dockyard voters, in the several boroughs of Chatham, Devonport, Greenwich, Portsmouth, and Pembroke, who would have been disfranchised had this bill become law, was 3,635. Commons Papers, 1866, No. 318.

[1] Campbell's Chancellors, vii. 335. May, Const. Hist. ii. 107.
[2] Parl. Deb. vol. xli. p. 102.

responsible advisers of the crown towards their subordinates in office. But it has been well remarked by Lord Grey, that 'it would be impossible to limit the power of dismissal to cases in which misconduct could be proved before a court of law, without incurring the risk of having the executive government paralysed by the passive resistance of persons holding these situations, and by the obstructions they would be able to throw in the way of ministers they wished to oppose. Law would be too clumsy an instrument for regulating the conduct of the ministers of the crown and the permanent civil servants of the state in their relations to each other. This is now far more effectually and far more safely accomplished by the power of public opinion. So great is the authority of public opinion, that no minister now ever thinks of dismissing a public servant from those offices which are regarded as permanent, unless for gross misconduct; but at the same time he has the power (and public opinion would support him in using it) of dismissing such a servant for misconduct, which it might be impossible for any law to define beforehand, and of which there might be no legal evidence, though there was a moral certainty.'[1] Lord Grey proceeds to point out that active opposition to their political chiefs for the time being, or attempts to embarrass them either by passive resistance or by putting difficulties in the way of their administration of office are just those kinds of misconduct which would be most dangerous, and yet most difficult to suppress or prevent by legal enactment.' 'The knowledge that there is no legal restriction on the power of dismissal to prevent a minister from dealing with such a case as it would deserve, has probably been the principal reason why such cases do not arise; and, by preventing the possibility

Exercise of the power of dismissal.

---

[1] Grey, Parl. Govt. new ed. pp. 326, 327.
[2] Ibid. p. 327. And see speeches of Earls Granville and Grey, in House of Lords, April 18, 1864, on the Education Committee and the vote of the House of Commons.

of a struggle between a government and its servants, has kept up the good feeling which has hitherto existed between them.'

Pensions and retiring allowances.

Whenever it is deemed advisable, in furtherance of proposed reforms or retrenchments in the public service, to dispense with the services of any particular class of public *employés*, it has always been customary to respect the claims of existing incumbents, by allotting to them suitable pensions or retiring allowances. It was well said by Edmund Burke, whose patient labours in the cause of national retrenchment were so eminently successful, that it was neither wise, expedient, or just to interfere retrospectively with places or pensions; that reform ought to be prospective; that the duration of the life of a nation was not to be compared with the short duration of the life of an individual; that an individual hardship, and especially an injustice, ought not to be committed for the sake of arriving a few years sooner at the object Parliament had in view, namely, economical reform. It is to the credit of the imperial government that they have invariably acted upon this magnanimous principle. Authority has been given to the Treasury, by a general Act of Parliament, to make suitable compensation to all persons whose offices may be abolished; and in cases which do not come within the purview of this Act, special provision is made by Parliament for the purpose. When the new Divorce and Probate Court was established, in 1857, provision was made to compensate the proctors who had practised in the old court, which was then abolished. This compensation amounted to the enormous sum of 116,000*l*. per annum.

---

* Grey, Parl. Govt. new ed. p. 327.
* Mirror of Parl. 1830, p. 1047.
* Act 4 & 5 Will. IV. c. 24. And see Commons Papers, 1852-3, vol. lvii. p. 717.
* 6 & 9 Vict. c. 78. See the case of Sir Richard Bromley, in 1865, wherein the government and the House of Commons vied with each other in the determination to deal as liberally as possible with a valued public servant upon his retirement. Hans. Deb. vol. clxxx. pp. 400-508.
* Hans. Deb. vol. cliv. p. 1045. Commons Papers, 1861, vol. II. p. 405.

As with the appointment and dismissal, so also in regard to the remuneration of public *employés*, it should be left to the government to determine the amount of pay to be allotted to all public servants, of whatever grade or position. Those who serve the crown should look directly to the crown for compensation and reward. The salaries and allowances of all public servants, in every department of state (with the exception of those functionaries whose salaries are fixed by Act of Parliament),¹ are regulated by the Lords Commissioners of the Treasury, and determined by Treasury minutes. It is competent for the official head of every public department to recommend to the Treasury the alteration or increase of salaries to his own subordinates. But every such recommendation is subjected to the closest scrutiny by the Treasury, who possess supreme control in all financial matters, over every other branch of the public service.² The salaries and expenses of the public departments are annually submitted to the review of the House of Commons in the estimates, and a separate vote is taken for the amount required to defray the same, in each department. Appended to the estimate for every vote, a list is given of the different items of expenditure included therein; but although it is within the power of the House of Commons, in committee of supply, to reduce any such vote by omitting the amount of any particular salary, or other item, this power is rarely exercised, and only upon grave and urgent considerations. It is perfectly competent for either House of Parliament, and more particularly for the House of Commons, to subject the conduct of the executive government towards the subordinate officers and servants of the crown to free enquiry and criticism; but there should be no attempt to interfere with the discretion of responsible ministers, in regulating

Salaries, &c., of public officers to be regulated by the Treasury.

And voted by Parliament.

---

¹ The officers of the two Houses of Parliament are also an exception to this rule; see *post*, pp. 402-400.

² Hans. Deb. vol. lxxiii. p. 1002. *Ibid.* vol. cxvii. p. 614. And see vol. ii. c. 2. On the Treasury.

the pay and allowances of public *employés*, except in cases where it is apparent that injustice and oppression have been exercised.[1]

Pecuniary details should be left to the Treasury.

While every salary, and the classification of every office is (with trifling exceptions) duly submitted in the annual estimates for the criticism and sanction of Parliament, it is the peculiar duty of the executive government and of the heads of the several departments to enter into the particular and minute considerations by which the rate of salaries, the annual increments, and the prospect of promotion are adjusted. This duty is discharged by the Lords of the Treasury, and should be left to their unfettered discretion, inasmuch as they are responsible for the expenditure incurred in every branch of the public service.

Applications for increase of salary.

By a Treasury minute, dated February 26, 1866, which embodies the substance of regulations previously established in various departments of the civil service, it is provided that henceforth, as a general rule, no application in relation to increased pay or allowances (or for promotion, where such rests with the Treasury) will be entertained by the board unless transmitted through the head of the department to which the applicant belongs. But in the event of the departmental head refusing to forward any such application, the Treasury will receive it direct from the subordinate officer, if it be accompanied by a copy or statement of the refusal, and will determine whether or not the communication was one which should have been addressed to them.

This minute has originated in consequence of a practice recently introduced by *employés* in the civil service of memorialising the Treasury for increase of salary or im-

---

[1] In 1850, upon motion of the prime minister (Lord John Russell), a select committee of the House of Commons was appointed to enquire into the salaries and emoluments of public officers. (Hans. Deb. vol. cx., p. 210.) But the government reserved to themselves the right of dealing with the recommendations of this committee as they thought fit. *Ibid.* vol. cxvii. pp. 804-807.

proved departmental position through members of Parliament or other influential persons, or by direct petition to the board itself.

In enforcing a stricter rule upon the service, the Treasury expressly disclaim the desire to debar any classes or individuals in the public service from making a respectful complaint of any matter of personal grievance. Still less do they intend to offer any obstacle to the most free action of members of the legislature who, on public grounds, may consider it their duty, whether in Parliament or by communications to the Treasury, to call attention to cases of grievance on the part of individuals, or who may think fit to enter upon the investigation of questions affecting the remuneration and other conditions of service under which classes of public officers are employed. It is equally the duty and the desire of the Treasury to afford every proper facility for such representations, and to give them their impartial attention.

But, on the other hand, a due regard to the principles of subordination, and the maintenance of proper relations between the various officers employed in the civil service, requires that for the future the Treasury should insist upon the observance of the rule which forbids subordinate officers from seeking advancement by means of pressure put upon the executive government by persons whose only knowledge of the circumstances of the case is derived from the *ex parte* representation of the applicants themselves.* Political influence forbidden.

All pensions and retiring allowances to public servants, although payable under the authority of an Act of Parliament, are awarded by the Lords of the Treasury, pursuant to regulations they are empowered to make from time to time, for that purpose.' Formerly, great irregu- Pensions how granted.

---

* Copy of Treasury Minute concerning Customs' Clerks, &c. Commons Papers, 1860, No. 83. And see Hans. Deb. vol. clxxxi. p. 1800.

' 57 Geo. III. c. 65, extended by 4 & 5 Will. IV. c. 24. If the government should refuse to allow to a public officer his just claims under

larities prevailed in the granting of pensions by the crown, and it became necessary for Parliament to interpose its authority to regulate and restrict the exercise of this function. Prior to the reign of Queen Anne, the crown had assumed the right of charging its hereditary revenues with pensions and annuities; and it had been held that the king had power in law to bind his successors. But, on the accession of Queen Anne, an Act was passed, forbidding the alienation of any portion of the hereditary revenues for any term beyond the life of the reigning monarch. On the accession of George III. the most part of the hereditary revenues of the crown being surrendered in exchange for a fixed civil list, the pensions which had previously been paid out of these revenues were henceforth paid out of the civil list. There was no limit to the amount of pensions so long as the civil list could meet the demand; and no principle on which the grant of them was regulated, save the discretion of the crown and its advisers.*

Abuses of the pension list. The abuses of the pension list, and the enormous facilities it afforded for corrupt purposes, frequently engaged the attention of Parliament during the reign of George III., and several Acts were passed at different periods to regulate the grant of pensions. The constitutional right of Parliament to investigate this matter, and to control the crown in respect thereto, was fully asserted and secured by Burke's Act in 1782,* which forbade the granting of secret pensions, upon the principle that Parliament had a right to be informed of every instance of the exercise of this prerogative in order to ensure and enforce the responsibility of the ministers of the crown.* This Act further acknowledged the principle that pensions ought to

---

the superannuation Act, he could apply to the court of Queen's Bench for a mandamus to compel the Treasury to pay him whatever he was entitled to receive. Hans. Deb. vol. clxxx. p. 502.

* May, Const. Hist. vol. 1. pp. 214, 215.
* 22 Geo. III. c. 82.
* Burke's Works, vol. iii. pp. 304–307. And see Hans. Deb. vol. clxxxiii. p. 423.

be granted for two causes only; namely, as a royal bounty to persons in distress, or as a reward for desert.

The interference of Parliament to restrain abuses in the grant of pensions continued during the succeeding reigns of George IV. and William IV.,[a] and finally, upon the accession of her present Majesty an Act was passed, which limited the right of the crown to grant additional pensions on the civil list to the sum of 1,200*l.* a year. This sum is granted to her Majesty, for each and every successive year of her reign, cumulatively for the payment of pensions. Such pensions, pursuant to a resolution of the House of Commons of February 18, 1834, to be awarded only to 'such persons as have just claims on the royal beneficence, or who, by their personal services to the crown, by the performance of duties to the public, or by their useful discoveries in science and attainments in literature and the arts, have merited the gracious consideration of their sovereign and the gratitude of their country.'[a] It is further required, that a list of the pensions granted shall be laid before Parliament from time to time, so as to enable the House of Commons to give its advice in regard to their bestowal should it desire to do so. The prime minister, and not the Chancellor of the Exchequer, is the responsible minister upon whose advice these pensions are conferred.[b]

Restrained by Parliament.

It is now recognised as a constitutional rule, that the grant of pensions should always come under the cognisance of the House of Commons. Even in the case of pensions and retiring allowances awarded, according to established practice, under the provisions of the Superannuation Acts, the money to defray the same must be annually voted by the House of Commons, although the faith of

All pensions to come under cognisance of House of Commons.

---

[a] May, Const. Hist. vol. i. pp. 217, 218. And see Hans. Deb. vol. clxxvi. p. 358.
[a] 1 & 2 Vict. c. 2. Report on Civil List, Dec. 5, 1837. Report on Official Salaries, 1850. Evid. 202-204.
[b] Mirror of Parl. 1840, pp. 1327, 1347.

Parliament might be virtually considered as pledged to their continuance."

Widows and orphans of civil service;
Neither the Superannuation nor the Pension Acts confer upon the Treasury any authority to grant an allowance to the widows and families of deceased public officers in the civil service, howsoever strong the claim may be in any particular instance. The only fund out of which such a pension could be granted would be from the limited amount above mentioned, which is payable out of the civil list.^d This has been occasionally resorted to for such a purpose in cases of peculiar hardship and desert.

Of army and navy officers.
The widows and orphans of officers in the army and navy are entitled to pensions under certain regulations; but a similar bounty is not extended to the families of deceased adjutants and quartermasters of militia regiments, because these officers 'are not liable to the dangers of foreign service common to officers in the line.'^e

Summary.
We have now completed our review of the royal prerogative in relation to office-holders. We have seen that the constitution has vested in the sovereign the right of appointing, controlling, remunerating, and dismissing all the public servants of the crown, with an exception in the case of certain functionaries whose tenure of office has been made that of 'good behaviour,' and who can only be dismissed from their employments upon an address of the two Houses of Parliament. By this means, the dignity and independence of the crown in the choice of its officers and the efficiency of the public service are secured. At the same time, adequate protection is afforded against abuse in the distribution of patronage and the control and dismissal of public *employés* by the responsibility of ministers to Parliament for the faithful

---

^c Attorney-General, in Hans. Deb. vol. clxxix. p. 1320. In the annual estimates the sum required under the Superannuation Acts is included in one vote, but the names, &c. of all the pensioners are appended thereto, and a list of new pensions is given.
^d Hans. Deb. vol. clxxix. p. 788.
^e Lord Hartington, Secretary of State for War. Hans. Deb. vol. clxxxiii. p. 683.

exercise of this prerogative. Ministers are directly accountable for maintaining the public service in a proper state of efficiency, for selecting qualified persons to fill all subordinate offices under the crown, for awarding to such persons adequate remuneration, and for granting them protection against oppression or dismissal upon insufficient or unwarrantable grounds.

The authority that appoints to office is necessarily competent to dismiss any insufficient or untrustworthy servants. It is also the proper judge of their qualifications and of the remuneration they should receive. In all such matters Parliament has no right to interfere except in cases of manifest abuse or corruption, when it may be called upon to exercise its inquisitorial power.' Upon such occasions, however, the Houses of Parliament are constitutionally empowered to institute investigations, to declare their opinion as to the manner in which this prerogative has been exercised in any particular instance, and, if need be, either to appeal to the crown to redress the grievance, or to proceed to remedy it themselves by an act of legislation. *Right of Parliament to investigate,*

It is also quite in accordance with constitutional usage for either House to address the crown or to record their opinion by resolution upon the existing state of the various public departments generally, and to advise the adoption of such reforms as may be calculated to increase the efficiency of administration.ᵇ But when fundamental changes are sought to be effected, whereby the crown would be deprived of any of its prerogative rights, or which transcend the scope of the lawful authority of an order in council the proper course would be to bring in a Bill, embodying the substance of the proposed regulations, in order that the same may receive the concurrence of the whole *and to advise the crown, in respect to this prerogative.*

ᶠ See precedents, *post*, pp. 408–418.
ᵍ See Debates in Parliament on Motions for Administrative Reform, on June 15, 18, and 21, 1855. Proposed resolutions in regard to the constitution of the Office of Works, submitted to the House of Commons in 1800, 1803, and 1806.

VOL. I.   D D

legislature.ᵇ This was the plan pursued by Mr. Burke, in 1780, in carrying out his proposed œconomical reforms in the various departments of state.¹

Control exercised by Parliament.

Another indirect but powerful influence possessed by Parliament in the control of the public service arises from the necessity for obtaining the sanction of the legislature to the supplies required for carrying on the government and defraying the salaries of all the public *employés*. 'Thus without touching the prerogative itself its exercise is moderated. The effect of this check upon the exercise of the royal prerogative is, that the responsible ministers of the crown usually take care not to advise the sovereign to do any act requiring to be supported by supplies, unless they believe that it will meet with the approbation of Parliament, especially that of the lower House, which is invested by the constitution with the principal control over the public purse. It is indeed very usual, in cases which admit of delay, to obtain the previous sanction of Parliament to the erection of new offices; and thus the influence of that assembly as a council of advice and deliberation is materially extended.'ʲ

Parliamentary addresses for contingent expenses.

Moreover, by the usage of Parliament, it has always been considered allowable for either House to address the crown for funds to defray the salaries and other expenses of their own establishments, pursuant to regulations they may themselves adopt in this behalf. Each House of Parliament is at liberty to determine the amount of remuneration to be allowed to their respective officers and servants;ᵏ although the salaries of the principal officers are fixed by statute, and are paid out of the Consolidated

---

ᵇ Hans. Deb. vol. cxxxix. pp. 605, 713. And see *ante*, p. 202, concerning the Minutes of Council on the Revised Code of Education.
¹ 22 Geo. III. c. 82. See other cases cited in Tomline's Law Dictionary, verbo *Office*, I.
ʲ Bowyer, 157. See the debates on the proposed additional judge in Chancery, Mirror of Parl. 1830, pp. 2289, 2420, 2500. And see an objection raised in Committee of Supply to an appointment of a certain person to be Inspector-General of Marines, and the debate thereon. *Ibid.* 1830-31, pp. 403, 405, 1008.
ᵏ Commons Journals, June 20, 1836; Lords Journals, April 23, 1850.

Fund. Formerly, addresses were passed by the House of Commons, at the close of every session, for advances of funds to defray the cost of maintaining the rest of the establishment.¹ But of late years these expenses are included in the estimates, and annually voted in Committee of Supply. And it is customary for the government, in their own discretion, to give effect to recommendations from Committees of the House of Commons, in favour of appropriations for particular parliamentary services, by inserting items in the supply estimates, to the required amount, without waiting for any formal application from the House itself." *Recommendations of Committees.*

Upon the retirement of the Speaker of the House of Commons from the chair, it has been the invariable usage for the House to address the crown, that 'some signal mark of royal favour' may be conferred upon him, on his 'ceasing to hold the office of Speaker.' The response to this application, on the part of the crown, is by conferring a peerage upon the retiring Speaker, and by a message recommending to the House to grant a suitable allowance for the support of the dignity." *Speaker of House of Commons.*

A similar practice formerly prevailed in the case of the Chaplain to the House of Commons. After a short term of service it was customary to vote an address to the crown, soliciting the bestowal of church preferment upon this functionary. When Parliaments were of triennial duration, such addresses were uniformly passed after a service of about two years and a half. After they became septennial, it was usual to allow the Speaker two chaplains during each Parliament. Since 1837, owing to the diminution of church patronage in the gift of the crown, an annual salary has been voted to this officer in supply, in lieu of an application for preferment. But on May 31, 1838, the House having, prior to the change of sys- *Chaplain.*

---

¹ Mirror of Parl. 1820, p. 1080. 1802-3. (Houses of Parliament.)
" See Estimates for Civil Services, * See *ante*, p. 317.

tem, addressed the crown in favour of three chaplains, and received favourable answers,.though (for the reason above mentioned) no preferment had been conferred upon them, an address, recapitulating these circumstances, and reiterating the request was agreed to. During the debate thereon, the Home Secretary (Lord John Russell), while defending the government from an intentional disregard of the wishes of the House, admitted that the House were justified in the course they had taken. But he afterwards observed ' that no address of the House can bind the crown in the disposal of its patronage, otherwise than according to the advice that may be given to it.'" In reply to the address, her Majesty stated that she would ' take into her consideration in what manner the wishes of her faithful Commons could be carried into effect.' In the course of the session, in Committee of Supply, an opinion being generally expressed in favour of a salary of 400*l*. a year being allowed to the chaplain, instead of 200*l*., as heretofore, the Chancellor of the Exchequer promised to consider the matter. Accordingly, the estimates in the following year, proposed to fix the salary at 400*l*., which has ever since been the recognised allowance of this dignitary: and from that time the situation has been held as a permanent appointment.'

Salaries, &c., of House of Lords.

The salaries and retiring allowances of the House of Lords' establishment, are fixed by the House itself." The fee fund of the House ordinarily suffices to pay all these demands;' but when a deficiency occurs, application is made by the clerk of the Parliament to the Treasury, to insert in the estimates a sufficient sum to cover the same. The Treasury have no knowledge or control over the fee fund of the House of Lords, or over the appropriation thereof. In 1865, however, they suggested

---

" Mirror of Parl. 1838, p. 4401.
* *Ibid.* p. 4541.
' *Ibid.* p. 5328; *Ibid.* 1839, p. 410. Parkinson's Under Government, p. 54.

' See Lords Journals, April 23, 1850.
' May, Parl. Prac. p. 622.

to the clerk of the Parliament the expediency of following the course adopted by the House of Commons, in regard to their fee fund, which is regularly paid over to the Consolidated Fund, and the charges upon the same included in the annual estimates, and voted by Parliament.[a] Applications for pensions by officers of the House of Lords are decided upon by the House itself; either directly, or upon a report from the select committee on the office of the Clerk of the Parliament and Usher of the Black Rod.[b]

The salaries, retiring allowances, and other disbursements on behalf of the establishment of the House of Commons, are settled by the commissioners appointed by statute[c] for regulating the offices of the House of Commons. The commissioners consist of the Speaker of the House of Commons, the Chancellor of the Exchequer, the Secretaries of State, and certain other functionaries, being members of the House of Commons. Practically, the actual business of the board is transacted by Mr. Speaker. But the board is always convened when there is anything important to be done. The salaries of officers of the House of Commons have been regulated, from time to time, upon reports from select committees of the House, from 1836 (up to which period they were paid by fees) to 1849. The establishment is divided into three branches or departments; which are under the clerk, the Speaker, and the sergeant-at-arms respectively. The head of each department sanctions the items which concern his own department, whether they be for salaries or contingent expenses; and the entire pay-list is submitted to the Speaker, for his sanction and signature. If the establish-

Salaries, &c., of House of Commons.

---

[a] Report Com. Pub. Accounts, 1865, p. 47. And see Hans. Deb. vol. clxxvii. p. 1123.

[b] Mr. Birch's case. Hans. Deb. Feb. 20, 1848. Mr. Edmunds' case, Lords Journals, Feb. 17 and 24, 1865. And see Mr. Gladstone's observations, in Hans. Deb. vol. clxxvii. p. 1370. The resolution granting Mr. Edmunds a pension was afterwards rescinded, on proof that he had been guilty of gross misconduct and malversation in office; see Hans. Deb. May 9, 1865.

[c] 52 Geo. III. c. 11; and 9 & 10 Vict. c. 77.

ment requires to be varied, or increased, the Treasury is not consulted, 'the Speaker's sanction would be sufficient; for instance, in 1865, there were two references of private bills put on, at 1,000*l.* each: that was done with the sanction of the Speaker.' By the Act 12 & 13 Vict. c. 72 the Speaker's audit in regard to all expenditure for the House of Commons is final. His order is the warrant to the Treasury to insert the amounts required to be voted by Parliament in the annual estimates. The Treasury adopt his return without examination, and include the amount in the estimates, because it concerns the internal economy of Parliament. There are, however, certain items of expenditure, which are common to both Houses, that are settled by the Treasury; such as the sums to be allowed for the payment of witnesses attending committees, the allowance for a shorthand writer, and other miscellaneous charges of inconsiderable amount. Retiring allowances to officers of the House of Commons are settled by the commissioners, on the basis of the Superannuation Acts.'

The foregoing particulars will show that, in matters affecting their own *employés*, the Houses of Parliament are privileged to intrench upon the royal prerogative to determine the remuneration to be allowed to public officers, to an extent that, in the case of other officials, would not be allowable."

But while, as a rule, any direct interference by Parliament with the exercise of the prerogative of the crown, in the appointment, control, or dismissal of public servants, would be unconstitutional, unless under the peculiar cir-

---

* See Rep. Com. on Public Accounts, 1865, Evid. 845, 977, &c. 1107, &c. 1121, &c. And see Hans. Deb. vol. clxxvii. p. 1123.

" But a motion to declare the opinion of the House as to the extent of remuneration that ought to be allowed by the Lords of the Treasury to Mr. Gurney for expenses of experiments in lighting the House of Commons, performed under the direction of a committee of the House, was pronounced by the Speaker to be informal, without the previous consent of the crown. Mirror of Parl. 1830, p. 5110.

cumstances already indicated, when it may become the *Enquiries of ministers.* duty of Parliament to tender advice upon the subject; it is nevertheless agreeable to usage for enquiries of ministers, or desultory discussions to take place, in either House, in reference to the appointment and control of office-holders, in particular instances, when a direct motion on the subject would be objectionable. In this way opportunity is afforded to the administration to explain and defend the propriety of appointments, which may have been subjected to misrepresentations by the press or the public at large."

The following precedents will serve to explain and confirm the statements made in this section; and will explain under what circumstances parliamentary interference with this branch of the prerogative has heretofore taken place:—

" On June 8, 1800, a member called the attention of the House of Commons (without making any motion) to the unfavourable position and inferior rate of pay of the civil assistants of the Ordnance Survey, compared with that of other public servants. His remarks were favourably received by the ministry, and the alleged grievance shown to have no real existence. (Hans. Deb. vol. clix. p. 508.) See the cases of Mr. Barker and of Mr. Jopp, in Commons' Debates of March 1, 1801. On March 4, 1801, enquiry was made of the ministry whether a person, recently appointed to a lucrative office, had received the same in acknowledgment of political services rendered by his father to the liberal party? Lord Palmerston replied that he was 'unable to answer the question.' (Hans. Deb. vol. clxi. p. 1307.) On May 2, 1802, a member having moved for and obtained a return of the services of the late barrack-master at Sheffield, and the retiring allowance granted to him, enquired why he and others similarly circumstanced had been allowed such a paltry pittance, when the Treasury had legal power to grant double the amount. In reply, the Secretary of the Treasury gave satisfactory explanations on the point. (Hans. Deb. vol. clxvi. p. 1185.) And see the enquiry, on Feb. 20, 1803, as to the intended appointment of Mr. Reed to an important office in the navy department, over the heads of persons of ability and long standing in the service. (*Ibid.* vol. clxix. p. 572.) This appointment afterwards gave rise to a motion for papers, in order 'to show to the country the facts connected therewith;' but, being opposed by government, the motion was negatived on division. *Ibid.* vol. clxxii p. 1189.

I. As to the Appointment, Dismissal, or Control of Public Officers.

Precedents

Mr. Spencer Perceval.

In 1807, in the interval between the resignation of the Grenville ministry, and the accession to office of that of the Duke of Portland, it was rumoured that it was the intention of the king to offer the situation of Chancellor of the Duchy of Lancaster to Mr. Spencer Perceval, as an inducement to that eminent statesman to accept office in the new ministry. It had been heretofore the usual (though not invariable) custom to confer this office during pleasure, but as a means of compensating Mr. Perceval for relinquishing a lucrative profession for the service of the crown, the king proposed that he should hold it for life. Whereupon, on March 25, a member of the House of Commons moved an address to the king that he would be graciously pleased not to grant the office in question, 'or any other office not usually granted for life, for any other term than during pleasure.' During the discussion of this motion, Mr. Perceval took the opportunity of stating that it was true the king had made him this offer under the circumstances alleged, but that in order to prevent his Majesty from being fettered by any advice the House of Commons might give, he had resolved not to take advantage of the offer, but that he should be prepared to give his services to the crown, in any political capacity, notwithstanding. The motion for the address was supported by the leading members of the late administration, who took the ground that it was not a restriction upon the royal prerogative, but rather in the interest of the king, who should not be advised to give any places for life, but to keep them at his own disposal to reward his faithful servants from time to time. The address was agreed to by a large majority, and ordered to be presented to his Majesty by such members of the House as were of the privy-council.⁷ Agreeably to constitutional usage, no reply was given by the king, until after the formation of his new ministry, when he was pleased to send down the following answer: 'His Majesty acquaints his faithful Commons that he will take the subject of their address into his most serious consideration, and thinks it proper, at the same time, to inform them that he has thought it fit to provide that in a grant now to be made of the office of Chancellor of the Duchy of Lancaster, the office shall be conferred only during his royal pleasure. His Majesty assures his faithful Commons that, in the execution of the powers with which he is intrusted by law to grant certain offices for life, as in the exercise of all the prerogatives of his crown, his conduct will at all times be governed by an anxious attention to the public interest

---

⁷ Parl. Deb. vol. ix. pp. 104-220.

and welfare.' ' 'Accordingly, Mr. Perceval, who had accepted office **Precedents** in the new ministry as Chancellor of the Exchequer, held the situation of Chancellor of the Duchy of Lancaster conjointly therewith, and also during pleasure.' Since that time, this office, which may be regarded as a sinecure, has been always held by a member of the administration.

In 1809, an enquiry was instituted by the House of Commons, **The Duke** upon the motion of Colonel Wardle, into the conduct of H.R.H. **of York.** the Duke of York, the then commander-in-chief, who was charged with conniving at the corrupt sale of military commissions for the advantage of a woman by the name of Clarke, with whom he had had a dishonourable connection. The Duke was defended by the prime minister, Mr. Perceval, who succeeded in carrying an amendment exculpating his Royal Highness from any guilty participation in Mrs. Clarke's proceedings. The Duke, however, resigned his command of the army; whereupon the House resolved to proceed no further in the matter.' But two years afterwards, in May 1811, the Duke was reappointed to office. This gave rise to a motion of censure which was submitted to the House of Commons on June 6. It was opposed by ministers, who pleaded his Royal Highness's fitness for the post, and his personal popularity with the army, and urged that the former proceedings of the House were not meant to operate as a perpetual disqualification, and did not, in fact, affix any stigma upon his character. The motion was accordingly negatived by a large majority.

Shortly before the meeting of Parliament, in 1812, the prince **Colonel** regent was advised to bestow upon his faithful servant, Colonel **McMahon.** McMahon the office of Paymaster of Widows' Pensions. The abolition of this office, as being in the nature of a sinecure, had been recommended, so far back as 1783, by the Commissioners for Public Accounts: and again by the Commissioners of Military Inquiry, in 1808. The House of Commons resolved, in 1810, that it was expedient to abolish all sinecures, and at the same time 'to enable his Majesty to reward in a different way those who had filled high effective civil offices.' Regarding Colonel McMahon as one whose services merited a public remuneration, and no other means having been provided by Parliament for the purpose, the ministry recommended that he should be appointed to the office in question; subject, however, to any decision that Parliament might come to for the reformation or abolition of the office. On January 9, 1812, the case was brought before the House of Commons, upon an amendment to postpone the motion to go into Committee of Supply, which, after a long debate, was negatived. On February 22, an amend-

---

' Commons Journals, vol. lxii. p. 305.   ' Parl. Deb. vol. xxiii. p. 210.
' *Ibid.* March 17 and 20, 1809.

ment was submitted in Committee of Supply, to reduce the proposed grant for pensions to officers' widows, by the amount intended to be given as salary to Colonel McMahon. This also was negatived by a majority of 16. But upon the report of the resolutions of Supply on the following day, the said amendment was again proposed and agreed to by a majority of 3.[c] This vote occasioned the abolition of the sinecure. The ministry then advised the appointment of Colonel McMahon to the office of Keeper of the Privy Purse, and private secretary to the prince regent, with a salary to be defrayed by the Treasury. On April 14, Mr. Wynn moved for a copy of this appointment with a view to proposing a resolution of censure thereupon, on the ground that it was unconstitutional for the reigning monarch to have a private secretary. The motion was negatived by a large majority. But, on June 15, ministers informed the House that the prince regent had directed the salary of Colonel McMahon to be paid out of his privy purse. Whereupon all further opposition to the appointment ceased, and the gallant colonel was permitted to retain it until the day of his death.[d]

Lt.-general of the Ordnance.

In 1823, a motion was made by Mr. Hume in the House of Commons to condemn the filling up of a vacancy in the office of lieutenant-general of the ordnance; the said office having been declared to be unnecessary by a royal commission; an amendment was proposed for the appointment of a select committee to enquire into the duties of this office, and the expediency of abolishing it, which was negatived; after which the main question was negatived on division.[e] On March 29, 1830, in Committee of Supply on the Ordnance Estimates, Sir James Graham moved an amendment, to reduce the vote to defray the ordnance salaries by the amount payable to the lieutenant-general, with a view to obtain the abolition of the said office; the amendment was negatived on division.[f] But in the following year the office was abolished.[g]

Colonial Secretary.

On April 16, 1832, an attempt was made to induce the House of Commons to interpose in a case where the Colonial Secretary (exercising the discretion vested in him by an Act of Parliament) had refused to grant an extension of leave of absence to a colonial clergyman. It was moved to resolve that, for certain reasons therein stated, it was the opinion of the House that this clergyman should be allowed an additional six months' leave, without prejudice to his

---

[c] Parl. Deb. vol. xxl. pp. 114, 606, 691.
[d] See *ante*, p. 102.
[e] Parl. Deb. N.S. vol. viii. pp. 110, 140–171.
[f] Mirror of Parl. 1830, pp. 1099–1113. See a similar motion on March 12, 1830, concerning the office of Treasurer of the Navy, which was negatived. *Ibid.* p. 735. In 1835, pursuant to the Act 5 & 6 Will. IV. c. 35, this office was merged into that of paymaster-general.
[g] Haydn, Book of Dignities, p. 102.

salary. The Under-Secretary for the Colonies opposed the motion; Precedents he showed that much indulgence had already been granted to this gentleman; and declared that it would be quite contrary to the practice of the House to interfere with the government in such a matter. Accordingly the motion was negatived.[b]

In 1837, Mr. Hume, being desirous of impugning the recent Commander-appointments of commander-in-chief and military secretary, pro- in-chief. posed, on the consideration of the report from the Committee of Supply on the Army Estimates, an amendment to reduce the vote by the amount of the respective salaries of these officers; but Mr. Wynn (a very high authority) declared that this course was neither 'regular nor constitutional;' and, if successful, would lead, not to the substitution of one individual for another as commander-in-chief, but to the abolition of the office. He considered that the object the mover had in view amounted to an improper interference with the prerogative of the crown in appointments to office; adding, that 'it is undoubtedly the right of the House to allot what sum it may think proper for the expenses of the army; but if a charge is intended against any individual, it ought to be stated intelligibly and directly, in the form of an address.' The amendment was then put and negatived.[i]

In 1841, objection being taken in the House of Commons to the Solicitor to creation of a new office, that of Solicitor to the Home Department, Home Department. and a resolution proposed that such an office was unnecessary; it was urged, in reply, that the proper time to make the objection would be in Committee of Supply, when a vote would be submitted to defray the salary of the same. Accordingly, the motion was withdrawn, and the objection renewed in the debate on the estimates. But the government having promised to enquire into the matter, no further action took place.[j]

In 1838, upon the appointment of the Earl of Durham to the Sir T. office of governor-general of Canada, his lordship was accom- T——. panied to Quebec by a gentleman named T—— (afterwards Sir T. T——), who had been convicted of adultery several years previously, but had since filled situations of honour and responsibility. In consequence of his high legal attainments and general ability, Lord Durham appointed Mr. T—— as one of his secretaries, and gave him a seat in the executive council. When his lordship's appointments generally came under review by the Home Government, they were all approved of with the exception of that of Mr. T——. Meanwhile,

---

[b] Mirror of Parl. 1831-2, p. 1862.
[i] Ibid. 1837, p. 801.
[j] Ibid. 1841, p. 1508. Ibid. 1841, sess. 2, p. 351. See also the case of the crown solicitor for the county of Meath. Hans. Deb. (3) vol. clix. p. 1533.

Precedents enquiry had been made in the House of Lords, whether it was true that this individual had been appointed to an office by Lord Durham. At first it was denied by the government, but when it was clear from the Canadian journals that such an appointment had taken place, the government declared that they had received the intelligence 'with surprise and regret.'[b] Subsequently, the government remonstrated with Lord Durham for what he had done, but his lordship replied that he took the whole responsibility upon himself and would rather resign his own office than suffer it to be cancelled. Thus far had the correspondence proceeded, the government being unwilling 'to disturb Lord Durham's government by actually insisting' on the rescinding of this appointment, when more serious events occurred in Canada, which led to the retirement of Lord Durham from his post. Mr. T—— accompanied his lordship home. But the matter was not allowed to drop here. The question was again brought under notice of the House of Lords after the Earl of Durham had resumed his seat in that assembly in 1839,[f] and a motion was made for an address to the crown for correspondence on the subject. Upon that motion the foregoing explanations took place; and the prime minister (Lord Melbourne) having stated that the correspondence in question had been principally private and unofficial, the mover expressed himself satisfied with the regret expressed on the part of the government that such an objectionable appointment should have been made, and withdrew his motion.[a]

Sir P. Maitland. On August 13, 1839, a motion in the House of Lords for the production (with other papers) of a letter from Sir Peregrine Maitland, tendering his resignation of the command of the Madras Army, and of his seat in the Indian Council, was objected to by the administration, because there was no charge against his 'character and conduct' of that officer, and nothing which called for a vindication of either. Whereupon the mover consented not to press his motion, so far as this letter was concerned.[b]

Mr. Heathcote. In 1844, a petition having been presented to the House of Commons from a Mr. Heathcote, complaining of his dismissal, by the Secretary of State, from the office of Sub-Inspector of Factories, upon a false charge, founded upon misapprehension, it was moved that the petition be taken into consideration. The mover admitted 'that in most cases it was inexpedient for the House to interfere with the exercise of that discretionary power which must be possessed by every government over its subordinate officers,' and that in his opinion, 'the only cases to justify the interference were when

---

[b] Mirror of Parl. 1838, pp. 5181, 5517.
[f] Ibid. 1839, p. 307.
[a] Ibid. pp. 339-350.
[b] Ibid. p. 4976.

the head of the department did not seem to have been in possession of **Precedents**
the facts of the case, or that he had laboured under some misapprehension.'[*] The Home Secretary (Sir James Graham) opposed the
motion; giving, however, explanations of the matter complained of;
while at the same time protesting against the House being 'converted
into a court of appeal against the executive: for if he were to be
responsible for the duties that he performed, he must exercise them
according to his own conscience and judgment with reference to the
dismissal of officers who held their offices during pleasure, and with
whose public conduct he was dissatisfied.'[b] Whereupon the motion
was negatived.

In 1848, the case of Sir J. T. Claridge, Recorder of Prince of **Sir J. T.**
Wales' Island, dismissed by order in council, 'on grounds of public **Claridge.**
policy,' was brought before the House of Commons, on motion for
an address to the crown, setting forth 'that no imputation rested
on the capacity or integrity of Sir J. T. Claridge,' and praying that
some other appointment might be conferred upon him. It was
alleged that while 'the independence of the judges in England was
secured by the fact of their holding their offices for life, in the
colonies they were liable to dismissal by the government,[c] and the
only security they had for the independence of the colonial judges,
was the appeal to the Committee of the Privy Council. The motion
however, was objected to by the President of the Board of Control
(Sir J. Hobhouse), as being an interference with the prerogative of
the crown, in regard to appointments to office, and it was withdrawn.[d] It was pertinently remarked, by the President of the India
Board: 'If the crown confers an appointment on Sir J. T. Claridge,
in compliance with an address of the House, who will be responsible
for the appointment to the House?'[e]

---

[*] Hans. Deb vol. lxxvi. p. 1623.
[b] *Ibid.* pp. 1634, 1640.
[c] In Canada, the judges are removable by the governor, upon the
address of both Houses of the provincial Parliament, with a right of
appeal within six months to the
privy-council. 12 Vict. c. 63, § 4.
So, also, the equity judges, by 12
Vict. c. 64, § 3.
[d] Hans. Deb. vol. c. pp. 812-816.
[e] *Ibid.* p. 815. See, also, the case
of Mr. Langslow, district judge in
Ceylon, Hans. Deb. (3) vol. xciv. pp.
278-305. The case of Mr. Stoner,
appointed by the Colonial Secretary
to be a judge in Victoria, but the
attention of government being called
to the fact that he had been charged
by a committee with bribery at an
election, his appointment was cancelled. *Ib.* vol. cxxxi. pp. 689-695,
836. And see *ib.* vol. cxxxii. pp.
810, 527-560. But upon further
inquiry into the case, the government were of opinion that Mr. Stoner
had been hardly dealt with, and that
his conduct had not been such as to
disqualify him for honourable employment. Accordingly, in 1858, he
was appointed judge of the West Indian Encumbered Estates Court, the
duties of which he discharged in the
most exemplary manner, and in 1865
he was permitted to exchange this
office for that of a judge of a county
court in England. The circumstances
attending these appointments were

Precedents

Patronage of Board of Admiralty.

On April 19, 1853, after the accession to office of the Aberdeen administration, the government acquiesced in a motion made by an independent member of the House of Commons, for the appointment of a select committee to 'enquire into the exercise of the influence and patronage of the Admiralty, in the dockyards, and public departments, connected with the several Parliamentary boroughs,' it having been alleged that this patronage had been made use of, for political purposes, by persons officially connected with the Derby administration.[t] The committee reported to the House on May 23, with minutes of evidence in regard to the several branches of the enquiry. They showed that, prior to the year 1847, corrupt practices in regard to appointments and promotions to office were very prevalent in the dockyards; but that, on February 27, 1847, an Admiralty order was issued, in the form of a circular, insisting upon the introduction and maintenance of a system of promotion, to depend solely upon merit and efficiency. This was followed up, in 1849, by another circular to the same general effect, which was backed by a personal appeal from Sir Francis Baring, the then first lord of the Admiralty, to the superintendents and principal officers of the dockyards, that they would give him an assurance that they would not interfere in politics. These measures seemed to have worked very successfully. But when the Derby ministry came into power, the circular of 1849 was cancelled, with a view to favour the interests of the party in power; and though but few political appointments appear to have been made, they were sufficient in number to 'subvert the confidence of the men, and render nugatory all the solemn assurances of circulars issued by the Admiralty, to the effect that men should rise by merit, and not by political influence.' The committee imputed blame for these transactions principally to Mr. Stafford, the then secretary of the Admiralty, to whom the first lord, upon his accepting office, had given up 'all the civil patronage, excepting the master shipwrights, and one class of messengers, which he reserved for deserving sailors and marines.' Recently, the circular of 1849 was restored, and its provisions rendered more secure by being embodied in an order in council. The committee concluded with a recommendation that should the system under which promotions in the dockyards are now again regulated, be hereafter altered, Parliament should be informed thereof as soon as possible.[u] On July 5, 1853, a motion was made

---

explained and justified by the government in the House of Commons. See Hans. Deb. vol. cxlv. p. 1212. Ibid. vol. clxxviii. p. 593. The case of Mr. Lawley, appointed governor of South Australia, on the recommendation of the Colonial Secretary, but proving afterwards to have been engaged in gambling speculations, his appointment was revoked before he had left England. Ib. vol. cxxxv. pp. 1225-1250.

[t] Hans. Deb. vol. cxxvi. pp. 33-122.
[u] Report on Dockyard Appoint-

in the House of Commons, that, referring to said report and evidence, 'this House is of opinion that, during the administration of the late Board of Admiralty, the patronage of dockyard promotions, and the influence of the Admiralty, were used and exercised for political purposes, to an extent, and in a manner calculated to reflect discredit upon that department of the government, and to impair the efficiency of the service.' In order to get rid of this charge, an amendment, implicating 'every administration of the Admiralty' in a similar offence, was proposed. After a short discussion, a motion to adjourn the House was carried, and the debate was never again resumed. On May 30, the Dockyard Committee were instructed by the House to consider the case of Lieutenant Engledue, R.N., who in 1840 had been struck off the list of lieutenants of the Royal Navy for an act of insubordination. Upon several occasions, afterwards, at different times, Mr. Engledue memorialised the Board of Admiralty to restore him to his former position, but was invariably refused. However, on November 30, 1852, he again renewed his application, and on December 22 he was informed that he was at liberty to memorialise the queen in council to be reinstated. This permission was given two days after the Derby ministry had announced that they only held office until their successors were appointed. The memorial was sent in, favourably entertained, and referred to the Admiralty. On January 4, 1853, the queen's approval was given to the restoration of Mr. Engledue. On the 6th inst. before the transaction was quite completed, a new Board of Admiralty was appointed. Nevertheless the appointment was confirmed. But soon afterwards papers in relation to this case were moved for in the House of Commons, and being transmitted, were referred to the Committee on Dockyard Appointments, it having been alleged that political influence had been made use of to procure the restoration of Mr. Engledue to his former rank in the service, notwithstanding the repeated refusals of the Admiralty to reinstate him. The committee carefully investigated the circumstances of the case, in view of which they reported, on July 26, their opinion 'that the restoration of Mr. Engledue to his former rank in the Royal Navy was not a judicious proceeding.' But they added, that notwithstanding their attention having been called to the peculiar time when the application was granted, 'they have not heard any evidence which shows that this favour was bestowed from any political or unworthy motives.'

Precedents

Case of Lt. Engledue.

---

ments: Commons Papers, 1852-3, vol. xxv. pp. 3-14. And see Hans. Deb. vol. cxxv. p. 505.

' Hans. Deb. vol. cxxviii. pp. 1200-1311.

" Ibid. pp. 1321-1326. See, also, in this connection, the Churchward case, which is described in another part of this chapter, post, p. 408.

' Hans. Deb. vol. cxxvi. p. 876.

' Commons Papers, 1852-3, vol. xxv. p. 471.

Precedents. In 1855, a motion was made in the House of Commons, for the
appointment of a committee to enquire into 'the grounds and jus-
Mr. T. F. tification of' the removal from office of the Right Hon. T. F.
Kennedy. Kennedy, a Commissioner of Woods and Forests, and a Privy
Councillor, who was dismissed from office by Mr. Gladstone,
Chancellor of the Exchequer, because 'he could not serve the public
with credit therein,' and had treated his subordinates improperly
and unfairly, so that the government could not be responsible for
his conduct.[a] The motion was opposed by Mr. Gladstone (though
he had, meanwhile, retired from office) on the ground that it was
'entirely contrary to Parliamentary usage and injurious to the
public service,' and that 'no *primâ facie* ground had been established for it.'[b] Admitting the abstract right of the House to
institute such an enquiry, in conformity with the resolution of
1784,[c] nevertheless 'he found that the practice of the House had
been uniformly to decline enquiring into the removal of public servants, when the removal had taken place according to law, and
according to the apparently conscientious judgment of those who,
by law, were made responsible for the conduct of such public servants.'[d] Viewing the motion as intended 'to impugn his conduct
while in office, in one of the most important functions belonging to a minister,' Mr. Gladstone declared that he should abstain
from voting on it. Accordingly, after an elaborate speech, he
withdrew.[d] The Secretary of the Treasury (Mr. Wilson) defended the dismissal, and said, 'it would be impossible to carry
on the work of government if the House were to assume a right to
review every transaction of this kind, although if a *primâ facie* case
of injustice was made out it ought not to be overlooked.'[e] Lord
Palmerston acquitted Mr. Kennedy of any conduct reflecting on
'his honour, his veracity, or his character,' but nevertheless resisted
the motion, as a dangerous precedent, and contended that 'a discretion must be left in the hands of the servants of the crown as to
removing from office those whom they thought incompetent' for
their duties; adding, that 'if the House were to establish as a precedent that any man removed from a situation was to appeal to his
friends in the House of Commons, and obtain a verdict as to the
propriety of his removal, there would be an end of all discipline in
the service of the state.'[f] Satisfied with the acknowledgment that
Mr. Kennedy's honour stood perfectly unimpeached, the mover
consented to withdraw his motion.[g]

---

[a] Hans. Deb. vol. cxxxvi. p. 1991.
[b] Ibid. p. 2010.
[c] See ante, p. 255.
[d] Hans. Deb. vol. cxxxvi. pp. 1996-2001.
[e] Ibid. pp. 1992-2011.
[f] Ibid. p. 2029.
[g] Ibid. p. 2031.
[h] Ibid. p. 2032. See also the discussion in the House of Commons on

PARLIAMENTARY CONTROL OF PUBLIC OFFICERS. 417

In 1860, a motion for papers was made in the House of Commons, which involved an attempt to induce the House to review the decision of the Civil Service Commissioners, in respect to a candidate rejected upon examination before them. The government protested against such an interference with public servants engaged in a judicial inquiry, as being unprecedented and unjustifiable. 'If,' it was said, 'it can be shown that the Commissioners were not worthy of the confidence of the government, or of this House, that they act with unfairness, or are incompetent, from literary or other disqualifications, then let the House interfere by an address to the crown to remove them from their offices.' The motion was negatived.[h] Subsequently the House refused to direct those Commissioners to publish certain information with their annual report, on the ground that they were not amenable to the jurisdiction of the House, but only to the crown itself.[i]

Precedents Civil Service Commissioners.

On March 4, 1861, it was moved in the House of Lords, that a select committee be appointed to inquire into the circumstances attending the appointment and resignation of Mr. Turnbull to a place in the Record Office; but the motion was opposed by the Government, and negatived.[j]

Mr. Turnbull.

On July 15, 1861, it was moved in the House of Lords to resolve that it is desirable, without delay, to restore the Consular

---

the case of Mr. Chisholm Anstey, who was removed from his office of Attorney-General of Hong Kong for 'his violent temper and want of discretion' in his conduct to his superior the governor of the island, to whom he had shown 'an excess of personal animosity and want of respect.' (H. D. vol. clxxii. pp. 1883-0180.) See also the debates in both Houses of Parliament, in 1863, upon the removal of two judges in the Ionian Islands, by the authority of the Lord High Commissioner, and with the sanction of the Secretary of State for the Colonies. Pursuant to an address of the House of Lords of April 17, papers on this subject were laid upon the table; but as the reasons for the removal of these functionaries did not clearly appear from the same, further papers containing 'any charges of conduct inconsistent with their judicial office,' were moved for in the House of Lords on July 9. This motion was opposed by the Government, on the ground that it was 'a most dangerous precedent' to authorise an appeal to Parliament from acts of responsible ministers in the execution of the law, and to require the production of confidential communications from the High Commissioner to his superiors in office, and of letters from other persons intended to be confidential, without their consent. Nevertheless, as the sense of the House was in favour of the motion, the government gave way, and allowed it to pass without a division. After the production of the papers, no further action was taken in the matter by either House.

[h] Hans. Deb. vol. clviii. pp. 802-007.
[i] *Ibid.* p. 2083. And see *Ibid.* vol. clxx. p. 23. See further, as to the interference of Parliament with Commissioners appointed by the crown to conduct an inquiry, *ante*, p. 200.
[j] Hans. Deb. vol. clxi. p. 1271. See also *Ibid.* p. 2101. And see the case of Mr. Reed's appointment, *Ibid.* vol. clxxii. p. 1138.

VOL. I. E E

418   THE ROYAL PREROGATIVE

Precedents. Consul at Mozambique. authority at Mozambique, in order to aid in repressing the slave-trade on the eastern coast of Africa. [In the previous session the House had addressed the crown, requesting that a consul might be re-appointed at this place; but as yet the government had not done so.] The aforesaid motion was opposed by the Under Secretary for Foreign Affairs, on the ground that it was an undue encroachment on the functions of the executive, and not a case in which Parliament should interfere. He added that the address last year had been carried by surprise, and because the ministry, not anticipating a division, had allowed their supporters to leave the House. After these explanations, the motion was withdrawn.[a]

Irish Court of Chancery. A bill, introduced by Mr. Whiteside, in 1865, to alter the constitution, &c. of the Irish Court of Chancery, contained a clause providing that certain judicial offices in the said Court should be conferred upon persons at present holding other offices of high position. This was opposed by the Attorney-General, who said that it would not be 'for the public advantage to set the example of naming in Acts of Parliament the persons who were to be appointed to particular posts about to be created, instead of leaving the appointments to the crown, acting under the guidance of its responsible advisers. He did not think it advisable that these appointments should be made in the House of Commons, because nothing could be more invidious than to invite personal discussions as to the fitness of individuals for particular offices.'[b] The bill was shortly afterwards withdrawn.

II. As to the Remuneration of Public Employés.

Pensions. On May 20, 1828, a motion was made in the House of Commons for a return of Pensions granted on the English Civil List; but the motion was opposed by the ministry, on the ground that it was a principle to maintain inviolate the arrangements made with the crown respecting the Civil List, which had been granted for the lifetime of the sovereign; and that unless the Civil List shall become in such state as to render it necessary to apply to Parliament for assistance, or unless some special case of abuse is made out, the House have no right to inquire into details of this kind. On division, the motion was negatived.[m]

The next case that will engage our attention under this head is one which occurred in 1830, when the Grey Ministry, immediately

---

[a] Hans. Deb. vol. clxiv. p. 855. See a similar proceeding in the House of Commons, in the case of the consulship at Pesth. *Ibid.* p. 1001.

[b] Hans. Deb. vol. clxxvii. p. 311. See also Mr. Walpole's observations on this point, *Ibid.* vol. clxxviii. p. 525. And see *Ibid.* vol. clxxxiv. p. 520. And *ante*, p. 77 n.

[m] Mirror of Parl. 1828, pp. 1585–1593.

upon their appointment to office, took the initiative, and invited the House of Commons to appoint a committee to consider the amount of the salaries and emoluments payable to members of the administration holding seats in either House of Parliament; pledging themselves to abide by the recommendations of the committee on the subject. The Chancellor of the Exchequer (Lord Althorp), in moving for this committee, on December 9th, stated that, while it was necessary, in point of form, that his name, as the mover, should be included, he hoped he would be excused for non-attendance, as the government were desirous that the committee should be exclusively composed of independent members, and altogether free from the suspicion of government influence.* His lordship cited a precedent for this course, in 1806, when the then Chancellor of the Exchequer, in appointing a committee to inquire into the state of the finances, selected no one to serve thereon who was an officeholder under the crown. Lord Althorp's committee reported on March 30, 1831, recommending very considerable reductions in official salaries, which were agreed to by the government.° But it would appear that this inquiry was not regarded as sufficiently complete, for on April 12, 1850, Lord John Russell (the First Lord of the Treasury) moved for the appointment of a similar committee, who should also be empowered to consider of the diplomatic establishments, and the salaries and retiring allowances of the judges. The proposal to refer the question of official salaries to a select committee, instead of determining upon them in council, with the experience and on the responsibility of the government, was strenuously opposed in the House, but the motion was finally agreed to. The only member of the ministry who sat upon the committee was the mover himself. The committee reported on July 25th: their recommendations in regard to official salaries were few and unimportant, as in their opinion the reductions formerly made, upon the report of the committee in 1831, had gone far enough.°

Precedents. Official salaries.

---

* Mirror of Parl. 1830, p. 430. Two members of the late ministry were placed on the committee in order that they might be able to give details as to official business. They consented to attend for this purpose, but refused to act as ordinary members of the committee. *Ibid.* pp. 619, 1285.

° The committee having recommended a reduction of the salary of the President of the Board of Control, which had been acquiesced in by the Government, an independent member of the House of Commons, on Sept. 20, 1831, moved a series of resolutions declaring the inexpediency of reducing this salary from 5,000*l*. per annum at which it had been fixed since 1810, to 3,500*l*. as proposed by the committee. The government, however, opposed this motion, and the previous question was put thereon and negatived. (Mirror of Parl. 1831, pp. 2531-2539.) But in 1853 the salary was again raised to 5,000*l*. per ann., by the Act 16 & 17 Vict. c. 85, sec. 31, in order that this office might be on a similar footing with other Principal Secretaries of State.

° Com. Papers, 1850, vol. xv. p. 170.

Precedents

Upon the other branches of inquiry several important recommendations were made. The report was ordered to lie on the table and be printed. Before the next meeting of Parliament, the government undertook, upon their own responsibility, and according to their own judgment, to decide upon the manner in which they would deal with the various recommendations contained therein.³

Lord Douglas.

On May 8, 1833, Mr. Hume moved an address to the crown, praying that the law-officers might be instructed to inquire into the validity of a pension or sinecure office granted by his late Majesty George IV. to Lord Douglas, contrary (as he alleged) to an agreement between the Crown and Parliament: with the consent of the government the motion was agreed to.⁴ Ministers afterwards intimated their intention to apply to the Court of Session to set aside the grant.⁵

Customs salaries.

On July 30, 1834, a petition was presented to the House of Commons from certain commissioners of customs, complaining of the reduction of their salaries under a treasury minute. The petitioners admitted that 'the question of salaries rests exclusively with the executive, and ought not to be brought before Parliament,' but they claimed that theirs was an exceptional case, and one of peculiar hardship. The Chancellor of the Exchequer characterised this as 'a most unusual and extraordinary proceeding,' but proceeded to show that the petitioners had no just grounds of complaint in the present instance. Members generally acknowledged 'the extreme inexpediency' of 'making the House a court of appeal in questions of this sort.' Even Mr. Hume, that staunch supporter of the people's rights, declared that 'he could not conceive anything more mischievous' than for the House to interfere where it had not a right to do so; and that the House was 'called upon to decide whether the legislature or the executive should determine what salaries are to be given to the servants of the public.' The petition was by leave withdrawn.⁶

Pension to King of Hanover.

On May 1, 1838, Mr. Hume moved for leave to bring in a bill to suspend the payment of the annuity granted by Act of Parliament to H.R.H. the Duke of Cumberland, so long as he should continue King of Hanover, being of opinion that it was inexpedient and uncalled-for to continue a pension granted to an English prince after he had become an independent sovereign. The motion was opposed by the Chancellor of the Exchequer (Mr. T. Spring Rice), on the ground that the annuity had been granted for the term of 'the natural life' of His Royal Highness, and that Parliament had

---

³ Hans. Deb. vol. cxvi. p. 518.   ⁵ *Ibid.* p. 3582.
⁴ Mirror of Parl. 1833, p. 1681.   ⁶ *Ibid.* 1834, pp. 3101-3104.

no right to put a new construction on the grant, so as to deprive him of it. This view was sustained by the House, and the motion rejected. Similar motions were again proposed by Mr. Hume, on March 27, 1840, and on June 30, 1843, but were opposed by the ministry on the same grounds as before, and negatived by the House.

Precedents

On February 27, 1840, the attention of the House of Commons was directed to the grant of a pension to Sir John Newport, on his retirement from the office of Comptroller of the Exchequer. This was an office which was held under a statute 'during good behaviour.' It was wholly independent of the crown, and did not entitle the incumbent to receive a pension on his relinquishing office. It had been held by Sir John Newport for five years only, previous to which he had performed various public services during a long public career, but none of them of a nature that authorised him to claim a retiring allowance. The government, however, being desirous of rewarding Sir John's long and faithful services, determined upon his retirement from the Comptrollership to allow him a pension of 1,000l. a year out of the Royal Bounty Fund, which was set apart, under the Act 1 & 2 Vict. c. 2, to enable the crown to reward persons who had just claims on the royal beneficence for discoveries in science, &c., or the performance of special duties to the crown or public. This proceeding was called in question in a series of resolutions submitted to the House, setting forth that the peculiar office lately held by Sir John Newport disqualified him from the receipt of a pension from the crown; that it was contrary to the spirit and intent of Parliament in respect to Civil Service pensions to allot him an annuity for public political services out of a fund set apart for the reward of merit of a different kind; and that, for these and other reasons set forth, the House deems it expedient to express its decided opinion that the pension in question *ought not* to be drawn into precedent. The ministry met these resolutions by an amendment, asserting the nature and value of Sir John Newport's services upon which his claim to a retiring allowance was based, and declaring that, on reviewing the whole case, 'this House is satisfied that the grant of a pension to a retired Comptroller of the Exchequer, in circumstances so peculiar, *cannot* be drawn into precedent.' The House, however, was not satisfied with the explanations and excuses of ministers, but passed the original resolutions by a majority of twenty-eight.[1]

Sir John Newport.

In 1840, a retired public servant petitioned the House of Commons, complaining of the insufficiency of his superannuation allowance, and declaring that he was legally entitled to a larger amount. A

Superannuation allowance.

---

[1] Mirror of Parl. 1840, p. 1323.

Precedents   motion to refer this petition to a committee was opposed by the Chancellor of the Exchequer, who explained the merits of the case, and said that 'it would have a very bad effect on the public service if the House should interfere with the retired allowances of public officers.' The motion was negatived on a division.^a

Rev. Dr. Morrison.   On March 26, 1844, a motion was made in the House of Commons for an address to the queen, requesting that a suitable provision might be made for the widow and children of the late Rev. Dr. Morrison, on account of the eminent public services in China of the doctor and of his eldest son, both deceased. The prime minister (Sir R. Peel) fully admitted the value of the services rendered to the country by the Morrisons, but declared that the rule in respect to pensions to civil servants could not be extended to this family, and that there were no other means available for the purpose; adding that 'the House should be exceedingly cautious how they established a precedent in such a case of special interference with the conduct of the executive government, and in some degree with the prerogative of the crown.' The motion was accordingly withdrawn.^t

Officers of Insolvent Debtors Court.   On April 8, 1862, the attention of the House of Commons was called to the case of the clerks and officers of the late Insolvent Debtors Court, whose interests had been injuriously affected by the operation of the Bankruptcy Act of 1861. The ministry stated that it was not their intention to introduce any measure for the relief of these persons, but that they would offer no objection to the reference to a select committee of any petition setting forth their claims; and that they would agree to carry out any recommendation from such committee as to the amount of compensation which should be awarded to these persons. Whereupon a select committee was appointed accordingly, which reported on July 9. Pursuant to this report, a bill for the relief of these complainants was introduced, and passed into a law.^v

Post Office employés.   On July 22, 1862, Sir George Bowyer moved the House of Commons for the appointment of a committee to inquire into alleged grievances complained of in a petition from upwards of 1,500 persons in the Post Office department. The Chancellor of the Exchequer (Mr. Gladstone) opposed the motion, 'as being of a most dangerous character, not only to the good order of the Post Office department, but to the entire public service.' 'The question had been settled by competent authority, namely, the executive government.' 'If the House thought the executive government to

---

^s Mirror of Parl. 1840, p. 1810.
^t Hans. Deb. vol. lxxiii. p. 1582. See, also, a discussion in the House of Commons, on Feb. 26, 1861, on an address to the queen respecting forage allowances to cavalry officers.
^v 25 & 26 Vict. c. 99. See the case of Divorce Court proctors, *ante*, p. 304.

blame, let them take the proper course and pronounce their censure upon them; but he was satisfied that no worse policy could be adopted than for the House to take into its own hands the management of the public services.' Sir S. Northcote (a leader of the Opposition) 'entirely assented to this doctrine, that it was most mischievous for the House of Commons to take out of the hands of the government the details of arrangements made in the various departments.' The motion was accordingly withdrawn.[s]

Precedents

On March 6, 1865, Mr. Ferrand (who represented a large dockyard constituency) called the attention of the House to the great inequality and inadequacy of the wages paid to men employed in the Royal Dockyards, with a view 'to elicit an expression of opinion by the House which would induce the Admiralty—who had hitherto refused redress—to take their most reasonable claims into consideration.' The alleged grievances were explained away by the Secretary to the Admiralty, who called upon the House not to countenance the principle of interference with the discretion of government in the remuneration of public servants, at the instigation of members whose constituents were in the receipt of wages from the public treasury. The subject was then dropped.[y]

Dockyard labourers

On April 28, 1865, a motion was made in the House of Commons to refer a petition from certain merchants of Liverpool complaining of the inadequate remuneration of the out-door officers of Customs, to a select committee to inquire into the alleged grievances. The Chancellor of the Exchequer (Mr. Gladstone) admitted that if any public servant could complain of any grievance by reason of the acts of the government, 'it was the duty of the government to render an account of their proceedings to the House, and it would be perfectly within the rules of prudence to risk an inquiry by a committee.' Nevertheless, the executive government should be held responsible for the regulation and the pay of the public servants, and nothing would tend so much to the disorganisation of the public service, or do more to lower the character of the House of Commons, than any attempt to take this duty out of the hands of government. Upon an assurance that the grievance complained of should receive the attention of government, the motion for a committee was negatived on division.[z]

Customs officers.

On May 12, 1865, a motion was made in the House of Commons to declare the expediency and propriety of increasing the salaries of postmasters, upon whom additional labour had been imposed by the establishment of Post Office Savings Banks. The Secretary of the Treasury and the Chancellor of the Exchequer explained that

Postmasters.

---

[s] Hans. Deb. vol. clxvii. p. 672.
[y] Ibid. vol. clxxvii. p. 1130.
[z] Ibid. vol. clxxviii. p. 1205; and see Ibid. vol. clxxx. p. 671.

424   THE ROYAL PREROGATIVE

Precedents   the Government were considering all cases of hardship arising from
             this cause, and were dealing with them equitably; but that they
             were not prepared to introduce any wholesale and sweeping change
             in the present system. Whereupon the motion was withdrawn.ᵃ
Registrar   On May 15, 1865, inquiry was made of the Attorney-General as
of Leeds   to the circumstances attending the resignation by Mr. H. S. Wilde
Bank-   of the office of Registrar of the Court of Bankruptcy at Leeds,
ruptcy   and the appointment of his successor, and in regard to the act
Court.   of Lord Chancellor Westbury in sanctioning the grant of a retiring
             pension to Mr. Wilde, though his conduct in office had dis-
             entitled him to any such advantage.ᵇ On the following day, the
             papers connected with Mr. Wilde's resignation of office were ordered
             to be laid before the House,ᶜ and on May 19 were ordered to be
             printed. On May 23, with the consent of the government, and
             especially of the Lord Chancellor, who caused it to be stated that
             he courted inquiry into the matter, a select committee was appointed
             to inquire into all the circumstances attending Mr. Wilde's resigna-
             tion of office, the grant to him of a pension, and the appointment of
             his successor. Subsequently it was agreed that this committee
             should be nominated by the General Committee of Elections, and
             should consist of five ordinary members, and two additional mem-
             bers being lawyers, who should be empowered to examine witnesses
             and conduct the case on either side, but should not have a right to
             vote.ᵈ On June 22, the report of this committee was brought up,
             and ordered to lie upon the table, and to be printed. The report,
             which was accompanied by copious evidence, acquitted the Lord
             Chancellor of all charge but that of haste and want of caution in
             granting a pension to Mr. Wilde. Nevertheless the committee
             recorded their opinion, that the general impression created by the
             sudden retirement of Mr. Wilde, and the pecuniary transactions which
             took place between Mr. Bethell (the eldest son of the Lord Chancel-
             lor) and Mr. Welch, who was appointed to succeed Mr. Wilde, ' were
             calculated to excite the gravest suspicions,' and that their investi-
             gation had been 'highly desirable for the public interests.'ᵉ On
             July 3, a motion, to resolve that the conduct of the Lord Chancellor
Mr. L.   in reference to the appointments in the Leeds Bankruptcy Court and
Edmunds.   in the case of Leonard Edmunds,ᶠ which had been reported upon by

ᵃ Hans. Deb. vol. clxxix. pp. 104–200.
ᵇ Hans. Deb. vol. clxxix. p. 293, and see p. 440.
ᶜ Commons Journals, May 16.
ᵈ Hans. Deb. vol. clxxix. pp. 781–785. The committee decided upon conducting their inquiry with closed doors. Ibid. vol. clxxx. p. 881.

ᵉ Rep. Com. Leeds Bankruptcy Court, Commons Papers, 1865, p. x.
ᶠ On Feb. 14, 1865, Leonard Edmunds, Reading Clerk and Clerk of Committees of the House of Lords, petitioned the House for leave to resign his office, and for the grant of a retiring allowance. The petition was presented by the Lord Chancel-

a committee of the House of Lords, a copy of whose report had Precedents been laid before this House—was 'highly reprehensible, and calculated to throw discredit on the administration of the high offices of state,' was moved by Mr. Hunt: to this an amendment (of which no notice had been given) was proposed by the Lord Advocate, acquitting the Lord Chancellor from all charge except that of haste and want of caution in granting a pension to Mr. Wilde, but declaring the opinion of the House that some further check should be placed by law upon the grant of pensions to the holders of legal offices. Previous to the commencement of the debate, Mr. Bouverie had given notice that he should move, as an amendment to the main motion, to resolve, that this House, having considered the report of the committee on the Leeds Bankruptcy Court, and the evidence, &c., are of opinion that, while the evidence discloses the existence of corrupt practices with reference to the appointment of P. R. Welch to the office of registrar of the said court, they are satisfied that no imputation can fairly be made against the Lord Chancellor with regard to this appointment; and that such evidence and also that taken before the Lords' committee on the circumstances connected with the resignation by Mr. Edmunds of the offices held

by, upon whose motion the resignation was accepted, and the petition referred to the select committee on the Office of the Clerk of the Parliaments, &c. On Feb. 17, the Lord Chancellor acquainted the House that he had appointed his second son, (the Hon. Slingsby Bethell) to the office vacated by Mr. Edmunds, which appointment was approved of by the House. On the same day, the committee reported in favour of allowing to Mr. Edmunds the usual retiring pension, which report was agreed to by the House on Feb. 24. On March 7, the Lord Chancellor, being moved thereto by various discreditable rumours which were afloat, informed the House of certain circumstances connected with the conduct of Mr. Edmunds while holding a situation in the Patent Office, and subsequently when in the employ of the House, which demanded investigation. Whereupon, on his lordship's motion, a select committee was appointed to inquire into all the circumstances connected with Mr. Edmund's resignation of both the said offices, and with the grant of a retiring pension to him by the House. This committee reported on May 2. On May 9, on motion of Lord Redesdale, a member of 'the Pension Committee,' a passage from the report of the committee of inquiry was read, which appeared to reflect upon the previous committee for recommending a pension to Mr. Edmunds, without duly considering the imputations upon his conduct. Lord Redesdale then moved two resolutions, to exonerate the 'Pension Committee' from all blame in the matter. After a long debate, the previous question was put thereon, and negatived; and the resolution of the House of Feb. 24, agreeing to the recommendation of the committee in favour of a retiring allowance of 800£ per annum to Mr. Edmunds, was rescinded. Before putting this motion to the vote, a petition was presented to the House from Mr. Edmunds that he might be first heard, by counsel, in his defence; but Earl Granville (the leader of the House) said that he felt it impossible to accede to this request. See Lords Journals and debates of the dates aforesaid. And see post, p. 505.

by him, 'show a laxity of practice and a want of caution with regard to the public interests on the part of the Lord Chancellor in sanctioning the grant of retiring pensions to public officers against whom grave charges were pending, which, in the opinion of this House, are calculated to discredit the administration of his great office.' The Lord Advocate's amendment was first proposed; but although Mr. Bouverie's amendment was not technically before the House and could not be discussed until it should be moved, its terms were known, and generally preferred by those who took part in the debate, including Mr. Hunt, the mover of the main motion.ᵉ The question, 'That the words proposed to be left out [i.e. Mr. Hunt's motion] stand part of the question,' was therefore put and negatived without a division. On the question that the Lord Advocate's amendment be then added, Lord Palmerston (the premier) moved, that the debate be now adjourned. This was negatived on division by a majority of 14. Lord Palmerston thereupon agreed to accept this division as conclusive in favour of Mr. Bouverie's amendment. The Lord Advocate's amendment was accordingly put and negatived, and then Mr. Bouverie's amendment was agreed to without a further division. On the following day, Lord Palmerston announced that, owing to this vote, Lord Chancellor Westbury had tendered his resignation, which had been accepted, and that he would merely retain the seals for a few days for the convenience of public business.ʰ On July 5, the Lord Chancellor informed the House of Lords of his resignation. He added that, had he followed his own judgment, he would have retired from office when the charges were first raised against him, as he felt that the holder of the Great Seal ought never to be in the position of an accused person. But he had been dissuaded from this step by the prime minister, who said it would not do to admit this as a principle of public conduct, for the consequence would be that whoever brought up an accusation would at once succeed in driving the Lord Chancellor from office. Since then he had repeatedly pressed his resignation upon Lord Palmerston but without satisfying him that the time had come when it should be accepted, until after the vote of the House of Commons on July 3, which had determined him no longer to consent to retain office.ⁱ In the session of 1866 an Act was passed requiring the Lord Chancellor to transmit to the Lords of the Treasury all applications for

---

ᵉ Hans. Deb. vol. clxxx. pp. 1002, 1117.
ʰ Ibid. p. 1161.
ⁱ Ibid. p. 1174. On Feb. 13, 1860, the Attorney-General informed the House that, in accordance with the recommendation of the Leeds Bankruptcy Court Committee in the previous session, criminal informations had been filed against Mr. Welch and the Hon. R. Ibbetholl for corrupt practices in obtaining, or attempting to obtain, a judicial appointment.

superannuation allowances on retirement of which he may approve, from any officer connected with the Court of Chancery, or in Bankruptcy or Lunacy, or any of the superior Courts of Common Law, and empowering the Treasury to decide thereon.[j] This statue is intended to take away from the Lord Chancellor the absolute right which he had hitherto enjoyed, and to give to the Treasury the power of determining upon the report of the Lord Chancellor the amount of pension to which any such officer is entitled by law upon his retirement.[k]

Precedents

We have next to consider the prerogative of the crown in regard to Supply and Taxation, and the constitutional rights of Parliament in reference thereto.

Prerogative in regard to Supply and Taxation.

The true doctrine on this head has been briefly stated by May, in the following words: 'The crown, acting with the advice of its responsible ministers, being the executive power, is charged with the management of all the revenues of the country, and with all payments for the public service. The crown, therefore, in the first instance, makes known to the Commons the pecuniary necessities of the government, and the Commons grant such aids or supplies as are required to satisfy these demands; and provide by taxes, and by the appropriation of other sources of the public income, the ways and means to meet the supplies which are granted by them. Thus the crown demands money, the Commons grant it, and the Lords assent to the grant. But the Commons do not vote money unless it be required by the crown; nor impose or augment taxes unless they be necessary for meeting the supplies which they have voted, or are about to vote, and for supplying general deficiencies in the revenue. The crown has no concern in the nature or distribution of taxes; but the foundation of all Parliamentary taxation is, its necessity for the public service, as declared by the crown through its constitutional advisers.'[l]

---

[j] 29 & 30 Vict. c. 68.
[k] Hans. Deb. vol. clxxxiii. p. 1038.
[l] May, Parl. Prac. p. 512. See also Mill, Rep. Gov. p. 90.

In entering upon a more detailed investigation of the relative functions of the crown and of Parliament in the matter of Supply, it is proposed to divide the subject into two parts, and to consider, first, the constitutional restrictions upon Parliament in respect to (*a*), Supply and Taxation ; and, secondly (*b*), the Rights and Privileges of Parliament, and especially of the House of Commons, in the grant of money for the public service ; and in the oversight and control of the public expenditure.

I. a. *The Restrictions upon Parliament in matters of Supply.*

No supply to be granted but on demand of the crown:

According to ancient constitutional doctrine and practice, no moneys can be voted by Parliament for any purpose whatsoever, except at the demand and upon the responsibility of ministers of the crown.*

In former times, when any aids and supplies were required for the public service, the crown made known its wants to the House of Commons by message ; this message was taken into consideration by the Commons, and the necessary supplies were voted by that House, according to its discretion. This mode of procedure in obtaining grants of money admitted of no exception. It therefore left no opportunity to any private member to introduce any scheme of his own whereby any charges would be made upon the people. But in the beginning of the last century, a specious evasion of this constitutional rule crept in. The wholesome system of exchequer control, in the custody of public moneys—which afforded protection alike to the crown and to the Parliament against illegal appropriations—was made the occasion of attempts to induce the crown, by the exercise of Parliamentary influence, to sanction expenditures that were extravagant and unjustifiable. Finding that there was generally a

---

* See Mr. Gladstone's speeches, Hans. Deb. vol. clxxxi. p. 1131; *Ibid.* vol. clxxxii. p. 507.

balance of public money remaining in the exchequer, as yet unappropriated to any specific service, there was a growing disposition on the part of private members to regard this money as available for any purpose they might be disposed to favour. Petitions were presented to the House from various persons claiming pecuniary assistance or relief; which being often promoted by members who were friends to the parties, and carrying with them the appearance of justice or of charity, induced the House to approve, or at utmost to be indifferent to their success. By this means large sums were granted to private persons improvidently, and sometimes upon insufficient grounds." In the year 1705 this abuse became so notorious, that early in the next session, on December 11, 1706, before any petitions of this sort could be again offered, the House resolved, 'That they would receive no petition for any sum of money relating to public service, but what is recommended from the crown.' This resolution was made a standing order on June 11, 1713, and amended, June 25, 1852, to bring it into conformity with existing practice, by the substitution of a new order to declare, 'That this House will receive no petition for any sum of money relating to public service, or proceed upon any motion for granting any money, but what is recommended from the crown.'° The uniform practice of the House has construed this rule to extend to any motion which involves the expenditure of public money, even though it may not directly propose a grant.ᵖ It has

marginalia: Or petitions for pecuniary relief received; Or motions for grant of money entertained;

---

* Hats. Prec. vol. lii. p. 242. Mr. Ayrton's speech on proposing the new Supply Order, on March 20, 1861. Hans. Deb. vol. clxxxii. p. 591.

° For cases illustrating the strictness with which the House of Commons adheres to this rule, see Mirror of Parl. 1837, p. 259. Ibid. 1837-8, p. 2020; 1839, p. 123. The standing order of June, 1852, was extended to charges upon the Indian revenues, by standing order of July 21, 1859. The House was informed by a member of the Petitions Committee, on March 20, 1860, 'that there was hardly a meeting of that committee at which petitions were not rejected, on account of their praying for a grant of public money, or some similar informality.'—Hans. Deb. vol. clxxxii. p. 601.

ᵖ May, Parl. Prac. 514; 3 Hats.

430   THE ROYAL PREROGATIVE.

On reports of committees.

even been held to preclude a select committee from recommending that public compensation should be given to individuals for losses incurred, unless the same had been previously sanctioned by the crown.[a] This is a striking proof of the strictness with which this rule is enforced; as the mere report of a committee, though entitled to respectful consideration, does not bind the House to anything, unless it be formally agreed to by the House itself.

Bills imposing public charges:

But while the House of Commons has invariably maintained the principle embodied in the foregoing standing order, so far as it was directly applicable, the ingenuity of members has discovered a way of practically evading it. Of late years a practice has arisen of permitting the introduction of bills by private members which, though not professedly in the nature of money bills, do yet necessitate, to a greater or less extent, the imposition of new charges upon the people, the precise extent of which cannot always be estimated at the outset. These bills have been either for the construction of certain public works, or for the establishment or encouragement of certain new institutions, or they have proposed to grant new salaries to officials to be appointed under the bill, or to grant compensation or aid to individuals, or associations for various causes assigned. But whatever may be the precise object of these bills, inasmuch as they establish grounds of expense, they are an evasion of the constitutional rule which forbids the grant of money by

---

105. The consent of the crown is understood to have been given, whenever a pecuniary proposition is introduced into the House by a minister of the crown. Hans. Deb. vol. cv. p. 471.

[a] May, 514, citing Fourdrinier's case, June 15, 1837; and see Hans. Deb. vol. clxvi. p. 710. In several similar instances committees have evaded the rule by the use of general terms in favour of the relief they desired to recommend. But the rule does not apply to select committees on public questions, appointed at the instigation, or with the consent, of government. Such committees may recommend the adoption of anything within their order of reference, notwithstanding that their recommendations may involve the expenditure of money. See the Report of the Select Committee on Dockyards, of July 15, 1864.

Parliament, except at the application of the crown. In order to admit of the proposed grant without a direct violation of constitutional practice, bills of this description invariably contain a clause to the effect that the necessary expenses to be incurred thereby should be 'defrayed out of moneys to be hereafter voted by Parliament.' The facilities attending the introduction of such bills has frequently induced the government themselves to take advantage of this mode of obtaining the sanction of Parliament to their legislative measures. Moreover, under certain circumstances, and with a view to facilitate the progress of public business, bills of this class have even been permitted to originate in the House of Lords.[t] It is of course obvious that the introduction of such bills on the part of the crown is not open to the same objections as when they are brought in by private members; nevertheless, even in the case of government bills, it is most desirable that such measures should be subjected to careful scrutiny, and that the probable expense they would entail should be duly estimated, and made known to the House by a responsible minister, before it is called upon to sanction them.[u]

But where such bills have originated with private members, they have, as a general rule, been productive of great abuse, by encouraging injudicious and extravagant expenditure. If the principle of the bill obtains the sanction of Parliament, the faith of Parliament becomes pledged to the outlay involved, and ministers are obliged

Have been productive of great abuse.

---

[t] Provided that any clauses which infringe upon the privileges of the Commons are formally struck out of the bill before it is sent to that House. But for the sake of convenience, and to make the measure intelligible, such clauses may be either written, or printed in red ink, in the copy of the bill which is sent down from the Lords; in which case they are understood not to form part of the bill, but to be merely suggestions, to be offered for the acceptance of the Commons in committee. See May, Parl. Prac. p. 500. And see the proceedings on the Divorce Court Bill, on August 20 and 23, 1860. Han. Deb. vol. clx. pp. 1628, 1744, 1765.

[u] See, in regard to the Kensington Road Hill, Smith, Parl. Rememb. 1862, p. 25. See the debate in the Commons, on the Public Offices (Site and Approaches) Bill, on March 7, 1865.

to include, in future estimates, distinct provision for the same; and when the particular grant that is required to carry out any such measure is brought forward in Committee of Supply, any objection to its principle is commonly met by the assertion that it is useless, if not unfair, to oppose it at this stage, inasmuch as Parliament has already agreed that the proposed expenditure ought to be incurred. So long as private members are permitted to initiate measures which involve the expenditure of public money without the previous consent of the crown, it would be in vain to expect an economical administration of the public funds. These considerations were brought under the notice of the House of Commons by a private member (Mr. Ayrton) on May 16, 1862, when, after a short debate upon the subject, the Chancellor of the Exchequer promised that it should receive the attention of government, and that hereafter a committee should be appointed to review the whole question, and to recommend rules to remedy the evils arising from this objectionable practice.' No such committee having been proposed, the subject was again brought up, by Mr. Ayrton, on March 20, 1866. After adverting to the consequences which had arisen from the introduction of this novel and unconstitutional practice, he proposed—in the interest of economy, and in order that 'the whole responsibility of increasing the public expenditure should be thrown upon her Majesty's ministers'—that 'The standing order of June 25, 1852, relating to applications for public money, be repealed, and, in lieu thereof, that this House will receive no petition for any sum relating to

New standing orders to require the previous consent of the crown to such bills or motions.

' Hans. Deb. vol. clxvi. pp. 1831-1848. The attention of the House was again directed to the injurious consequences of this practice in a speech of the Chancellor of the Exchequer, on May 22, 1865, in regard to a proposition emanating from a private member, to transfer an annual expenditure of upwards of two millions on behalf of the poor, from local to public revenues, and to provide that this enormous amount should be thenceforth defrayed 'out of moneys provided by Parliament,' instead of being chargeable upon parochial poor rates. *Ibid.* vol. clxxix. pp. 685-690. See also Mr. Gladstone's speech on Feb. 20, 1866, *Ibid.* vol. clxxxi. p. 1132.

public service, or proceed upon any motion for a grant or charge upon the public revenue, whether payable out of the Consolidated Fund, *or out of moneys to be provided by Parliament,* unless recommended from the crown;' and that the further standing order of the same date, relating to public aids or charges upon the people, be repealed, and that, in lieu thereof, it be resolved—'That if any motion be made in the House for any aid, grant, or charge upon the public revenue, whether payable out of the Consolidated Fund, or out of moneys to be provided by Parliament, or for any charge upon the people, the consideration and debate thereof shall not be presently entered upon, but shall be adjourned till such further day as the House shall think fit to appoint; and then it shall be referred to a committee of the whole House, before any resolution or vote of the House do pass therein.' The proposed new orders were thankfully accepted by the Chancellor of the Exchequer, on the part of government, approved of by experienced members generally, and agreed to by the House."

And here it may be noticed, that the practice of the House of Lords, in these particulars, is less stringent than that of the House of Commons. There is no rule or usage of the House of Lords to forbid the presentation and discussion of a petition for pecuniary redress or compensation, provided it be couched in general terms." And although the House of Lords have no right to initiate measures of taxation, or propositions for increasing the pecuniary burdens of the people, yet they are not constitutionally debarred from instituting inquiries, by their own committees, into financial matters, or into questions which involve the expenditure of public money." The consent of the Lords is indispensable to every legislative

Practice of House of Lords less stringent.

" Hans. Deb. vol. clxxxii. pp. 601–603.
" *Ibid.* vol. clxxiii. p. 1022; vol. clxxiv. p. 602.
" See May's Parl. Prac. p. 511. Lords Committees were appointed in 1858, on spiritual destitution in populous places; and in 1860, on the levying and assessment of church rates.

measure, whether of supply or otherwise, and it is desirable that they should be prepared, by full investigation and free inquiry, to give or withhold their assent intelligently."

Precedents

Thus, in 1852, the House of Lords appointed a select committee to inquire into the claims of Baron de Bode for pecuniary relief, in respect to a certain claim against the government; and in the following year Lord Lyndhurst moved a resolution, based upon the report of this committee, 'earnestly recommending this claim to the favourable consideration of the government.' The motion was negatived on its own merits, but its regularity was not disputed.' In 1860, a Lords Committee upon Floating Breakwaters, &c. recommended 'that a sum not exceeding 10,000l. be placed at the disposal of the Admiralty,' to enable that department to test any plans for the suitable construction of such works.* On July 5, 1861, Lord Shaftesbury moved an address to the queen, in favour of the extension, throughout India, of the best systems of irrigation and internal navigation. The previous question was proposed on this motion, on the ground that the government were themselves prepared to carry out the principle advocated, as fully as possible, but would consider 'the adoption of such an abstract resolution to be inconvenient.'*

Wise restraint imposed by House of Commons upon themselves.

The House of Commons, in forbidding, by their standing orders and uniform practice interpreting the same, the reception of petitions for pecuniary aid, and the presentation of reports from select committees recommending the expenditure of public money, have voluntarily assumed a restraint which goes beyond the positive obligation of the constitutional rule that requires all grants of money by Parliament to be made only upon the application of the crown. Nevertheless, they have wisely imposed upon themselves this restriction, in order to guard against importunate demands from without, and as a check upon the too easy liberality of their own members. The re-

---

* See further on this subject, *post*, p. 457, where the relative position of the two Houses, in regard to questions of supply and taxation, is discussed.

' Hans. Deb. vol. cxxix. p. 1007.

* See *Ibid.* vol. clxvii. p. 232.

* *Ibid.* vol. clxiv. pp. 394, 401. And see a discussion in the House of Lords, on June 30, 1865, upon a peer calling attention to the claims of naval captains on the reserved pay-list under certain orders in council. *Ibid.* vol. clxxx. p. 675.

sponsibility of recommending applications for pecuniary redress or relief to the consideration of Parliament should rest solely upon the executive government, who are strictly accountable for every item of public expenditure, and who possess peculiar facilities for investigating into the merits of all pecuniary claims. It is, moreover, a waste of time to encourage premature debates in Parliament upon questions involving a grant of money, whether for public or private purposes, before the attention of government has been directed to the merits of the application.

Should any case arise wherein it may appear to be the duty of the House to point out to the government public charges which ought to be incurred, they have still undoubted authority to do so, either by the adoption of a resolution,[b] expressing an abstract opinion in favour of a proceeding which will necessitate a future grant of money, or by agreeing to address the crown to incur certain expenditure, with an assurance of their readiness to make good the same,—the House is free to approach the crown with their constitutional advice in this, as in any other matter of prerogative. This method of procedure does not finally bind the House to make the grant, and it throws upon the government the responsibility of either accepting or rejecting the recommendation. But this is a right which the House exercises, and should exercise, with very great reserve, and only under peculiar and exceptional circumstances.[c] The adoption of an abstract resolution, however, for the express purpose of evading a wholesome rule in matters affecting the public expenditure, should be discouraged as much as possible.[d]

Resolution or address of the House in favour of a particular expenditure.

Addresses from the House of Commons to the crown, requesting an issue of public money for some particular purpose, with the assurance 'that this House will make good the same,' are perfectly regular, and agreeable to

---

[b] See cases cited in May, Parl. Prac. ed. 1863, p. 648. a.
[c] Mr Gladstone's speech on Mr. Ayrton's motion, March 20, 1860.
[d] May, Parl. Prac. p. 648. And see ante, p. 262.

precedent. But such addresses are only justifiable when there is no reason to apprehend that the supposed advance would be disapproved of by the other House of Parliament, whose concurrence is necessary to give legal effect to any measure of supply or appropriation. Such addresses have generally been adopted upon occasions of urgency which have arisen after the committee of supply has closed its sittings—as, in order to submit to the crown a proposal to confer a pecuniary benefit on a particular person; or to show respect to the memory of some illustrious person lately deceased, by the erection of a monument to his honour; or for the purpose of obtaining the co-operation of the crown in a matter affecting the privileges of the House.* But it is always presumed that the proposed advance would meet the approval of the Lords, when afterwards included in the bill of supply.

When an address is objectionable.

This mode of obtaining the issue of money has been improperly resorted to, for the express purpose of escaping the necessity for appealing to the House of Lords for their concurrence; and also in order to compel the government, contrary to their own judgment, to incur expenditure at the mere request of the House of Commons. In any such cases it is the duty of the ministry to interpose, and, by asserting the prerogative of the crown, to protect the privileges of the House of Lords from violation, and the public revenue from an unwarrantable outlay.'

If a proposition be submitted to the House of Commons,

---

* See 3 Hats. 178–180. n. May's Parl. Prac. ed. 1863, p. 578.

' After the battle of Navarino, a private member succeeded in inducing the House of Commons, notwithstanding the opposition of the government, to pass an address to the king, that he would graciously consider the claims of the officers and men who fought in this engagement to head-money. These claims had been investigated by the government, and rejected on grounds of public policy; but after the adoption of this address, by a nearly unanimous vote, the government agreed to propose a grant for this purpose in Committee of Supply; reiterating, however, their conviction of its inexpediency. (Mirror of Parl. 1834, pp. 2258, 2644, 2458.) See also the case of the Chinese prize-money in 1845, but which was successfully resisted by the government. Hans. Deb. vol. lxxxii. p. 681.

on behalf of the crown, for a supply for a particular ser- *Opinion of the Commons in favour of a larger grant than that recommended by the crown.* vice, and an opinion should be generally expressed by the House in favour of a more liberal appropriation on this behalf, than that which has been asked for by the government, while it is confessedly beyond the power of the House to vote a larger sum of its own accord, the ministry, in deference to the opinion of members, will sometimes agree to submit a motion for the increased amount suggested;[a] or will undertake to reconsider the matter, and to apply to Parliament for a further grant, at a future period, should it appear expedient so to do.[b]

And in order to elicit an expression of parliamentary *Formal motions to take the sense of Parliament.* opinion upon some doubtful question involving pecuniary outlay, or to justify their own decision on some application for pecuniary aid, the ministry will occasionally communicate the formal consent of the crown to the discussion, by the House, of a motion concerning the same, without contemplating any further proceedings in the case. Or, a desultory debate may be permitted to take place, in either House of Parliament, upon a question of this kind, without any formal motion. Or, a motion may be proposed, to express in general terms the opinion of the House upon the merits of the case, without directly asserting that any grant of money is required.[c] By such

---

[a] As in the case of the proposed grant for the purchase of an annuity for the Duke of Wellington. The government recommended a vote of 300,000l., but, in deference to the wishes of the House, they consented to ask for 400,000l. for this purpose. (Hans. Deb. vol. xxvii. p. 871.) See also the case of Sir Henry Havelock, *Ibid.* vol. cli. p. 2456. But no grant recommended, salary proposed, or item in the estimates can be increased, except upon the recommendation of the crown. (*Ibid.* vol. cxliii. p. 700. And see May, Parl. Prac. p. 529.) It may be reduced in Committee of Supply, or by the House itself, as in the case of Prince Albert's annuity. Mirror of Parl. 1840, pp. 304, 380, 440.

[b] In 1832, the government proposed, in supply, a vote of 10,000l. for the relief of the distressed Poles. An opinion in favour of a larger amount was unanimously expressed by the committee, but it was admitted that constitutional usage forbade a motion to that effect being made, except by the ministry. The Chancellor of the Exchequer at first defended the smaller sum, but finally agreed to re-consider the question. (Mirror of Parl. 1838, p. 5875.) Accordingly, the estimates next year included an additional sum of 15,000l. for this service.

[c] See the case of Sir A. B. King, in Mirror of Parl. 1831, pp. 223, 440, 477. While on this occasion the

THE ROYAL PREROGATIVE.

a course, the constitutional oversight of Parliament in all pecuniary transactions of the government may be exercised, consistently with a due regard for the prerogative of the crown.

Precedents

The following precedents may serve to illustrate this branch of our inquiry.

Mr. Palmer.

The first case that will claim our notice is that of Mr. Palmer, which engaged the attention of Parliament for a number of years.

This gentleman, originally the manager of a country theatre, conceived a plan for the improvement of postal communication throughout the kingdom, which, being communicated to Mr. Pitt, he appointed him Comptroller-General of the Post-Office, with full power to carry out his proposed reforms. These were so successful that in a few years the postal system was greatly benefited, and the revenues from the same largely increased. It was at first agreed to reward Mr. Palmer by a grant for life of two and a-half per cent. on a certain proportion of the increased net revenue, which would eventually have given him some 10,000l. per annum. But, after a time, Mr. Palmer's conduct in office became insubordinate and objectionable, and the government were obliged to dismiss him. In so doing, they cancelled the agreement under which the percentage on the increased postal revenues had been awarded to him, and gave him, in lieu thereof, a pension of 3,000l. a-year. Not satisfied with this amount, and claiming the continuance for his lifetime of the per-centage in question, he appealed to the House of Commons, by petition, in the year 1807. Government allowed the king's recommendation to the petition to be signified, for the purpose of obtaining an inquiry into the case by a committee of the House. A favourable report thereon was made, on July 13, but nothing further was done until the next session, when, by permission of the government (who continued, however, to oppose the claim), a bill was introduced into the House of Commons to secure to Mr. Palmer his *future* per-centage on the net increased postal revenues. The bill was passed, notwithstanding the opposition of the govern-

---

ministry successfully opposed a motion in favour of compensation to Sir A. D. King for the loss of an office, it appears by the estimates in the following year, that they ultimately consented to his indemnification, by recommending an annual grant of 2,500l. for this purpose, which he received for several years. (Index, Com. Journ. 1820-1837, p. 1067.) See the case of the lessees of Mr. Speaker Manners Sutton by the burning of the Houses of Parliament in 1837; Mirror of Parl. 1837-8, p. 402; the case of Fourdrinier's patent, *Ibid.* 1839, p. 2007; the case of the Distressed Letter Carriers, Hans. Deb. vol. cxxiv. p. 841; and the motion for a committee to inquire into the claims of J. Clare for compensation for an invention, Hans. Deb. vol. clxxiv. p. 1400.

ment, but was rejected in the House of Lords.ʲ Meanwhile, a *Precedents*
supply resolution, granting a certain sum to defray *arrears* of per-
centage claimed by Mr. Palmer, was reported, agreed to, and a bill
ordered thereupon. But as the Lords had thrown out the prospective bill in favour of Mr. Palmer, it was proposed by the Chancellor
of the Exchequer, and agreed to by the House, that the grant of
arrears should not be included in the General Appropriation Act,
but in a separate bill, 'for the avowed purpose of affording to the
Lords an opportunity of considering that grant distinctly from the
other grants of the year.'ᵏ The bill was not proceeded with in that
session, but Mr. Palmer's friends determined to persevere, and on
May 21, 1811, they induced the House of Commons to pass an
address to the prince regent, beseeching him to advance the sum of
54,000l. to Mr. Palmer, 'being the amount of arrears due to him
out of the Post Office revenues, and assuring his royal highness
that the House will make good the same.' The House of Lords
greatly resented this address, and a warm debate took place therein
on the subject on the following day, but no proceedings were had.
Two days after, the premier assured the House of Lords that he
should not recommend his royal highness to sanction a claim which
their lordships considered to be unfounded.ˡ Accordingly, the
reply of the prince regent, as sent down to the House of Commons,
stated, That it must at all times be the prince regent's desire to
attend to the wishes of the House of Commons, ' and that he shall
be ready to give effect to them in this instance whenever the means
shall have been provided by Parliament;' in other words, by a
legislative act, which should have received the concurrence of both
Houses.ᵐ An attempt was made to induce the House to agree to a
motion that this answer tended to create a misunderstanding between the crown and the Commons, but it was negatived by a large
majority. The opposers of the motion allowed the existence of the
right of addressing the crown for money, but justified the answer in
this instance, because the regent must have known that what the
Commons had resolved to be due as of right, had been denied to be
due by the Lords, after an inquiry into the facts of the case.ⁿ In
the following session, with the formal consent of the crown, a
further attempt was made to indemnify Mr. Palmer. A bill was
passed by the House of Commons for securing to him his future
per-centage, and for granting nearly 80,000l. as arrears due. The
government, as heretofore, continued to oppose the measure, and it
was rejected, upon the third reading, in the Lords. Next session a

ʲ See Parl. Deb. vol. xl. pp. 101–
252, 950–973. Encyc. Brit. xviii. 407.
ᵏ 3 Hats. 203. n. Parl. Deb. xl.
pp. 1010–1042.

ˡ *Ibid.* vol. xx. p. 290.
ᵐ See *Ibid.* pp. 347, 350.
ⁿ *Ibid.* pp. 343–365.

Precedents

similar bill was passed by the Commons, and rejected by the Lords. Finally, and in the same session, the matter was compromised by the introduction of another bill, granting the sum of 50,000*l.* to Mr. Palmer, 'in consideration of public services performed by him,' to which bill the Lords agreed, and it received the royal assent.[a]

Baron de Bode

Our next case will be that of the Baron de Bode, whose claims for pecuniary indemnification have been urged for upwards of forty years upon successive administrations, and still remain unsettled. The baron alleged that he was born a British subject, and originally possessed a large property in France, but which had been confiscated by the government of that country during the Revolution. After the peace a treaty was made between France and Great Britain, under which a large sum of money was paid over to the British government for the purpose of indemnifying British subjects whose property had been confiscated by the French authorities at that period. Under this treaty the baron (and subsequently his son and heir) made various applications to the government, to the legal tribunals, and to both Houses of Parliament for payment of his claim, which had been pronounced invalid. In 1834, a committee of inquiry into the same was appointed by the House of Commons, notwithstanding the opposition of the ministry. Being unable to complete the investigation in that year, a motion was made in the following session for the re-appointment of the committee. The motion was again opposed by the ministry, who declared it to be an attempt to convert the House into a Court of Appeal, and was negatived.[b] In 1852, Lord Lyndhurst induced the House of Lords to appoint a committee of inquiry into the claims of the baron, as set forth by him in a petition to that House, and which reported in favour of the same.[c] Whereupon, on August 1, 1853, his lordship moved a resolution, based upon the report of the committee, 'earnestly recommending the petitioner's claim to the favourable consideration of her Majesty's government;' but after a long debate, the motion was negatived on the ground that it had already been decided by competent tribunals, and ought to be regarded as conclusively disposed of.[d] On June 20, 1854, a resolution was proposed in the House of Commons, 'that the national good faith requires that the just claims of the Baron de Bode, established after protracted investigations, should be satisfied.' The government, however, continued to deny the justice of the claim, and the motion was rejected.[e] At

---

[a] General Index, Commons Journ. 1801–1820, p. 700.
[b] Mirror of Parl. 1834, p. 1438; 1835, p. 1002. In 1845 the case was argued before the Court of Queen's Bench, upon a petition of right, and decided against the baron. See Q. B. Rpts. viii. 208.
[c] Hans. Deb. vol. cxxii. p. 478.
[d] *Ibid.* vol. cxxix. p. 1007.
[e] *Ibid.* vol. cxxxiv. pp. 392–425.

RESTRICTIONS UPON PARLIAMENT AS TO SUPPLY. 441

length on June 4, 1801, on a further petition from the baron, the **Precedents** House of Commons was again moved to appoint a committee to consider and report on this case; but the Attorney-General re-argued the question, and declared that the petitioner was not in reality a British subject, and therefore had no claim upon the fund above mentioned. The Chancellor of the Exchequer urged that it would be cruel to the petitioner himself to do anything to keep alive his claim, and desired to know, if the committee reported favourably thereon, how such a report 'could justify the executive government in acting against an opinion of all the law advisers of the crown for the last thirty years?' But notwithstanding the opposition of government the committee was appointed.¹ The committee took voluminous evidence, but were unable to conclude their inquiry; they therefore, on August 1, reported to the House their proceedings and the evidence they had taken.² Since then, nothing more has been done in Parliament in this case.

Our next leading precedent is that which arose out of the much-litigated Danish claims. During the war with France in 1807, **Danish claims.** Great Britain, having reason to suspect that Denmark, although nominally a neutral power, was secretly favouring the designs of the French ruler, suddenly captured the Danish fleet while it was lying in the harbour of Copenhagen. By way of reprisal, the Danish government seized and confiscated the property of the British merchants who were trading in the Baltic sea. As Great Britain was not actually at war with Denmark at this time, it was contended that she should be answerable for the consequences of her act of aggression towards that kingdom, and should compensate the British merchants for their losses by the act of reprisal. This was acknowledged, and a large portion of these claims was paid by the government. But others, to a considerable amount, remained unliquidated. Accordingly, the merchants who conceived themselves aggrieved by the non-recognition of their claims, petitioned the House of Commons for indemnification. Whereupon, on May 24, 1838, an address to the crown was moved for an inquiry into the rest of these claims, with a view to their being satisfied. The government opposed the motion, on the ground that all the debts which by the law of nations were justly due had been paid by Great Britain, and that the remainder of the claims were untenable. Nevertheless, the motion for the address was carried.³ After the vote had been taken, the Chancellor of the Exchequer declared that his opinion on the matter remained unaltered, and that 'considering the serious consequences which may be produced by such a vote, he begged to say that he undertook no further responsibility on the

¹ Hans. Deb. vol. clxiii. pp. 571–607.
² Com. Papers, 1801, vol. xi. p. 515.
³ Mirror of Parl. 1838, p. 4247.

Precedents question.'" The government, however, upon further consideration, agreed to pay a portion of the remaining claims." This being deemed insufficient, in the following session a similar address was moved and carried, against the government.' Whereupon the government consented to pay an additional number of the claims.' The claimants being still unsatisfied, a third address was passed on June 10, 1841, for the liquidation of the remainder, assuring her Majesty that the House would make good the same.' Upon this the government took a stand, and declared that they would not consent to any further expenditure on this account. The Chancellor of the Exchequer stated that the crown had no fund out of which a further payment could be made, and that it was therefore no use for the House to ask it to do so. Accordingly, on June 21, the following reply to the address was reported: That it must at all times be the most earnest desire of her Majesty to attend to the wishes of the House of Commons, and that she shall be ready to give effect to them in this instance, whenever the means shall have been provided *by Parliament*. No action was taken by the House upon this answer. But similar addresses were again proposed and negatived by the House on June 20, 1843, July 9, 1844, and June 26, 1851; after which no further application to Parliament on behalf of the Danish claimants was made until July 12, 1861, when the attention of the House of Commons was again called to the subject by a member, who recapitulated the arguments in favour of the claimants, but contented himself with laying the matter before the House without making any motion. The Attorney-General and the Chancellor of the Exchequer resisted any renewed agitation of the question, the latter asserting that whereas the Constitution required the concurrence of the executive government and of the House of Commons, in any money appropriation, governments of various politics had repeatedly denied the justice of these claims, and for the last fifteen years the House of Commons, though often appealed to, had equally repudiated the demand, it would be therefore wrong to give further encouragement to their discussion in Parliament. The subject was then dropped, and has not since been renewed.

Duke of Sussex.
On July 6, 1838, Mr. Gillon moved an address to the crown to consider the parliamentary grant of an annuity to H.R.H. the Duke of Sussex, 'with a view to recommend to the House some addition thereto.' The Home Secretary (Lord John Russell) resisted the motion on the ground that the matter was properly cognizable by the government, whose duty it was to advise an increase of the allowance if necessary, but who had not thought fit to do so. Sir

---

" Mirror of Parl. 1838, p. 4235.
' Ibid. p. 5883.
' Ibid. 1839, pp. 3051-3056.
' See Ibid. pp. 4083, 4710; and 1841, p. 2250.
' Ibid. 1841, p. 2240.

R. Peel agreed in this doctrine, and asserted that the interference of the House would be 'an exceedingly dangerous precedent.' Accordingly the motion was negatived on division.[b]

Precedents

On June 30, 1840, Sir R. H. Inglis moved for a committee to consider of an address to the crown, declaring the readiness of the House to make a grant to supply the deficient church accommodation throughout the kingdom; and on June 16, 1842, Mr. Ferrand moved for an address for the advance of one million pounds to relieve the distress prevailing in the manufacturing districts: both these motions, notwithstanding the opposition of government, were debated, but they were each negatived on division.

Church accommodation in England.

On February 4, 1847, Lord George Bentinck moved for leave to bring in a bill to raise a loan of sixteen million pounds, to encourage the construction of railroads in Ireland, and to give prompt employment to the suffering poor in that country. Lord John Russell (the prime minister) opposed the bill, but did not object to its introduction, understanding from the Speaker that, 'in point of form, no objection existed thereto provided it did not include those money clauses which would require a previous committee.'[c] It was afterwards stated, on the part of government, that the prerogative of the crown should not be made use of in any way 'to interfere with the full discussion of the measure.'[d] Accordingly the bill proceeded to a second reading, when, on the motion of the Chancellor of the Exchequer, it was postponed 'for six months.'[e]

Railroads in Ireland.

On July 22, 1862, the case of Captain Grant, who had rendered great benefits to the army by the introduction of an improved system of cooking, in barrack and in camp, was brought before the House of Commons on a motion that his services were 'entitled to recognition.' This was considered by the government, and was in fact intended, to be equivalent to a recommendation for a grant of money to this officer; but the motion had been drawn up in these vague terms in order to admit of its being discussed without an infringement of the standing orders. The Secretary of State for War objected to the motion as being an evasion of the standing orders, and also on its own merits, contending that the services of Captain Grant were not of a nature to justify a compensation from the public purse. On division, the motion was negatived, but only by a majority of one. A few days afterwards the Secretary for War informed the House that, 'in consequence of the opinion expressed by a nearly equal division, the subject should be further investigated by the government.'[f] Being dissatisfied with the amount proposed to be given by the government to Captain Grant, a motion

Captain Grant.

---

[b] Mirror of Parl. 1838, p. 5400.
[c] Hans. Deb. vol. lxxxix. p. 608.
[d] Ibid. p. 657.
[e] Ibid. vol. xc. p. 123.
[f] Ibid. vol. clxviii. p. 855.

Precedents   was made in the House of Commons on May 20, 1864, for an address to her Majesty to render him 'some suitable reward for his services;' but, after explanations from the Under Secretary for War, the motion was negatived on division.[a]

Yeomanry Cavalry.   In 1864, the government having determined from motives of economy to refrain from submitting to Parliament the usual vote (of about 40,000*l*.) to defray the cost of assembling the Yeomanry Cavalry for the accustomed period of six days' training on permanent duty, an amendment was moved on March 8 to the motion that the Speaker do leave the chair for the House to go into Committee of Supply on the army estimates, to resolve that the discontinuance of the drill would be detrimental to the efficiency of the force, inexpedient, and contrary to the recommendations of a departmental committee in 1861. The government opposed the motion, and contended that the efficiency of the force would be in no wise impaired by the temporary suspension of active training. On a division, the amendment was negatived by a majority of one. On May 5 following, the Under Secretary for War submitted to the Committee of Supply a vote of 39,200*l*. for the training of the Yeomanry, alleging that since the aforesaid division the unexpected advices from New Zealand had enabled the government to effect a saving in the estimate on account of the war in that island, and they were therefore in a position to continue the usual grant on behalf of the Yeomanry Cavalry. On division, the vote was agreed to by a large majority.[b]

I. b. *The Restrictions upon Parliament in matters of Taxation.*

Propositions concerning taxes should emanate from ministers.   As a proposed grant of money cannot be increased, nor a new grant made, except upon the recommendation of the crown, in like manner any proposition for the levy of a new tax or duty—or even for the repeal of an existing impost—should emanate from the government.[c]

On March 25, 1830, Mr. Poulett Thomson moved for the appointment of a committee to consider of revising and re-arranging the general system of taxation. The motion was strenuously and successfully opposed by Mr. Secretary Peel, as being an unprecedented attempt to deprive the ministers of the crown of one of their most important and peculiar functions. He remarked that pro-

---
[a] Hans. Deb. vol. clxxv. p. 523.
[b] *Ibid.* p. 45.
[c] Hans. Deb. vol. clxxxii. p. 502. See the debates on motions for the repeal of the taxes on knowledge, in the House of Commons, on June 14, 1832, and April 14, 1853.

posals for the imposition of taxes belonged peculiarly to the crown; custom and sound policy having long ago devolved upon ministers the duty of submitting such questions to the consideration of Parliament.ʲ So, also, a motion on March 14, 1844, by a private member for a committee to consider of imposing a certain probate duty on real estate, was objected to by the Speaker and by Sir Robert Peel (the prime minister), on the ground that it ought not to be offered, except in Committee of Ways and Means, nor unless it could be shown that the public exigencies required it. After some debate the motion was withdrawn.ᵏ

While the strict right of a private member to introduce a bill or resolution for the modification or repeal of an existing tax cannot be denied, and has been acknowledged of late years by leading statesmen,ˡ it is nevertheless in the highest degree inexpedient for private members to take the initiative in proposing such questions to Parliament. It is an important financial principle, that 'the House should not be called upon to condemn taxes which they are not prepared on the instant to repeal,'ᵐ as by so doing they unsettle the minds of commercial men in their business transactions, and occasion embarrassment to the government in their plans for the regulation of the public finances. Abstract resolutions in regard to particular branches of taxation have been not infrequently submitted to the House of Commons by private members, but they have been uniformly resisted by the government as being inexpedient and impolitic. *Inexpedient for private members to introduce such questions.*

Abstract resolutions on particular taxes.

The following examples may be referred to, as having an important bearing on this branch of our inquiry. *Precedents*

First, in regard to the question of the Income Tax. The attention of the House has been frequently invited to the consideration of this question, by private members, who from time to time have propounded various schemes to relieve certain classes of the community from the unequal operation of this impost. On May 2, 1851, Mr. *Income Tax.*

ʲ Mirror of Parl. 1830, p. 1032. See also similar motions, proposed and negatived, on March 20, 1843; on August 7, 1848; on May 10, 1849; and on May 10, 1864.

ᵏ Hans. Deb. vol. lxxlii. p. 1052.

ˡ By Mr. Disraeli, in Hans. Deb. vol. cxxv. p. 1174. By Mr. Gladstone, *Ibid.* vol. clxi. p. 1047.

ᵐ Mr. Gladstone, *Ibid.* vol. cxxv. p. 1140; vol. clxxiii. p. 1482.

Precedents Hume induced the House to agree to an amendment to a government bill for continuing the Property Tax for three years, whereby its operation was limited to one year, with an express view to an inquiry into the mode of assessing and collecting the Income Tax. Such a committee was formally appointed on May 8, with authority to consider whether a more equitable mode of levying this tax could be devised. Both the premier (Lord John Russell) and Mr. Disraeli expressed their disapprobation of this committee as an unwise interference with the functions of government; but, nevertheless, consented to its appointment, in order to carry out the previous determination of the House.[a] The committee encountered great difficulties in the investigation of this question, and, after devoting two years to the subject, confined themselves to reporting the evidence they had taken to the House, without expressing any opinion thereupon.[b] On February 19, 1861, on the motion of Mr. Hubbard, a select committee was again appointed, to consider of some more equitable mode of levying the Income and Property Tax. The motion was opposed by the Chancellor of the Exchequer (Mr. Gladstone), and by Sir Stafford Northcote, an eminent leader of the Opposition, but was carried by a majority of four. After full inquiry, the committee reported to the effect, that the objections to this tax were rather to its essence and nature than to its incidence; and that it would be unjust to reconstruct its mode of operation without at the same time revising other parts of our fiscal system.[c] Notwithstanding the adverse report of this committee, Mr. Hubbard, on May 13, 1862, submitted to the House a resolution in favour of a re-adjustment of the Income Tax, in respect to certain alleged abuses. The motion was opposed by the Chancellor of the Exchequer, and negatived by a large majority. Nothing daunted by this defeat, Mr. Hubbard renewed his attack in the following session, by moving, on March 24, 1863, a similar resolution for the re-adjustment of this impost. The motion was again opposed by the Chancellor of the Exchequer, who characterised Mr. Hubbard's scheme as being visionary and impracticable, and as affording no adequate remedy for the admitted irregularities of the Income Tax. Without any further debate, the motion was then put and negatived.[d] On April 23 following, Mr. Roebuck moved to resolve that on a

---

[a] Hans. Deb. vol. cxvi. pp. 720-732.

[b] Commons Papers, 1851, vol. x. p. 330; 1852, vol. ix. pp. 1, 461. See also Poto on Taxation, p. 90.

[c] Commons Papers, 1861, vol. vii. p. 4.

[d] Hans. Deb. vol. clxix. p. 1848. On June 14, 1864, Mr. Hubbard again moved a resolution, condemnatory of the inequalities and injustice attending the operation of the existing property and income tax; but it was negatived on division. See Mr. Hubbard's observations on this tax, on May 4, 1865. Ibid. vol. clxxviii. p. 1501.

renewal of this tax, a lower charge should be imposed on precarious incomes than on permanent incomes. The motion was opposed by the Chancellor of the Exchequer, and, after a short debate, was withdrawn. *Precedents*

In 1850, and again in 1851 and in 1853, Lord R. Grosvenor brought in a bill to abolish the annual duty payable on Attorneys', &c. Certificates. The principle of this bill was affirmed by the House, on division; but the government succeeded in delaying its passage. On May 19, 1865, on motion of Mr. Denman, an abstract resolution in favour of the abolition of this duty was agreed to by the House, notwithstanding the 'stout resistance of the government,' both on the ground of principle and expediency.[a] *Duty on Certificates.*

On April 14, 1853, Mr. Milner Gibson moved the House of Commons to declare that the Advertisement Duty ought to be repealed. The Government opposed the motion, but it was agreed to on division.[b] Nevertheless, the Chancellor of the Exchequer refused to give way. Some days afterwards the House went into Committee of Ways and Means, when the Chancellor of the Exchequer proposed to fix the rate of this duty at sixpence. The opponents of the duty again succeeded: the proposed rate was struck out, and no other amount inserted in the resolution.[c]. After this, the government acquiesced in the abolition of the duty.[d] *Advertisement Duty.*

On the same occasion (April 14, 1853), and as a part of his scheme for the abolition of taxes on knowledge, Mr. Milner Gibson moved a resolution condemning the continuance of the Paper Duty as a permanent source of revenue, as being impolitic and inconsistent with the efforts of Parliament for the encouragement of education. The previous question was proposed on this resolution, and negatived. On June 21, 1858, Mr. Gibson again brought forward the question, upon a motion 'That this House is of opinion that the maintenance of the excise on paper, as a permanent source of revenue, would be impolitic; and that such financial arrangements ought to be made as will enable Parliament to dispense with that tax.' The Chancellor of the Exchequer (Mr. Disraeli) stated his readiness to agree to the repeal of this tax when a favourable opportunity should arise, but he strongly objected to the latter part of the motion, as being a 'highly impolitic and inexpedient' endeavour to hamper the government by an abstract resolution concerning a tax, at a time when it would be impossible to act upon it. He suggested the withdrawal of the latter part of the motion, from the word 'impolitic,' which was also advised by Lord John Russell and other leading members, on the same ground. This *Paper Duty.*

---

[a] Hans. Deb. vol. clxx. pp. 614–625.
[b] Ibid. vol. clxxix. pp. 551–577.
[c] Ibid. vol. cxxv. p. 1187.
[d] Ibid. vol. cxxviii. p. 1128.
[e] Ibid. vol. clii. p. 1008.

440   THE ROYAL PREROGATIVE.

Precedents being consented to by Mr. Gibson, the former part of the motion, condemning the permanent continuance of the paper duties, was agreed to without a division.* In 1860, Mr. Gladstone (the then Chancellor of the Exchequer) included the abolition of the paper duty in his financial measures for the year, and a bill for that purpose passed the House of Commons, but was rejected by the Lords." Next session a similar proposition was inserted in a bill respecting customs and inland revenue, which passed both Houses, and became law.

Hop Duty. On March 5, 1861, Mr. Dodson moved to resolve 'that the maintenance of any duties upon Hops is impolitic; and that in any remission of taxation or adjustment of financial burdens, provision should be made for the removal of such duties.' The Chancellor of the Exchequer (Mr. Gladstone) asked no one to give an opinion on the merits of this duty, but objected to the motion on the ground that it was an abstract resolution relating to the matter of finance. Without denying the right of the House, under any circumstances, to pass such a resolution, he characterised the same as being a rash innovation on the practice of the House in former times. He held up the paper duty resolution as an example which ought to be a warning to the House not to commit itself to a similar proceeding, but to await the proper time when the financial condition of the country could be considered as a whole in connection with the fiscal propositions to be submitted to it by the government. Acquiescing in these views, the House negatived the motion by a large majority." The budget laid before the House by the Chancellor of the Exchequer in the following session contained a proposal for the repeal of the hop duties, so that the sentiments entertained by the House on this question ultimately prevailed.

Fire Insurance Duty. On May 4, 1860, and again on March 8, 1861, Mr. H. B. Sheridan moved for leave to bring in a bill to reduce the duty on Fire Insurance. On both occasions the motion was opposed by the ministry, and negatived by the House. In 1860, the motion was made after the budget had been opened by the Chancellor of the Exchequer, and he objected to it because it was ill-timed, as it would effect a considerable loss of revenue that could not be spared, and because, even if its operation should be postponed, no tax ought to be condemned until the House is prepared to reduce or abolish it." In 1861, the Chancellor of the Exchequer objected to the motion on the ground that no proposal should be made to reduce a tax until after the budget had been brought forward, when, if it should appear that

---
* Hans. Deb. vol. cli. pp. 110-135.
" Lords Debates, May 21, 1860. A narrative of this celebrated case will be given in the next section of this chapter, post, p. 450.
' Hans. Deb. vol. clxi. pp. 1448-1457.
" Ibid. vol. clviii. p. 728.

there was a surplus revenue sufficient to justify an abatement of tax- Precedents
ation, the proposed claim for relief could be put into competition
with similar demands, and be fairly considered by the House.[a] On
April 1, 1862, Mr. Sheridan again proposed his bill. This time, as
on the previous occasion, the budget had not been submitted to the
House. The Chancellor of the Exchequer, in opposing the motion,
said that it was 'the duty of every government—a duty always
acted upon—to object to any individual and isolated proposals for the
repeal of taxes before the House had within its view the general
state of the revenue and charges of the country.' 'The popular
principle of government, and the control of it by the House of Commons, depend on nothing so much as this,—that it should narrow
into a single measure the financial operations of the year.' If brought
forward after the introduction of the budget, the same objections to
this motion would not apply. On this point it was also contended
by the premier (Lord Palmerston) that it was a principle of our
constitutional system, that the discretion of proposing to Parliament
the necessary financial arrangements for the year should be left to
the Chancellor of the Exchequer, as the organ of the administration,
and that any objections to be offered, or alterations to be proposed,
should be reserved until after the opening of the budget. Nevertheless the motion for leave to bring in the bill was carried against the
government.[b] Subsequently, on introducing the budget, the Chancellor of the Exchequer briefly explained the impossibility of carrying out the reduction of this tax, stating that there was no surplus
revenue available for the purpose. He added that he was sorry to
reflect that the only security for a Chancellor of the Exchequer lay
in his utter destitution. 'If he does not possess a surplus you cannot take it from him; or, according to an old proverb current in the
northern portion of this kingdom, which I will translate for fear of
offending Scottish ears by a defective accent, "It is difficult to deprive a Highlander of a particular garment which he does not wear."'[c]
Accordingly the bill, though formally presented on April 10, was
not proceeded with, because the mover 'took the vote of the House
to imply rather a recognition of the principle of reduction than the
empowering a private member to interfere with the financial arrangements of the government.'[d] On July 14, 1863, the subject was
again submitted to the House of Commons by Mr. Sheridan, in the
shape of an abstract resolution, recording the opinion of the House
that the duty upon fire insurances is 'excessive in amount, that it
prevents insurance, and should be reduced at the earliest opportunity.' The motion was opposed by Mr. Gladstone on the general

---

[a] Hans. Deb. vol. clxi. p. 1007; and
see vol. clxxii. p. 813.
[b] Ibid. vol. clxvi. pp. 385-500.
[c] Ibid. p. 404.
[d] Ibid. vol. clxxii. p. 700.

Precedents

grounds of constitutional practice previously urged by him, but was nevertheless carried against the government by a majority of thirty-six. On March 15, 1864, Mr. Sheridan declared his intention of again taking the sense of the House in regard to this tax, but would defer so doing until after the budget had been opened. On April 7, in his budget speech, the Chancellor of the Exchequer stated that, 'in deference to the convictions entertained by the House, the government had determined to recommend that the duty on fire insurances should be reduced one-half.'[e] Dissatisfied with this concession, Mr. Sheridan moved to resolve, upon going into Committee of Ways and Means, that a further reduction would be more in accordance with the wishes of the House in agreeing to the foregoing resolution. He was opposed by the Chancellor of the Exchequer; and, upon division, the motion was negatived.[f] On March 21, 1865, Mr. Sheridan again submitted to the House a motion to declare the expediency of reducing this duty to a uniform standard of one shilling and sixpence on all descriptions of insurable property. It was strenuously opposed by the Chancellor of the Exchequer, who moved the previous question; but on division the previous question was carried, and the main question agreed to. On proposing the budget on April 27 following, the Chancellor of the Exchequer announced that, in deference to the unmistakable expression of opinion by the House on this subject, the government had decided to recommend a reduction of this duty to a uniform rate of one shilling and sixpence, from June 25.[a] This concession, however, failed to satisfy Mr. Sheridan and his friends. Accordingly, in the session of 1866, both Mr. Sheridan and Mr. Hubbard gave notice of separate motions regarding this tax. Mr. Hubbard's motion, which was first proposed as an amendment to the motion for the second reading of the Customs and Inland Revenue Bill, was to declare the inexpediency of retaining, as part of the Inland Revenue for the service of the year, the present duties on fire and marine insurances, for certain reasons alleged. After a short debate the amendment was negatived without a division.[b]

Malt Tax.

On June 24, 1864, Mr. Morritt moved, as an amendment upon going into Supply, to resolve that in case of any modification of the indirect taxation of this country, the Excise on Malt requires consideration. The motion was opposed by the Chancellor of the Exchequer upon similar grounds of objection to those made use of in regard to former motions of this description, and was negatived on division. On March 7, 1865, a similar resolution was proposed by Sir Fitzroy Kelly. After an amendment had been proposed thereto and withdrawn, the previous question was put and negatived. But on proposing his budget on April 27 following, the Chancellor of

---

[e] Hans. Deb. vol. clxxiv. p. 600.
[f] Ibid. p. 1431-1450.
[a] Ibid. vol. clxxviii. pp. 1120-1124.
[b] Ibid. vol. clxxxiii. pp. 1100-1202, 1407.

the Exchequer intimated that he was prepared to offer a partial relief to the opponents of this duty by giving the maltster the option of having the duty charged by weight instead of by measure.¹ This trifling concession was of no avail to satisfy the opponents of the malt tax. Accordingly on April 17, 1866, Sir F. Kelly again submitted a resolution in favour of the speedy reduction and ultimate repeal of this duty. After a long debate, the motion was negatived on division.

Precedents

It is also an invariable rule of constitutional practice that ministers are not required to answer questions involving an explanation of their intentions as to matters of taxation, until they may deem it expedient to the public interests to declare them.²

Enquiries of ministers concerning taxes.

The general question of a revision of the Customs duties having been submitted to the House by the crown, it is perfectly competent to any member, in committee of the whole House upon the Customs Acts, to offer an amendment to a particular rate of duty proposed to be levied, either for the increase or diminution of the same: it may even be proposed to insert in the schedule a new rate of duty, provided it relates to an article which is already included therein.³ And when the House resolves itself into a Committee of Ways and Means to consider of raising supplies for the service of the current year, it is competent for any member to propose another scheme of taxation for the same purpose, as a substitute for the government plan.⁴ But a proposition made by the Chancellor of the Exchequer, in Committee of Ways and Means, to require licenses to be taken out by brewers, cannot be amended, upon the motion of a private member, by extending such licenses to other manufacturers, iron-masters, and coal-owners; inasmuch as this would be a new and

Amendments to government scheme of taxation.

---

¹ Hans. Deb. vol. clxxviii. p. 1120 b.; Act 28 & 29 Vict. c. 90.
² Mirror of Parl. 1840, p. 1209. Hans. Deb. vol. clviii. p. 1870; vol. clxxxi. p. 968.
³ New Commons Journals, 1842, p. 307; Hans. Deb. vol. lxxv. p. 1020.
⁴ Mirror of Parl. 1840, p. 3042. And see a case on June 20, 1830, where a member proposed a reduction of the soap duties in lieu of the government scheme for a reduction of the duty on newspaper stamps. Ibid. 1830, p. 1963.

distinct tax, and not the mere increase of a duty upon an article already recommended by government for taxation."

Upon one occasion, in committee of the whole House on the Stamp Duties, the opponents of a proposed rate of duty on Advertisements succeeded in negativing the government proposition altogether.º And on May 12, 1862, in committee on the Customs and Inland Revenue Bill, so much thereof as imposed a tax for brewing beer in private houses was struck out; the government agreeing to the same, in deference to the wishes of the House.º And if a proposed tax which has been announced in the budget excites general dissatisfaction, it is not unusual for the government to acquaint the House, at a subsequent stage of proceeding, that they have resolved to abandon it.ᵖ

In another part of this section (*post*, p. 518) precedents will be found, showing the extent to which the financial propositions of the government have been modified by the House of Commons since the Reform of Parliament in 1832.

We have now to consider,

II. THE RIGHTS AND PRIVILEGES OF PARLIAMENT, AND ESPECIALLY OF THE HOUSE OF COMMONS, IN THE GRANT OF MONEY FOR THE PUBLIC SERVICE; AND IN THE OVERSIGHT AND CONTROL OF THE PUBLIC EXPENDITURE.

A. *As to Parliamentary Control over the Grant of Supplies.*

Grant of supplies by Parliament.

From a very early period in the history of England the principle has been established, that the right of tax-

---

ᵐ May, Parl. Prac. ed. 1863, p. 505. In committee upon the Stamp Duties Bill, on August 4, 1850, a private member having proposed a clause to extend the probate duty upon property above the value of one million, the government consented to this impost. But, in point of form, it was considered necessary for a resolution to this effect to be proposed by the Chancellor of the Exchequer, in Committee of Ways and Means, and afterwards introduced into the bill. See *Ibid.*; Hans. Deb. vol. clv. p. 991; Com. J. vol. cxiv. p. 348.

º Hans. Deb. vol. cxxvii. p. 1120.

º *Ibid.* vol. clxvi. p. 1574.

ᵖ Proposed duties on club-houses and on charities, in 1863. Hans. Deb. vol. clxx. pp. 840, 1102, 1125, 1305, 1395.

ation, and the granting supplies for the public service, belong exclusively to Parliament.

The old prerogative claim of the sovereign to levy taxes on the subject at his own will and pleasure, was first expressly restrained by the declaration, in Magna Charta, that 'no scutage or aid shall be imposed in our kingdom unless by the general council of our kingdom;' with certain exceptions peculiar to the person and family of the king himself.

This concession lies at the foundation of our parliamentary institutions, and especially of the House of Commons as a distinct branch of the legislature. The growth of the Commons in power and influence was strikingly exemplified by the statute *De tallagio non concedendo*, in the 25th Edward I., by which it was declared, 'That no tallage or aid shall be taken or levied without the good will and assent of the archbishops, bishops, earls, barons, knights, burgesses, and other freemen of the land.'

Concurrently, however, with parliamentary taxation, other imposts used to be levied by royal prerogative,[a] independently of the action of Parliament; but none of these survived the Revolution of 1688. It was guaranteed by the Bill of Rights that henceforth 'no man be compelled to make any gift, loan, or benevolence, or tax, without common consent by Act of Parliament.' And it was finally established by the Act of Settlement, 'That levying money for or to the use of the crown by pretence and prerogative, without grant of Parliament, for longer time or in other manner than the same is or shall be granted, is illegal.'

Since that memorable period the crown has been entirely dependent upon Parliament for its revenues, which are derived either from annual grants for specific public services, or from payments already secured and appropriated by Acts of Parliament, and which are

No supplies to be used unless granted by Parliament.

---

[a] See *ante*, p. 285; Cox, Inst. pp. 000–003.

commonly known as charges upon the Consolidated Fund.'

On this principle—while ordinary prize-money, obtained through the valour of the army and navy, is distributed by the crown itself, by virtue of its prerogative*—it has been acknowledged that money received by the government for the ransom of the city of Canton, during the war with China, could not be appropriated to public uses, without the authority of Parliament.¹ And the principle which forbids gifts or loans of money to be solicited by the government has been further extended, to forbid any person from voluntarily lending money to the crown, or to any department of state, for public purposes, without the sanction of Parliament, under penalty of a misdemeanour.* The charter of the Bank of England contains a clause forbidding money transactions between the Bank and the Treasury, that have not received express parliamentary authority.*

A discussion arose in the House of Commons on April 28, 1862, in reference to the Military Reserved Fund, a fund which had accumulated from the proceeds of the sale of army commissions, and now amounted to a very considerable sum.* This fund had been appropriated, under the authority of the Secretary of State for War, to 'facilitate and remove the friction from the working of the system of purchase,' and it was admitted that no fault could be found with

---

* Broom, Const. Law, pp. 368–402.
* Hans. Deb. vol. lxxi. p. 352; vol. lxxxi. p. 682. And yet in 1863 the government undertook to make no final arrangement in regard to certain Indian prize-money, until papers on the subject had been communicated to the House of Commons, 'so as to give that House the opportunity of intercepting the proposed distribution, if it thought proper to do so.' Hans. Deb. vol. clxxii. pp. 240, 817, 1475. See further on this subject, ante, p. 430, note (f).
* Ibid. vol. lii. p. 424.
* See debates in the Commons on Mr. Sheridan's motion respecting voluntary aids for public purposes without the consent of Parliament, Parl. Hist. vol. xxxi. pp. 83, 97; and in the Lords, Ibid. p. 122. See Lord Brougham's comments on this case, Hans. Deb. vol. lxxxiii. p. 37; and Mr. Massey's valuable observations thereupon in his George III. vol. iv. p. 77.
* Hans. Deb. vol. clxii. p. 687; and see Report of the Comptroller of the Exchequer, in Rep. Committee on Public Moneys, Commons Papers, 1857, Sess. 2, vol. ix.
* The Commons committee on military organisation, of 1860, first directed the attention of the House to the existence of this anomalous fund. (Report, pp. xi. xii.; Evid. pp. 471–479.) And see Smith's Parl. Rememb. 1862, p. 70.

the practice. Nevertheless, grave constitutional objections were urged against the existence of a fund not voted by Parliament, or subject to parliamentary control, but which was expended at the discretion of government. The Secretary for War confessed that these objections were well-founded, and promised that the attention of the government should be directed to the question, with a view to this fund being brought under parliamentary examination and audit.[z]

The constitutional principle of parliamentary control is also applicable to advances, loans, or gifts of public money, to foreign powers, corporations, or private persons; to the remission of debts due to the crown by any such persons or powers; and even to the sale of property by one department of the state, and its purchase by another department, for public uses.[y] *Loans. Debts due to the crown. Government sales.*

Advances out of the public funds, for whatsoever purpose, should ordinarily be made only by express authority of Parliament. But in urgent cases, requiring immediate relief, or when, on grounds of public policy, secrecy is advisable, the government can have recourse in the first instance to the 'Civil Contingencies,' or the 'Treasury Chest' funds, the nature of which will be hereafter explained. But they are strictly accountable to Parliament for all such transactions, and the advances so made out of these funds must be replaced out of moneys voted by Parliament for that service.[z] *Advances of public money.*

---

[z] Hans. Deb. vol. clxvi. p. 685; and see vol. clxviii. p. 730.

[y] The question of sales of public property between different public departments will be considered in *post*, p. 552, when treating of unauthorised expenditure.

[z] See Mr. Pitt's advance to Messrs. Boyd, Benfield and Co. in 1796, Parl. Deb. vol. v. pp. 385-424. Also Hans. Deb. vol. lxiii. pp. 1130, 1314; Peel's Memoirs, vol. ii. p. 174; Knight's Hist. of Engl. vol. viii. p. 548; Rep. on Public Moneys, 1857, p. 121. See the comments of Mr. Toulmin Smith on the unauthorised donation by the Commissioners of Woods and Forests, on April 20, 1865, of the sum of 15,000*l.* to 'the Bishop of London's Fund,' out of the land revenues of the crown, 'as a contribution in the name and on the part of her Majesty.' These revenues (under the Civil List Act) form part of the Consolidated Fund, and can only be appropriated by Parliament. The queen had already made a liberal contribution to the bishop's fund from her privy purse; but this act of the Commissioners of Woods was illegal without the previous sanction of Parliament. Smith's Parl. Rememb. 1865, p. 60.

Remission of loans or debts, &c., require the sanction of Parliament.

Loans to foreign powers.

No remission by government of loans, or of debts due to the crown, whether by foreign powers, corporations, or individuals, is justifiable without the knowledge and consent of Parliament;[a] and the surrender of the rights of the crown in cases of 'Treasure Trove,' by relinquishing the same to the finders, would be unjustifiable, had it not been authorised by the Civil List Act.[b] So far as loans to foreign powers are concerned, the practice of government has been heretofore somewhat irregular and objectionable, as the following cases will show.

In 1863, when the Ionian Islands were ceded by the British government to the kingdom of Greece, a portion of certain arrears, due by the said islands to the imperial treasury, was remitted, without the previous authority of Parliament.[c] This proceeding gave rise to a motion of censure in the House of Commons, on June 27, 1864. The Chancellor of the Exchequer defended the course taken by the government, by reference to former precedents; but at the same time he admitted that it was questionable whether it might not be possible to improve the established practice in such cases. In 1823, the government, by a convention with the Emperor of Austria, agreed to accept the sum of 2,500,000l. in lieu of a much

[a] S. O. II. of C. March 25, 1715, and March 20, 1707. Compounding debts due to the crown. Com. Journ. vol. lxxv. p. 107; vol. lxxxi. p. 60. Case of the Crinan Canal Co. Ibid. vol. lxxxiii. pp. 213, 210, 251. By Act 11 & 12 Vict. c. 54, this canal was assumed by government, because the company were unable to repay the sums advanced to them by the treasury. See also the case of the Leith Docks, &c. By the Act 23 & 24 Vict. c. 48, the Lords of the Treasury were authorised to accept the sum of 50,000l. in full satisfaction for a debt of 228,374l. 0s. 8d., incurred by the city of Edinburgh for advances made by the treasury on behalf of the harbour and docks of Leith; this debt having been secured by bonds to the said amount, granted by the corporation of Edinburgh. The bill was brought in by Mr. Laing, the secretary to the Treasury; it elicited no debate in the House of Commons, but was referred to a select committee, before whom Mr. Laing appeared, and showed that the proposed arrangement was the best bargain that could be made by the government. (Commons Papers, 1860, vol. xv. p. 32.) Whereupon the bill was reported and agreed to by both Houses. See also the Dominica Hurricane Loan Act, 23 & 24 Vict. c. 57.

[b] 1 & 2 Vict. c. 2, sec. 12. Hans. Deb. vol. clxxx. p. 440.

[c] Hans. Deb. vol. clxxiii. p. 1083; vol. clxxvi. p. 608.

larger amount due by Austria, under previous engagements with the British crown. This proceeding was not submitted to Parliament until the following year, when it was sanctioned by the Act 5 Geo. IV. c. 9. A debt due by Portugal was remitted, by treaty, in 1815, without any application to Parliament upon the subject. In brief, the constitutional practice in such cases was thus defined by the Chancellor of the Exchequer. When a sum of money, to which the British crown was entitled, was surrendered, it was customary to surrender the same by treaty, which was not made contingent on the assent of Parliament. He admitted that, in a constitutional point of view, the assent of Parliament was necessary,[d] but it was not usual to make it a condition precedent in the treaty itself. But when the crown undertook to pay a sum of money, it was customary to make such payment conditional upon the assent of Parliament. After these explanations the motion of censure was withdrawn.[e] A bill to carry out an 'unconditional agreement' made by treaty with Greece, to remit 4,000l. a year, as a personal dotation to George I., king of the Hellenes, out of the debt due by Greece to Great Britain, was introduced by government, and passed without amendment.[f]

In proceedings in Parliament upon matters of supply and taxation, the two Houses do not stand on precisely the same footing. Although the consent of both Houses is indispensable to give legal effect and validity thereto, yet, from a very early period, the Commons have succeeded in maintaining their exclusive right to originate all measures of this description. They have gone further, and have claimed that such measures should be simply affirmed or rejected by the Lords, and should not be amended by that House in the slightest particular. The Lords have practically acquiesced in this restriction;

Rights of the Commons in the grant of supply.

---

[d] In fact he had distinctly admitted this necessity upon a former occasion. Hans. Deb. vol. clxxii. p. 251.
[e] Ibid. vol. clxxvi. pp. 301, 405.
[f] Act 27 & 28 Vict. c. 40.

although they have never formally consented to it."
The questions in controversy between the two Houses in
matters of supply have been elaborately discussed in the
3rd vol. of Hatsell's Precedents, and in May's Treatise on
the Practice of Parliament; it would therefore be superfluous to enter upon them here; suffice it to say that the
proceedings between the two Houses on this subject are
now in strict conformity with the resolution of the Commons on July 3, 1678, which declared that 'all aids and
supplies, and aids to his Majesty in Parliament, are the
sole gift of the Commons; and all bills for the granting
of any such aids and supplies ought to begin with the
Commons, and that it is the undoubted and sole right of
the Commons to direct, limit, and appoint in such bills
the ends, purposes, considerations, conditions, limitations,
and qualifications of such grants; which ought not to be
changed or altered by the House of Lords.'

Practice of the Lords in supply.
Without abandoning the abstract right of dealing with
bills of supply and taxation as they may think fit, the
Lords seldom attempt to make any but verbal alterations,
in which the sense or intention is not affected; but even
in regard to these, when the Commons have accepted
them, they have made special entries in their journal
recording the character and object of the amendments,
and their reasons for agreeing to them.[b]

Of late years an attempt has been made, by an ingenious
process of reasoning, to establish a distinction between the
right of the Lords to reject a bill imposing a tax and
one repealing a tax. But this distinction is fallacious,
and is not warranted either by precedent,[1] or by constitutional authority.[j] The only ground for such a difference is the fact that taxes being levied on behalf of the
sovereign, when she, by her responsible financial advisers,
is desirous of renouncing any specific tax, and the Com-

---

[a] Hans. Deb. vol. clxiii. pp. 720, 722.
[b] See May's Parl. Prac. ed. 1883, p. 535, citing precedents.
[i] Report of Committee of Commons on Tax Bills, 1860, pp. 75–84.
[j] See Cox, Institutions, p. 188.

mons assent to the repeal of the same, it is not customary, under ordinary circumstances, for the Lords to oppose the wishes of the sovereign and of the other House. The control of the public finances by the House of Commons is a constitutional right, and they are presumed to be the best judges of the financial condition of the state, its obligations and requirements. Nevertheless, every bill to impose or repeal a tax involves other considerations besides those which are purely questions of revenue; it necessarily includes principles of public policy, or of commercial regulation, and on points of this kind the Lords, as a co-ordinate branch of the legislature, are constitutionally free to act and advise as they may judge best for the public interests. It is true that the peculiar privileges of the Commons in regard to supply and taxation should ordinarily restrain the Lords from intermeddling with the details of financial schemes propounded by the government and agreed to by the popular branch, but circumstances may occur when the exercise by the House of Lords of their right to accept or reject any measure affecting the finances of the nation may be most beneficial to the interests of the community at large; and it would be unwarrantable to deny them the possession of this right because it might be expedient that it should be resorted to only upon extraordinary occasions.

The relations between the two Houses in matters of supply and taxation will be further illustrated by a narrative of the Paper duties case. We have already seen [b] that in the year 1858 the House of Commons, by the adoption of an abstract resolution, condemned the continuance of the paper duty as a permanent source of revenue. Accordingly, in 1860, a measure for the repeal of this impost was submitted by the Chancellor of the Exchequer in his budget, and in due course was sent up to the House of Lords in a separate bill. The paper duty yielded a revenue of 1,300,000l. per annum, to make up for the loss of which it was proposed to add a penny in the pound to the Income tax. This recommendation was agreed to by both Houses; but the Lords refused to concur in the remission of the paper duties, on the ground that the state of the public finances,

Paper duties case.

---

[b] See *ante*, p. 447.

Paper duties case.
and the condition of the country, then on the eve of war with China, did not warrant the sacrifice of such a large amount of revenue. Other injurious consequences were also predicted as likely to result from a repeal of the duty on this article of manufacture. Whereupon the second reading of the bill was postponed for six months. After the House of Commons became officially cognisant of this fact, by the report of a committee appointed to ascertain the fate of the bill, they appointed a committee to search the Journals of both Houses, in order to ascertain the practice of Parliament with regard to the several descriptions of bills imposing or repealing taxes. On June 29, this committee reported numerous precedents, which were set forth with great care and perspicuity; but they refrained from offering any opinion, or from making any comments upon the practice of each House, except to illustrate and explain. On July 5, Lord Palmerston (the premier) proposed to the House of Commons the following resolutions:—

'1. That the right of granting aids and supplies to the crown is in the Commons alone, as an essential part of their constitution; and the limitation of all such grants, as to the matter, manner, measure, and time, is only in them. 2. That although the Lords have exercised the power of rejecting bills of several descriptions relating to taxation by negativing the whole, yet the exercise of that power by them has not been frequent, and is justly regarded by this House with peculiar jealousy, as affecting the right of the Commons to grant the supplies and to provide the ways and means for the service of the year. 3. That to guard for the future against an undue exercise of that power by the Lords, and to secure to the Commons their rightful control over taxation and supply, this House has in its own hands the power so to impose and remit taxes, and to frame Bills of Supply, that the right of the Commons as to matter, manner, measure, and time may be maintained inviolate.'

It was not proposed to follow up these abstract propositions with any action in reference to the bill for the repeal of the paper duties, because the legal and technical right of the Lords to refuse their assent to that bill was not disputed by the government, who nevertheless thought it necessary that the protest implied in the adoption of these resolutions should be recorded. They were accordingly agreed to by the House, on July 6, without a division, but after a full debate. In the course of the discussion, the following points were strongly insisted upon. The first resolution, it was remarked, seems to have been copied from an ancient precedent on the Commons Journals for 1692, the language whereof, though correct in the main, has been noticed by Hallam, in his Constitutional History, as that which cannot be precisely vindicated or approved, for it appears (however unintentionally) to deny the right of the Lords to a free concurrence in matters of supply; which is contrary to the express admissions of the second resolution.[1] It is well known that the Lords have never formally acknowledged any farther privilege to the Commons than that of originating Bills of Supply; and although in practice they have for a long period acquiesced in the claim of the Commons that they should not alter or amend any Money Bill, yet their right to reject such measures as a whole is as undoubted as their right to express agreement therein. It is granted that the power of taxation is one that peculiarly appertains to the House of Commons; and that it is their privilege, in providing supplies for the service of the year, should they think fit, 'to combine the whole into one scheme,' that must be accepted or rejected by the Lords, without any attempt to alter or vary the details of the financial arrangements composing the same.[2] Yet the propriety and expediency of such a course, in every instance, may be seriously impeached. We have already seen,[3] in the case of Palmer, when the Commons proposed to grant a sum of money to a person whose claims to compensation were open to dispute, that they included the appropriation in a separate bill, for the avowed purpose of affording to the Lords an opportunity of considering that grant distinctly from the other grants of the year. In like manner, in the immeasurably more important instance of the financial propositions of the government, it properly belongs to the Lords to judge, not merely of the general expediency of the proposed scheme, when regarded as a whole, and of its probable results upon the country at large, but also to consider the various questions of commercial legislation and public policy that may be involved in its details. The House of Lords has an onerous duty to perform in respect to every bill, financial or otherwise, that may be sent to it from the other chamber, in submitting the same to careful revision, for the purpose of restraining hasty or improvident legislation, and sanctioning by its wisdom, influence, and authority whatsoever may be necessary to promote the public good. This can only be adequately performed when full opportunity is afforded for pronouncing an independent judgment upon every separate question which the Lords may be called upon to decide.[4]

Paper duties case.

[1] Hans. Deb. vol. clix. pp. 1419, 1487.
[2] Ibid. pp. 1380, 1505.
[3] See ante, p. 430.
[4] In support of this view, see Jurist. N. S. vi. pt. ii. pp. 235, 290. See also Edinburgh Review, January, 1862, art. viii. For a reference to ancient precedents, and an able and ingenious argument in opposition to the claims and proceedings of the Lords on this occasion, see various articles in Smith's Parl. Remembrancer, 1860, pp. 123-162, 172, 179, 184. And see the speech of Lord R. Montagu, in the House of Commons, on March 20, 1863, in reference to the conduct of the House of Assembly of the colony of Victoria, in claiming the right to tack a Tariff Bill to the Appropriation Bill, with a view to compel the Legislative Council to accept the same, contrary to the instructions laid down by the Secretary

462   THE ROYAL PREROGATIVE.

Paper duties case.   On July 17, Lord Fermoy moved the House of Commons to resolve 'that the rejection by the Lords of the bill for the repeal of the paper duties is an encroachment on the rights and privileges of the House of Commons; and it is therefore incumbent upon this House to adopt a practical measure for the vindication of its rights and privileges.' He based this proposition on the erroneous construction of the first resolution moved by Lord Palmerston, and which Hallam by anticipation had condemned, and also on the alleged necessity for following up the foregoing resolutions with some decisive action. But the ministry opposed this motion, and the previous question was proposed thereon and negatived.[r]

In the following session (1861), the Chancellor of the Exchequer, conformably to the principle asserted in the third resolution aforesaid, embodied his whole budget propositions, including resolutions for the repeal of the paper duty, in one bill. Great exception was taken to this course by a powerful minority in the House of Commons, and it underwent considerable discussion on May 13 and 16. It was urged that although such a proceeding was undeniably in accordance with some former precedents, and a strictly allowable method of disposing of the financial measures of the year, yet that the practice for the last thirty or forty years had been to insert the propositions of the budget in several bills; that it was not desirable to include multifarious matters, such as the repeal and the imposition of taxes, in one bill, even though the subjects were cognate; that the Lords have never formally abandoned their right to amend Money Bills, though leading members of that House may have done so, when speaking in its behalf; that admitting such a claim to be inconsistent with the privileges of the Commons in regard to Supply, yet that the balance of the Constitution requires that the Lords should possess a controlling power in all matters of legislation, whether financial or otherwise, and that they ought not to be driven to the alternative of rejecting the whole supplies for the year—and thereby jeopardising the public credit, the existence of the ministry, and the welfare of the state—or of being obliged to agree to a bill containing many distinct and separate provisions, all of which they were not disposed to accept; that while the extreme right of the Commons may be held to justify the embodying of all the budget resolutions in one bill, yet that this power should not be exercised except on extraordinary occasions, and that ordinarily no proceedings should be resorted to that would deprive the Lords of the

of State for the Colonies, that Revenue and Appropriation Bills should invariably be distinct and separate measures. See also the 'Correspondence,' and 'Further Correspondence,'

'respecting the non-enactment of the Appropriation Act in Victoria,' presented to Parliament in 1866.

[r] Hans. Deb. vol. clix. pp. 2078–2100.

opportunity of exercising a deliberate judgment on every distinct Paper legislative proposition, until after continued provocation, and the duties case. repeated exercise, by the Lords, of their right to reject measures forming part of the financial scheme agreed to by the Commons; which extreme right of the Lords ought to be reserved for rare and exceptional occasions; and, finally, that it was quite unprecedented for a financial bill which had been rejected by the Lords to be afterwards embodied in another bill, sent up and passed by them in that shape; so that, at all events, the course now proposed was premature, and ought not to have been adopted until after successive failures to induce the Lords to agree to the repeal of the paper duty in a separate bill. Nevertheless, the bill was sent to the Lords in the shape it had been introduced by the government. Its second reading was moved in that House on June 7. In the course of the debate thereon, Lord Derby, while asserting that the bill was open to objection in point of form, did not attempt to dispute the strict right of the Commons to include all the financial arrangements of the year in one measure, alleging that the Lords could, if they deemed it expedient, vindicate their privileges by dividing the bill into two or more parts. He also clearly showed that the Lords had never formally abandoned their right to amend a Money Bill, and that in the opinion of eminent constitutional authorities, they would be warranted in such an act, should it be necessary to vindicate their freedom of deliberation, and to prevent the enacting of a measure which they regarded as objectionable.[q] He added that there were 'repeated cases of financial measures being amended by the House of Lords, and the amendments being accepted by the House of Commons' (after, of course, the formal assertion of their privileges, by laying aside the bill, and re-introducing it, as amended). Notwithstanding these objections, no attempt was made to oppose the passing of this bill, or to introduce any amendments therein; its opponents contenting themselves with recording, in an able and elaborate protest, all the arguments that had been adduced against it.[r] Toulmin Smith, in his Parliamentary Remembrancer for 1861, although he had sided against the Lords in the beginning of the controversy, condemned the present proceeding of the Commons, as betokening a lack of 'ordinary courtesy and self-respect,' 'really amounting to a declaration that the House of Lords shall be overridden, without scruple, whenever the Commons want to pass a bill that cannot be safely trusted on the stage of fair discussion.'[s]

Following the precedent so successfully established,

---

[q] Hans. Deb. vol. clxiii. p. 720.
[r] Ibid. p. 1144. Lords Journals, vol. xciii. p. 378.
[s] Parl. Rememb. 1861, p. 88; and see pp. 100, 101, 118.

Commons include the whole budget resolutions in one bill.
the Chancellor of the Exchequer determined to introduce the budget propositions of 1862 in one general bill.¹ Leading members of the Commons strenuously protested against this course, as being a serious restriction upon the opportunities for discussing these important financial measures, but without avail.² This was probably the largest 'Money Bill' ever passed, as it dealt with between twenty-two and twenty-three million pounds of public taxation. It was commented upon somewhat severely in the House of Lords on this ground, but the Colonial Secretary (the Duke of Newcastle) contended that the new practice of combining the whole budget resolutions in one bill was merely a resort to former constitutional usage, and was sanctioned by high authority. Lord Derby considered that this course was more open to objection on the part of the Commons than of the Lords, inasmuch as it 'deprives the House of Commons of some of the most valuable means which they have at their disposal of duly debating and fully considering the financial measures of the government.' So far as the Lords were concerned, 'the one course interposes to us no greater obstacle than the other; because, as it is perfectly within our province and our right to reject a particular proposition in a single bill, so it is equally within our competence to reject that same proposition when incorporated with others,'* and leave to the Commons the consequences of their own proceeding. After some further debate, the bill was concurred in without amendment. In like manner, the financial propositions of government in each of the sessions of 1863, 1864, 1865, and 1866, were all included in one bill, although on May 17, 1866, Mr. Disraeli took occasion to reiterate his conviction that this course was attended with considerable inconveniences.*

Having briefly noticed the relative position of the two

---

¹ Hans. Deb. vol. clxvi. p. 772.
² Ibid. pp. 1501–1507.
* Hans. Deb. vol. clxvii. p. 180.
* Ibid. vol. clxx. p. 851; vol. clxxxiii. p. 1128.

branches of the legislature in regard to matters of supply, we will now proceed to consider, more particularly, the course pursued in submitting to the House of Commons the pecuniary necessities of the state, and in obtaining the sanction of Parliament to the expenditure required on behalf of the same.

Directly the House of Commons have agreed to the Address in answer to the speech from the throne, they order the speech to be taken into consideration on a future day. When that day arrives, so much of the speech as relates to 'the Estimates' is read by the Speaker. A motion is then made 'that a supply be granted to her Majesty,' and the House resolve that, on a future day, they will go into committee to consider of that motion, to which committee the royal speech is referred. It has been ruled by the Speaker that no amendment can be made to the motion, 'That a supply be granted,' and that it is not debatable when first proposed, but only on the day appointed for its consideration.* On the day appointed, the committee sit, the speech is considered, and they agree to a resolution, 'That a supply be granted to her Majesty,' which, being reported on a future day, is agreed to by the House, *nem. con.* Until this resolution has been adopted, ministers are unable to submit the estimates to the House.'

Grant of supply.

The general question in favour of a supply having been determined, the House appoint another day on which to resolve themselves into committee to consider of the supply granted, or, as it is commonly called, the Committee of Supply. They then order the estimates for the Army and Navy to be laid before them, and address the crown to give directions accordingly.

Appointment of Committee of Supply.

When the first report of the Committee of Supply has been received by the House, and agreed to, a day is appointed for the House to resolve itself into a committee

---
* May, Parl. Prac. ed. 1851, p. 548; Mirror of Parl. 1834, p. 67.
' *Ibid.* 1830, p. 147.

Committee of Ways and Means.
The Budget.

'to consider of ways and means for raising the supply' granted.

It is in the Committee of Ways and Means that the Budget, or financial statement of the Chancellor of the Exchequer, is usually made. In 1833, Mr. Hume moved an amendment to the motion for the Speaker to leave the chair to go into Committee of Supply, the object of which was to compel the Chancellor of the Exchequer to open the budget before the Army and Navy estimates were voted, but the amendment was negatived without a division.[a] But several instances are cited by May wherein the budget was brought forward in Committee of Supply, or of Ways and Means, before the usual votes for the service of the year had been taken.[b]

The introduction of the budget has been thus described:—'Before, or soon after the close of each financial year, the Chancellor of the Exchequer submits to the House of Commons a general statement of the results of the financial measures of the preceding session, and gives a general view of the expected income and expenditure of the ensuing year; he intimates at the same time whether the government intends to propose the repeal of any taxes, or the raising of money by the imposition of taxes, or by loan, or otherwise. This exposition of the state of the finances for the past and ensuing year gives the House of Commons all the necessary information to enable them to exercise an important check upon the minister, by limiting his means of raising money to the sums actually required for the public expenditure. If his statement shows a larger surplus revenue than the House of Commons considers it prudent to leave as a margin to the government, pressure is immediately brought to bear upon it to procure a reduction of taxation; if, on the other hand, the minister shows that the revenue will be insufficient to meet the expenditure, it rests exclusively

---

[a] Mirror of Parl. 1833, p. 004.
[b] May, Parl. Prac. ed. 1854, p. 550; and see post, p. 510.

with the House of Commons to grant or to refuse the demands which may be submitted to them for meeting that deficiency. The intention of this budget statement is not only to lay before the House of Commons the scheme of taxation for the ensuing year, but to satisfy them that the public income to be raised in the year will be sufficient, and no more than sufficient, to meet the expenditure which the government proposes to incur within the year."[b]

After the Chancellor of the Exchequer has concluded his financial statement, it is customary for members to rise and put questions to the finance minister with respect to any point which may require further explanation. This is a convenient practice, and is much to be preferred to that of raising, at once, a general debate upon the budget, as it enables the whole ministerial scheme to be laid before the country in a complete and intelligible shape.[c]

{{Questions upon the Budget.}}

Before proceeding to point out the constitutional practice in the grant of supplies and ways and means for the service of the crown, it will be necessary to show the various sources from whence the public revenue is derived, and the extent to which the revenue is subjected to the periodical revision and control of the House of Commons.

{{Public revenue.}}

The revenues of the crown in Great Britain were anciently derivable from the hereditary lands of the crown, and from the operation of various prerogative rights. But since the establishment of parliamentary government, these revenues have been mostly surrendered to the control of Parliament, in exchange for a permanent civil list.[d] The public revenues of the country are now chiefly obtained from taxes and other imposts, which are levied under the authority of Acts of Parliament. The whole revenue, from whatever source derived, is now (with some trifling

---

[b] Rep. on Public Moneys, Commons Papers, 1857, sess. ii. vol. ix.; Memo. on Financial Control, by Sir G. C. Lewis (Chanc. of Excheq.), p. 25. For the derivation of the word

[c] 'Budget,' see Statistical Journal, vol. xxix. p. 325.
[c] Gladstone (Chanc. of Excheq.), Hans. Deb. vol. clxxxiii. pp. 105, 411.
[d] See May, Const. Hist. vol. i. ch. iv.

exception) paid into the Bank of England or Ireland to the account of her Majesty's Exchequer. The old system of retaining public money at the Exchequer itself has been entirely abolished, and this great department remodelled, by recent legislation, as will hereafter appear, when we consider the manner in which the control of Parliament is exercised over the issue of public money.

The revenues which are thus paid into the Bank of England, to the account of the Exchequer, comprise all the principal revenues of the kingdom, including the Customs and Inland Revenue, and the receipts from the Post Office.

Consolidated Fund. Formerly, the proceeds of parliamentary taxes constituted separate and distinct funds, but, by the Act 27 Geo. III. c. 47, it was directed that the various duties and taxes should be carried to and constitute a fund, to be called 'The Consolidated Fund.'*

Gross receipts to be paid into the Exchequer. Until the year 1854, the charges of collection and management of the revenue of Customs, Inland Revenue, and the Post Office, were payable out of the gross receipts of these imposts, respectively, and only the net revenue, after these and other deductions, was paid into the Consolidated Fund. The constitutional objections to this practice were repeatedly pressed upon the attention of successive administrations without effect. At length, on April 29, 1847, Dr. Bowring submitted to the House of Commons a series of resolutions—based upon the report of the Commissioners of Public Accounts in 1831—recommending the adoption of an improved system for the security of the public revenue, and for ensuring greater accuracy, simplicity, and completeness, in the public accounts; and requiring that the gross revenue of the country, without any deduction whatever, should be paid into the public chest, and be subjected to the surveillance

---

* The Consolidated Funds of England and Ireland were united by 56 Geo. III. c. 98; and by 1 Vict. c. 2, various hereditary revenues of the crown were carried to this fund.

and control of Parliament. After some debate, the motion was withdrawn. But, on April 30, 1848, the discussion was again renewed, and Dr. Bowring succeeded in carrying his resolutions by a bare majority. When questioned upon the subject in the following session, the Chancellor of the Exchequer informed the House that steps had been taken by the government to carry out in part the reforms proposed by the resolutions.[f] But it was not until 1854 that the great object aimed at by Dr. Bowring was sought to be accomplished, by the passing of a Bill, which was introduced into Parliament by Mr. Gladstone, 'to bring the gross income and expenditure of the United Kingdom, &c. under the more immediate view and control of Parliament.'[g] By this Act, it was intended that the whole of the gross revenues of the country, derived from the Customs, Excise, (with the exception of certain drawbacks, discounts, and repayments,) and other taxes (not including the land revenues of the crown, which are otherwise provided for), should be paid into the Exchequer, and the cost of collection be defrayed out of votes in supply.[h] Besides the cost of collection, the revenue was formerly chargeable with certain judicial and other salaries, pensions, and other payments, under the authority of various Acts of Parliament. By Mr. Gladstone's Act, these charges were transferred either to the Consolidated Fund or to the annual supplies to be voted by Parliament.[i] Under the authority of this Act, moreover, a very large number of charges, previously paid out of the Consolidated Fund, were placed, thenceforth, in the annual estimates.[j] And, by the Act 19 & 20 Vict. c. 59, certain superannuations and other charges which still remained payable out of the gross revenues were directed to be removed from the

---

[f] Hans. Deb. vol. cii. p. 490.
[g] Act 17 & 18 Vict. c. 94.
[h] Mr. Gladstone's speech, in Hans. Deb. vol. cxxx. p. 216; see also Ibid. vol. cxxxv. p. 801.
[i] As to the results which have followed from this improved system, see Peto on Taxation, ch. ix. 'On the Collection of the Revenue;' and Northcote on Financial Policy, p. 238.
[j] Mr. Gladstone, in Hans. Deb. vol. clxix. p. 1049.

same, and placed upon the Consolidated Fund, &c. The only payments remaining which could be legally charged upon the gross revenues were the charges on the land revenues of the crown—the net receipts only of which are payable to the Consolidated Fund, under the statute 10 Geo. IV. c. 50, sect. 113, and the Civil List Act of 1 & 2 Vict.—and the drawbacks, bounties, repayments, and discounts, aforesaid.

Gross revenues.

But notwithstanding the Acts of 1854 and 1856, the intention whereof was clearly to require the payment of the whole revenue, minus the drawbacks, &c. above-mentioned, into the Exchequer, this result was not obtained, owing to an omission in the Acts of any provision to render such a course compulsory. Accordingly, the attention of the Committee on Public Moneys, in 1857, was directed to the matter, and they recommended the passing of a law to make it imperative on the government to pay the gross revenues to the Exchequer, without any other deductions than those above mentioned, in order that all issues for the public service might receive the previous sanction of Parliament. They also suggested that, if possible, the charges on the land revenues should be brought under the same parliamentary control.[1] By Treasury minutes, dated February 15 and December 23, 1858, the government agreed to this recommendation, excepting so far as the land revenues were concerned, which, for reasons stated, could not be carried out until a new civil list should be under consideration.[2] But although the Treasury undertook to submit to Parliament a Bill to effect this desirable improvement, no such measure was brought forward, and this great reform remained partially uncompleted until the passing of the Exchequer and Audit Departments Act, in 1866, the tenth clause of which has made the practice obligatory. Before the passing of this Act, the cost of collection was

---

[1] Rep. Com. Pub. Moneys, 1857, p. 4. xxxiv. p. 380; and 1860, vol. xxxix.
[2] Commons Papers, 1857-8, vol. pt. i. p. 174.

still deducted in some cases from the gross revenue; in other instances part of the cost was paid out of the gross revenue, and another part voted by the House of Commons in the supplies of the year."

For considerations of public convenience, it has been customary, in the case of the revenue departments generally, to pay the salaries of employés, in the first instance, out of revenue receipts, and afterwards to repay these advances to the Exchequer out of the parliamentary votes for the said departments. This practice has been tacitly approved by the Committee of Public Accounts, and is sanctioned by the tenth clause of the Exchequer Act. But it is open to abuse, and has been objected to by the Secretary of the Board of Audit.^a

Salaries in revenue departments.

With this exception, therefore, the whole public revenue of the country, together with moneys received from loans, is placed to the account of the Consolidated Fund, out of which all public payments are made. Such payments are twofold: 1. By authority of permanent grants, under Acts of Parliament. 2. Pursuant to annual votes in Committee of Supply, payable out of the Consolidated Fund by ways and means annually provided.

The services provided for by permanent grants are in the proportion of about thirty millions to seventy millions of revenue. They are as follows:—

Permanent grants.

1. The Funded Debt;^b 2. The Civil List; 3. Annuities to the Royal Family, and Pensions; 4. Salaries and Allowances of certain independent Officers, including the higher class of Diplomatic Functionaries;^c 5. Courts of Justice;

---

^a Peto on Taxation, p. 210. But see Earl Grey on Parl. Gov. (new ed. pp. 85-90) for some weighty remarks on the evil effects attending this change of system.

^b Rep. Com. Public Accounts, 1865, p. 142; and see post, p. 655.

^c For an interesting account of the precautions taken to secure the punctual payment of interest to the national creditor, and also the payment of other fixed charges by the Bank of England, on behalf of the government, see an article in the Shilling Magazine (for May, 1866), vol. iv. p. 44.

^d On March 20, 1863, it was moved in the House of Commons to resolve that the whole cost of the diplomatic service ought to be provided for by annual estimates submitted to Parliament, instead of, as at present, one-

6. Certain Miscellaneous Services, comprising Interest and Sinking Fund of the Russian, Dutch, and Greek Loans, Compensations, &c. These charges are made payable out of the Consolidated Fund, by permanent statutes, from year to year, without any renewal of parliamentary authority. The principle of not subjecting to the uncertainty of an annual vote the provision for the security of the public creditor, the dignity of the crown, annuities and pensions to royal and distinguished persons, the salaries of judges and other officers in whose official character independence is an essential element, compensations for rights surrendered, and like charges, is one the soundness of which is generally admitted, although it may have been in certain cases carried too far.

Annual charges.

The annual charges for the payment of interest on the unfunded debt, for the maintenance of the naval and military forces, for the collection of the revenue, and for the various civil services, are prepared in the respective departments of state to which they severally belong, and are afterwards revised and approved by the Treasury, in the manner described in the chapter of this work which treats of the functions of that branch of the executive government. They are then submitted to the House of Commons by command of the crown in very detailed estimates.

---

half the amount being payable out of the Consolidated Fund by a fixed annual charge under an Act of Parliament. The Chancellor of the Exchequer opposed the motion, on grounds of expediency, and it was negatived on division.

Rep. on Pub. Moneys, 1857, p. 20.

The 'unfunded debt' consists principally of Exchequer bills, which are in the nature of temporary loans to the government. Every year, during the sitting of the Committee of Supply, grants are made from time to time of money on account, to be raised by Exchequer bills or loans. This supply of credit is voted in Committee of Supply, after which a resolution is reported from the Committee of Ways and Means that a sum equal to that amount be raised by loans or Exchequer bills, to be charged on the next aids to be granted by Parliament. Cox, Inst. 163; and see Hans. Deb. vol. clxi. p. 1309.

It is not customary to send the estimates to the House of Lords. In 1788 they applied for a copy, and were refused by the Commons. In 1830 they succeeded in obtaining a copy, 'almost for the first time in their history.' Hans. Deb. vol. clix. pp. 1440, 1563.

Until the year 1848, there was one exception to this rule, in respect

In order that the House may be informed, as early as possible, of the expenditure for which they will have to provide, the following resolution was agreed to on February 19, 1821, and has ever since been complied with:—

Presentation of the estimates.

'That this House considers it essentially useful to the exact performance of its duties, as guardians of the public purse, that, during the continuance of the peace, whenever Parliament shall be assembled before Christmas, the estimates for the Navy, Army, and Ordnance Departments should be presented before January 15 then next following, if Parliament be then sitting; and that such estimates should be presented within ten days after the opening of the Committee of Supply, when Parliament shall not be assembled till after Christmas.'

The estimates for Civil Services, commonly called the Miscellaneous estimates, and those for the Revenue departments, have been usually presented somewhat later in the session.* The Committees on Public Moneys, on Miscellaneous Expenditure, and on Public Accounts, appointed within the last ten years, have all recommended that these estimates should be laid on the table every session, as soon as possible after the meeting of Parliament, but as yet the government, though they have expressed a desire to do so, have found great difficulty

---

to the Disembodied Militia estimates, which used to be formally prepared by a committee of the House of Commons. In former times, the privilege of the direct control of the House over the expenditure upon the Militia was highly prized, as one of the safeguards of the liberties of the country, the Militia being considered a constitutional force, as distinguished from the regular Army. Of late years that feeling has been entirely changed, in consequence of the control acquired by the House over the regular Army in Committee of Supply; the Militia estimates had come to be in fact prepared in the War Office, and to be merely formally assented to by the committee charged to prepare them. It was accordingly agreed to abandon this ancient usage, and to permit these estimates to be henceforth prepared by the executive government, and to be presented to Parliament simultaneously with the ordinary Army estimates, as in the case of the expenses of the Embodied Militia and the Yeomanry and of the Volunteers. Hans. Deb. vol. clxviii. p. 682. And see Mirror of Parl. 1828, p. 1221; Hans. Deb. vol. clxix. p. 198.

* May, Parl. Prac. ed. 1863, p. 550.

in expediting their delivery.' On March 21, 1862, complaint was made of this to the House of Commons; but the Chancellor of the Exchequer (Mr. Gladstone) replied that, while he admitted that it was most desirable to carry out this recommendation as strictly as possible, these estimates could not be presented with the same regularity as those for military and naval services; their preparation depended so much, not merely on other public departments, but upon members of commissions, governing bodies of institutions, and even on others who gave gratuitous services to the public, that it was impossible to expedite them as much as could be wished; and that, if the House laid down any fixed rule on the subject it would be complied with, 'but the effect would be that the miscellaneous estimates would be imperfect, and the practice of presenting supplementary estimates—one of the greatest financial evils the House could endure—would of necessity prevail.' Nevertheless, the Civil Service estimates for 1866-67 were laid upon the table, in an improved shape, on February 16, 1866, being within sixteen days of the meeting of Parliament. This desirable arrangement having been once accomplished, it will probably be adhered to in future.

Supplementary estimates.

The objection urged by Mr. Gladstone in the foregoing remarks against the practice of Supplementary Estimates, is one that he has repeatedly pressed upon the attention of Parliament. In his evidence before the Committee on Public Accounts, in 1862, he stated that he regarded such estimates 'with great jealousy. Though very plausible in theory, he thought that in practice nothing tended so much to defeat the efficacy of parliamentary control as the easy resort to supplementary estimates. To render this control effectual, it was necessary that the House of Commons should have the money transactions of the year presented to it in one mass, and in one account. If it is to be a set of current transactions,

---

' Treasury minute of December 23, 1858, in Commons Papers, 1860, vol. xxxix. pt. i. p. 170.
* Hans. Deb. vol. clxv. p. 1030.

with a balance varying from time to time, the House would never know where it was. If supplementary estimates were easily and frequently resorted to, the House would be obliged, in self-defence, to appoint a permanent Finance Committee.'"

The great and increasing expenditure of government has given rise to various expedients, on the part of financial reformers, to effect reductions in the same. The constitutional course of appointing a Committee of Public Accounts will be noticed in its proper place. Such committees, however, are necessarily limited to the investigation of past transactions, and to the consideration of questions arising out of the management of financial matters by the executive government. Not content with such legitimate enquiries, attempts have occasionally been made to induce the House of Commons to appoint select committees to revise the estimates before they should be submitted to the Committee of Supply; but these attempts have been uniformly unsuccessful. In one or two instances, during the reign of William III., we read of the estimates, with other accounts, being referred to a select committee;' but since the doctrine of ministerial responsibility has been properly understood, no such proceedings have been permitted, as the following cases will show :—

Proposed reductions in the public expenditure.

Committee to revise the estimates.

Precedents

On March 16, 1835, Mr. Hume moved to refer the Navy estimates to a select committee, prior to their being submitted to the committee of supply. The Chancellor of the Exchequer (Sir Robert Peel) opposed the motion, declaring that 'it is for the executive government, from the information it receives from all quarters, diplomatic and otherwise, to judge of what the country ought to bear, and then to submit that opinion to the approbation of the House. The government might be required to form their judgment upon facts which it might not be consistent with their duty publicly to disclose, and they are bound to ask, in some instances, for not personal but political confidence from the House. To entrust all this to a finance committee would be to transfer

---

* Com. on Pub. Accts. 1862. Evid. 1571. See also his remarks in Hans. Deb. vol. clxix. p. 1840. And in the debate on the supplementary estimates submitted by Mr. Disraeli, in 1867, *ibid.* vol. clxxxiv. pp. 1202, 1073.

' Hans. Deb. vol. clxv. p. 1325.

Precedents the duty of the monarchy to the House of Commons.' Sir James Graham, a leader of the Opposition, also opposed the motion, and it was negatived by a large majority. A few days afterwards Mr. Hume moved that the Army and Ordnance estimates be referred to a select committee, with a view to the reduction of expenditure, and for other purposes. The motion was opposed by Lord John Russell, the leader of the Opposition, and it was resisted by Sir Robert Peel on the ground that the executive government commands means of information which neither the House of Commons nor a select committee can have access to, and it is their constitutional province, on their own responsibility, to propose what the exigencies of the public service may require. Mr. Hume expressed his willingness to concede to the discretion of the government the amount of force to be maintained, but this did not satisfy Sir R. Peel, who pointed out the serious objections which existed to a transference of the constitutional revision of the whole House over the estimates to a committee of a few members, who could not exercise an efficient control, and whose assumed jurisdiction would nevertheless practically operate to withdraw the supply votes from the beneficial scrutiny of the committee of the whole House. After some further discussion the motion was withdrawn.

In 1857, a similar motion, to refer the Army estimates to a select committee, not being seconded, fell to the ground.

In 1847, notice being taken that 'a constant increase was going on in the Miscellaneous estimates, which required some efficient check,' the government were asked to consent to the appointment of 'a committee, or other tribunal, to which the said estimates could be submitted, previously to the House being called upon to vote them in committee of supply.' The First Lord of the Treasury (Lord John Russell) admitted that ' there was great room for enquiry, and early in the next session he hoped that a select committee would lay down some principles on which in future it would be safe to proceed.' Accordingly, on February 22, 1848, Lord John Russell himself moved for the appointment of two committees, one to enquire into the expenditure of the Navy, Army, and Ordnance, the other into the Miscellaneous expenditure of the country. These committees were restricted in their enquiries within constitutional limits; the government did not propose to abandon their discretion and responsibility in regard to the force required to be maintained in any department of the public service,

---

* Mirror of Parl. 1835, p. 314. And see similar remarks by Mr. Disraeli, when in opposition, in 1857. Hans. Deb. vol. cxlvi. p. 64. See also Grey, Parl. Gov. p. 78; Mill, Rep. Gov. p. 90.
* Mirror of Parl. 1835, pp. 802–802.
* Hans. Deb. vol. cxlv. p. 843.
* Ibid. vol. xciv. p. 185.

but, with this proviso, they invited the fullest investigation into the details of the public expenditure, with a view to reductions to be made in future estimates.[d] Notwithstanding the difference of origin, these two committees were substantially the same as the finance committees which are now annually appointed by the House of Commons, and which have never sought to interfere with the estimates for the ensuing year, as laid upon the table of the House by command of the sovereign. Nevertheless, great public advantages have resulted from the labours of these committees, in the simplification and improvement of the estimates in future years, as well as in the reduction of the public expenditure.

On March 11, 1862, another attempt was made to induce the House of Commons to control the estimates, by Lord Robert Montagu, who moved to resolve that, in order to strengthen the check upon the government in regard to issues of money for any public service whatever, in excess of the sums voted by Parliament, as well as to secure the just appropriation of every payment voted by Parliament to its proper account, a committee be appointed, to be annually nominated by the Committee of Selection, for the purpose of revising all estimates or accounts laid before Parliament, with instruction to consider of improving the present system of audit, and also to report to the House the exact period of the financial year when it would be desirable that the annual estimates should be presented to Parliament, so as to enable the necessary examination of such estimates or accounts to be completed and reported upon by the said committee before this House proceeds to sanction such estimates, &c. by a vote of payment in supply. This proposal that the estimates should undergo revision by a select committee was strenuously resisted by the government, as cutting at the root of our present political system. Any such committee would either supersede the House, in its duty of examining and passing the accounts, or it would supersede the government in its duty of submitting them. It would lead to a transference of the responsibility of the government for the estimates to an irresponsible body. The motion was negatived, on division, by a large majority.'[e]

And here it may be suitable to refer to a class of motions

---

[d] Hans. Deb. vol. xcvi. pp. 1057-1070; vol. ci. p. 713.

[e] Ibid. vol. clxv. pp. 1300-1350. See also General Peel's remarks on the question of referring the estimates to a select committee, Ibid. p. 940. On April 13, 1863, a motion to refer part 1. of the Civil Service estimates (on Public Works) to a select committee was negatived. See a similar case on May 20, 1864. On April 3, 1865, a motion to refer the whole Civil Service estimates to a select committee was proposed, and withdrawn after a few remarks from the Secretary of the Treasury. Hans. Deb. vol. clxxviii. p. 717.

which, although they do not concern the estimates for the current year, are, nevertheless, intended to effect a prospective reduction of the annual estimates, and to express the constitutional opinion of the House of Commons in regard to the increase of the public expenditure.

Motions for reduction of expenditure.

Precedents

On July 10, 1849, it was moved by Mr. Henley to resolve, that a reduction of ten per cent. be made in all salaries in all the departments of government, at home and abroad. The motion was opposed by the Chancellor of the Exchequer, who contended that the public servants were not more highly paid than was necessary to their adequate remuneration. After debate, the motion was negatived by a large majority. But on April 12, 1850, on motion of Lord John Russell (the Prime Minister), a select committee was appointed to enquire into the salaries and emoluments of offices held, during the pleasure of the crown, by members of Parliament, and also into the salaries, fees, and pensions of judicial officers, and into the cost of the diplomatic service. This committee made a valuable report on the duties of official persons of the highest rank, but generally adverse to a reduction of salaries.[f]

On March 10, 1857, Mr. Gladstone moved to resolve that, 'in order to secure to the country that relief from taxation which it justly expects, it is necessary, in the judgment of this House, to revise and further reduce the expenditure of the state.' The House of Commons had, a few days previously, censured the government (which otherwise possessed the confidence of the House) for the conduct of affairs in China, and the government had determined to appeal to the country by a dissolution of Parliament. In order to enable them to carry on the public service until the assembling of a new Parliament, ministers applied to the House of Commons for a 'vote on account,' for four months. Having no objection to this course, and admitting it to be just and customary, Mr. Gladstone was yet of opinion that the proposed estimates were excessive. He accordingly sought, by this motion, to compel the government to re-consider their estimates before the re-assembling of Parliament, and to submit them, with considerable reductions, to the judgment of the new House of Commons. The House did not concur with Mr. Gladstone as to the propriety or expediency of this motion, and it was negatived without a division.

On June 3, 1862, Mr. Stansfeld moved to resolve, that the national expenditure is capable of reduction, without compro-

---

[f] Commons Papers, 1850, vol. xv. p. 170. See Treasury minute of May 20, 1851, recording the steps which have been taken for giving effect to the recommendations of this committee. *Ibid.* 1851, vol. xxxi. p. 379.

mising the safety, independence, or legitimate influence of the country. In amendment, Lord Palmerston (the Prime Minister) moved that the House, sensible of the necessity of economy, is at the same time mindful of its obligation to provide for the security of the country at home and the protection of its interests abroad, and that it observes with satisfaction the decrease already effected in the national expenditure, and trusts such further diminution may be made in it as the future state of things may warrant. Besides this amendment, no less than five other amendments, either to Mr. Stansfeld's, or to Lord Palmerston's motion, stood upon the notice paper. One of them (Mr. Walpole's) was regarded by Lord Palmerston as equivalent to a vote of want of confidence; he therefore suggested that it should have the priority. The members who were about to propose the other amendments agreed to withhold them; but Mr. Walpole declared that he did not intend a vote of censure by his motion, yet, after Lord Palmerston's statement respecting it, he was not prepared to encounter the responsibilities which would be entailed by the success of his amendment, and therefore he would not move it. Lord Palmerston, in justifying his own amendment, said that he hoped that the government would next year be able to present diminished estimates to Parliament. After a long debate, Lord Palmerston's amendment was carried, by a large majority. In the two following sessions, upon opening the budget, the Chancellor of the Exchequer referred to this resolution, and showed that the government had succeeded in effecting considerable reductions in the estimates for the ensuing year, with a reasonable hope of further retrenchment in future.[a] Upon the accession of the Derby administration to office, in 1866, Mr. Disraeli, the new Chancellor of the Exchequer, took occasion to advert to this resolution, and to assure the House that the financial policy of the government would be framed in accordance therewith.[b]

On February 11, 1864, Sir H. Willoughby called the attention of the House to the enormous increase of taxation and expenditure within the last few years. The annual average of the public expenditure during the years 1842 to 1846 was 50,250,000l., whilst in 1864 it amounted to nearly 70 millions. This amount of taxation was levied in a time of peace, and was entirely independent of the local taxation, which amounted to nearly twenty millions additional! In giving his explanations on this subject, the Chancellor of the Exchequer stated that, owing to the great increase in the items of the civil expenditure, the task of the Treasury in controlling the same had become increasingly onerous and difficult, and could only be

---

[a] Hans. Deb. vol. clxx. p. 200; Ibid. vol. clxxiv. p. 688.
[b] Ibid. vol. clxxxiv. p. 1280.

450   THE ROYAL PREROGATIVE.

Precedents. effectually performed when the government was sustained by the House of Commons in its efforts to resist additional expenditure.'[1]

On March 1, 1864, Mr. Marsh moved that the Civil Service and Miscellaneous Estimates had been, for many years, rapidly increasing, and ought to be reduced. After explanations from the Secretary of the Treasury as to the causes which had occasioned this increase, and rendered it unavoidable, a brief debate ensued, which ended in the withdrawal of the motion.

On February 26, 1866, Mr. White moved to resolve, that the expenditure of the government has, of late years, been excessive; that it is taken in great measure out of the earnings of the people, &c. After a long debate, the motion was withdrawn.

Contents of the estimates.
The estimates of the supplies required by government for the service of the ensuing year are at present (1866) divided into about 170 separate votes, or resolutions, which appropriate specified sums for services specially defined, and for the period of one year. Some of the votes are for very large amounts, but, practically, there is no more difficulty in dealing with such votes than with any others, inasmuch as each vote is accompanied, in the printed estimates, with a list of the particular items, or heads, of expenditure, which are intended to be defrayed out of the same. In addition to the information thus afforded in regard to the proposed expenditure, the printed estimates contain numerous explanatory notes, and, occasionally, an appendix of official correspondence in relation to particular branches of expenditure. The estimates are now submitted to the House of Commons in much greater detail than formerly, in order to meet the increasing demand for full and accurate information upon all matters which concern the public expenditure.[2]

Army and Navy estimates.
Considerable improvements have recently been made in the framing of the Army and Navy estimates.[3] And, as a result of the passing of the Exchequer and Audit

---

[1] Hans. Deb. vol. clxxiii. p. 477.
[2] Ibid. vol. clxvii. p. 50; Ibid. vol. clxxi. p. 322.
[3] Reports, Sel. Committ. on Navy, Army, and Ordnance Estimates, in Commons Papers, 1847-48, vol. xxi.; 1849, vol. ix.; 1850, vol. x. Reports, Com. on Pub. Accounts, 1864, Evid. p. 2; 1865, p. 31.

Departments Act of 1866, it has been proposed, by the Treasury, to re-model the classification of the estimates for Miscellaneous Civil Services. At present these estimates are arranged under seven heads, or classes, of subjects, viz.:—1. Public Works and Buildings; 2. Salaries and Expenses of Public Departments; 3. Law and Justice; 4. Education, Science, and Art; 5. Colonial, Consular, and other Foreign Services; 6. Superannuation and Retired Allowances, and Gratuities for Charitable and other purposes;[1] 7. Miscellaneous, Special, and Temporary Objects. The Lords of the Treasury are of opinion that henceforth it will be more convenient, not only as a means of facilitating discussion on the estimates in the House of Commons, but also in the subsequent preparation and audit of the appropriation accounts of the expenditure incurred, that the services conducted under the responsibility of distinct departments of the government should, as far as possible, be grouped together in a distinct series of votes. This opinion has been concurred in by the Committee of Public Accounts.[m]

Civil Service estimates.

A careful and discriminative classification of votes, and items of votes, in the annual estimates, materially facilitates the classification of payments, limits the discretion of accountants, and leaves less room for differences of opinion in regard to the vote to which a particular payment is chargeable.[n] It is therefore of great importance

Classification of estimates.

---

[1] It is worthy of remark that the English estimates, as a general rule, contain but few grants in aid of private charities or local benevolent institutions. It is considered that the practical result of governmental aid to such institutions would be to dry up the sources of private benevolence, upon which local charities must chiefly depend, and to weaken the motives for their economical management, thereby seriously injuring instead of promoting their welfare. Rep. Com. Misc. Exp. 1847-48, pp. 27, 35. Hans. Deb. vol. clxvi. p. 1003. Peto on Taxation, p. 303.

[m] Treasury minute, dated June 22, 1869. Commons Papers, 1869, No. 343. Rep. Com. Pub. Accts., 1866, pp. iii. 6. For an account of the Miscellaneous Civil Service estimates, their classification, gradual increase, and revision, with a view to reduction, see Peto on Taxation, p. 310; Reports of Committees on Misc. Exp. in 1847-8; and on Public Accts. in 1861 and 1862. Mr. Gladstone, in Hans. Deb. vol. clxxiv. p. 638.

[n] Rep. Com. Pub. Moneys, 1857, App. pp. 35, 83.

that no pains should be spared in the judicious preparation of the estimates.

When the estimates have been presented to the House, they are ordered to be printed for the use of members, and are referred to the Committee of Supply.

Committee of Supply.

The sittings of the Committee of Supply then commence. The member of the administration who is charged with the duty of representing the particular department on behalf of which the grants are proposed,[a] first explains to the committee whatever may be necessary to satisfy them as to the general expediency and propriety of the class of estimates under consideration, and then proceeds to propose each grant in succession. When the Navy or Army estimates are under the consideration of the committee, it is customary to permit members to animadvert upon the whole estimates, or upon naval or military matters generally, before the first vote is taken; and this opportunity is usually embraced, by the mover of the estimates, to review the general subject-matter of the same. But, after the first vote, the discussion is strictly confined to the particular vote before the committee.[b] The Civil Service estimates, however, are of too multifarious a description to be dealt with in a general statement.[c]

Each resolution of Supply is proposed from the chair in the following words: 'That a sum not exceeding £———

---

[a] Hans. Deb. vol. cxlv. p. 850. By the usage of Parliament, the estimates for the British Museum, after they have been approved by the Treasury, are invariably introduced and moved by some member of the governing body of that institution, irrespective of his political opinions, the preference being given to one who is not an ex-officio trustee. Mirror of Parl. 1840, p. 4537. Hans. Deb. vol. clv. p. 430. Ibid. vol. clxvii. p. 450. This is confessedly an anomalous practice (see Lord H. Lennox's motion on the subject in the Commons on March 18, 1862); but it has the advantage of ensuring, as the representative in the House of this great national collection, one who is familiar with its multifarious details, and able to afford minute information concerning its actual condition and requirements. On this account the administration have been hitherto unwilling to change this arrangement for one more in accordance with the principles of parliamentary government. Ibid vol. clxix. p. 1055; Ibid. vol. clxxvi. p. 1358; Ibid. vol. clxxxiv. pp. 1557, 1603.

[b] Ibid. vol. clxxxi. pp. 1321, 1626.

[c] Ibid. p. 1782.

be granted to her Majesty' for the object specified in the particular vote in the printed estimates. This motion may be either agreed to or negatived, but it is not competent for the committee to make any alteration therein which could change the destination of the vote,' or increase the amount proposed,' because the House of Commons can only vote money pursuant to the recommendation of the crown. In like manner, it is irregular to move an instruction to the Committee of Supply, as it is only competent for the committee to consider the estimates which have been submitted to the consideration of the House by the crown.'

On May 18, 1863, ministers proposed a vote in Committee of Supply on account of the packet service, to which was appended a proviso that no part of the same should be applied to pay Mr. Churchward for postal services under a contract which had been condemned by the House itself. An amendment was offered to omit this proviso, but it was objected to as being irregular. The chairman, however, ruled that it was in order, inasmuch as ' it did not enlarge or divert the vote from any purpose.'⁷ In answer to an objection made to the proviso itself, the Chancellor of the Exchequer contended that, because a condition of this kind might be proposed on behalf of the crown, it did not follow that a similar proposal could be made by an independent member. Moreover, the proposal of the crown did not affect the service itself, and was no precedent for any vote which might limit or alter that service.⁷ The ministerial proposition was accordingly agreed to.

' The Speaker, Hans. Deb. vol. lxxi. p. 206. *Ibid.* vol. clxix. p. 1774; vol. clxxiii. p. 1282.
' *Ibid.* vol. calviii. p. 392. So a motion to increase the number of men in a vote on the Army estimates, though professedly intended merely to rectify an error in the calculations of ministers, was declared to be irregular. *Ibid.* vol. clxix. p. 1207; and see *ante*, p. 437.
' The Speaker, Mirror of Parl. 1828, p. 1972. But see the proceedings in the case of Capt. Ross, the Arctic navigator, to obtain for him a grant of 5,000*l.* Upon his petitioning the House of Commons, with the consent of the crown, his petition was referred to a select committee, reported upon favourably, and then, his petition having been previously referred to the Committee of Supply, a vote was agreed to in supply on motion of a private member, to grant him the sum recommended by the select committee. *Ibid.* 1834, pp. 608, 797, 843, 2804. And see a similar case in regard to a vote proposed by Mr. Hume, in Committee of Supply, for the purchase of 1250 copies of Marshall's Digest of Statistics. *Ibid.* 1853, p. 1513.

* See the particulars of this case, *post*, p. 408.
' Hans. Deb. vol. clxx. p. 1884.
⁷ *Ibid.* p. 2038.

Votes in Supply.

The votes in Committee of Supply are usually proposed for large sums for particular heads of services, but as the separate items for which the supply is required are detailed in the estimates, the practice of the House (as altered in 1857) permits of a question being put that any item objected to 'be omitted from the proposed vote,' or, 'be reduced by the sum of £——,' as the case may be. Where a general reduction of a particular vote is proposed, the question is first put upon the smallest amount proposed to be granted; and, in like manner, if more than one amendment be offered, conformably to the ancient order of the House, 'That where there comes a question between the greater and lesser sum, or the longer and shorter time, the least sum and the longest time ought first to be put to the question.' [a] After a motion for the reduction of a particular item in a vote has been proposed from the chair, it is not competent to propose a motion in relation to, or to debate, a previous item,[b] but any question in regard to the same may be raised upon the report of the resolutions to the House.

It is irregular to move in Committee of Supply for the adoption of a general resolution in regard to any particular vote,[c] or to move that a particular vote be referred to a select committee.[d] But a vote can be reduced, with the ulterior object of moving in the House for the appointment of a select committee to enquire into the question connected therewith.[e]

A vote proposed in Committee of Supply may not, in point of form, be postponed, because there is no period to which it can be postponed.[f] But the mover may, with the consent of the committee, withdraw it, and submit it again on another day, with or without alteration, and either as a distinct vote, or in separate items.[g]

---

[a] May, Parl. Prac. ed. 1863, pp. 550–562. Hans. Deb. vol. clxxii. p. 1020.
[b] Ibid. vol. clxxix. p. 1280.
[c] Mirror of Parl. 1831, p. 1826;
[d] Ibid. 1831-2, p. 3472.
[e] Hans. Deb. vol. clxxii. p. 131.
[f] Ibid. vol. clix. p. 549.
[g] Mirror of Parl. 1840, p. 1498; Ibid. 1840, p. 2307.

On June 15, 1863, Lord Palmerston moved, in Committee of Supply, for the adoption of a vote of 67,000*l.* to purchase land at South Kensington. This formed part of a general proposition for the purchase of the International Exhibition building, the entire cost of which had been stated in the estimates at 484,000*l.* Of this amount, the one item of land alone had been estimated at 172,000*l.*; and objection was taken that the government had no right, suddenly, and without previous notice, to ask for a *less sum* than they had proposed in the estimates to apply for. But it was ruled by the chairman, and subsequently by the speaker, that there was nothing irregular in this proceeding.[d] On June 8, 1865, the vote for temporary commissions was taken for 30,702*l.*, being 5,000*l. more* than was set down in the estimates. No explanation was given as to the reason for this alteration.[e]

The Committee of Supply considers the money to be voted for the *current year*. Where the proposed grant is not part of the service of the current year—as, for instance, a permanent increase to judges' salaries—it is more regular to propose it in any other committee of the whole House than the Committee of Supply, provided the queen's recommendation is first signified, and on their report a Bill is ordered, or a clause inserted in a Bill already before the House.[f]

In Supply money is voted only for the current year.

The entire sums proposed to be granted for particular services are not always voted at the same time, but a certain sum is occasionally voted either 'on account' or as a vote of credit. Votes of credit are usually asked

Votes of credit.

---

[d] Hans. Deb. vol. clxxi. p. 937. *Ibid.* vol. clxxii. p. 74. On another occasion, the government, without previous notice, reduced an intended vote by 33,000*l.* on account of circumstances which had transpired since the framing of the estimates. *Ibid.* vol. clxxiv. p. 830. Again, on May 9, 1864, the vote for Miscellaneous Services (Army) was taken for 5,000*l.* less than the original estimate, but the proceeding excited no remark. Smith's Parl. Rememb. 1864, p. 81.

[e] *Ibid.* 1865, p. 81.

[f] See May's Prac. ed. 1863, p. 577.

486   THE ROYAL PREROGATIVE.

Votes 'on account.'

for on behalf of contemplated war expenditure, when it is necessary to have ample funds on hand, and impossible to determine beforehand the exact amount required.[a] Votes 'on account' have, until lately, been restricted to occasions of unexpected emergency, arising out of ministerial changes, when it has been desirable to place at the disposal of government funds for the public service without specifically appropriating the same to particular items of expenditure. In such cases it is usual to vote a portion only of the yearly estimates, and in the following session to enquire into the expenditure thereof, in order to ascertain that it was duly appropriated to legitimate purposes.[b] When Parliament is about to be dissolved, upon a ministerial crisis, it is obviously improper to call upon the House of Commons to vote either the full amount or all the details of the proposed estimates, and so commit the country to the financial policy of ministers whose fate is about to be determined by a general election. The duty of finally deciding upon these estimates should be reserved for the new House of Commons. Meanwhile the supply of credit should be restricted to such an amount as may be absolutely required for the public service, until the re-assembling of Parliament, and the vote 'on account' should not be regarded as in any degree pledging the House to an approval of the entire estimates.[c]

Surrender of unexpended balance.

Within the last few years, however, the practice of taking votes 'on account' has become more general.[d] This is owing to the gradual introduction of a new rule, requiring the government to surrender into the Exchequer, at the end of the year, all unexpended balances. This change of system was completely effected at the expiration of the financial year terminating on March 31, 1863,

---

[a] May's Pract. ed. 1863, p. 668.
[b] See 3 Hatsell, pp. 213–215.
[c] Hans. Deb. vol. cxliv. p. 2170. Ibid. vol. clviii. p. 1047. This course was followed, upon pending ministerial changes, in 1841, 1857, and 1859. See May's Prac. p. 507.
[d] Smith's Parl. Rememb. 1860, p. 135. Hans. Deb. vol. clxiii. p. 1536.

when, 'for the first time in our financial history, all the services were required to surrender the balances standing to their credit.'[k] This arrangement has necessitated an application to Parliament, before the close of the first quarter of the new financial year, for a vote 'on account,' to meet the ordinary charges accruing therein. But this practice is not altogether free from objection. When such a vote is submitted, it is always for one large sum 'on account of certain Civil Services;' and the House is deprived of the opportunity of considering, adequately, the particular items of any vote included therein, until, on a future occasion, definitive votes are taken for the balances required for each particular service.[l] And when the completion of the vote is asked for, it has been urged that it may be late in the session, when the attendance of members is thin, and the disposition of the House adverse to minute investigation.[m] But it is probable that the government will be able to meet this objection by a timely introduction of votes for balances. On March 27, 1863, the Chancellor of the Exchequer said, 'The practice to vote "on account" was entirely novel, because it was incident to a system which had been adopted for the purpose of giving effect to an important administrative improvement. It was necessary to prepare a list of

Votes 'on account.'

[k] Chanc. of Exch. in Hans. Deb. vol. clxx. p. 209. It appears, however, that, in regard to the Civil Service expenditure, the Treasury have resolved to retain any unexpended balances of 'the last year's votes,' to be used towards payments falling due in the first quarter of the next financial year. So much of the ordinary expenses of the quarter as cannot be met from this source is defrayed out of a 'vote on account,' which is taken early in the session. Hans. Deb. vol. clxxviii. p. 733. And this vote evidently includes the amount remaining over from the previous year; otherwise an unauthorised expenditure would be incurred. See Ibid. p. 851.

[l] On July 10, 1863, on a vote for 3,781l. to complete a large amount voted 'on account' for civil contingencies, an item of 6,000l. was objected to, and the government consented to its being omitted. But as they could not reduce a smaller sum by a larger, the vote for 3,781l. was withdrawn altogether. Hans. Deb. vol. clxxii. p. 544. See also a discussion on 'votes on account,' in Hans. Deb. vol. clxxviii. p. 733, &c.

[m] See Mr. A. Smith's motion, on June 20, 1861, deprecating this practice, and observations thereon in T. Smith's Parl. Rememb. 1861, p. 135.

Votes 'on account.'

votes on which probable advances would be required before there was an opportunity of bringing them definitively before the House.' That ' was a practice to which recurrence would necessarily have to be had in future years.'ᵃ Again, on March 8, 1866, it was stated by the Secretary to the Treasury (Mr. Childers) that it was understood that the vote ' on account' should involve no new principle, but should be only in conformity with the votes taken for similar services during the previous year; and that the rule had been never to take more than a fourth part of the vote for the year, except in certain particular cases of public emergency; so that the committee, in agreeing to votes ' on account,' would not pledge themselves to the estimates for the year, in anticipation of the opportunity to be afterwards afforded of voting them in detail.ᵇ

Responsibility for grant of supply.

While the government are solely responsible for the propriety and extent of any application to the House to grant supplies, the Commons are themselves responsible for voting the same. The House looks to the executive to state what is wanted, and to make known to them all that is necessary to satisfy them of the expediency of the grant. If the information communicated be not full and satisfactory, it is always in the power of the House to withhold the grant of any particular item until they are satisfied with the reasons given for it.ᶜ

It is the peculiar province of the government to decide upon the several amounts required to carry on the public service, and to maintain the credit of the country at home and abroad. None others are equally competent to form a judgment on this question. On the other hand, the

---

ᵃ Hans. Deb. vol. clxx. p. 108. On this occasion, through some casual inadvertence, it happened that later on at the same sitting of the committee in which votes ' on account' of certain services were taken, definitive votes of the balances themselves were passed through Committee of Supply. This gave rise to much angry comment. Ibid. vol. clxix. pp. 1055, 1007; vol. clxx. pp. 105-106.

ᵇ Ibid. vol. clxxxi. p. 1780; and see Ibid. vol. clxxviii. p. 740.

ᶜ See Smith's Parl. Rememb. 1802, p. 111.

vigilant oversight which is constitutionally exercised by the House of Commons over the public expenditure is a continual check upon ministers, and serves to prevent profligate and extravagant outlay,^a which, in times past, when this control was less stringently applied, was of too frequent occurrence. The debates on the estimates, though generally but thinly attended, have been productive of incalculable public advantage.^b For, while it is impossible for a numerous representative assembly to scrutinise details of expenditure, and to form an accurate opinion in regard to all the items embraced in the estimates, equally devoid of extravagance or parsimony, nevertheless the moral influence which is exercised over the government by criticising the votes submitted for adoption in Committee of Supply is a more efficient and desirable restraint upon improper expenditure than even the formal rejection of particular votes.^c The function of the House of Commons, in matters of supply, is to exert a watchful but general control over the executive government, with a view to prevent unnecessary outlay, and to check abuses in the public expenditure; leaving to the ministers of the crown the responsibility, which properly

Effects of debates in Supply on the public expenditure.

---

^a See Smith's Parl. Rememb. 1801, p. 154; and *Ibid.* p. 140, Chatham Dockyard.

^b The late Joseph Hume was pre-eminently distinguished, throughout his long parliamentary career, for his untiring vigilance, and patient labour, in the cause of economy and retrenchment. Adequately to fulfil such a duty, 'time, energy, and labour must be devoted to the wearying, irksome, and self-denying work of becoming thoroughly acquainted with a vast mass of details, by following from point to point every item of public expenditure, and bringing to bear upon it the force of independent judgment and the light of public opinion.' Mr. Gladstone's eulogy upon Mr. Hume, Hans. Deb. vol. clxxxi. p. 1134. In commemoration of Mr. Hume's great public services, the House of Commons voted in favour of placing his bust within the precincts of the House. *Ibid.* vol. clxxxiv. pp. 485–494, 2168.

^c Sir S. Northcote, in Hans. Deb. vol. clxv. p. 800. Thus, on February 20, 1863, the government would have been defeated on an amendment to omit an item of 134,000*l.* for iron to armour-plate wooden ships, had not Lord Palmerston given a distinct pledge that no more of such ships should be built without the express sanction of the House. *Ibid.* vol. clxix. p. 853. See a further discussion on the same subject on March 12, 1863. And see Sir R. Peel's remarks on the Irish 'Agricultural vote.' *Ibid.* vol. clxxix. p. 1251.

belongs to their position, of asking for such supplies as the necessities of the state require, and of enforcing to the utmost a strict economy in the use of the funds entrusted to them.'

Items in the estimates rejected by the Commons.

In point of fact, since the introduction of parliamentary government, it has only been on rare and comparatively unimportant occasions that the demands of the crown for supplies for particular services have not been complied with. As a general rule, whatever sums ministers have stated to be required for the use of the state, the Commons have freely granted.

In proof of this the following instances may be cited from the parliamentary proceedings of the last eight years, as being the only cases wherein particular items in the annual estimates have been rejected by the House of Commons in Committee of Supply:—
In 1858, the salary of the travelling agent of the National Gallery, amounting to 300*l*., was disallowed; in 1859, the salary of the Registrar of Sasines; but on recommitment this was agreed to.* On August 1, 1859, the vote of 2,361*l*. for the Statute Law Consolidation Commission was rejected.* In 1860, the following items were rejected: On July 23, 1,200*l*. for erecting a building to hold the Wellington funeral car; on August 3, 1,600*l*. for two statues of British sovereigns in the new House of Parliament; on August 14, 800*l*. for extra clerks at the Board of Trade; and on August 15, the vote to defray the salary of Paymaster of Civil Services in Ireland was reduced by 1,000*l*., but this was agreed to by the government, as they contemplated the abolition of the office." In 1861, the government submitted a smaller vote (340*l*.) for the removal of the Wellington car to the crypt of St. Paul's, which was agreed to. The vote for the statues in the new Houses

---

' See Grey, Parl. Gov. new ed. p. 88. In the new edition of this valuable essay, Lord Grey (pp. 115, 221) points out the evils arising from the weakness of ministers in the House of Commons, as exemplified in the extent to which votes in supply have become less the expression of the deliberate views of the servants of the crown as to what would be best for the public service than of the opinion entertained at the moment by a fluctuating majority, a state of things which must unavoidably engender jobbery and reckless expenditure of the public treasury. And see Lord Grey's speech in Hans. Deb. vol. clxi p. 180. See also *Ibid.* vol. clxv p. 940.

* May, Const. Hist. vol. i. p. 470.
* Smith's Parl. Rememb. vol. ii. p. 150.
" Hans. Deb. vol. clx. p. 1325. And see Parl. Rememb. 1861, p. 132

of Parliament was also again submitted and agreed to." In the same year, on June 6, the Navy estimates were reduced by 3,225*l.*, being an item for the extension of the Chatham dockyard, a work which, if sanctioned by the House, would have occasioned an ultimate expenditure of over 900,000*l.* In 1862, on March 6, a vote of 10,787*l.* for enlarging the Royal Military College at Sandhurst was negatived, but afterwards, on March 13, reconsidered, and, on satisfactory explanations from government, agreed to: on April 28, a vote of 5,000*l.* for Highland roads and bridges was negatived. In 1863, on June 4, an item of 400*l.* for a clerk of the works at Constantinople was rejected; on July 2, a vote of 105,000*l.* for the purchase, &c. of the Exhibition buildings at South Kensington was negatived; on July 10, a proposed item of 6,000*l.* for expenses connected with the Thames Embankment Bill of 1862, being objected to, was withdrawn. In 1864, on May 2 (upon motion of the Secretary of the Admiralty), an item of 5,000*l.*, intended to be applied towards the construction of a dock at Malta, was negatived, to admit of further information being obtained as to the proper site of the dock, agreeably to suggestions made by Opposition members in the House of Commons;[?] on May 30, a vote of 4,000*l.* for the erection of a lunatic asylum in the Isle of Man (but in the following session this vote was again proposed and agreed to),[3] and on June 6, a vote of 10,000*l.* (on account of a total estimate of 150,000*l.*) towards the erection of a new National Gallery at Burlington House, were severally negatived. In 1865, and in 1866, all the supply votes submitted by government were agreed to by the House of Commons.

Independently, in the first instance, of the Committee of Supply, there is another mode of initiating proceedings for the grant of public money—namely, by the introduction of Bills for the construction of public works, the establishment of new institutions, or for other purposes, that necessitate, to a greater or less extent, new charges upon the people. Sometimes the government is authorised by such Bills to undertake the construction of certain public works, the cost of which is to be defrayed out of the Consolidated Fund.[a] But usually such Bills

Bills involving money charges.

---

[a] Hans. Deb. vol. clxiv. pp. 151, 170.
[?] See *Ibid.* vol. clxxvii. pp. 1104, 1173.
[3] *Ibid.* vol. clxxix. p. 507.
[a] See the Fortifications Expenses Acts, 23 & 24 Vict. c. 109; 25 & 26 Vict. c. 78; 26 & 27 Vict. c. 80; 27 & 28 Vict. c. 100; 28 & 29 Vict. c. 61. But on July 30, 1860, in deference to objections made by members of the House of Commons to the

contain a clause providing that the charges in question shall be defrayed 'out of moneys to be voted by Parliament.' Hitherto it has been customary to permit Bills of this description to be introduced by private members, without reference to the government; but this practice led to so much irregularity that, in the session of 1866, a new standing order was adopted, requiring the recommendation of the crown to be given before the House will entertain any motion that will involve a charge upon the public revenue, whether direct or out of moneys to be provided by Parliament.[b] The effect of this order will be to place the introduction of such Bills hereafter under the direct control of the government. But, under any circumstances, it will be incumbent upon the House of Commons to exercise a strict oversight and control over measures of this kind, as well as over the direct financial propositions of ministers. In the session of 1862, two such Bills, introduced by members of the administration, were rejected by the House on account of the excessive expenditure they would occasion.[c]

Must be recommended by the crown.

Addresses for advance of money.

Sometimes the House of Commons, either with or without the previous recommendation of the crown, as the case may be, agrees to address the crown to advance money for some particular purpose, with an assurance that the expenses to be incurred will be afterwards made good by the House. But this practice is only justifiable under peculiar circumstances, which have already engaged our attention in a former part of this chapter.[d]

---

introduction, late in the session, of a Bill to provide for the construction of certain additional works connected with this great scheme of national defence, the government withdrew the Bill, and agreed to proceed next year in the ordinary form of presenting an estimate for these works, and voting the same in Committee of Supply. See *post*, p. 401.
[b] See *ante*, p. 472.
[c] The motion, on February 25, 1862, for leave to bring in a Bill to construct a permanent road between Kensington and Bayswater, which, on account of the opposition it gave rise to, was withdrawn, and an estimate promised for a temporary road instead. The British Museum Bill, the motion for the second reading whereof was postponed on May 19, for 'three months.' See Smith's Parl. Rememb. 1862, pp. 25, 101.
[d] See *ante*, p. 415.

There is yet another method whereby it has been customary for public expenditure to be either pledged or actually incurred by government to amounts in excess of that which has been actually voted by Parliament— namely, by means of contracts, or other engagements, entered into for the construction of public works, or the performance of particular services for the public benefit. Such contracts necessarily pledged the government to prospective payments for a series of years, while the funds required could only be obtained by annual votes in Committee of Supply, or by special Acts passed from time to time, granting the necessary sums, the consent of Parliament to the continuance of the contract being assumed from their concurrence in the initial payment proposed, while their vote has been given, perhaps, in total ignorance of the terms of the contract itself.* The attention of Parliament was first directed to the irregularity of this practice, and to the necessity for the exercise of a more rigid control over this branch of expenditure, in the year 1859, in consequence of certain objectionable transactions regarding contracts for postal and telegraphic services that then transpired. A committee was appointed by the House of Commons on the subject, and their reports led to the adoption by the House of various resolutions and standing orders, to be hereafter enumerated, which were intended to assert and maintain the right of the House to control the execution of such contracts. By these rules, ample provision has been made to secure that full information shall be given to the House when any such contracts have been entered into, and that they shall invariably contain a clause declaring that the consent of the House, either expressed or implied, is necessary to give them validity. Although at present these rules merely extend to the case of certain specified contracts, it has been admitted, by the highest authority,

<small>Contracts for public services.</small>

<small>Require the approval of the House of Commons.</small>

---

* See Hans. Deb. vol. clxxi. pp. 402–400.

that the executive has no constitutional right to make a contract which shall be binding on the House of Commons.' It may, therefore, be safely assumed that hereafter no contracts, involving any considerable amount of public expenditure beyond that which has been granted for the service of the current year will be carried out until the sanction of Parliament has been obtained on behalf of the same.

Contracts for military works.

In fact, in the session of 1862, the constitutional control of the House of Commons over contracts received a still more extended application, and was embodied in an Act of Parliament. In a previous session (that of 1860), the House had resolved to grant the sum of two million pounds to construct necessary works for the fortification of the British coast; and, in 1862, a Bill was brought in to provide for a large portion of this expenditure. On July 10, in committee on the Bill, a clause was proposed by Sir Stafford Northcote to declare that any contracts to be entered into by government for this service which involved the expenditure of a greater sum than that which had been already voted by Parliament must be previously approved of by the House of Commons. The ministry, at first, opposed this clause. The Chancellor of the Exchequer remarked that 'the practical wisdom and the good or bad economy of such contracts was a matter on which the House of Commons, as a deliberative assembly, had not the opportunity of forming an opinion in the same way as the executive government; and it was not according to usage that the government should be able to relieve itself of its special responsibility with regard to these contracts by a resolution of the House of Commons. The responsibility of the government would be better preserved by giving the House the power of interfering with these contracts before they became valid than by asking the House to approve each of them by a resolution.'

' Mr. Gladstone in Hans. Deb. vol. clvii. p. 1412. And see *ante*, p. 290.
' Hans. Deb. vol. clxviii. p. 109.

On a division, the clause was negatived by a majority of five. On July 14, however, the ministry announced their acceptance of this provision.[h] It accordingly appears in the statute to the following effect: That it shall not be lawful for the Secretary of State to enter into any contract involving the expenditure of any sum greater than that for which the authority of Parliament has been specifically obtained, without inserting therein a clause requiring that such contract shall not be binding until it has lain for one month on the table of the House of Commons without disapproval, or be formally approved of within that period.[i] The object of this clause is not to insist that every contract entered into by government for the construction of these works shall be first submitted for the approval of Parliament, but that no such contract shall be made for a greater sum than has been actually voted without the previous knowledge and consent of the House of Commons, so that the government may not be able to bind the House in such a way as to prevent entire freedom of action whenever a further appropriation is required.[k]

To be laid before Parliament.

Moreover, in regard to the expenditure to be incurred on behalf of these fortifications, it has been distinctly acknowledged by the government that, while they would be fully authorised to enter into contracts to amounts not exceeding the total estimated cost of the works, the general scheme of which had been sanctioned by Parliament, yet that the carrying out of any such contracts must depend upon the consent of Parliament to vote the sums required to make good the same, from time to time. And in a debate on a Bill to make further provision for these fortifications, it was stated by ministers that, with this additional grant, '*no new works*' as to the principle of which the House had not already pronounced

Contracts for new works.

---

[h] Hans. Deb. vol. clxviii. pp. 200, 635.
[i] 25 & 26 Vic. c. 78, sect. 2. See Smith's Parl. Rememb. 1862, p. 149.
[k] See Hans. Deb. vol. clxviii. pp. 187-203; Ibid. vol. clxxvi. p. 1533.
[l] Ibid. vol. clxxii. p. 688.

would be undertaken; and furthermore that, when the schedule of the Bill was under consideration, it would be competent for any member to move 'that a particular work should not be continued.'[a] The cost of these fortifications, as originally estimated by the Palmerston administration, was a little over five million pounds. From time to time, fresh grants, to make up the appropriation for this service to the required amount, were voted by Parliament. Meanwhile, the estimated cost of the works grew to between six and seven millions. But though additional sums of money were asked for to execute the works, 'the number and nature of the works to which the assent of Parliament had been given' remained unaltered. In 1866, however, the new Derby government were of opinion that some extension of the works was desirable. Accordingly, towards the close of the session, they submitted a Bill to the House of Commons to sanction the commencement of a new work, and to authorise the expenditure of 50,000*l.* on behalf of the same. The money itself was not required, inasmuch as there were sufficient funds in hand, which had been saved from former grants for fortifications. But it was necessary to obtain the sanction of Parliament to this new appropriation. The ex-Chancellor of the Exchequer, and other leading members, strongly objected to this Bill, for various reasons, but principally on the ground that 'the proposal should have been made in the estimates, at a time when the House was able to give its full mind to a matter of such importance.' Whereupon the Government agreed to withdraw the Bill, and 'to proceed next year in the ordinary and convenient form of presenting an estimate for these works, so that the House could have a fair opportunity of discussing the necessity for them.'[b]

Fortifications Bill of 1866.

In 1865, pursuant to the recommendations of the Select Committee on the Royal Dockyards in 1864, and with a

---

[a] Hans. Deb. vol. clxxvi. pp. 1583, 1873.   [b] *Ibid.* vol. clxxxiv. p. 1000, &c.

view to the more economical and expeditious completion of the works for the extension of the dockyards at Portsmouth and Chatham, the government obtained authority from Parliament for the Admiralty to enter into contracts for a term not exceeding five years, the maximum sum to be payable on behalf of any such contract not to exceed 250,000*l.* in any one year; the same to be defrayed out of moneys to be voted by Parliament, year by year, during the continuance of the contract; a copy of every contract entered into under this Act to be laid before both Houses of Parliament within thirty days after it has been made, or within thirty days after the next meeting of Parliament, if such contract was made during the recess.[*]

Dockyard works.

On March 20, 1865, the House of Commons was informed, in answer to a question, that the new contract with the West India and Pacific Steamship Company, for carrying mails to Jamaica, &c. being terminable at six months' notice, had no clause suspending its operation until it had been one month before the House. A copy of the contract was nevertheless laid upon the table.[†]

Postal contracts.

The following narrative of the proceedings of the Committee on Packet and Telegraphic Contracts in 1859 and 1860, and of the action of the House on their reports, will throw additional light upon this subject, and will also point out the steps that have been taken by the House to impeach the validity or expediency of any contract.

It was on July 7, 1859, that, upon motion of the Chancellor of the Exchequer, a select committee was appointed to enquire into and report on the manner in which contracts, extending over periods of years, have, from time to time, been formed or modified by her Majesty's government with various steam-packet companies for the conveyance of the mails by sea; and likewise into any agreements, actual or prospective, which have been adopted at the public charge for the purposes of telegraphic communications beyond sea; together

Packet and Telegraphic Contracts Committee.

---

[*] By Act 28 & 29 Vict. c. 51. And *Ibid.* vol.clxxix. p. 540.
see Hans. Deb. vol. clxxvii. p. 1161. [†] Hans. Deb. vol. clxxvii. p. 1021.

Churchward case.

with any recommendations as to rules to be observed hereafter by the government in making contracts for services which have not yet been sanctioned by Parliament, or which extend over a series of years. Owing to the late period of the session at which they commenced their labours, it was impossible for the committee to complete their enquiry before the prorogation. They accordingly confined their attention and devoted their first report to the circumstances under which the contract between the executive government and Messrs. Churchward and Jenkings for conveying the mails between Dover and the French coast had been renewed.[a] The extension had twice taken place, the last time on April 26, 1859, when the contract (which would expire in 1863) was further extended until 1870. This was done upon the recommendation of the Board of Admiralty, and in opposition to the views of the Postmaster-General.

It appeared in evidence before the committee, that on the eve of the last general election, when the extension of his contract was under consideration at the Treasury, Mr. Churchward volunteered his support, as an influential elector for Dover, to Captain Carnegie, one of the lords of the Admiralty, if he should become a candidate for that borough. He did this on the expectation that his contract was to be renewed. The committee, however, fully exonerated all the officers, both of the Admiralty and of the Treasury, with whom the decision in regard to this contract rested, from being influenced by any corrupt or political motive in granting the same. They did, indeed, consider that the conduct of Mr. Murray, the private secretary to the First Lord of the Admiralty, was open to grave censure; but they had not sufficient evidence to show that any member of the government was cognisant of the communications between Mr. Murray, Mr. Churchward, and Captain Carnegie.

While declaring themselves most anxious for the fulfilment of all engagements entered into in good faith between the government and private individuals, the committee, nevertheless, submitted to the House ' whether Mr. Churchward, in having resorted to corrupt expedients affecting injuriously the character of the representation of the people in Parliament, has not rendered it impossible for the House of Commons, with due regard to its honour and dignity, to vote the sums of money necessary to fulfil the agreement, to extend his contract from June 20, 1863, to April 26, 1870.'

A change of ministry having taken place since the last renewal of this contract, the incoming administration, in deference to the foregoing report, and to the general opinion of the House, tacitly con-

---

[a] Report on Post Office and Telegraphic Contracts, Commons Papers, 1860, sess. ii. vol. vi. p. 1.

curring therein, refused to recognise the amended contract, which Churchward case.
entitled Mr. Churchward to a fixed sum per annum, but permitted
him to continue to conduct his postal service under the former contract, under which he was ordinarily allowed a smaller amount
but was authorised to make extra charges for certain special services.
This contract would remain in force until June 1863, and was free
from objection of any kind, it not having been included in the censure of the committee.[r]

The friends of Mr. Churchward, however, were not willing that
his last contract should be thus set aside without a struggle. Accordingly, on March 27, 1860, Captain L. Vernon, who had been a
member of the afore-mentioned committee, moved to resolve that
this House, having considered the report and evidence presented by
the committee on packet contracts, is of opinion that the contract
entered into on April 26, 1859, between the Lords of the Admiralty
and J. G. Churchward ought to be fulfilled. The Chancellor of the
Exchequer (Mr. Gladstone) opposed this motion, declaring that the
impartial finding of the committee was entitled to respect; that
independently of their report it was clear from the evidence that
corrupt expedients, affecting injuriously the dignity of Parliament,
had been resorted to to obtain a renewal of this contract. Under
these circumstances, he added, the present ministry were under no
obligation to carry out the new contract, and the House were not
bound to vote the money, for 'the executive has no constitutional
authority to make a contract binding on the House of Commons.'[s]
Whereupon the motion was negatived on division.

Mr. Churchward strenuously remonstrated against the repudiation of his last contract, and applied for leave to have the case
between himself and the Admiralty argued before the Court of
Queen's Bench; but the Admiralty refused their consent to this
plan, declaring that they would do nothing that would admit the
validity of his claims or prejudice the decision of the House of Commons. The government also informed Mr. Churchward that they
would only undertake to propose and support in Parliament votes
for his services up to June 1863.

As a final effort, Mr. Churchward notified the Postmaster-General, in February 1863, that he had submitted his case to eminent
counsel, who had advised him that his last contract was good and
valid; and that, in the event of the department persisting in refusing to recognise it, he was at liberty to proceed, by petition of right,
to recover compensation for damages thereby sustained. In making
this communication, he expressed his desire to avoid being placed
in antagonism with the government, and expressed his willingness

---

[r] Hans. Deb. vol. clvii. pp. 1370, 1408.   [s] Ibid. p. 1412.

Churchward case.

either to leave his case to a court of law or to the decision of arbitrators. The department took no notice of this offer, but informed Mr. Churchward that his contract would terminate on June 20, 1863, and that tenders for the future conduct of the services in question had been accepted, subject, however, to a provision that, if Parliament should still vote the moneys which would be required to pay Mr. Churchward, under the proposed extension of his contract to April 26, 1870, the new arrangements were not to take effect. In reply, Mr. Churchward reiterated his remonstrances against the conduct of the government in treating his last contract as non-existent, and repeated his assurances of his readiness and ability to perform the same with efficiency up to its final termination.[t]

In order to bring this controversy to a definite conclusion, the government took the unusual course of appending to a vote on account of the packet service, proposed in Committee of Supply on May 18, 1863, a statement that the same included provision for payments to Mr. Churchward for postal services to June 20, 1863, and a proviso that no part of the vote should be applied towards any further payment to him, by virtue of his last contract with the Admiralty, in respect to the period subsequent to that date. This condition gave rise to a very animated debate, not only in committee, but also on the reception of the report by the House on May 29.[u] It was objected that it was quite unprecedented and foreign to the proper functions of the Committee of Supply to submit to it any motion other than one to agree to, reject, or reduce, a proposed grant; and that any such innovation in practice would be likely to lead to very serious consequences, affecting the constitutional relations of the House with the crown and with the Lords in the matter of supply. On the other hand, it was urged that this proceeding, if new, was not necessarily irregular; that it was one which the administration had chosen as being the most fitting method of carrying out the recorded opinion of the committee of 1859, and of the House in 1860, on Mr. Churchward's contract; that it was impossible the form of motion used on this occasion could be drawn into precedent to justify a departure, under different circumstances, from the recognised usage of Parliament in supply votes, inasmuch as the proviso in question was proposed by the government itself as a condition under which it asked for the money, and could not warrant a private member in attempting to limit or change the application of a proposed grant for a particular service. 'It does not follow,' said the Chancellor of the Exchequer, 'because a proposal of this kind

---

[t] Papers on Packet Service (Dover and Calais, &c.), Commons Papers, 1863, vol. xxx. p. 607. Report of Postmaster-General for 1862, p. 10.
[u] And see Hans. Deb. vol. clxxi. p. 1020.

may be made by the crown, therefore a similar proposal may be made by an independent member.' Moreover, 'the proposal of the crown refers to the exclusion of a particular individual from the performance of a stipulated service. It has no bearing on the service itself. It does not limit or alter the service, and, consequently, it is no precedent for any vote which might limit or alter that service.'[v] After much debate, the ministerial proposition was agreed to upon a division. It was afterwards inserted in the Appropriation Bill, and received the full sanction of law. As a further security to government against any claims that Mr. Churchward might continue to urge, similar clauses were inserted in the Appropriation Acts of 1864, 1865, and 1866.[w] Nevertheless, Mr. Churchward commenced proceedings in the Court of Queen's Bench against the Board of Admiralty by a petition of right, claiming damages to the extent of 120,000*l*. for injuries sustained by the cancelling of his contract. The case was ably argued on behalf of the plaintiff, but the court (in November 1865) decided against him, on the ground that it would be unjust and unwarrantable that the Admiralty should be obliged to carry out a contract after Parliament had refused to make provision for the same.[x]

To return to the proceedings of the Committee on Packet and Telegraphic Contracts. Having been unable to complete their enquiry in 1859, the committee was reappointed in the following session, and made three reports.

In their first report, the defects in the existing practice in regard to contracts for postal services entered into by the executive departments were pointed out, and the necessity for a more efficient control over the same by Parliament was strongly insisted upon. The practice, introduced by the Derby administration, of inserting words in postal contracts declaring the subsidies to be payable 'out of moneys to be voted by Parliament,' although it introduced no new principle in regard to the funds applicable to this service, distinctly recognised that all such contracts were subject to the approval of the House of Commons.[y] From the want, however, of early information as to the terms of existing contracts, and the fact that, until called upon, in Committee of Supply, to vote money on behalf of the

Control of Parliament over postal contracts.

---

[v] Hans. Deb. vol. clxx. p. 2090.
[w] 26 & 27 Vic. c. 119, sect. 18; 27 & 28 Vic. c. 73, sect. 17; 28 & 29 Vic. c. 123, sect. 24. 29 & 30 Vic. c. 91, s. 24.
[x] Law Times Reports, N. S. vol. xiv. p. 57.
[y] Hans. Deb. vol. clvii. pp. 1397, 1400. Sir Stafford Northcote informed the House that he had introduced these words when he was Financial Secretary of the Treasury in 1859, for the first time, into the Galway postal contract, in order 'to save the members of the government personally from actions which might otherwise be brought against them, in the event of Parliament, for any reason, declining to sanction the contract.' *Ibid.* vol. clx. p. 1001; and see *ibid.* vol. clxiii. p. 1103.

same, the House was ignorant of the nature and extent of agreements entered into by the executive government, it was obviously impossible for the House to exercise its right of control with that freedom which is absolutely essential for the right performance of its high functions. In the interval between the execution of a contract and the application to Parliament for a vote in supply on account thereof, heavy expenses and liabilities are necessarily incurred by the contractors, so as to render it a matter of peculiar hardship and difficulty for the House, in the absence of any charge of fraud, misrepresentation, or corrupt proceedings, to interpose and refuse to vote the moneys required to carry out a contract which has been entered into by government within the limits of its own authority.[a] Parliamentary control is thereby practically excluded in regard to an important branch of public expenditure. While it seems repugnant to the principles of our constitution that the executive government should be free to enter into contracts binding the country for prolonged periods, and by anticipation, to the payment of vast sums, without the possibility of any effective parliamentary check beyond the disapproval after the evil had been accomplished, and when perhaps the ministers by whom the contract was made were no longer in office, nevertheless the committee were fully sensible of the difficulties attending any change of system, which might result in a parliamentary canvass on behalf of competing candidates for a public contract. They accordingly recommended that these transactions should remain altogether in the hands of the executive, who should be free to execute any contract according to their own discretion and responsibility, but that a clause should be inserted in all new contracts for the conveyance of mails by sea, or for the purpose of telegraphic communications beyond sea, requiring that they shall not be binding until they have lain on the table of the House of Commons for one month, without disapproval, unless sooner approved of by a resolution of the House.[b]

Postal and Telegraphic contracts.

On July 24, the foregoing recommendation was embodied in a resolution, which was agreed to by the House of Commons, together with two other resolutions, providing (1) for the early transmission to the House of any such contracts, accompanied by a Treasury minute, setting forth the grounds on which the same have been executed,

---

[a] See Hans. Deb. vol. clvii. p. 1304.
[b] First Report of Sel. Com. on Packet and Telegraphic Contracts, 1860, pp. xiii.-xv. (in Com. Papers, 1860, vol. xiv. For precedents of proceedings had in the approval or disapproval of contracts by the House of Commons, see *ante*, p. 294.

and declaring (2) that, when any such contracts require to be confirmed by Act of Parliament, they should not be dealt with as private Bills, and that power to the government to enter into agreements by which obligations at the public charge shall be undertaken should not be given in any private Act.' So far as Bills relating to government contracts are concerned, these resolutions would appear to have been superseded by a new standing order, adopted by the House on March 4, 1861, and which, without taking such measures out of the category of private Bills, ensures that due attention shall be directed to them by requiring that the Chairman of the Committee of Ways and Means shall make a special report to the House previously to the second reading of any private Bill by which it is intended to authorise, confirm, or alter, any contract, with any department of the government, whereby a public charge has been or may be created, and providing for the due consideration of such report by the House." [Control of Parliament over contracts.]

The recommendations of the Packet and Telegraphic Contract Committee of 1860, in their first report, were principally founded upon the proceedings of government in reference to the Galway contract; and as a brief narrative of this case will contribute to elucidate the subject of parliamentary control over transactions of this description, it is here subjoined.

In 1858, a private company, of which Mr. Lever was the managing director, established a line of steamers for commercial purposes, to ply between the ports of Galway, in Ireland, and New York, in the United States. This scheme excited considerable interest, especially in Ireland, and several deputations waited upon the ministry, in the course of that year, urging the importance of its being encouraged by government. After much negotiation between the parties, it was at length agreed upon to allow this company a subsidy of 78,000l. per annum for seven years, on condition of its efficient performance of postal services between Ireland and America. The proposed contract was disapproved of by the Postmaster- [Galway contract.]

' Commons Journals, 1860, p. 413.   ' Standing Orders, 1862, No. 78.

Galway contract.

General for several reasons. But it was formally authorised by the Treasury for 'important considerations of commercial and social advantage, in relation chiefly to Ireland.' There appeared to be a general impression abroad, that political advantages to the party then in power had been a chief inducement in the grant of these privileges. Moreover, the contract was open to serious objection on other grounds. Accordingly, when a change of ministry occurred in the following year, one of the first acts of the new administration was to procure the appointment of the Committee on Packet and Telegraphic Contracts. As we have already seen, the committee were unable to enter into any enquiry respecting the Galway Company during that session; but upon their reappointment, in 1860, the subject of this contract immediately engaged their attention. Meanwhile the contract had gone into operation, but as it contained a clause expressly declaring that the subsidy was only payable 'out of moneys to be voted by Parliament,' there was still opportunity for its being set aside, if it were disapproved of by the House of Commons.

After careful investigation into the facts of the case, the committee, on May 22, reported their opinion that this contract had been unwisely entered into; that it had been given without sufficient regard to the interests of Canada, whose line of ocean steamers would have readily undertaken the new service on more favourable terms, and that it was altogether an impolitic and improvident arrangement. Nevertheless, as it was still open to the House, in its own discretion, to decline to vote the necessary funds to carry the contract into effect, the committee refrained from making any recommendation on the subject.[a]

On June 26, the committee presented a second report, stating that they had been compelled to resume their enquiries into the matter of the Galway subsidy, in consequence of the receipt of information pointing to the probability of a corrupt agreement having been made between certain parties, in order to procure the postal subsidy to the Galway line of steam-packets. They had accordingly instituted a searching enquiry into these transactions, but had been unable to convict the present contractors of any share therein. They therefore deemed it most advisable to inform the House of the whole particulars, and to leave the decision thereon entirely to the judgment of the House, without suggesting any opinion of their own.[b] No proceeding was taken by the House upon this report. But on July 16, 1861, a petition was presented from Mr. Irwin, one of the persons implicated by the committee in the fraudulent transactions therein referred to, complaining of the conduct of Mr. Lever (a

---

[a] First Report, Com. on Packet Contracts, Commons Papers, 1860, vol. xiv. pp. 12–14. [b] Second Report, ibid. p. 520.

member of the House) as managing director of the Galway Company. Mr. Lever not being in his seat, the petition was withdrawn, but it was again brought up on July 19, when Mr. Lever denied its allegations, and challenged enquiry. On this occasion the petition was ordered to be printed for the use of members only. On July 22, a motion was made that it be referred to a select committee, upon which Mr. Lever entered into a detailed refutation of the charges it contained against himself. The general sense of the House being against taking any further notice of the matter, the motion was then withdrawn.[f]

Meanwhile the government had determined that the Galway contract should proceed, and inasmuch as the select committee had abstained from recommending the cancelling thereof, notwithstanding the adverse conclusions they had arrived at respecting it, the Secretary of the Treasury, in Committee of Supply, on August 9, 1860, proposed a vote of 60,000*l.* as a first instalment upon the same. In submitting this motion, he frankly acknowledged the weight of censure resting upon the contract, from the terms of the report of the select committee, but nevertheless he expressed his 'strong feeling that arrangements of this kind could not be set aside on mere grounds of general policy or impolicy,' and declared that he did not believe the House had ever refused to vote the estimate for a contract merely on such grounds. To do so in the present instance, when more than a year had elapsed since the contract had been made, would, he contended, be unfair to the company. He further showed that the fraudulent transactions, adverted to in the second report of the committee, had taken place between parties who were no longer connected with the company, and therefore it would be wrong to visit the consequences of their misdoing upon the existing directors and shareholders, who were entirely blameless in the matter. The bargain made with the company might have been a bad one for the public, but it would be still worse for the House, under any pretence, to sanction a breach of faith, and establish a precedent of repudiating inconvenient obligations. This vote, notwithstanding considerable opposition, was finally passed, on division, by a large majority.

Their contract being thus acknowledged and confirmed by Parliament, the company endeavoured to fulfil their engagements. But they did not succeed in accomplishing that which they had undertaken, and after repeatedly receiving extensions of time, and other indulgences, they were at length informed by the Postmaster-General, that their contract was at an end. This decision naturally excited much dissatisfaction among the friends of the company, and

[f] Hans. Deb. vol. clxiv. pp. 977, 1178, 1280.

Galway contract.

on June 14, 1861, a committee was moved for, in the House of Commons, to enquire into the circumstances attending the termination of the contract. The ministry did not oppose this motion (although it was characterised by leading members on the other side of the House as an undue encroachment upon the functions of the executive government), and it was agreed to without a division.[f] The committee carefully investigated the case and, on July 23, made an elaborate report thereon. In it they expressed their opinion 'that the Postmaster-General was justified in declining to continue a contract which, in his judgment, at the time of its determination, the company could not carry out efficiently.' But, they added, they had reason to believe that ere long the company would be in possession of an efficient fleet of steamships, and should it be advisable to re-establish postal communication between the west of Ireland and America, they thought the Galway Company were deserving of the favourable consideration of the government.[h] This appears to have been agreed to by the government, for, on August 6, Lord Palmerston informed the House, that whenever there was a reasonable prospect of the company being able to fulfil their engagements, they would give a favourable consideration to their claims.[i] His lordship renewed these assurances on June 24, 1862,[j] and again on February 9, 1863.[k] Whereupon, on March 20, 1863, Mr. Baxter moved a resolution, declaring that the House was not prepared to grant a sum of money to the Galway Packet Company. He grounded his motion upon the allegation that the renewal of the contract was wholly uncalled for, and could only have proceeded from corrupt political motives. Lord Palmerston repudiated this accusation, and contended that there had been sufficient public reasons to justify the government in giving the company another trial. On division, the motion was negatived by a large majority.[l] On May 4, the government formally notified the company of their willingness to renew the contract. On July 21, on motion of Mr. Peel (the Secretary of the Treasury), it was resolved, without debate, that the said contract be approved.[m]

Having disposed of the subject of postal contracts, the committee of 1860 turned their attention to the remaining branch of enquiry, concerning telegraph lines, to which their third report is devoted. It briefly describes the various lines of Ocean telegraphs, on behalf of which the executive government had entered into pecuniary agreements. One of these was the Red Sea and India Tele-

Ocean Telegraph.

[f] Hans. Deb. vol. clxiii. pp. 1071–1130.
[h] Report on Royal Atlantic Steam Navigation Company, Commons Papers, 1861, vol. xli. p. 13.
[i] Hans. Deb. vol. clxiv. p. 1891.
[j] Ibid. vol. clxvii. p. 1023.
[k] Ibid. vol. clxix. p. 187.
[l] Ibid. p. 1891.
[m] Ibid. vol. clxxii. pp. 93, 1202; but see ibid. vol. clxxiii. p. 1450.

graph line, which was incorporated in 1859, and afterwards attained such an unenviable notoriety. The committee explained the circumstances under which the government had undertaken to assist this company. They arose out of the political importance attributed to the project, and its uncertainty as a commercial speculation. This induced the government to guarantee 4½ per cent. on the capital of 800,000*l.* for a period of fifty years. Unfortunately, whether intentionally or otherwise does not clearly appear, this guarantee was not made conditional on success, as in similar cases, but was absolute. It was stipulated, however, that an Act of Parliament should be obtained to confirm and carry out the agreement. This Act was brought in, proceeded upon, and passed as a private Bill.ᵃ As originally introduced, there was nothing in the Bill to show the nature and extent of the pecuniary obligations incurred by the government. It is true that in the House of Lords a copy of the agreement was afterwards added to the Bill, by way of schedule; but whilst under consideration in the Commons, it contained no information as to the conditions of the agreement, whereby members could judge of its propriety or sufficiency.ᵇ The line had scarcely gone into operation before it was evident that it was a complete failure, and all attempts to remedy the disaster proved ineffectual. In taking notice of this result, the committee abstained from commenting upon the mode of constructing the telegraphic cable, and confined themselves to an investigation of the contract itself. As to the conditions under which such contracts should be entered into, the committee would not venture to make any suggestions. But they pointed out that it was obviously not in the form of a private Bill that agreements of this kind could be effectually brought under the notice and control of Parliament; and they were of opinion that no power to guarantee dividends or interests, on the part of government, should in any case be given by a private Act.ᶜ As the line continued inoperative, and as doubts were entertained whether the government was strictly bound to continue their annual payments to the shareholders under such circumstances, the government, actuated by a high sense of honour, and bearing in mind that, without doubt, the public had understood that the agreement was unconditional, the possibility of entire failure, after completion, having been overlooked on all sides, introduced a Bill to declare 'that the guarantee contained in the said agreement was not intended to be and is not conditional on the line of telegraph of the company being in working order.' The law officers of the crown had given their opinion that, under the

Red Sea and India Telegraph.

ᵃ 22 & 23 Vict. c. iv.
ᵇ Third Report of Contracts, Commons Papers, 1860, vol. xiv. pp. 605,
606. Hans. Deb. vol. clxi. p. 250.
ᶜ Third Report, p. vi.

circumstances of the case, the government were wholly exonerated from continuing to pay the money; nevertheless, as a question of good faith, ministers persevered in the Bill, and it became law.

After the introduction of this Bill, the House proceeded to give effect to the recommendations of the committee, though not precisely in the manner they had suggested, by the adoption of the standing order already noticed, which prescribed the course of procedure in respect to private Bills which are intended to authorise, confirm, or alter, any contracts with government, so as to ensure that the attention of Parliament shall be formally directed thereto.

Right of the House to refuse the supplies.

The foregoing cases afford ample illustration of the effectual control which is constitutionally exercised by the House of Commons over the grant of public money. But these examples have been confined to particular items of proposed expenditure. There still remains an undisputed right, on the part of the House of Commons, to withhold altogether the supplies asked for on the part of the crown. Before the introduction of parliamentary government, this formidable instrument of attack was often made use of to wrest from an arbitrary monarch the redress of grievances. But now there is no longer any need to resort to such an extreme measure, and this once dreaded weapon 'lies rusty in the armoury of constitutional warfare.' In 1781, Mr. Thomas Pitt proposed to delay the granting of the supplies for a few days, in order to extort from Lord North a pledge regarding the war in America. It was then admitted that no such proposal had been made since the Revolution; and the House resolved to proceed with the Committee of Supply by a large majority. In the same session, Lord Rockingham moved, in the House of Lords, to postpone the third reading of a Land Tax Bill, until explanations had been given regarding the causes of Admiral Kempenfeldt's retreat, but did not press it to a division.

On February 22, 1864, Mr. Bernal Osborne moved

---

* Hans. Deb. vol. clxl. p. 2152. 24 Vic. c. 4.
* Ante, p. 503.
* Parl. Hist. vol. xxii. p. 751.
* Ibid. p. 805.

to postpone the consideration of the Navy Estimates for three weeks, until the papers relating to the Schleswig-Holstein question had been laid on the table, the production of which he was of opinion had been unwarrantably delayed. But the leaders of the Opposition were not prepared to justify this extreme proceeding, though agreeing that these papers ought to have been sooner produced, and the motion was negatived on division.

'The precedent of 1784 is the solitary instance in which the Commons have exercised their power of delaying the supplies. They were provoked to use it by the unconstitutional exercise of the influence of the crown; but it failed them at their utmost need,* and the experiment has not been repeated. Their responsibility, indeed, has become too great for so perilous a proceeding. The establishments and public credit of the country are dependent on their votes, and are not to be lightly thrown into disorder. Nor are they driven to this expedient for coercing the executive, as they have other means, not less effectual, for directing the policy of the state.'[†]

The resolutions of the Committee of Supply are reported to the House on a future day, they are then agreed to, disagreed to, or re-committed, as the case may require. If, on consideration of the report, it be thought necessary to increase the sum granted by the Committee of Supply, the resolutions proposed to be increased must be re-committed. The House may indeed *lessen* the sum proposed to be granted without re-committal, but to increase the amount would be to impose a charge not previously sanctioned by the committee.

'But these resolutions, although they record the sanction of the House of Commons to the expenditure submitted to them, and authorise a grant to the crown for the objects specified therein, do not enable the govern-

Resolutions of Committee of Supply.

---

* See *post*, p. 532. May, Const. Hist. vol. i. p. 64.
† *Ibid.* pp. 470–472.

ment to draw from the Consolidated Fund the money so appropriated. A further authority is required, in the shape of a resolution in Committee of Ways and Means, which must be embodied in a Bill, and be passed through both Houses of Parliament, before practical effect can be given to the votes in supply, by authorising the Treasury to take out of the Consolidated Fund, or, if that fund be insufficient, to raise by Exchequer bills ᵛ on the security of the fund, the money required to defray the expenditure sanctioned by such votes. The votes in Committee of Supply authorise the expenditure; the votes in Committee of Ways and Means provide the funds to meet that expenditure.

'The manner in which this provision is made is as follows: As soon after the commencement of the session as possible, when votes on account of the great services have been reported,ˣ a resolution is proposed in Committee of Ways and Means for a general grant out of the Consolidated Fund towards making good the supply granted to her Majesty. This grant never exceeds the amount of the votes actually passed in Committee of Supply; upon this resolution a Bill is founded, which passes through its various stages, and finally receives the royal assent, at a very early period of the session; and then, but not before, the Treasury are empowered to direct an issue of the Consolidated Fund to meet the payments authorised by the vote in supply of the House of Commons.ʸ The constitutional effect of this proceed-

---

ᵛ For the origin, history, and practice, in regard to Exchequer bills, see Hans. Deb. vol. clxi. p. 1340; vol. clxv. p. 131; vol. clxxx. p. 285; and Report on Public Moneys, 1857, pp. 32–44.

ˣ 'It is the salutary, judicious, and almost invariable rule of the House not to enter upon questions of Ways and Means until the House has passed its judgment upon those items of the expenditure of the year which are at once the greatest and most variable— viz. the Naval and Military Estimates;' and the Chancellor of the Exchequer ordinarily refrains from making his financial statement until these estimates have been passed. (Gladstone, (Ch. of Exch.) Hans. Deb. vol. cliv. p. 800. Concerning the exceptions to this practice, see *ante*, p. 400.

ʸ May's Parl. Pract. ed. 1863, p. 632. Hans. Deb. vol. cxxxvi. pp.

ing is that, until the queen and the House of Lords have assented to the grant of ways and means, the appropriation of the public money directed by the vote in supply of the House of Commons is inoperative. These general grants of ways and means, upon account, provided by successive Acts of Parliament during the session, in anticipation of the specific appropriations embodied in the Appropriation Act passed at the close of the session, may be viewed as the form in which Parliament considers it most convenient to convey their sanction to the ad interim issue of public money upon the appropriation directed by the Commons alone, relying upon their final confirmation being obtained at the close of the session. The final grant of ways and means to cover the whole of the supplies voted in the session is always reserved for the Appropriation Act; thus, although the House of Commons at an early period of the session might have voted the whole of the supplies of the year, they could still hold their constitutional check upon the minister by limiting the grant of ways and means to an amount sufficient only to last such time as they might think proper to give him the means of carrying on the public service, and they are by such limited grants at all times enabled to prevent the minister from dissolving or proroguing Parliament."*

Ad interim advances of money.

All taxes are not necessarily proposed in the Committee of Ways and Means. Though the distinction is not always observed, it is the usual practice to confine the

---

1310, 1305. Second Rep. Com. of Pub. Accounts, 1857, p. iii. See the Exchequer Act, 4 Will. IV. c. 15, sect. 11. And for examples of Sessional Ways and Means Acts, see 13 Vict. c. 3, sect. 7; 21 Vict. c. 6, &c. It is one of the especial duties of the Speaker of the House of Commons to see that no Ways and Means Bill covers a larger amount than has been already voted in Committee of Supply, and agreed to by the House. After the votes in supply have been agreed to, the Speaker officially transmits a copy of them to the Comptroller of the Exchequer, to acquaint him for what purposes, and in what amounts, the Commons have sanctioned the outlay of public money. Mem. on Financial Control, pp. 5, 27. Shilling Magazine, vol. iv. p. 48.

* Report on Public Moneys, Commons Papers, 1857, sess. ii. vol. ix. Memo. on Financial Control, pp. 20, 27. See the Chanc. of Excheq. observations in Hans. Deb. vol. cxxxvi. pp. 1310–1320, 1305.

Taxes voted in Committee of Ways and Means, or otherwise.

deliberations of this committee to such taxes as are more distinctly applicable to the immediate exigencies of the public income; and to consider, in other committees of the whole House, all fiscal regulations, and alterations of permanent duties, not having directly for their object the increase of revenue.[a] Accordingly, it is irregular to move, in Committee of Ways and Means, a general motion concerning taxation—as, 'that it is expedient to equalise the duties levied on the descent of real and personal property;' or, an amendment deprecating an addition to the funded debt—though it is quite competent for a private member to propose a scheme of taxation, to raise the supplies required for the service of the year, by way of amendment to the government proposition.[b]

It is the invariable course, in Committee of Ways and Means, to submit to the House resolutions which impose taxation before those which are intended to repeal taxation.[c]

Annual and permanent taxation.

Duties are either annually voted, upon the recommendation of the Chancellor of the Exchequer, in his budget, or they are made permanent, by special Acts of Parliament. Occasionally certain duties heretofore voted annually are made permanent;[d] but while it is in the discretion of government to propose to Parliament a greater or less amount of permanent taxation, from time to time, it is not desirable ' to vary the constitutional practice of always maintaining some large amount of taxation to be annually voted by the House.'[e] It is right that the great bulk of the revenue arising from taxation should be levied under permanent Acts, in order to maintain the public credit on a firm footing, and for the security of the commercial

---

[a] May, Parl. Pract. Ed. 1863, p. 570.
[b] Mirror of Parl. 1840, p. 3042; and ibid, 1841, sess. ii. p. 408. As to the right of members to propose schemes of taxation by way of substitute to the government plan, see *ante*, p. 451.
[c] Hans. Deb. vol. clxii. p. 1330.
[d] For example, the sugar duties, in 1864. See Hans. Deb. vol. clxxiv. pp. 1180, 2021. See Smith's Parl. Rememb. 1864, p. 77.
[e] Hans. Deb. vol. xc. p. 1343.

interests of the country, which would suffer if existing imposts were liable to frequent change.'

It is an important privilege of the House of Commons that sufficient time should be allowed for deliberation upon any proposition submitted by government relative to taxation or public expenditure.^g No resolutions of the Committee of Ways and Means should be reported to the House on the same day on which they were agreed upon in committee; except upon 'urgent occasion.'^h When reported, they may be agreed to, negatived, or re-committed. It is customary to report such resolutions, and move the concurrence of the House thereto, upon the day following that upon which they have been agreed to in committee, in order to avoid loss to the revenue by further delay.ⁱ Bills are then ordered to be brought in to give effect to the same, and every exertion is made by the government to pass such bills with as little delay as possible.

Time to be allowed to consider all financial questions.

Pending the ultimate decision of Parliament upon any bill for the imposition or alteration of taxes, it is customary for the executive government, upon their own responsibility, to give immediate effect to resolutions altering existing rates of duty, or imposing new duties, as soon as they have been reported from committee, and agreed to by the House.^j But this does not prevent the substance of such resolutions from being again discussed, at future parliamentary stages, with a view to their amendment or rejection.^k Meanwhile, the new taxes are authorised to be collected by government, from the day named in the resolution, or from the date of passing the

New rates of duty immediately enforced.

---

^f Hans. Deb. vol. cxxviii. p. 951. Lord Derby, *Ibid.* vol. clxiii. p. 724. Sir S. Northcote, *Ibid.* vol. clxvi. p. 1391. But see Mr. Disraeli's observations on this point, *Ibid.* vol. clix. p. 1480.
^g Hans. Deb. vol. cxxxvii. pp. 1030, 1048.
^h *Ibid.* vol. clviii. pp. 1101, 1208.

Toulmin Smith, Parl. Rememb. 1860, p. 123.
ⁱ Hans. Deb. vol. cxxxiii. p. 40.
^j May, Parl. Prac. ed. 1863, p. 574. Hans. Deb. vol. clxv. p. 631.
^k Hans. Deb. vol. cxvii. p. 1416; *Ibid.* vol. clviii. p. 980, &c.

same, because it is not doubted that the bill which imposes them, as from the date of the resolution whereon it is founded, will become law, by the concurrence of the two other branches of the legislature. If such concurrence be withheld, the resolution becomes inoperative, and the duties levied by anticipation must be repaid to the parties from whom they had been collected.[1]

New rates of duty: how levied. It is the invariable practice, when the duty on any particular article is raised, to levy the new rate of duty on stocks in bond, and cargoes afloat, when they are entered for consumption. This sometimes operates prejudicially to the interests of merchants who have imported largely of the article in question, with the expectation that the duty will remain unchanged. But the hardship is unavoidable, as it would not be consistent with usage, or with the policy of government, to announce beforehand their intentions in such a matter.[m]

Whenever the duty on spirits is increased by resolution of the House, it is customary to charge the increased rate of duty upon all spirits in the hands of distillers, whether they hold it in bond or duty paid; but not to charge the additional rate on spirits which have passed into the hands of wholesale dealers, even though they may have taken large and unusual quantities out of bond in anticipation of the increased duty. In 1855 the government desired to subject the article in the hands of dealers to the increased rate of duty; but precedents were

---

[1] See the Attorney-General's observations, Hans. Deb. vol. xcix. p. 1310. See also *Ibid.* vol. clvi. p. 1274, vol. clx. p. 1827.

[m] Chan. of the Excheq. Hans. Deb. vol. xcix. p. 1315. The United States Tariff Act of 1861, which was passed on March 2, and imposed new duties from April 1 of that year, contained a clause (sec. 33), exempting 'merchandise in deposit in warehouse or public store on April 1,' and merchandise 'actually on shipboard, and bound to the United States, within 15 days after the passing of the Act,' from the additional duties. See also similar (though not identical) provisions in the United States Statutes for August 1861, ch. 45, sec. 5. By the U. S. Tariff Act of 1862, ch. 163, sec. 21, goods in bonded warehouses, &c. were exempted from additional duty, but not goods on shipboard. So also the Tariff Act of 1864, ch. 171, sec. 10.

against it, and they abandoned the attempt." On the other hand, if the duty on an article be reduced, it is customary for the reduction of duty to come into operation the day after the adoption of the resolution by the House; and it is entirely foreign to the usage of Parliament to allow any drawback upon stocks of the article in the hands of dealers.*

On May 4, 1865, the case of the retail tea-dealers,—who are obliged to keep large stocks on hand of duty-paid tea, and who would be great sufferers by the sudden reduction of duty thereon, and the consequent influx of fresh stocks of tea at the reduced rate of duty,—was brought before the House. The Chancellor of the Exchequer declared that, 'as a general principle, the time at which a reduction of duty shall come into operation is regulated by large considerations of public policy, and not by the convenience of retail dealers;' and that he knew of 'no case, during the last twenty years, in which, in regard to any article not about to undergo a process of manufacture, but simply to be distributed to the customers, time had been given to get rid of the stocks of the retailers.' Nevertheless, as in the present instance there had been an expectation to the contrary, specially founded upon a declaration of the government in 1853 in respect to the tea duty, he would consent to postpone the reduction from May 6 to June 1, with an entry on the Journals that the delay had been granted 'on special grounds.' The resolution was amended accordingly.*

Case of the tea-dealers.

The financial operations of government are not confined to propositions concerning supply and taxation, but necessitate various proceedings in the money market for raising the supplies voted by Parliament, as well as for the regulation and management of the public debt. But the spirit of the constitution requires that all important operations which a finance minister may undertake for the public service should come under the review of Parliament before they are carried into effect. Until the year 1861 the government had the power, through the medium of the Commissioners for the Reduction of the National Debt,

All financial operations to be laid before Parliament.

---

* Hans. Deb. vol. cxxxvii. p. 1780; clxxviii. p. 1241.
Ibid. vol. cxl. p. 1831.   * Ibid. vol. clxxviii. pp. 1471-1500.
* Ibid (Chan. of the Excheq.) vol.

of funding and re-funding Exchequer bills of every description (including Supply Exchequer Bills, Deficiency Bills, and Ways and Means Bills), without the cognizance of Parliament; thus converting an instrument which had been issued, under the sanction of Parliament, for a temporary purpose, in anticipation of the produce of the ordinary public revenue for the year, into a part of the funded debt of the country. In 1861, however, a measure was passed, at the instigation of the government, and in conformity with the recommendations of the Public Moneys Committee of 1857, to do away with this objectionable practice by amending the law in regard to Exchequer Bills.[a] This Act, together with an amending statute, passed in the following year,[r] has deprived the government of the power of making any addition to the funded debt without the authority of Parliament; and it virtually requires the Chancellor of the Exchequer to submit to the judgment of Parliament all his financial transactions which may effect any change in the condition of the funded or unfunded public debt.[s]

Loans and financial contracts.

Whenever a loan, or financial contract, which has been entered into by government upon its own responsibility, is submitted for the approval of Parliament, the sense of the House in regard to the same should be expressed with as little delay as possible.[t]

Stocks.

It is the practice to give immediate effect to resolutions of the House of Commons with regard to the commutation and redemption of public stocks; and the Speaker notifies parties concerned as soon as the resolutions have been agreed to.[u]

In the exercise of their constitutional functions, the House of Commons not infrequently dissent from the financial propositions of ministers. In 1767, on a proposal

---

[a] 24 Vict. c. 5. And see Mr. Gladstone's speech on introducing the Bill, in Hans. Deb. vol. clxi. p. 1300.
[r] 25 Vict. c. 3. And see Hans. Deb. vol. clxv. p. 131.
[s] Mr. Gladstone, in Hans. Deb. vol. clxx. p. 104.
[t] Hans. Deb. vol. cxxxii. p. 1400.
[u] Ibid. vol. cxxvi. p. 321.

to continue the land tax of four shillings in the pound for one year, an amendment, to reduce the tax to three shillings, was carried. This was the first occasion, since the Revolution, on which a minister had been defeated on any financial measure.* Throughout the French war, the Commons, with singular unanimity, agreed to every grant of money, and to every new tax and loan, proposed by successive administrations." But in 1816, after the close of the war with France, when the government were desirous of continuing the Property Tax for a longer term, in order to get rid of a portion of the burthens occasioned by that protracted struggle, the feeling of the House was so strongly opposed to the continuance of war taxes after peace had been obtained, that the Chancellor of the Exchequer was defeated, on the 18th March, in Committee of Ways and Means, upon his motion for the renewal of the Property Tax. After this, he voluntarily abandoned the war duties upon malt, amounting to about 2,700,000*l*. Altogether it has been computed that the government lost, on this occasion, about twelve millions of anticipated revenue.ᵗ

Budgets rejected or amended by the House

It is somewhat remarkable that the great ministerial defeat, recorded in the preceding paragraph, was so quietly accepted by the government, and did not lead to a ministerial crisis. But the true doctrine on this point is that which was expressed by Lord John Russell, in 1851, after the government had sustained a defeat on some financial proposition. He remarked that 'questions of taxation and burdens are questions upon which the House of Commons, representing the country, have peculiar claims to have their opinions listened to, and upon which the executive government may very fairly, without any loss of its dignity,—provided they maintain a sufficient revenue for the credit of the country and for its establishments,—

Do not necessitate a change of ministry.

---

* Parl. Hist. vol. xvi. p. 502. p. 451. Knight, Hist. of England, vol.
" May, Const. Hist. vol. i. p. 471. viii p. 53. See also *Edinb. Rev.* vol.
ᵗ Hans. Deb. (1816), vol. xxxiii. cix. p. 184.

reconsider any particular measures of finance they have proposed." To the same effect, Mr. T. Baring, the Under Secretary for War in Lord Palmerston's administration, said, in 1861, after the rejection by the House of Lords of the Bill for the repeal of the Paper Duties,—which formed part of the financial measures of government for that year,—'I am happy that we live at a time when experience has shown that a budget may be modified or rejected without any change in the position of the ministry. I am glad that we have seen budgets withdrawn, and fresh ones introduced. We have seen taxes remitted, or taxes, the remission of which, when proposed, has been refused, without any effect upon the cabinet. In fact, a change of the budget does not involve a change of ministry, and I rejoice that it is so, because I think it would be most unpardonable obstinacy on the part of public men to adhere to the terms of a budget which was opposed to the wishes and feelings of Parliament. It would be unfortunate for the free exercise of the judgment of this House, if the rejection of any portion of a budget were to be construed into a vote of want of confidence.'

Precedents of budgets amended or rejected by the House of Commons.

In proof of the extent to which the financial measures of government have been subjected, from time to time, to modification at the hands of Parliament—and to point out under what circumstances the rejection of their financial policy has been regarded by an administration as a token of their having forfeited the confidence of the House of Commons—the following particulars are given of the various budgets which have been amended or rejected by the House, from the epoch of the Reform of Parliament in 1832.

The first budget submitted to a reformed House of Commons was opened by the Chancellor of the Exchequer on April 19, 1833. Its details gave rise to no discussion at the time; but shortly after-

⁷ Hans. Deb. vol. cxvi. p. 634.   ⁸ Ibid. vol. clxii. p. 991.

wards several motions, on behalf of the agricultural interest, were introduced and debated. One of them was, at the first, successful. This was a motion proposed on April 26, by Sir W. Ingilby, to reduce the malt tax from 20s. 8d. to 10s. per quarter. Notwithstanding the opposition of ministers, the motion was carried by a majority of ten.[a] On the next sitting day the Chancellor of the Exchequer informed the House that this vote had considerably embarrassed the government, the more so as its success might probably lead the House to agree to another motion, about to be submitted, for the repeal of the assessed taxes; and that it would occasion a loss of revenue amounting to 2,500,000l. Accordingly, the government determined to afford the House an opportunity of reconsidering their vote, by moving (in amendment to the motion to repeal the house and window taxes), on April 30, to resolve 'That a great deficiency of revenue would be occasioned by the reduction of the malt tax to 10s. per quarter, and by the repeal of the taxes on houses and windows, which could only be supplied by the substitution of a general tax upon property; and that as the effect of that course would be to change the whole financial system of the country, it would at present be inexpedient to adopt it.'[b] At the time appointed this motion was proposed and agreed to; an amendment to omit therefrom so much as related to the malt tax being negatived by 285 to 191. Whereupon Sir W. Ingilby moved that the previous resolution be read, and that leave be given to bring in a bill pursuant to the same. But on a division of 76 to 238, leave was refused.[c] On May 21 a motion for the repeal of the taxes upon houses and windows was negatived by a large majority.

None of the budgets presented to the House of Commons from 1833 to 1841 underwent any material alteration at the hands of the House of Commons. But on April 30, 1841, Mr. F. T. Baring, Chancellor of the Exchequer in Lord Melbourne's administration, submitted his budget to the House. One of its most prominent features was a proposal to reduce the duty on foreign (or slave-grown) sugar from 63s. to 36s. per cwt. The government at the same time announced their intention to propose an alteration in the corn laws by a reduction of the amount of protection then afforded to the agriculturists of Great Britain. On May 7, Viscount Sandon, on going into Committee of Ways and Means, moved to resolve that the House was not prepared to consent to the proposed reduction of the duty on slave-grown sugar, in view of the immense sacrifices heretofore made for the abolition of slavery and the slave-trade, and

Precedents

1833.

1841.

[a] Mirror of Parl. 1833, p. 1480.
[b] Ibid. p. 1502.
[c] Ibid. p. 1548. See the observations of Mr. Disraeli on this proceeding, when it was cited as a precedent on a similar occasion. Hans. Deb. vol. lxxv. p. 1028.

Precedents in prospect of a supply of free-labour sugar from the British colonies. After a protracted debate from May 7 to May 18, Lord Sandon's resolution was carried. The government, instead of regarding this defeat as decisive of their fate, gave notice of their intention to move for the adoption of the usual annual sugar duties. Sir Robert Peel, not wishing to offer any factious opposition to the government, or to stop the supplies, supported this motion; but, in order to elicit the opinions of the House in regard to the ministry upon a direct issue, he proposed a vote of want of confidence, which being agreed to on June 4, led to the dissolution of Parliament. A majority adverse to the ministry were returned to the new House of Commons; they were again defeated upon an amendment to the address, when they retired from office, and were replaced by the administration of Sir Robert Peel as First Lord of the Treasury, the Right Hon. Henry Goulburn being Chancellor of the Exchequer.

Sir R. Peel continued in office for five years, but he was so uniformly unsuccessful in his financial policy that the progress of his financial measures through Parliament seldom gave rise to any formidable opposition. But an exception must be made to the budget of 1844, which excited great hostility, and was nearly the occasion of the overthrow of the government.

1844. The annual financial statement for the year 1844 was made by Mr. Goulburn on April 29. He adverted therein to the question of the sugar duties; but it was not until June 3 that the proposed alteration in these duties was formally submitted to the House. On the eve of the expiration of a treaty with the slave-holding state of Brazil, which, while it lasted, bound Great Britain to admit Brazilian sugar on as favourable terms as that of the free countries of Java or Manilla, the government proposed a 24s. duty on British, and a 34s. duty on foreign free-grown sugar. These rates did not satisfy the West India interest, who (after an amendment had been proposed, and negatived, for the admission of slave-grown sugar on the same footing with free) contended for a proportionate reduction of duty on sugars from the British colonies, so as to leave the present relative rates unchanged. Accordingly, on June 14, in committee on the Sugar Duties Bill, an amendment was proposed by Mr. Miles, to reduce the relative rates above mentioned from 24s. and 34s. respectively, to 20s. and 30s.; and further, to impose a discriminating duty in regard to certain descriptions of foreign free-grown sugar of 14s. This amendment was carried against the government by a majority of 20. The vote was taken on the question, 'That the words proposed to be left out [i. e. the government scheme] stand part of the clause,' which was negatived. The committee then reported progress. On the next sitting-day the committee again sat, and Sir R. Peel announced the intentions of government. He stated that ministers felt it necessary, on grounds of commercial and financial policy, to adhere to their original proposition, and that he must ask the committee to re-consider their vote. He therefore moved,—as an amendment to the motion, that the words proposed by Mr. Miles, in lieu of those struck out of the clause by the vote of June 14, be inserted,—that the rates of duty originally proposed by government be substituted. In the course of the debate which ensued, Sir R. Peel having intimated that, if defeated upon this occasion, ministers would consider that they had lost the confidence of the House, the government amendment was agreed to.[e] Objections were taken to this proceeding on the point of form, but they were overruled.[a]

On February 18, 1848, Lord John Russell being the First Lord of the Treasury, and Sir Charles Wood Chancellor of the Exchequer, the budget was brought forward by Lord John Russell. His scheme was received with great disfavour by the House of Commons, and by the public at large, especially the proposed renewal and increase of the income tax. Though an adverse motion on this subject, by Mr. Hume, was negatived, the feeling in the House against the increase of this tax was too strong to be disregarded. Accordingly, on February 28, the Chancellor of the Exchequer made a new financial statement, in which he announced that the government, in deference to the wishes of the House and the country, would not press for an increase of the income tax. Later in the session, on June 30, Sir Charles Wood made another statement, consequent upon the great loss of anticipated revenue by the withdrawal of the proposed additional income tax, without the adoption of other measures for making up the deficiency. Finally, on August 25, he produced what was called his 'fourth budget,' in which he reviewed at length the financial prospects of the year.[f]

The budget of 1850 was brought forward by Sir Charles Wood on March 14. It included a proposal for the revision of the stamp duties, which, although intended to reduce this tax as a whole, would have the effect of increasing it in certain cases. In consequence of the opposition which this part of his financial scheme encountered, the Chancellor of the Exchequer was induced to agree to a material reduction of his proposed rates; but this concession failed to satisfy his opponents, who carried an amendment for a further reduction of the duty. After this defeat, the government took no more steps in the matter for about a month, when Sir Charles Wood stated that they were prepared to proceed with the bill, with a small advance on the proposed rate, as amended.

1848.

1850.

---

[e] Hans. Deb. vol. lxxv. pp. 997, 9-8, 1011, 1002, 1102. Commons Journals, June 14, 17; and 20, 1844.
[f] Hans. Deb. vol. lxxv. p. 1010.
[f] Northcote, Financial Policy, pp. 100-110.

Precedents. This arrangement was accepted by the House.[a] Besides their defeat on this question, the government were defeated in respect to two other questions of taxation, by the introduction of bills for the repeal of the duty on attorneys' and proctors' certificates, and in relation to the duty on bonded spirits in Ireland. The first-mentioned bill was carried through to a third reading, notwithstanding the opposition of the government, but was finally thrown out at this stage. The other bill did not proceed beyond a first reading, owing to the lateness of the session. Both these measures were again brought forward in the following session, but, through the exertions of the government, were finally rejected.[b]

1851. Next year, the budget was introduced on February 17, 1851. It met with an unfavourable reception from the public. February 21 was fixed upon for its discussion in committee, but, before that day arrived, the government sustained a defeat on Mr. Locke King's County Franchise Bill, and resigned office. Their retirement was, however, attributed, at least in part, to the unpopularity of their financial policy. Owing to the inability of the Conservative party to form an administration, the late ministers resumed their places. On April 4, Sir Charles Wood again brought forward his budget in nearly the same shape as before. But, on May 2, Mr. Hume succeeded in carrying an amendment, to limit the duration of the income tax to one year, instead of three years as proposed in the budget. He afterwards obtained the appointment of a select committee to inquire into the mode of assessing and collecting this impost. Twice during this session the ministry sustained defeats upon a motion of Lord Naas respecting the mode of levying the duty on home-made spirits when taken out of bond. But at a subsequent stage they retrieved their position, and succeeded in negativing the bill introduced by Lord Naas to carry out his project.[c] Notwithstanding these defeats, the government remained in office until their final overthrow in February 1852, when they were replaced by a Conservative ministry.[d]

1852. On December 3, 1852, the budget was introduced by the new Chancellor of the Exchequer, Mr. Disraeli. It met with formidable opposition at the outset, and although an attempt, on the part of Mr. Thomas Duncombe, to dispose of it as a whole, on the question that the Speaker do now leave the Chair, was unsuccessful; yet, as soon as the House went into committee, and the first resolution by which it was proposed to double the existing house tax was sub-

---

[a] The total loss of revenue by the remissions of this Bill amounted to about half-a-million per annum, being 200,000l. more than had been contemplated by Government when they introduced the measure. Annual Register, 1850, pp. 110-123.
[b] Northcote, Financial Policy, pp. 124, 165.
[c] Annual Reg. 1851, p. 102. Hans. Deb. vol. cxvi. p. 631.
[d] Northcote, pp. 142-165.

mitted, all the opposing parties combined against it. Rival sections Precedents found themselves able to join in defeating the ministerial scheme in the aggregate, though differing amongst themselves as to the merits of its several parts. After a protracted debate, the government were defeated on December 16, by a majority of 19, whereupon they retired from office, and were succeeded by the administration of Lord Aberdeen.[k]

On April 18, 1853, Mr. Gladstone, as Chancellor of the Exchequer, 1853. introduced his first budget. Though full of startling conceptions and new financial ideas, it was received on the whole with considerable favour. In one or two particulars, however, Mr. Gladstone was compelled to modify his scheme. A proposition for the revision of licenses upon certain trades, though not rejected by the House, met with so much opposition out of doors that it was ultimately abandoned. Mr. Gladstone was also unsuccessful in his endeavour to effect a re-adjustment of the advertisement duty. Before the budget was brought in, a resolution had been carried, in opposition to the government, in favour of the total repeal of this duty. In consequence of this defeat, the government were obliged to give way, and consent to the abandonment of this duty. The bill for the repeal of the attorneys' certificate duty was again introduced, notwithstanding the resistance of government, but it was defeated at a subsequent stage. In other respects the financial measures of the government were passed through the House of Commons without much difficulty.[l]

The budget for 1854 was introduced by Mr. Gladstone on March 1854. 6, but the growing demands of the war with Russia rendered it necessary for him to bring forward a second financial scheme on May 8. These measures gave rise to much debate, but were not subjected to any alteration.

Nothing occurred in respect to any of the budgets of the succeeding years to call for remark until that of February 10, 1860, 1860. which was presented by Mr. Gladstone. It included a proposal for the repeal of the paper duty, thereby remitting taxation to the amount of more than one million pounds.[m] The bill to give effect to this measure was strenuously opposed in its passage through the House of Commons, and was thrown out in the House of Lords.[n] This circumstance had no other remarkable result except that it led to the adoption, in 1861, of different arrangements in reference to the fiscal legislation required for the service of the year. Instead of introducing several distinct bills upon the resolutions reported from the Committee of Ways and Means for the imposition of taxes, the several propositions were all included in one bill. In this way the

---

[k] Northcote, pp. 174-181.
[l] Ibid. pp. 183-217.
[m] Hans. Deb. vol. clxii. p. 008.

[n] For a narrative of the proceedings in both Houses in regard to this case, see ante, p. 450.

524   THE ROYAL PREROGATIVE.

Precedents government were enabled to renew their measure for the repeal of the paper duties, and to carry it successfully through both Houses. Much dissatisfaction, however, was expressed at the magnitude and complexity of this bill, and at the curtailment of the opportunities for discussing the various points involved therein, on account of their being all embraced in one measure. Accordingly, in committee on the bill, it was agreed that it should be divided into three, namely, the Inland Revenue, Stamp Duties, and Spirits Sale Bills, all of which received the concurrence of the House of Lords.

1862. In 1862 the budget propositions were again included in one bill, which was probably the largest 'Money Bill' that had ever been introduced into the Imperial Parliament, as it dealt with between twenty-two and twenty-three million pounds of public taxation. On this occasion no attempt was made to alter the form of procedure, though it was severely commented upon in both Houses.[a] The only alteration that was made in this budget was by the introduction in the House of Commons, on May 12, of an amendment in respect to beer and spirit licenses, to which the government gave their consent.

1863. The budget of 1863 contained two proposals which encountered serious opposition within and without the walls of Parliament. Of these one was a provision to subject charities to the operation of the income tax, from which they had been previously exempt. Mr. Gladstone defended this item of his budget with great skill, in an elaborate argument. Nevertheless, he declared at once that the government had no wish or intention to press its acceptance upon the House ' by the means which a government may exert.' ' The House must be responsible for its rejection.' After a full debate, in which no 'independent member declared himself' favourable to the scheme, Mr. Gladstone withdrew this provision without taking the sense of the committee upon it.[b] The other obnoxious recommendation in this budget was a proposal to impose a license duty upon clubs. In deference to the requests that were made to him 'from all quarters,' Mr. Gladstone consented to withdraw this item.[c]

The financial proposals of the government contained in the budget of 1864 were adopted substantially as they were submitted to the House of Commons.[d]

1865. The budget of 1865 contained propositions affecting the stamp duties, income tax, and the duties on tea and on fire insurances. These were severally agreed to by the House of Commons. But a question arose in regard to the time when the proposed reduction

---

[a] See Hans. Deb. May 12 and 30, 1862; and ante, p. 464.
[b] Hans. Deb. vol. clxx. pp. 1102, 1125. He also withdrew a resolution to impose a Legacy Duty on Charitable Bequests in Ireland. Ibid. p. 1773.
[c] Ibid. pp. 840, 1303, 1305.
[d] Ibid. vol. clxxvi. p. 1858.

of the duty on tea should take place. The government proposed that the new duty should go into operation on May 6; but a strong case was made out for delaying the time until June 1; and although opposed on general principle to the amendment, the Chancellor of the Exchequer finally consented to the adoption of a proviso, to be added to the resolution, 'That, on special grounds, the said reduction shall not take effect until June 1, 1865.'ᵃ

The budget of 1866 was introduced by Mr. Gladstone, the Chancellor of the Exchequer, on May 3. In the month of July a change of ministry took place. On July 23, the new finance minister, Mr. Disraeli, informed the House, that in order to raise the necessary funds to meet certain supplementary estimates which the incoming administration had felt it their duty to submit to Parliament, they had resolved upon relinquishing the bill, which had passed its second reading, for the conversion of certain terminable annuities towards the liquidation of a portion of the national debt. This was the only alteration effected in the financial proposals of the ex-ministry.

We will now proceed to consider the subject of Money Bills, which are of three kinds, viz. Tax Bills, Bills of Supply, and Bills of Appropriation. All these bills have a peculiar form of preamble, which intimates that the revenue or grant of money is the peculiar gift of the House of Commons, and such bills are invariably presented for the royal assent by the Speaker of the House of Commons.ᵇ

Tax Bills, for raising revenues to be applied towards the services of the current year, are founded upon resolutions of the Committee of Ways and Means.

In like manner, Bills of Supply, or rather of Ways and Means, authorising an advance out of the Consolidated Fund, or the issue of Exchequer Bills, towards making good supplies which have been voted by the House of Commons for the service of the year, emanate from the Committee of Ways and Means, in the way which has been already described.ᶜ

When the Committees of Supply and Ways and Means have finished their sittings, a bill is ordered, which enu-

---

ᵃ Hans. Deb. vol. clxxviii. pp. 1471-1500. See ante, p. 515.
ᵇ Cox, Inst. 108.   ᶜ See ante, p. 510.

528   THE ROYAL PREROGATIVE.

Appropriation Bill.

merates every grant that has been made during the session, appropriates the several sums, as voted by the Committee of Supply, which shall be issued and applied to each separate service, and directs that the said supplies shall not be used for any other than the purposes mentioned in the said act. This is known as the Consolidated Fund Bill, or, more generally, as the Appropriation Bill. By this act, which completes the financial proceedings of the session, the supply votes, originally passed by the Commons only, receive full legislative sanction. The appropriation is always reserved for the end of the session, and it is irregular to introduce any clause of appropriation into a bill passing through Parliament at an earlier period.*

Duty of the Speaker in matters of supply.

By constitutional practice, the Speaker of the House of Commons, as the guardian of its privileges, is required to take oversight of the financial proceedings of the House during the session, and it is his duty to ascertain that every bill for giving ways and means to the Treasury is kept within the amount of the votes in supply already granted. At the close of the session he checks the final balance between the full amount of the votes in supply and the ways and means previously authorised, and limits the final grant of ways and means in the Appropriation Act to that amount."

Appropriation clauses in bills of supply.

The constitutional rule, now so well understood and acknowledged, 'That the sums granted and appropriated by the Commons for any special service should be applied by the executive power only to defray the expense of that service,'" although not wholly unrecognised in earlier times,' was first distinctly enunciated and partially enforced soon after the Restoration. But it was not until the

---

* The Speaker, in Mirror of Parl. 1841, p. 611; and see Hans. Deb. vol. clxx. pp. 1807, 1914. But this was not formerly the case: see Parl. Deb. vol. ix. p. 632.

" Report on Pub. Moneys, Commons Papers, 1857, sess. 2, vol. ix. Mem. on Financial Control, pp. 5, 27, 70.

¹ 9 Hatsell, 210.

ʲ See Hargrave's Judicial Arguments, vol. i. pp. 397–402.

Revolution of 1688 that this great principle was finally established and incorporated into the system of parliamentary government.ᵃ At this epoch Solicitor-General (afterwards Lord) Somers and Mr. Sacheverel, by special direction of the House of Commons, framed some appropriation clauses with great care, which were included in the statute 1 Wm. & Mary, s. 2, c. 1, and are given in full in Hatsell, vol. iii. Appendix, No. 15. These clauses were not formally repeated in subsequent Bills of Supply, but they are referred to as to be 'put in force and practised' in various succeeding statutes. Thenceforth it became the established and uniform practice, 'that the sums granted by the House of Commons for the current service of the year should, by a special appropriation, either in the act for levying the aid or in some other act of the same session, be applied only to the services which they had voted.' This doctrine has been enforced, from time to time, by penalties imposed by Acts of Parliament upon officers of the Exchequer and others who should divert or misapply the moneys granted to any other purpose; and a violation of the same is a misdemeanour, that has been declared to be a sufficient ground for a parliamentary impeachment.ᵇ

Form of the appropriation clause.

The modern form of the appropriation clause, after enumerating the grants of the session, and applying them to their respective services, is as follows: 'That the said aids and supplies shall not be issued or applied to any use, intent, or purpose, other than those before mentioned, or for the other payments, &c., directed to be satisfied by any Acts of Parliament, &c., of this session.'ᵇ This clause is invariably inserted in the annual Appropriation Act. On two occasions, in 1857 and in 1859, where two sessions were held in one year, it was omitted in the acts of the second session on technical grounds, arising from

---

ᵃ 3 Hats. 202.
ᵇ Ibid. 201. Cases cited in Lord Monteagle's Report, Commons Papers, 1857, sess. 2, vol. ix. p. 507; and see Hans. Deb. vol. clxiv. p. 1740.
ᵇ May, Prac. ed. 1863, p. 575.

the fact of two Parliaments being convened in each of those years. But, in point of fact, it has been authoritatively stated, that though, as a declaration of constitutional principle, the said clause might reasonably be inserted in any Appropriation Bill, yet that 'it was in point of law mere surplusage, because the government had no authority to appropriate those moneys to any other purposes than those for which Parliament had appropriated them.'^c

<small>Authority given to the surpluses of army and navy grants to make good deficiencies therein.</small>

The Appropriation Act also contains a provision, that the expenditure for navy and army services shall be confined to those services respectively, but that 'if a necessity shall arise for incurring expenditure not provided for in the sums appropriated' for the said services, 'and which it may be detrimental to the public service to postpone until provision can be made for it by Parliament in the usual course,' application shall be made to the Treasury, who are empowered to authorise such additional expenditure to be temporarily defrayed out of any surpluses which may have accrued by the saving of expenditure upon any votes within the same departments; provided that the House of Commons shall be duly informed thereof, in order to make provision for such deficient expenditure as may be determined; and provided also, that the aggregate grants for the navy and army services shall not be exceeded.^d

<small>Subject to approval of the House of Commons.</small>

The manner in which the observance of the Appropriation Act is secured, and the circumstances under which any deviation from the strict rule of parliamentary appropriation is permissible, will engage our attention in the next section.

It only remains, in this branch of our enquiry, to add a few remarks upon the progress of the Appropriation Bill through Parliament.

The constitutional restrictions upon the grant of money

<small>c Mr. Gladstone, in Hans. Deb. vol. clxiv. p. 1745.   d 26 & 20 Vic. c. 71, sec. 20. See Hans. Deb. vol. cxliii. p. 603.</small>

otherwise than through the Committee of Supply, necessarily confine the action of the House of Commons in respect to money votes to the proceedings of this committee, and to the decision upon their resolutions, when reported to the House. A motion to address the crown, that a vote which had been reported from Committee of Supply, and agreed to by the House, should not be expended, was declared by the Speaker to be irregular and out of order.* Technically, such vote could, of course, be struck out of the Appropriation Bill.† But in practice this Bill has been defined by Lord Palmerston to be 'simply a form that is required by the Constitution, and not a Bill to give rise to any discussion.' And while he did not 'dispute the power or right of the House to make any alteration it pleased in a Bill as it passed through its several stages, it had never been a custom, by alterations in the Appropriation Bill, to rescind the previous acts and votes of this House.'‡ Amendments which did not affect the determinations of the Committee of Supply have, though very rarely, been made in the Appropriation Bill during its progress through the House.§

Procedure upon the Appropriation Bill, at its various stages.

It has also been ruled that debates and amendments upon the several stages of the Appropriation Bill are to be governed by the same rules as those applicable to other Bills, and must therefore be relevant to the Bill, or some part of it, and should not be allowed the same latitude as that practised on going into Committees of Supply and of Ways and Means.‖ This rule, however, does not preclude a member from bringing a question of foreign or domestic policy before the House, upon the motion for going into committee on this Bill, or upon the second or third reading, if it be a question that 'arises out' of any of the votes thereby appropriated.¶

---

* Hans. Deb. vol. clxiv. p. 1500.
† Ibid. p. 1502.
‡ Ibid. pp. 1750, 1751; and see vol. clxxvi. p. 1800.
§ See Commons Journals, July 22, 1858.
‖ Hans. Deb. vol. cxliii. pp. 500, 641; Ibid. vol. clxxx. p. 830.
¶ Ibid. vol. cxliii. p. 643; vol. clxxvi. p. 1859.

330   THE ROYAL PREROGATIVE.

Final statement of estimated revenue and expenditure for ensuing year.

In 1863 the Chancellor of the Exchequer (Mr. Gladstone) introduced the practice of submitting to the House, upon the third reading of the Appropriation Bill, a rectified statement of the estimated revenue and expenditure for the ensuing year. He pointed out the alterations which had been made in the original estimates since they had been introduced, in consequence of certain items of revenue which had been asked for by government not having been granted by the House; and noticed the effect of certain items of expenditure which had been authorised pursuant to supplemental estimates upon the general balance, as stated on the opening of the budget.[h] In 1864 Mr. Gladstone made a similar statement, upon the motion for going into Committee on the Appropriation Bill;[i] but not in 1865. On July 23, 1866, Mr. Disraeli informed the House of the altered position of the public finances since the budget of his predecessor in office had been submitted.

Appropriation Bill to be printed.

On account of the formal character of the Appropriation Bill, it had been customary to abstain from printing it for the use of members. But as complaints were made of alterations in the wording of the Bill having been occasionally made which were unknown to members generally, it was resolved, on March 24, 1863, that henceforth a sufficient number of copies of all Appropriation Bills should be printed, and delivered to members applying for the same, in time for consideration before the committal of such Bills.[k] In 1865, the Appropriation Bill was presented to the House in a much improved shape.[l]

To be presented by the Speaker for the royal assent.

When the Appropriation Bill has passed both Houses, and is ready for the royal assent, it is returned into the charge of the Commons until the time appointed for the prorogation of Parliament, when it is carried by the Speaker to the bar of the House of Peers, and there

---

[h] Hans. Deb. vol. clxxii. p. 1268.
[i] *Ibid.* vol. clxxvi. p. 1857.
[k] *Ibid.* vol. clxix. pp. 730, 1631.
[l] *Ibid.* vol. clxxx. p. 717.

received by the Clerk of the Parliament, for the royal assent. When the sovereign is present in person, the Speaker prefaces the delivery of the Money Bills with a short speech. 'The main criterion by which the topics of these speeches have been selected appears to have been the political importance of the measures which have employed the attention of the House of Commons during the preceding session, unlimited by any consideration of their progress or their failure.' Even 'the peculiar privilege and concern of the House of Commons' has been noticed in such addresses.° On one occasion, some observations of Sir Fletcher Norton, in his speech on presenting the Supply Bill, became the subject of remark and complaint in the House of Commons, on account of their uncourtly style; but his friend Mr. Fox, having come to the rescue, Sir Fletcher was formally thanked by the House for his speech.ᵖ At the close of the Speaker's address, the Money Bills are tendered for the royal assent, which they receive before any of the other Bills awaiting the royal sanction, and in a peculiar form of words, which acknowledge the supply to be the free gift of the Commons.ᵠ

Speech of the Speaker on presenting Money Bills.

Any deviation from the constitutional rule of parliamentary appropriation of supplies granted for the public service is to be regarded with great jealousy.ʳ Nevertheless it will sometimes occur, as when a ministerial crisis has necessitated a speedy dissolution of Parliament,

---

° Speaker Abbott, in defence of a speech of his own, delivered in 1813; Parl. Deb. vol. xxvii. pp. 479, 481. May, referring to this defence, characterises Speaker Abbott's speech as 'an act of indiscretion, if not disorder, which placed him in the awkward position of defending himself, in the chair, from a proposed vote of censure. From this embarrassment he was delivered by the kindness of his friends, and the good feeling of the House, rather than by the completeness of his own defence.' Const. Hist. vol. ii. p. 376, n.

ᵖ May, Const. Hist. vol. i. p. 200.

ᵠ May, Parl. Prac. ed. 1863, p. 570.

ʳ See the proceedings had, in both Houses, when at a period of public emergency, in 1794, the Commons were induced to empower the crown to apply out of the aids of the year such sums as the exigency of public affairs might require. The Act 7 Geo. II. c. 12, sec. 12, containing this provision, was protested against by the House of Lords, and is censured by Hatsell as a measure entirely subversive of the rules of Parliament in the grant of supplies. 3 Hats. pp. 190, 218.

332   THE ROYAL PREROGATIVE.

Votes of credit.

or when military operations on a large scale are about to be undertaken for the defence of the empire, or the prosecution of a foreign war—that it is deemed expedient to entrust the government with means for carrying on the public service, for a limited period, by votes of credit for large sums, instead of by specific appropriations for the several branches of public expenditure, as in the case of the ordinary supplies. But this proceeding is only justifiable upon occasions of great and unforeseen emergency, which do not admit of delay; or which may render it inexpedient for the House to commit itself to the details of expenditure included in the estimates prepared by an existing ministry whose tenure of office has been condemned. It is incumbent upon the House, under such circumstances, to limit the supply of credit to the bare necessity of the state, for the period which must elapse before the reassembling of Parliament; and to require the sums so granted to be properly accounted for at the earliest possible period.*

Whether supply is voted en bloc or in detail, an Appropriation Act is equally necessary.

But whether the supplies are voted in large sums or in detail, it is equally necessary that they should be included in an Act of Appropriation, whereby the sanction of the three branches of the legislature is given to the expenditure of the money voted by the House of Commons.

No Appropriation Act in 1784.

In 1784 a case occurred which it was feared would have led to serious consequences. The prime minister, Mr. Pitt, was in a minority in the House of Commons, and it was well known that he was only waiting for the supplies in order to dissolve Parliament. The estimates had passed through the Committee of Supply, when, on January 12, the House of Commons resolved that any public officer who, in reliance upon the votes in supply, should cause to be paid any sums of money for the public service, after the prorogation of Parliament, and without the express authority of an Act of Appropriation, would be guilty of a 'high crime and misdemeanor, a daring breach of a public trust, derogatory to the fundamental privileges of Parliament, and subversive of the constitution.' Nevertheless, the prorogation and dissolution of Parliament took place before the passing of the Appropriation Act. The new House

---

* See *ante*, p. 480.

of Commons was favourable to Mr. Pitt's administration, and it appearing, by returns furnished to the House, that ministers had abstained from using any moneys not actually granted by law, but such as the exigencies of the state imperatively required, no further proceedings were had upon the matter.[t] The supplies in question were however re-voted in the next session, and included in the Appropriation Act 24 Geo. III. sess. 2, c. 44.

There have been only one or two other instances since the revolution of the prorogation of Parliament before an Act of Appropriation had been passed. One took place in 1807, when a new Parliament which had been in existence only about four months was dissolved, in the midst of the session, for the purpose of strengthening the government by an appeal to the country on the question of the Roman Catholic claims. On this occasion the ordinary supplies had been voted by the House of Commons, but 'the Irish Money Bills had not been passed,' and 'none of the sums which had been voted for the public service were appropriated, for no Appropriation Act had been passed.' The dissolution of Parliament under these circumstances was severely commented upon by constitutional authorities in the new Parliament.[u] The Chancellor of the Exchequer, in defending the course pursued by ministers, declared that during this interval there had been no irregular issue of public money, for that 'the public expenditure had been maintained out of the sums appropriated by Parliament;' clauses of appropriation having been inserted in certain Bills passed in the previous session, although there had been no general Appropriation Act. 'In the issues that had taken place, therefore, the government had acted according to law, and under the authority of Parliament.'[v] On the death of George III. in 1820, the Commons, in anticipation of a dissolution of Parliament, voted certain temporary supplies, which were not appropriated by Act of Parliament in that session. Objections were raised to these votes in the House of Lords, as being an infringement of the right of their Lordships to assent to the grant of supplies; but it was ultimately resolved 'that this House, from the state of public business, acquiesce in these resolutions, although no Act may be passed to give them effect.'[w] Again, in 1831, owing to the excitement occasioned by the rejection of the Reform Bill in the House of Lords, Parliament was hurriedly dissolved in April, before the passing of an Appropriation Act. The new Parliament met on June 14, when all the grants of the former session were re-voted in Committee of Supply.[x]

Or in 1807.

Or in 1820.

Or in 1831.

[t] 3 Hatsell, 200-209. See the comments and explanations of Mr. Perceval, Chancellor of the Exchequer in 1807, on this case. Parl. Deb. vol. ix. p. 611.

[u] Parl. Deb. vol. ix. p. 618.
[v] Ibid. p. 631.
[w] Hans. Deb. vol. xli. pp. 1031-1035.
[x] May's Prac. ed. 1863, p. 534, n.

B. *As to Parliamentary Control over the Issue and Expenditure of Public Money.*

<small>Parliamentary control over issue and expenditure of public money.</small>

Having explained the constitutional procedure in respect to the grant of public money for the service of the state, we have next to consider the regulations which have been established by law for the purpose of preventing the illegal issue or expenditure thereof.

Strange as it may appear, 'there has always been a marked contrast between the jealous susceptibility displayed by the House of Commons in asserting their exclusive right to grant the supplies, and the indifference with which (until very lately) they have abandoned the final appropriation of the supplies, when granted, to the unchecked discretion of the executive government.'[1]

At the present time, however, the constitutional control of Parliament over the public expenditure is exercised with great vigilance and effect. In the fulfilment of this important function, the House of Commons is assisted by three distinct tribunals, each of which has appropriate duties to discharge. These are: 1. The department of the Exchequer and Audit; 2. The Treasury; and 3. The Standing Committee on Public Accounts. The sphere of action which belongs to these several departments has recently engaged the attention of Parliament and of the executive government, and is still, to some extent, in process of adjustment. But the relative position of each towards the others will be apparent, as we proceed to consider their respective functions.

The subject will naturally divide itself into four heads. 1. The control which is exercised over the public revenue, its receipt, custody, and issue, by the department of the Exchequer and Audit; an office which has been newly consolidated and regulated by the Act 29 & 30 Vict. c. 39, passed in 1866. 2. The control which is

---

[1] Rep. Com. Pub. Accts. 1865, Appx. p. 115.

exercised over every branch of the public expenditure of the Lords Commissioners of her Majesty's Treasury. 3. The operation of the system of Audit, which is now applicable to all accounts of past expenditure, in every department of state. 4. The supervision over the issue and expenditure of public money which is exercised by the Standing Committee on Public Accounts.

1. *The Control over the Public Revenue by the Department of Exchequer and Audit.*

The check upon unauthorised expenditure is primarily effected by vesting the power of issue in the Exchequer, an office which is quite independent of the Treasury, and is presided over by a Comptroller-General, who is appointed during good behaviour, and is in fact a parliamentary officer, responsible to both Houses, and liable to impeachment, as well as to dismissal, upon their joint address.[a]

Control over the issue of public money by the Exchequer department.

The office of the Receipt of Her Majesty's Exchequer has, from time immemorial, been regarded as a check upon the Treasury, and a protection both to the sovereign and to the subject, in the custody and payment of the public money. The whole revenue of the country, with the exception of certain deductions from the gross receipts which are authorised by law, is required to be paid directly into the Bank of England, or of Ireland, to the 'Account of Her Majesty's Exchequer;'[b] and from this office authority is given to issue money, in conformity with the appropriations of Parliament. The Comptroller-General himself has no power of making issues from the Bank; his duty is confined to the granting of credits, or

---

[a] Act 4 & 5 Will. IV. c. 15, sec. 2. This statute, under which the ancient office of the Exchequer was remodelled and reformed, was passed at the recommendation of a Commission of Inquiry into the Public Accounts, in 1831. Rep. Com. on Pub. Moneys, 1857, Appx. p. 75. And see a debate in the House of Commons, on the office of Comptroller of the Exchequer, on February 27, 1840.

[b] Treasury Minute, December 23, 1858. Commons Papers, 1860, vol. xxxix. pt. 1, p. 174.

making transfers to the accounts of persons named in the Treasury warrants. Returns are made daily to the Treasury, showing all the sums paid to the Exchequer account at the banks aforesaid. These banks also send to the Treasury daily accounts of their receipts and issues, in pursuance of Exchequer credits and transfers. With this complete information, the Treasury can exercise a daily check over all Exchequer transactions; which has heretofore rendered it unnecessary to subject the Exchequer accounts to the special examination of the Board of Audit.[b]

Functions of the Exchequer. The functions of the Exchequer, as defined by the Commissioners of Public Accounts in 1831, consist in— (1) the receipt and safe custody of the public treasure; (2) a control over the crown and its ministers in relation thereto; (3) the duty of record.[c]

Formerly, the exercise of the functions of the Exchequer was a very complex affair, owing to the excessive number of officers, and the cumbrous forms which had to be resorted to, in order to put its authority in operation. But in 1834, pursuant to the recommendations of the commissioners aforesaid, a statute was passed which abolished several of the subordinate officers, simplified the machinery of business, and transferred to the Comptroller-General all the prescriptive powers and duties previously exercised by other functionaries in this department.

The essential powers which are now possessed by the Exchequer have been thus described—'It is the great conservator of the revenues of the nation. It does not exercise any authority over the administrative departments of receipt, nor over the departments of payment further than to guard against the illegal application of

---

[b] Com. Papers, 1802, vol. xxxix. pt. 1, p. 180. Second Rep. Com. Pub. Accts. 1849, p. 25. But under the Exchequer and Audit Act of 1846, the accounts of money paid into the Exchequer must be examined by the Commissioners of Audit. Rep. Com. Pub. Accts (Exchequer, &c. Bill), 1849. Evid. 241, &c.
[c] Rep. Com. of Pub. Accounts, on the Exchequer, Commons Papers, 1831, vol. x. p. 10.

any portion of the public income. The constitutional functions of its officers, who hold their situations for life, are to provide for the safe keeping and proper appropriation of the public money. For this purpose it is charged with the receipt of the revenues, which are vested in its name, and deposited in its care, until issued under the authority of Parliament for the service of the state; and it is armed with a power of denying its sanction to any demands upon it, from whatever minister or department they may be made, unless those demands are found in accordance with the determinations of the legislature.'[d]

Moreover, the office of Comptroller of the Exchequer renders it absolutely necessary that Parliament should be assembled at least once in every year, and that it should not be prorogued before the passing of an Act of Appropriation; because it is the duty of this high functionary to refuse to permit the issue of any public money except under the authority of an Act of Parliament.

In the year 1857, Sir G. C. Lewis (the then Chancellor of the Exchequer) laid before the Committee of the House of Commons on Public Moneys a proposal that the office of the Receipt of Her Majesty's Exchequer should be abolished, and its functions of control transferred to the Commissioners of Audit, with additional powers; in order that one department, responsible to Parliament, and reporting directly to Parliament, should henceforth control the original issue, and, both by concurrent and final audit, superintend the application of the public moneys to the services for which they were voted by Parliament.[e] This proposal, however, drew forth a strong remonstrance from Lord Monteagle, the then Comptroller of the Exchequer, who pointed out, in an elaborate

Proposed union of the Exchequer and Audit offices.

---

[d] Rep. Com. on Pub. Moneys, Commons Papers, 1856, vol. xv. Evid. p. 2; Mem. on Financial Control, Commons Papers, 1857, Sess. 2, vol. ix. p. 75; Act 4 & 5 Will. IV. c. 15, secs. 11-13. Other duties of the Exchequer, which are not material to the present inquiry, are described in Murray's Hand-book of Church and State, p. 135.

[e] Rep. Com. Pub. Moneys, 1857, p. 34.

memorandum, the beneficial results of Exchequer control over the issues of public money, and the constitutional importance of his office in the guardianship of the public revenues. This induced the government to abandon their scheme, and led to the withdrawal of resolutions for the abolition of the Exchequer office which had been submitted to the committee.[f] The committee, however, recommended the reorganization of the Board of Audit, with higher powers, so as to make it rank with the principal departments of state, and to interpose an effective check on existing abuses, thereby rendering the control of Parliament over the details of the public expenditure effectual and complete.[g] This recommendation was not regarded, at the time, with much favour, either by the government or by the House of Commons.[h]

<small>Partially effected in 1866.</small>

But in 1865 Lord Monteagle announced his intention of retiring from office. Whereupon the administration submitted to Parliament a Bill to unite the offices of Comptroller of the Exchequer and Chairman of the Board of Audit, which became law.[i] It was alleged, in behalf of this Bill, that while 'Exchequer control had become inefficient, anomalous, and unreal, to a very great degree,' and not sufficiently important to justify the maintenance of a separate establishment,' it was not intended to alter the duties then performed by the Comptroller of the Exchequer, but merely to assign the same to the Chairman of the Board of Audit until Parliament should be enabled to consider the question in all its bearings, and to decide whether any further changes were desirable. Meanwhile, the Chairman of the Audit Board, in holding both offices, would be elevated, in point of salary and tenure, to the highest position of dignity and independence.

A very short time sufficed to satisfy the Government

<small>
[f] Rep. Com. Pub. Moneys, 1857, p. 10.
[g] Ibid. p. 5.
[h] Commons Deb. March 11, 1862; Hans. Deb. vol. clxv. p. 1350.
[i] Act 28 & 29 Vic. c. 93.
[j] Chanc. of Excheq. Hans. Deb. vol. clxxx. p. 303.
</small>

as to the necessity for further legislation on this subject. Accordingly, early in the following session, a Bill was brought into the House of Commons, by the Chancellor of the Exchequer, to consolidate the duties of the Exchequer and Audit departments, to regulate the receipt, custody, and issue of public moneys, and to provide for the audit of the accounts thereof. This Bill was referred to the Standing Committee of Public Accounts, by whom it was subjected to the most careful examination. The committee took evidence in regard to the Bill from the principal officers of the Board of Audit, of the Exchequer, and of other administrative departments. Finally, they reported it to the House, with considerable amendments; and with a recommendation that, when it became law, a standing order should be adopted, requiring that all reports on Appropriation and Consolidated Fund accounts, and Treasury minutes to extend the principle of the Appropriation audit to other services than those to which it has been heretofore applicable, should be regularly referred to the Committee on Public Accounts.[a] The Exchequer and Audits Department Bill passed through both Houses with very little opposition, and notwithstanding the change of ministry which took place during this session, it was freely accepted by the new administration, and became law.[b] *Exchequer and Audit departments consolidated in 1866.*

Such of the provisions of this Act as materially modify the constitutional practice which heretofore prevailed in relation to its subject-matter will be noticed in their appropriate places in this section. But beyond the change effected by the consolidation of two offices which were formerly distinct, and of widely different importance, the alterations made by this Act in the existing practice are comparatively few, and of minor consequence. *Provisions in the new Consolidation Act.*

As regards the receipt of public moneys by the Exchequer, no change in the existing regulations has been *As regards receipt of*

---

[a] Special Rep. Com. Pub. Accounts, 1866, p. lii.
[b] Act 29 & 30 Vict. c. 39.

made, except to render it compulsory upon the government to pay to the Exchequer account the gross revenues, after deducting certain charges enumerated in section 11. But this had been already the practice, under the authority of a Treasury minute, ever since the year 1854, when the charges for the collection of the revenue were first voted.[a]

As regards custody of public moneys. As regards the custody of public moneys in the Exchequer, the new Act introduced no change whatever. It requires all public moneys to be paid, as heretofore, to the account of the Exchequer at the Bank of England, or of Ireland, and to remain there, subject to the provisions of the Act. The moneys are to be placed to the account, not of the Treasury, or of the government, but of 'her Majesty's Exchequer,' as represented by an independent officer, called the Exchequer and Audit Commissioner.[b]

As regards issue of public moneys. As regards the issue of public moneys from the Exchequer account, there is substantially no difference in the control to be exercised by the Exchequer and Audit Commissioner over the issues, over that which heretofore prevailed; but there is a different machinery resorted to, as will appear from the following account of the successive steps required to give effect to a parliamentary appropriation.

Procedure to give effect to a parliamentary appropriation.
1. It is necessary that there should be votes of the House of Commons, in Committee of Supply, granting money, for certain specified services, to the crown. These votes to be subsequently confirmed by the Appropriation Act, and substantiated by an Act of Parliament placing at the disposal of the Treasury ways and means to satisfy the same. 2. One or more royal orders, authorising the Treasury to apply the supplies granted to her Majesty (by the Ways and Means Act covering the same), in conformity to the votes of Parliament in the Appropri-

---

[a] See *ante*, p. 470; Rep. Com. Hill, 1860, Evid. 10-16. Pub. Accts. on Excheq. and Audit   [b] *Ibid.* Evid. 37-41.

ation Act.* 3. To enable the Treasury to meet these payments, it applies to the Comptroller and Auditor General for a general credit, to an amount not exceeding that of the available ways and means, and in accordance with the votes in supply; whereupon the said officer grants to the Treasury credits, on the Exchequer accounts at the Bank, not exceeding the amount of the ways and means granted by an Act of Parliament.† 4. This having been obtained, the Treasury will then operate upon that credit, by transfers to the Paymaster-General's account, to enable him to meet the payments for the different services. When the Treasury have issued their daily orders to the Bank of England to transfer money to the Paymaster-General's account, the Bank is required to advise the auditors thereof immediately, in order that they may have the materials for checking the accounts which they are called upon, by the audit clauses of the Exchequer Act, to check before they are submitted to Parliament by the Treasury.‡

By these constitutional forms, the principle of the monarchy is asserted as fully, in respect to the issue of moneys voted to the sovereign for the public service, as

Monarchical principle fully asserted.

---

* The orders are under the royal sign-manual, countersigned by the Lords of the Treasury. Formerly the royal authority was conveyed by a writ under the Privy Seal. During the mental incapacity of George III. the deputy clerks of the Privy Seal declined to prepare warrants to pass the Privy Seal for the want of a warrant signed by the king himself; and the auditor of Exchequer refused to issue money under Treasury warrants merely. But the difficulty was overcome by both Houses of Parliament agreeing to resolutions authorising the Exchequer to obey the Treasury warrants. (May, Const. Hist. i. 179.) Before the passing of the Exchequer Act of 1866, the royal orders were addressed to the Comptroller of the Exchequer, authorising him to issue the full amount of the supplies voted, on receiving directions from the Treasury. This necessitated a Treasury warrant to the Exchequer, delegating authority to the Secretary of the Treasury to apply, from time to time, for the issues required; and an issuing letter, from the Secretary to the Exchequer, directing that the special issue required should be placed to the credit of the Paymaster-General. This is now much simplified, and the royal orders are sent to the Treasury direct, because the ways and means are granted, by the Act, to the Lords of the Treasury.

† Act 29 & 30 Vict. c. 39, sec. 15.

‡ Rep. Com. Pub. Accts. (Exchq. and Audit Bill) 1866, Evid. 40, 62-64, compared with the Mem. on Financial Control (Commons Papers, 1857, sess. ii. vol. ix.) pp. 30, 70.

by the use of the sign manual in all other affairs of state: and the independent control of the Exchequer is maintained by the power of suspending or refusing the grant of credit to the Treasury until, in the words of the Act 4 & 5 Will. IV. c. 15, sec. 11, the Comptroller-General shall have first satisfied himself that 'the royal order has been made in conformity with, and has not exceeded, the amount of the grant of Parliament.' Nor is this a mere fiction. The control of the Exchequer was exercised in upwards of one hundred cases, between 1834 and 1857, and has proved effectual for the purposes designed.[1]

There is a difference in regard to Supply charges and Consolidated Fund charges. The actual amounts of the former are specified in the votes, and in the Appropriation Act. The amounts of the latter are not specified in the Act, and must be made up by the Treasury. Before the Exchequer permits the insertion of any new charge on the Consolidated Fund, the warrant or other instrument creating the office, or making the grant, is called for, examined, and recorded. If found correct, the charge is allowed; if not, its amount would be deducted from the total, and not issued.[2]

Money only to be applied to services sanctioned by Parliament.

The Exchequer and Audit Act of 1866 expressly forbids the Treasury, or any subordinate authority, from directing the payment of expenditure which has not been sanctioned either by an Act whereby services are or may be charged on the Consolidated Fund, or by a vote of the House of Commons.[3] The ways and means are general, and may be applied to any services voted. But no money voted can be issued until the Ways and Means Act is passed; and the amount of supply voted is limited in the issue by the amount of ways and means. It is only by authority of the Ways and Means Act—which always contains a clause stating that the ways and means

---

[1] See Mem. on Fin. Control, pp. 78, 80, 84, 114. And see Lord Monteagle's Ev. before Com. on Pub. Moneys, Com. Papers, 1856, vol. xv.

[2] Mem. Fin. Control, p. 78; Rep. Com. Pub. Accts. (Excheq. Bill) 1866, Evid. 173-180.

[3] Act 29 & 30 Vict. c. 39, sec. 11.

therein granted may be applied to any services voted by the House of Commons—that the resolutions of supply can be acted upon.*

In case of a deficiency of funds to meet the permanent charges on the Consolidated Fund, the Act of 1866 empowers the Treasury to apply to the Bank of England to make advances to the extent of that deficiency, on the security of Deficiency Bills, which are chargeable upon the growing revenue of the quarter. A similar provision is contained in the Ways and Means Acts, in respect to services to be provided for by those Acts. The only point wherein this differs from the old practice is, that formerly such Bills were issued by the Exchequer, but now by the Treasury. Under no circumstances would the Comptroller of the Exchequer grant a credit in excess of his balance at the Bank.*

{Deficiency Bills.}

To revert, however, to the control which is exercised by the department of the Exchequer over the issue of public money. After all, that control is only effective in guarding against issues contrary to the expressed will of Parliament, or in excess of the total amount of the ways and means granted to make good the supplies voted. It cannot follow the amount authorised to be advanced under the Treasury warrant, and guard against the future misapplication thereof. If such misapplication does occur, it is evidently the department by whom the money is received, and not the Comptroller-General, who is responsible for the same. In the opinion of the law officers of the crown, the Exchequer check, even before the Act of 1866, was distinctly limited to the great heads of expenditure, such as army, navy, works, &c., and did not extend to their subsidiary votes; which is a matter resting between the Treasury and the departments charged with the details of public expenditure.* For

{Exchequer control over issue of money will not prevent illegal expenditure.}

---

* Rep. Com. Pub. Accts. (Excheq. and Audit Bill) 1860, Evid. 50–61.
* Ibid. 64–78, 82.
* Ibid. pp. 62, 63. And see Report of Committee on Public Accounts, 1862, Min. of Ev. 100; Rep. Com. Pub. Accts. 1865, pp. 117, 118.

example, it would be 'impossible for the Exchequer to keep a check upon the appropriation of the separate naval votes, in which a large portion of the expenditure is incurred abroad, and upon imprests (i. e. advances) which cannot be assigned to a vote at the time of issue.'

Funds in the hands of the Paymaster-General are all used as 'one balance.'

Once the public money has been formally transferred from the credit of the Exchequer to that of the Paymaster-General, it is 'the usual practice, authorised by the Treasury, and in conformity with the recommendations of the Public Moneys Committee' of 1857, for the Pay Office to 'apply the moneys in the hands of the Paymaster to the general expenditure, without reference to the Exchequer credits from which the moneys have been transferred, provided the service had been voted by Parliament, and the vote was not exceeded;' in other words, for the Paymaster-General 'to use all his balances as one balance,' re-distributing the whole of the aggregate sum in his Exchequer Credit Account, 'according to the demands of the different departments of the public service, irrespective of the particular titles under which the sums may have been assigned to his credit in the books of the Bank.' This arrangement has been formally approved of by the Committee on Public Accounts, and it is attended with the great advantage that it prevents the loss that would be occasioned by having useless balances lying at the Bank of England.'

By the eleventh clause of the Exchequer Act of 1866, this practice has been distinctly legalised. But though the Paymaster is at liberty to use all the money that comes into his hands as one fund, it is a mere matter of account, and by way of an advance. The purpose for which the money is issued will be that to which it is to be finally appropriated, and it will be so appropriated in his books. With the safeguard which will be hereafter

---

* Rep. Com. Pub. Accts. 1862, Evid. 1740; Rep. of said Com. on Excheq. Bill, 1866, Evid. 127, 128.

⁷ Second Report, Public Accounts Committee, 1862, pp. 3, 4, 15; Rep. Com. Pub. Accts. 1865, Appx. p. 130.

afforded to Parliament by the universal operation of the Appropriation Audit, there can be no objection to make the moneys at the disposal of the Paymaster-General applicable to defray all the services which have been voted by Parliament.' To prevent abuses, however, the suggestion of the Public Moneys Committee has been followed, and an adjustment of accounts takes place at the pay-office at the end of every month, when a statement of balances, showing the credit standing to each separate vote and account is forwarded to the Treasury.ᵃ

Nevertheless, the system of Exchequer control, while it effectually prevents the unauthorised *issue* of public money, is powerless of itself to prevent irregular *expenditure*.

The control of the Exchequer over the issues of public money is based upon an admitted principle of our constitutional system, that no money is legally available for public purposes but that which has been placed at the disposal of government by Parliament. The government, in fact, are unable, under the laws now in force, to obtain from the Exchequer any money but what is drawn against some specific parliamentary grant. The issue of money by the Comptroller of the Exchequer is, moreover, accompanied by what is substantially an authoritative direction to the proper officers to apply such money to the particular service for which it was granted by Parliament, and the annual Appropriation Acts have always strictly forbidden any misapplication of the funds granted therein. But these stringent requirements, though they have undoubtedly served to restrain unauthorised expenditure, have not sufficed to prevent it altogether. The 'systematic appropriation' of funds granted by Parliament for specific purposes is an abuse which has existed for centuries, and which has continued to be practised to some extent even in our own day, notwithstanding frequent resolutions of

Principle of Exchequer control over issue of money.

ᵃ Rep. Com. Pub. Accts. (Excheq. Bill) 1866, Evid. 70-80, 127-131.   ᵇ Second Rep. Pub. Accts. Com. 1863, pp. 7, 15.

the House of Commons, and penalties imposed by legislative enactment upon all public officers who should presume to divert or misapply the public revenues to any other uses than those for which they had been appropriated by Parliament.[b]

Impossibility of wholly preventing unauthorised expenditure.

It is therefore erroneous to suppose that the government can be absolutely *prevented* from any misapplication of the parliamentary grants. Even were it possible to do so, it would not be politic to restrain the government from expending money, under any circumstances, without the previous authority of Parliament. In the words of Mr. Macaulay (Secretary to the Board of Audit), 'cases must constantly arise, in so complicated a system of government as ours, where it becomes the duty of the executive authorities, in the exercise of their discretionary powers, boldly to set aside the requirements of the legislature, trusting to the good sense of Parliament, when all the facts of the case shall have been explained, to acquit them of all blame; and it would be, not a public advantage, but a public calamity, if the government were to be deprived of the means of so exercising their discretionary authority.'[c] To the same effect, we have a declaration by a Committee of the House of Commons, that 'in special emergencies expenditure unauthorised by Parliament becomes absolutely essential. In all such cases the executive must take the responsibility of sanctioning whatever immediate urgency requires; and it has never been found that Parliament exhibited any reluctance to supply the means of meeting such expenditure.'[d]

Discretionary powers vested in government.

Remedy against unauthorised expenditure.

The best remedy against unauthorised and unjustifiable expenditure is to be found in the vigilant exercise of the inquisitorial powers of Parliament, through the Standing Committee on Public Accounts. Mr. Macaulay is indeed

---

[b] 3 Hatsell, 200, &c. Debate in the Commons, June 23, 1828, on 'the misappropriation of public funds.' Rep. Com. on Public Moneys, 1857, pp. 31, 81.

[c] Rep. Com. Pub. Accts. 1865, apx. p. 140.

[d] First Report, Com. on Packet and Telegraphic Contracts, p. xv. Commons Papers, 1860, vol. xiv.

of opinion that the government should be left free to do as they thought fit with the parliamentary grants, being responsible to Parliament for all that they might do; and that the Appropriation Audit should be relied upon to keep Parliament fully informed as to how the several issues from the Exchequer had been actually applied, and as to the circumstances under which the requirements of the Appropriation Act had been departed from, in any particular instance.' But such a proceeding would be derogatory alike to the judgment of the executive government—who should be able to foresee and apply for the necessary provision to meet all ordinary expenditure likely to occur within the fiscal year—and to the authority of Parliament itself, as the keeper and guardian of the public purse. Ample provision has been made by Parliament to meet the case of extraordinary and unforeseen items of expenditure, by placing at the disposal of government the necessary funds to defray the same, by means of the 'Treasury Chest,' and the 'Civil Contingencies' Funds, the nature and extent of which will be presently explained. *Mr. Macaulay's opinion on this head.*

But before entering upon this topic, it may be appropriate to notice some remarkable instances wherein the government have assumed the responsibility of incurring expenditure without the previous sanction of Parliament, and to point out the proceedings taken by the House of Commons in regard to the same. *Instances of expenditure by government without authority of Parliament.*

At the commencement of the French revolutionary war, Mr. Pitt advanced enormous sums, amounting to upwards of 1,200,000*l.* to the Emperor of Germany, to aid in the defence of the 'general interests of Europe,' without the previous sanction of Parliament. Upon the attention of the House of Commons being directed to this affair, it was proposed to pass a vote of censure on the minister, but his friends interposed, and induced the House to agree to an amendment, declaring that the proceeding in question, 'though not to be drawn into precedent, but upon occasion of special necessity, was, under the peculiar circumstances of the case, a justifiable and proper *Mr. Pitt's advances to Germany.*

---

* Rep. Com. Pub. Accounts, 1865, p. 140.

exercise of the discretion vested in his Majesty's ministers' by a former vote of credit.

Excess of naval and military expenditure.

Again, so recently as March 7, 1859, resolutions were submitted to the Committee of Supply for the grant of 1,050,000l. to make good a deficiency in the appropriations for the army, and for the grant of 133,930l. 8s. 9d. to defray an excess in the naval expenditure, over and above the sums voted for the service of the preceding year. This deficiency arose out of the emergencies of the Indian mutiny and the Chinese war. A large proportion of the liability incurred on behalf of the army was by way of an advance, to be repaid out of the Indian revenue: and the actual deficiency for the army service would have only amounted to about 180,000l. if the surpluses on certain other army votes could have been taken in aid; but owing to an alteration made in the Appropriation Act of 1856-7, these surpluses were obliged to be repaid into the Exchequer. Anyhow, a very considerable expenditure, in excess of the Appropriation Act of the year, had been incurred upon the responsibility of ministers. This proceeding did not give rise to any formal discussion in the House of Commons, but it was severely animadverted upon in the 'Parliamentary Remembrancer.'

China war.

In the following year a similar occurrence took place, the history of which is especially noteworthy, as it points out the securities which have been devised, by the wisdom of Parliament, to ensure that no extraordinary responsibility in regard to the expenditure of money should be assumed by the government without the attention of the House of Commons being called thereto by accountable officers. The circumstances were as follows: Soon after the meeting

---

Parl. Hist. November 13, 1760. See also the proceedings of the House of Commons, in 1805, in regard to Mr. Pitt's conduct in loaning public money to Boyd, Benfield & Co., public contractors, to enable them to fulfil their engagements with government. (Parl. Deb. vol. v. pp. 385-424.) But when, in 1840, after the prorogation of Parliament, the government ordered an increase to be made to the navy, beyond that authorised by the legislature—although the circumstances which induced the government to assume this responsibility were exceptional and peculiar—great objection was taken in the House of Commons to the act, and it was declared by Sir R. Peel and other leading members that either a supplementary vote of credit, in anticipation of the emergency, should have been asked for, or else the special attention of the House should have been directed thereto by the crown, at the re-assembling of Parliament, in order to obtain indemnification for the transaction, either by a special Act of Indemnity, or in some other way, so as to prevent its being hereafter drawn into precedent. It was finally agreed to introduce a clause into the Appropriation Bill, for the purpose of recording the sense of the House on this proceeding. (Mirror of Parl. 1841, pp. 481, 931; 4 & 5 Vict. c. 59, sec. 11, 12.) See also a debate in the Commons, on unauthorised expenditure of public money, in Hans. Deb. April 12, 1851.

See Commons Papers, 1859, sess. 1, vol. xix. p. 580.

Hans. Deb. vol. clii. p. 1403.

Parl. Rememb. 1859, p. 57.

of Parliament, in 1860, the government—being aware that an expenditure had been incurred by the naval and military departments, on account of the China war, for which no provision had been made in the ordinary grants for those services in the preceding session—submitted an estimate to the House of Commons, on February 21, to enable them to meet the anticipated excess of expenditure. On March 19, a vote of credit for 850,000*l.* for this service was reported from Committee of Supply. But ' under the legal restrictions applicable to votes in supply, no actual issue out of the vote of credit could be made at the Exchequer until Parliament had appropriated ways and means from which the issue could be legally met. It became necessary, therefore, to vote a sum in ways and means' to cover this vote. Accordingly, on March 21, such a vote was reported. ' Votes of ways and means (which are authorities to take moneys out of the Consolidated Fund), unlike votes in supply, have not legal effect until an Act has been passed confirming the grant of ways and means. The delay which was occasioned by the necessity of obtaining a Ways and Means Act to sanction the issue of the amount of the vote of credit out of the Consolidated Fund in the year for which it was granted, postponed the day on which the issue could be legally made at the Exchequer until March 31, 1860, the last day of the financial year 1859-60.[j] Owing to this delay, the vote in supply became in effect a deficiency vote, and therefore applicable to make good an expenditure already defrayed, and not, as in all ordinary cases, a provision to meet prospective expenditure.' Accordingly, on receipt of advice of the Exchequer credit for the amount voted, the Paymaster-General placed that amount to the credit of the 'Treasury Chest' in his books: from whence, agreeably to usage, the moneys required for the navy and army services in China had been advanced. This transaction was carefully investigated by the Committee on Public Accounts, in 1863, who did not see cause to question the regularity of the proceedings of any public department in respect thereto. But, in order to strengthen the check upon the government, and to prevent unauthorised expenditure, they reiterated a recommendation of the Committee on Public Moneys, in 1857, that ' all payments of the Paymaster-General should be checked from day to day in the department in which they are authorised or made, by an officer appointed by the Commissioners of Audit,' whose duty it should be ' to follow from day to day the appropriation of every payment to its proper account, and to report immediately to the commissioners any excess of the vote sanctioned by Parliament, or other irregularity.' [k]

[j] The Ways and Means Act referred to did not receive the royal assent until March 31.

[k] Second Rep. of Com. on Pub. Accounts, 1863, pp. iii.–vii.

Funds out of which unauthorised expenditure is defrayed.

And here it may be asked, Out of what fund are the government able to make these enormous advances? If the Comptroller-General is empowered, as we have seen, to interpose his authority, and forbid the issue of any money, except such as may be asked for by the Treasury under the express authority of Parliament, how is it that the government have been able to obtain possession of the means to incur such extraordinary expenditure, without a previous Act of Appropriation? To this it is replied, that the wisdom of Parliament has itself provided for this contingency. 'The public interests require that the government should possess the power of incurring expenses of indispensable necessity, although Parliament may not have previously provided for them. . . . Unforeseen events may happen, and lead to an expenditure beyond the provision made by Parliament for the ordinary service of the year; and it must be for the interest of the public, that no delay should occur in taking the necessary measures, and in defraying the expenses which such events may entail.' There is, accordingly, a fund called the 'Treasury Chest Fund,'

Treasury Chest Fund.

which is maintained for the purpose of supplying the specie required for the 'Treasury Chests' in the several colonies, and for making the necessary advances for carrying on the public service at the various naval and military stations. By the Act 24 & 25 Vict. c. 127, this fund is limited to 1,300,000*l.*; and is authorised to be employed by the Treasury 'as a Banking Fund, for facilitating remittances, and for temporary advances for public and colonial services; to be repaid out of the moneys appropriated by Parliament, or otherwise applicable to those services.' The governors of colonies have authority, in cases of emergency, to pay advances out of the Treasury Chest, to be made good out of votes in supply. This unavoidably occasions an expenditure, in certain cases, which has not been authorised by Parliament, but the earliest opportunity is taken to explain the transaction to the House of Commons. There is also another fund, which was created in

1861, pursuant to the recommendations of the Committee on Public Accounts, in their fourth report in that year. It is called the 'Civil Contingencies Fund,' and is limited to 120,000*l*. The Treasury are empowered to draw upon this fund, from time to time, to defray new and unforeseen expenditure for civil services at home, for which no votes had been taken, or to meet deficiencies on ordinary votes. But every advance made from these funds must be repaid out of votes to be taken in Parliament, in the following year, on behalf of the services for which such advances had been made. No expenditure whatever is allowed to be finally charged against either of these funds. The 'Civil Contingencies Fund' has been set apart by the Treasury as a substitute for the irregular items annually included in the estimates under the head of 'Civil Contingencies,' and which had frequently to be voted after the expenditure had been incurred. The creation of this fund has been formally approved of by the Committee on Public Accounts; and there is no reason to doubt that the sanction of the legislature, which is certainly required to make it legally available for public purposes, would, if applied for, be readily granted.[1]

<small>Civil Contingencies Fund.</small>

There is yet another fund, that for 'Secret Services,' the disposal of which is in the hands of government, although the greater part of the amount is annually voted in supply. The vote in supply for this service usually amounts to between thirty and forty thousand pounds. But this does not include the whole amount at the disposal of government for secret services. On the contrary, the distinction has been uniformly maintained, that while it is proper to come to Parliament to make a general grant for such purposes, it is right that government should have at their disposal a fixed amount for the same which is independent of an annual parliamentary vote. Accordingly, the Civil

<small>Secret Service expenditure.</small>

---

[1] Rep. Com. Pub. Accounts, 1862, Appx. p. 102; Hans. Deb. vol. clxix. p. 1859; Ibid. vol. clxxvi. p. 1702. (Vote for Ashantee War.) Accounts relating to Civil Conting. Fund, 1864–5; Commons Papers, 1865, No. 374; Rep. Com. Pub. Accounts, 1865; Evid. 31–37; and see Appx. p. 140.

List Act, which is passed upon the accession of the sovereign to the throne, sets apart the sum of 10,000*l.* per annum, which is payable out of the Consolidated Fund, for 'Home Secret Service.' The annual vote in supply is intended to supplement the deficiency of this grant.* The Secretaries of State, and others, who may draw upon this fund, are bound by oath not to use any of it for purposes which do not legitimately appertain to their several departments. And the names of all persons receiving secret service money, with the sums paid to them, must be entered in a book, in order to be produced in either House of Parliament if required. It is not usual, however, to give information to Parliament, in regard to the expenditure out of this fund.*

Increasing strictness in regard to unauthorised expenditure.

The increasing strictness of the House of Commons, in regard to the appropriation of public moneys to the sole uses for which they have been voted by Parliament, is remarkably exemplified in two cases which engaged the attention of the Committee on Public Accounts, in 1864:—

Sale of public lands, and purchase of other lands with the price thereof.

1. A negotiation between the War Office and the Office of Woods and Forests, for the exchange of certain public lands. This negotiation finally resulted, not in the mere exchange of land for land—which is not an uncommon occurrence, and could always be effected between public departments, with the sanction of the Treasury—but in the sale of lands at Brighton, no longer wanted for military purposes, to private parties; and the purchase with the

---

* Act 1 & 2 Vict. c. 2, sec. 15; Chanc. of Excheq. in Mirror of Parl. 1837-8, p. 123.

* 22 Geo. III. c. 82, secs. 24-29; Mirror of Parl. 1831, p. 650; 1834, p. 2010; 1837, p. 1080; Hans. Deb. vol. lxv. p. 182; vol. clix. p. 1628. The mode in which the Secret Service Vote is audited is described in the Rep. Com. Pub. Accounts, 1865, Evid. 1800-1821. For the year ending March 31, 1867, the vote was 32,000*l.* This amount has not varied for several years past, but the money is only paid out as required by a Secretary of State. Secret Service expenditure is chiefly incurred by the Foreign Office. The balance not required remains in the Treasury, and is surrendered to the Exchequer at the end of the year: considerable sums have thus been surrendered from time to time. (Mr. Under-Secretary Peel, Hans. Deb. vol. clxxix. p. 1130; *Ibid.* vol. clxxx. p. 601.)

proceeds thereof of land in Woolmer Forest from the Office of Woods and Forests. 'This was, technically and substantially, not an exchange of land, but a sale of land by the War Office, and a subsequent purchase of land from the Woods and Forests.' The committee agree in opinion with the Board of Audit, through whose report the transaction was brought under the notice of Parliament, 'that the produce of this sale of land at Brighton ought to have been paid into the Exchequer as an extra receipt, and that, if it was requisite to make a purchase of land in Woolmer Forest, the proposal to do so should have been submitted in the regular way to the House of Commons.'*

2. A practice which had prevailed for a number of years in the War Office, of making purchases of army supplies for the Indian and Colonial Governments, out of moneys voted in supply for similar services for the imperial army. These purchases had been made for reasons of public convenience, and were considered as advances to the governments aforesaid, to be repaid by them to the War Office. The money had been punctually repaid; nevertheless, the committee were of opinion that such a practice unavoidably occasioned great perplexity and derangement in the accounts, and was, moreover, open to the objection made to it by the Accountant-General of the Army, that it is 'wrong in principle, that money distinctly granted for one purpose by Parliament should be appropriated without parliamentary sanction or knowledge to another purpose.' The committee accordingly recommended the subject to the consideration of her Majesty's

<small>Advances for the purchase of certain army supplies.</small>

<small>* Rep. Com. Pub. Accounts, 1864, p. vi.; and Evid. pp. 31-34. Adverting to this transaction in the following year, the committee were informed by an officer of the government, that the objection taken by the committee was considered as 'perfectly valid, and it will be our future law.' The proceeding complained of 'will never be repeated.' (Ibid. 1865, Evid. 1470.) Accordingly, in 1863, when it was desired to appropriate 71 tons of old gun-metal (valued at 4,170l.), the property of the War Department, towards the construction of the National Memorial to the Prince Consort, an estimate for this expenditure was submitted to the House, and the amount voted in Committee of Supply. (See Hans. Deb. vol. clxxiv. pp. 1551, 1604.)</small>

government; observing that 'if it be thought necessary that these stores and other advances should be supplied out of moneys voted by Parliament,' they consider 'that distinct provision should be made for them in the estimates, and that all receipts on account of such advances should be paid into the Exchequer.'*

There still remain two unauthorised sources of supply, which, however convenient in practice, and unobjectionable, or even expedient, in the abstract, are nevertheless, until sanctioned by Parliament, opposed to an admitted constitutional principle. The one is the 'cash account' of the paymaster-general, which is the receptacle of various sums and deposits which, though not placed by Parliament at the disposal of the government, are regarded in practice as available sources of supply for the working accounts of the paymaster. For instance, sums realised from the sale of old stores, sums which are deposited with the paymaster for safe keeping or investment—as, for example, moneys paid in respect of the Crown's Nominee Fund, or the Mercantile Marine Fund—sums remitted home on account of fees received by consuls abroad, or in respect of the obligations of certain colonies to the mother country for military protection, &c.; all such sums and deposits are carried to the credit of the paymaster's cash account, and are used to supply his working account with funds; which are not legally available for public purposes. The Committee on Public Accounts has suggested that such moneys should be transferred to the Exchequer, or invested, or kept in deposit, as the circumstances of each case might require; and that they should in no case be used for public purposes.*

The other instance of money being used to defray voted services without the sanction of the legislature, is that

margin: Cash account of the paymaster-general.

* Rep. Com. Pub. Accounts, 1856, pp. vi., vii. And see Exid. pp. 18, 24.
* Mr. Macaulay's Paper, Rep. Com. on Pub. Accounts, 1865, p. 141. See further, as to 'extra receipts,' and money realised from sale of old stores, Rep. Com. Pub. Accts. 1860; Evid. 441-518.

of the receipts of revenue. The salaries of the various revenue departments are never paid, in the first instance, out of the votes, but out of the revenue: such advances being afterwards repaid from the votes. This practice is pursued by collectors of revenue throughout the kingdom in reference to certain payments on account of the public service at the several localities in question; the advances being subsequently repaid to the revenue from the votes applicable to such services. The Committee on Public Accounts, though cognisant of the mode in which these temporary advances are made from the revenue, do not appear to have objected to it; and the existing practice, both as regards the receipts of revenue and the paymaster's cash account, has always been defended by the government as tending to economy, to the security of the public money, and to simplicity of account. This may be a sufficient reason for adhering to the present practice; nevertheless, it is equivalent to the establishment of so many additional Treasury Chest Funds, of indefinite extent, without any parliamentary authority whatever. Provided proper steps are taken to insure an efficient appropriation audit of all the parliamentary grants, there is no reason to fear that a continuance of this practice would facilitate abuse, or misappropriation. But it will be hereafter an important point to determine the conditions under which the government should be authorised by law to use for public purposes moneys derived from other sources than the grants of Parliament and the Treasury Chest Fund.'

Salaries in the revenue departments.

We now proceed to consider the second branch of our enquiry, viz., the mode in which the constitutional control of Parliament over the public expenditure is conducted, through the instrumentality of the responsible department of the Treasury.

' Mr. Macaulay's Paper, appended to Rep. Com. on Pub. Accounts, 1865, p. 142. And see *ante*, p. 471.

2. *The Functions of the Treasury in relation to the Public Expenditure.*

Functions of the Treasury in controlling public expenditure.

By immemorial custom, the Lords Commissioners of the Treasury have been constitutionally empowered to control all the other departments of the state, in matters of finance and public expenditure. In various Acts of Parliament, and reports of committees of the House of Commons, this authority has been from time to time recognised and enforced. By degrees, however, this wholesome control had been gradually relaxed, and the various public departments, more particularly those in charge of naval and military affairs, had begun to act independently of the Treasury, incurring expenses beyond the votes of Parliament, without previous reference to this supreme authority. In order to check the growing extravagance in the public service, and to introduce a proper responsibility in regard to public expenditure, committees of the House of Commons recommended that the ancient control of the Treasury should be again exercised. In 1817, the Finance Committee adverted to the subject in the following terms: 'Feeling, as your committee do strongly, the necessity of bringing all financial subjects officially within view of the Treasury,' they suggest whether—in addition to the ' unrecorded and confidential intercourse which must at all times exist on the part of the First Lord of the Admiralty, and the Master-General of the Ordnance, and the Chancellor of the Exchequer respectively, on all matters which they may feel it their duty to bring under the consideration of their colleagues in the cabinet,'—it might not be advisable that it should be made a rule of the Privy Council, whenever orders in council are in contemplation to regulate the establishment of any public department, 'that every proposition involving an increase of public expense should, according to the nature of the case, either be submitted to a Committee of Council, consisting of such members as may be connected with the Treasury, or be made by the Council Office the subject of a direct reference to, and report from, the Treasury to that office before it is presented to his Majesty for his final approbation. By this arrangement, which will combine the forms which have from the earliest times prevailed in the practice of our government, with that essential control which your committee judge it necessary to place in the financial ministers alone, they hope that the results which they have so often recommended may be attained.'

Pursuant to the foregoing report, a Treasury Minute was issued on March 13, 1818, embodying a memorandum agreed upon by the Earl of Liverpool (First Lord of the Treasury), the First Lord of the Admiralty, and the Master-General of the Ordnance, and approved of by the prince regent, ' to carry into effect the recommendation of the Finance Committee, in their fourth and sixth reports, that no department of large expenditure ought ever to be placed beyond the controlling superintendence of the Board of Treasury.' That minute established various regulations for checking naval and military expenditure which are now obsolete, one of which required the working heads of the army and navy departments to attend the Treasury whenever that Board wished for verbal in addition to written information on any financial subject connected with their departments.'

Ten years afterwards, a committee of the House of Commons called the attention of the House to the fact, ' that the ancient and wise control vested by our financial policy in the hands of the Treasury over all the departments connected with the public expenditure has been in a great degree set aside. Although it is the practice to lay the annual estimates before the Board of Treasury, the subsequent course of expenditure is not practically restrained as it ought to be by one governing and respon-

---

' Sixth Rep. Com. on Finance, Accounts, 1802, Ev. 665, 700, 643. 1817, quoted in Rep. of Com. on Pub. ' Ibid. Min. of Evid. 643.

Functions of the Treasury in controlling public expenditure.

sible power, but remains too much under the separate management of the departments. The want of a constant check over the expenditure, which is the consequence of the departure from the old and constitutional course, has established a scale of expense greatly beyond what existed during the former periods of peace. Each department naturally endeavours to exalt its own importance, and wishes to promote its general efficiency, and to have everything in it complete and perfect; hence the desire to secure these objects, rather than the exigency of the public service, has had too much influence over a great part of the public expenditure.' Again: 'The establishment of an effectual control in the hands of the Treasury is nothing more than the restoration to the Treasury of its ancient authority. It is necessary that this control should be constantly exercised in determining the amount of expenditure to be incurred by each department, in securing the application of each sum voted in the annual estimates to the service for which it has been voted, in regulating any extraordinary expenditure which, upon an emergency, may be deemed necessary within the year, although not included in the estimates; and in preventing any increase of salary or extra allowance, or any other emoluments, being granted without a minute expressive of the approbation of the Board of Treasury. The committee have further to observe, that it is expedient not only to restore this control, but to secure it from being again set aside, which cannot be effected, except by the House of Commons constantly enforcing its application, by holding the Treasury responsible for *every act of expenditure*" in each department.'"

" This expression must not be taken too literally. The Treasury authorities consider that it merely claims for the Treasury 'a certain degree of responsibility for every excess or surplus in the estimate sanctioned by Parliament'; requiring that every such excess should be made known to the Board. (Com. of Pub. Accounts, 1862; Min. of Evid. 964, 970.) The Chancellor of the Exchequer is the minister who is responsible to Parliament for the entire estimates, and who is liable to censure if the calculations in his budget, though founded in great measure

THE TREASURY AND PUBLIC EXPENDITURE.   539

The foregoing recommendations set forth, with sufficient clearness, the nature and extent of Treasury control which would appear to be necessary to insure a proper responsibility in financial matters, and to check extravagant and unauthorised expenditure.¹ They were not, however, attended with any immediate result. Nevertheless, in the time which has elapsed since the date of these reports, they have mostly been adopted, so far as is consistent with the freedom of action that properly belongs to the great executive departments.

The first reform which was effected was at the instance of Sir James Graham, who, when First Lord of the Admiralty, in 1832, introduced and caused to be embodied in the Act 2 & 3 Will. IV. c. 40, sec. 30, what is termed the Appropriation Check. This valuable departmental reform will be fully discussed in the following section (*post*, p. 578). It will suffice here to state that the Appropriation Check, or Audit, was a regulation requiring the Admiralty to make up an annual account of expenditure under the several heads of service specified in the Appropriation Act, and submit the same to the Commissioners of Audit, to be compared with the vouchers. The commissioners to certify the correctness of the said accounts, and to note under each head whether the expenditure had exceeded or fallen short of the vote of Parliament. The certified account to be annually laid before the House of Commons.

Appropriation Audit of naval expenditure.

Up to 1845, none of the departments appear to have applied to the Treasury for authority to exceed any vote included in their estimates. In that year, a Treasury Committee on Ordnance Expenditure reported an opinion

---

upon the proceedings of other departments, should prove deficient. Nevertheless, the heads of other departments of expenditure, e.g. the Naval Minister, or the Secretary for War, are called to account in the House for their several estimates, when they are under discussion. *Ibid.*

1001-1003.
¹ Finance Report of 1828, pp. 5, 9.
² Further recommendations, with a view to enforce the superintending control of the Treasury, were made by the Committee on Navy, &c., Estimates, in 1848. Commons Papers, 1847-8, vol. xxi. p. 35.

that efficient control over the public expenditure could only be established by the examination of the audited accounts by a Committee of the House of Commons; but that, in the absence of such a committee, they considered that a control should be exercised by the Treasury, as being the department primarily responsible for the regularity of the public finances. Parliament, in assigning to the Commissioners of Audit the duty of reporting on the public accounts, had reserved to itself a right of revision; but hitherto no action had been taken by the House of Commons on these reports; it was therefore expedient to consider whether this task ought not to be undertaken by the Treasury. This recommendation was concurred in by the Lords of the Treasury, who, on January 13, 1846, issued a minute, declaring that 'No executive department is authorised to exceed the sum appropriated by Parliament under each general head or vote in their respective estimates, or to apply any surplus which may exist under one vote to supply the deficiency on others, without the express previous sanction of the Treasury, to be given on a written representation of the circumstances which render the adoption of such a course indispensable for the public service.' This opinion was endorsed by the House of Commons in a resolution of March 30, 1849, that 'when a certain amount of expenditure for a particular service has been determined upon by Parliament, it is the bounden duty of the department which has that service under its charge and control, to take care that the expenditure does not exceed the amount placed at its disposal for that purpose.' And by a clause which was first introduced into the Annual Appropriation Act for the year 1846-7, the Treasury are empowered to meet emergencies in the navy and army departments by authorising the appropriation of any surpluses or grants

---

* See General Balfour's Paper, in Statistical Journal, vol. xxix. p. 392. See also the Annual Appropriation Acts; Smith's Parl. Rememb. 1857-8, p. 145; Rep. of Com. on Misc. Expenditure, 1860; Min. of Evid. p. 6.

in the same department towards making good any deficiency caused by such emergencies, provided that the aggregate sum voted for each department for the year be not exceeded. This Act was followed up by Treasury minutes, intended to explain more minutely the manner of giving effect to the same, and of ensuring to the Treasury the right of appeal and ultimate control in all cases of unforeseen and unprovided expenditure.[a]

And army departments to use their surplus funds to make good deficiencies.

The appropriation clause above cited was, until recently, so framed as to confer on the Treasury the power of *finally* appropriating surpluses on particular grants to cover deficiencies on others within the same department. It so continued from 1846 to 1861. Meanwhile much controversy arose as to the true intent and meaning of the clause itself. Notwithstanding the obvious meaning of the Act of Parliament, the Board of Admiralty have, as a general rule, refused to recognise the supreme authority of the Treasury, and have claimed the right, under their own patent, of directing their own expenditure.[b] In complying with the directions of the statute, and seeking the formal sanction of the Treasury to transfers of votes, the Board does not, in point of fact, afford to the Treasury sufficient information to enable them to exercise a proper control. Their applications, moreover, are usually made after the unauthorised expenditure has been incurred.[c] The Treasury have refrained from the attempt to compel a recognition of their right to control this department in the details of expenditure. A large proportion of almost every vote consists of expenditure abroad, so that it is impossible to know beforehand whether any

Practice of the Admiralty in this matter.

---

[a] See Rep. of Com. on Pub. Accounts, 1862, Evid. 640-664. And see Chanc. of Exchequer's observations in Hans. Deb. vol. clxix. pp. 1800, 1863. But the Treasury were required, by a clause in the Appropriation Act, to inform the House of Commons of all such transactions, and to lay before the House copies of applications for transfers, in order to afford to members an opportunity of canvassing any breach of the strict rules relating to the appropriation of public money. See 21 & 22 Vic. c. 107, sect. 20; and Hans. Deb. vol. clxii. p. 1540; ibid. vol. clxv. p. 801.

[b] Rep. on Pub. Accounts, 1862, Min. of Evid. 750-760, 788.

[c] Ibid. 664, 823-828.

vote will be exceeded or not. Experience has shown 'that, unless the Treasury are prepared to take the whole responsibility of the conduct of the Navy, they cannot possibly take such management of the details.'[d] The First Lord of the Admiralty recently declared his view of the matter to be 'that the Admiralty should have the power of spending under each *vote* (the naval estimates being ordinarily divided into seventeen separate votes) the whole of the sum taken under that vote; that, if we want to transfer from one vote to another, we should go as we have gone at the time, and submit it to the Treasury.'[e]

---

[d] Rep. on Pub. Accounts, 1862, Min. of Evid. 1442, 1435.

[e] *Ibid.* 1440, 1510. In this view the Treasury have not altogether concurred. In recent cases they have required that even the separate *items of a vote*, corresponding with the detailed estimates submitted to the House of Commons, shall not be exceeded without their express sanction. See the debate on Sir H. Willoughby's motion respecting the appropriation of public moneys, on March 11, 1861. And this has been made imperative by a Treasury minute, dated January 27, 1863. (Rep. Com. on Pub. Accounts, 1861, Evid. pp. 40, 41; see also the Report for 1862, Evid. p. 42.) In the controversy between the Naval Department and the Treasury on this subject, previous to the issue of this minute, it was admitted by the Admiralty that they had no right to exceed the amount of their original estimate for any particular work, or to commence any new item of expenditure, without the authority of the Treasury and the knowledge of Parliament. When using surpluses to supply deficiencies within a particular 'vote,' it is agreed that they must strictly confine themselves to continuing expenditure previously commenced under the authority of Parliament. This rule was adopted in 1858, and sanctioned by a departmental committee of accounts and audit. (*Ibid.* 1206–1208.) It was under this rule that the First Lord of the Admiralty justified his conduct in 1860, when he applied a large sum voted by Parliament for the express purpose of building iron ships to the purchase of timber for stores, without applying for the Treasury sanction to the transaction. (See Mr. Disraeli's observations on this proceeding, in Hans. Deb. vol. clxvii. p. 342; also *Ibid.* vol. clxix. pp. 811–853; and Smith's Parl. Rememb. 1862, pp. 30, 32.) The Chancellor of the Exchequer appears inclined to agree in the main, in this interpretation of the relative duties of the Admiralty and the Treasury, in the matter of transfers, but without having arrived at any definite conclusions thereon. While questioning how far the principle of subdividing votes is one that ought to be recognised, as a means of avoiding Treasury control, he did not think that any government would establish, or that Parliament would sanction, the doctrine that in every case of excess under every head of each vote the Admiralty should be obliged to go to the Treasury. Where there was an excess upon the whole vote, the Treasury would require the Admiralty to submit to Parliament a supplementary estimate. (Mr. Gladstone's evidence, *ibid.* 1553–1562.) And the power of transfer should not be exercised to sanction expenditure for services which had been undertaken, without the previous authority of Parliament. Case of the German settlers at the Cape. See Hans. Deb.

But even so, it is contended that 'the previous sanction' required from the Treasury must be understood to mean a formal sanction to the transfer, which is not necessarily or usually given before the expenditure has been incurred. It is urged that no other construction of the rule is practicable or consistent with the secrecy and despatch so often necessary in carrying out the directions of government, conveyed through a Secretary of State.' If the First Lord of the Admiralty were to shrink from the responsibility of exceeding his estimates, in obeying such directions, he would have to request the First Lord of the Treasury to convene a cabinet in order that the point might be discussed. Should a disagreement arise between the Treasury and the Admiralty on a financial question, they would appeal to the cabinet.^a

Construction of the rule requiring Treasury sanction to all extra expenditure.

The Treasury, as a general rule, invariably gives way when applied to by any board or other department presided over by a cabinet minister for their sanction to spend money. They may delay at first, and if a sufficiently plausible reason for the application be not given, the Secretary of the Treasury may appeal to the Chancellor of the Exchequer, and a correspondence may ensue between the departments, but the Treasury invariably gives way in the end. The Chancellor of the Exchequer, if he disapproved of the proposal, would decide whether it would be desirable to submit it for the opinion of the cabinet, or to settle it himself with the political head of the department concerned.^b Nevertheless, the necessity for coming to the Treasury does operate, to some extent, as a check; first, it gives the Treasury an opportunity of calling the atten-

---

vol. clxix. pp. 1253, 1852; Rep. Com. Pub. Accounts, 1804, evid. p. 5.
^z Rep. Com. Pub. Accounts, 1862, Evid. 1520–1522.
^a *Ibid.* 1624, 1502.
^b *Ibid.* 108, 720, 1340, 2056. The same principle prevails in communications between the Treasury and the Foreign Office in regard to matters of expenditure. Theoretically, the Treasury is presumed to have control, but practically the Secretary of State would not permit of any interference in the detail expenditure of his own office. See special Rep. Com. of Pub. Accounts, 1861, on Excheq. and Audit Depts. Bill, Evid. 351–356. And see *post*, p. 578, note ^t.

tion of (for example) the Admiralty to points that seem to require further consideration; and, secondly, it leads the department in question to be careful in framing its proposals, with a view to their undergoing parliamentary investigation. If the consent of the Treasury to a transfer were refused, on the ground that the expenditure sought to be sanctioned was improper, the department would have to go to Parliament for a vote for the excess.¹

Extension of the appropriation audit to Army expenditure.

In 1846 the system of appropriation audit in force in the Navy was introduced into the Army departments. Each of those departments, namely, the Ordnance and the War Office, presented separate estimates. They had, within their respective grants, the same power of transfer as the Admiralty, but no transfer could be made from a vote under one department in aid of a deficiency in that of another. In 1856–57 these departments, together with the Commissariat, were consolidated under the Secretary of State for War. In the Appropriation Act the sums given for the Army were divided into two aggregate grants— one, in round numbers, for six million pounds, and the other for nine millions. At first, the power of transfer was confined to the separate grants; 'but in 1858 it appears that a change was made in the wording of the Appropriation Act, so as to give to the War Department the power, with Treasury consent, to transfer the surplus on a vote within one grant to the deficiency on a vote included in the other grant. The change thus introduced has been continued in subsequent Acts.' Viewing this alteration as defeating the intention of the House and of the government, in dividing the votes into two aggregate grants, and as affording to the government a very extended power of transfer, the Committee on Public Accounts, in 1862, recommended that the Appropriation Act should be so framed in future as to limit the power of

¹ Rep. Com. Pub. Accounts, 1862, Evid. 148, 1601, 2355. Mr. Gladstone quoted an instance wherein, upon a remonstrance from the Treasury, the Admiralty agreed to reduce their application for authority to build twenty gunboats for service in China, to one half that number. 1601.

transfer to the extent of the particular grant.ʲ It should be observed, however, that the Army department, unlike the Admiralty, invariably obtains Treasury sanction before applying the surplus of one vote to the exigencies of another. And any correspondence that may have arisen in consequence of the necessity for such transfer is required to be published with the Army estimates for the following year.ᵏ

[margin: Treasury sanction to all extra Army expenditure.]

In the preparation of their original estimates, the same difference is noticeable between the practice of the Army and Navy departments. The Admiralty forward the Navy estimates to the Treasury, for formal sanction, so short a time before they must be presented to Parliament as to render a detailed examination of their contents impossible. But that is not the case with the War Office.ˡ

[margin: Army and Navy estimates.]

The value of the appropriation clause above mentioned, the true intent and meaning of which has given rise to so much controversy, was questioned, on the ground that it 'loosens the control of Parliament over the separate grants for naval and military services, by giving a power to the Treasury to vary the appropriation specially directed by Parliament itself;' and it was recommended that this clause should be expunged from the Appropriation Act.ᵐ The annual appointment by the House of Commons of a committee of enquiry into the audited accounts undoubtedly affords facilities for securing more effectually than by Treasury control the strict appropriation of public money to the purposes for which it has been voted.ⁿ The Committee on Public Accounts in 1862

[margin: Value of the clause authorising the Treasury to deviate from the appropriation in certain cases.]

ʲ Second Rep. Com. Pub. Accounts, 1862, pp. iv. v. And see Hans. Deb. vol. clxix. p. 1840. But though in the new Appropriation Act of 1862-63 these two great heads have been maintained, they are practically useless, because the power of the Treasury to appropriate the savings, without consulting Parliament, was done away with by that Act. Rep. Com. Pub. Accts. 1864, Evid. p. 7.

ᵏ Rep. Com. Pub. Accounts, 1863, Evid. 1884-1898, 2202.

ˡ Ibid. 950, 970.

ᵐ Memo. by Mr. Anderson, the sole surviving member of the Treasury Committee of 1845, in app. to Rep. on Pub. Accounts, 1862, p. 102.

ⁿ Ibid. Min. of Evid. 1730. See also cases cited of the abuses arising from the want of a sufficient check over the departments by whom the

bestowed great attention to this point, and unanimously resolved that the power of transfer, in relation to Army and Navy appropriations, ought to be subjected to some further check. In view of the resolution of the House of Commons, on March 30, 1849, setting forth the duty of all public departments to confine their expenditure within the amount placed at their disposal by Parliament, the committee declared it to be the duty of each department, with the assistance of the Treasury, so to frame their estimates as to provide as far as possible for all anticipated expenditure; and that, if additional outlay should unexpectedly become necessary, the department ought to communicate with the Treasury thereupon without delay. The Treasury should then determine whether Parliament should be applied to for a supplementary vote, or whether it would be more expedient to meet the additional expenditure by an advance from the surplus on hand from other votes. If the latter, the Treasury should authorise the same in writing. At the making up of the final accounts, copies of all such applications, and of the Treasury letters and warrants thereupon, should be presented to Parliament. A vote should then be proposed in supply to meet any deficiencies, and all surpluses should be surrendered to the Exchequer. By this plan the government would be at liberty to exercise its discretion in providing for unexpected emergencies, by permitting transfers of surpluses to meet deficiencies, and the House of Commons would possess an opportunity of reviewing such transactions, when transfers that had been made were submitted for their approval in the shape of a vote.* These recommendations were sanctioned by Parliament and by the government. A new appropriation clause was inserted in the Appropriation Act of the year, which, instead of authorising the Treasury to determine

New regulations on this subject recommended.

---

power of transfer is exercised,—in Lord R. Montagu's speech, Hans. Deb. March 24, 1863. And see Rep.

Com. Pub. Accts. 1864, Evid. p. 9. * Second Rep. Com. of Pub. Accounts, 1862, pp. vii. viii.

finally on applications for transfers, merely empowered them to authorise the temporary use of surpluses, in order that the advances thus made might be submitted for the sanction of Parliament, and the deficiencies in question be provided for 'in such manner as Parliament might direct.'[*] A Treasury minute, to give effect to the new arrangements, was issued on January 27, 1863. It prescribed the circumstances under which the naval and military departments should be at liberty to apply for the Treasury sanction to expenditure for services unforeseen and unprovided for; and the forms to be observed in such applications, with a view to enable the Treasury to submit to the House of Commons all needful information in relation thereto.[†]

<small>New form of appropriation clause, enabling the Treasury to give a temporary sanction to the use of surpluses.</small>

A statement of savings and deficiencies upon the grants for Army services for the year 1862-63—together with copies of the correspondence between the War Office and the Treasury for authority to incur expenditure that would occasion an excess on a particular vote—was communicated to the Committee on Public Accounts for 1864. These accounts are the first that were prepared under the altered system introduced by the Appropriation Act of 1862, by which the Treasury were empowered to give a temporary sanction only to applications for leave to make use of surpluses to defray excesses upon other services, and were required to submit to the consideration of Parliament the final determination thereupon. The committee reported that the effect of this change had been very beneficial to the public service, and that the great object of the alteration in the Appropriation Act had been accomplished. Heretofore it had not been customary for the departments to apply to the Treasury to authorise transfers until the time for closing the account was at hand, which afforded no opportunity to the Treasury of exercising any judgment upon such applications. 'Now,

<small>Benefits of this change.</small>

---

[*] 25 and 26 Vict. c. 71, sect. 20.
[†] Commons Papers, 1863, vol. xxix. p. 173.

before any excess of expenditure is incurred, the departments apply to the Treasury for their sanction as soon as the necessity for it arises.' But in many cases it is impossible to tell, until the account is squared, what the amount of excess or deficiency will be; the application for the Treasury sanction is therefore ordinarily deferred until the account is made up. But any large excess must be foreseen, and no excess would be sanctioned which could not be covered by the aggregate vote.'

All temporary advances to be submitted to the sanction of the House of Commons.

The committee carefully considered the important constitutional point, as to the mode in which these 'temporary advances' should be submitted for the subsequent sanction of the House of Commons. They declared their opinion that, as soon as the accounts ascertaining the deficiencies and savings on the votes for Army and Navy services had been laid before the House, no time should be lost in seeking the sanction of Parliament to the 'temporary advances' authorised by the Treasury, by a vote, 'which ought to receive the most formal consideration and sanction of the House.' 'A vote in the form of a resolution of a committee of the whole House would be the proper mode of effecting this object, and of complying with the provisions of the Appropriation Act.' This resolution to be embodied as a clause in the Appropriation Act.°

In the manner following.

Accordingly, on July 18, 1864, the reports of the Navy and Army expenditure, for the year ending March 31, 1863, were considered in committee of the whole House, and resolutions agreed to—(1) setting forth the savings effected in the grants on behalf of these services, and also the amounts of expenditure in excess of the said grants, which had been 'temporarily defrayed,' under the authority of the Treasury, out of the surpluses; and (2)

° Rep. Com. of Pub. Accounts, 1863, Evid. 400–420.
° Rep. Com. of Pub. Accounts, 1864, p. v. And see Evid. pp. 52–54. But it would appear to be still under the consideration of the government, as to what course should be taken to obtain the sanction of Parliament to the temporary use of the surpluses. See Rep. Com. of Pub. Accts. 1865, Evid. 1507–1522.

'That the application of so much of the said surpluses be sanctioned.' The effect of asking the House to pass these resolutions was explained by the Chancellor of the Exchequer as intended 'simply to give them the opportunity, if they thought fit, of disapproving of any of these transfers from one vote to another;' and that, if the House did not approve of the manner in which the government had exercised the discretionary power entrusted to them, they might pass 'a vote of censure.'ᵇ The resolutions above mentioned were afterwards embodied in the Appropriation Act for 1864.ᶜ Similar proceedings took place, in the following sessions, in regard to the transfers of Army and Navy expenditure for the years ending March 31, 1864 and 1865. The resolutions passed through the House without debate,ᵛ and were included in the Appropriation Acts.ʷ

In the case of expenditure on behalf of the *Civil Services*, the Treasury have no authority to apply any surplus from one Civil Service vote to meet deficiencies in another. All surpluses are obliged to be surrendered to the Exchequer, and all deficiencies to be voted by Parliament. Each vote has its own special account in the books of the Paymaster-General, and a balance of debit and credit is struck every week. When an issue is applied for, the votes on account of which the issue is required are always specified. The consequence is, that a Civil Service vote can never be exceeded, the balances at the end of the year are surrendered, and there are no transfers.ˣ At the same time, there is a fund, called the

No transfers allowed on the Civil Service votes.

ᵃ Hans. Deb. vol. clxxvi. p. 1080.
ᵇ 27 and 28 Vict. c. 73, sect. 20.
ᶜ Hans. Deh. vol. clxxx. p. 331; *ibid.* vol. 184, p. 1830.
ᵛ 28 and 29 Vict. c. 123, sect. 20.
ˣ Nevertheless, in the matter of the grants for educational purposes, by a system of minutes in council, issued without the cognisance of Parliament, it was, until very recently, in the power of the crown to enter into engagements which would have the effect of involving Parliament in additional expenditure beyond the sums actually voted on behalf of education, and from which the House could not honourably extricate itself. But in 1862, the subject was brought under the notice of Parliament, and regulations adopted to prevent the continuance of this objectionable practice. See *ante*, p. 204.

'Civil Contingencies Fund,' to meet unforeseen civil expenditure in special cases, pursuant to the recommendations contained in the Fourth Report of the Committee on Public Accounts in 1861; which fund is limited, as has been already stated, to the sum of 120,000*l*.[r]

The whole sum voted need not be expended.

A vote in Committee of Supply is in the nature of a *maximum*. It is not incumbent on the government to spend the whole of the amount granted, but it is a matter of discretion.[s]

Balances not expended within the year to be surrendered to the Exchequer.

So far as relates to the Army and Navy estimates, it has for a length of time been the rule and practice that, if the money voted for any particular service be not expended within the year, the power of expenditure granted by the vote ceases, and the money cannot afterwards be made use of until it is revoted by Parliament.[t] This rule has been carried out of late years very strictly. For example, in 1861, out of 15,000*l*. voted to enlarge the Military College at Sandhurst, 5,000*l*. only was expended within the year. Accordingly, next session, the balance of 10,000*l*. was again included in the estimates. This time the House of Commons refused to vote the money. Some days afterwards, however, the government induced the House to recommit the resolution, for the purpose of reconsidering their decision. Upon this occasion the vote was agreed to.[u] It is only very lately that the Civil Service votes and Miscellaneous Estimates have been subjected to the same rule. In 1857 the Committee on Public Moneys reported a recommendation, that 'all unexpended balances should be surrendered, and grants unapplied, but required for the completion of the services

---

[r] See *ante*, p. 551.
[s] Hans. Deb. vol. clxv. p. 1100.
[t] *Ibid.* vol. cxli. p. 181; vol. clxv. pp. 1850, 1889. But see as to unexpended balances on the 'China Vote of Credit,' *ibid.* vol. clxx. p. 1051; vol. clxxv. p. 1572; Commons Papers, 1861, No. 314. The rule does not apply to cases such as the grant for the construction of fortifications, which was made by special Act of Parliament, and did not come out of the year's income, but was raised by annuities, as an addition to the national debt. *Ibid.* vol. clxxii. p. 339; Act 26 and 27 Vict. c. 80.
[u] Hans. Deb. vol. clxv. pp. 1124, 1410, 1554.

to which they had been appropriated, should be revoted.' The Committee on the Miscellaneous Estimates in 1860 made a similar recommendation; as also did the Committee on Public Accounts, in 1861, in their fifth report. On June 24, 1861, the Under-Secretary to the Treasury informed the House that the government were making arrangements to carry out these suggestions. The new system was partially introduced in the same year, but it was not universally adopted until the following session. On March 31, 1863, 'for the first time in our financial history, all the services were required to surrender the balances standing to their credit' into the Exchequer. The votes are now taken 'for services coming in course of payment during the year,' instead of, as heretofore, 'for the services of the year.' By this means, the highly objectionable system of allowing running balances to go from year to year has been stopped, and the control of Parliament over the public expenditure has been practically guaranteed.

Votes now taken for payments within the year.

On April 3, 1865, the Secretary of the Treasury is reported as having informed the House that, in regard to the Civil Service Estimates, the Treasury had decided to surrender to the Exchequer all unexpended balances of former years, 'except the last year's balances!' He then proposed a vote 'on account,' in anticipation of the ordinary estimates, 'for the necessary charges of the first quarter of the current financial year,' inasmuch as the 'balances in the Exchequer, to the credit of the different services, were merely the balances of last year's votes, and were not sufficient without this vote on account.'

' Rep. Com. on Pub. Moneys, 1857, p. 7. See observations thereon in Ty. minute of February 15, 1858, in Commons Papers, 1857-8, vol. xxxiv. p. 341.

ᵈ Hans. Deb. vol. clxiv. p. 315.

ᵉ Ibid. vol. clxvi. p. 900.

ᶠ Chanc. of Exchq. in ibid. vol. clxx. p. 200.

ᵍ First Rep. Com. on Pub. Accts. 1862, p. iv.

ʰ Hans. Deb. vol. clxxviii. p. 733. But as there was no parliamentary authority to expend any portion of the last year's votes, except for 'payments during the year,' it is evident that there is some technical error in this statement. Probably the balances were retained as a matter of convenience, but there is no doubt that they must have been revoted, by including their several amounts in the 'vote on account.' See ibid. p. 851; and the Secretary of the Treasury's (Mr. Peel) own statement afterwards. Ibid. vol. clxxix. p. 600.

Difference between the Board of Audit and Board of Works on this point.

Inasmuch as the Appropriation Act of 1862 was the first Act in which the votes were taken to meet the expenditure coming in course of payment within the financial year, it is worthy of mention that there was a difference of opinion between the Board of Audit and the Board of Works as to the interpretation which should be put upon this Act. The Board of Works held that it was not intended to deprive them of the power of using balances which had accrued upon votes of Parliament anterior to 1862. On the other hand, the Board of Audit contended that all such balances should be surrendered, and that no credits but those granted in 1862 were available for expenses coming in course of payment in the year 1862–63. The adjustment ultimately made by the Treasury in regard to these accounts fell very far short of that which, in the opinion of the Board of Audit, should have taken place. This adjustment, however, was based on the assumption that the estimates presented to Parliament by the Board of Works for the year 1862–63, were framed on the principle of appropriating to the service of the year the balances remaining on account of former grants—that the sums voted represent only the estimated expenditure founded on that principle—and therefore that it was the intention of Parliament that the new arrangement for the surrender of balances remaining at the close of the financial year should take effect from March 31, 1863. But it appears that the Board of Works have continued to spend their arrears of balances, which had accrued before 1862, up to 1865, thereby making use of money without a parliamentary vote. These facts were communicated to the Committee of Public Accounts in 1865 by the Secretary of the Board of Audit.

Duty of the House of Commons.

In communicating the foregoing particulars to the Committee, Mr. Macaulay remarked that it was 'the natural and proper function of the House of Commons to see that the adjustment of the account as proposed by government is in accordance with the requirements of the

Appropriation Act.' But up to the present time no such adjustment has ever been made by the House of Commons.¹

3. *The Application of the System of Audit to the Public Accounts.*

a. THE ORDINARY DUTIES OF THE BOARD OF AUDIT.

We now proceed to consider the provision which has been made by Parliament for the examination and audit of the public accounts.

Origin of the system of audit.

Previously to 1785, certain officers of the Exchequer fulfilled the duties of auditors; but in that year a permanent board of commissioners for auditing the public accounts was constituted by the Act 25 Geo. III. c. 52. The duties of the board were defined and enlarged by several subsequent statutes.¹

Nevertheless, up to the time of the recent change in the constitution of the board by its amalgamation with the Exchequer department, its position and functions were confessedly anomalous and unsatisfactory. Presided over by commissioners who were nominally independent of the Treasury, the duties of the board were discharged, not by the auditors themselves, but by clerks appointed by the Treasury, and subject to the direction and control of that department—a position which naturally unfitted them for exercising an impartial investigation into the operations of the Treasury itself. It has, indeed, been alleged that the Treasury refrained from any interference with the board in the fulfilment of the duties assigned to it by statute;² and that with regard to accounts examined under the 'Appropriation Audit,' which is conducted on behalf of Parliament, the Treasury and the Board of Audit are equally convinced that the latter should receive no

Defective system at first established.

---

¹ Rep. Com. Pub. Accounts, 1865, Evid. 70–140, 270, &c. And see *ante*, p. 547.
² See Cox, Eng. Govt. p. 001.

² See Treasury minute, Commons Papers, 1857-58, vol. xxxiv. p. 385. Rep. Com. Pub. Accts. 1862, Evid. p. 37.

instructions from the former, which would be inconsistent with the performance of their duty to Parliament.¹

Board of Audit dependent on the Treasury.

But notwithstanding its parliamentary origin and peculiar responsibilities, the Board of Audit has been hitherto regarded as a department of the executive government, dependent upon the Treasury exclusively for the regulation of its strength, resources, and organisation; and as regards the examination of accounts under the administrative audit, it is strictly dependent upon the Treasury. The gradual extension of the principle of the appropriation audit, however, has been the means of elevating the Board of Audit into a more independent position. As soon as the main functions of the auditors shall be, not to act on behalf of the Treasury as a check upon the transactions of Treasury accountants, but on behalf of the House of Commons as a check upon the pecuniary transactions of the Treasury itself, of the other great departments of state, and of the executive government generally, the auditors will probably become, in fact as well as in theory, the servants of the House of Commons, and dependent upon the House, not only for guidance as to what duties they should perform but for the means of performing those duties efficiently.ᵃ

Is in fact a mere Board of Verification.

Still, it is important to remember that the Board of Audit was never designed to exercise any direct control over the public expenditure. In the words of Mr. Gladstone, 'it is a board to ensure truth and accuracy in the accounts of the public expenditure, and might properly be termed a board of verification.' To attempt to confer upon it coercive and controlling powers would be to transfer to it what strictly belongs to the House of Commons.ᵇ It is as an auxiliary to the labours of the Standing Committee on Public Accounts that the investi-

---

¹ Rep. Com. Pub. Accts. 1865, Evid. 1101–1200.
ᵃ Ibid. observations of Mr. Macaulay, Secretary Bd. of Audit, p. 168.
ᵇ Hans. Deb. vol. clxv. p. 1370.

gntions of the Board of Audit are mainly important, and are capable of being made increasingly valuable.°

By the Act of 1866, for consolidating the duties of the Exchequer and Audit departments, the duties and responsibilities of the commissioners of audit are considerably increased. They will now be required to examine the accounts connected with the permanent charges on the Consolidated Fund, the accounts relating to the receipts of money payable into the Exchequer, and the whole of the accounts relating to the voted services. In addition to this, it is provided by section 33 of the said Act, that the Treasury shall have the power, in case of any other accounts coming before them which, on public grounds, they might consider it desirable to subject to revision, to refer the same to the commissioners of audit for examination, even though they did not relate to the receipt and expenditure of public imperial funds. It has been suggested, however, by officers of the board and others, that this power should only be exercised in rare and peculiar cases, and that as a rule the labours of the commissioners should be as much as possible confined to the business of examining accounts relating to the receipt, issue, and expenditure, of imperial funds.ᵖ *(Enlarged functions of the Audit Board.)*

It is furthermore provided by section 34 of this Act, that all public officers who are in the receipt of fees shall account for the same to the audit office. But this security is confessedly inadequate as a means of ascertaining whether all the fees received in any public department are brought to credit. All it can accomplish is to provide that all the fees brought to credit are duly accounted for. The check upon receipts must necessarily be conducted by some efficient system of check and countercheck in the department itself.ᵠ *(Audit of fees.)*

This Act will undoubtedly impart new life and vigour

° Rep. Com. Pub. Accts. 1864, 1866, Evid. 241–257. Evid. pp. 9, 35, 65. ᵠ Ibid. 233–240.
ᵖ Ibid. (Excheq. and Audit Bill)

Independent position of the Audit Board under the new Act.

into the system of auditing the public accounts. Independently of the advantages to be anticipated from the general application of the appropriation audit to every branch of the public expenditure, a point to be hereafter specially noticed, much benefit will result from the greater degree of independence assigned to the audit officers over that which they previously enjoyed. It is true that the Treasury is still empowered to appoint, from time to time, such officers as may be required for conducting the business of the department, and to regulate their number and salaries. But this power is conferred upon the Treasury expressly in order that there may be some member of the government, having a seat in the House of Commons, responsible for such appointments.' And, on the other hand, the Comptroller and Auditor General is authorised to promote, suspend, or remove, any of the *employés* in his department; to make rules for the conduct of business therein; and (subject to the approval of the Treasury) to establish regulations for the guidance of all public accountants.'

Departmental Audit.

In proceeding to define, more particularly, the functions which appertain to the Board of Audit, as a department for examining and verifying the public accounts, it should be premised that, irrespective of the operations of this board, every department in the state is bound to apply to their expenditure some sort of check or departmental audit, whether their accounts are examined by independent auditors or not.'

And in addition to the check to which public accounts

' Hans. Deb. vol. clxxxii. p. 1804.
' Rep. Com. Pub. Accts. (Exchequer and Audit Bill), 1860, Evid. 201–303.
' Ibid. 1865, Evid. 290. Thus the accounts of the Foreign Office have not hitherto been audited by the Audit Board, but by the permanent Under-Secretary of State for Foreign Affairs. Hans. Deb. vol. clxxix. p. 1100. But under the provisions of the Public Moneys and Accounts Act of 1866, it is provided that, from April 1, 1867, these accounts shall be subjected to the Appropriation Audit, and to the revision of the Comptroller and Auditor General. See Special Report from Com. on Pub. Accts. 1866, on the Exchequer and Audit Departments Bill, Evid. 314–353.

may be subjected in the department to which they relate, all accounts of public expenditure are liable to two kinds of audit—1. The administrative audit; 2. The appropriation audit.

The administrative audit, as its name imports, is conducted on behalf of the Treasury, with a view to purposes which are purely administrative. Until recently, this was the only kind of audit applied to the public accounts; and it is still (1866) the only check which is applied to the miscellaneous civil service accounts, with certain exceptions to be hereafter noticed. This audit may be conducted by any persons whom the Treasury shall appoint; in fact, it is sometimes conducted by the Paymaster in Scotland, by the Paymaster-General, by the Board of Trade, and even by the Treasury itself. But, in general, it is conducted by the Board of Audit, acting exclusively on behalf of the Treasury, and with a view to enable the Treasury to maintain their legitimate authority and control over the various departments of expenditure.* The board has no authority to apply this audit to the public expenditure generally, but only to such accounts as they may be directed by the Treasury to examine. Apart from the mere business of checking the accounts, it is the main duty of the board, in conducting this audit, to determine whether the departmental expenditure has been in accordance with Treasury instructions, whether special or general. After receiving the auditor's report, it becomes the duty of the Treasury to decide what should be done in respect to any irregularity, or departure from the directions of the Treasury, that may be pointed out therein.†

It is not a little curious, that amongst the numerous statutory provisions relating to the administrative audit, none can be found which imposes on the auditors the duty

---

* Appended to the Fifth Report of the Pub. Accounts Com. for 1861 is a table of the accounts which are audited by the Audit Board, and of those which are audited by other departments.
† Rep. Com. Public Moneys, 1857, p. 14; Rep. Com. Pub. Accounts, 1865, Evid. 3, 4, 118, 252, &c.; and App. p. 119.

Imperfection of the administrative audit.

of questioning, or even of noticing, any expenditure that may have been incurred in excess of a parliamentary vote, or in respect of a service for which no appropriation whatever had been made." This left the door open for much abuse, and enabled the Treasury to expend money which had been granted for one service for entirely different purposes, without fear of detection or censure by Parliament. Sometimes it happened, however, that such reckless and extravagant expenditure was incurred, more particularly on behalf of the army or navy, as to call for the special interposition of Parliament.* For example, the Admiralty account, for a series of years prior to 1831, was systematically misappropriated.' It was not until the year 1832 that a partial remedy was found for this evil, by the introduction of a new description of audit, which will now engage our attention.

b. The Nature and Operation of the Appropriation Audit.

Origin of the appropriation audit.

It reflects the highest credit upon the government, that we are indebted, for this important administrative reform, to one who held at the time a prominent office in the state.

In the year 1832, Sir James Graham, who was at that time First Lord of the Admiralty, introduced into the House of Commons a Bill for the better regulation of the naval accounts, the most prominent feature of which was a provision empowering the commissioners of audit to examine the accounts and vouchers of naval expenditure, side by side with the votes and estimates for the naval service; and to report the result of the comparison annually to the House of Commons. This Bill became law; and, pursuant to its requirements, the votes for naval services were, for the first time, arranged under distinct heads, or branches of expenditure, in the annual Appropriation

---

" Rep. Com. Pub. Accounts, 1865, App. p. 110.
* 3 Hatsell, pp. 209-211.
' Rep. Com. Pub. Accounts, 1865, p. 110.

Act; in a form which, with some slight alterations, has been observed ever since.[a]

Prior to the introduction of this reform, the several amounts voted in supply for various navy services were added together, and included in the Appropriation Bill in a bulk sum, to the credit of the naval service generally. This practice was justified by the presumed impossibility of estimating beforehand, with any certainty, the probable sum required for each service. So long as it continued, the whole of the naval money, except that voted to defray the navy debt, could be legally applied to any one service; subject, of course, to future enquiry by the House of Commons, as to the expediency of such an appropriation. *Its peculiar benefits.*

The appropriation audit cured this evil; and, in spite of some defects of detail, it has worked well. In 1846 a new Act was passed (the 9 & 10 Vict. c. 92), which extended the operation of the audit to the accounts of military as well as naval expenditure. This Act also establishes the principles which shall govern the Board of Audit in applying the appropriation check to such other departments as may, from time to time, be brought within its operation, by direction of Parliament.[b] *Extended to army accounts.*

The efficiency of the new scheme of audit was further secured by the government not merely taking the votes for the distinct and separate naval services for which they were granted in committee of supply, but also restricting the application of the grants to payments actually made on behalf of the particular service within the period of the financial year.[c]

It should be observed, however, that the appropriation audit was not intended to limit the discretion of the responsible departments of state entrusted with naval or military expenditures, so as to prevent them from deviating

---

[a] For full particulars of this change, see Rep. Com. Pub. Accounts, 1862, Evid. pp. 1–4, &c.
[c] Rep. Com. Pub. Accounts, 1865.
Evid. 227.
[b] See *ante*, p. 570; and see Rep. Com. Pub. Accounts, 1865, p. 120.

from the directions of the Appropriation Act in cases of necessity, but merely to secure such a revision of their accounts, by an independent authority, as would suffice to detect any departure from the particular application of the votes which had received the sanction of Parliament.^c

Power of using surpluses. Both the Admiralty and the War Departments still retain the power of making use of the surplus of one vote to meet any deficiency in another, provided the aggregate grant for naval or military services is not exceeded. This power, as we have already stated,^d is exercised with the knowledge and consent of the Treasury.

Further extension of the appropriation audit. In 1851, by the Act 14 & 15 Vict. c. 42, the appropriation audit was directed to be applied to the newly-created departments of the Board of Woods and the Board of Public Works.

In 1856, the Committee on Public Moneys was appointed. They sat for two sessions; and their report, in 1857, 'has formed the text of all that has been subsequently said or written on the subject of the appropriation audit.' They recommended that it should be applied to the 'accounts of income and expenditure kept at the Treasury, to the accounts of the revenue departments, and to the various accounts comprising the expenditure of the votes for civil services, including civil contingencies.'^e The government, by Treasury minutes dated February 15 and December 23, 1858, agreed to the principle of this recommendation, but pointed out certain practical difficulties in the way of its immediate adoption.^f

In 1860, by the Act 24 & 25 Vict. c. 93, the appropriation audit was extended to the expenditure of the customs, the inland revenue, and the post-office departments;

---

^c Rep. Com. Pub. Moneys, 1857, p. 6. The nature, scope, and mode of applying the appropriation audit are described in the Rep. Com. Pub. Accounts, 1862, Evid. pp. 34–41. See further, on this subject, Rep. of Committee in 1865, p. 17, &c. and App. pp. 115–148.

^d *Ante*, p. 560.

^e Report, 1857, p. 6.

^f Commons Papers, 1857–8, vol. xxxiv. p. 382; 1860, vol. xxxix. pt. i. p. 175.

and in 1861 (pursuant to the report of the Committee on Public Accounts of that year), to payments out of the civil contingencies fund. It only remained that it should be applied to the miscellaneous civil service expenditure; and, although this extension has been repeatedly urged upon the government by the Committee on Public Accounts,[a] the undertaking was found to be attended with so many difficulties, that, until the present year (1866), no provision has been made for giving effect thereto.

In a memorandum submitted to the Committee on Public Accounts in 1865, by Mr. Macaulay, the Secretary of the Board of Audit, three distinct proposals for accomplishing this desirable object, which have emanated from very high authority, are discussed; but each of them are shown to be open to serious objections. Another plan, which he considers to be free from defect, is suggested by Mr. Macaulay himself. A brief notice of these different schemes may not be unprofitable.

Projects for applying it to all the voted services.

The first proposal was that made by the Committee on Public Moneys, in 1857, to the effect that the appropriation check should be applied, day by day, to the accounts of civil service expenditure, by means of audit-office clerks, stationed in the pay-office. This plan Mr. Macaulay shows to be quite impracticable.[b]

The second proposal emanated from the Treasury, and is explained in a Treasury minute which was laid before Parliament in February 1858 (Parl. Paper, No. 94). This minute sets forth the peculiar difficulties attending an application of the appropriation audit to the civil service accounts, over that of other branches of the public expenditure, and proceeds to suggest—1. That an annual account of the sums voted, and the expenditure incurred in the financial year, under each miscellaneous civil service vote, and of the balances remaining on hand, shall be

---

[a] See Report of 1862, p. lii. and App. p. 2; Report of 1864, App. Nos. 3 and 4. [b] Rep. Com. Pub. Accounts, 1865, App. pp. 120-123.

prepared in the finance department of the Treasury. 2. That this account shall be transmitted to the commissioners of audit for their examination and report. 3. That said account, with the auditors' report thereon, shall be laid before Parliament. But there are serious defects in this scheme. Although the Treasury is the ultimate source of authority for all public expenditure, the cases wherein votes are charged with expenditure under the direct orders of the Treasury are very few. And it is obvious that the department which undertakes to lay before Parliament the appropriation account of a vote should be in a position to certify, of its own knowledge, that the account is accurate, and that the expenditure recorded in it is properly chargeable to the vote. The Treasury have admitted the insufficiency of this scheme by withdrawing it.

In lieu thereof a third proposal has been made by the Treasury, that a consolidated account of the appropriation of all the miscellaneous votes should be prepared by the commissioners of audit, for submission to Parliament, after the several accounts of expenditure had been examined by the board in detail. This proposal is open to the obvious objection that it requires the audit office to examine and audit an account which had been prepared by themselves. In such a case the several departments concerned would be entitled, not only to question the fairness and accuracy of the accounts, but to reject them altogether. The existing relations between the Board of Audit and the executive departments would thereby be entirely inverted, for while the former would cease to be appropriation auditors, and would become the accountants general of the civil service, the latter would appear before the House of Commons, by their representatives, not as the responsible accountants for the money entrusted to their management, but as auditors, or, at all events, as critics of accounts prepared for them by the Board of Audit.[1]

---

[1] Rep. Com. Pub. Accounts, 1865, App. pp. 123-127.

The defects in the foregoing schemes are all distinctly traced by Mr. Macaulay to the neglect of the essential principle, that those who accept the management of trust money are the proper persons to account for it. The trustees, in the present instance, are the several departments who are called upon by the Treasury to administer the sums granted by Parliament for particular services. These departments must be severally held responsible for seeing that the vote they administer is spent in accordance with the intentions of Parliament. The only reasons which have yet been urged to exempt the departments from this responsibility are derived from the existence in the civil service of certain anomalous practices, which are themselves highly objectionable. These practices should be abolished.[1]

Defects in these projects for applying the appropriation check to all the voted services.

It should also be remembered that the Board of Audit is merely a board of verification, not of control. Its proper function is to insure truth and accuracy in the public expenditure. It should never be required to advise, control, or remonstrate with, any executive department in regard to expenditure. Its business is simply to report to Parliament every infraction of the law relating to the appropriation of public money; leaving it to the departments concerned to give such explanations as may be necessary, to the Committee on Public Accounts, to investigate and report their opinions on the financial transactions of the government, and to the House of Commons to determine thereupon.[b]

The scheme which Mr. Macaulay himself suggests for the due application of the appropriation audit to all the parliamentary grants, is based upon the principle above contended for, that every parliamentary vote should be placed by the Treasury under the immediate superintendence and control of some one responsible officer or department known to the House of Commons, and held

Another scheme suggested.

---

[1] Rep. Com. Pub. Accounts, 1865, App. pp. 128, 129.
[b] *Ibid.* pp. 130, 131.

responsible for the proper application thereof; that regular 'appropriation accounts' should be annually prepared by each department for submission to the House of Commons, which accounts should be rendered to the Board of Audit to be examined and reported upon; that the board should report to the House every case in which it may appear to them that a vote has been exceeded, or a sum charged against a vote which is not supported by proof of payment, or wherein a payment charged did not take place within the period of the account, or cannot be charged against a particular vote consistently with the requirements of Parliament.[1]

Clauses in the Act of 1866 on this subject.
At length, in 1866, by the Act to which our attention has been already directed, for the reorganisation of the exchequer and audit departments, provision has been made for the accomplishment of this important reform. In the clauses of this Act which relate to the audit of accounts all existing enactments for the application of the appropriation audit to the several branches of the public expenditure to which it had been previously applied are consolidated. No alteration is made in the practice in regard to the army and navy accounts. But the Act proceeds to provide for the extension of the appropriation audit to the whole of the grants for civil services, including every item that is voted in committee of supply.[2]

Opinion of the Committee of Public Accounts thereon.
The precise mode in which the foregoing provisions are to be carried out has not yet been communicated to Parliament. The Exchequer and Audit Departments Bill, however, was referred to the Committee on Public Accounts, who, after a thorough scrutiny of its details, reported it to the House, with some amendments, but with a decided approval of its general purport. In evidence before this committee, the Chairman of the

---

[1] Full details of this scheme are given by Mr. Macaulay, in a series of proposed regulations, with explanatory notes. Rep. Com. Pub. Accounts, 1865, App. pp. 131-139.

[2] Act 29 & 30 Vict. c. 39, sec. 22-32.

Board of Audit, and Mr. Macaulay, the secretary, agreed in the opinion that the Bill embraced the leading principles in regard to audit for which the audit-office had been long contending; namely—1. That the department which is entrusted with the administration of a vote shall be responsible for the preparation of the appropriation account thereof; that is to say, an account showing how the trust which has devolved upon the department has been discharged.* 2. That the department which shall be entrusted with the administration of each vote shall be appointed by the Treasury. 3. That the auditors shall be responsible to Parliament only.* It is further provided by the 23rd clause of the said Act, that the Treasury shall prepare a plan of account-books and accounts adapted to the requirements of each branch of the public service, and which shall exhibit in a convenient form the whole of the receipts and payments, &c., on behalf of the same, with a view to the appropriation audit thereof. By a Treasury minute, dated June 22, 1866, a departmental committee has been nominated to devise the plan of these books and accounts, which, when finally agreed upon, will be adopted under the sanction of an order in council.*

<small>New arrangements under this Act.</small>

It is undoubtedly of the first importance that the appropriation audit should be extended to every branch of the public expenditure, inasmuch as the financial accounts which are annually presented to Parliament do not as yet exhibit the precise relation between the grants and the expenditure for each particular service; and

<small>Anticipated advantages therefrom.</small>

---

* This will necessitate a re-casting of the estimates, so that it may appear upon the face of the vote what department is responsible for its administration. Rep. Com. Pub. Accts. (Exch. and Audit Bill), 1860, Evid. 101, 104, 207. Arrangements have already been made by the Treasury, with the approval of the Committee of Public Accounts, for this new classification of the estimates. See ante, 481.

* Rep. Com. Pub. Accts. (Exch. and Audit Bill), 1860, Evid. 181–192, 300–313. For a discussion of certain points of difficulty in the application of these principles, see Ibid. 195–211.

* For a copy of this minute, see Commons Papers, 1866, No. 301.

Parliament has no means of comparing the expenditure actually incurred with any vote to which the appropriation audit has not been applied.

Under the new system of taking the votes for those issues only which will come in course of payment during the year, the appropriation audit is more especially valuable. Without it, the departments having no direct interest in looking after their unexpended balances, such balances, instead of being surrendered to the Exchequer, could easily be applied, by direction of the Treasury, to some service not authorised by Parliament; and it being no one's business to call attention to the irregularity, it might escape notice.[a]

Manner of conducting the appropriation audit.

The appropriation audit is conducted exclusively by the commissioners of audit, acting in concert with an officer from the accountant's branch of the department whose accounts are under examination. Every account is examined by the commissioners, on behalf of the House of Commons, in accordance with the rules prescribed by the Exchequer and Audit Act of 1866.

Results thereby obtained.

The object of this audit, and its precise difference from a mere administrative audit, have been thus explained. The appropriation audit is intended to ascertain what payments are properly chargeable to a particular parliamentary vote. It accordingly determines—1. Whether the expenditure incurred is verified by regular vouchers. 2. Whether it has been sanctioned by the proper departmental authority. 3. Whether it has been distinctly authorised by Parliament. The administrative audit is confined to the two first enquiries, but the appropriation audit determines all three.[b] Accordingly, whenever any particular accounts are directed by the Treasury to be subjected to the appropriation audit, the mere administrative audit to which such accounts may have been

---

[a] Rep. Com. Pub. Accts. 1865, Evid. 45–67, 252–257. [b] Ibid. Evid. 202, App. pp. 142–147.

previously subjected is necessarily merged in the larger enquiry.'

When the accounts for the past financial year to which the appropriation audit is applied have been duly examined, the commissioners are required to embody the result of such examination in reports for the information of the House of Commons. Their report is sent, first of all, to the Treasury, in order that that department may interpose its authority to rectify any irregularity pointed out therein; and also that the Treasury, in transmitting the report of the auditors to the House of Commons, may accompany it with any observations they may think fit to make upon it.' It is the duty of the commissioners to direct the attention of Parliament, in their reports, to every departure from the provisions of the Appropriation Act. These reports should make mention not merely of any cases of positive irregularity on the part of any department of the state in the expenditure of public money placed in their hands for particular purposes, but also of any cases wherein, with the sanction of the Treasury, surpluses of certain votes had been used to defray the deficiencies of other votes, in conformity with the provisions in the recent Appropriation Acts, permitting the Treasury to authorise such an arrangement 'temporarily,' and subject to the future approbation of Parliament." And it is here that the appropriation check ceases to be operative, and that the interference of the House of Commons becomes indispensable if it be intended to make the control of Parliament over the public expenditure paramount and effectual.

Reported to the House of Commons.

Who should finally determine on such reports.

Thus far it has been remarked that in no one instance has the House of Commons decided what should be done in respect to any irregularity which has been pointed out by the Board of Audit.' Where questions have occurred

---

* Rep. Com. Pub. Accounts, 1865, Evid. 24, 235, &c.
* Ibid. (Exch. and Audit Bill), 1860, Evid. 214–228.
* See ante, p. 508.
* Rep. Com. Pub. Accounts, 1865, Evid. 270.

between the Treasury and other departments regarding the surrender of unexpended balances, the adjustment ultimately directed to be made by the Treasury has been tacitly accepted by Parliament, notwithstanding that the Board of Audit have pointed out that it fell very far short of what should have been made. And even when it has been necessary to take a vote of the House of Commons to confirm a grant which had been temporarily made by the Treasury of surpluses to meet deficiencies in certain cases, the departments concerned or the Treasury have come before the House and made their own statement of the case, and the House has always adopted the account without a word." In fact, 'no Appropriation Act has ever been adjusted under parliamentary impulse in any way, and it is there that the appropriation check is really defective.'[a]

Direct interference of Parliament in financial matters unnecessary.

It may be questioned, however, whether it is either necessary or expedient for Parliament to interfere, in a formal and direct manner, with the responsible departments entrusted with the management of the public expenditure. The increasing publicity which is now given to all the transactions of government, especially where the outlay of public money is concerned, and the good understanding which happily prevails between the Treasury and the House of Commons upon financial matters, have hitherto rendered it unnecessary for Parliament to do more than call the attention of Government to any irregular or objectionable practice, in order to insure its being remedied with the least possible delay. And this brings us to the mention of the crowning act whereby the House of Commons has been enabled to exercise a constitutional control over the public expenditure, without infringing upon the functions of responsible ministers ; that is to say, through the instrumentality of

Control exercised by means of the Public Accounts Committee.

" Rep. Com. Pub. Accounts, 1865, Evid. 70-140, 272-288.
[a] Ibid. Evid. of Mr. Macaulay,
140. And see Lord Robert Montagu's speech, Hans. Deb. vol. clxxx. p. 792.

a standing committee of its own members. In the year 1845, as we have already seen, a departmental committee of the Treasury reported their opinion that efficient control over the public expenditure could only be secured by the examination of the audited accounts by a committee of the House of Commons.' But this recommendation was not carried out; and the country is mainly indebted for the introduction of this important feature into the political system of England to the timely counsels of the Committee on Public Moneys, who, in their report in 1857, advised that the principle of the concurrent audit, or appropriation check, should be extended to all accounts of public income and expenditure to which it had not yet been applied; that the whole of the public accounts finally audited should be presented to Parliament before the close of the year succeeding that to which they relate; and that these audited accounts should be annually submitted to the revision of a committee of the House of Commons.'

Origin of this committee.

We have now, therefore, to consider the origin and functions of the last tribunal by means of which Parliament, and more especially the House of Commons, is enabled to exercise its constitutional control over the public expenditure with vigilance and success, viz.:—

4. *The Standing Committee on Public Accounts.*

With a view to obtain the co-operation of the House of

' See *ante*, p. 540.
' Rep. Com. on Pub. Moneys, p. 0. In taking leave of this committee, from whose report so much valuable information has been drawn to elucidate this branch of our subject, it may be observed that they submitted to the House recommendations on several points of detail, which have not been noticed in these pages, but which they commended to the continued attention of Parliament and of the executive government, until it might be found practicable to carry them into effect. *Ibid.* p. 8. Treasury minutes were issued on February 15 and December 23, 1858, reviewing the several recommendations of the committee, and announcing the intentions of government in regard to the same. Commons Papers, 1857-8, vol. xxxiv. p. 377; 1860, vol. xxxix. pt. i. p. 173. See also later intimations of the intentions of government on this subject in Hans. Deb. vol. clxi. pp. 1300-1331; vol. clxv. p. 1020.

Finance committees.

Commons in the important task of economical retrenchment and reform, it had been long the practice for the government from time to time to call upon the House to appoint what were termed finance committees, with authority to enquire into the revenue and expenditure of the country in every branch of the public service. The first instance of the appointment of such a committee was during the administration of Mr. Pitt, in 1786. From this date, similar committees, composed of men selected for their talents and knowledge of finance, without distinction of party, but including some members of the existing ministry,[a] were appointed about once in every ten years, until 1828, when twenty years—to 1848—elapsed without the nomination of such a committee, if we except one in 1834, which was confined to colonial military expenditure.[b] On February 22, 1848, on motion of the Chancellor of the Exchequer, two select committees were appointed, one on military expenditure, and the other to enquire into the expenditure for miscellaneous services.

Such committees, though not professedly secret, being intended to receive information from government which it would not be expedient to divulge to members generally, have been usually empowered to conduct their enquiries in secret, and to exclude from publicity any evidence which it might be important to abstain from disclosing.[c] And, in consenting to the appointment of these committees, the government have been careful to stipulate that their enquiries should be restricted within

---

[a] Mirror of Parl. 1828, pp. 100, 203.

[b] Hans. Deb. vol. xcvi. pp. 991, 1056. A committee on a portion of the public expenditure was obtained in 1778, on motion of a private member. Parl. Hist. vol. xix. p. 972. See also, in 3 Hats. p. 187, notice of a similar committee in 1070. But these were partial in their operation, and did not review the entire finances of the country. When Sir R. Peel was requested, in 1835, to consent to the appointment of a finance committee, he replied that, while he did not object to such committees, 'he was certainly of opinion that they ought not to be too frequently appointed.' Mirror of Parl. 1835, p. 302.

[c] Peel, in Hans. Deb. vol. xcvi. pp. 1007, 1063.

constitutional limits, and that, while reporting their opinions in regard to retrenchments in the public expenditure and economical reforms, they must not encroach on the functions of the executive government, who are alone responsible for deciding as to the number of men required for the army or navy, or any other branch of the public service, in order to maintain due efficiency therein.[d]

<small>Beneficial if confined within proper limits.</small>

On February 2, 1860, a motion was carried in the House of Commons against the government, 'that it would be desirable to appoint, every year, a select committee to enquire into the miscellaneous civil service expenditure of the preceding year; into the payments made out of the Consolidated Fund; and into those on account of the woods, forests, and land revenues.' But, doubtless through the influence of government, no such committee was nominated. Nevertheless, on March 29 following, the government consented to the appointment of a committee whose powers should be limited to an enquiry into 'the expenditure for miscellaneous services, and to report whether any reduction could be effected therein.' This committee made a report on July 25, strongly recommending that they should be re-appointed in the next session. On February 21, 1861, enquiry was made of ministers in the House of Commons whether they had taken any steps to give effect to the recommendations of the Committee on Public Moneys of 1857, that the principle of audit should be applied to the miscellaneous expenditure, and that a committee on the public accounts should be annually appointed, &c. In reply, the Chancellor of the Exchequer stated that the government were willing to accede to the appointment of a committee to review the audited accounts from year to year, but that for the present year the army and navy expenditure alone could be subjected to such scrutiny, as the miscellaneous

<small>Consent of government to appointment of a public accounts committee.</small>

---

[d] Peel, in Hans. Deb. vol. xcvi. p. 1073; and vol. ci. p. 713.

Committee first appointed in 1861.

expenditure had not as yet been brought under the system of audit. On April 9 following, upon motion of the Chancellor of the Exchequer, a select committee was appointed for the examination, from year to year, of the audited accounts of the public expenditure; and the Chancellor intimated his intention of moving that the appointment of such a committee should be a standing order." On March 31, 1862, this promise was fulfilled by the appointment of a standing committee, styled 'The Committee of Public Accounts,' for the examination of the accounts, showing the appropriation of the sums granted by Parliament to meet the public expenditure, to consist of nine members, who shall be nominated at the commencement of every session, of whom five shall be a quorum. On April 3 this was made a standing order.

Use of this committee.

This committee has been characterised by Mr. Gladstone as ' an institution well founded on the principles of parliamentary government,' it being intended 'to give completeness to our system of parliamentary control over the public moneys;'' and as affording to the House of Commons, through its investigations, ' the best security for the due, speedy, and effectual examining and rendering of the public accounts.'' An excellent understanding prevails between the government and this committee; and its proceedings have been invariably characterised by moderation and impartiality. The secretary of the Treasury is always a member of the committee, and reports to it officially every session the steps which have been taken during the past year to give effect to its recommendations. If any particular recommendation proves impracticable or

---

* Hans. Deb. vol. clxii. pp. 318, 773; vol. clxv. p. 1027.
† Ibid. vol. clxxvii. p. 450; Second Rep. Com. Pub. Accounts, 1868, p. 21.
* Hans. Deb. vol. clxv. p. 1351. The form in which the public accounts are now prepared for presentation to Parliament was first arranged by a committee of the House of Commons in 1797, and afterwards simplified by another committee in 1822. The form then adopted, with some alterations and additions, is still adhered to.—Balfour, on the Budgets and Accounts of England and France, in *Statistical Journal*, vol. xxix. p. 344.

inexpedient, reasons are given why it has not been carried out.

Great care is taken in the choice of members to compose this important committee. It was at first proposed that it should be chosen by the Committee of Selection; but they declined to undertake the duty, and the committee is now nominated by government, in concert with such members of the House as are of the greatest weight and authority upon financial questions.[b] This is in conformity with the practice which formerly prevailed in the appointment of finance committees.[i] The same gentlemen are re-appointed every session; and hitherto the government have successfully resisted all attempts to alter the composition of the committee.[1]

Selection of its members.

The Committee on Public Accounts in 1861 made five reports, containing various recommendations, some of them in furtherance of the conclusions of the Committee on Public Moneys in 1857, and all designed to remedy existing abuses, and to make the control of Parliament over the public finances more effectual. They specially recommended the extension of the appropriation audit to all accounts of public expenditure, and improvements in the existing system of audit. Also, that votes for public works should be taken 'for services coming in course of payment during the year,' instead of 'for the services of the year.' And finally the adoption of measures for the proper regulation and audit of the Treasury Chest Fund, and the Civil Contingencies Fund. The Treasury agreed to all these suggestions, and two Acts were passed (the 24 & 25 Vict. cc. 93 and 127) to give effect to the same.

Reports of the Committee in 1861.

The Committee on Public Accounts was re-appointed in 1862, pursuant to the standing order above mentioned. Their first report reviewed the recommendations of the previous years, and pointed out the extent to which they

Its reports in 1862.

---

[b] Hans. Deb. vol. clxv. p. 1350.   [i] Hans. Deb. vol. clxvi. pp. 330, 528; vol. clxix. p. 715.
[1] Mirror of Parl. 1828, pp. 189, 203.

had been carried out by the government. It also made known to the House an important decision of the Treasury, that 'this year all the votes for the civil service are being taken for payments within the year,' without which no satisfactory appropriation account could be submitted to Parliament. The second report concerned the question of transfers from army and navy surpluses, which has been already discussed in a former page (*ante*, p. 566). The third report contained suggestions for improvements in regard to the army and navy estimates. All these recommendations were favourably entertained by the government.

Its reports in 1863.

The committee was reappointed in 1863. The first report recapitulated the action taken by the government upon the reports of previous sessions. The second (and final) report was confined to an examination into the proceedings of government in relation to the vote of credit of March 19, 1860, to defray the expenses of the war in China.[h]

Its report in 1864.

In 1864 the committee made but one report. It treated of the new accounts of army and militia expenditure, prepared in conformity with the amended Appropriation Act, whereby the ultimate consent of Parliament was required to transfers of surpluses under certain votes to defray excesses under other votes, which had been temporarily authorised by the Treasury; and pointed out the proper mode of indicating the sanction of Parliament to such transactions. It discussed the expediency of improving the practice of the naval and military departments in respect of debit and credit accounts concerning the transactions of past years. It directed the attention of the House to the circumstances attending the sale of certain lands by the War Office, and the purchase of other lands from the office of Woods and Forests; also, to the practice of the army department in purchasing army

---

[h] See *ante*, p. 549.

supplies for the Indian and Colonial governments out of moneys voted for similar services for the British army; and recommended that in future the strict rule of Parliamentary appropriation, applicable to such cases, should be adhered to.¹

In 1865 the committee made one report only. It referred to certain proposed changes in the arrangement of the navy estimates, of which they expressed a general approval. Also, to the mode of accounting for fees received in certain public departments. It had been stated by the Chancellor of the Exchequer (Mr. Gladstone), in evidence before a select committee of the House of Lords, upon the malversation in office of Mr. Edmunds, Clerk of the Patents, that 'the present state of the law is very deficient indeed with respect to the miscellaneous heads of receipt, relating to a great variety of funds which come into the hands of public officers.' The Lords' committee had expressed their opinion that this deficient state of the law should not be allowed to continue, as it not only imperilled the custody of public money, but offered to various persons employed in the public service temptation to misconduct.ᵐ Accordingly, the Committee on Public Accounts directed their attention to this subject, and reported their opinion that the system of account in regard to these receipts was not satisfactory; but that they desired to institute further inquiries into the matter before offering any general recommendation thereupon. Meanwhile, they commended the evidence they had taken to the attention of government.ⁿ The minutes of

Its report in 1865.

---

¹ See a letter from the Secretary of the Treasury, stating what steps had been taken by the Treasury in accordance with these recommendations.—Rep. Com. Pub. Accounts, 1865, p. 160.

ᵐ Rep. Sel. Com. on Resignation of Mr. Edmunds, Lords Papers, 1865. And see Mr. Gladstone's remarks on this subject in the House of Commons, Hans. Deb. vol. clxxix. p. 637.

ⁿ By the Public Offices Fees Act, 1865 (29 and 30 Vict. c. 76), it is provided that the Treasury shall be authorised to direct that from and after a time to be specified by public notice, all or any of the fees payable in money in any public office, shall be collected by means of stamps, to be issued by the Commissioners of evidence and appendix to this report contain much information—to which attention has been directed in the preceding pages—respecting the origin, nature, and objects of the appropriation audit, with the outline of a scheme (prepared by the Secretary of the Board of Audit) for carrying into effect the proposed extension of the same to the votes for miscellaneous civil services.

Its reports in 1866.

On March 1, 1866, the Bill to consolidate the duties of the exchequer and audit departments, to regulate the receipt, custody, and issue of public moneys, and to provide for the audit of the public accounts, was referred to the consideration of this committee. On March 15 the committee made a special report upon this Bill, with the evidence taken thereon. They had agreed to the Bill, with some amendments; and they recommended that, in the event of its becoming law, it should be made a standing order that all reports from the exchequer and audit departments, on appropriation and consolidated fund accounts, and Treasury minutes in relation to appropriation accounts, should be referred to this committee. On August 4, the committee made a short general report on the proposed re-classification of the estimates, and on certain minor matters of account.

Attempt to obtain a committee to revise the estimates, &c.

The Committee on Public Accounts is of immense utility in bringing the entire revenue and expenditure of the country under the control of the House of Commons; in pointing out abuses in the management of the public finances; and in suggesting remedies. The cordial co-operation of the government with this committee has materially facilitated its labours, and enhanced its means of usefulness. Nevertheless, there are some who are still of opinion that enough has not been done to establish the supremacy of Parliament in financial matters. This sentiment found expression in a resolution proposed to the

---

Inland Revenue. The money received for such stamps, after deducting certain charges, to be carried to the Consolidated Fund; and annual accounts thereof to be laid before Parliament.

House of Commons on March 11, 1862, by Lord Robert Montagu, who moved for the annual appointment of a select committee to revise all estimates and accounts presented to Parliament ; to consider of the improvement and extension of powers of the Board of Audit ; and to determine the exact period of the financial year when it would be desirable that the annual estimates should be presented to the House of Commons, with a view to their undergoing examination by the said committee previous to the action of the Committee of Supply thereupon. The motion was opposed by the government, by whom it was urged that the several committees of public moneys and of public accounts had suggested numerous important reforms, which had been carried out by the government ; and that the existence of the last-named committee afforded the surest guarantee for the speedy and effectual carrying out of every proposition that was calculated to secure the constitutional rights of the House of Commons as the guardian of the public purse. After a short debate, the motion was negatived, on division, by a large majority. For further particulars on this subject, see *ante*, p. 477.

It would be superfluous to follow the course adopted in treating of other prerogatives, and to supplement this section with a narrative of precedents illustrative of the control of Parliament over the public expenditure, inasmuch as the principal cases of this description have been already noticed in the progress of our inquiry, and may be readily referred to by consulting the Index.

The remaining branches of the royal prerogative, which will engage our attention in the present chapter, are those wherein the sovereign represents the state in its dealings with foreign nations. They will naturally admit of the following classification :—1. The right of declaring war and making peace. 2. Intercourse with foreign powers. 3. The right of making treaties. 4. Interference in the internal concerns of foreign nations. Under each head the

Prerogative in relation to foreign powers.

constitutional limits of parliamentary interference with the prerogative in question will be briefly stated.

(1.) *The Right of declaring War and making Peace.*

Right of declaring war, and making peace.

The Constitution has vested this right exclusively in the crown, to be exercised according to the discretion of the sovereign, as he may judge the honour and interests of the nation to require. But this, like all other prerogatives, must be exercised by the advice and upon the responsibility of ministers, who are accountable to Parliament, and are liable to parliamentary censure or impeachment for the improper commencement, conduct, or conclusion of a war.[o]

How far subject to parliamentary control.

The previous consent of Parliament, either to the commencement of a war, or the conclusion of a peace, is not formally required by the Constitution. The necessity for obtaining adequate supplies for the prosecution of a contest with any foreign power, and the control possessed by Parliament over the army and navy by means of the annual Mutiny Acts, coupled with the existence of ministerial responsibility, constitute a sufficiently powerful check against the improper use of this prerogative. Nevertheless, if the hostilities about to be entered into are likely to involve serious consequences, it would be the duty of ministers, before engaging therein, to summon Parliament, to communicate to it the reasons for resorting to arms, and to ask for its advice and co-operation in carrying on the war.[p] If Parliament be in session at the time, it is customary for a royal message to be sent down, announcing the commencement of hostilities; but this form has not been invariably observed.[q]

---

[o] Cox, Inst. Eng. Govt. 500. Bowyer, Const. Law, 100.

[p] Macaulay, in Hans. Deb. vol. lxxxiv. p. 880. Palmerston, *Ibid.* vol. cxliv. p. 108, and vol. cxlvi. p. 1638. See also *Ibid.* vol. cxliv. pp. 72, 2475. For precedents of parliamentary interference in questions of war and peace, see May, Const. Hist. vol. i. p. 458. Smith's Parl. Rememb. 1859, p. 95; 1860, p. 1.

[q] Commons Journ. Feb. 11, 1793. May 22, 1815. March 27, 1854. No message was sent upon the com-

RIGHT OF DECLARING WAR AND MAKING PEACE. 599

The crown, in communicating to Parliament the breaking out of hostilities, the existence of a state of war, or the commencement of negotiations for peace,[a] thereby invites an expression of opinion upon the same. The advice tendered by Parliament may be unfavourable to the policy of ministers, and its indispensable assistance withheld. Thus, the American war was brought to a close, against the will of the king, by the interposition of the House of Commons.[b] In 1791, Mr. Pitt was obliged to abandon an intended war with Russia, which he deemed essential to the preservation of the balance of power in Europe, in deference to the adverse opinion of the House of Commons, expressed indirectly but unmistakeably, after a royal message on the subject had been transmitted to Parliament.[c] After the escape of Napoleon from Elba, in 1815, a message was sent to both Houses by the prince regent, informing them of the measures undertaken by government for securing the peace of Europe. In the Commons, on April 7, in amendment to an address of thanks in answer to this message, Mr. Whitbread moved that the prince regent should be requested to exert his most strenuous endeavours to secure to the country the continuance of peace. This was negatived

Interference of Parliament with this prerogative.

---

mencement of the China war; see Mirror of Parl. 1840, p. 2584. As regards the Persian war, see Parl. Deb. July 10, 1857. And as to wars in India, *Ibid.* July 6, 1858. The 54 clause of the India Government Act, 21 & 22 Vict. c. 106, expressly directs that when any order to commence hostilities is sent to India the fact shall be communicated to Parliament within three months, if Parliament be sitting, or within one month after its next meeting. The China war (1857–1860), was 'begun and finished without the servants of the crown thinking fit to ask for a direct approval of their policy by Parliament,' although resolutions condemnatory of the war were proposed in both Houses and carried in the House of Commons. Hans. Deb. vol. clxi. p. 546.

[a] C. Journals, Decem. 8, 1795, Oct. 29, 1801, January 31, 1850. When negotiations for peace have failed, Parliament should be immediately informed thereof, in order that some action should be taken thereupon, if necessary. Hans. Deb. vol. cxxxviii. pp. 105, 181, 500, 830, &c.

[b] On March 4, 1782, the House resolved, that 'all those who should advise the continuance of the American war were to be considered as enemies to the king and country.' This brought the war to an end, despite the wishes and intentions of George III. See May, Const. Hist. vol. i. p. 458.

[c] Stanhope's Pitt, vol. ii. p. 113.

by a large majority. Again, on April 28, he moved an address to the prince regent, entreating him to take measures to prevent the renewal of war on the ground of the executive power of France being vested in any particular person. This also was opposed by government, and negatived by a large majority. On March 3, 1857, the House of Commons condemned the policy of the war with China. This occasioned a dissolution of Parliament, which resulted in favour of ministers.

<small>Parliament is bound to sustain the crown, in a foreign war.</small>

But if the government, on their own responsibility, and with a knowledge of the international relations of the kingdom, which it would have been impolitic to have fully disclosed to Parliament beforehand, should have found it necessary, in defence of the honour or the interests of the state, to engage in a foreign war, it becomes the duty of Parliament, in the first instance, to afford the crown an adequate support. Thus, Mr. Disraeli, the leader of the Opposition, upon the declaration of war with Russia, in 1854, said, 'If her Majesty sends a message to Parliament, and informs us that she has found it necessary to engage in war, I hold that it is not an occasion when we are to enter into the policy or impolicy of the advice by which her Majesty has been guided. It is our duty, under such circumstances, to rally round the throne, and to take subsequent and constitutional occasions to question the policy of her Majesty's ministers, if it be not a proper one.' In a former part of this chapter—when treating of the prerogative in regard to the direction and control of the army—various precedents were adduced, pointing out the manner in which Parliament should exercise its constitutional right of inquiry into the prosecution of foreign wars; and the case of the China war, above cited, is a memorable example of the condemnation by Parliament of a

---

<small>* Hans. Deb. vol. cxxxii. p. 281. *Ibid.* vol. clxxiii. p. 97.
For similar remarks by Mr. Disraeli See *ante*, pp. 330-334.
in reference to this prerogative, see</small>

war which it regarded as unwise and inexpedient, while, at the same time, it did not refuse to furnish the means of bringing it to a successful issue.

(2.) *Intercourse with Foreign Powers.*

The sovereign is the constitutional representative of the nation in its intercourse with foreign powers. The transaction of affairs of state with other nations appertains exclusively to the executive government, which is always in existence, ready for the discharge of its functions, and constantly assisted by experienced advisers in the performance of its discretionary powers. *{Intercourse between the crown and foreign powers.}*

The medium of communication between the sovereign of Great Britain and the accredited representatives of foreign nations is the Secretary of State for Foreign Affairs. It is his duty, in official interviews with foreign ministers, and by means of written despatches, to convey the views, opinions, and conclusions of the government upon matters arising out of the relations of the British crown with other countries.

It is a necessary rule that the substance of all personal communications between the representatives of the British crown and the ministers of any foreign country, upon matters of public concern, should be committed to writing, in order that a fair and complete record of the transactions between Great Britain and other states may be preserved in the Foreign Office, and, in due course, submitted to Parliament.* The English constitutional system requires that Parliament should be informed, from time to time, of everything which is necessary to explain the conduct and policy of government, whether at home or abroad,' in order that it may interpose with ad- *{Information thereof to be given to Parliament.}*

---

* See Mr. Disraeli's speech, in Hans. Deb. vol. clvii. p. 1179.
' Lord Palmerston, *Ibid.* vol. clxxiii. p. 1104. In 1810 the House of Commons passed a resolution of censure upon the Earl of Chatham (the Master-General of the Ordnance and a cabinet minister), who had com-

vice, assistance, or remonstrance, as the interests of the nation may appear to demand. It is unquestionably of immense advantage to the country, that the diplomatic transactions and proceedings of government abroad should be freely communicated to Parliament, for thereby the foreign policy of the crown ordinarily receives the approbation of Parliament, and is sustained by the strength of an enlightened public opinion.' This in itself confers an additional weight to our policy and opinions abroad. On the other hand, it is notorious that the English system of giving publicity to information obtained by government, in regard to occurrences in foreign countries, is viewed with great disfavour on the Continent. A knowledge of the fact that all information procured by our foreign agents is liable to be made public, militates somewhat against their usefulness, and tends to place them occasionally in an embarrassing position. It induces towards them, moreover, a feeling of reserve on the part of the representatives of other governments; and necessitates that our ministers should resort, more than they would otherwise do, to the practice of private correspondence.*

Advantage of communicating to Parliament information on foreign policy.

Discretion in withholding what ought not to be divulged.

But a certain amount of discretion must always be allowed to the government in respect to communicating or withholding documents and official correspondence which may be asked for by either House of Parliament. While it is necessary that Parliament should be informed of all matters which are essential to explain or defend the policy of government, it is equally necessary that a minister should be able, upon his own responsibility, to

---

manded a military expedition to the Scheldt, on account of his having presented to the king a secret report of the expedition, without communicating the same to his colleagues, or causing it to be considered as a public document. (See *ante*, p. 170.) It was justly contended, that if such a proceeding were permitted, it would strike at the root of ministerial responsibility. Parl. Deb. vol. xvi. p. 9 **.

' See Earl of Clarendon, on the increasing power of public opinion over the foreign policy of the government, Hans. Deb. vol. clxxxiii. p. 572.

* Rep. of Commons Committee on the Diplomatic Service, 1861, pp. 50, 110, 324, 372.

withhold from the public such information as he may judge could not be afforded without detriment to the public service. Ministers are sometimes obliged to give 'extracts' only from official papers, in certain cases; but Parliament is bound to receive what is communicated upon the faith and credit of the administration in whom their general confidence is reposed, unless they are prepared to question the personal integrity of ministers, or to pronounce a verdict of censure upon their public conduct.[a]   *'Extracts' given in certain cases.*

Thus, it is generally inexpedient, and highly impolitic, to communicate to Parliament papers concerning diplomatic negotiations which are still pending; and 'nothing is more prejudicial to the action and efficiency of the diplomatic service than the perpetual motions for the production of papers, which are made by a certain class of politicians,' who insist upon the fullest information on questions of foreign policy, at unseasonable times.[b]   *Papers concerning pending negotiations.*

It has occasionally happened, however, that the government, in the exercise of their own discretion, have laid before Parliament papers in regard to disputes with foreign nations, whilst the negotiations are still pending, expressly in order that the opinion of Parliament may be announced, so as to influence the course of events.[c] But in 1860 a motion in the House of Commons, for the production of a copy of a despatch received from abroad (upon a subject on which negotiations were pending), and before it had been answered, was successfully opposed by the

---

[a] See a debate in the House of Commons on March 19, 1861, on a motion for a committee to consider the discrepancies between the copies of certain correspondence relating to Afghanistan, which was presented to Parliament in 1859, and again (in a different shape) in 1858; and to report thereon with a view to secure that all copies of documents presented to the House shall give a true representation of the originals. After explanations on the part of Lord Palmerston, against whose official conduct the motion was directed, it was negatived. But see Smith's Parl. Rememb. 1861, p. 45. See also the case of the China Despatches, noticed in Smith's Parl. Rememb. 1860, p. 35.

[b] Rep. Com. Diplomatic Service, Commons Papers, 1861, vol. vi. p. 344.

[c] Mr. Disraeli, citing case of Crimean War, in 1854. Hans. Deb. vol. clxiii. p. 803.

Foreign Secretary (Lord John Russell), on the ground that 'such a course would not only be contrary to precedent, but contrary to every principle recognised by the Constitution:' it 'would be like inviting the House to dictate the answer.'[d]

Count Walewski's despatch in 1858.

In 1858, a despatch was received from Count Walewski, Foreign Secretary to the French Government, referring to a recent attempt upon the life of the French Emperor, which had been plotted in England, and angrily remonstrating against the alleged impunity of assassins in England. Instead of replying to this despatch, the government laid it before Parliament, and made it the foundation of a Bill, which they introduced into the House of Commons, to amend the law concerning conspiracy to murder. But the Commons, indignant at the imputations contained in this despatch, and at the conduct of the ministry in relation thereto, rejected the Bill upon its second reading, by the adoption of a resolution, expressing their regret that the government, 'previously to inviting the House to amend the law of conspiracy, had not felt it to be their duty to make some reply' to Count Walewski's despatch.[e] This resolution led to a change of ministry.

Drafts of despatches.

It is a common practice, in order to save time, to send on a despatch, intended for presentation to a foreign court, by the British minister abroad, with instructions to withhold the delivery thereof until all the parties concerned had agreed upon it. If afterwards the despatch is not agreed to, it is simply cancelled. It then has no existence; and government have uniformly refused to communicate to Parliament the original draft of any such despatch.[f]

Private and confidential correspondence.

Any attempt to coerce the government into producing to Parliament all the papers they may possess upon a matter of foreign policy, without regard to their being confidential, or unsuitable for general publication, could only result in compelling the agents of government to have recourse to 'private correspondence' for the communication of everything but mere ordinary information.

---

[d] Hans. Deb. vol. clvii. p. 1177. And see post, p. 612.
[e] Ibid. vol. cxlviii. p. 1758.
[f] Lord Palmerston, Ibid. vol. clxxlii. p. 640. (Layard), Ibid. vol. clxxv. p. 602.

This would occasion not only immediate public loss, but also permanent injury to the state; for when one administration succeeded another, it would be unable to discover, amongst the official records of the public departments, the real grounds of action, and motives for decisions, upon great public questions. In communications between the Imperial Government and its agents abroad, private and confidential letters are necessarily frequently made use of. These letters refer to circumstances not sufficiently certain, or sufficiently important, to be placed in the formal shape of a despatch; or it may be that they communicate circumstances which have been learnt from conversations, and which it would be impossible to lay before Parliament without placing the writer in a position that would exclude him thereafter from all means of information which it is essential he should obtain. Such letters it is the duty of the Foreign Secretary to receive, and it is equally his duty not to lay them before the House.[a]

It is contrary to the etiquette observed towards sovereign princes to communicate to Parliament autograph letters addressed by them to the monarch of Great Britain. The practice is, for the Secretary of State to refer to the substance of such letters in an official despatch, acknowledging the receipt thereof, whereby an official record is preserved of their contents.[b] Nor is it proper, or consistent with practice, to lay before Parliament a letter from a foreign monarch to one of his ministers of state, even though a copy of the same may have been transmitted to the Foreign Office by our own ambassador.[c]

Etiquette towards foreign sovereigns.

It is also unusual to lay before Parliament any commu-

---

[a] Lord Palmerston, Hans. Deb. vol. clvii. p. 1182. For further particulars in regard to the practice of private correspondence between the foreign secretary and the diplomatic servants of the crown, see vol. ii. c. 2, on Members of the Ministry (the Secretary of State for Foreign Affairs).
[b] Mr. Canning, in Parl. Deb. vol. xxxvi. p. 187.
[c] Hans. Deb. vol. clxxxiv. p. 351.

nications between ambassadors and ministers abroad and the sovereign to whom they are accredited. Such documents are regarded as 'confidential,' for the obvious reason that their production 'might lead to serious consequences.'[1]

Appointment of ambassadors.

The sovereign, considered as the representative of her people, has the exclusive right of sending ambassadors to foreign states, and receiving ambassadors at home.[2] This prerogative should be regarded as inviolate, and should not be interfered with by either House of Parliament,—except in cases of manifest corruption or abuse; else the responsibility for its faithful exercise by the minister of state who is properly accountable for the same would be impaired, if not destroyed.

Not to be controlled by Parliament.

In 1814, the Right Hon. George Canning was appointed ambassador extraordinary at the Court of Lisbon, for the purpose of congratulating the Prince of Brazil upon his return to Portugal. The salary and allowances to Mr. Canning were on the scale ordinarily allowed to such functionaries; but a few months previously, it appears that the Foreign Secretary had written to the resident minister at Lisbon, requiring him, as a matter of economy, to reduce the expenses of the mission. The subsequent appointment of Mr. Canning, at a greatly increased rate of expenditure, led to the imputation that he owed his nomination to corrupt influences, and that his appointment was, in fact, 'a pecuniary and profitable party job.' Accordingly, on May 6, 1817, after Mr. Canning had returned home, Mr. Lambton moved in the House of Commons a series of resolutions reciting the particulars of the case, and asserting the appointment to have been inconsistent with the previous declarations of government in regard to this mission, uncalled for, and resulting in an 'unnecessary and unjustifiable waste of the public money.' The Foreign Secretary (Lord Castlereagh) defended the conduct of the government, and afterwards Mr. Canning himself gave full and satisfactory explanations, which entirely exonerated all parties from corrupt or improper conduct in the matter. Nevertheless, the motion was pressed to a division, but it was negatived by a large majority.[3]

Upon the accession to office of Sir Robert Peel, in 1835, he selected the Marquis of Londonderry to be ambassador at St. Peters-

[1] Lord John Russell, Hans. Deb. vol. xxxi. p. 702.
[2] Bowyer, Const. Law, pp. 157, 158.
[3] Parl. Deb. vol. xxxvi. pp. 100-211.

burg. This choice was unpopular in the House of Commons, and on March 13, 1835, a motion was made for an address 'for a copy of the appointment, if any, of an ambassador to St. Petersburg, together with a return of the salary and emoluments attached thereto.' No vote was taken on this motion, it being stated that the appointment, although intended, had not yet been made. But the adverse feeling towards Lord Londonderry on the part of the House of Commons was so very apparent, that his lordship, without communicating with any member of the government, declared in the House of Lords that he would not accept the mission.[m] Both the Duke of Wellington and Lord John Russell protested against the unconstitutional invasion by the House of Commons of the royal prerogative;[n] and Sir R. Peel, who had announced his intention of adhering to the choice he had made,[o] afterwards stated that he had been no party to Lord Londonderry's withdrawal, and that had the address passed, he should have resigned office.[p]

It would be a manifest breach of this prerogative to permit either House of Parliament to communicate directly with any foreign prince or power. All such communications must be made officially through the government, and by a responsible minister of the British crown.

Houses of Parliament may not communicate directly with foreign powers.

In 1836, the French government made a valuable present of books to the libraries of the Houses of Lords and Commons. The fact was duly reported to each House, by their respective library committees. In the House of Lords, a resolution, expressing grateful satisfaction for this donation, was adopted; but it was admitted that no precedent existed to warrant the House in transmitting the same direct to the French Chamber of Peers. After a short discussion on the point of form, it was agreed that the resolution should be forwarded through the Secretary of State for Foreign Affairs, without any further action on the part of the House.[q] It was decided in the Commons, that, after the session, their Speaker should make some arrangements for conveying an expression of thanks for this donation to the French authorities, without the adoption by the House of any formal vote thereupon.[r]

Upon the occasion of the successes of the allied armies of England and France, during the Crimean war, in 1854, the thanks of Parliament were voted to the French commander and his army, 'for their gallant and successful co-operation' with our troops, and

---

[m] Mirror of Parl. 1835, p. 350.
[n] Ibid. pp. 350, 358.
[o] Ibid. p. 345.
[p] Ibid. 1841, p. 1834. Peel's Memoirs, vol. ii. p. 88.
[q] Mirror of Parl. 1836, p. 1330.
[r] Ibid. p. 2830.

the English commander, Lord Raglan, was desired to convey to them this resolution. But this vote was admitted by Lord John Russell to be 'unusual, and perhaps unprecedented;' and grave doubts were expressed by Earl Derby, whether such a proceeding on the part of the House towards the troops of a foreign power was not irregular and unbecoming. Nevertheless, the unanimity of feeling which generally prevailed at the time towards our French ally caused the point of form to be overruled.[a]

On May 1, 1865, Addresses to the queen were voted in both Houses of Parliament, to convey to her Majesty the expression of the deep sorrow and indignation with which the intelligence of the assassination of Mr. Lincoln, President of the United States, had been received, and praying her Majesty to communicate the abhorrence of the House, and their sympathy with the government and people of the United States, upon this occasion, to the American government. These addresses were agreed to, *nemine dissentiente*; although, in the House of Lords, Earl Derby took exception upon formal grounds, and suggested that the more regular course would have been 'simply to move a resolution of this, in conjunction with the other House of Parliament,' expressing the feelings proposed to be embodied in the Address to the crown. No reply was made by the mover of the Address (Earl Russell, the Foreign Secretary) to this point.[b]

And ought to receive no communications from foreign princes.

On June 30, and July 10 and 13, 1863, a singular and unprecedented occurrence took place in the House of Commons. Two members, Messrs. Roebuck and Lindsay, in the course of debate upon the expediency of recognising the Southern American Confederacy, communicated to the House an opinion of the Emperor of the French upon the subject, which his Imperial Majesty, they stated, had authorised them to make known to the House of Commons. This proceeding gave rise to a very lively discussion, and elicited from Lord Palmerston (the premier) some very pertinent remarks. 'The British Parliament,' he said, 'is in no relation to, has no intercourse with, no official knowledge of, any sovereign of any foreign country. Therefore it is no part of our functions to receive communications from the sovereign or government of any foreign state, unless such communications are made by the responsible minister of the crown, in consequence of official communications held by order of a foreign government with the British government.' After further observations on this point, his lordship declared that he thought it right to place on record, so far as could be done by a statement in the House, that the proceeding in question

---

[a] Hans. Deb. vol. cxxxvi. pp. 320, 381.   [b] *Ibid.* vol. clxxviii. p. 1223.

was 'utterly irregular, and ought never to be drawn into precedent.'

The principle involved in the foregoing cases admits, moreover, of a more extended application, and forbids of any formal communications between the Houses of Lords and Commons and other legislatures in the British empire, except through the medium of the executive officers of the Imperial Government.

Houses of Parliament can only communicate with other legislative bodies through the imperial executive.

Thus, on March 1, 1855, inquiry was made of ministers, in the House of Lords, whether they intended to propose that the thanks of Parliament should be given to the several colonial legislatures who had liberally evinced their sympathy with the mother country during the Russian war, by large contributions to the Patriotic Fund. It was replied, that no precedent existed for such a communication, and that 'it was a matter of grave doubt whether a precedent should be now set, recognising an intercommunication between the Imperial Parliament and the Legislatures of the Colonies in matters pertaining to the crown, which would set the crown altogether aside.' In this view all the leading statesmen of the House concurred.

(3.) *The Right of making Treaties.*

It is a peculiar function of sovereignty to make treaties, leagues, and alliances with foreign states or princes; and by the law of nations it is essential to the validity of a treaty that it be made by the sovereign power, for then it binds the whole community. In England the sovereign power is vested exclusively in the crown, acting under the advice of its responsible ministers. Whatever engagements or contracts the sovereign enters into, no other power within the kingdom can legally delay, resist, or annul; although the king's ministers are responsible to Parliament for their participation in the conclusion of any

Right of making treaties.

---

* Hans. Deb. vol. clxxii. p. 600.
* Ibid. vol. cxxxvi. pp. 2073–2084. See also the course taken by the House of Lords, in 1856, upon the occasion of the gift by the widow of the late Lord Chancellor Truro of his collection of law books, as a donation to the library. Ibid. vol. cxli. p. 131. Lords Journals, 1856, pp. 74, 95.

treaty derogatory to the honour and interest of the nation."

Power of Parliament in respect to treaties. The constitutional power appertaining to Parliament in respect to treaties is limited. It does not require their formal sanction or ratification by Parliament, as a condition of their validity.[y] The proper jurisdiction of Parliament in such matters may be thus defined: First, it has the right to give or withhold its sanction to those parts of a treaty that require a legislative enactment to give it force and effect; as, for example, when it provides for an alteration in the criminal or municipal law, or proposes to change existing tariffs or commercial regulations.[y] Secondly, either House has the right to express to the crown, by means of an address, its opinion in regard to any treaty, or part of a treaty, that has been laid before Parliament.[z] Thirdly, it is in the power of either House, if it disapproves of a convention or treaty, to visit the ministers of the crown who are responsible for the same with censure or impeachment, as the case may be.[a]

If a treaty requires legislative action, in order to carry it out, it should be subjected to the fullest discussion in Parliament, and especially in the House of Commons, with a view to enable the government to promote effectually the important interests at stake, in their proposed alterations in the foreign policy of the nation.[b] But while

---

[w] Bowyer, Const. Law, p. 100. 1 Blackstone, ch. vii. Lord Palmerston, in Hans. Deb. vol. clxxiv. p. 787.

[x] Hans. Deb. vol. clvi. p. 1301.

[y] See cases in Hertslet's Treaties, vol. ix. p. 1034, &c.

[z] Mr. Pitt's dictum, quoted in Smith's Parl. Rememb. 1800, p. 32. Lord Aberdeen's motion in House of Lords, January 20, 1832, for an address to the king, to cause certain alterations to be made in the project of a treaty respecting Holland, which had been made public, with a view to the honour of Great Britain and the just claims of Holland. (Mirror of Parl. 1831-2, pp. 310, 2823.) Mr. B. Cochrane's motion, in House of Commons, on July 13, 1860, in regard to an article in the treaty with China, respecting the residence of a British Plenipotentiary at Pekin; and Lord John Russell's observations thereupon. Hans. Deb. vol. clix. p. 1880.

[a] Mr. Gladstone, in Hans. Deb. vol. clvi. p. 1380. Lord H. Petty's motion of censure in regard to the Convention of Cintra. Parl. Deb. Feb. 21, 1809. For older cases, see Cox, Inst. Eng. Govt. p. 600. And *ante*, p. 42.

[b] Hans. Deb. vol. clvi. pp. 1256, 1326.

Parliament may refuse to agree to measures submitted to them for the purpose of giving effect to any treaty, they have no power to change or modify, in any way, a treaty itself.'

It is not usual to lay before Parliament treaties which have not been ratified by the government;ᵈ nor treaties between foreign powers, to which Great Britain is not a party; although copies thereof may have been communicated to the British Government.ᵉ

It is unnecessary and inexpedient for the House of Commons to interfere in any way, or declare its opinion, on any matter of alleged violation of treaty, or which concerns the foreign relations of Great Britain with other countries; unless at the instigation of the executive government, and with a view to powers or opinions sought for by the executive; as matters affecting our relations with foreign countries are prerogative.ᶠ But questions may be put to the administration in Parliament, in reference to alleged infractions of treaties by foreign powers, and for the purpose of directing the attention of government thereto.ᵍ

Alleged violations of treaties.

Moreover, 'it is neither regular to ask, nor is it convenient to answer, questions relative to treaties which are yet pending.'ʰ The initiation of a foreign policy and the

Treaties still pending.

ᶜ Mr. Gladstone, Hans. Deb. vol. lxxl. p. 548.

ᵈ Mirror of Parl. 1839, pp. 6009, 6105. But, in 1846, the government submitted to the House of Commons a 'Sugar Duties and Drawback Bill,' the object of which was, 'to give effect to a treaty which had not yet been ratified, and therefore could not be presented to the House in the usual form, by command of her Majesty; but for the information of the House, as the treaty required legislation, a copy had been presented as a return from the Treasury.' Chan. of the Excheq. Hans. Deb. vol. clxxx. p. 280.

ᵉ Mirror of Parl. 1834, p. 2858.

ᶠ Lord John Russell, Hans. Deb. (3) vol. xc. pp. 800, 801. See the discussion, in the House of Commons, on June 28, 1861, on an abstract resolution proposed in reference to the Garibaldi fund, for the liberation of Italy. And on the motion in the House, on April 28, 1864, to resolve that certain instructions issued to a colonial governor, in regard to the observance of neutrality in the American Civil War, were 'at variance with the principles of international law.'

ᵍ See *Ibid.* vol. clvii. pp. 740, 757; vol. clviii. pp. 1100, 1120.

ʰ Mirror of Parl. 1841, p. 1032.

conducting of negotiations with foreign powers appertains exclusively to the executive government, who are responsible for the course and issue of the same; and should not be interfered with by Parliament, who necessarily can only possess imperfect information upon the subject, either by advice or by vote. So long as Parliament is satisfied with the general principles upon which negotiations are being conducted, and approves of the general policy of the government, it should abstain from all interference with pending negotiations.[1]

Parliament ought not to legislate in matters proper for negotiation.

So strictly is this rule observed, that, in 1839, a Bill introduced by government for the Suppression of the Portuguese Slave Trade was rejected by the House of Lords, at the instigation of the Duke of Wellington, Lord Lyndhurst, and other eminent statesmen, expressly on the ground that Parliament ought not to be called upon to act in a matter which should properly be effected by negotiation and by the action of the executive government on their sole responsibility. After the rejection of the Bill, an Address to the crown was adopted by the House of Lords, urging negotiations with foreign powers to suppress the traffic in slaves, and the adoption of other measures by government to that end, especially as regards the Portuguese slave trade, and giving assurances of the readiness of the House to concur with the Commons in whatever measures might be necessary to bring about such a desirable result. To this Address a suitable reply was given by the crown. At the same time, the ministry introduced another Bill on the subject, which was free from the principal objections pointed out in the former measure. The Duke of Wellington, however, was still dissatisfied, and adhered to his opinion that the objects intended ought to be effected by order in council, without the intervention of Parliament. In its progress through the Lords, the Bill underwent some important alterations, rendering it more conformable to constitutional law and usage; and it was finally agreed to by both Houses.[2]

---

[1] See the speeches of Mr. Disraeli and of Lord Palmerston, in Hans. Deb. vol. clxxv. pp. 1279, 1280. And of Earls Derby and Russell, *Ibid.* pp. 1024, 1028. Papers regarding pending negotiations with foreign powers are only communicated to Parliament at the discretion of the crown, and so far as they can be produced without public injury or inconvenience; see Mirror of Parl. 1830, p. 671; 1840, pp. 2047, 2040; 1841, p. 1507. And see *ante*, p. 603.

[2] See Parl. Debates, 1839, *passim*. Annual Register, 1839, pp. 242–253.

After the conclusion of important negotiations with the representatives of any foreign state or states, it is usual for the government to communicate the result to Parliament, and to declare what is the course which the government propose to take in regard to the questions involved therein. If either House should be of opinion that the government has failed in its duty in any respect, it is competent for them to take any line of conduct they may think proper, in order to make known to the crown their opinions upon the subject.[k] For, while the initiation of a foreign policy is the prerogative of the crown, to be exercised under the responsibility of constitutional ministers, it is the duty of Parliament, when the result of the negotiations conducted by ministers has been communicated to them, to criticise, support, or condemn that policy, as they may deem the interests of the nation shall require.[l]

Result of negotiations to be made known to Parliament.

Thus, on July 4, 1864, after the protocols of the conference held in London, in the summer of 1864, between the representatives of European powers, to consider of the dissensions between Denmark and Germany, had been laid before Parliament, Mr. Disraeli moved in the House of Commons a vote of censure upon ministers, in the shape of an Address to the queen, to represent that the course pursued by the government had failed to maintain their avowed policy of upholding the integrity and independence of Denmark, had lowered the just influence of this country in the counsels of Europe, and thereby diminished the securities for peace. An amendment, to declare that the independence of Denmark and the security of its possessions in Schleswig-Holstein ought to be guaranteed, was negatived without a division. Another amendment, approving of the conduct of government in abstaining from armed interference in the war, for the defence of Denmark, was put, and agreed to. On July 8, a similar vote of censure was proposed in the House of Lords; an amendment, to modify the terms thereof, was put, and negatived, and the main question was agreed to. It is noteworthy that this vote was carried by means of proxies, for, of the peers present, there were 123 non-contents to 119 contents; but, by the aid of proxies, this decision was reversed, and the total majority in

Invasion of Denmark in 1861.

---

[k] Earl Russell, Hans. Deb. vol. clxxvi. p. 323.
[l] Mr. Disraeli, Ibid. p. 740.

favour of the vote of censure was 9, there being 177 in favour and 168 against it.[m]

Right of the crown to dispossess itself of territory, without assent of Parliament.

For a discussion of the question as to how far it is competent for the crown to dispossess itself of any portion of its dominions, without the assent of Parliament, see the debate on the Address moved in the House of Commons, in relation to the Royal Proclamation issued in 1854, abandoning and renouncing all sovereignty over the Orange River territory and its inhabitants.[n] This question, so far as regards the right of the crown to surrender to a foreign state a part of its territory, was supposed to have been settled in the affirmative, on the authority of Lord Chancellor Thurlow, but Lord Campbell disputes the correctness of the dictum of his predecessor.[o] The point has again arisen in reference to the Ionian Islands, and has been argued by Earl Grey, in favour of the crown;[p] also by Lord Palmerston, and Sir R. Palmer (Solicitor-General), to a similar effect, with an exception in the case of newly-discovered territories which had been settled by British subjects, when the laws of this country having been introduced therein, the cession could not take place without the consent of Parliament. Or, in the case of conquered or ceded countries, if Parliament had legislated concerning them, the Solicitor-General was of opinion that the concurrence of Parliament might be necessary to their relinquishment.[q]

(4.) *Interference in the Internal Concerns of Foreign Nations.*

Interference in concerns of foreign nations.

The crown, acting through the Secretary of State for Foreign Affairs, is sometimes called upon to express its opinions in regard to the conduct of other powers, in

---
[m] Hans. Deb. vol. clxxvi. p. 1100.
[n] Ibid. vol. cxxxiii. pp. 59-87.
[o] Campbell's Chancellors, vol. v. pp. 555, 556 n. To the same effect, see Smith's Parl. Rememb. 1861, pp. 13, 141.
[p] Hans. Deb. vol. clxix. p. 57.
[q] Ibid. pp. 230, 1807; and see Ibid. vol. clxxiv. p. 378.

matters of internal or domestic concern. The interests of British subjects resident in foreign parts, or engaged in commercial transactions with foreign citizens, may require the interposition of the crown on their behalf; or a particular line of policy adopted by a foreign state towards its own subjects, or towards a neighbouring state, may be viewed by the British government as contrary to recognised principles of humanity, or of natural right, or as being likely to occasion a disturbance of the peace of nations. Under such circumstances, the crown is warranted by international usage, in offering friendly advice or remonstrance to a foreign government.[y] But great delicacy is necessary in all such acts of intervention, lest they should fail of their intended effect, and irritate instead of conciliating; thereby weakening the moral strength of the crown in its foreign relations, or necessitating a resort to arms.[z] It is obvious that, if any diplomatic interventions are called for, they can only be exercised through the recognised official channels of international communication. Direct interference by

Intervention in foreign affairs.

---

[y] See a number of instances, cited by Lord Palmerston, wherein the British government 'have interfered with great success in the affairs of other countries, and with great benefit to the countries concerned,' Hans. Deb. vol. clxxv. p. 532.

[z] 'All public writers have declared that a nation has the right to settle its own form of government, provided it does not injure other nations in its mode of doing so, just as every householder may regulate his own house, provided he does not cause a nuisance to the neighbourhood; but if one nation attacks another, all nations are at liberty to judge whether their interests and the general independence are affected thereby. Thus the first kind of intervention should, as a rule, be forbidden and avoided.' Of late years, the leading powers of Europe have abstained, as a general principle, from such intervention. 'But the case would be quite different if, when a great power attacks a small independent state, with a view to conquest, other powers were as a rule to remain quiescent.' 'It does not follow, however, that in every case of invasion with a view to interference in the internal concerns of a state, neutral powers are bound to resist the invader.'—Earl Russell (citing cases and authorities) in the new edition of his Essay on the English Constitution, pp. lxxxii.–xcvii. And see his speech in Hans. Deb. vol. clxxvi. p. 1178; the proposed votes of censure upon the policy of the government in regard to the Schleswig-Holstein question, in the House of Lords, on April 11, and in the House of Commons on July 4, 1864; and the discussion, in the Lords, on affairs of Austria, &c., May 8, 1866. For the opinions of Earl Derby, and Lord Stanley on non-intervention, see Hans. Deb. vol. clxxxiv. pp. 1154, 1218, 1263.

When Parliament may interpose in affairs of foreign powers.

either House of Parliament in the domestic or municipal concerns of a foreign country would be highly irregular and unconstitutional. If, however, by virtue of existing treaties with a foreign state, or for any other reason, the British crown possesses a distinct and formal ground for interposition in a domestic matter arising within a foreign territory, it would be perfectly regular for either House to address the crown to exercise that right. Such a proceeding could only be legitimately restrained by considerations of political expediency, but it should not be persevered in, if opposed, on this ground, by the responsible advisers of the crown.[t]

Lafayette, &c.

In the years 1794 and 1796,[u] the House of Commons was moved to address the crown to intercede with the government of Prussia for the liberation of General Lafayette and other Frenchmen, who had been captured during the war with France, and confined in Prussian prisons. The proposed addresses were supported by Fox and other leading Whigs, on the ground that Lafayette and his friends were not subjects either of Prussia or Austria; that they had not violated the laws of either country, but were mere prisoners of war, and that England, as an ally of Prussia, was entitled to intercede in their behalf. Mr. Pitt, however, successfully resisted the motions on constitutional grounds. He said, 'No instance of such interference as is now proposed has ever occurred at any former period . . . . . nor could such interference be attempted without establishing a principle of the most unwarrantable tendency; a principle inconsistent with the internal policy and independent rights of foreign states.' 'It would be improper for this House to take any share in a transaction which in no degree comes within their province, and on which their decision could have no influence.'[v]

Polignac, &c.

On a similar occasion, on May 31, 1836, a motion was made in the House of Commons for an Address to his Majesty to use his good offices with his ally, the king of the French, for the release of Prince Polignac and other state prisoners, formerly ministers of state of the late King Charles X., now confined in the fortress of Ham for attempting a revolution in France, which was afterwards

---

[t] Lord Palmerston, on proposed address for the recognition of the Southern American Confederacy, Hans. Deb. vol. clxxii. pp. 556, 608.

See Parl. Debates on General Fitzpatrick's motions on March 17, 1794, and Dec. 16, 1796.

[v] Parl. Hist. vol. xxxii. p. 1392.

successfully accomplished by others in July 1830, and by means of which the present king of the French was placed upon the throne. The Foreign Secretary (Lord Palmerston), though personally sympathising in the object sought to be obtained by the motion, declared that the House 'could take no step so inexpedient, or even dangerous, as to ask the King of England by address to interfere in matters connected with the domestic concerns of another country.'* After a short debate, the motion was withdrawn.

On March 5, 1839, a member moved an Address for correspondence between the Foreign Office and the British minister at Stockholm relative to the erection of Slite, in Gottland, into a free-port, to the manifest advantage of British interests. Lord Palmerston opposed the motion, because no sufficient parliamentary grounds for it had been shown; and because neither 'this House nor the English government has any business to meddle with the internal affairs of the government of Sweden,' as would be done were this motion to prevail. It was accordingly negatived.ˣ

Port of Slite.

But there is a manifest difference between an unauthorised interference in the municipal proceedings of a foreign country and interference with a specific object, under a specific treaty.ʸ Recognising this distinction, the government acquiesced in motions made in the House of Commons, both in 1832 and 1842, for Addresses for copies of manifestoes and ukases issued by the Russian government, and relating to the administration of the kingdom of Poland; England having been party to a treaty, in 1815, by which the condition of Poland had been regulated, and subsequent acts of the Russian government towards the Poles having taken place, in alleged contravention of that treaty, so that the Parliament of England possessed a right to information as to the grounds upon which that condition had been changed, and were justified in expressing their sympathy with the sufferings of Poland, although it might not be

Affairs in Poland.

---

* Mirror of Parl. 1830, p. 1011.
ˣ Ibid. 1830, pp. 789–792; see also Ibid. p. 2702. And on May 10, 1861, a motion for copies of despatches from our ambassador at Vienna, describing the constitution lately granted by the Emperor of Austria to his subjects, was withdrawn; on its being stated by the Foreign Secretary (Lord John Russell) that, 'although there is no secret about the matter,' it was not desirable to produce papers 'which relate so entirely to the internal affairs of Austria.' Hans. Deb. vol. clxii. p. 1870.

ʸ But in any case it is not regular to lay before Parliament copies of official documents of foreign countries, unless they are in the formal and official possession of government. Hans. Deb. (3) vol. lxxxiii. p. 428. And it is a rule which, as a matter of courtesy, is always observed, that, when documents have been communicated to the British government by foreign powers, they are not laid before Parliament without first consulting said powers as to whether or not they desire them to be published. Ibid. vol. clxxiii. pp. 830, 861.

Poland.

expedient for the government to take any formal steps that would be regarded as hostile or offensive by Russia.*

But, on March 17, 1865, Lord Palmerston opposed a motion condemnatory of the conduct of Russia towards Poland, on the ground that the records of Parliament already contained a deliberate expression of opinion on the subject, and that it was not desirable to weaken this proceeding by any mere repetition of similar opinions. Such motions, he contended, should only be resorted to in order to obtain from the House once and for all a decisive expression of opinion, which may have the effect of influencing events, or, if necessary, of obtaining from government some action with a view to give effect to the same. The motion was accordingly withdrawn.

Sound dues.

On March 16, 1841, a member moved to resolve that, in the opinion of the House of Commons, certain tolls, known as the Sound dues, levied by the King of Denmark on British (and other) shipping were unjust, and required revision. The Foreign Secretary admitted the fact, and the truth of the general statements urged in its behalf; also, that the grievance was one of long standing; but he declared that negotiations had been recommenced for the removal of the tolls, and that it was therefore inexpedient for the House to interfere. Sir R. Peel (in Opposition at the time) concurred in the inexpediency of interference by the House in foreign negotiations, but considered that, if the crown should be unable to procure redress, the House might properly and advantageously interpose, and fortify the crown by a temperate expression of opinion on the subject, which would doubtless have weight with the Danish government. By general consent, the present motion was set aside by the previous question, to be renewed at another time, if necessary.* The House was afterwards informed, in reply to a question, of the satisfactory progress of the negotiations.*

Bearing in mind the constitutional limits wherein the active interference of Parliament in the affairs of foreign nations is necessarily restrained, there is, nevertheless, an important function fulfilled by the British legislature, as

---

* Sir R. Peel, in Hans. Deb. (3) vol. lxiv. pp. 823–826. A motion for an Address to the crown for a copy of the instructions by the government of the United States to its officers for the suppression of the slave trade was opposed by the administration, because, although the instructions had been communicated to the British government under a recent treaty, yet it was no part of the duty of the British government to communicate them to Parliament, but rather for the United States government to determine whether they should publish them or not. *Ibid.* vol. lxxi. p. 541.

* Mirror of Parl. 1841, pp. 700–709.

* *Ibid.* p. 2304.

the mouthpiece of an enlightened public opinion, which calls for special remark. When events are transpiring abroad upon which, in the interest of humanity, or of the peace and good government of the world, it is desirable that British statesmen should have an opportunity of declaring their sentiments, from their place in Parliament—whether by so doing they merely express, with the weight due to their personal character and high official position, the general feelings of the country, or whether they aim at influencing public opinion itself by intelligent and authoritative explanations upon points concerning which they possess peculiar facilities for instructing the public mind—it is customary for some member to call the attention of the House and of the government thereto, in an informal way, or upon a motion for papers.* But, while important beneficial results may follow from the temperate use of this practice, it is liable to great abuse. Discussions upon topics which are beyond the jurisdiction of Parliament to determine should not be provoked except upon grave and fitting occasions. When by the operation of existing treaties, the position and duties of England may be affected by events transpiring in other countries⁴—or where there is a reasonable probability that the observations of statesmen and politicians in the British legislature will have a beneficial influence upon the fortunes of the country to which they refer*—they would not be unsuitable, or out of place. But whenever the ministers of the crown discourage or deprecate the expression of opinions in Parliament upon the course of affairs in other countries, it is safer to defer to

Opinions expressed in Parliament on foreign affairs.

---

* E. g. see the observations of Sir R. Peel and of Lord John Russell on religious intolerance in Spain, Hans. Deb. vol. clxi. pp. 2064, 2072; discussion on the affairs of Denmark, and Holstein, in the House of Lords on March 18, 1861; and on the Pope and the Kingdom of Italy, in the Lords, on April 19, 1861; debates on the affairs of Poland, in the Lords, on July 19, 1861, and in the House of Commons, on Feb. 27, 1863.

⁴ Hans. Deb. vol. clxix. p. 884.

* Sir F. Goldsmid and Lord Palmerston, Ibid. vol. clxvii. pp. 1171, 1195.

their guidance, and to refrain from utterances that may be hurtful to the cause which it is desired to promote, and that might even operate prejudicially upon the interests of the British nation.

Concluding remarks.

We have now passed under review the principal prerogatives of the British crown, and have endeavoured to point out, in the light of precedent, and with the help of recognised authority in the interpretation of constitutional questions, the proper functions of Parliament in relation thereto. We have shown that the exercise of these prerogatives has been entrusted, by the usages of the Constitution, to the responsible ministers of the crown, to be wielded in the king's name and behalf, for the interests of the state; subject always to the royal approval, and to the general sanction and control of Parliament. Parliament itself, we have seen, is one of the councils of the crown, but a council of deliberation and advice, not a council of administration. Into the details of administration a parliamentary assembly is, essentially, unfit to enter; and any attempt to discharge such functions, under the specious pretext of reforming abuses, or of rectifying corrupt influences, would only lead to greater evils, and must inevitably result in the sway of a tyrannical and irresponsible democracy. 'Instead of the function of governing, for which,' says Mill,' 'such an assembly is radically unfit, its proper office is to watch and control the government; to throw the light of publicity on its acts; to compel a full exposition and justification of all of them which anyone considers questionable; to censure them if found to merit condemnation; and if the men who compose the government abuse their trust, or fulfil it in a manner which conflicts with the deliberate sense of the nation, to expel them from office'—or, rather, compel them to retire, by an unmistakable expression of the will of Parliament. Instead of attempting to decide

---

' Mill, Rep. Govt. p. 104.

upon matters of administration by its own vote, the proper duty of a representative assembly is 'to take care that the persons who have to decide them are the proper persons,' 'to see that those individuals are honestly and intelligently chosen, and to interfere no further with them; except by unlimited latitude of suggestion and criticism, and by applying or withholding the final seal of national assent.'*

---

* Mill, Rep. Govt. pp. 94, 104. Functions of Representative Bodies' The whole chapter 'On the Proper is deserving of a careful study.

INDEX.

ABERDEEN, Lord, his administration, 148
Abstract resolutions, 252
Act of Uniformity, 318
Addington, Mr., his administration, 80
Addresses for advance of public money, 435, 442
Administrations, annals of, 72
 — — tabular view of, 162
Administration in Parliament, 7, 24
 — — how to increase its strength, 23
 — — ought not to have seats *ex officio*, 26
Administrative audit, 577
Admiralty, Board of, its conduct investigated, 330, 336, 414
 — — practice in regard to surplus money-grants, 541
Albert, Prince, appointed the Queen's Private Secretary, 124
 — — his character and public conduct, 126
 — — vote in aid of the National Memorial to, 553 n.
Ambassadors, appointment of, 606
Anne, Queen, her character and conduct, 176
Appropriation Act, 526, 529
 — clauses in Bill of Supply, 528
 — — new form of, 586
 — — prorogation of Parliament before passing an, 532
Appropriation audit, 559, 564
 — — its nature and operation, 578, 586
 — — its application to all parliamentary grants, 581
Army and Navy, appointments in, how made, 382
 — — pensions to widows and orphans in the, 400
 — — prerogative in relation to the, 320
 — — subject to ministerial control, 56, 321

Army and Navy subject to parliamentary oversight, 326
 — — surplus grants for, used to make good deficiencies, 528, 540, 568
 — — *See also* Troops
Articles of War, framing of the, 294 n.
Attorney-General, ordered to prosecute offenders, 356
Audit, Board of, its ordinary duties, 578
 — *See* Exchequer and Audit Department
Australia, democratic institutions in, 17

BARBER, Mr. W. H., case of, 381
 Beales, Mr. Edmund, case of, 392
Bedchamber question, 120
Bethell, Mr., case of, 424
Bewicke, Mr., case of, 355
Bills in Parliament, imposing public charges, 430, 431
 — — suspended and renewed at next session, 217 n.
Birth of eminent statesmen, dates of, 236 n.
Bishops.—*See* Church of England
Bode, Baron de, case of, 440
Boroughs, nomination, use of, 11
 — — in the hands of peers, &c., 62
Bribery practices, investigations into, 356
British Museum estimates, 482 n.
Brougham, Lord, on the kingly office, 204
Budget, introduction of the, 486
 — questions on the, 487
 — resolutions on the, included in one Bill, 484
 — rejected or amended by the House of Commons, 517
 — final statement of estimated revenue and expenditure, 530

CAB

CABINET Council, 46, 217
— not attended by the Sovereign, 229
Cabinet secrets not to be divulged, 301
Canadian Episcopate, 312
Canning, Mr., his administration, 109, 221
Caroline, Queen, case of, 62
Cattle plague, legislation on the, 251
Chaplains to House of Commons, 403
Charters, how granted, 372
Chartist prisoners, case of the, 350
China, mortality of troops in, 310
Church of England, its legal position in England, 305
— — — the colonies, 308
— — — foreign countries, 317
— — — Act of Uniformity, 318
— — — patronage, how distributed, 382
Churchward, Mr., case of, 483, 488
Civ'l Contingencies Fund, 551
Civil Service.—See Public Officers
Colenso, Bishop, case of, 310
Colonial Bishops Bill, 316
Colonial Church, position of the, 308
Colonial defences, 279
Commissions of enquiry, 271
Committee of Supply.—See Supply
Consolidated fund, 468
Contracts, subject to parliamentary control, 286, 493-508
Convocations, 306
Corn law question, 110
Corporations, how created, 372
County families, influence of the, 10, 24. —See Whig Families
Courts martial, 327
Crimean expedition, 324
Crown, dormant powers of the, 8
— necessity for strengthening its influence in Parliament, 15, 19
— waning authority of the, 70
— may not dispense with existing laws, 287
— debts due to the, how remitted, 455, 456
— right to relinquish a portion of its dominions, 614.—See also Sovereign; Parliament; Prerogative
Customs' officers, remuneration of, 420, 423

DANISH Claims, case of the, 411
Debts due to the Crown, how remitted, 455, 456
Departmental audit, 576
Departmental regulations, 290
Derby, Lord, his first administration,146

FRA

Derby, Lord, his second administration, 153
— — his third administration, 160
— — on the influence of the Sovereign, 208
Despatches, when communicated to Parliament, 603
— confidential, 604
Diocesan Synods in England, 307
— — in the colonies, 313
Dispensing power of the Crown, 287

ECCLESIASTICAL matters.—See Church
Edmunds, Mr., case of, 421 n., 525
Education Office, Inspectors' Reports, 261
— — Minutes, to be laid before Parliament, 292
— — how submitted to the House of Commons, 295
Engledue, Lieut., case of, 415
Estimates.—See Supply
Exchequer, functions of the, 536
— united with the Audit Office, 537, 573
— functions of the new department, 539
— its control over the issue of money, 615.—See also Public Money
Exchequer Bills, 610 n.
Executive authority.—See Ministers
Extra receipts, 553, 5

FEES, public, audit of, 579
— collection of, 585
Finance committees, 590
Financial propositions.—See Budget; Supply
Foreign Office expenditure, how far subject to Treasury control, 563 n.
— — — audit of, 570 n.
Foreign policy, controlled by Parliament, 602
Foreign Powers, prerogative in relation to, 597
— — intercourse with, 601
— — interference in domestic concerns of, 611
— — opinions in Parliament on foreign affairs, 612
— — etiquette towards foreign princes, 605.—See also Negotiations
Forestal inclosures, 276
Fortifications on the coast, proceedings in Parliament concerning, 263, 299, 494
Fox, C. J., as a minister, 56
France, democratic institutions in, 17
Franchise.—See Public Officers; Reform

GAL

GALWAY postal contract, 503
— George I. and II. as sovereigns, 177
George III., his character and conduct, 48, 180, 207
— — his personal influence, 58
— — proceedings upon his mental affliction, 235, 641 n.
George IV. as a sovereign, 61
Gladstone, Mr., his budgets, 523
Goderich, Lord, his administration, 111
Governing families, their influence, 59, 66
Grenville administration, 56, 68
Grey, second Earl, his administration, 118
Grey, third Earl, his suggestions on parliamentary reform, 20
— his plan to strengthen ministers in Parliament, 23
— on the kingly office, 208

HARBOUR at Holyhead, 277
Harbours of refuge, 274
Honours, the gift of the Crown, 365
— proceedings in Parliament in relation to, 367
House of Commons, its origin, 25
— — — introduction of ministers therein, 7, 45
— — — its constitutional position, 29
— — — difficulty of controlling it since the Reform Act, 66
— — — sanctions transfers of surpluses of Army and Navy expenditure, 582
— — — its duty to adjust accounts of public expenditure, 572, 587. — See also Parliament; Reform
Household (Royal), appointments in the, how made, 188
Hume, Mr. Joseph, his labours on behalf of economy, 589 n.

IMPEACHMENT of Ministers, 43
— Indian army, employment of, out of the East Indies, 321 n.
Indian army officers, grievances of, 339
Information to Parliament, when to be given or withheld, 278
Intervention and non-intervention of British Crown in foreign affairs, 615

JAMAICA, martial law in, 342
Jews, admission of, to Parliament, 250
Judges, proceedings against, in Parliament, 353, 358

VOL. I.

MIN

Judges in Ionian Islands, case of, 417 n.
Judicial appointments, how conferred, 383, 418
Justice, administration of, subject to parliamentary control, 332
— erroneous convictions, 364

KEMPENFELDT expedition, enquiry into, 330
Kennedy, Mr. T. F., case of, 416
King can do no wrong, how explained, 40
'King's Friends,' the, party of the, 42
Kingly office, its importance, 176, 201.
—See also Crown; Sovereign

LANDS.—See Public Lands
Life peerages, 368
Liverpool, Lord, his administration, 100
Loans by the Crown, how made and how remitted, 453, 466, 548 n.
— proceedings in Parliament respecting, 510
Lopez, Sir M., case of, 343
Lords, House of, its constitutional position, 27
— — — its dormant powers, 8
— — — important services, 29
— — — indifference of peers to their legislative duties, 30
— — — practice upon petitions for aid, and financial enquiries, 132.
—See Parliament
Lowe, Mr. R., enquiry into his administration of the Education department, 285

MMAHON, Colonel, case of, 409
Magistrates, proceedings in Parliament for removal of, 361
Mail contracts. — See Contracts
Martial law, 341
Melbourne, Lord, his first administration, 67, 122
— — his second administration, 128
— — acts as the Queen's Private Secretary, 191
Mercy, prerogative of, 343
Militia officers, dismissal of, 227 n.
Ministers, the channel of communication with the Crown, 170
— how they communicate with the Crown, 231
— their appointment and dismissal by the Crown, 210, 221, 227
— entitled to a fair trial from Parliament, 213

S S

MIN

Ministers accept office without a majority in the House of Commons, 214
— how far they are selected by the Sovereign, 218, 225
— must possess the confidence of Parliament, 223
— must have the implicit confidence of the Sovereign, 227
— their executive acts, how far subject to parliamentary control, 254
— abuse of executive authority, how to be dealt with, 284
— illegal or oppressive acts by individual ministers, 299, 303
Ministerial defeats in Parliament, 78, 120 n., 131-133
— — on financial propositions, 517
Ministerial interregnum, 107, 151, 228
Ministerial responsibility, origin of, 37
— — when first acknowledged, 41
— — progress and extent of, 46, 63, 169, 174, 245, 256, 325
— — is to Parliament, and to no other tribunal, 301
— — for the dismissal of their predecessors, 68, 124, 223
— — for the official acts of their subordinates, 288
Ministry.—*See* Ministers
Minister of Council, rightful limits of, 291
— — — on educational matters, 293
Money.—*See* Supply
Money Bills, 525
Muir, Palmer, &c., case of, 348
Mutiny Act, 321

NAVY.—*See* Army and Navy
Negotiations, papers concerning, when communicated to Parliament, 602, 612 n.
— matters proper for, should be left to executive action, 512
— result of, to be communicated to Parliament, 613
New Zealand episcopate, 314
North, Lord, his administration, 73

OATHS in Parliament, 250
Officers.—*See* Public Officers
Officers of Army and Navy, control of the Crown over, 326
Opinions, legal, confidential documents, 357
Orders in Council, 285-290

PALMER, Mr., case of, 438
Palmerston, Lord, his first administration, 150
— — his second administration, 158

PEN

Papers, when communicated to Parliament and when refused, 278, 602
— cost of furnishing to Parliament, 281
— concerning private affairs, 281
Paper-duties case, 459
Pardon, prerogative of, 343
Parliament advises the Crown on the formation of a ministry, 211
— may not interfere with the dismissal of a minister, 226
— its constitutional relation to the Crown, 248
— may advise the Crown upon any matter, 253
— may inquire into all acts of administration, 255
— representation of every public department therein, 388
— ought not to legislate on matters proper for negotiation, 512
— proper functions of, 620
— dissolution of, when justifiable, 134, 154, 209
— — cases of, from 1782 to 1866, 162
— prorogation of, its effect, 218
Parliament, Houses of, appointment of their officers and servants, 387
— — — contingent expenses, how provided for, 402
— — — salaries of employés in both Houses, 404
— — — may not communicate directly with foreign powers, 507
— — — or with other legislative bodies, 609.—*See* also Votes of Thanks
Parliamentary government defined, 1
— — to what it owes its success, 13
— — its peculiar advantages, 32
Partition Treaties, case of the, 42
Party government defined, 8
— — origin of, 47
Patronage in the hands of an out-going administration, 137
— abuse of, 376
— how dispensed, 380
— extent of, in Great Britain, 384
— of the Board of Admiralty, enquiry into its distribution, 414
Paymaster General, funds in his hands, how applied, 541, 549
— — cash account, 551
Peel, Sir R., his first administration, 66, 123
— his second administration, 139
Peers, creation of, 368
— life peerages, 368
— their interference at elections, 9
Pensions.—*See* Public Officers

Perceval, Mr., his administration, 83
— — his appointment to the Chancellorship of the Duchy of Lancaster, 408
Petition of Right, procedure on, 239
Petitions for aid to be recommended by the Crown, 429, 434
Pitt, William, his first administration, 74, 77
— — his second administration, 80
Portland, Duke of, first administration, 76
— — second administration, 90
Post office, opening letters at the, 272
— — Sunday labour in the, 282
Prerogative defined, 244
— in connection with Parliament, 244
— government defined, 3
— existed before the Revolution of 1688, 38
— its weakness, 39
Prime minister, the free choice of the Sovereign, 219
— — chosen by his colleagues, 221
— — empowered to select his own colleagues, 218, 225
— — the channel of communication between the Crown and the ministry, 228, 230
Prince Consort, position and duties of a, 195; and see Albert, Prince
Private correspondence on public matters, 611
Private Secretary to the Sovereign, 191
Privy Council, meetings of, 233
— — decisions of, questioned in Parliament, 260. See also Minutes of Council
Privy councillors, their appointment and responsibility, 42, 61, 217, 272, 273
Prize money, distribution of, 327 n. 367 n. 438 n. 451 n.
Proclamations, their constitutional limits, 288
Impory the basis of representation, 2
Public accounts, form of the, 692 n.
— — standing committee of, its origin and functions, 592
— — — its reports, 593
Public lands, sale or exchange of, when subject to parliamentary control, 552
Public money, parliamentary control over the grant of, 453
— — over the issue and expenditure of, 521
— — exercised by the Exchequer and Audit department, 625
— — proceedings to give effect to a parliamentary appropriation, 549

Public money to be expended only as Parliament may direct, 512, 543
— — unauthorised expenditure, 546
— — discretion of the government in emergent cases, 548
— — increasing strictures of Parliament in controlling expenditure, 552. See also Supply; Treasury
Public moneys' committee of 1857, 589 n.
Public officers, rights of the Crown in relation to, 375
— — political and non-political appointments, 377, 382
— — advantages of permanency in the civil service, 378
— — promotions not to be influenced by politics, 383, 397
— — competitive examinations, 385, 417
— — all subordinated to some political head, 388
— — for what cause they may be dismissed, 389, 393
— — should abstain from interference in politics, 391
— — their exercise of the franchise, 391 n.
— — pensions and retiring allowances, 394, 397
— — salaries how regulated, 398
— — — — of ministers of state, 419
— — — — of parliamentary officers and servants, 404
— — of revenue officers paid out of receipts, 471, 555
— — pensions to, how regulated, 398, 419, 421
— — their appointment, direction, and remuneration, how far subject to parliamentary control, 401, 407-427. See also Treasury
Public opinion in relation to Parliament, 14, 228 n.
— — on questions of foreign policy, 202 n.

QUEEN'S University, Ireland, charter, case of the, 373

RED Sea and India telegraph, case of the, 608
Reform Act of 1832, its enactment, 112
— — its effects, 13, 65, 70
Reform Bill of 1858, 144
— — of 1866, 149

INDEX

REF

Reform, parliamentary, Mr. Pitt's scheme, 60
— — probable consequences of further reform, 16, 18
Representative system, its origin, 35
Resolutions of either House, effect of a prorogation of Parliament on, 247
— how far binding, 250
— in favour of money grants, 431, 435
— in favour of the repeal, &c., of particular taxes, 446
— abstract, 252
Returns.—See Papers
Revenue, public, how derived, 467
— gross receipts paid into the Exchequer, 498
Revenue officers, their salaries paid out of receipts, 471, 555
Revolution of 1688, its effects, 3, 7, 26, 40
Rewards.—See Honours
Rockingham administration, 73
Roman Catholic question, 57, 85, 116
Russell, Lord, his first administration, 144
— — his second administration, 148

SALARIES.—See Parliament, Houses of; Public Officers
Secret service expenditure, 551
Secretary of State, office of, 172
Select committees not to encroach on administrative functions, 257
— — to consider administrative and other public questions, 270
Shelburne administration, 76
Sovereign, on the office of, 167
— personal irresponsibility of the, 168, 239, 242
— must act through a minister, 173
— personal acts of government, 176
— impersonality of the, 176
— may employ a private secretary, 181
— constitutional position defined, 201
— ceremonial functions, 201
— social pre-eminence, 205
— political influence, 210
— appointment and dismissal of his ministers, 210, 217, 225.—See also Prime Minister
— to be consulted on all state affairs, 230
— communications with his ministers, 231
— use of the royal sign-manual, 237, 238, 541 n.
— delegation of royal functions, 233
— absence from the realm, 234
— alterance of royal functions, 235

SUP

Sovereign as a witness, 213
— as a churchwarden, 212 n.
— royal prerogatives, 244
— in relation to Parliament, 216.—See also Crown; King
Speaker of the House of Commons, address to the Crown on his behalf, 367, 402
— his duty in regard to supply grants, 411 n. 528
— his speech on presenting money bills for the Royal assent, 531
Standing army, 322
Standing orders, their validity, 247 n.
Stocks, redemption of, 512
Sugar duties, case of the, 520
Superannuation allowances to public officers, 297
Supply, origin of parliamentary control over, 35
— cannot be raised by prerogative, 286
— prerogative in regard to, 427
— only granted on demand of the Crown, 428
— petitions or motions for aid to be recommended by the Crown, 454
— — exceptions to this rule, 425
— grant of, by Parliament, 453
— must be obtained by Parliamentary grant, 454
— Commons may refuse to grant, 502
— temporary advances on responsibility of government, 455
— peculiar rights of the Commons in the grant of, 457
— rights of the Lords, 458
— appointment of committee of supply, 465
— permanent grants, 471
— charges annually voted, 472
— presentation of the estimates, 473
— supplementary estimates, 474
— on the revision of the estimates by a select committee, 475, 587
— motions for reduction of expenditure, 478
— classification of the estimates, 480, 555 n.
— proceedings in committee of supply, 482
— votes of credit and votes on account, 485
— votes taken for payments within the year, 571
— effect of debates in committee of supply, 489
— items in the estimates rejected by the House, 490
— Resolutions reported from committee of supply, 499

SUP

Supply, votes in committee of ways and means, 510
— money advanced in anticipation of Appropriation Act, 511
— all financial operations to be submitted to Parliament, 515
— bills of supply and appropriation, 525
— surpluses on Army and Navy grants may be used for deficiencies on similar grants, 528
— *See also* Public Money; Taxation; Treasury
Supply Bills, proceedings on, 525

T

TAX Bills, proceedings on, 525
Taxation, prerogative in relation to, 427
— motions concerning, should proceed from ministers, 444
— abstract resolutions on, proposed by private members, 445
— Ministerial scheme amended by Parliament, 451
— may not be levied by prerogative, 286, 453
— consists of annual and permanent duties, 512
— when new rates of duty are to be levied, 513
Thom's case, 351
Transfers of army and navy grants.— *See* Treasury
— of civil service votes, not permissible, 569
Treasure trove, 440
Treasury regulates salaries and pensions of public officers, 325
— to apply to Exchequer for supplies granted by Parliament, 540
— functions of the, in controlling public expenditure, 558
— controls expenditure of all public departments, 560, 582
— empowers Army and Navy departments to use their surplus votes for deficiencies, 528, 580
— subject to the sanction of Parliament, 568
— its duties in auditing the public accounts, 571
Treasury Chest Fund described, 550
Treaties, right of making, 609
— function of Parliament in relation to, 610

TOR

Troops, their employment by the magistracy, 311 n.— *See also* Army and Navy; Indian Army

U

UNAUTHORISED expenditure by Government, how dealt with by Parliament, 448
Unexpended balances of supply grants to be repaid to Exchequer, 460, 569
— difference between the Board of Works and Board of Audit on this point, 572
United States of America, working of their democratic institutions, 17
— objectionable tenure of office therein, 319
— practice in regard to the time of levying new duties, 514 n.

V

VICTORIA, Queen, her conduct as a sovereign, 70, 187
Volunteer corps, formation and control of, 323
Votes ' on account,' 486
Votes of credit, 485
— to be included in an Appropriation Act, 521
Votes of thanks in Parliament, 368

W

WALCHEREN expedition, case of the, 232
War and peace, prerogative in relation to, 602
— how far controlled by Parliament, 603
Wellington, Duke of, his administration, 114
Westbury, Lord Chancellor, case of, 421
Whig families, their influence, 17
— claim to nominate the king's ministers, 60, 218, 220
Wilde, Mr. H. S., case of, 424
William III. as a constitutional king, 11
— appoints the first parliamentary administration, 15
William IV., his conduct as a sovereign, 185
— and the Reform Bill, 65, 120
— dismisses his ministers upon insufficient grounds, 67

Y

YEOMANRY Cavalry, vote to defray the cost of drilling, 411
York, Duke of, enquiry into his public conduct, 409

LONDON
PRINTED BY SPOTTISWOODE AND CO.
NEW-STREET SQUARE

₊ *Vol. II. of this work is now in the press, and will contain chapters on the following subjects:—*

I. The Cabinet Council: its origin, modern development, and present position in the English Constitution.

II. The several Members of the Administration; their relative position and political functions.

III. The Administration in Parliament: their conduct of public business, &c.

IV. Proceedings in Parliament against Judges for misconduct in office.

39 Paternoster Row, E.C.
London: January 1867.

GENERAL LIST OF WORKS

PUBLISHED BY

Messrs. LONGMANS, GREEN, READER, and DYER.

Arts, Manufactures, &c. 12	Miscellaneous and Popular Metaphysical Works 6
Astronomy, Meteorology, Popular Geography, &c. 7	Musical Publications 11
Biography and Memoirs 3	Natural History and Popular Science 7
Chemistry, Medicine, Surgery, and the Allied Sciences 9	Poetry and The Drama 17
Commerce, Navigation, and Mercantile Affairs 19	Religious and Moral Works 13
Criticism, Philology, &c. 4	Rural Sports, &c. 18
Fine Arts and Illustrated Editions 11	Travels, Voyages, &c. 15
Historical Works 1	Works of Fiction 16
Index 21–24	Works of Utility and General Information 19
Knowledge for the Young 20	

Historical Works.

Lord Macaulay's Works. Complete and uniform Library Edition. Edited by his Sister, Lady Trevelyan. 8 vols. 8vo. with Portrait, price £5 5s. cloth, or £8 8s. bound in tree-calf by Rivière.

The History of England from the Fall of Wolsey to the Death of Elizabeth. By James Anthony Froude, M.A. late Fellow of Exeter College, Oxford. Vols. I. to X. in 8vo. price £7 2s. cloth.

Vols. I. to IV. the Reign of Henry VIII. Third Edition, 54s.

Vols. V. and VI. the Reigns of Edward VI. and Mary. Second Edition, 28s.

Vols. VII. & VIII. the Reign of Elizabeth, Vols. I. & II. Fourth Edition, 28s.

Vols. IX. and X. the Reign of Elizabeth. Vols. III. and IV. 32s.

The History of England from the Accession of James II. By Lord Macaulay.

Library Edition, 5 vols. 8vo. £4.
Cabinet Edition, 8 vols. post 8vo. 48s.
People's Edition, 4 vols. crown 8vo. 16s.

Revolutions in English History. By Robert Vaughan, D.D. 3 vols. 8vo. 45s.

Vol. I. Revolutions of Race, 15s.
Vol. II. Revolutions in Religion, 15s.
Vol. III. Revolutions in Government, 15s.

An Essay on the History of the English Government and Constitution, from the Reign of Henry VII. to the Present Time. By John Earl Russell. Fourth Edition, revised. Crown 8vo. 6s.

The History of England during the Reign of George the Third. By the Right Hon. W. N. Massey. Cabinet Edition, 4 vols. post 8vo. 24s.

The Constitutional History of England, since the Accession of George III. 1760–1860. By Sir Thomas Erskine May, K.C.B. Second Edit. 2 vols. 8vo. 33s.

Brodie's Constitutional History of the British Empire from the Accession of Charles I. to the Restoration. Second Edition, 3 vols. 8vo. 36s.

Historical Studies. I. On Precursors of the French Revolution; II. Studies from the History of the Seventeenth Century; III. Leisure Hours of a Tourist. By Herman Merivale, M.A. 8vo. 12s. 6d.

Lectures on the History of England. By William Longman. Vol. I. from the Earliest Times to the Death of King Edward II. with 6 Maps, a coloured Plate, and 53 Woodcuts. 8vo. 15s.

History of Civilization in England and France, Spain and Scotland. By HENRY THOMAS BUCKLE. Fifth Edition of the entire work, complete in 3 vols. crown 8vo. price 24s. cloth; or 42s. bound in tree-calf by Rivière.

The History of India, from the Earliest Period to the close of Lord Dalhousie's Administration. By JOHN CLARK MARSHMAN. 3 vols. crown 8vo. [*Nearly ready.*

Democracy in America. By ALEXIS DE TOCQUEVILLE. Translated by HENRY REEVE, with an Introductory Notice by the Translator. 2 vols. 8vo. 21s.

The Spanish Conquest in America, and its Relation to the History of Slavery and to the Government of Colonies. By ARTHUR HELPS. 4 vols. 8vo. £3. VOLS. I. & II. 28s. VOLS. III. & IV. 16s. each.

History of the Reformation in Europe in the Time of Calvin. By J. H. MERLE D'AUBIGNÉ, D.D. VOLS. I. and II. 8vo. 28s. VOL. III. 12s. and VOL. IV. price 16s. VOL. V. in the press.

Library History of France, in 5 vols. 8vo. By EYRE EVANS CROWE. VOL. I. 14s. VOL. II. 15s. VOL. III. 18s. VOL. IV. 18s.

Lectures on the History of France. By the late Sir JAMES STEPHEN, LL.D. 2 vols. 8vo. 24s.

The History of Greece. By C. THIRLWALL, D.D. Lord Bishop of St. David's. 8 vols. fcp. with Vignette-titles, 28s.

The Tale of the Great Persian War, from the Histories of Herodotus. By GEORGE W. COX, M.A. late Scholar of Trin. Coll. Oxon. Fcp. 7s. 6d.

Greek History from Themistocles to Alexander, in a Series of Lives from Plutarch. Revised and arranged by A. H. CLOUGH. Fcp. with 44 Woodcuts, 6s.

Critical History of the Language and Literature of Ancient Greece. By WILLIAM MURE, of Caldwell. 5 vols. 8vo. £3 9s.

History of the Literature of Ancient Greece. By Professor K. O. MÜLLER. Translated by the Right Hon. Sir GEORGE CORNEWALL LEWIS, Bart. and by J. W. DONALDSON, D.D. 3 vols. 8vo. 36s.

History of the City of Rome from its Foundation to the Sixteenth Century of the Christian Era. By THOMAS H. DYER, LL.D. 8vo. with 2 Maps, 15s.

History of the Romans under the Empire. By CHARLES MERIVALE, B.D. Chaplain to the Speaker. Cabinet Edition, with Maps, complete in 8 vols. post 8vo. 48s.

The Fall of the Roman Republic; a Short History of the Last Century of the Commonwealth. By the same Author. 12mo. 7s. 6d.

The Conversion of the Roman Empire; the Boyle Lectures for the year 1864, delivered at the Chapel Royal, Whitehall. By the same. 2nd Edition. 8vo. 8s. 6d.

The Conversion of the Northern Nations; the Boyle Lectures for 1865. By the same Author. 8vo. 8s. 6d.

Critical and Historical Essays contributed to the *Edinburgh Review.* By the Right Hon. Lord MACAULAY.
LIBRARY EDITION, 3 vols. 8vo. 36s.
CABINET EDITION, 4 vols. post 8vo. 24s.
TRAVELLER'S EDITION, in 1 vol. 21s.
POCKET EDITION, 3 vols. fcp. 21s.
PEOPLE'S EDITION, 2 vols. crown 8vo. 8s.

History of the Rise and Influence of the Spirit of Rationalism in Europe. By W. E. H. LECKY, M.A. Third Edition. 2 vols. 8vo. 25s.

The History of Philosophy, from Thales to the Present Day. By GEORGE HENRY LEWES. Third Edition, partly re-written and greatly enlarged. In 2 vols. VOL. I. *Ancient Philosophy;* VOL. II. *Modern Philosophy.* [*Nearly ready.*

History of the Inductive Sciences. By WILLIAM WHEWELL, D.D. F.R.S. late Master of Trin. Coll. Cantab. Third Edition. 3 vols. crown 8vo. 24s.

Egypt's Place in Universal History; an Historical Investigation. By C. C. J. BUNSEN, D.D. Translated by C. H. COTTRELL, M.A. With many Illustrations. 4 vols. 8vo. £5 8s. VOL. V. is nearly ready, completing the work.

Maunder's Historical Treasury; comprising a General Introductory Outline of Universal History, and a Series of Separate Histories. Fcp. 10s.

Historical and Chronological Encyclopædia, presenting in a brief and convenient form Chronological Notices of all the Great Events of Universal History. By B. B. WOODWARD, F.S.A. Librarian to the Queen. [*In the press.*

NEW WORKS PUBLISHED BY LONGMANS AND CO.

History of the Christian Church, from the Ascension of Christ to the Conversion of Constantine. By E. BURTON, D.D. late Regius Prof. of Divinity in the University of Oxford. Eighth Edition. Fcp. 3s. 6d.

Sketch of the History of the Church of England to the Revolution of 1688. By the Right Rev. T. V. SHORT, D.D. Lord Bishop of St. Asaph. Seventh Edition. Crown 8vo. 10s. 6d.

History of the Early Church, from the First Preaching of the Gospel to the Council of Nicæa, A.D. 325. By the Author of 'Amy Herbert.' Fcp. 4s. 6d.

History of Wesleyan Methodism. By GEORGE SMITH, F.A.S. Fourth Edition, with numerous Portraits. 3 vols. crown 8vo. 7s. each.

The English Reformation. By F. C. MASSINGBERD, M.A. Chancellor of Lincoln. Fourth Edit. revised. Fcp. 7s. 6d.

Biography and Memoirs.

Life and Correspondence of Richard Whately, D.D. late Archbishop of Dublin. By E. JANE WHATELY, Author of 'English Synonymes.' With 2 Portraits. 2 vols. 8vo. 28s.

Extracts of the Journals and Correspondence of Miss Berry, from the Year 1783 to 1852. Edited by Lady THERESA LEWIS. Second Edition, with 3 Portraits. 3 vols. 8vo. 42s.

The Diary of the Right Hon. William Windham, M.P. From 1783 to 1809. Edited by Mrs. H. BARING. 8vo. 18s.

Life of the Duke of Wellington. By the Rev. G. R. GLEIG, M.A. Popular Edition, carefully revised; with copious Additions. Crown 8vo. with Portrait, 5s.

Life of the Duke of Wellington, partly from M. BRIALMONT, partly from Original Documents (Intermediate Edition). By Rev. G. R. GLEIG, M.A. 8vo. with Portrait, 15s.

Brialmont and Gleig's Life of the Duke of Wellington (the Parent Work). 4 vols. 8vo. with Illustrations, £2 14s.

Life of Robert Stephenson, F.R.S. By J. C. JEAFFRESON, Barrister-at-Law; and WILLIAM POLE, F.R.S. Member of the Institution of Civil Engineers. With 2 Portraits and 17 Illustrations on Steel and Wood. 2 vols. 8vo. 32s.

History of my Religious Opinions. By J. H. NEWMAN, D.D. Being the Substance of Apologia pro Vitâ suâ. Post 8vo. 6s.

Father Mathew: a Biography. By JOHN FRANCIS MAGUIRE, M.P. Popular Edition, with Portrait. Crown 8vo. 3s. 6d.

Rome; its Rulers and its Institutions. By the same Author. New Edition in preparation.

Letters and Life of Francis Bacon, including all his Occasional Works. Collected and edited, with a Commentary, by J. SPEDDING, Trin. Coll. Cantab. VOLS. I. and II. 8vo. 24s.

Some Account of the Life and Opinions of a Fifth-Monarchy Man, chiefly extracted from the Writings of JOHN ROGERS, preacher. Edited by the Rev. EDWARD ROGERS, M.A. Student of Christ Church, Oxford. Crown 4to.
[*Nearly ready.*

Life of Amelia Wilhelmina Sieve- king, from the German. Edited, with the Author's sanction, by CATHERINE WINKWORTH. Post 8vo. with Portrait, 12s.

Mozart's Letters (1769-1791), translated from the Collection of Dr. LUDWIG NOHL by Lady WALLACE. 2 vols. post 8vo. with Portrait and Facsimile, 18s.

Beethoven's Letters (1790-1826), from the Two Collections of Drs. NOHL and VON KÖCHEL. Translated by Lady WALLACE. 2 vols. post 8vo. Portrait, 18s.

Felix Mendelssohn's Letters from Italy and Switzerland, and Letters from 1833 to 1847, translated by Lady WALLACE. With Portrait. 2 vols. crown 8vo. 5s. each.

Recollections of the late William Wilberforce, M.P. for the County of York during nearly 30 Years. By J. S. HARFORD, F.R.S. Second Edition. Post 8vo. 7s.

Memoirs of Sir Henry Havelock, K.C.B. By JOHN CLARK MARSHMAN. Second Edition. 8vo. with Portrait, 12s. 6d.

NEW WORKS published by LONGMANS and CO.

Essays in Ecclesiastical Biography. By the Right Hon. Sir J. STEPHEN, LL.D. Fourth Edition. 8vo. 14s.

Biographies of Distinguished Scientific Men. By FRANÇOIS ARAGO. Translated by Admiral W. H. SMYTH, F.R.S. the Rev. B. POWELL, M.A. and R. GRANT, M.A. 8vo. 18s.

Vicissitudes of Families. By Sir BERNARD BURKE, Ulster King of Arms. FIRST, SECOND, and THIRD SERIES. 3 vols. crown 8vo. 12s. 6d. each.

Maunder's Biographical Treasury. Thirteenth Edition, reconstructed and partly rewritten, with above 1,000 additional Memoirs, by W. L. R. CATES. Fcp. 10s. 6d.

Criticism, Philosophy, Polity, &c.

The Institutes of Justinian; with English Introduction, Translation, and Notes. By T. C. SANDARS, M.A. Barrister-at-Law. Third Edition. 8vo. 15s.

The Ethics of Aristotle with Essays and Notes. By Sir A. GRANT, Bart. M.A. LL.D. Director of Public Instruction in the Bombay Presidency. Second Edition, revised and completed. 2 vols. 8vo. price 28s.

On Representative Government. By JOHN STUART MILL, M.P. Third Edition. 8vo. 9s. crown 8vo. 2s.

On Liberty. By the same Author. Third Edition. Post 8vo. 7s. 6d. crown 8vo. 1s. 4d.

Principles of Political Economy. By the same. Sixth Edition. 2 vols. 8vo. 30s. or in 1 vol. crown 8vo. 5s.

System of Logic, Ratiocinative and Inductive. By the same. Sixth Edition. 2 vols. 8vo. 25s.

Utilitarianism. By the same. 2d Edit. 8vo. 5s.

Dissertations and Discussions. By the same Author. 2 vols. 8vo. 24s.

Examination of Sir W. Hamilton's Philosophy, and of the Principal Philosophical Questions discussed in his Writings. By the same. Second Edition. 8vo. 14s.

The Elements of Political Economy. By HENRY DUNNING MACLEOD, M.A. Barrister-at-Law. 8vo. 16s.

A Dictionary of Political Economy; Biographical, Bibliographical, Historical, and Practical. By the same Author. Vol. I. royal 8vo. 30s.

Lord Bacon's Works, collected and edited by R. L. ELLIS, M.A. J. SPEDDING, M.A. and D. D. HEATH. VOLS. I. to V. Philosophical Works, 5 vols. 8vo. £4 6s. VOLS. VI. and VII. Literary and Professional Works, 2 vols. £1 16s.

Bacon's Essays, with Annotations. By R. WHATELY, D.D. late Archbishop of Dublin. Sixth Edition. 8vo. 10s. 6d.

Elements of Logic. By R. WHATELY, D.D. late Archbishop of Dublin. Ninth Edition. 8vo. 10s. 6d. crown 8vo. 4s. 6d.

Elements of Rhetoric. By the same Author. Seventh Edition. 8vo. 10s. 6d. crown 8vo. 4s. 6d.

English Synonymes. Edited by Archbishop WHATELY. 5th Edition. Fcp. 3s.

Miscellaneous Remains from the Common-place Book of RICHARD WHATELY, D.D. late Archbishop of Dublin. Edited by E. JANE WHATELY. Post 8vo. 7s. 6d.

Essays on the Administrations of Great Britain from 1783 to 1830. By the Right Hon. Sir G. C. LEWIS, Bart. Edited by the Right Hon. Sir E. HEAD, Bart. 8vo. with Portrait, 15s.

By the same Author.

Inquiry into the Credibility of the Early Roman History, 2 vols. 30s.

On the Methods of Observation and Reasoning in Politics, 2 vols. 28s.

Irish Disturbances and Irish Church Question, 12s.

Remarks on the Use and Abuse of some Political Terms, 9s.

The Fables of Babrius, Greek Text with Latin Notes, PART I. 5s. 6d. PART II. 3s. 6d.

An Outline of the Necessary Laws of Thought: a Treatise on Pure and Applied Logic. By the Most Rev. W. THOMSON, D.D. Archbishop of York. Crown 8vo. 5s. 6d.

The Elements of Logic. By THOMAS SHEDDEN, M.A. of St. Peter's Coll. Cantab. 12mo. 4s. 6d.

Analysis of Mr. Mill's System of Logic. By W. STEBBING, M.A. Second Edition. 12mo. 3s. 6d.

The Election of Representatives, Parliamentary and Municipal; a Treatise. By THOMAS HARE, Barrister-at-Law. Third Edition, with Additions. Crown 8vo. 6s.

Speeches on Parliamentary Reform. By the Right Hon. B. DISRAELI, M.P. Chancellor of the Exchequer. 1 vol. 8vo. [*Nearly ready.*

Speeches of the Right Hon. Lord MACAULAY, corrected by Himself. Library Edition, 8vo. 12s. People's Edition, crown 8vo. 3s. 6d.

Lord Macaulay's Speeches on Parliamentary Reform in 1831 and 1832. 16mo. 1s.

A Dictionary of the English Language. By R. G. LATHAM, M.A. M.D. F.R.S. Founded on the Dictionary of Dr. S. JOHNSON, as edited by the Rev. H. J. TODD, with numerous Emendations and Additions. Publishing in 36 Parts, price 3s. 6d. each, to form 2 vols. 4to. VOL. I. in Two Parts, now ready.

Thesaurus of English Words and Phrases, classified and arranged so as to facilitate the Expression of Ideas, and assist in Literary Composition. By P. M. ROGET, M.D. 18th Edition, crown 8vo. 10s. 6d.

Lectures on the Science of Language, delivered at the Royal Institution. By MAX MÜLLER, M.A. Taylorian Professor in the University of Oxford. FIRST SERIES, Fifth Edition, 12s. SECOND SERIES, 18s.

Chapters on Language. By F. W. FARRAR, M.A. F.R.S. late Fellow of Trin. Coll. Cambridge. Crown 8vo. 8s. 6d.

The Debater; a Series of Complete Debates, Outlines of Debates, and Questions for Discussion. By F. ROWTON. Fcp. 6s.

A Course of English Reading, adapted to every taste and capacity; or, How and What to Read. By the Rev. J. PYCROFT, B.A. Fourth Edition, fcp. 5s.

Manual of English Literature, Historical and Critical: with a Chapter on English Metres. By THOMAS ARNOLD, M.A. Second Edition. Crown 8vo. 7s. 6d.

Southey's Doctor, complete in One Volume. Edited by the Rev. J. W. WARTER, B.D. Square crown 8vo. 12s. 6d.

Historical and Critical Commentary on the Old Testament; with a New Translation. By M. M. KALISCH, Ph. D. VOL. I. *Genesis*, 8vo. 18s. or adapted for the General Reader, 12s. VOL. II. *Exodus*, 15s. or adapted for the General Reader, 12s.

A Hebrew Grammar, with Exercises. By the same. PART I. *Outlines with Exercises,* 8vo. 12s. 6d. KEY, 5s. PART II. *Exceptional Forms and Constructions,* 12s. 6d.

A Latin-English Dictionary. By J. T. WHITE, D.D. of Corpus Christi College, and J. E. RIDDLE, M.A. of St. Edmund Hall, Oxford. Imp. 8vo. pp. 2,128, price 42s.

A New Latin-English Dictionary, abridged from the larger work of *White* and *Riddle* (as above), by J. T. WHITE, D.D. Joint-Author. 8vo. pp. 1,048, price 18s.

The Junior Scholar's Latin-English Dictionary, abridged from the larger works of *White* and *Riddle* (as above), by J. T. WHITE, D.D. surviving Joint-Author. Square 12mo. pp. 662, price 7s. 6d.

An English-Greek Lexicon, containing all the Greek Words used by Writers of good authority. By C. D. YONGE, B.A. Fifth Edition. 4to. 21s.

Mr. Yonge's New Lexicon, English and Greek, abridged from his larger work (as above). Square 12mo. 8s. 6d.

A Greek-English Lexicon. Compiled by H. G. LIDDELL, D.D. Dean of Christ Church, and R. SCOTT, D.D. Master of Balliol. Fifth Edition, crown 4to. 31s. 6d.

A Lexicon, Greek and English, abridged from LIDDELL and SCOTT's *Greek-English Lexicon*. Eleventh Edition, square 12mo. 7s. 6d.

A Sanskrit-English Dictionary, The Sanskrit words printed both in the original Devanagari and in Roman letters; with References to the Best Editions of Sanskrit Authors, and with Etymologies and Comparisons of Cognate Words chiefly in Greek, Latin, Gothic, and Anglo-Saxon. Compiled by T. BENFEY. 8vo. 52s. 6d.

A Practical Dictionary of the French and English Languages. By L. CONTANSEAU. 11th Edition, post 8vo. 10s. 6d.

Contanseau's Pocket Dictionary, French and English, abridged from the above by the Author. New Edition, 18mo. price 3s. 6d.

New Practical Dictionary of the German Language; German-English, and English-German. By the Rev. W. L. BLACKLEY, M.A. and Dr. CARL MARTIN FRIEDLÄNDER. Post 8vo. 11s.

Miscellaneous Works and Popular Metaphysics.

Recreations of a Country Parson. By A. K. H. B. First Series, with 41 Woodcut Illustrations from Designs by R. T. Pritchett. Crown 8vo. 12s. 6d.

Recreations of a Country Parson. Second Series. Crown 8vo. 3s. 6d.

The Commonplace Philosopher in Town and Country. By the same Author. Crown 8vo. 3s. 6d.

Leisure Hours in Town; Essays Consolatory, Æsthetical, Moral, Social, and Domestic. By the same. Crown 8vo. 3s. 6d.

The Autumn Holidays of a Country Parson; Essays contributed to Fraser's Magazine and to Good Words. By the same. Crown 8vo. 3s. 6d.

The Graver Thoughts of a Country Parson, Second Series. By the same. Crown 8vo. 3s. 6d.

Critical Essays of a Country Parson, selected from Essays contributed to Fraser's Magazine. By the same. Post 8vo. 9s.

Sunday Afternoons at the Parish Church of a University City. By the same. Crown 8vo. 3s. 6d.

A Campaigner at Home. By Shirley, Author of 'Thalatta' and 'Nugæ Criticæ.' Post 8vo. with Vignette, 7s. 6d.

Studies in Parliament: a Series of Sketches of Leading Politicians. By R. H. Hutton. (Reprinted from the Pall Mall Gazette.) Crown 8vo. 4s. 6d.

Lord Macaulay's Miscellaneous Writings.
Library Edition, 2 vols. 8vo. Portrait, 21s.
People's Edition, 1 vol. crown 8vo. 4s. 6d.

The Rev. Sydney Smith's Miscellaneous Works; including his Contributions to the Edinburgh Review. People's Edition, 2 vols. crown 8vo. 8s.

Elementary Sketches of Moral Philosophy, delivered at the Royal Institution. By the same Author. Fcp. 8s.

The Wit and Wisdom of the Rev. Sydney Smith: a Selection of the most memorable Passages in his Writings and Conversation. 16mo. 5s.

Epigrams, Ancient and Modern: Humorous, Witty, Satirical, Moral, and Panegyrical. Edited by Rev. John Booth, B.A. Cambridge. Second Edition, revised and enlarged. Fcp. 7s. 6d.

The Folk-Lore of the Northern Counties of England and the Borders. By William Henderson. With an Appendix on Household Stories by the Rev. S. Baring-Gould. Crown 8vo. with Coloured Frontispiece, 9s. 6d.

From Matter to Spirit: the Result of Ten Years' Experience in Spirit Manifestations. By Sophia E. De Morgan. With a Preface by Professor De Morgan. Post 8vo. 8s. 6d.

Essays selected from Contributions to the Edinburgh Review. By Henry Rogers. Second Edition. 3 vols. fcp. 21s.

Reason and Faith, their Claims and Conflicts. By the same Author. New Edition, revised and extended, and accompanied by several other Essays, on related subjects. Crown 8vo. 6s. 6d.

The Eclipse of Faith; or, a Visit to a Religious Sceptic. By the same Author. Eleventh Edition. Fcp. 5s.

Defence of the Eclipse of Faith, by its Author. Third Edition. Fcp. 3s. 6d.

Selections from the Correspondence of R. E. H. Greyson. By the same Author. Third Edition. Crown 8vo. 7s. 6d.

Fulleriana, or the Wisdom and Wit of Thomas Fuller, with Essay on his Life and Genius. By the same Author. 16mo. 2s. 6d.

Occasional Essays. By Chandos Wren Hoskyns, Author of 'Talpa, or the Chronicles of a Clay Farm,' &c. 16mo. 5s. 6d.

An Essay on Human Nature; showing the Necessity of a Divine Revelation for the Perfect Development of Man's Capacities. By Henry S. Boase, M.D. F.R.S. and G.S. 8vo. 12s.

The Philosophy of Nature; a Systematic Treatise on the Causes and Laws of Natural Phenomena. By the same Author. 8vo. 12s.

The Secret of Hegel: being the Hegelian System in Origin, Principle, Form, and Matter. By James Hutchison Stirling. 2 vols. 8vo. 28s.

An Introduction to Mental Philosophy, on the Inductive Method. By J. D. Morell, M.A. LL.D. 8vo. 12s.

Elements of Psychology, containing the Analysis of the Intellectual Powers. By the same Author. Post 8vo. 7s. 6d.

NEW WORKS PUBLISHED BY LONGMANS AND CO.   7

Sight and Touch: an Attempt to Disprove the Received (or Berkeleian) Theory of Vision. By THOMAS K. ABBOTT, M.A. Fellow and Tutor of Trin. Coll. Dublin. 8vo. with 21 Woodcuts, 5s. 6d.

The Senses and the Intellect. By ALEXANDER BAIN, M.A. Prof. of Logic in the Univ. of Aberdeen. Second Edition. 8vo. 15s.

The Emotions and the Will, by the same Author. 8vo. 15s.

On the Study of Character, including an Estimate of Phrenology. By the same Author. 8vo. 9s.

Time and Space: a Metaphysical Essay. By SHADWORTH H. HODGSON. 8vo. pp. 588, price 16s.

The Way to Rest: Results from a Life-search after Religious Truth. By R. VAUGHAN, D.D. Crown 8vo. 7s. 6d.

Hours with the Mystics: a Contribution to the History of Religious Opinion. By ROBERT ALFRED VAUGHAN, B.A. Second Edition. 2 vols. crown 8vo. 12s.

The Philosophy of Necessity; or, Natural Law as applicable to Mental, Moral, and Social Science. By CHARLES BRAY. Second Edition. 8vo. 9s.

The Education of the Feelings and Affections. By the same Author. Third Edition. 8vo. 3s. 6d.

On Force, its Mental and Moral Correlates. By the same Author. 8vo. 5s.

Christianity and Common Sense. By Sir WILLOUGHBY JONES, Bart. M.A. Trin. Coll. Cantab. 8vo. 6s.

Astronomy, Meteorology, Popular Geography, &c.

Outlines of Astronomy. By Sir J. F. W. HERSCHEL, Bart. M.A. Eighth Edition, revised; with Plates and Woodcuts. 8vo. 18s.

Arago's Popular Astronomy. Translated by Admiral W. H. SMYTH, F.R.S. and R. GRANT, M.A. With 25 Plates and 358 Woodcuts. 2 vols. 8vo. £2 5s.

Saturn and its System. By RICHARD A. PROCTOR, B.A. late Scholar of St. John's Coll. Camb. and King's Coll. London. 8vo. with 14 Plates, 14s.

The Handbook of the Stars. By the same Author. Square fcp. 8vo. with 3 Maps, price 5s.

Celestial Objects for Common Telescopes. By T. W. WEBB, M.A. F.R.A.S. With Map of the Moon, and Woodcuts. 16mo. 7s.

A General Dictionary of Geography, Descriptive, Physical, Statistical, and Historical; forming a complete Gazetteer of the World. By A. KEITH JOHNSTON, F.R.S.E. 8vo. 31s. 6d.

M'Culloch's Dictionary, Geographical, Statistical, and Historical, of the various Countries, Places, and principal Natural Objects in the World. Revised Edition, with the Statistical Information throughout brought up to the latest returns. By FREDERICK MARTIN. 4 vols. 8vo. with coloured Maps, £4 4s.

A Manual of Geography, Physical, Industrial, and Political. By W. HUGHES, F.R.G.S. Prof. of Geog. in King's Coll. and in Queen's Coll. Lond. With 6 Maps. Fcp. 7s. 6d.

Hawaii; the Past, Present, and Future of its Island-Kingdom: an Historical Account of the Sandwich Islands. By MANLEY HOPKINS, Hawaiian Consul-General, &c. Second Edition, revised and continued; with Portrait, Map, and 8 other Illustrations. Post 8vo. 12s. 6d.

Maunder's Treasury of Geography, Physical, Historical, Descriptive, and Political. Edited by W. HUGHES, F.R.G.S. With 7 Maps and 16 Plates. Fcp. 10s. 6d.

Physical Geography for Schools and General Readers. By M. F. MAURY, LL.D. Fcp. with 2 Charts, 2s. 6d.

Natural History and Popular Science.

The Elements of Physics or Natural Philosophy. By NEIL ARNOTT, M.D. F.R.S. Physician Extraordinary to the Queen. Sixth Edition, rewritten and completed. 2 Parts, 8vo. 21s.

Volcanos, the Character of their Phenomena, their Share in the Structure and Composition of the Surface of the Globe, &c. By G. POULETT SCROPE, M.P. F.R.S. Second Edition. 8vo. with Illustrations, 15s.

Rocks Classified and Described. By BERNHARD VON COTTA. An English Edition, by P. H. LAWRENCE (with English, German, and French Synonymes), revised by the Author. Post 8vo. 14s.

⁎ Lithology, or a Classified Synopsis of the Names of Rocks and Minerals, also by Mr. LAWRENCE, adapted to the above work, may be had, price 5s. or printed on one side only (interpaged blank), for use in Cabinets, price 7s.

Sound: a Course of Six Lectures delivered at the Royal Institution of Great Britain. By Professor JOHN TYNDALL, LL.D. F.R.S. 1 vol. crown 8vo.
[*Nearly ready.*

Heat Considered as a Mode of Motion. By Professor JOHN TYNDALL, LL.D. F.R.S. Second Edition. Crown 8vo. with Woodcuts, 12s. 6d.

A Treatise on Electricity, in Theory and Practice. By A. DE LA RIVE, Prof. in the Academy of Geneva. Translated by C. V. WALKER, F.R.S. 3 vols. 8vo. with Woodcuts, £3 13s.

The Correlation of Physical Forces. By W. R. GROVE, Q.C. V.P.R.S. Fifth Edition, revised by the Author, and augmented by a Discourse on Continuity. 8vo.

Manual of Geology. By S. HAUGHTON, M.D. F.R.S. Fellow of Trin. Coll. and Prof. of Geol. in the Univ. of Dublin. Second Edition, with 66 Woodcuts. Fcp. 7s. 6d.

A Guide to Geology. By J. PHILLIPS, M.A. Prof. of Geol. in the Univ. of Oxford. Fifth Edition. Fcp. 4s.

A Glossary of Mineralogy. By H. W. BRISTOW, F.G.S. of the Geological Survey of Great Britain. With 486 Figures. Crown 8vo. 12s.

The Elements: an Investigation of the Forces which determine the Position and Movements of the Ocean and Atmosphere. By WILLIAM LEIGHTON JORDAN. VOL. I. royal 8vo. with 13 maps, price 8s.

Phillips's Elementary Introduction to Mineralogy, re-edited by H. J. BROOKE, F.R.S. and W. H. MILLER, F.G.S. Post 8vo. with Woodcuts, 18s.

Van Der Hoeven's Handbook of Zoology. Translated from the Second Dutch Edition by the Rev. W. CLARK, M.D. F.R.S. 2 vols. 8vo. with 24 Plates of Figures, 60s.

The Comparative Anatomy and Physiology of the Vertebrate Animals. By RICHARD OWEN, F.R.S. D.C.L. 3 vols. 8vo. with upwards of 1,700 Woodcuts. VOLS. I. and II. price 21s. each, now ready. VOL. III. in the Spring.

The First Man and His Place in Creation, considered on the Principles of Common Sense from a Christian Point of View; with an Appendix on the Negro. By GEORGE MOORE, M.D. M.R.C.P.L. &c. Post 8vo. 8s. 6d.

The Lake Dwellings of Switzerland and other Parts of Europe. By Dr. F. KELLER, President of the Antiquarian Association of Zürich. Translated and arranged by J. E. LEE, F.S.A. F.G.S. Author of 'Isca Silurum.' With several Woodcuts and nearly 100 Plates of Figures. Royal 8vo. 31s. 6d.

Homes without Hands: a Description of the Habitations of Animals, classed according to their Principle of Construction. By Rev. J. G. WOOD, M.A. F.L.S. With about 140 Vignettes on Wood (20 full size of page). Second Edition. 8vo. 21s.

The Harmonies of Nature and Unity of Creation. By Dr. G. HARTWIG. 8vo. with numerous Illustrations, 18s.

The Sea and Its Living Wonders. By the same Author. Third Edition, enlarged. 8vo. with many Illustrations, 21s.

The Tropical World. By the same Author. With 8 Chromoxylographs and 172 Woodcuts. 8vo. 21s.

Manual of Corals and Sea Jellies. By J. R. GREENE, B.A. Edited by J. A. GALBRAITH, M.A. and S. HAUGHTON, M.D. Fcp. with 39 Woodcuts, 5s.

Manual of Sponges and Animalcule; with a General Introduction on the Principles of Zoology. By the same Author and Editors. Fcp. with 16 Woodcuts, 2s.

Manual of the Metalloids. By J. APJOHN, M.D. F.R.S. and the same Editors. 2nd Edition. Fcp. with 38 Woodcuts, 7s. 6d.

Sketches of the Natural History of Ceylon. By Sir J. EMERSON TENNENT, K.C.S. LL.D. With 82 Wood Engravings. Post 8vo. 12s. 6d.

Ceylon. By the same Author, 5th Edition; with Maps, &c. and 90 Wood Engravings. 2 vols. 8vo. £2 10s.

The Wild Elephant, Its Structure and Habits, with the Method of Taking and Training It in Ceylon. By the same Author. Fcp. 8vo. with Illustrations.

A Familiar History of Birds. By E. STANLEY, D.D. late Lord Bishop of Norwich. Fcp. with Woodcuts, 3s. 6d.

Kirby and Spence's Introduction to Entomology, or Elements of the Natural History of Insects. Crown 8vo. 5s.

Maunder's Treasury of Natural History, or Popular Dictionary of Zoology. Revised and corrected by T. S. COBBOLD, M.D. Fcp. with 900 Woodcuts, 10s.

The Elements of Botany for Families and Schools. Tenth Edition, revised by THOMAS MOORE, F.L.S. Fcp. with 154 Woodcuts, 2s. 6d.

The Treasury of Botany, or Popular Dictionary of the Vegetable Kingdom; with which is incorporated a Glossary of Botanical Terms. Edited by J. LINDLEY, F.R.S. and T. MOORE, F.L.S. assisted by eminent Contributors. Pp. 1,274, with 274 Woodcuts and 20 Steel Plates. 2 Parts, fcp. 20s.

The British Flora; comprising the Phænogamous or Flowering Plants and the Ferns. By Sir W. J. HOOKER, K.H. and G. A. WALKER-ARNOTT, LL.D. 12mo. with 12 Plates, 14s. or coloured, 21s.

The Rose Amateur's Guide. By THOMAS RIVERS. New Edition. Fcp. 4s.

The Indoor Gardener. By Miss MALING. Fcp. with Frontispiece, 5s.

Loudon's Encyclopædia of Plants; comprising the Specific Character, Description, Culture, History, &c. of all the Plants found in Great Britain. With upwards of 12,000 Woodcuts. 8vo. 42s.

Loudon's Encyclopædia of Trees and Shrubs; containing the Hardy Trees and Shrubs of Great Britain scientifically and popularly described. With 2,000 Woodcuts. 8vo. 50s.

Bryologia Britannica; containing the Mosses of Great Britain and Ireland, arranged and described. By W. WILSON. 8vo. with 61 Plates, 42s. or coloured, £4 4s.

Maunder's Scientific and Literary Treasury; a Popular Encyclopædia of Science, Literature, and Art. New Edition, thoroughly revised and in great part rewritten, with above 1,000 new articles, by J. Y. JOHNSON, Corr. M.Z.S. Fcp. 10s. 6d.

A Dictionary of Science, Literature, and Art. Fourth Edition, re-edited by the late W. T. BRANDE (the Author) and GEORGE W. COX, M.A. 3 vols. medium 8vo, price 63s. cloth.

Essays on Scientific and other subjects, contributed to Reviews. By Sir H. HOLLAND, Bart. M.D. Second Edition. 8vo. 14s.

Essays from the Edinburgh and Quarterly Reviews; with Addresses and other Pieces. By Sir J. F. W. HERSCHEL, Bart. M.A. 8vo. 18s.

Chemistry, Medicine, Surgery, and the Allied Sciences.

A Dictionary of Chemistry and the Allied Branches of other Sciences. By HENRY WATTS, F.C.S. assisted by eminent Contributors. 5 vols. medium 8vo. in course of publication in Parts. VOL. I. 31s. 6d. VOL. II. 26s. VOL. III. 31s. 6d. and VOL. IV. 24s. are now ready.

A Handbook of Volumetrical Analysis. By ROBERT H. SCOTT, M.A. T.C.D. Post 8vo. 4s. 6d.

Elements of Chemistry, Theoretical and Practical. By WILLIAM A. MILLER, M.D. LL.D. F.R.S. F.G.S. Professor of Chemistry, King's College, London. 3 vols. 8vo. £2 13s. PART I. CHEMICAL PHYSICS, Third Edition, 12s. PART II. INORGANIC CHEMISTRY, 21s. PART III. ORGANIC CHEMISTRY, Third Edition, 24s.

A Manual of Chemistry, Descriptive and Theoretical. By WILLIAM ODLING, M.B. F.R.S. PART I. 8vo. 9s.

A Course of Practical Chemistry, for the use of Medical Students. By the same Author. Second Edition, with 70 new Woodcuts. Crown 8vo. 7s. 6d.

Lectures on Animal Chemistry Delivered at the Royal College of Physicians in 1865. By the same Author. Crown 8vo. 4s. 6d.

The Toxicologist's Guide: a New Manual on Poisons, giving the Best Methods to be pursued for the Detection of Poisons. By J. HORSLEY, F.C.S. Analytical Chemist. Post 8vo. 3s. 6d.

The Diagnosis and Treatment of the Diseases of Women; including the Diagnosis of Pregnancy. By GRAILY HEWITT, M.D. &c. New Edition, with Woodcut Illustrations. In the press.

Lectures on the Diseases of Infancy and Childhood. By CHARLES WEST, M.D. &c. 5th Edition, revised and enlarged. 8vo. 16s.

Exposition of the Signs and Symptoms of Pregnancy; with other Papers on subjects connected with Midwifery. By W. F. MONTGOMERY, M.A. M.D. M.R.I.A. 8vo. with Illustrations, 25s.

A System of Surgery, Theoretical and Practical, in Treatises by Various Authors. Edited by T. HOLMES, M.A. Cantab. Assistant-Surgeon to St. George's Hospital. 4 vols. 8vo. £4 13s.

Vol. I. General Pathology, 21s.

Vol. II. Local Injuries: Gun-shot Wounds, Injuries of the Head, Back, Face, Neck, Chest, Abdomen, Pelvis, of the Upper and Lower Extremities, and Diseases of the Eye. 21s.

Vol. III. Operative Surgery. Diseases of the Organs of Circulation, Locomotion, &c. 21s.

Vol. IV. Diseases of the Organs of Digestion, of the Genito-Urinary System, and of the Breast, Thyroid Gland, and Skin; with APPENDIX and GENERAL INDEX, 30s.

Lectures on the Principles and Practice of Physic. By THOMAS WATSON, M.D. Physician-Extraordinary to the Queen. Fourth Edition. 2 vols. 8vo. 31s.

Lectures on Surgical Pathology. By J. PAGET, F.R.S. Surgeon-Extraordinary to the Queen. Edited by W. TURNER, M.D. 8vo. with 117 Woodcuts, 21s.

A Treatise on the Continued Fevers of Great Britain. By C. MURCHISON, M.D. Senior Physician to the London Fever Hospital. 8vo. with coloured Plates, 18s.

Anatomy, Descriptive and Surgical. By HENRY GRAY, F.R.S. With 410 Wood Engravings from Dissections. Fourth Edition, by T. HOLMES, M.A. Cantab. Royal 8vo. 28s.

The Cyclopædia of Anatomy and Physiology. Edited by the late R. B. TODD, M.D. F.R.S. Assisted by nearly all the most eminent cultivators of Physiological Science of the present age. 5 vols. 8vo. with 2,853 Woodcuts, £6 6s.

Physiological Anatomy and Physiology of Man. By the late R. B. TODD, M.D. F.R.S. and W. BOWMAN, F.R.S. of King's College. With numerous Illustrations. Vol. II. 8vo. 25s.

Vol. I. New Edition by Dr. LIONEL S. BEALE, F.R.S. in course of publication; PART I. with 8 Plates, 7s. 6d.

Histological Demonstrations; a Guide to the Microscopical Examination of the Animal Tissues in Health and Disease, for the use of the Medical and Veterinary Professions. By G. HARLEY, M.D. F.R.S. Prof. in Univ. Coll. London; and G. T. BROWN, M.R.C.V.S. Professor of Veterinary Medicine, and one of the Inspecting Officers in the Cattle Plague Department of the Privy Council. Post 8vo. with 223 Woodcuts, 12s.

A Dictionary of Practical Medicine. By J. COPLAND, M.D. F.R.S. Abridged from the larger work by the Author, assisted by J. C. COPLAND, M.R.C.S. and throughout brought down to the present state of Medical Science. Pp. 1,560, in 8vo. price 36s.

The Works of Sir B. C. Brodie, Bart. collected and arranged by CHARLES HAWKINS, F.R.C.S.E. 3 vols. 8vo. with Medallion and Facsimile, 48s.

Autobiography of Sir B. C. Brodie, Bart. printed from the Author's materials left in MS. Second Edition. Fcp. 4s. 6d.

A Manual of Materia Medica and Therapeutics, abridged from Dr. PEREIRA's Elements by F. J. FARRE, M.D. assisted by R. BENTLEY, M.R.C.S. and by R. WARINGTON, F.R.S. 1 vol. 8vo. with 90 Woodcuts, 21s.

Dr. Pereira's Elements of Materia Medica and Therapeutics. Third Edition, by A. S. TAYLOR, M.D. and G. O. REES, M.D. 3 vols. 8vo. with Woodcuts, £3 15s.

Thomson's Conspectus of the British Pharmacopœia. Twenty-fourth Edition, corrected and made conformable throughout to the New Pharmacopœia of the General Council of Medical Education. By E. LLOYD BIRKETT, M.D. 18mo. 5s. 6d.

Manual of the Domestic Practice of Medicine. By W. B. KESTEVEN, F.R.C.S.E. Second Edition, thoroughly revised, with Additions. Fcp. 5s.

Sea-Air and Sea-Bathing for Children and Invalids. By WILLIAM STRANGE. M.D. Fcp. 3s.

The Restoration of Health; or, the Application of the Laws of Hygiene to the Recovery of Health: a Manual for the Invalid, and a Guide to the Sick Room. By W. Strange, M.D. Fcp. 6s.

Manual for the Classification, Training, and Education of the Feeble-Minded, Imbecile, and Idiotic. By P. Martin Duncan, M.B. and William Millard. Crown 8vo. 5s.

The Fine Arts, and Illustrated Editions.

The Life of Man Symbolised by the Months of the Year in their Seasons and Phases; with Passages selected from Ancient and Modern Authors. By Richard Pigot. Accompanied by a Series of 25 full-page Illustrations and numerous Marginal Devices, Decorative Initial Letters, and Tailpieces, engraved on Wood from Original Designs by John Leighton, F.S.A. 4to. 42s.

The New Testament, Illustrated with Wood Engravings after the Early Masters, chiefly of the Italian School. Crown 4to. 63s. cloth, gilt top; or £5 5s. morocco.

Lyra Germanica; Hymns for the Sundays and Chief Festivals of the Christian Year. Translated by Catherine Winkworth; 125 Illustrations on Wood drawn by J. Leighton, F.S.A. Fcp. 4to 21s.

Cats' and Farlie's Moral Emblems; with Aphorisms, Adages, and Proverbs of all Nations; comprising 121 Illustrations on Wood by J. Leighton, F.S.A. with an appropriate Text by R. Pigot. Imperial 8vo. 31s. 6d.

Shakspeare's Sentiments and Similes printed in Black and Gold, and Illuminated in the Missal style by Henry Noel Humphreys. In massive covers, containing the Medallion and Cypher of Shakspeare. Square post 8vo. 21s.

Half-Hour Lectures on the History and Practice of the Fine and Ornamental Arts. By W. B. Scott. Second Edition. Crown 8vo. with 50 Woodcut Illustrations, 8s. 6d.

The History of Our Lord, as exemplified in Works of Art. By Mrs. Jameson and Lady Eastlake. Being the concluding Series of 'Sacred and Legendary Art.' Second Edition, with 13 Etchings and 281 Woodcuts. 2 vols. square crown 8vo. 42s.

Mrs. Jameson's Legends of the Saints and Martyrs. Fourth Edition, with 19 Etchings and 187 Woodcuts. 2 vols. 31s. 6d.

Mrs. Jameson's Legends of the Monastic Orders. Third Edition, with 11 Etchings and 88 Woodcuts. 1 vol. 21s.

Mrs. Jameson's Legends of the Madonna. Third Edition, with 27 Etchings and 165 Woodcuts. 1 vol. 21s.

Musical Publications.

An Introduction to the Study of National Music; Comprising Researches into Popular Songs, Traditions, and Customs. By Carl Engel, Author of 'The Music of the most Ancient Nations.' With Frontispiece and numerous Musical Illustrations. 8vo. 16s.

Six Lectures on Harmony. Delivered at the Royal Institution of Great Britain before Easter 1867. By G. A. Macfarren. 8vo. [In the press.

Lectures on the History of Modern Music, delivered at the Royal Institution. By John Hullah. First Course, with Chronological Tables, post 8vo. 6s. 6d. Second Course, the Transition Period, with 26 Specimens, 8vo. 16s.

Sacred Music for Family Use; A Selection of Pieces for One, Two, or more Voices, from the best Composers, Foreign and English. Edited by John Hullah. 1 vol. music folio, 21s. half bound.

Hullah's Part Music, Sacred and Secular, for Soprano, Alto, Tenor, and Bass. New Edition, with Pianoforte Accompaniments, in course of publication in Monthly Numbers, each number in Score, with Pianoforte Accompaniment, price 1s. and in separate Parts (Soprano, Alto, Tenor, and Bass), uniform with the Score in size, but in larger type, price 3d. each Part. Each Series (Sacred and Secular) to be completed in 12 Numbers, forming a Volume, in imperial 8vo.

Arts, Manufactures, &c.

Drawing from Nature; a Series of Progressive Instructions in Sketching, from Elementary Studies to Finished Views, with Examples from Switzerland and the Pyrenees. By GEORGE BARNARD, Professor of Drawing at Rugby School. With 18 Lithographic Plates and 108 Wood Engravings. Imp. 8vo. 25s.

Gwilt's Encyclopædia of Architecture. New Edition, revised, with alterations and considerable Additions, by WYATT PAPWORTH. With above 850 New Engravings and Diagrams on Wood by O. JEWITT, and upwards of 100 other Woodcuts. 8vo. [*Nearly ready.*

Tuscan Sculptors, their Lives, Works, and Times. With 45 Etchings and 28 Woodcuts from Original Drawings and Photographs. By CHARLES C. PERKINS. 2 vols. Imp. 8vo. 63s.

The Grammar of Heraldry; containing a Description of all the Principal Charges used in Armory, the Signification of Heraldic Terms, and the Rules to be observed in Blazoning and Marshalling. By JOHN E. CUSSANS. Fcp. with 196 Woodcuts, 4s. 6d.

The Engineer's Handbook; explaining the Principles which should guide the young Engineer in the Construction of Machinery. By C. S. LOWNDES. Post 8vo. 5s.

The Elements of Mechanism. By T. M. GOODEVE, M.A. Prof. of Mechanics at the R. M. Acad. Woolwich. Second Edition, with 217 Woodcuts. Post 8vo. 6s. 6d.

Ure's Dictionary of Arts, Manufactures, and Mines. Re-written and enlarged by ROBERT HUNT, F.R.S., assisted by numerous Contributors eminent in Science and the Arts. With 2,000 Woodcuts. 3 vols. 8vo. [*Nearly ready.*

Treatise on Mills and Millwork. By W. FAIRBAIRN, C.E. F.R.S. With 18 Plates and 322 Woodcuts. 2 vols. 8vo. 32s.

Useful Information for Engineers. By the same Author. FIRST, SECOND, and THIRD SERIES, with many Plates and Woodcuts. 3 vols. crown 8vo. 10s. 6d. each.

The Application of Cast and Wrought Iron to Building Purposes. By the same Author. Third Edition, with 6 Plates and 118 Woodcuts. 8vo. 16s.

Iron Ship Building, its History and Progress, as comprised in a Series of Experimental Researches on the Laws of Strain; the Strengths, Forms, and other conditions of the Material; and an Inquiry into the Present and Prospective State of the Navy, including the Experimental Results on the Resisting Powers of Armour Plates and Shot at High Velocities. By W. FAIRBAIRN, C.E. F.R.S. With 4 Plates and 130 Woodcuts, 8vo. 18s.

Encyclopædia of Civil Engineering, Historical, Theoretical, and Practical. By E. CRESY, C.E. With above 3,000 Woodcuts. 8vo. 42s.

The Practical Mechanic's Journal: An Illustrated Record of Mechanical and Engineering Science, and Epitome of Patent Inventions. 4to. price 1s. monthly.

The Practical Draughtsman's Book of Industrial Design. By W. JOHNSON, Assoc. Inst. C.E. With many hundred Illustrations. 4to. 28s. 6d.

The Patentee's Manual: a Treatise on the Law and Practice of Letters Patent for the use of Patentees and Inventors. By J. and J. H. JOHNSON. Post 8vo. 7s. 6d.

The Artisan Club's Treatise on the Steam Engine, in its various Applications to Mines, Mills, Steam Navigation, Railways, and Agriculture. By J. BOURNE. C.E. Seventh Edition; with 37 Plates and 546 Woodcuts. 4to. 42s.

A Treatise on the Screw Propeller, Screw Vessels, and Screw Engines, as adapted for purposes of Peace and War; illustrated by many Plates and Woodcuts. By the same Author. New and enlarged Edition in course of publication in 24 Parts, royal 4to. 2s. 6d. each.

Catechism of the Steam Engine, in its various Applications to Mines, Mills, Steam Navigation, Railways, and Agriculture. By J. BOURNE. C.E. With 199 Woodcuts. Fcp. 9s. The INTRODUCTION of 'Recent Improvements' may be had separately, with 110 Woodcuts, price 3s. 6d.

Handbook of the Steam Engine, by the same Author, forming a KEY to the Catechism of the Steam Engine, with 67 Woodcuts. Fcp. 9s.

The Art of Perfumery; the History and Theory of Odours, and the Methods of Extracting the Aromas of Plants. By Dr. Piesse, F.C.S. Third Edition, with 53 Woodcuts. Crown 8vo. 10s. 6d.

Chemical, Natural, and Physical Magic, for Juveniles during the Holidays. By the same Author. Third Edition, enlarged with 38 Woodcuts. Fcp. 6s.

Talpa; or, the Chronicles of a Clay Farm. By C. W. Hoskyns, Esq. With 24 Woodcuts from Designs by G. Cruikshank. Sixth Edition. 16mo. 5s. 6d.

History of Windsor Great Park and Windsor Forest. By WILLIAM MENZIES, Resident Deputy Surveyor. With 2 Maps and 20 Photographs. Imp. folio, £8 8s.

Loudon's Encyclopædia of Agriculture: Comprising the Laying-out, Improvement, and Management of Landed Property, and the Cultivation and Economy of the Productions of Agriculture. With 1,100 Woodcuts. 8vo. 31s. 6d.

Loudon's Encyclopædia of Gardening: Comprising the Theory and Practice of Horticulture, Floriculture, Arboriculture, and Landscape Gardening. With 1,000 Woodcuts. 8vo. 31s. 6d.

Loudon's Encyclopædia of Cottage, Farm, and Villa Architecture and Furniture. With more than 2,000 Woodcuts. 8vo. 42s.

Bayldon's Art of Valuing Rents and Tillages, and Claims of Tenants upon Quitting Farms, both at Michaelmas and Lady-Day. Eighth Edition, revised by J. C. Morton. 8vo. 10s. 6d.

Religious and *Moral Works*.

An Exposition of the 39 Articles, Historical and Doctrinal. By E. HAROLD BROWNE, D.D. Lord Bishop of Ely. Seventh Edition. 8vo. 16s.

The Pentateuch and the Elohistic Psalms, in Reply to Bishop Colenso. By the same. Second Edition. 8vo. 2s.

Examination-Questions on Bishop Browne's Exposition of the Articles. By the Rev. J. GORLE, M.A. Fcp. 3s. 6d.

The Acts of the Apostles; with a Commentary, and Practical and Devotional Suggestions for Readers and Students of the English Bible. By the Rev. F. C. Cook, M.A., Canon of Exeter, &c. New Edition. 8vo. 12s. 6d.

The Life and Epistles of St. Paul. By W. J. CONYBEARE, M.A. late Fellow of Trin. Coll. Cantab. and J. S. HOWSON, D.D. Principal of Liverpool Coll.

LIBRARY EDITION, with all the Original Illustrations, Maps, Landscapes on Steel, Woodcuts, &c. 2 vols. 4to. 48s.

INTERMEDIATE EDITION, with a Selection of Maps, Plates, and Woodcuts. 2 vols. square crown 8vo. 31s. 6d.

PEOPLE'S EDITION, revised and condensed, with 46 Illustrations and Maps. 2 vols. crown 8vo. 12s.

The Voyage and Shipwreck of St. Paul; with Dissertations on the Ships and Navigation of the Ancients. By JAMES SMITH, F.R.S. Crown 8vo. Charts, 10s. 6d.

Fasti Sacri, or a Key to the Chronology of the New Testament; comprising an Historical Harmony of the Four Gospels, and Chronological Tables generally from B.C. 70 to A.D. 70: with a Preliminary Dissertation and other Aids. By THOMAS LEWIN, M.A. F.S.A. Imp. 8vo. 42s.

A Critical and Grammatical Commentary on St. Paul's Epistles. By C. J. ELLICOTT, D.D. Lord Bishop of Gloucester and Bristol. 8vo.

Galatians, Third Edition, 8s. 6d.
Ephesians, Third Edition, 8s. 6d.
Pastoral Epistles, Third Edition, 10s. 6d.
Philippians, Colossians, and Philemon, Third Edition, 10s. 6d.
Thessalonians, Second Edition, 7s. 6d.

Historical Lectures on the Life of Our Lord Jesus Christ: being the Hulsean Lectures for 1859. By the same Author. Fourth Edition. 8vo. 10s. 6d.

The Destiny of the Creature; and other Sermons preached before the University of Cambridge. By the same. Post 8vo. 5s.

The Broad and the Narrow Way; Two Sermons preached before the University of Cambridge. By the same. Crown 8vo. 2s.

The Greek Testament; with Notes, Grammatical and Exegetical. By the Rev. W. WEBSTER, M.A. and the Rev. W. F. WILKINSON, M.A. 2 vols. 8vo. £2 4s.

Vol. I. the Gospels and Acts, 20s.
Vol. II. the Epistles and Apocalypse, 24s.

Rev. T. H. Horne's Introduction to the Critical Study and Knowledge of the Holy Scriptures. Eleventh Edition, corrected, and extended under careful Editorial revision. With 4 Maps and 22 Woodcuts and Facsimiles. 4 vols. 8vo. £3 13s. 6d.

Rev. T. H. Horne's Compendious Introduction to the Study of the Bible, being an Analysis of the larger work by the same Author. Re-edited by the Rev. John Ayre, M.A. With Maps, &c. Post 8vo. 9s.

The Treasury of Bible Knowledge; being a Dictionary of the Books, Persons, Places, Events, and other Matters of which mention is made in Holy Scripture; intended to establish its Authority and illustrate its Contents. By Rev. J. Ayre, M.A. With Maps, 15 Plates, and numerous Woodcuts. Fcp. 10s. 6d.

Every-day Scripture Difficulties explained and illustrated. By J. E. Prescott, M.A. Vol. I. *Matthew and Mark*; Vol. II. *Luke and John*. 2 vols. 8vo. 9s. each.

The Pentateuch and Book of Joshua Critically Examined. By the Right Rev. J. W. Colenso, D.D. Lord Bishop of Natal. People's Edition, in 1 vol. crown 8vo. 6s. or in 5 Parts, 1s. each.

The Pentateuch and Book of Joshua Critically Examined. By Prof. A. Kuenen, of Leyden. Translated from the Dutch, and edited with Notes, by the Right Rev. J. W. Colenso, D.D. Bishop of Natal. 8vo. 8s. 6d.

The Church and the World: Essays on Questions of the Day. By various Writers. Edited by Rev. Orby Shipley, M.A. Second Edition, revised. 8vo. 15s.

The Formation of Christendom. Part I. By T. W. Allies. 8vo. 12s.

Christendom's Divisions; a Philosophical Sketch of the Divisions of the Christian Family in East and West. By Edmund S. Ffoulkes, formerly Fellow and Tutor of Jesus Coll. Oxford. Post 8vo. 7s. 6d.

Christendom's Divisions, Part II. *Greeks and Latins*, being a History of their Dissensions and Overtures for Peace down to the Reformation. By the same Author. [*Nearly ready.*]

The Life of Christ, an Eclectic Gospel, from the Old and New Testaments, arranged on a New Principle, with Analytical Tables, &c. By Charles De La Pryme, M.A. Revised Edition. 8vo. 5s.

The Hidden Wisdom of Christ and the Key of Knowledge; or, History of the Apocrypha. By Ernest De Bunsen. 2 vols. 8vo. 28s.

The Temporal Mission of the Holy Ghost; or, Reason and Revelation. By the Most Rev. Archbishop Manning. Second Edition. Crown 8vo. 8s. 6d.

Essays on Religion and Literature. Edited by the Most Rev. Archbishop Manning. 8vo. 10s. 6d.

Essays and Reviews. By the Rev. W. Temple, D.D. the Rev. R. Williams, B.D. the Rev. B. Powell, M.A. the Rev. H. B. Wilson, B.D. C. W. Goodwin, M.A. the Rev. M. Pattison, B.D. and the Rev. B. Jowett, M.A. 12th Edition. Fcp. 5s.

Mosheim's Ecclesiastical History. Murdock and Soames's Translation and Notes, re-edited by the Rev. W. Stubbs, M.A. 3 vols. 8vo. 45s.

Bishop Jeremy Taylor's Entire Works: With Life by Bishop Heber. Revised and corrected by the Rev. C. P. Eden, 10 vols. £5 5s.

Passing Thoughts on Religion. By the Author of 'Amy Herbert.' New Edition. Fcp. 5s.

Thoughts for the Holy Week, for Young Persons. By the same Author. Third Edition. Fcp. 8vo. 2s.

Self-examination before Confirmation. By the same Author. 32mo. 1s. 6d.

Readings for a Month Preparatory to Confirmation from Writers of the Early and English Church. By the same. Fcp. 4s.

Readings for Every Day in Lent, compiled from the Writings of Bishop Jeremy Taylor. By the same. Fcp. 5s.

Preparation for the Holy Communion; the Devotions chiefly from the works of Jeremy Taylor. By the same. 32mo. 3s.

Principles of Education drawn from Nature and Revelation, and Applied to Female Education in the Upper Classes. By the same. 2 vols. fcp. 12s. 6d.

The Wife's Manual; or, Prayers, Thoughts, and Songs on Several Occasions of a Matron's Life. By the Rev. W. Calvert, M.A. Crown 8vo. 10s. 6d.

Lyra Domestica; Christian Songs for Domestic Edification. Translated from the *Psaltery and Harp* of C. J. P. Spitta, and from other sources, by Richard Massie. First and Second Series, fcp. 4s. 6d. each.

Spiritual Songs for the Sundays and Holidays throughout the Year. By J. S. B. MONSELL, LL.D. Vicar of Egham. Fourth Edition. Fcp. 4s. 6d.

The Beatitudes: Abasement before God; Sorrow for Sin; Meekness of Spirit; Desire for Holiness; Gentleness; Purity of Heart; the Peace-makers; Sufferings for Christ. By the same. Third Edition. Fcp. 3s. 6d.

Lyra Sacra; Hymns, Ancient and Modern, Odes, and Fragments of Sacred Poetry. Edited by the Rev. B. W. SAVILE, M.A. Third Edition, enlarged. Fcp. 5s.

Lyra Germanica, translated from the German by Miss C. WINKWORTH. FIRST SERIES, Hymns for the Sundays and Chief Festivals; SECOND SERIES, the Christian Life. Fcp. 3s. 6d. each SERIES.

Hymns from Lyra Germanica. 18mo. 1s.

The Chorale Book for England; a complete Hymn-Book in accordance with the Services and Festivals of the Church of England; the Hymns translated by Miss C. WINKWORTH; the Tunes arranged by Prof. W. S. BENNETT and OTTO GOLDSCHMIDT. Fcp. 4to. 12s. 6d.

Congregational Edition. Fcp. 2s.

Lyra Eucharistica; Hymns and Verses on the Holy Communion, Ancient and Modern; with other Poems. Edited by the Rev. ORBY SHIPLEY, M.A. Second Edition. Fcp. 7s. 6d.

Lyra Messianica; Hymns and Verses on the Life of Christ, Ancient and Modern; with other Poems. By the same Editor. Second Edition, enlarged. Fcp. 7s. 6d.

Lyra Mystica; Hymns and Verses on Sacred Subjects, Ancient and Modern. By the same Editor. Fcp. 7s. 6d.

The Catholic Doctrine of the Atonement; an Historical Inquiry into its Development in the Church; with an Introduction on the Principle of Theological Developments. By H. N. OXENHAM, M.A. formerly Scholar of Balliol College, Oxford. 8vo. 8s. 6d.

From Sunday to Sunday; an Attempt to consider familiarly the Weekday Life and Labours of a Country Clergyman. By R. GEE, M.A. Fcp. 5s.

Our Sermons: an Attempt to consider familiarly, but reverently, the Preacher's Work in the present day. By the same Author. Fcp. 6s.

Paley's Moral Philosophy, with Annotations. By RICHARD WHATELY, D.D. late Archbishop of Dublin. 8vo. 7s.

Travels, Voyages, &c.

Ice Caves of France and Switzerland; a narrative of Subterranean Exploration. By the Rev. G. F. BROWNE, M.A. Fellow and Assistant-Tutor of St. Catharine's Coll. Cambridge, M.A.C. With 11 Woodcuts. Square crown 8vo. 12s. 6d.

Village Life in Switzerland. By SOPHIA D. DELMARD. Post 8vo. 9s. 6d.

How we Spent the Summer; or, a Voyage en Zigzag in Switzerland and Tyrol with some Members of the ALPINE CLUB. From the Sketch-Book of one of the Party. Third Edition, re-drawn. In oblong 4to. with about 300 Illustrations, 15s.

Beaten Tracks; or, Pen and Pencil Sketches in Italy. By the Authoress of 'A Voyage en Zigzag.' With 42 Plates, containing about 200 Sketches from Drawings made on the Spot. 8vo. 16s.

Map of the Chain of Mont Blanc, from an actual Survey in 1863—1864. By A. ADAMS-REILLY, F.R.G.S. M.A.C. Published under the Authority of the Alpine Club. In Chromolithography on extra stout drawing-paper 28in. x 17in. price 10s. or mounted on canvas in a folding case, 12s. 6d.

Transylvania, its Products and its People. By CHARLES BONER. With 5 Maps and 43 Illustrations on Wood and in Chromolithography. 8vo. 21s.

Explorations in South-west Africa, from Walvisch Bay to Lake Ngami and the Victoria Falls. By THOMAS BAINES, F.R.G.S. 8vo. with Maps and Illustrations, 21s.

Vancouver Island and British Columbia; their History, Resources, and Prospects. By MATTHEW MACFIE, F.R.G.S. With Maps and Illustrations. 8vo. 18s.

History of Discovery in our Australasian Colonies, Australia, Tasmania, and New Zealand, from the Earliest Date to the Present Day. By WILLIAM HOWITT. With 3 Maps of the Recent Explorations from Official Sources. 2 vols. 8vo. 20s.

The Capital of the Tycoon; a Narrative of a 3 Years' Residence in Japan. By Sir RUTHERFORD ALCOCK, K.C.B. 2 vols. 8vo. with numerous Illustrations, 42s.

Florence, the New Capital of Italy. By C. R. WELD. With several Engravings on Wood, from Drawings by the Author. Post 8vo.

The Dolomite Mountains. Excursions through Tyrol, Carinthia, Carniola, and Friuli in 1861, 1862, and 1863. By J. GILBERT and G. C. CHURCHILL, F.R.G.S. With numerous Illustrations. Square crown 8vo. 21s.

A Lady's Tour Round Monte Rosa; including Visits to the Italian Valleys. With Map and Illustrations. Post 8vo. 14s.

Guide to the Pyrenees, for the use of Mountaineers. By CHARLES PACKE. With Maps, &c. and Appendix. Fcp. 6s.

A Guide to Spain. By H. O'SHEA. Post 8vo. with Travelling Map, 15s.

Christopher Columbus; his Life, Voyages, and Discoveries. Revised Edition, with 4 Woodcuts. 18mo. 2s. 6d.

Captain James Cook; his Life, Voyages, and Discoveries. Revised Edition, with numerous Woodcuts. 18mo. 2s. 6d.

The Alpine Guide. By JOHN BALL, M.R.I.A. late President of the Alpine Club. Post 8vo. with Maps and other Illustrations.

Guide to the Eastern Alps. [Just ready.

Guide to the Western Alps, including Mont Blanc, Monte Rosa, Zermatt, &c. price 7s. 6d.

Guide to the Oberland and all Switzerland, excepting the Neighbourhood of Monte Rosa and the Great St. Bernard; with Lombardy and the adjoining portion of Tyrol. 7s. 6d.

Humboldt's Travels and Discoveries in South America. Third Edition, with numerous Woodcuts. 18mo. 2s. 6d.

Narratives of Shipwrecks of the Royal Navy between 1793 and 1857, compiled from Official Documents in the Admiralty by W. O. S. GILLY; with a Preface by W. S. GILLY, D.D. 3d Edition, fcp. 5s.

A Week at the Land's End. By J. T. BLIGHT; assisted by E. H. RODD, R. Q. COUCH, and J. RALPH. With Map and 96 Woodcuts. Fcp. 6s. 6d.

Visits to Remarkable Places: Old Halls, Battle-Fields, and Scenes Illustrative of Striking Passages in English History and Poetry. By WILLIAM HOWITT. 2 vols. square crown 8vo. with Wood Engravings. 25s.

The Rural Life of England. By the same Author. With Woodcuts by Bewick and Williams. Medium 8vo. 12s. 6d.

Works of Fiction.

Atherstone Priory. By L. N. COMYN. 2 vols. post 8vo. 21s.

Ellice: a Tale. By the same. Post 8vo. 9s. 6d.

Stories and Tales by the Author of 'Amy Herbert,' uniform Edition, each Tale or Story complete in a single volume.

AMY HERBERT, 2s. 6d.	KATHARINE ASHTON, 8s. 6d.
GERTRUDE, 2s. 6d.	
EARL'S DAUGHTER, 2s. 6d.	MARGARET PERCIVAL, 5s.
EXPERIENCE OF LIFE, 2s. 6d.	LANETON PARSONAGE, 4s. 6d.
CLEVE HALL, 3s. 6d.	URSULA, 4s. 6d.
IVORS, 3s. 6d.	

A Glimpse of the World. By the Author of 'Amy Herbert.' Fcp. 7s. 6d.

The Six Sisters of the Valleys: an Historical Romance. By W. BRAMLEY-MOORE, M.A. Incumbent of Gerrard's Cross, Bucks. Fourth Edition, with 14 Illustrations. Crown 8vo. 5s.

Gallus; or, Roman Scenes of the Time of Augustus: with Notes and Excursuses Illustrative of the Manners and Customs of the Ancient Romans From the German of Prof. BECKER. New Edit. Post 8vo. 7s. 6d.

Chariclos; a Tale Illustrative of Private Life among the Ancient Greeks: with Notes and Excursuses. From the German of Pr. BECKER. New Edition, Post 8vo. 7s. 6d.

Icelandic Legends. Collected by JON ARNASON. Selected and Translated from the Icelandic by GEORGE E. J. POWELL and E. MAGNUSSON. SECOND SERIES, with Notes and an Introductory Essay on the Origin and Genius of the Icelandic Folk-Lore, and 3 Illustrations on Wood. Crown 8vo. 21s.

The Warden; a Novel. By ANTHONY TROLLOPE. Crown 8vo. 2s. 6d.

Barchester Towers: a Sequel to 'The Warden.' By the same Author. Crown 8vo. 3s. 6d.

Tales from Greek Mythology. By GEORGE W. COX, M.A. late Scholar of Trin. Coll. Oxon. Second Edition. Square 16mo. 3s. 6d.

Tales of the Gods and Heroes. By the same Author. Second Edition. Fcp. 5s.

Tales of Thebes and Argos. By the same Author. Fcp. 4s. 6d.

The Gladiators; a Tale of Rome and Judæa. By G. J. WHYTE MELVILLE. Crown 8vo. 5s.

Digby Grand, an Autobiography. By the same Author. 1 vol. 5s.

Kate Coventry, an Autobiography. By the same. 1 vol. 5s.

General Bounce, or the Lady and the Locusts. By the same. 1 vol. 5s.

Holmby House, a Tale of Old Northamptonshire. 1 vol. 5s.

Good for Nothing, or All Down Hill. By the same. 1 vol. 6s.

The Queen's Maries, a Romance of Holyrood. By the same. 1 vol. 6s.

The Interpreter, a Tale of the War. By the same Author. 1 vol. 5s.

Poetry and The Drama.

Goethe's Second Faust. Translated by JOHN ANSTER, LL.D. M.R.I.A. Regius Professor of Civil Law in the University of Dublin. Post 8vo. 15s.

Tasso's Jerusalem Delivered, translated into English Verse by Sir J. KINGSTON JAMES, Kt. M.A. 2 vols. fcp. with Facsimile, 14s.

Poetical Works of John Edmund Reade; with final Revision and Additions. 3 vols. fcp. 18s. or each vol. separately, 6s.

Moore's Poetical Works, Cheapest Edition, complete in 1 vol. including the Autobiographical Prefaces and Author's last Notes, which are still copyright. Crown 8vo. ruby type, with Portrait, 6s. or People's Edition, in larger type, 12s. 6d.

Moore's Poetical Works, as above, Library Edition, medium 8vo. with Portrait and Vignette, 14s. or in 10 vols. fcp. 3s. 6d. each.

Moore's Lalla Rookh, Tenniel's Edition, with 68 Wood Engravings from Original Drawings and other Illustrations. Fcp. 4to. 21s.

Moore's Irish Melodies, Maclise's Edition, with 161 Steel Plates from Original Drawings. Super-royal 8vo. 31s. 6d.

Miniature Edition of Moore's Irish Melodies, with Maclise's Illustrations, (as above) reduced in Lithography. Imp. 16mo. 10s. 6d.

Southey's Poetical Works, with the Author's last Corrections and copyright Additions. Library Edition, in 1 vol. medium 8vo. with Portrait and Vignette, 14s. or in 10 vols. fcp. 3s. 6d. each.

Lays of Ancient Rome; with Ivry and the Armada. By the Right Hon. LORD MACAULAY. 16mo. 4s. 6d.

Lord Macaulay's Lays of Ancient Rome. With 90 Illustrations on Wood, Original and from the Antique, from Drawings by G. SCHARF. Fcp. 4to. 21s.

Miniature Edition of Lord Macaulay's Lays of Ancient Rome, with Scharf's Illustrations (as above) reduced in Lithography. Imp. 16mo. 10s. 6d.

Poems. By JEAN INGELOW. Twelfth Edition. Fcp. 8vo. 5s.

Poems by Jean Ingelow. A New Edition, with nearly 100 Illustrations by Eminent Artists, engraved on Wood by the Brothers DALZIEL. Fcp. 4to. 21s.

Poetical Works of Letitia Elizabeth Landon (L.E.L.) 2 vols. 16mo. 10s.

Playtime with the Poets: a Selection of the best English Poetry for the use of Children. By a LADY. Crown 8vo. 5s.

Bowdler's Family Shakspeare, cheaper Genuine Edition, complete in 1 vol. large type, with 36 Woodcut Illustrations, price 14s. or, with the same Illustrations, in 6 pocket vols. 3s. 6d. each.

Arundines Cami, sive Musarum Cantabrigiensium Lusus Canori. Collegit atque edidit H. Drury, M.A. Editio Sexta, curavit H. J. Hodgson, M.A. Crown 8vo. price 7s. 6d.

The Æneid of Virgil Translated into English Verse. By John Conington, M.A. Corpus Professor of Latin in the University of Oxford. Crown 8vo. 9s.

The Iliad of Homer Translated into Blank Verse. By Ichabod Charles Wright, M.A. late Fellow of Magdalen Coll. Oxon. 2 vols. crown 8vo. 21s.

The Iliad of Homer in English Hexameter Verse. By J. Henry Dart, M.A. of Exeter College, Oxford; Author of 'The Exile of St. Helena, Newdigate, 1838.' Square crown 8vo. price 21s. cloth.

Dante's Divine Comedy, translated in English Terza Rima by John Dayman, M.A. [With the Italian Text, after Brunetti, interpaged.] 8vo. 21s.

Rural Sports, &c.

Encyclopædia of Rural Sports; a Complete Account, Historical, Practical, and Descriptive, of Hunting, Shooting, Fishing, Racing, &c. By D. P. Blaine. With above 600 Woodcuts (20 from Designs by John Leech). 8vo. 42s.

Notes on Rifle Shooting. By Captain Heaton, Adjutant of the Third Manchester Rifle Volunteer Corps. Fcp. 2s. 6d.

Col. Hawker's Instructions to Young Sportsmen in all that relates to Guns and Shooting. Revised by the Author's Son. Square crown 8vo. with Illustrations. 18s.

The Rifle, its Theory and Practice. By Arthur Walker (79th Highlanders), Staff, Hythe and Fleetwood Schools of Musketry. Second Edition. Crown 8vo. with 125 Woodcuts, 5s.

The Dead Shot, or Sportsman's Complete Guide; a Treatise on the Use of the Gun, Dog-breaking, Pigeon-shooting, &c. By Marksman. Fcp. with Plates, 5s.

Hints on Shooting, Fishing, &c. both on Sea and Land and in the Freshand Saltwater Lochs of Scotland. By C. Idle, Esq. Second Edition. Fcp. 5s.

A Book on Angling: being a Complete Work on every branch of Angling practised in Great Britain. By Francis Francis. With numerous Explanatory Plates, coloured and plain, and the largest and most reliable List of Salmon Flies ever published. Post 8vo.

The Art of Fishing on the Principle of Avoiding Cruelty; being a brief Treatise on the Most Merciful Methods of Capturing Fish; describing certain approved Modes in Fishing, used during 60 Years' Practice. By the Rev. O. Haymond, LL.B. Fcp. 8vo.

Handbook of Angling: Teaching Fly-fishing, Trolling, Bottom-fishing, Salmon-fishing; with the Natural History of River Fish, and the best modes of Catching them. By Ephemera. Fcp. Woodcuts, 5s.

The Fly-Fisher's Entomology. By Alfred Ronalds. With coloured Representations of the Natural and Artificial Insect. Sixth Edition; with 20 coloured Plates. 8vo. 14s.

The Cricket Field; or, the History and the Science of the Game of Cricket. By James Pycroft, B.A. 4th Edition. Fcp. 5s.

The Cricket Tutor; a Treatise exclusively Practical. By the same. 18mo. 1s.

Cricketana. By the same Author. With 7 Portraits of Cricketers. Fcp. 5s.

Youatt on the Horse. Revised and enlarged by W. Watson, M.R.C.V.S. 8vo. with numerous Woodcuts, 12s. 6d.

Youatt on the Dog. (By the same Author.) 8vo. with numerous Woodcuts, 6s.

The Horse-Trainer's and Sportsman's Guide: with Considerations on the Duties of Grooms, on Purchasing Blood Stock, and on Veterinary Examination. By Digby Collins. Post 8vo. 6s.

Blaine's Veterinary Art: a Treatise on the Anatomy, Physiology, and Curative Treatment of the Diseases of the Horse, Neat Cattle, and Sheep. Seventh Edition, revised and enlarged by C. Steel, M.R.C.V.S.L. 8vo. with Plates and Woodcuts, 18s.

On Drill and Manœuvres of Cavalry, combined with Horse Artillery. By Major-Gen. Michael W. Smith, C.B. commanding the Poonah Division of the Bombay Army. 8vo. 12s. 6d.

NEW WORKS PUBLISHED BY LONGMANS AND CO.   19

The Horse's Foot, and how to keep it Sound. By W. MILES, Esq. 9th Edition, with Illustrations. Imp. 8vo. 12s. 6d.

A Plain Treatise on Horse-shoeing. By the same Author. Post 8vo. with Illustrations, 2s. 6d.

Stables and Stable Fittings. By the same. Imp. 8vo. with 13 Plates, 15s.

Remarks on Horses' Teeth, addressed to Purchasers. By the same. Post 8vo. 1s. 6d.

The Dog in Health and Disease. By STONEHENGE. With 70 Wood Engravings. New Edition. Square crown 8vo. 10s. 6d.

The Greyhound. By the same Author. Revised Edition, with 24 Portraits of Greyhounds. Square crown 8vo. 21s.

The Ox, his Diseases and their Treatment; with an Essay on Parturition in the Cow. By J. R. DOBSON, M.M.C.V.S. Crown 8vo. with Illustrations, 7s. 6d.

Commerce, Navigation, and Mercantile Affairs.

The Commercial Handbook of France; Furnishing a detailed and comprehensive account of the Trade, Manufactures, Industry, and Commerce of France at the Present Time. By FREDERICK MARTIN. With Maps and Plans, including a Coloured Map showing the Seats of the Principal Industries. Crown 8vo.

Banking, Currency, and the Exchanges; a Practical Treatise. By ARTHUR CRUMP, Bank Manager, formerly of the Bank of England. Post 8vo. 6s.

The Theory and Practice of Banking. By HENRY DUNNING MACLEOD, M.A. Barrister-at-Law. Second Edition, entirely remodelled. 2 vols. 8vo. 30s.

A Dictionary, Practical, Theoretical, and Historical, of Commerce and Commercial Navigation. By J. R. M'CULLOCH. New Edition in preparation.

Practical Guide for British Shipmasters to United States Ports. By PIERREPONT EDWARDS, Her Britannic Majesty's Vice-Consul at New York. Post 8vo. 6s. 6d.

A Manual for Naval Cadets. By J. M'NEILL BOYD, late Captain R.N. Third Edition; with 240 Woodcuts, and 11 coloured Plates. Post 8vo. 12s. 6d.

The Law of Nations Considered as Independent Political Communities. By TRAVERS TWISS, D.C.L. Regius Professor of Civil Law in the University of Oxford. 2 vols. 8vo. 30s. or separately, PART I. Peace, 12s. PART II. War, 18s.

A Nautical Dictionary, defining the Technical Language relative to the Building and Equipment of Sailing Vessels and Steamers, &c. By ARTHUR YOUNG. Second Edition; with Plates and 150 Woodcuts. 8vo. 18s.

Works of Utility and General Information.

Modern Cookery for Private Families, reduced to a System of Easy Practice in a Series of carefully-tested Receipts. By ELIZA ACTON. Newly revised and enlarged; with 8 Plates, Figures, and 150 Woodcuts. Fcp. 7s. 6d.

On Food and its Digestion; an Introduction to Dietetics. By W. BRINTON, M.D. Physician to St. Thomas's Hospital, &c. With 48 Woodcuts. Post 8vo. 12s.

Wine, the Vine, and the Cellar. By THOMAS G. SHAW. Second Edition, revised and enlarged, with Frontispiece and 31 Illustrations on Wood. 8vo. 16s.

A Practical Treatise on Brewing; with Formulæ for Public Brewers, and Instructions for Private Families. By W. BLACK. Fifth Edition. 8vo. 10s. 6d.

How to Brew Good Beer: a complete Guide to the Art of Brewing Ale, Bitter Ale, Table Ale, Brown Stout, Porter, and Table Beer. By JOHN PITT. Revised Edition. Fcp. 4s. 6d.

The Billiard Book. By Captain CRAWLEY, Author of 'Billiards, its Theory and Practice,' &c. With nearly 100 Diagrams on Steel and Wood. 8vo. 21s.

Whist, What to Lead. By Cam. Third Edition. 32mo. 1s.

Short Whist. By Major A. The Sixteenth Edition, revised, with an Essay on the Theory of the Modern Scientific Game by Prof. P. Fcp. 3s. 6d.

Two Hundred Chess Problems, composed by F. Healey, including the Problems to which the Prizes were awarded by the Committees of the Era, the Manchester, the Birmingham, and the Bristol Chess Problem Tournaments; accompanied by the Solutions. Crown 8vo. with 200 Diagrams, 5s.

The Cabinet Lawyer; a Popular Digest of the Laws of England, Civil, Criminal, and Constitutional. 22nd Edition, entirely recomposed, and brought down by the Author to the close of the Parliamentary Session of 1868. Fcp. 10s. 6d.

The Philosophy of Health; or, an Exposition of the Physiological and Sanitary Conditions conducive to Human Longevity and Happiness. By Southwood Smith, M.D. Eleventh Edition, revised and enlarged; with 113 Woodcuts. 8vo. 15s.

Hints to Mothers on the Management of their Health during the Period of Pregnancy and in the Lying-in Room. By T. Bull, M.D. Fcp. 5s.

The Maternal Management of Children in Health and Disease. By the same Author. Fcp. 5s.

Notes on Hospitals. By Florence Nightingale. Third Edition, enlarged; with 13 Plans. Post 4to. 18s.

The Executor's Guide. By J. C. Hudson. Enlarged Edition, revised by the Author, with reference to the latest reported Cases and Acts of Parliament. Fcp. 6s.

Hudson's Plain Directions for Making Wills. Fcp. 2s. 6d.

The Law relating to Benefit Building Societies; with Practical Observations on the Act and all the Cases decided thereon, also a Form of Rules and Forms of Mortgages. By W. Tidd Pratt, Barrister. 2nd Edition. Fcp. 3s. 6d.

C. M. Willich's Popular Tables for Ascertaining the Value of Lifehold, Leasehold, and Church Property, Renewal Fines, &c.; the Public Funds; Annual Average Price and Interest on Consols from 1731 to 1861; Chemical, Geographical, Astronomical, Trigonometrical Tables, &c. Post 8vo. 10s.

Thomson's Tables of Interest, at Three, Four, Four and a Half, and Five per Cent., from One Pound to Ten Thousand and from 1 to 365 Days. 12mo. 3s. 6d.

Maunder's Treasury of Knowledge and Library of Reference; comprising an English Dictionary and Grammar, Universal Gazetteer, Classical Dictionary, Chronology, Law Dictionary, Synopsis of the Peerage, useful Tables, &c. Fcp. 10s. 6d.

Knowledge for the Young.

The Stepping Stone to Knowledge: Containing upwards of 700 Questions and Answers on Miscellaneous Subjects, adapted to the capacity of Infant Minds. By a Mother. 18mo. price 1s.

The Stepping Stone to Geography: Containing several Hundred Questions and Answers on Geographical Subjects. 18mo. 1s.

The Stepping Stone to English History: Containing several Hundred Questions and Answers on the History of England. 1s.

The Stepping Stone to Bible Knowledge; Containing several Hundred Questions and Answers on the Old and New Testaments. 18mo. 1s.

The Stepping Stone to Biography; Containing several Hundred Questions and Answers on the Lives of Eminent Men and Women. 18mo. 1s.

Second Series of the Stepping Stone to Knowledge; containing upwards of Eight Hundred Questions and Answers on Miscellaneous Subjects not contained in the First Series. 18mo. 1s.

The Stepping Stone to French Pronunciation and Conversation; Containing several Hundred Questions and Answers. By Mr. P. Sadler. 18mo. 1s.

The Stepping Stone to English Grammar; containing several Hundred Questions and Answers on English Grammar. By Mr. P. Sadler. 18mo. 1s.

The Stepping Stone to Natural History; Vertebrate or Backboned Animals. Part I. Mammalia; Part II. Birds, Reptiles, Fishes. 18mo. 1s. each Part.

INDEX.

ABBOTT on Sight and Touch 7
ACTON'S Modern Cookery 19
ALCOCK'S Residence in Japan 16
ALLIES on Formation of Christianity 14
Alpine Guide (The) 16
APJOHN'S Manual of the Metalloids 8
ARAGO'S Biographies of Scientific Men .. 4
———— Popular Astronomy 7
ARNOLD'S Manual of English Literature .. 5
ARNOTT'S Elements of Physics 7
Arundines Cami 19
Atherstone Priory 16
Autumn Holidays of a Country Parson ... 6
AYRE'S Treasury of Bible Knowledge 14

BACON'S Essays, by WHATELY 4
———— Life and Letters, by SPEDDING . 3
———— Works 4
BAIN on the Emotions and Will 7
———— on the Senses and Intellect 7
———— on the Study of Character 7
BAIKIE'S Explorations in N.W. Africa ... 15
BALL'S Guide to the Central Alps 12
———— Guide to the Western Alps 12
———— Guide to the Eastern Alps 16
BARNARD'S Drawing from Nature 12
BAYLDON'S Rents and Tillages 13
Beaten Tracks 15
BECKER'S Charicles and Gallus 16
BEETHOVEN'S Letters 4
BENFEY'S Sanskrit-English Dictionary 5
BERRY'S Journals 3
BLACK'S Treatise on Brewing 19
BLACKLEY and FRIEDLANDER'S German
and English Dictionary 5
BLAINE'S Rural Sports 19
———— Veterinary Art 19
BLIGHT'S Week at the Land's End 16
BOOLE'S Essay on Human Nature 8
———— Philosophy of Nature 6
BOKER'S Transylvania 15
BOOTH'S Epigrams 4
BOURNE on Screw Propeller 12
BOURNE'S Catechism of the Steam Engine 12
———— Handbook of Steam Engine ... 12
———— Treatise on the Steam Engine 12
BOWDLER'S Family SHAKSPEARE 19
BOYD'S Manual for Naval Cadets 19
BRAMLEY-MOORE'S Six Sisters of the Valleys 16
BRANDE'S Dictionary of Science, Literature, and Art 9
BRAY'S (C.) Education of the Feelings .. 7
———— Philosophy of Necessity 7
———— On Force 7
BRITTON on Food and Digestion 19
BRISTOW'S Glossary of Mineralogy 8
BRODIE'S Constitutional History 3

BRODIE'S (Sir C. B.) Works 10
———— Autobiography 12
BROWNE'S Ice Caves of France and Switzerland 15
———— Exposition 39 Articles 13
———— Pentateuch 13
BUCKLE'S History of Civilisation 9
BULL'S Hints to Mothers 20
———— Maternal Management of Children 20
BUNSEN'S Ancient Egypt 9
BUNSEN on Apocrypha 14
BURKE'S Vicissitudes of Families 4
BURTON'S Christian Church 3

Cabinet Lawyer 20
CALVERT'S Wife's Manual 14
Campaigner at Home 6
CATS and FARLIE'S Moral Emblems 11
Chorale Book for England 15
CLOUGH'S Lives from Plutarch 3
COLENSO (Bishop) on Pentateuch and Book
of Joshua 14
COLLINS'S Horse Trainer's Guide 19
COLUMBUS'S Voyages 16
Commonplace Philosophy in Town and
Country 6
CONINGTON'S Translation of Virgil's Æneid 19
CONTANSEAU'S Two French and English
Dictionaries 5
CONYBEARE and HOWSON'S Life and Epistles
of St. Paul 13
COOK'S Acts of the Apostles 13
———— Voyages 16
COPLAND'S Dictionary of Practical Medicine 10
COX'S Tales of the Great Persian War . 17
———— Tales from Greek Mythology . 17
———— Tales of the Gods and Heroes 17
———— Tales of Thebes and Argos .. 17
CRAWLEY'S Billiard Book 19
CRESY'S Encyclopædia of Civil Engineering 11
Critical Essays of a Country Parson 6
CROWE'S History of France 3
CROWE on Banking, &c. 19
CUSSANS'S Grammar of Heraldry 19

DART'S Iliad of Homer 19
D'AUBIGNÉ'S History of the Reformation in
the time of CALVIN 3
DAYMAN'S Dante's Divine Commedia ... 19
Dead Shot (The), by MARKSMAN 19
DE LA RIVE'S Treatise on Electricity ... 8
DESMARRE'S Village Life in Switzerland 15
DE LA PRYME'S Life of Christ 14
DE MORGAN on Matter and Spirit 6
DE TOCQUEVILLE'S Democracy in America 3
DISRAELI'S Speeches on Reform 3
DOBSON on the Ox 19

NEW WORKS published by LONGMANS and CO.

Duncan and Millard on Classification, &c. of the Idiotic	11
Dyer's City of Rome	2
Edwards's Shipmaster's Guide	19
Elements of Botany	9
Ellice, a Tale	16
Ellicott's Broad and Narrow Way	13
—— Commentary on Ephesians	13
—— Destiny of the Creature	13
—— Lectures on Life of Christ	13
—— Commentary on Galatians	13
—— —— Pastoral Epist.	13
—— —— Philippians,&c.	13
—— —— Thessalonians	13
Engel's Introduction to National Music	11
Essays and Reviews	14
—— on Religion and Literature, edited by Manning	15
Fairbairn's Application of Cast and Wrought Iron to Building	12
—— Information for Engineers	12
—— Treatise on Mills & Millwork	12
Fairbairn on Iron Ship Building	11
Farrar's Chapters on Language	5
Froude's Christendom's Divisions	14
Francis's Fishing Book	18
Froude's History of England	1
Gee's Our Sermons	15
—— Sunday to Sunday	15
Gilbert and Churchill's Dolomite Mountains	16
Gilly's Shipwrecks of the Navy	16
Goethe's Second Faust, by Anster	17
Goodeve's Elements of Mechanism	12
Goold's Lectures on Brown's Exposition of the 39 Articles	13
Grant's Ethics of Aristotle	5
Graver Thoughts of a Country Parson	5
Gray's Anatomy	10
Greene's Corals and Sea Jellies	9
—— Sponges and Animalcules	9
Grove on Correlation of Physical Forces	9
Gwilt's Encyclopædia of Architecture	12
Handbook of Angling, by Ephemera	18
Hare on Election of Representatives	5
Harley and Brown's Histological Demonstrations	10
Hartwig's Harmonies of Nature	9
—— Sea and its Living Wonders	9
—— Tropical World	9
Haughton's Manual of Geology	8
Hawker's Instructions to Young Sportsmen	18
Heaton's Notes on Rifle Shooting	18
Healey's Chess Problems	20
Helps's Spanish Conquest in America	3
Henderson's Folk-Lore	6
Herschel's Essays from Reviews	9
—— Outlines of Astronomy	7
Hewitt on the Diseases of Women	10
Hind on Time and Space	7
Holland's Essays on Scientific Subjects	9
Holmes's System of Surgery	10

Hooker and Walker-Arnott's British Flora	9
Hopkins's Hawaii	2
Horne's Introduction to the Scriptures	14
—— Compendium of the Scriptures	14
Horsley's Manual of Poisons	9
Hosking's Occasional Essays	6
—— Talpa	19
How we Spent the Summer	15
Howitt's Australian Discovery	16
—— Rural Life of England	18
—— Visits to Remarkable Places	16
Hudson's Directions for Making Wills	20
—— Executor's Guide	20
Hughes's (W.) Manual of Geography	7
Hullah's History of Modern Music	11
—— Transition Musical Lectures	11
—— Part Music	12
—— Sacred Music	11
Humboldt's Travels in South America	15
Humphreys's Sentiments of Shakspeare	11
Hutton's Studies in Parliament	6
Hymns from Lyra Germanica	14
Ingelow's Poems	17
Icelandic Legends, Second Series	17
Idle's Hints on Shooting	18
Jameson's Legends of the Saints and Martyrs	12
—— Legends of the Madonna	12
—— Legends of the Monastic Orders	12
Jameson and Eastlake's History of Our Lord	12
Johnson's Patentee's Manual	12
—— Practical Draughtsman	12
Johnston's Gazetteer, or General Geographical Dictionary	7
Jones's Christianity and Common Sense	7
Jordan's Elements	5
Kalisch's Commentary on the Bible	5
—— Hebrew Grammar	5
Kellen's Lake Dwellings of Switzerland	2
Kesteven's Domestic Medicine	10
Kirby and Spence's Entomology	9
Kuenen on Pentateuch and Joshua	14
Lady's Tour round Monte Rosa	15
Lawson's (L. E. L.) Poetical Works	17
Latham's English Dictionary	5
Lawrence on Rocks	8
Lecky's History of Rationalism	3
Leisure Hours in Town	6
Lewes's Biographical History of Philosophy	4
Lewin's Fasti Sacri	13
Lewis on Early Roman History	4
—— on Irish Disturbances	4
—— on Observation and Reasoning in Politics	4
—— on Political Terms	4
Lewis's Essays on Administrations	4
—— Fables of Babrius	4
Liddell and Scott's Greek-English Lexicon	5
—— Abridged ditto	5
Life of Man Symbolised	12
Lindley and Moore's Treasury of Botany	9

NEW WORKS PUBLISHED BY LONGMANS AND CO.

LONGMAN's Lectures on History of England	1
LOUDON's Encyclopædia of Agriculture	13
———— Gardening	13
———— Plants	9
———— Trees and Shrubs	9
———— Cottage, Farm, and Villa Architecture	13
LOWNDES's Engineer's Handbook	12
Lyra Domestica	16
——— Eucharistica	16
——— Germanica	11, 16
——— Messianica	15
——— Mystica	16
——— Sacra	16
MACAULAY's (Lord) Essays	2
———— History of England	1
———— Lays of Ancient Rome	17
———— Miscellaneous Writings	6
———— Speeches	6
———— Works	1
MACFARREN's Lectures on Harmony	11
MACLEOD's Elements of Political Economy	4
———— Dictionary of Political Economy	4
———— Theory and Practice of Banking	10
McCULLOCH's Dictionary of Commerce	7
———— Geographical Dictionary	7
MACVIE's Vancouver Island	16
MAGUIRE's Life of Father Mathew	3
———— Rome and its Rulers	3
MALING's Indoor Gardener	9
MANNING on Holy Ghost	16
MARSHMAN's History of India	2
———— Life of Havelock	3
MARTIN's Commercial Handbook of France	10
MASSEY's History of England	1
MASSINGBERD's History of the Reformation	16
MAUNDER's Biographical Treasury	7
———— Geographical Treasury	7
———— Historical Treasury	2
———— Scientific and Literary Treasury	9
———— Treasury of Knowledge	10
———— Treasury of Natural History	9
MAURY's Physical Geography	7
MAY's Constitutional History of England	1
MELVILLE's Digby Grand	17
———— General Bounce	17
———— Gladiators	17
———— Good for Nothing	17
———— Holmby House	17
———— Interpreter	17
———— Kate Coventry	17
———— Queen's Maries	17
MENDELSSOHN's Letters	5
MESSIAH' Windsor Great Park	13
MERIVALE's (H.) Historical Studies	1
———— (C.) Fall of the Roman Republic	2
———— Romans under the Empire	2
———— Boyle Lectures	2
MILES on Horse's Foot and Horse Shoeing	19
———— on Horses' Teeth and Stables	19
MILL on Liberty	4
———— on Representative Government	4
———— on Utilitarianism	4
MILL's Dissertations and Discussions	4
———— Political Economy	4
———— System of Logic	4
———— Hamilton's Philosophy	4

MILLER's Elements of Chemistry	9
MONSELL's Spiritual Songs	16
———— Beatitudes	15
MONTGOMERY on Pregnancy	10
MOORE's Irish Melodies	11, 17
———— Lalla Rookh	17
———— Journal and Correspondence	5
———— Poetical Works	17
———— (Dr. G.) First Man	2
MORELL's Elements of Psychology	6
———— Mental Philosophy	6
MOSHEIM's Ecclesiastical History	16
MOSLEY's Letters	5
MÜLLER's (Max) Lectures on the Science of Language	5
———— (K. O.) Literature of Ancient Greece	2
MURCHISON on Continued Fevers	10
MURE's Language and Literature of Greece	2
New Testament Illustrated with Wood Engravings from the Old Masters	11
NEWMAN's History of his Religious Opinions	5
NIGHTINGALE's Notes on Hospitals	20
ODLING's Animal Chemistry	9
———— Course of Practical Chemistry	9
———— Manual of Chemistry	9
O'HEA's Guide to Spain	18
OWEN's Comparative Anatomy and Physiology of Vertebrate Animals	8
OXENHAM on Atonement	15
PACKE's Guide to the Pyrenees	18
PAGET's Lectures on Surgical Pathology	10
PEREIRA's Elements of Materia Medica	10
———— Manual of Materia Medica	10
PERKINS's Tuscan Sculptors	11
PHILLIPS's Guide to Geology	8
———— Introduction to Mineralogy	8
PIESSE's Art of Perfumery	13
———— Chemical, Natural, and Physical Magic	13
PITT on Brewing	19
Playtime with the Poets	17
Practical Mechanic's Journal	13
PRATT's Law of Building Societies	20
PRESCOTT's Scripture Difficulties	16
PROCTOR's Handbook of the Stars	7
———— Saturn	7
PYCROFT's Course of English Reading	5
———— Cricket Field	18
———— Cricket Tutor	18
———— Cricketana	18
RAYMOND on Fishing without Cruelty	18
READE's Poetical Works	17
Recreations of a Country Parson	6
REILLY's Map of Mont Blanc	18
RIVERS's Rose Amateur's Guide	9

NEW WORKS PUBLISHED BY LONGMANS AND CO.

Rogers's Correspondence of Greyson	6
——— Eclipse of Faith	6
——— Defence of ditto	6
——— Essays from the *Edinburgh Review*	6
——— Reason and Faith	6
——— (E.) Fifth Monarchy Men	3
Roget's Thesaurus of English Words and Phrases	5
Ronalds's Fly-Fisher's Entomology	19
Rowton's Debater	5
Russell on Government and Constitution	7
Sandars's Justinian's Institutes	4
Scott's Handbook of Volumetrical Analysis	9
——— Lectures on the Fine Arts	11
Scrope on Volcanos	7
Sewell's Amy Herbert	16
——— Cleve Hall	16
——— Earl's Daughter	16
——— Experience of Life	16
——— Gertrude	16
——— Glimpse of the World	16
——— History of the Early Church	8
——— Ivors	16
——— Katharine Ashton	16
——— Laneton Parsonage	16
——— Margaret Percival	16
——— Passing Thoughts on Religion	16
——— Preparation for Communion	16
——— Principles of Education	16
——— Readings for Confirmation	16
——— Readings for Lent	16
——— Examination for Confirmation	16
——— Stories and Tales	16
——— Thoughts for the Holy Week	16
——— Ursula	16
Shaw's Work on Wine	19
Sheddon's Elements of Logic	4
Shipley's Church and the World	16
Short Whist	20
Short's Church History	8
Southey's (Caroline) Life, by Warter	
Smith's (Southwood) Philosophy of Health	20
——— (J.) Paul's Voyage and Shipwreck	19
——— (G.) Wesleyan Methodism	5
——— (Sydney) Miscellaneous Works	5
——— Moral Philosophy	6
——— Wit and Wisdom	6
Smith on Cavalry Drill and Manoeuvres	18
Southey's (Doctor)	6
——— Poetical Works	17
Stanley's History of British Birds	9
Stebbing's Analysis of Mill's Logic	4
Stephen's Essays in Ecclesiastical Biography	4
——— Lectures on History of France	2
Stephenson's Life, by Jeaffreson and Pole	5
Stepping-Stones (The) to Knowledge, &c.	20
Stirling's Poetry of Hegel	6
Stonehenge on the Dog	19
——— on the Greyhound	19
Strange on the Air	10
——— Restoration of Health	10
Sunday Afternoons at the Parish Church	6

Tasso's Jerusalem, by James	17
Taylor's (Jeremy) Works, edited by Eden	16
Tennent's Ceylon	8
——— Natural History of Ceylon	8
——— Wild Elephant	8
Thirlwall's History of Greece	2
Thomson's (Archbishop) Laws of Thought	4
——— (J.) Tables of Interest	20
——— Conspectus, by Birkett	10
Todd's Cyclopaedia of Anatomy and Physiology	10
——— and Bowman's Anatomy and Physiology of Man	10
Trollope's Barchester Towers	17
——— Warden	17
Twiss's Law of Nations	19
Tyndall's Lectures on Heat	8
——— Lectures on Sound	8
Ure's Dictionary of Arts, Manufactures, and Mines	12
Van Der Hoeven's Handbook of Zoology	8
Vaughan's (R.) Revolutions in English History	3
——— (R. A.) Hours with the Mystics	7
——— Way to Rest	7
Walker on the Rifle	18
Watson's Principles and Practice of Physic	10
Watts's Dictionary of Chemistry	9
Webb's Objects for Common Telescopes	7
Webster & Wilkinson's Greek Testament	15
Weld's Florence	16
Wellington's Life, by Brialmont and Gleig	9
——— by Gleig	2
West on Children's Diseases	9
Whately's English Synonymes	4
——— Life and Correspondence	3
——— Logic	4
——— Remains	4
——— Rhetoric	4
——— Paley's Moral Philosophy	15
Whewell's History of the Inductive Sciences	3
Whist, what to lead, by Cam	20
White and Riddle's Latin-English Dictionaries	5
Wilberforce (W.) Recollections of, by Harford	5
Willich's Popular Tables	20
Wilson's Bryologia Britannica	9
Windham's Diary	3
Wood's Homes without Hands	8
Woodward's Historical and Chronological Encyclopaedia	3
Wright's Homer's Iliad	16
Yonge's English-Greek Lexicon	5
——— Abridged ditto	5
Youle's Nautical Dictionary	19
Youatt on the Dog	19
——— on the Horse	19

www.ingramcontent.com/pod-product-compliance
Lightning Source LLC
Chambersburg PA
CBHW021219300426
44111CB00007B/363